Journalism Today

SIXTH EDITION

Donald L. Ferguson

Jim Patten

Bradley Wilson

National Textbook Company
a division of NTC/CONTEMPORARY PUBLISHING GROUP
Lincolnwood, Illinois USA

Interior and cover design: Think Design

Cover illustration: Jeff Berlin

Reviewers
Richard Johns, Executive Director,
Quill and Scroll Society

Laura Schaub, Executive Director,
Oklahoma Interscholastic Press Association

Pat Gathright
MacArthur High School, San Antonio, Texas

Susan Komandowsky
Round Rock High School, Round Rock, Texas

Lorraine Liverpool
Cooper City High School, Cooper City, Florida

Carolyn Phipps
Woodale High School, Memphis, Tennessee

Acknowledgments begin on page 563, which is to be considered an extension
of this copyright page.

ISBN: 0-658-00404-2

Published by National Textbook Company, a division of NTC/Contemporary Publishing Group, Inc.
4255 West Touhy Avenue, Lincolnwood (Chicago), Illinois 60712-1975 U.S.A.

Contents

SECTION TWO

Gathering News for the School Newspaper   56

SECTION THREE

Writing and Delivering the News 124

SECTION FOUR

Writing Features, Sports, and Editorials 264

SECTION FIVE

Other Aspects of Scholastic Journalism   332

SECTION SIX
Photography   434

SECTION SEVEN

Computers and Desktop Publishing   480

Stylebook 505

Appendix 541

Glossary 551

Acknowledgments 563

Index 565

About the Authors

Donald L. Ferguson has taught high school journalism in his native Nebraska and college journalism at Ohio State and Baylor Universities. Currently, he is a partner/owner of a global communications and media-consulting firm headquartered in New York City. Ferguson holds degrees in journalism from the University of Nebraska and the Medill School of Journalism, Northwestern University. He is coauthor of four books; active in professional journalism, public relations, and community affairs; and is a recipient of the President's Award for Service to Education, given by the National School Public Relations Association.

Jim Patten is head of the Journalism Department at the University of Arizona in Tucson. As a professional journalist, both before and after beginning a teaching career in 1967, he has worked at nine newspapers in a variety of positions including reporter, copy editor, columnist, editorial writer, photographer, and sportswriter. The winner of many teaching awards, including the Annis Chaiken Sorensen Award for Distinguished Teaching in the Humanities, Patten is a graduate in journalism from the University of Nebraska. He also holds a master's degree in journalism from Iowa State University. He has served as writing coach for newspapers in California, Texas, Pennsylvania, Nebraska, and Arizona.

Bradley Wilson has taught photojournalism and journalism and advised high school publications in Texas. He served as the president of the Association of Texas Photography Instructors from 1993 through 1996. Also the author of two other journalism books, one on desktop publishing and one on photography for high school students, Wilson is active in state and national journalism-related associations for which he has written numerous articles. He has taught workshops on photography and on being a journalism adviser, as well as on student newspapers, yearbooks, and desktop publishing, for various schools and associations nationwide. He is currently editor of *Journalism Education Today,* the magazine of the Journalism Education Association. Wilson holds a bachelor of journalism degree from The University of Texas-Austin and was a recipient of the Medal of Merit from the Journalism Education Association. He also holds the highest award for Excellence in Communications from the Texas School Public Relations Association.

Introduction

The book you have in your hands reflects deeply held philosophies about both yesterday and tomorrow. A great deal of new material in the book stems from the dawn of the Information Age and the incredible impact of the Internet. Technology continues to boom, and we urge you to get in on the action. Computers, on-line resources, and improving techniques are woven into the discussion throughout the book.

No one, however, should mistake journalism for mere computer keystrokes. The news, as you will read, does not gather itself. There will always be a need for reporters and editors, even though they may not be called that in the future. The world will always need people who can identify society's information needs and fulfill them. In other words, someone will always have to cover the city council, and it doesn't matter a great deal whether news of that meeting appears in a newspaper, on a TV news program, on a web site, or even beamed directly into the audience's brain by some yet-undiscovered means. That's just the delivery system. The information itself is what counts.

Good journalism necessarily entails good writing. Bad writing, whether in cyberspace, on the air, or on paper, has a damaging effect on your audience. It pays to learn how to write well, and the instruction and exercises in this book are designed to help you develop your newswriting skills.

Contents

Journalism Today is divided into seven sections. The first section, "Journalism in a Democracy," covers the rise and responsibilities of American media. Chapter 1, "Looking Back: The History of American Media," covers the development of journalism in America. The roles and responsibilities of journalists are covered in Chapter 2, "Meeting Ethical and Legal Responsibilities."

Sections Two, Three, and Four are "how-to" chapters, with an emphasis on newspapers. Section Two, "Gathering News for the School Newspaper," focuses on student publications. In Chapter 3, "Deciding What Is News," you will learn what makes a good story. Chapter 4, "Organizing the Staff to Capture the News," covers new ways to structure your staff. How to conduct an interview and then write it up are the focus of Chapter 5, "Making the Interview Work."

Section Three, "Writing and Delivering the News," covers writing good news stories. You will learn how to best capture your audience's attention in Chapter 6, "Writing News Story Leads." The body of the story is the focus of Chapter 7, "Writing News Stories and Headlines." In Chapter 8, "Handling Quotes Fairly and Accurately," you will learn how to use quotes correctly and to your best advantage. Chapter 9, "Doing In-Depth Reporting," teaches you how to do substantive stories. Chapter 10, "Design and Layout," gives numerous examples of how to produce effective pages.

Section Four, "Writing Features, Sports, and Editorials," focuses on more specialized areas of journalism. Chapter 11, "Writing Feature Stories," Chapter 12, "Writing Sports Stories," and Chapter 13, "Writing for the Editorial Page," address effective writing in these areas.

Section Five, "Other Aspects of Scholastic Journalism," covers a variety of journalism-related topics. Chapter 14, "Producing the Yearbook," covers the elements of producing a yearbook from planning to page layout. Chapter 15, "Writing for Radio and Television," focuses on broadcast journalism. In Chapter 16, "Understanding and Using Public Relations," you will learn about public relations, both what it is and how to use it. The business aspects of journalism, such as budgeting and advertising, are found in Chapter 17, "Handling Finances: Advertising and Business."

Section Six, "Photography," covers both practical and aesthetic aspects of photography. Chapter 18, "Taking and Using Effective Photographs," shows you how to shoot and then use good photographs. In Chapter 19, "Understanding Technical Aspects of Photography," you will learn about the practical side of photography: how cameras work, how to control exposures, and how to work in a darkroom.

Section Seven, "Computers and Desktop Publishing," covers the technological resources available. The final chapter, "The Impact of Technology," offers an overview of desktop publishing and on-line resources in journalism.

A variety of other features are included to help you learn about journalism. The On Display features show examples from student newspapers and yearbooks from around the country. Seeing samples of what other students are doing can inspire and encourage you. The end-of-chapter material includes summary material and both individual and team activities to help you practice what you have just learned. A final activity encourages you to explore the Internet in understanding and applying journalistic concepts and skills.

In addition, each chapter contains a Trends and Issues feature. Each of these presents an issue at stake in journalism, from on-line resources to invasion of privacy. The Career Profile at the end of each chapter high-lights a well-established journalist discussing his or her career path as well as offering advice for up-and-coming journalists.

Journalism Today and in the Future

The craft of journalism today demands that you maintain a balance between yesterday and tomorrow. As a journalist, you should cherish the traditional values—ethics, concern for the community, hard work, honesty, and the craft of true journalism. The examination of ethical issues will always be critical, from how a criminal case is handled in the press to the way guests on talk shows are treated. The Appendix in this edition contains ethical standards that journalists are expected to live up to.

As you develop your journalistic skills and techniques, remember to stay flexible about the inevitable stream of change—from how the news is researched to how it's delivered. Journalists and scholars are concerned with a number of issues at the beginning of the new century. Will the new media kill print media? Is there a future for newspapers? Most believe that newspapers will survive well into the 21st century and beyond. On-line distribution may even help newspapers. Generally, new media supplement the current media, rather than replace them. Radio and TV have not driven out newspapers, although they have brought about certain changes. The point is that no one can predict the future.

As the lines between print, TV, cable, and cyberspace blur, journalists need to remain open to new ideas about packaging and delivering information. However, good journalists must also remain true to the essentials of journalism: to report the news fairly, accurately, and well. As Katherine Fulton advised, "The wisest strategy . . . is to remain committed to high-quality reporting and storytelling—and to invest seriously in understanding new media" (*Columbia Journalism Review,* March/April 1996).

A final word of advice to those who want to become journalists: Start reading. Put down that joystick, turn off the TV and the computer, and grab a book. Read it, then read another one. Read the recipes on the cereal box at breakfast and the signs on the bus. This text will teach you the essential journalistic skills, but you can't become a journalist solely by reading this book—or any other, for that matter. You learn journalism by doing journalism. The doorway to journalism is closed, however, to all but the truly literate. And that means devouring the written word.

SECTION ONE

CHAPTER 1

Looking Back: The History of American Media

partisan press		yellow journalism	global village
penny press		muckraking	computer-assisted repo...
wire service		shock jock	

KEY CONCEPTS

After reading this chapter, you will

▶ understand how the printed press in America developed

▶ know how the American concept of freedom of the press came into being

▶ understand the development and impact of radio and television

▶ know how the Internet became a tool for gathering and disseminating information

▶ recognize some of the issues facing journalism at the beginning of the 21st century

The Information Age has dawned—with a bang.

Millions—soon to be billions—of people around the planet are electronically linked, building virtual communities with little regard for international boundaries.

Fiercely independent, sometimes chaotic, always resistant to government regulation, the Internet appears to have changed communication as much as any development in history. In its impact on the way human beings communicate, the Internet ranks with the invention of movable type; the advent of the telegraph, telephone, radio, and television; and the creation of satellite technology—or so it seems.

The true significance of the Internet is unknown. Journalists and communication scholars struggle to glimpse the ultimate impact of the changes it has brought. Some think the world of news and information has been altered in a fundamental way.

Others think the electronic changes merely affect the delivery system for news: Your newspaper is delivered on line instead of being tossed onto your porch.

Although no one can yet guess where we're going with new technology, one thing is certain: We're not going backward.

The amount of information available on line is staggering. Some of it's excellent—and some of it's trash. That just about describes information as it has always been. Somebody has to sort it out, make sense of it, organize it, judge it, and interpret it.

That's what journalists do—and have always done, whether with quill pens, typewriters, or computers. They scan the environment, picking from thousands of news items those that are the ... or that affect the most people. ... gathered, facts are weighed, and ... written, packaged, and delivere...

To do this, journalists need... skills they've always needed. T... be broadly educated. They nee... about everything, because that... cover: everything. They need p... and language skills.

Journalists also need to dem... good sense, good judgment, goo... poise under pressure, and ethical... moral standards. These fundamen... apply whether information is deli... the audience on line or in the trad... fashion.

Acce...
a perr...
peopl...

2

Journalism
in a
Democracy

CHAPTER 1

Looking Back: The History of American Media

KEY CONCEPTS

After reading this chapter, you will

▶ understand how the printed press in America developed

▶ know how the American concept of freedom of the press came into being

▶ understand the development and impact of radio and television

▶ know how the Internet became a tool for gathering and disseminating information

▶ recognize some of the issues facing journalism at the beginning of the 21st century

The Information Age has dawned—with a bang.

Millions—soon to be billions—of people around the planet are electronically linked, building virtual communities with little regard for international boundaries.

Fiercely independent, sometimes chaotic, always resistant to government regulation, the Internet appears to have changed communication as much as any development in history. In its impact on the way human beings communicate, the Internet ranks with the invention of movable type; the advent of the telegraph, telephone, radio, and television; and the creation of satellite technology—or so it seems.

The true significance of the Internet is unknown. Journalists and communication scholars struggle to glimpse the ultimate impact of the changes it has brought. Some think the world of news and information has been altered in a fundamental way.

Accessing the Internet is a part of daily life for many people today.

Others think the electronic changes merely affect the delivery system for news: Your newspaper is delivered on line instead of being tossed onto your porch.

Although no one can yet guess where we're going with new technology, one thing is certain: We're not going backward.

The amount of information available on line is staggering. Some of it's excellent— and some of it's trash. That just about describes information as it has always been. Somebody has to sort it out, make sense of it, organize it, judge it, and interpret it.

That's what journalists do—and have always done, whether with quill pens, typewriters, or computers. They scan the environment, picking from thousands of news items those that are the most important or that affect the most people. Information is gathered, facts are weighed, and stories are written, packaged, and delivered.

To do this, journalists need the same skills they've always needed. They need to be broadly educated. They need to know about everything because that's what they cover: everything. They need people skills and language skills.

Journalists also need to demonstrate good sense, good judgment, good writing, poise under pressure, and ethical and moral standards. These fundamentals apply whether information is delivered to the audience on line or in the traditional fashion.

The Internet and the technology that accompanies it have created new and different opportunities for journalists, but the standards remain unchanged: Be fair. Get it right. And don't expect the technology to do the journalist's work. As former NBC President Bob Mulholland told a 1995 gathering on the future of communication, "The news does not gather itself."

Not that it ever did. Think for a moment about communication and information in "the old days." If you had lived in colonial America—indeed if you had lived only 50 years ago—you would recognize how far the world has come in journalism and in information processing.

The colonists and Native Americans of the 17th century were information paupers who rarely saw a newspaper. Communication was by letter and word of mouth. In contrast, most people today have access to thousands of information sources—including newspapers, which is how it all began.

Publick Occurrences, Both Foreign and Domestick, **the first attempt at a newspaper published in the American colonies, was suppressed by the British after only one issue.**

America's history is inseparable from the history of its journalism. Early newspapers printed essays that stirred the revolutionaries and that chronicled the historic break from England. Today, journalists still help set the agenda. They help a democratic nation make historic decisions by providing the facts and opinions needed to elect the leaders who decide national policy.

America's First Newspapers

The first American newspapers didn't look like the huge papers you see today. Often they were only one sheet long and contained little of what you think of as news. Letters, essays, and material borrowed from whatever source an editor could find made up the journalistic fare.

The first attempt, *Publick Occurrences,* was published in Boston in 1690 by Benjamin Harris. After only one issue, the British colonial authorities suppressed the paper because they didn't like what Harris printed.

Fourteen years later the colonies had their first continuously published newspaper: the *Boston News-Letter,* started by John Campbell in 1704. It was published "by authority," meaning it had the government's approval. As pioneers moved south and west, more newspapers cropped up. Most carried the "by authority" tag and were closely supervised by the British government.

Establishment of Freedom of the Press

In the early days newspapers that criticized the government were guilty of sedition—the stirring of rebellion. The truth of statements was no defense. The principle then was "The greater the truth, the greater the libel." The government figured that false criticism (which is how libel is defined today) was easier to turn aside than well-founded criticism.

A case in 1735 established truth as a defense against libel charges. In the *New York Weekly Journal* John Peter Zenger printed articles critical of Governor William Cosby. Zenger wrote few of the articles himself, but as the publisher he was arrested on a charge of seditious libel and jailed. The case was considered open and shut. If Zenger printed attacks on the British crown, he was guilty of libel, even if his statements were true.

Andrew Hamilton of Philadelphia, considered by many the finest attorney of the period, defended Zenger. Then in his eighties, Hamilton was still brilliant and forceful. He stunned the crowd when he said: "I do confess (for my client) that he both printed and published the two newspapers set forth in the information. I hope in so doing he has committed no crime."

To the court this seemed in effect a guilty plea, since its only concern was to prove that Zenger was responsible for publishing the articles in question. But Hamilton continued, "I hope it is not our bare printing

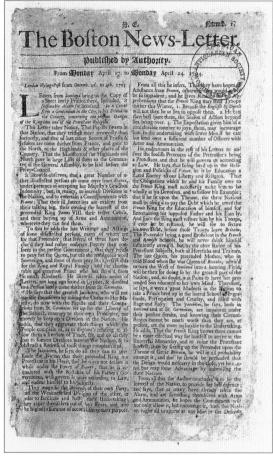

The *Boston News-Letter* has the distinction of being the first continuously published newspaper in the United States.

or publishing a paper that will make it a libel. For the words themselves must be libelous—that is, false, malicious, and seditious—or else we are not guilty."

The judge denied Hamilton the right to prove the facts in the papers, so Hamilton appealed to the jury: "Every man who prefers freedom to a life of slavery will bless and honor you as men who have baffled the attempt of tyranny; and by an impartial and uncorrupt verdict, have laid a noble foundation for securing to ourselves, our posterity, and our neighbors, that to which nature and the laws of our country have given us a right—the liberty both of exposing and opposing arbitrary power (in these parts of the world, at least) by speaking and writing—Truth."

The Crown had not counted on the will of people—in this case represented by the jurors—struggling to be free. They deliberated only briefly before shouting "not guilty," and the celebrations began.

The Birth of the Nation

The Zenger trial, and other instances of press suppression at the time, fanned the flames of freedom that were beginning to burn in the colonies. The colonial press of the day played a vital role in the birth of the nation. By 1775, when the Revolution began, 37 newspapers were being published. These newspapers generally allied themselves with the patriots, at least partly because of their anger over the Stamp Act, which imposed a tax on periodicals. They backed the Revolution and printed the cries to battle that rallied the rebels. Some historians believe that there would not have been a Revolution without the support of the press.

Newspapers then, and for the next century, lined up deliberately with political parties: This was the era of the partisan press. Readers who supported the fight for independence bought a Whig newspaper; those who were loyal to the British Crown bought a Tory paper. (Most papers today try to report political news objectively, although some ally themselves with a particular party on the editorial page.)

QUOTES

worth quoting

Were it left to me to decide whether we should have a government without newspapers or newspapers without a government, I should not hesitate to prefer the latter.

—Thomas Jefferson (1743–1826), U. S. President

When the war ended and the Constitutional Convention met in Philadelphia, the framers did not, as many people believe, spend much time on the question of freedom of the press. The Constitution made no mention of a free press because most state constitutions had already covered the matter. But the Bill of Rights—the first 10 amendments to the Constitution—addressed the issue. The First Amendment, ratified in 1791, guarantees a free press with the words "Congress shall make no law . . . abridging the freedom of speech, or of the press."

After the Revolution the young nation grew rapidly, and so did the newspaper industry. Hundreds of newspapers opened all over the new land. The first daily, the *Pennsylvania Post,* was founded in 1783. The first student newspaper, the *Students Gazette,* was founded even earlier at the Friends Latin School in Pennsylvania, in 1777.

Even small towns had papers. Like those in the big cities, they were published by printers who had to set the type by hand, one letter at a time, and print them on clumsy presses. The Industrial Revolution, however, was at hand, and soon newspapers joined in the never-ending race for better technology.

Student newspapers appeared in the new United States remarkably early. The oldest of these, the *Students Gazette,* published its first issue in 1777. It was handwritten by Quaker students of the Friends Latin School in Pennsylvania.

The Penny Press

Early newspapers carried little actual news. They were filled largely with opinions in the form of essays, letters, and editorials, plus a few advertisements. Then in 1833, Benjamin Day founded the *New York Sun,* filled it with news, and sold it for only a penny. Day's staff covered the police beat, wrote about tragedies and natural disasters, and toned down the opinions. Thus was born the "penny press," probably more truly the forerunner of today's newspapers than either *Publick Occurrences* or the *Boston News-Letter.*

An important publisher during the penny press era, Horace Greeley established the *New York Tribune* in 1841 and advocated many reform causes in its pages.

Because it was so inexpensive and distributed by street sales rather than subscription, the penny press achieved a mass audience, made up primarily of the new working class of the Industrial Revolution.

With such a large audience, advertising took on a major role. (To this day, it's advertising that pays the cost of producing newspapers and getting newscasts on the air.)

Two years later James Gordon Bennett started the *New York Morning Herald.* Although it sold for two cents, it continued the newsy ways of the *Sun.* Similar papers were soon founded in Boston, Baltimore, Philadelphia, and other cities.

One of the most influential penny presses was the *New York Tribune,* founded in 1841 by social reformer Horace Greeley. The *Tribune's* daily circulation never matched that of the *Sun* or the *Herald,* but its weekly edition had 200,000 subscribers—more readers than any other publication of that time.

Since colonial times, women had contributed to the growth and development of American journalism, operating newspapers and print shops. They continued to do so during the expansion of newspapers in the 1800s. Cornelia Walter was editor of the *Boston Transcript* in the 1840s, and in 1850 Jane Grey Swisshelm, who worked for Greeley's *Tribune,* became the first woman to cover Congress.

In cities such as Pittsburgh, Chicago, New Orleans, Atlanta, St. Louis, and Louisville, the penny press grew and prospered. Headlines became larger and designs better as newspapers competed for street sales. By the mid-1800s, it was not at all unusual for a major city such as New York to have eight or nine competing newspapers.

The *New York Times,* which today is considered by many professional journalists the best newspaper in the country, was founded in 1851 by Henry Raymond. From the beginning it set a standard for fairness and accuracy in reporting, a standard that has been widely imitated but rarely equaled. Adolph Ochs bought the paper in 1896. It was he who gave it the motto "All the News That's Fit to Print," which reflects the paper's long-standing attitude to cover legitimate news in a tasteful way.

The Effect of the Telegraph

Newswriting and news coverage began to change in 1861, when reporters at Civil War battle sites made use of the telegraph (invented 18 years before) to transmit their stories. To ensure that the outcome of a battle got into the story in case the telegraph broke down during transmission, reporters became more concise and developed the inverted-pyramid format of writing: giving the most important facts in the first few sentences.

Shortly after the telegraph began to speed the reporting of news, the first news-gathering service was formed: the Harbor News Association. This service, a forerunner of the Associated Press, began selling news to client papers in 1849. Other such wire services, including United Press International, soon sprang up. By 1910 there were 2,600 daily newspapers in the United States; some of them had bureaus in the nation's capital and around the world. The information explosion was beginning.

Yellow Journalism

The late 19th century saw an era most journalists would rather forget: the age of "yellow journalism." The term refers to an unethical, irresponsible brand of journalism involving hoaxes, altered photographs, screaming headlines, "scoops," frauds, and endless self-promotions by the papers. *Yellow journalism* derives from the name of the Yellow Kid, a cartoon character that appeared in the *Sunday World* during the 1890s.

The most notable of the yellow journalists were William Randolph Hearst, publisher of the *New York Journal,* and Joseph Pulitzer, publisher of the *New York World.* Like their predecessors, the "penny press," these newspapers attracted huge audiences, and their competition for readers, advertisers, and each others' most talented writers was fierce. Color

HISTORY worth remembering

Pulitzer and Hearst. The names of yellow journalists Joseph Pulitzer and William Randolph Hearst are today still known in association with newspapers, but also with journalism education and awards. Pulitzer founded the Columbia School of Journalism, the first of its kind, and endowed the Pulitzer Prizes, awarded annually for excellence in specific areas of journalism, literature, and music. The Hearst Foundation makes a valuable contribution to journalism education through newswriting, broadcasting, and photography contests for college journalism students.

supplements, numerous illustrations, cartoon strips, and dramatic coverage of wars and sporting events sent the papers' circulations soaring.

Nellie Bly

The period was perfect for the circulation-building exploits of Nellie Bly, the name used by Elizabeth Cochrane, the most famous of the women journalists beginning to make names for themselves. Bly worked for Pulitzer's *World* and was noted for her "stunts," stories in which she made the news herself. Once she pretended to be mentally ill and was committed to New York's Blackwell Island Asylum. When she was released after 10 days, she wrote a story exposing the asylum's poor conditions. The story sparked reform around the country.

Bly's most famous story was about her trip around the world. A book of that period, Jules Verne's *Around the World in Eighty Days,* was very popular. Bly set out to circle the globe in fewer than 80 days, and as readers everywhere followed her adventures, she did it—in 72 days.

Spanish-American War

During the yellow journalism period a movement began in Cuba to seek independence from Spain. Beginning in 1895, the *World* and the *Journal* whipped up a war climate in support of the Cuban nationalists and tried to lure the United States into the conflict. One famous story of the time was about a *Journal* artist in Cuba who cabled Hearst that there was no war and he was coming home. Hearst is said to have wired back, "Please remain. You furnish the pictures, and I'll furnish the war."

Newspaper reporter Nellie Bly, working for the *New York World*, was willing to travel anywhere to get— or create—a story.

$50,000 REWARD.—WHO DESTROYED THE MAINE?—$50,000 REWARD.

EDITION FOR GREATER NEW YORK

NEW YORK JOURNAL

AND ADVERTISER.

NO. 5,572.   Copyright, 1898, by W. R. Hearst.—NEW YORK, THURSDAY, FEBRUARY 17, 1898.—16 PAGES.   PRICE ONE CENT in Greater New York and Jersey City. Two Cents Elsewhere

DESTRUCTION OF THE WAR SHIP MAINE WAS THE WORK OF AN ENEMY.

$50,000!

$50,000 REWARD!
For the Detection of the Perpetrator of the Maine Outrage!

Assistant Secretary Roosevelt Convinced the Explosion of the War Ship Was Not an Accident.

The Journal Offers $50,000 Reward for the

$50,000!

$50,000 REWARD!
For the Detection of the Perpetrator of the Maine Outrage!

When the battleship U.S.S. *Maine* blew up in Havana harbor in 1898, the Hearst paper featured a huge illustration and this headline: DESTRUCTION OF THE WAR SHIP MAINE WAS THE WORK OF AN ENEMY. Congress demanded that Spain leave the island, and war resulted. While the press was not solely to blame for the Spanish-American War, the yellow journalism of the time certainly contributed to an atmosphere of suspicion and conflict.

Yellow journalism reached its peak during the late 1800s. The headline on this paper exploited the sinking of the battleship U.S.S. *Maine* and whipped up public sentiment to go to war.

Muckraking

The end of yellow journalism ushered in a period during which American newspapers developed a significant social consciousness. Many papers crusaded for child-labor laws, promoted hospitals and tuberculosis sanitariums, collected money for the needy, and exposed public graft. Critics of the crusading journalists called them *muckrakers*, a term coined by Theodore Roosevelt, which the reformers came to think of as a term of praise.

A new medium came into its own during the late 19th and early 20th centuries: the magazine. Such publications as *McClure's, Collier's, Munsey's,* and the *Saturday Evening Post* joined the fight for social justice that the newspapers had initiated. They had circulations in the hundreds of thousands, and they battled corruption in all of its forms. Patent medicine companies, child labor, the status of African Americans, and the meat-packing industry all came under scrutiny. The Pure Food and Drugs Act of 1906 grew out of the crusades, as did many other reforms. Ida Tarbell's series on "The History of the Standard Oil Company" in *McClure's* was one of the first attacks on big business. Her investigative reporting put John D. Rockefeller, Standard Oil's president, on the defensive for years to come.

The Development of Minority Media

As founder of the *Chicago Defender*, Robert S. Abbott was the first to give African Americans a public forum for addressing civil rights and other issues.

As the nation progressed, minority groups began taking on important roles in American journalism. The *Chicago Defender,* one of the nation's largest and most influential African-American newspapers, was founded in 1905 by Robert S. Abbott, whose parents had been slaves. The *Defender* took the lead in encouraging Southern blacks to move to the North in search of better jobs in that region's growing industries. The *Defender* became a daily in 1956 under Abbott's nephew, John H. Sengstacke, who built a large chain of African-American newspapers.

African-American magazines, too, have prospered. One of the most famous, *Ebony,* has been in circulation since 1945. *Essence* and *Black Enterprise,* though newer, exhibit similar staying power; and on television, the Black Entertainment Network has also made its presence felt.

Hispanic media have taken their place on the American media scene as well. Two of the largest Hispanic-American newspapers are *El Diario–La Prensa* in New York City and *Diario Los Americas* in Miami. Hispanic-American papers are also published in Washington, D.C., San Francisco, Dallas, Houston, Los Angeles, Chicago, and many other cities. One of the highest-rated FM stations in Los Angeles is Spanish-language KLVE; and *Hispanic Online,* the electronic version of *Hispanic Magazine,* can be found on the Internet.

The first Native-American newspaper was the *Cherokee Phoenix,* which appeared in 1828. It was shut down by the government five years later for publishing ideas seen as antigovernment. Today the independent (from tribal control) *Lakota Times* is perhaps the most prominent

Native-American newspaper; and its publisher, Tim Giago, is probably the most prominent Native-American journalist. Giago also publishes *Indian Country Today* in Rapid City, South Dakota.

Asian-American interests are covered by such publications as *Sampan* in Boston, the *Filipino Reporter* in New York City, *Pacific Citizen* in Los Angeles, and *Korea Times* in Chicago—as well as by many smaller papers around the nation.

News-industry leaders place great emphasis on attracting minorities to news work. The National Association of Hispanic Journalists, Native American Journalists Association, National Association of Black Journalists, Asian American Journalists Association, and similar groups are active in the cause of diversifying newsrooms. Additionally, many colleges and universities offer special job fairs and scholarships designed to make young people aware of journalism opportunities. These practices not only open career doors; they improve the sensitivity of news organizations covering stories involving ethnic issues.

MEDIA worth mentioning

The top five. The five largest newspapers, in terms of circulation, in the United States today are the following:

The Wall Street Journal

USA Today

The New York Times

The Los Angeles Times

The Washington Post

All but the *Washington Post* have daily circulations of more than one million.

The Advent of Radio

At the turn of the century, a development was looming that would change the nature of the news—and of the world—forever. In 1906 Dr. Lee De Forest made improvements in the vacuum tube that made possible the new medium of radio. Although no one person invented radio, De Forest's vacuum tube was the key breakthrough.

De Forest made the first newscast in 1916, when he broadcast presidential election returns over a limited area. Regular daily programs started in Detroit in 1920. That same year station KDKA in Pittsburgh, Pennsylvania, broadcast the Harding-Cox presidential election returns of 1920, considered a milestone in radio journalism.

Radio brought many American families together in the 1930s and 1940s through its mix of comedy, sports, and news.

The National Broadcasting Company (NBC) was formed in 1926 and the Columbia Broadcasting System (CBS) in 1927. The Mutual Broadcasting System went on the air in 1934, and when part of NBC's network was sold in 1945, it was renamed the American Broadcasting Company (ABC).

It soon became clear that the airwaves, which legally belong to the public, had to be regulated. Stations were saturating them and interfering with each other's broadcasts. In 1912 a law was passed that empowered the Department of Commerce to assign wavelengths to license applicants. The Radio Act of 1927 broadened this power and created the Federal Radio Commission. This was the forerunner of today's Federal Communications Commission (FCC), which has jurisdiction—though not censorship power—over both radio and television.

Radio fascinated the American public in the 1920s, 1930s, and 1940s. Comedians such as Jack Benny, Bob Hope, and Fred Allen drew huge audiences, and sporting events such as football and baseball became widely accessible. Today, more than 500 million radios are in use. In the United States alone there are about 5,000 AM stations and almost as many FM stations.

Shock Jocks and Radio Talk Shows

Radio still occupies an important place among the media. Most stations play music mixed with news, and millions of Americans get their first word of major news events from radio as they drive to or from work or school. In the 1990s, though, radio took an unusual turn. So-called shock jocks and call-in talk shows began to dominate the air waves, especially on AM radio. Shock jocks—Howard Stern is one of the best known—make careers out of being insulting and outrageous, saying whatever comes to their minds, apparently in the hope that their comments will offend.

Radio talk shows also have wide appeal—and stir wide controversy. Millions have tuned in to such outspoken conservative hosts as G. Gordon Liddy, a convicted Watergate figure, and commentator Rush Limbaugh. Some people find their criticism of the country's leaders and other high-ranking officials disrespectful and offensive. Others argue that their outspokeness is in the finest tradition of American irreverence toward its leaders.

It's important to distinguish legitimate journalism from the work of shock jocks and radio talk-show hosts. Journalism is devoted to providing accurate, objective, untainted information that the public can use personally in decision making, particularly political decision making. Part of the role of the journalist is to entertain, of course, but that is the exclusive aim of the jocks and hosts. They're not journalists; they're entertainers. They stimulate conversation and debate, and that's good, but what they say should be taken with a grain of salt.

The Impact of Television

The first television newscast took place in the late 1940s. Early television pictures were snowy, and transmission facilities were erratic. Both color and sound quickly improved. By the mid-1960s, more than 60 million TV sets were in use. Thirty years later, the number exceeded 90 million.

Television dramatically changed radio and newspapers. It took much of the entertainment role away from radio and claimed much of the spot-news, or breaking-news, role traditionally held by newspapers. Today newspapers deemphasize breaking news; it makes no sense for a newspaper to announce dramatically that an event occurred when most readers probably saw an account of it hours earlier on television. Modern newspapers

Information in Wartime

Should news coverage be censored in periods of war?

The relationship among the press, the public, and the government in periods of war has varied, depending on the times and public sentiment. By the late 1800s newspapers such as the *New York Journal* were not above creating stories to incite the public and so help force the government into conflict, as in the Spanish American War. In the 20th century the media developed ways to gain quicker, more accurate, access to wartime information. The government's reactions to having that information made public seemed to vary from war to war.

During the Vietnam War telejournalists brought graphic news of the war from the frontlines to the homefront almost immediately.

During World Wars I and II, the press and the government enjoyed generally friendly relations. World War II, in particular, regarded by many Americans as "the good war," had widespread support, and war correspondents such as Ernie Pyle became public heroes. Radio came into its own during this war, when President Franklin D. Roosevelt used the medium not only to pass along selected battle information but to exhort the public to cooperation and steadfastness.

In both world wars, information and images transmitted from the battlefield were carefully censored. Most noncombatants remained unaware of the brutality and horror of war.

The widespread availability of television in the 1960s had a great influence on the public perception of war. During the Vietnam War, for the first time, correspondents going into battle areas had their stories conveyed to the public almost immediately. If an ambush occurred, the correspondent could tape and record it as it happened. If soldiers were carried back from the battlefield bloody and bandaged, or even dead, the public could see that too. Television brought the horror of war home, often in living color.

Largely because of its effect on public sentiment, unrestricted wartime coverage essentially ceased after Vietnam.

In October 1983, when U.S. forces invaded the island of Grenada, no reporters were allowed on the island for two days after the invasion. This was the first time in U.S. history that journalists were not permitted to accompany soldiers into battle zones. Press restrictions were felt again in 1991 when combined U.S. and U.N. forces went to war with Iraq. During this so-called Gulf War, journalists were allowed limited access to combatants and sensed that they were receiving incomplete information from official sources.

In 1999 the trend changed a bit. In building acceptance for its action against the Serbs in Kosovo, the government again encouraged the press to convey the full horror of war. Images of atrocities committed against the Muslim population, including views of mass graves and grieving families, helped convince the public that military intervention was necessary.

As the 21st century begins, it appears that the government's position on wartime coverage will fluctuate depending on circumstances. Both the government and the media now recognize that even one strong wartime image can vastly influence public opinion. When and how both sides will use this information remains to be seen.

FOLLOW-UP

1. Find and interview someone who recalls watching television reports on the Vietnam War. How did the reporting affect their feelings about the war? What news stories do they remember as specifically influencing them?
2. Graphic images telecast from Somalia in the fall of 1993 effectively ended U.S. involvement in the conflict in the area. What exactly was broadcast, and what were the repercussions?

put more emphasis on examining the background of current news events and covering trends and lifestyles in depth.

In the 1930s President Franklin Roosevelt reached the American people through radio with his fireside chats. Today's presidents come to us in color through live news conferences, and presidential candidates debate each other as the voters watch. Press conferences also give the public a close-up look at news reporters in action.

During a major news event such as the impeachment of President Bill Clinton in 1998, the nation stopped to watch television. Competitions such as the Olympic Games are viewed simultaneously around the world. Communications philosopher Marshall McLuhan called this phenomenon the "global village."

Today the traditional major television networks—ABC, CBS, and NBC—have seen their audiences fragmented by the growth of other programming. The new networks include Cable News Network (CNN), an around-the-clock news service that is often first with breaking news; Fox, which scored a coup when it acquired the rights to NFL football telecasts; C-Span, which provides gavel-to-gavel coverage of many government and related public-affairs meetings and conferences; and MSNBC, which appears on cable and the Internet. Most U.S. cities also receive good programming through Public Broadcasting Service (PBS) stations, although periodic cuts in government support are a threat to that programming. Additionally, the hundreds of cable TV stations provide alternatives to the networks by broadcasting shows that appeal to smaller, more specific audiences.

Sensationalism on TV

In some ways television, like radio, reverted in the 1990s to yellow journalism practices of 100 years ago. Daytime talk shows featuring dysfunctional guests with unconventional relationships and lifestyles helped revive the sensational practices of the past. So, too, did some network television shows with the look and feel of news documentaries that actually focused mainly on the exploits of the rich and famous. Serious news became hard to find. "If it bleeds, it leads" expressed the unspoken philosophy of many local television news shows. A careful look would reveal that even traditional newspapers and magazines began running more "trash" news at the expense of serious news.

Yet as the new century begins, there is reason to hope. Interest in sensational programming seems to be waning. Television may present saturation coverage of the 1999 Littleton, Colorado, high school shootings, but it also promotes serious discussion of changes needed to prevent such events. Always sensitive to criticism (and the possibility of lower ratings), television news seems to be examining its practices as never before.

The Effects of Technology

The Internet was the last great media advance of the 20th century. It has made the transmission of information both amazingly quick and exceedingly efficient.

The Internet began to develop in the 1960s, as scientists at research institutions all over the world constructed independent computer networks that could convey information in the event of a nuclear holocaust. The Net came into popular use in the early 1990s, when commercial services such as CompuServe, Prodigy, and America Online made access to it available to anyone with a computer and a modem. The development of the graphical World Wide Web browser allowed users to access the Internet by categorizing much of the information on it, and computer programs like Mosaic, Microsoft Internet Explorer, and Netscape Navigator made surfing the Net not only popular but downright easy.

An Internet user can send a message virtually instantaneously to thousands of people all over the world by using mailing lists, or can chat via modem in real time with people everywhere. Material can be read and downloaded at the stroke of a key.

News on the Net

The news is "up there" too. The development of hypertext links, or easy ways to make connections from one article to another, allows access to newspapers, magazines, government reports, census data, texts of presidential speeches—literally millions and millions of words, pictures, and sounds about everything under the sun. Not surprisingly, this vast array of information includes high school and college on-line publications.

The Internet has changed the ways news is presented and read. For example, it has freed print journalists from the constraint of space. In traditional newswriting, stories are brief because space is limited. There's no shortage of space in cyberspace, however, so sometimes stories get too long (and some are worthless). News stories used to be simply linear—that is, read from beginning to end. Today readers may continue until they find a link that interests them, at which point they leave the original story and go surfing for related information. A click of a key returns them to the original document.

On-line publications offer, in addition to traditional news, links to restaurant reviews, travel tips, e-mail addresses of columnists and editorial writers so readers can provide instant feedback, and even community forums where readers can debate and discuss ideas—just as in the old days of town meetings. School newspapers are getting on line too, as evidenced by the sample in the following **ON DISPLAY** feature.

ON DISPLAY

On-Line Student Newspaper

Inklings, Staples High School, Westport, Connecticut

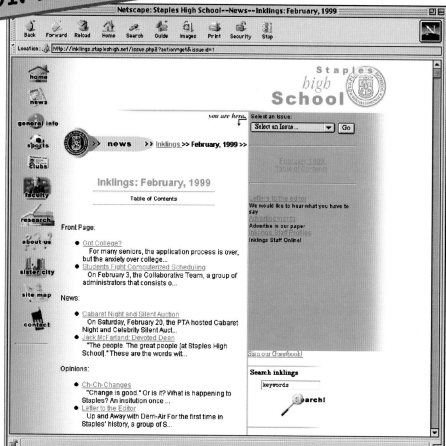

On-line newspapers, such as this student paper, offer interactive capacity and may reach a broader audience than traditional paper copies can.

Computer-Assisted Reporting

Computers have led to another change in journalism. It's called computer-assisted reporting, and it's a valuable new tool for digging out complicated information in a hurry.

It works this way: Suppose a reporter wants to check police performance in responding to calls for help. Maybe the hunch is that police respond more quickly to calls from affluent neighborhoods than from poor ones. The reporter could pore over hundreds of paper records to dig out information, but he or she could also access the police database and probably find the answer in minutes.

Databases all over the world are accessible to journalists. Government agencies make information available on crops, educational trends, health threats, crime, and a host of other issues. Private agencies and foundations provide other reliable data. Electronic bulletin boards on various topics convey not only information but also a sense of how users feel about it. Listservs bring together people who are interested in the same subject, including many high school and college journalists. Because anyone can publish on the Net, journalists have learned to be selective and verify the reliability of the sources.

Although a great deal of information can be accessed on line, it's not clear where the future of newspapers lies in providing information in this way. Newspapers on line find it difficult to turn a profit. One thing is certain: It's not sufficient just to dump the newspaper into cyberspace. That may have a satisfying and modern feeling to it, but it's difficult to see how readers are served any better than in the old, traditional way (although trees are saved, and that's important too). No, the on-line publication is just a start.

Journalism Today

Only a little more than a generation ago, it was common for families to subscribe to two newspapers a day, one in the morning and one in the evening. (Today only 46 American cities have two newspapers.) Whole families spent large parts of their day reading newspapers. People today, however, don't buy and read newspapers in the same numbers as their parents did, a development that has leaders in journalism alarmed. To interest younger readers, in particular, they are responding with special youth pages; with more stories and features that appeal to a younger audience; and with a program called "Newspapers in Education," in which many newspapers provide discounted copies and special services to schools and journalism educators. They are also striving to make newspapers more appealing—with charts, graphics, and color illustrations—to a visually oriented population.

The efforts are paying off. The number of young people reading newspapers and watching television newscasts is rising steadily. Among 18- to 24-year-olds, 52 percent read a daily newspaper and 62 percent read a Sunday paper. About 60 million newspapers are sold every day—and 2.29 people read each paper. Newspapers continue to lure more advertising dollars than any other medium, and they lead all media in providing on-line services.

It's important that the audience keep up with the news; a less-informed electorate combined with a media trend away from reporting on government and toward less serious news creates a potentially alarming situation. Good citizens should keep abreast of the news . . . and journalism students *must* do so.

Today, students are flocking in record numbers to the schools and departments of journalism on college and university campuses. Some of the very best minds are being educated for journalism careers. The job market is crowded but not impossible, and journalism educators remain confident that jobs will always be there for students who are well-educated and enthusiastic. The future of American journalism rests in the hands of people like you.

The reporters of tomorrow are being trained in high school and college journalism classes today.

Wrap-up

The dawn of the Information Age has changed the world and journalism dramatically. Millions of people are connected to each other via the Internet. Information on virtually every topic is readily available. Journalism will be affected, but the basic skills and attitudes journalists need to do their jobs will not change.

The Internet is the latest in a series of important changes in communication. Over the past 50 years the processing of information has speeded up to the point that important events are known around the world within minutes of their happening. By comparison, the people who lived in colonial America were information paupers.

The history of journalism in America cannot be separated from the history of the country. The first American newspaper, *Publick Occurrences,* was suppressed after only a single issue in 1690 because the British authorities disapproved of it. In 1735 the authorities tried to suppress John Peter Zenger's *New York Weekly Journal* because of its criticism of the government. A jury acquitted Zenger, finding that truth, not government approval, was the standard for publication.

The press was instrumental in the colonial drive for independence from England, and the First Amendment to the Constitution of the new country guaranteed freedom of the press.

In the 1800s newspapers began to devote more space to events and less to opinion and, because they cost only about a penny each, newspapers became immensely popular. The mass audience attracted more advertisers.

Technology, in the form of the telegraph, accelerated the transmission of news during the Civil War and led eventually to the establishment of news wire services such as the Associated Press.

The close of the 19th century saw the era of "yellow journalism," sensational stories and screaming headlines aimed at boosting circulation. Joseph Pulitzer's *New York World* and William Randolph Hearst's *New York Journal* helped incite the Spanish-American War and prompt the U.S. invasion of Cuba.

Gradually, sensationalism gave way to reform. Magazines such as *Collier's* and the *Saturday Evening Post* tried, often successfully, to better society and its institutions.

The improvement of the vacuum tube in 1906 led to the development of radio, the founding of the networks, and the creation of an instant news source for the American public. Television added pictures to sound, and a new medium was born.

Because of television, newspapers figure less prominently in the lives of students than they once did; however, this appears to be changing. Young people are returning to the printed page, and this encourages journalistic leaders. They know that the responsibilities of citizenship, of keeping fully informed, require a deeper understanding than TV alone can provide.

The Internet is a rich new source of information. Hundreds of newspapers—including school papers—are on line, along with every other type of information, all available at a keystroke. Reporters using databases for their research have created a whole new category of reporting, computer-assisted reporting, a major development in news gathering.

On Assignment

INDIVIDUAL ACTIVITIES

1. Write a brief definition of each of these terms:

computer-assisted reporting	penny press
global village	shock jock
muckraking	wire service
partisan press	yellow journalism

2. From this list of journalists associated with early newspapers in America, select two. Write a brief biography of each and discuss his or her role in the history of journalism.

Robert S. Abbott	Margaret Fuller
James Gordon Bennett	Benjamin Harris
Nellie Bly	Jane Grey Swisshelm
Benjamin Day	Cornelia Walter
Benjamin Franklin	Ida B. Wells

3. From this list of 20th century journalists, select three. Write a brief biography of each and discuss his or her role in the history of journalism.

Carl Bernstein	Molly Ivins
Margaret Bourke-White	Marshall McLuhan
David Brinkley	Edward R. Murrow
Christine Craft	John Quiñones
Katharine Graham	Gloria Steinem
Bryant Gumbel	Helen Thomas
Bill Hosokawa	Walter Winchell

4. Research the history of a newspaper in your area. Find out who founded the paper and when. Was it ever affiliated with a political party? Who owns the paper? Write a summary of your findings.

5. Research the history of a radio or television station in your area. Use the same questions as in activity 4. Write a summary of what you find out.

6. The following newspapers have interesting histories. Choose one and do some research into its background. Write a brief report on what makes it interesting.

The Philadelphia Inquirer
The Des Moines Register
Chicago Defender
Berkeley Barb
Milwaukee Journal Sentinel
USA Today
Alton (Illinois) *Observer*
The Wall Street Journal
Lakota Times (Indian Country Today)
The Tombstone (Arizona) *Epitaph*

7. Research the development of cartoon strips in American newspapers. Who produced the first one? Which newspaper carried it? Write an account of your findings.

8. Test your critical thinking. Take either side of the following question and write an essay: Should the American press be restricted by the government? Consider these related questions:
   a. If it should be restricted, who decides what the restrictions would be?
   b. What would the penalty be for violating the restrictions?
   c. Would such restrictions change the nature of American life? How?
   d. Are such changes good or bad? Why?
   e. Television is to some extent a controlled industry. Is that good or bad? Why?

TEAM ACTIVITY

9. Work with a team of three or four classmates. Each of you is to interview two or three students in your school to get answers to the following questions. Choose students from all different grade levels.

   a. What newspapers, if any, do you read? Which newspapers do members of your family read?

   b. Which news programs, including specials, have you watched recently?

   c. Where do you get your information about world and local events?

   d. Do you use the Internet? If so, what do you use it for primarily?

   e. How well informed about what's going on in the world would you say you are?

    Compile the information from all team members and summarize it in a report. If you wish, use graphs to clarify points. Compare your results with those of other teams in a class discussion.

SURF THE NET

10. How different are newspapers' print stories from those they run on the Internet? Choose a good-sized paper with a web site, and find two or three stories that appear in both the print and on-line editions. What similarities and differences exist in the coverage? in the writing style? What might account for the differences? Present your findings and conclusions to the class.

career profile

Journalism Professor and Critic

en Bagdikian began his newspaper career by chance. A chemistry major in college, he was on his way to a job interview in Springfield, Massachusetts, when he passed the *Springfield Morning Union* newspaper office and noticed a "Help Wanted" sign in the window.

"I wasn't crazy about chemistry anyway, so I went in and asked about the reporter job," he said. Bagdikian got the job, and this changed the course of his life.

"I loved it right away," he said. "It's a kind of license to look into all parts of society. Reporters are given access to people and circumstances most people never see, from the poor, drunk, and thieves to the governor."

Bagdikian went to work for the *Providence* (Rhode Island) *Journal and Evening Bulletin,* the *Washington Post,* and the *Columbia Journalism Review* before becoming a journalism professor at the University of California at Berkeley Graduate School of Journalism. He taught from 1977 to 1990 and was dean of the graduate school from 1985 to 1988.

He has been project director for the Mass Media Technology Study by Rand, project director for the Markle Foundation's Newspaper Survival Study, and president of the Mallett Fund for a Free and Responsible Press. Bagdikian has also written several books and received numerous honors, including the George Foster Peabody Award, the Sigma Delta Chi National Journalism Award, and a citation of merit from the American Society of Journalism School

Ben Bagdikian

Administrators as "journalism's most perceptive critic."

Bagdikian believes that the media need to do a better job. Most of the media, he says, are aimed at the middle class, depriving other socioeconomic sectors of the population systematic coverage of issues that affect their lives.

"The media are the only view that most people have of issues and events that citizens need to decide on," Bagdikian said. "The media have to do a better job to make sure the citizens get all the information they need to make informed decisions."

The media's role is more important today than it's ever been, Bagdikian believes.

"Life was not as complicated 50 years ago as it is now," he said. "People didn't have to make the decisions then that they have to make now. Most people only had

to make one career choice and lived in one town their whole life. But the whole world changed after World War II and there is so much going on now that people have to know about. The media are better today than they were 50 years ago, but they still fall short of what the citizens need."

Being a member of the press demands a responsibility for fairness, thoroughness, and accuracy, he said. The public places a trust in the media that cannot be betrayed.

"Getting the story means getting it right, complete, and fair," he said. "It does not mean getting a sexy quote or a sound bite."

Journalism is not an exotic profession, he said. "If you're looking for a trench coat and a job that's filled with romance, forget it," he said.

Nonetheless, to students considering journalism Bagdikian asks the following question: "Do you really care about how your communities work? Because if you don't really care, you shouldn't go into journalism."

FOLLOW-UP

1. Do you agree with Bagdikian that most media are aimed at the middle class? Bring in specific examples from newspapers, radio, and television to support your opinion.
2. How might the media do a better job of helping the public make what Bagdikian calls "informed decisions"? Present your ideas in a class discussion.

CHAPTER 2

Meeting Ethical and Legal Responsibilities

KEY CONCEPTS

After reading this chapter, you will

▶ understand the functions the media must fulfill in modern society

▶ know criteria to evaluate the performance of the various media

▶ understand the ethical principles of journalism

▶ recognize some of the major criticisms of the press

▶ understand libel laws and what defenses journalists have

▶ be familiar with major court rulings regarding the scholastic press

The *Columbia Journalism Review (CJR)*, produced at Columbia University in New York City, is a highly regarded publication devoted to covering the press. In December 1995, Joan Konner, then publisher of *CJR*, wrote the following:

One of the most awesome changes of our time is the increase in the power and pervasiveness of the news media. That's why the question of standards is so important. Around the world there is growing public concern about the performance and behavior of the news media. The bottom line is that the public no longer trusts us. And for journalism, that is critical. Trust is our most important product.

Konner is right. Journalists increasingly find themselves under a public microscope, their motives and sometimes even their morals questioned. Poll results vary, but by and large it's true that what used to be a

ethics	credibility	objectivity	slander	fair comment	KEY TERMS
"composite characters"	libel	right of reply	privileged statements	*in loco parentis*	
	prior restraint	plagiarism		forum theory	

Being well-informed about the news is essential to many people. Vast numbers start their day by reading a paper.

healthy relationship with the audience ("If you see it in the newspaper it must be true") has deteriorated. Trust has been lost.

Increasingly, journalists are viewed by many people as rude, arrogant, uncaring individuals who think only about "getting the story." People object to intrusive behavior by journalists—for example, taking photographs of people during grief-sticken moments. Such behavior probably is not as common as people may believe—but it happens more than journalists like to talk about.

Preoccupation with the trivial or the bizarre, insensitivity to minority groups or issues, bias, and flagrant inaccuracies—the criticism is widespread.

The media are also criticized for their size, especially large media chains that own newspapers, TV networks, magazines, and radio stations. These media conglomerates are seen as pervasive and powerful.

Some criticism is well deserved—and taken seriously by journalists. Some is misplaced. Scandal, crime, rapid social change—this turbulence is the daily fare of consumers of the mass media. Journalists are at the center of these events; they carry the message and often bear the brunt of the frustrations such messages arouse.

The public bears some responsibility, too. Americans criticize what some consider excessive coverage of sensational or tragic events—such as the death of John F. Kennedy, Jr., in 1999—but they tune in to such coverage by the millions. Similarly, many Americans criticize those elements of the press that demonstrate a disturbing return to old-time sensational journalism—while regularly watching the very shows and buying the very publications they criticize.

As a citizen, you can become a more discerning consumer of news. As a journalist, you can work to ensure that you properly use the power a free society entrusts to you.

The Functions of a Journalist

There are ways to determine how well journalists do their jobs. Traditionally, journalists in a free society are charged with the following responsibilities or functions.

The Political Function

Freedom always carries with it certain responsibilities; the guarantee of a free press carries the obligation of providing the audience with information upon which to base political decisions. Thus, the press (by which we mean radio, television, newspapers, magazines, and all other news-gathering and disseminating agencies, including the Internet) is regarded as the watchdog of government.

A news organization doing its job properly will cover in detail the activities of government. It will fight attempts by the government to do the public's business behind closed doors. It will watch for scandal and wrongdoing. It will scrutinize budgets and programs to see if the public's tax money is being spent properly. This function is the foremost of the press's responsibilities.

Unfortunately, there has been a noticeable decline in press coverage of government. So-called soft news (features, "news you can use") dominates many newscasts and newspapers.

The Economic Function

The public needs information about products, goods, and services in addition to events. Business, industrial, and agriculture news conveys this information, but so does advertising. Although much maligned by consumers, advertising pays the bills. Without it, there would be no independent newspapers or broadcasts to convey other information.

Advertising often is criticized for being in bad taste, and some of it is. You might, for example, find a commercial for a laxative offensive, but the presentation probably is not. The big question about advertising is this: Can advertising techniques be used to sell ideas as well as automobiles? To put it another way, Can advertising cause people to buy something they don't need or to vote for one candidate rather than another? Despite disagreement, most people subscribe to the "limited effects" notion of mass media. That is, consumers have psychological defenses through which they resist and mold messages from the mass media, including political and product advertising, to fit their own needs. Consumers are neither children, unable to understand a commercial, nor zombies, powerless to resist.

The Sentry Function

The press watches society's horizons. What is peeking over the horizon to challenge us tomorrow? Issues of brutality on the part of some police, the insurance and health needs of an aging population, and hate groups on the Internet all became public knowledge because the press brought them to people's attention. In other words, the press must report not only what is happening today but also what is likely to happen tomorrow.

In its sentry function, the media's responsibility is to keep the public informed of current and upcoming problems. The rise in homelessness beginning in the 1980s, for example, was brought to many people's attention through the media.

When the United States became involved in the social and political difficulties of Central America in the 1980s, many experts thought the press had failed in its duties as a sentry. They believed that journalists who lacked understanding of the region's culture, history, politics, and economics had not alerted the nation to the true extent of the problems there. On the other hand, in pointing out environmental threats, the press did better in the 1990s.

The Record-Keeping Function

The mass media should reflect an accurate record of local, national, and world news. Who was elected to the school board? What bills passed Congress? What happened to the price of oil? Who died? Who won and lost in sports? Who filed for bankruptcy? This function, too, is basic. The journalism of big headlines and splashy news programs depends on the underpinning of record keeping. Consumers need to know many basic things, including the data often found tucked away in the back of the paper.

The Entertainment Function

Mass media consumers need diversion as well as information. The comics, entertaining feature stories, and feature photos help meet this need. The business of the press is serious, of course, but the audience is made up of people of all ages and interests. Few newscasts or newspapers should be without an entertaining or light element.

The Social Function

In times long past, people got their news from their neighbors on a person-to-person basis. Passing along the news created a social situation in which people discussed their world. Today the mass media perform this function. "Did you read about the new civic center in the *Tribune* yesterday?" is a reflection of the social function.

The Marketplace Function

The press provides the forum in which all sorts of ideas are presented; it becomes the marketplace of ideas. If the audience is concerned about the environment and conveys this concern through the press, perhaps something will be done. If citizens don't want their trees cut down for a street-widening project, they turn to the forum of the mass media to generate support. Thus, a city's agenda is reviewed: Do we want wider streets for more efficient moving of traffic, or do we want the trees to remain and the automobile's dominance of our lives to be curtailed?

The Agenda-Setting Function

Scholars of the media have added another function to the list: the agenda-setting function. Although journalists don't tell us what to think, they do tell us what to think about. This concept suggests that far from dictating our thoughts—a power once attributed to the mass media— the media have the power to determine what we talk about as individuals and address as a nation. If the media place environmental issues on the agenda, people will begin to pay more attention to those issues.

It's almost impossible to isolate the effects of the mass media, because certain causes are too complex to trace. In a drought, for example, the media may emphasize that responsible citizens conserve water. Water usage may drop. No one will know, however, exactly what is cause and what is effect.

Here's another provoking question: Who sets the agenda for the mass media? Can the government place an item on the media's agenda (the war on drugs, perhaps) and then have the media place it before the public?

The media sometimes use their agenda-setting function to place certain issues, such as the need to protect the environment, before the public.

Evaluating the Media

How well is the press performing its agreed-upon functions? No one can read every newspaper and magazine; no one can listen to every radio and television newscast. You can, however, monitor your own news agencies. Try this system of evaluation.

Evaluating the media in your city or community can make you aware of how well they perform their various functions.

Newspapers

Study your local newspaper. Is it choked with self-seeking news releases sent to the media by publicity departments of various organizations? Are local issues and problems, as well as local government, covered thoroughly? Does the editorial page contain a lively and readable forum through a letters-to-the-editor column? Is an occasional longer and more thoughtful letter published with special prominence? Do the editorials treat local issues, candidates, and problems, or do they comment only on national and international issues? Do the sportswriters cover the sports scene with probing stories and questions, or are they cheerleaders for the athletic programs? Are "minor" sports covered? Are the same people in the paper every day, with little coverage of minority or low-income groups? Does the paper have in-depth or investigative stories? How much space is devoted to stories of crime and violence? How much is devoted to trivia: bridge columns, advice columns, and the like?

Radio

Listen to your local radio station or stations. Is the news mostly noisy bulletins and yesterday's stories culled from a newspaper? If the city faces a storm emergency or national disaster, does the station provide continuous, up-to-the-minute information? Are the news reporters real journalists, or do they just read wire-service reports? Is the amount of sports reporting excessive? Are there special programs centered on critical local issues? Are in-depth interviews ever aired? Do all talk shows represent just one side of the political spectrum? Is a forum provided for opposing viewpoints?

Television

Watch your local television newscasts. How much of a 30-minute newscast is devoted to commercials? How much local news is presented? How much sports? How much weather? Does the station use its newscast to entertain you or to inform you? Do the anchors and reporters devote precious minutes to inane chatter? Are there any in-depth or investigative stories? How much time is devoted to such trivia as shopping-center promotions, key-to-the-city presentations, and parades? Do the stations save their best—or most preposterous—stories for ratings-sweeps periods?

Magazines

The big-circulation, general-interest magazine is a thing of the past. *Life, Collier's, Redbook, Look*—names out of journalism history—folded or dramatically changed their formats. Except for the news magazines *Time, Newsweek,* and *U.S. News & World Report,* today's magazine is apt to appeal to a narrow, special interest. Magazines abound for every hobby and line of work, from coin collecting to journalism (*Quill,* for example). Judging their performance requires special expertise, but some observations can be made. For example, is the magazine fair even when it has a preconceived position? A magazine promoting hunting should be fair to opponents of hunting, and vice versa. Are the articles varied in nature—some light, some serious? Are the graphics up-to-date? Does the writing fit the overall tone of the publication?

As for the three major news magazines, they are prime targets for study. Identify one important issue and read the coverage it receives in each publication. What can you conclude about the magazine from what you read, especially regarding its fairness? Does it seem to have a political bias? What differences in tone can you identify among the three magazines?

Application to Scholastic Journalism

Many of the questions just raised apply to school, or scholastic, journalism as well. As you work on your school paper, yearbook, news bureau, or broadcast, give some thought to how these questions pertain to you.

The Ethics of Journalism

Throughout society, value is placed on right over wrong. Journalists are no exception to these expectations, nor should they be. Just as people expect their politicians to be honest and the Sunday afternoon football game to be fairly refereed, they also expect honesty from the press. More and more, however, polls indicate that the audience is wondering just how fair and honest journalists are.

The 1980s brought an outbreak of unusual violations to journalism. In one well-publicized case Janet Cooke of the *Washington Post* had to give back a Pulitzer Prize, journalism's highest honor, when it was discovered that the main character in her prize-winning story, an eight-year-old heroin addict, didn't exist. In the 1990s at least two prestigious journalists were found to be making up some of their information. There were also incidents of "composite characters," fictional characters a journalist had created by using characteristics of several real people. These problems eroded public confidence in the press to the point that some citizens want to pass laws regulating journalists' behavior.

Credibility

Thoughtful journalists are alarmed too. They know that the press must have credibility—that is, the ability to be believed and trusted. To restore that credibility, journalists today are putting more emphasis than ever on their ethical standards. Erring journalists find their colleagues in no mood to tolerate or forgive unprofessional conduct.

Many things govern journalists: time, space, economics, competition, geography, and the law. Above all else, however, it is the journalist's ethics that provide the daily working guidelines for deciding what gets into print or onto the airwaves. The ethical, responsible journalist tries to serve the audience's best interest.

Various codes of ethics have been written and agreed upon by journalists. None, however, is enforceable by law. Because the Constitution's First Amendment states, "Congress shall make no law . . . abridging the freedom of speech, or of the press," it would be unconstitutional to jail a journalist who violated ethical codes. A journalist who violates the law, of course, faces the same penalties as any other citizen.

Nor is it possible to require licensing or exams for journalists such as those that doctors and lawyers must pass. Licensing laws also run afoul of the Constitution. You can stop buying an unethical newspaper or watching an unethical newscast, but you can't lock up a journalist for an ethics violation unless he or she has actually broken the law.

The framers of the Constitution believed a free press, even though occasionally irresponsible, is vastly preferable to a government-controlled press. Does that mean that newspapers, for example, may print anything they please, without regard to consequences? No. The law does play a role. If a newspaper prints libel (false defamation), it may be required to pay money to the libeled person—but note that this penalty comes after publication, not before. Prior restraint, the halting or forbidding of publication, is not permitted in the United States except under the rarest of circumstances, usually pertaining to national security in wartime. Government censorship is against the law.

With the Constitution and long tradition protecting the right to publish, what keeps journalists honest? The only answer is ethics.

Accuracy

To the ethical journalist, accuracy has a special meaning. Close doesn't count. Names must be spelled exactly right, down to the middle initial. A journalist can't say that a person lives at 1010 Sycamore Street if the address is really 1010 Sycamore Drive. There is no such thing as a small error. No one lacking a sense of detail should go into journalism. It's not sufficient to bat .300 or even .400, averages that would get a baseball player into the Hall of Fame. For journalists, the batting average must be 1.000. They must be accurate, in every detail, all the time.

How often does the press achieve this "super-accuracy"? Not often enough, of course. If you have ever been the subject of a news story, you may have observed an error. Maybe your name was misspelled, or your year in school was wrong. What was the effect, for you, the next time you read a story in this paper? Of course, you questioned what you read. Even the smallest mistake reduces credibility. Check. Double-check. Ask the source another question. Never guess about anything. Always verify or confirm your information with at least one or more sources.

Objectivity

Another of the journalist's highest principles is objectivity, the state of mind that journalists acquire to make them fair, neutral observers of events and issues. Journalists do not permit their personal feelings, their likes or dislikes, to color news stories. You may not like a speaker or what is said, but you report it straight, without any hint of your own feelings. You may think environmentalists or Ku Klux Klan members or any other group is wrong, but you report what they do and let the audience decide. (Opinion, of course, is to be desired in columns and editorials.)

Some people say that objectivity is impossible, that it's impossible to have opinions and not let them show. Regardless, the journalist still must strive for that ideal.

If you find the idea of objectivity hard to grasp, think in terms of neutrality, fairness, impartiality, balance (telling all sides of a story), and honesty. Whatever you call it, journalists must set aside personal feelings. Always seek to provide unbiased accounts of the news for the audience. The journalist who vows to do this has taken a long first step on the road to professionalism.

The news article in the **ON DISPLAY** feature on page 37 demonstrates objectivity in reporting by presenting both sides of a volatile school issue in an evenhanded, nonjudgmental way.

Other Ethical Principles

Accuracy and objectivity are perhaps the two most important ethical principles journalists try to live by, but they are by no means the only ones. Some other important precepts follow.

Objective Reporting

The Tower, Grosse Pointe South High School, Grosse Pointe Farms, Michigan

Seniors Demand Sophomore Disqualification

by Tim Nicholson

Stating that the Sophomore Class utilized adult help in the construction of certain Homecoming decorations, the officers of the Senior Class have submitted an appeal which has delayed the announcement of Spirit Week winners.

Senior Class officers submitted an official letter of appeal at 10:30 a.m. Saturday. Because of the protest, all the Homecoming and Spirit Day awards were given to the Senior Class except for the best banner award, which is involved in the appeal. The announcement that an investigation was pending was made during halftime of the football game.

Specifically, the letter of appeal charges the Sophomore Class with not adhering to the Homecoming by-law stating that "All Spirit Week projects should be the work of the students." The by-law also states that "Any other [than the students] will result in disqualification."

The Senior Class officers claim that the sophomores hired Kinko's Copy Center to assist in their outside banner production. The seniors also point out that since the sophomore outside banner was produced with the aid of a professional, the inside banner may have also been produced in such a manner.

Members of the Sophomore Class were outraged.

"It really takes the heart out of everyone who put hard work into Spirit Week," said Sophomore Class President Cheryl MacKechnie.

MacKechnie said that she worked on the outside banner and no outside help of any kind was utilized. According to MacKechnie, the banner was drawn on graph paper and then scaled up until it fit the banner. She does not understand where anybody would get the idea that Kinko's had anything to do with it.

She did say, however, that the devil which adorned both banners and the sophomore Spirit Day shirts was a non-original tattoo adapted for their purposes.

Eric Shulte said he was in charge of the four artists who designed the inside banner for the sophomores. He also expressed anger.

"I have drawn and done artwork since I was a kid. This is a real insult to me. The seniors just can't handle the fact that sophomores beat them," said Shulte.

Senior Class officers said they are simply asking for an investigation.

"I think it's important that all the classes follow the Homecoming by-laws. I know for a fact that everything the seniors made for Homecoming was made by seniors only. It upsets me that our senior artists worked hard all summer preparing for Homecoming when other classes may not have been in compliance with the by-laws. My hope is that the right and just decision is made in this matter," Senior Class President Gretchen Carter said.

The investigation itself will be led by Assistant Principal Paul Pagel, according to Student Association (SA) Adviser Rod Scott. According to the Homecoming by-laws the SA president, adviser and proper administrator are in charge of any disqualification. Scott said who has the final say on the issue is not clear.

Pagel would not comment on the issue.

Christine Galnore, SA president, said that the SA is not trying to accuse the sophomores of cheating. She said that "we (the SA) are just trying to be fair to everyone and find out what really happened."

Galnore stressed that a decision cannot be made on hearsay and she, Pagel and Scott will only go with what they positively know is fact.

Scott said that the investigation will most likely take a few days and all parties involved are being met with in order to establish factual information.

Good taste. Avoid sensationalism and stay away from sexually explicit material. Sex and crime are subjects that require extreme caution in reporting and editing. Seek understatement, not overstatement. Never glorify bad behavior. Do not invade the privacy of others. Avoid profanity and anything else that might be considered obscenity.

Right of reply, or simultaneous rebuttal. If you must print or air criticism of someone, permit that person to respond to the criticism in the same story. It's not enough to run the criticism this week and the response next week. The response may never catch up with the original criticism.

Fairness to all. Everyone in your audience—regardless of race, color, philosophy, religion, gender, age, or economic status—has an equal right to fair treatment. Do not apply different standards to different people or groups. In school, no organization or group of any kind should be either favored or disfavored.

Plagiarism. Do not pass off the work of others as your own. No matter how much you like someone else's lead or phrase or story, you may not publish it as if you had written it. This is an absolute. You may quote from others' work, but you must give credit. In most classrooms students are failed for this offense; in the newsroom, reporters are fired for it.

Attribution. Identify where the information came from ("the President said today . . .") so the audience can judge for itself the value of the information. Do not use anonymous sources.

The truth. Never fake anything—your identity as a journalist, a quote, a photograph, a detail. Report only what you know beyond a doubt. Never speculate or guess.

    This list is incomplete and is, in some ways, abstract. It is, however, sufficient to make the point: Journalists must play fair.

    To reinforce these principles, the Society of Professional Journalists (SPJ) has created a code of ethics, which appears in the Appendix on pages 541–543. Based in Indiana, SPJ is the nation's largest journalistic group, including professional and student chapters all over America.

Libel Law

"If you print that, I'll sue you for everything you own!"

Gulp.

Hearing someone threaten to sue you is an unpleasant experience. Stay in journalism long enough, however, and chances are fair that it will happen. If you are sued, the case will be likely to involve libel—or at least an accusation of libel.

Libel is printed false defamation of character. (Spoken false defamation is slander, which we include under the general heading of libel.) To defame a person or organization is to reduce their reputation. For libel to have occurred, you must have written something false.

Falsely accused of planting a bomb at the 1996 Summer Olympics, security guard Richard Jewell sued, among others, the *Atlanta Journal-Constitution* for libel. Although Jewell was cleared of any wrong doing, he still feels his good name has been destroyed.

Should an accusation of libel arise, the journalist—and that includes the scholastic journalist—needs to be prepared. The student press is not exempt from libel law.

Libel laws are complex and changeable. Each court ruling provides subtle shifts in the law. One year it seems the press can print almost anything; the next year the law seems very restrictive. Libel laws vary from state to state and often involve whether the person libeled is a private person, a public figure, or an elected official. What follows is a general overview. Note that this general overview cannot touch on all the minute details of the law of libel, which fill whole libraries and have broad constitutional implications.

First, libel is seldom considered a crime. It's usually a civil action, heard in a civil court. Commit burglary, and you go to a criminal court, where the docket says, "State v. John Smith." Libel cases are actions between citizens; in civil cases the docket says, "Johnson v. Jones." The person asserting that libel has occurred, that his or her reputation has been damaged, is the plaintiff. The person accused is the defendant. The penalty involves a money judgment, which can run into millions of dollars, awarded to the plaintiff.

What can reduce the reputation of a person or organization? "She cheats on exams." "He is immoral." "She is a liar." "They falsified lab reports." The possibilities are endless. Certainly, the gravest libels occur when the basic morality, decency, or wholesomeness of a person or organization is questioned. Any publication of information that harms a person or organization requires the greatest of care. In scholastic situations it should be avoided virtually all the time.

Assertions that someone is dishonest, associates with criminals, has committed a crime, has a loathsome disease, or has general low character are dangerous. Proceed with special care. Remember that even if you *may* print or air such a story, you may decide *not* to for ethical reasons. Be aware that there is often a distinction between what you can get away with and what is right.

Also, although by definition libel is *printed* defamation, the laws and principles regarding libel and its defenses apply not only to print media—such as newspapers, yearbooks, and magazines—but to broadcasts, interactive multimedia projects, and on-line material.

worth quoting

As the free press develops, the paramount point is whether the journalist, like the scientist or scholar, puts the truth in the first place or in the second.

—Walter Lippmann (1899–1974), columnist and media critic

QUOTES

Defenses Against Libel

The best defense against a successful libel suit is good reporting. Check all facts. Get the other side. Let the accused person respond to any charge. Run corrections quickly and prominently.

In the event you are sued, these are other potential defenses:

Truth. The courts have made it clear that no publication will be held responsible for libel if the story in question is true.

You must, however, be able to prove to a jury that the information is true. What you know to be true may not seem so to the jury. Your witness may not be believed or may refuse to testify. Your documents may not be admitted into evidence. Be careful.

For example, suppose that you are writing a story about a well-known merchant, and you learn that 30 years ago he was convicted of burglary. He spent one year in prison for it. If you decide to include that item in your story, and are able to convince a jury that it's true, you are almost certainly safe from successful libel action.

But that's only part of the story. You may not be safe from an invasion-of-privacy suit. That is a suit in which the plaintiff in the example says, "Yes, that's true about the burglary charge, but since then I have had no further trouble with the law. In fact, I went to college, earned two degrees, and have been a successful merchant and civic leader since then. I have a family and attend church regularly. To dredge up that old case invades my right to be left alone and to live in peace."

You probably would lose a privacy suit.

Legal questions aside, be aware that in such cases responsible journalists will ask themselves the right question: Is any good served by bringing up such an old case? For a fair, honest, and ethical journalist, legal questions usually take care of themselves.

Another possible trap is the misconception that attribution is always a defense in libel cases. You cannot duck a libel charge merely by saying that all you did was report accurately what someone else said.

Let's say your track coach accused his assistant of stealing expensive supplies from his office and you report it this way: "The track coach said his assistant was stealing supplies." Your sentence is true; the track coach did say that about his assistant. Since truth is a defense, can you be sued successfully? The answer is yes—if the charge is false—because you published the libelous statement. The assistant can therefore recover damages from you. The principle is, The one who publishes pays. Attribution is no defense.

Privilege. There are some exceptions to the claim that attribution is not a defense. You may report whatever is said in an official legislative or judicial session without fear of a successful libel suit, provided your account is accurate and fair.

> Under the concept of privilege, anything said on the floor of Congress, in the state legislature, or in a court is immune from a libel suit.

What is said on the floor of Congress or the state legislature or in a courtroom is privileged, meaning that publication of such statements is immune from a libel suit. If the track coach accuses his assistant of stealing in an open courtroom, you may print it without fear of a successful libel suit. If one senator says that another is

a liar on the floor of the state senate, you may print that statement (with attribution, of course). Here the principle is that the public has a large stake in knowing what goes on in a courtroom or in the legislature. The press, therefore, may report such activities without the chilling effect that the fear of a suit can have.

It may seem to you that the laws favor the journalist, but this country has a deep, fervent commitment to open public debate. Our courts have a general fear of anything that restricts the information needed for that debate to be successful. Freedom of the press, properly handled, protects everyone, not just the person who owns the medium.

Fair comment. Another defense against successful libel suits is known as fair comment and criticism.

You are free to venture any opinion in reviewing books or records, theatrical events, movies, and the like. This is because a person who, for example, makes a movie is thrusting himself or herself onto the public stage and virtually asking for comment. If you review this book and say that it's bad, the authors won't sue. If you say that it's bad because it doesn't have a chapter on the responsibilities of the media, however, the authors may sue, because it does. Thus, you may express a negative opinion, but the facts you state must be true. For a fair-comment defense to convince a jury, you must explain the facts upon which your opinion is based. If your facts are proven true, your opinion is protected. Of course, you must limit your comment to the public part of a performance or creative work. You cannot claim the defense of fair comment if you say that a singer's record album is bad and he is also a thief.

Admission of error. A prompt correction of a published article that has been shown to be false is both a legal and an ethical responsibility. To do so in a libel case can help if you go to court. In effect, you are saying to the judge, "Yes, there may be libel here but it wasn't malicious. As soon as we found out we were wrong, we ran a correction." This may reduce the money judgment against you. In some states, special statutes make it a better defense.

Don't overlook the dangers presented by careless layout. For example, you could be in trouble if you have a photograph of the homecoming queen above a story on drug use or drunken driving. The implications would be read by all. As with printed errors, if such a mistake slips through, you should run a correction as soon as possible.

Public officials and public figures. When it comes to libel, some plaintiffs have a tougher time winning their case in court than others. Elected public officials—for example, the President, a U.S. senator, or the mayor—must show a greater degree of fault by the press in order to win a libel suit. Even nonelected public officials, such as public school principals, may be regarded in this category by a court of law. Thus, the senator who thinks he or she has been libeled must not only show the damage (as all plaintiffs must) but must also show that the press either knew it was printing a falsehood or exercised reckless disregard for the truth.

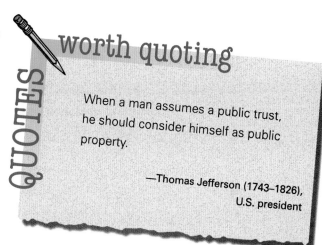

QUOTES

worth quoting

When a man assumes a public trust, he should consider himself as public property.

—Thomas Jefferson (1743–1826), U.S. president

Both of these circumstances are rare, for the press generally does not knowingly print lies or recklessly disregard the truth. Again, the idea here is the country's commitment to open debate. The courts have said that, for such debate to occur, the man or woman who has sought office or who accepts a position of trust in a public institution must accept the criticism and attention that come with it.

The courts are continuing to define others besides public officials who must show a high level of fault by the press in order to win libel suits. These people may be defined as public figures—those who thrust themselves into the public eye on a regular basis. Famous basketball players and movie stars fall into this category, as do some religious leaders.

The lines that separate public officials, public figures, and private citizens are sometimes fuzzy. The police chief is a public official even if not elected, but what about the beat-patrol officer? Such distinctions are difficult and should never be decided without the aid of legal counsel. The best thing is never to get into libel trouble. The worst is to try to handle it without expert help.

"Successful" Libel Suits

The alert reader may have noticed that virtually every reference to a libel suit has been qualified by calling it a *successful* libel suit. If you have an absolutely airtight defense, you won't lose the suit, but that doesn't mean you won't be sued in the first place. Anyone can sue anyone, and lawsuits are financially and emotionally draining.

Wise journalists avoid lawsuits even if they think they can win. Exercise extreme care as reporters, editors, and photographers. (Yes, pictures can be libelous, and they can invade privacy.) Avoiding suits and being ethical are better than counting on legal technicalities. Also, get the other side in the initial story. People who see their side in print seldom sue.

Finally, who can sue? Anyone, as we have said. And who can be sued? The editor? The publisher? The answer is that anyone involved in producing the libelous material may be sued—the reporter who wrote the story, the editor who assigned the story, the editor who drew the layout, even the copy editor who wrote the headline or caption. All these people can be sued—for everything they own.

Limits on Scholastic Journalism

On January 13, 1988, the U.S. Supreme Court handed down a decision involving the censorship of a school publication. An excerpt from the Associated Press report on the case, known as *Hazelwood School District v. Cathy Kuhlmeier,* appears below.

> The Supreme Court on Wednesday gave public school officials broad new authority to censor student newspapers and other forms of student expression.
>
> The court, by a 5–3 vote, ruled that a Hazelwood, Mo., high school principal did not violate students' free-speech rights by ordering two pages deleted from an issue of a student-produced, school-sponsored newspaper.
>
> "A school need not tolerate student speech that is inconsistent with its basic educational mission even though the government could not censor similar speech outside the school," Justice Byron R. White wrote for the court.
>
> He said judicial intervention to protect students' free-speech rights is warranted "only when the decision to censor a school-sponsored publication, theatrical production, or other vehicle of student expression has no valid educational purpose."
>
> The dissenting justices accused the court of condoning "thought control," adding, "such unthinking contempt for individual rights is intolerable."

This carefully worded report gave no hint of the debate and confusion that the court's decision would create in the ensuing years. Generally referred to today as "Hazelwood," the case and the ruling remain at the center of debate over student expression in secondary schools. There are strong arguments on both sides.

One side says, "The First Amendment of the Constitution applies to all citizens, including high school students, and therefore school administrators have no right to interfere with what's published in a school newspaper."

The other side says, "The school newspaper is a school-sponsored activity, and the principal is the publisher of the paper, acting on behalf of the citizens of the school district, and therefore has the ultimate, legal control over what's published in the paper."

Before examining in detail the many issues raised by Hazelwood, it's helpful to understand the thinking and legal decisions that predate it.

The Tinker Decision

Until about 30 years ago, most people assumed that control of student expression naturally rested with school authorities. The concept of *in loco parentis* seemed to cover the question. Under this legal idea, school authorities acted "in the place of the parent" and assumed a parent's rights, duties, and responsibilities. Some people accepted this idea. Some still do. Some do not.

In 1969, during the uneasy years of the Vietnam War, the U.S. Supreme Court addressed the question of student expression, if not the entire concept of *in loco parentis,* in the case of *Tinker v. Des Moines Independent School District.* Before Hazelwood the ruling in the case was the court's major statement on student expression.

In the case, three students in Des Moines, Iowa, decided to wear black armbands to protest the war. School administrators suspended the students, and the students sued. They lost in district and appeals courts but won when their case reached the U.S. Supreme Court. That court expressed the following:

> First Amendment rights, applied in light of the special characteristics of the school environment, are available to teachers and students. It can hardly be argued that either students or teachers shed their constitutional rights to freedom of speech or expression at the schoolhouse

gate. . . . In our system, . . . school officials do not possess absolute authority over their students. Students in school as well as out of school are "persons" under our Constitution.

Later, the court added that students and teachers "are possessed of fundamental rights which the state must respect, just as they themselves must respect their obligations to the State."

Although the Tinker case did not involve student journalists or free-press questions, subsequent court rulings made it clear that the principles applied to student journalists. Prior restraint (censorship) of student journalists was held to be illegal unless the material to be censored was libelous, obscene, an invasion of privacy, or "materially and substantially" disruptive of the school.

The Tinker ruling meant that student editors had the legal right to decide what would go into the paper, the yearbook, or the broadcast. If the students wanted to print obscene material, however, they could be stopped. Libelous stories or stories that invaded someone's privacy were not protected either. Advisers or administrators spotting this sort of material had the right to overrule the students. This also was true if the students printed material that threatened to disrupt the school environment.

Still, as today, it was not the law that truly governed behavior. Ethics (what is right, not just what is legal), compromise, experimentation, teaching-and-learning tactics—the whole array of elements at work in a school environment came into play. Most principals and advisers and most students worked within a reasonable framework, and legal difficulties were rare.

That brings us to the Hazelwood decision.

The Hazelwood Decision

Here are the facts of the case: In 1983 staff members of the *Spectrum,* the student newspaper of Hazelwood East High School in Missouri, prepared a series of stories about student pregnancy and the effects of divorce on students. The principal, Robert Reynolds, deleted the two pages of the paper on which the stories were to have appeared. Reynolds said he blocked the stories because they invaded the privacy of the students involved, even though they were unnamed. He feared they could be identified anyway.

"He also believed," the Supreme Court said in its ruling, "that the article's references to sexual activity and birth control were inappropriate for some of the younger students at the school."

Following the Supreme Court decision in his favor, Hazelwood East High School principal Robert Reynolds speaks to a journalism class.

Reynolds took the position that he was publisher of the newspaper and as such could determine its contents.

The students sued. A federal trial judge ruled in favor of the school district. But the Eighth U.S. Circuit Court of Appeals ruled for the students.

When the U.S. Supreme Court came down on the side of school authorities, it said: "A school may in its capacity as publisher of a school newspaper or producer of a school play 'disassociate itself' not only from speech that would 'substantially interfere with its work . . . or impinge upon the rights of other students' but also from speech that is, for example, ungrammatical, poorly written, inadequately researched, biased or prejudiced, vulgar or profane, or unsuitable for immature audiences." The court said only that censorship must be "reasonably related" to educational goals.

The language was too broad for some people, and reaction came swiftly.

Mark Goodman, executive director of the Washington, D.C.–based Student Press Law Center, an organization that provides legal help to students in censorship cases, said that within hours of the decision he received two calls from students complaining of censorship where none had existed before. Both cases involved stories about AIDS.

Many, but by no means all, school administrators responded favorably. So did many commercial newspapers, which appeared to favor the argument that the principal of a school has the same power to control content as the publisher of a commercial newspaper. Others argued that this is a bad analogy. They said that what a publisher does is his or her business because the newspaper is part of private enterprise; but, they said, what a principal does is society's business and cannot be capricious or arbitrary, any more than police officers or judges can. The difference between a commercial and a student newspaper, this reasoning goes, is that in a school the publisher is the government—and the United States has never permitted government control of the press.

Arguments for and against. What follows is a look at some of the specific arguments on either side of the Hazelwood dispute.

Some people say school administrators should have the final say about what goes into the newspaper or yearbook because, if there is a successful libel suit, the school will have to pay. Others argue that lawsuits are extremely rare in a school setting. Nevertheless, the other side responds, should a suit occur—rare event or not—it's the school that pays.

Student advocates say this: If schools grant students the responsibility for what they print, the students inherit the responsibility to pay any libel judgments. Naturally, it's pointed out that students do not usually have money to pay such judgments, but nowhere is it written that only the well-to-do have the right to publish.

This argument (who has the ultimate legal responsibility?) remains unsettled. It should be pointed out, however, that a principal who watches carefully what his or her students are printing may be doing so out of concern for the school's legal liability.

Another argument is that students are too young and too inexperienced journalistically to make mature judgments about what to print. For some, this is a compelling argument. There are, indeed, risks in permitting student journalists the power of the press. Apart from legal problems, feelings and reputations can be damaged. People in the news are not abstractions; they're human beings, and they need to be handled with care.

On the other hand, many student journalists are surprisingly sophisticated and, if they receive proper guidance from well-trained and well-educated advisers, usually can be trusted to do the right thing. Students who embark on irresponsible paths often can be convinced of the error of their ways by their advisers. Many educators believe it is better to teach,

Responses to Hazelwood

Whose opinion on the Hazelwood decision do you agree with?

"The Hazelwood case . . . involve[s] two separate and very distinct issues. One is a constitutional question, the right of a public school to control its own publication. The other is an educational question, the wisdom of exerting such control in ham-handed fashion."

—*Roanoke* (Virginia) *Times & World-News*

"[I]f we're preparing students . . . to face the real world and to be productive citizens . . . they have to be exposed to as much reality as they can handle."

—Edmund J. Sullivan, Director, Columbia Scholastic Press Association

"[Hazelwood] has caused us to be more careful. It's going to be on our shoulders to prove that we're responsible enough to handle the rights."

—Linda Puntney, Executive Secretary, Journalism Education Association

"As a teacher I don't think I can realistically teach what the First Amendment is and what it means unless I can turn around and practice it . . ."

—John Bowen, high school journalism adviser

"Do we want a generation of potential journalists coming through a system that doesn't encourage freedom of the press? What's going to happen ten years down the road from here?"

—Richard Johns, Executive Director, Quill and Scroll, International Honorary Society for High School Journalists

"Justice White said the courts may intervene when censorship serves no 'valid educational purpose.' If this decision brings gross abuses, then student journalists will be back in court with justice on their side."

—*Saginaw* (Michigan) *News*

Student Tammy Hawkins, editor of the Hazelwood East High School paper, displays the issue announcing the Supreme Court decision.

"[W]hat is a student to believe when taught about a free press and the First Amendment in class if the free expression of the school's own journalists is suppressed?"

—Henry Reichman, *Censorship and Selection: Issues and Answers for Schools*

"The 5–3 majority is basically correct in upholding the authority of educators over students of this age. But . . . [i]t's a pity that the justices . . . could not find space to admonish school systems to wield their power with wisdom, care, and restraint."

—*The New York Times*

"The reality of newspaper publishing includes making responsible decisions about what to print, in order to avoid unnecessary lawsuits. . . . To assume that these decisions are most appropriately left to the student journalist escapes all reason."

—National School Boards Association/National Association of Secondary School Principals

"[I]f there is no educational, scholastic freedom . . . then all [students] learn is to bow down to whatever particular governmental authority happens to be in charge of the rules at the time."

—Jack Harkrider, high school journalism adviser

"The real world is different. In a grown-up world, an editor is subject to a publisher. If the publisher says, 'Kill the piece,' that's it, sweetheart, the piece is killed."

—James Kilpatrick, syndicated columnist

FOLLOW-UP

1. As a class, discuss the quotes and categorize them according to whether they support or question Hazelwood. Which side appears to have the stronger case?

2. Check back issues of your school newspaper for as far back as they are available. Do you think that the types of stories and the way they are covered would have been different before Hazelwood? Why or why not?

to tell why something is wrong and should not be printed, than it is to issue a direct order against publication.

Some people say control of yearbooks and newspapers belongs exclusively to the school because the classes that produce the papers and books are just that: classes. Student activities. Just as the biology teacher controls her class and the history teacher controls his—both guided by the principal—the journalism teacher also exercises control. This is a good argument, all the better in schools where the publications are financed by the school and credit is granted for working on them.

Hazelwood has caused other controversies as well. How, ask critics of the decision, is it possible to teach First Amendment values in a school where students are censored? What of the educational value of good journalism classes? Aren't they meant to be learning experiences, and doesn't Hazelwood undermine them? These questions worry not only journalism advisers and students but school administrators too.

Limits on Hazelwood. If a publication is exclusively a class project and is used only for training and practice by student journalists, it's difficult to argue for student control—but not even this issue is totally black or white.

The *Spectrum,* the student newspaper in the Hazelwood case, was determined by the Supreme Court not to be an open forum. Had it been ruled a forum, the court's decision might very well have gone the other way. Under forum theory, once the government creates a forum, it cannot control the ideas expressed there. A forum is a place where ideas are exchanged. A city park, where people climb on soapboxes and say what they think, is a forum. Many universities have a mall or a "speaker's corner" where people may speak. These areas are protected by society, and the ideas expressed there are protected as well. If a school newspaper is a forum, Hazelwood probably does not apply.

Thus a school newspaper that has been declared a place where members of the school community exchange ideas—through columns, letters to the editor, guest columns—may be in a different legal position from that of a pure lab newspaper produced by students for practice and training. This in no way should affect student conduct or judgment, of course. Again, it's ethics, not the law, that governs student journalists.

Some states question Hazelwood itself. The Arkansas, Colorado, Iowa, Kansas, and Massachusetts legislatures have passed bills that, in effect, sidestep Hazelwood. Even before Hazelwood, California had a statute protecting student-press rights. Such legislation has been introduced in several other states and is in various stages of the legislative process. Many individual school districts also have made it clear that they will stick with the Tinker rules despite the Hazelwood ruling.

How can this be? Isn't federal law the last word? Yes. States may, however, grant more freedom than the federal government; they just can't grant less. So in this case, state and local rules can prevail—if that's what local citizens want.

The research shows without a doubt that there has been a large increase in censorship in high schools since Hazelwood. Some people remain unconvinced, however, about Hazelwood's effect. Although many advisers express dismay over the decision, others say, "This case is no big deal."

One of the most sensible reactions to the decision came from journalism professor and student-press scholar Bob Trager. In a speech just two months after the Hazelwood decision, Trager urged the following course of action:

> In the majority of schools, where teachers, administrators and students have been uncertain about the place of journalism in the curriculum and the extent to which students should be able to exercise their First Amendment rights, Hazelwood may spur additional discussion and reflection on these matters. And that can be to the good.
>
> Students, the publications adviser and school administrators should exchange views on freedom of expression. Ultimately, maybe they can reach a consensus, one that can be put into a formal, written policy. It should include a recognition of students' freedom to report, write and express their views. Remember, Hazelwood didn't prohibit that—it just said administrators could censor student-written material if they choose to. The goal here is to give them a reason not to.
>
> The policy also should make the adviser's role clear—to teach, guide and be a sounding board for student journalists.
>
> If administrators do review material before publication, they should commit to discussing with the students any concerns they have, so they can be resolved in a timely manner, and so students can learn from the experience. And there should be a means to appeal unfavorable decisions.
>
> Discussions leading to such a policy could begin by focusing on the Hazelwood decision itself.

 Wrap-up

Public confidence in the press has fallen. Journalists are often seen as rude and insensitive, at least in part because they are the bearers of unavoidable bad news.

Journalists have many roles assigned to them by society. Their coverage of government fulfills the political function expected of a constitutionally protected free press. Advertising provides information about products and services. As the press surveys the horizon and alerts the public to what's "out there," it fulfills the sentry function. Sports scores, birth announcements, and such information keep society's records. Comics, feature stories, and other light fare entertain people. Information in the mass media provides daily material for conversation and thus enhances people's social lives. The media also help set society's agenda, which can lead to solutions.

Various ways exist to evaluate the media. Interested citizens can compare newspapers, radio, television, and magazines with professional standards.

Journalists try to meet the ethical standards that, even more than the law, guide their work. Journalists are expected to be accurate and objective. Their standards emphasize good taste, fairness, care with attribution, and a devotion to truth.

A large problem for journalists is libel. Publishing material that is both false and damaging to someone's reputation can lead to a lawsuit with heavy financial penalties. Truth is the best defense for journalists. There is no libel without falsehood.

The legal situation for scholastic journalists changed greatly in 1988 with the U.S. Supreme Court's ruling in the Hazelwood case. In that case, the court said school officials can legally censor student newspapers and other forms of student expression if the censorship is related to educational needs. The decision tightened up scholastic journalism freedoms from censorship implied in the 1969 Tinker decision.

Educators and journalists are divided over whether the Hazelwood decision was good or bad, and there is disagreement over its long-term effects on scholastic journalism.

The decision permits a school principal to assume the role of publisher of the student newspaper. In that position the principal can control the paper's content. Nothing in the decision requires censorship, and many school districts continue to grant students and advisers final say over the paper. Some states have passed legislation reaffirming this freedom. School newspapers that are open forums for the exchange of ideas are generally considered exempt from the Hazelwood ruling.

People on both sides of the Hazelwood controversy agree that the responsibility of student journalists is unchanged. The emphasis must remain on accuracy, fairness, objectivity, balance, good taste, good judgment, and good sense.

On Assignment

INDIVIDUAL ACTIVITIES

1. Write a brief definition of each of these terms:

   "composite characters"   objectivity
   credibility   plagiarism
   ethics   prior restraint
   fair comment   privileged statements
   forum theory   right of reply
   in loco parentis   slander
   libel

2. Test your critical thinking. Have a class discussion about the following news issues. If possible, invite local news executives to class to join the discussion.
   a. Is the press really preoccupied with "bad news"? If not, why do so many people think this? What dilemmas do news people face in trying to balance news that the audience wants with news that it needs?
   b. In what kind of a climate do your local media operate? For example, do the owners of radio and TV stations also own a newspaper? Is there only one local paper? Are the media locally owned or part of a larger conglomerate? What conclusions can be drawn about media independence and competitiveness?
   c. What dilemmas do journalists face because of lack of time and space? Are there any solutions?
   d. Is it always the fault of the newspaper or station when the facts come out wrong in a story? Might it be the fault of the news source? Might the "error" be in the minds of the audience?
   e. When is it right for reporters to use anonymous sources? What ethical questions are involved?

3. Write a critique of the On Display article on page 37. Include specific examples of what makes it objective. Make your critique about one page long.

4. Write a brief essay on each of the following situations. Be prepared to discuss your position in class.
   a. As a school reporter, you're covering a meeting of the board of education. Suddenly the president of the board turns to you and says, "I'm sorry, but this part of the meeting is off the record. Please stop taking notes and do not report any of this in the paper." What do you do? Why?
   b. You're in the school cafeteria and you overhear two school administrators discussing "the massive number of students who cheat." Do you have a story? How would you proceed? Why?

5. Assume that you're a high school principal and have learned that the school paper intends to publish the following stories. In each case, tell what you would do and why.
   a. A student created a disturbance in the cafeteria, turning over tables, throwing food, and upsetting an urn of hot coffee. He was subdued and taken to a local hospital for psychiatric observation. The story being planned by the school newspaper is to include the student's name and photographs of the damage.
   b. The newspaper staff plans an editorial that criticizes the football coach for pressuring the parents of the students he coaches into buying kitchen appliances from him.
   c. Newspaper staff members investigating the all-school activities fund—money intended to support all the school's clubs and organizations—have discovered that school administrators have spent the entire fund to support the basketball team.
   d. Members of the student council have circulated a petition in the school to have the council's faculty advisor replaced.

6. Assume that you're the editor of the school newspaper for which the articles in activity 5 are planned. In each case, tell what you would do and why.

TEAM ACTIVITY

7. Working in teams, prepare a code of standards for the publications in your school. Compare your code to the code of ethics of the Society of Professional Journalists reprinted in the Appendix (pages 541–543). Review the codes prepared by the teams. Working as a class, prepare a code for your school.

SURF THE NET

8. Examine the Internet site for one or more of these organizations: the Journalism Education Association, the Student Press Law Center, and the Freedom Forum. Write a brief summary of how the site might be helpful in dealing with freedom of the press and censorship issues.

career profile

Media Lawyer

Jane Kirtley

The calls for legal help came to Jane Kirtley at all hours of the day—and night.

Kirtley, a former reporter turned lawyer, served until 1999 as executive director of the Reporters Committee for Freedom of the Press, a voluntary, unincorporated association of reporters and editors devoted to protecting the First Amendment. The committee assists reporters and media organizations whenever their ability to report the news is threatened.

"It's the kind of job that can take over your life," Kirtley said of her work for the Reporters Committee. "But the rewards far outweigh the negatives. It's a perfect job for anybody who loves the First Amendment and journalism."

Kirtley believes the responsibility of the media is to act as watchdog, looking out for readers' best interests. Any attempt to limit or control the ability of the press to do that must be fought.

"The overriding journalistic ethic is to inform the public," she said. As a journalist, one must "tell the truth as best that you determine it at the time, and trust the public to have the judgment and the sense to take the actions that are necessary to ensure preservation of our democratic system."

Kirtley began overseeing the legal defense and publications efforts of the Reporters Committee in 1985. She also edited the group's quarterly newsletter, the *News Media & the Law.* Earlier, she worked as a reporter for the *Evansville Press,* the *Oak Ridger,* and the *Nashville Banner.*

Kirtley warns of hard times ahead for the media if the public doesn't change its attitude toward the press.

"There is a lack of public understanding of the importance of the media," Kirtley said. "We're on the cusp of radical change. For the last ten to twelve years or so the public has felt it had no stake in press freedom. They felt the media was part of the problem and not the solution."

The public is starting to demand restrictions, she said, that go against the principles of the First Amendment. "If the members of the public don't see a relationship between free speech and free press, then we have a major problem," she said.

Kirtley continues to be concerned that as new communication technology, such as the Internet, is developed, government officials will find less resistance from the public to attempts to regulate it.

"I do worry that since the new technology vendors are not traditional media, the public won't look at regulation the same way it would if it were CBS News or the *New York Times* being regulated," she said.

Kirtley has served on many advisory boards and committees, including the First Amendment Congress, the Libel Defense Resource Center, and the Student Press Law Center. Presently she is Silha Professor of Journalism at the University of Minnesota and writes a monthly column for the *American Journalism Review.*

FOLLOW-UP

1. Do some research on what kinds of cases a media lawyer such as Kirtley might be involved in. Prepare a report on one such case and present it to the class.
2. Is Kirtley's belief in the sacredness of the First Amendment supported by the Supreme Court? Find out to what degree, if any, First Amendment privileges of free speech have been restricted by the Court.

SECTION TWO

CHAPTER 3

Deciding What Is News

The three chapters in this section are about gathering the news. That's a more elusive activity than it once was.

We used to think of news in relatively simple terms. News equaled events. News was automobile accidents, airplane crashes, violent weather, earthquakes, fires, slayings. News was meetings, press conferences, speeches, births, marriages, deaths. Known today as "hard news," its boundaries were not hard to define.

Then life became more complex, and the nature of news changed. The press moved away from events and concentrated on trends, on in-depth coverage of major issues. News was intricacies of government, damage to the environment, the changing family, population control, educational reform, automobile safety, health care.

At the same time another change started to take place. The news began shifting away from government, social issues, and the question. Where are we going in this society? Several factors account for this change of direction: declining literacy, loss of young readers, a drop in circulation generally, the

news judgment   proximity

advance   prom

timeliness   co

CHAPTER 4

Organizing the Staff to Capture the News

Change—some would say a revolution—has hit the news industry's organizational styles in the last decade or so.

New ways have been devised to organize, and therefore to improve, coverage. Traditional beat systems in which each reporter covered a specific area have given way to what one newspaper describes as "topical bear clusters." From the creation of the story idea through the reporting, photo, design, and production phases, teams often work together in an effort not just to capture the superficial day-to-day material but to get at the heart of readers' information needs. What follows may serve as a guideline.

The Newspaper Staff

Although staff organization has changed at the newsroom level, the lines of authority

mobile w
here. Th
cil"), te
conseo
specta
had e
and

Co
T
p
i

82

sts bec...
ernment news, with e....

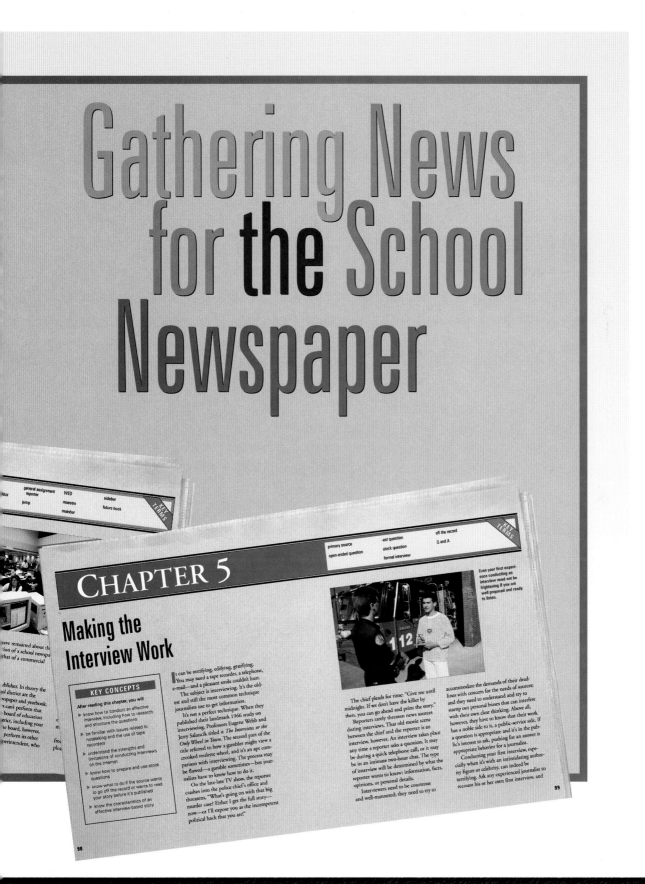

Gathering News for the School Newspaper

KEY TERMS

general assignment reporter	WED	sidebar
jump	maestro	future book
	mainbar	

KEY TERMS

primary source	-est question	off the record
open-ended question	stock question	Q and A
	formal interview	

CHAPTER 5

Making the Interview Work

KEY CONCEPTS

After reading this chapter, you will

▶ know how to conduct an effective interview, including how to research and structure the questions

▶ be familiar with issues related to notetaking and the use of tape recorders

▶ understand the strengths and limitations of conducting interviews on the Internet

▶ know how to prepare and use stock questions

▶ know what to do if the source wants to go off the record or wants to read your story before it's published

▶ know the characteristics of an effective interview-based story

It can be terrifying, edifying, gratifying. You may need a tape recorder, a telephone, e-mail—and a pleasant smile couldn't hurt.

The subject is interviewing. It's the oldest and still the most common technique journalists use to get information.

It's not a perfect technique. When they published their landmark 1966 study on interviewing, Professors Eugene Webb and Jerry Salancik titled it *The Interview, or the Only Wheel in Town*. The second part of the title referred to how a gambler might view a crooked roulette wheel, and it's an apt comparison with interviewing. The process may be flawed—a gamble sometimes—but journalists have to know how to do it.

On the late-late TV show, the reporter crashes into the police chief's office and threatens, "What's going on with that big murder case? Either I get the full story now—or I'll expose you as the incompetent political hack that you are!"

The chief pleads for time: "Give me until midnight. If we don't have the killer by then, you can go ahead and print the story."

Reporters rarely threaten news sources during interviews. That old movie scene between the chief and the reporter is an interview, however. An interview takes place any time a reporter asks a question. It may be during a quick telephone call, or it may be in an intimate two-hour chat. The type of interview will be determined by what the reporter wants to know: information, facts, opinions, or personal details.

Interviewers need to be courteous and well-mannered; they need to try to accommodate the demands of their deadlines with concern for the needs of sources; and they need to understand and try to stamp out personal biases that can interfere with their own clear thinking. Above all, however, they have to know that their work has a noble side to it, a public-service side. If a question is appropriate and it's in the public's interest to ask, pushing for an answer is appropriate behavior for a journalist.

Conducting your first interview, especially when it's with an intimidating authority figure or celebrity, can indeed be terrifying. Ask any experienced journalist to recount his or her own first interview, and

Even your first experience conducting an interview need not be frightening if you are well prepared and ready to listen.

98

99

CHAPTER 3

Deciding What Is News

KEY CONCEPTS

After reading this chapter, you will

▶ understand how definitions of news have changed over time

▶ recognize the influence of *USA Today* on modern news approaches

▶ be able to measure news values by audience interest and need

▶ recognize the classic elements of news: timeliness, proximity, prominence, consequence, human interest, and conflict

▶ know how to generate ideas by brainstorming

▶ understand the basics of obtaining information by polls

The three chapters in this section are about gathering the news. That's a more elusive activity than it once was.

We used to think of news in relatively simple terms. News equaled events. News was automobile accidents, airplane crashes, violent weather, earthquakes, fires, slayings. News was meetings, press conferences, speeches, births, marriages, deaths. Known today as "hard news," its boundaries were not hard to define.

Then life became more complex, and the nature of news changed. The press moved away from events and concentrated on trends, on in-depth coverage of major issues. News was intricacies of government, damage to the environment, the changing family, population control, educational reform, automobile safety, health care.

At the same time another change started to take place. The news began shifting away from government, social issues, and the question, Where are we going in this society? Several factors account for this change of direction: declining literacy, loss of young readers, a drop in circulation generally, the

Stories about calamities such as tornadoes or hurricanes are always of interest to readers.

mobile society ("Everybody just moved here. They don't care about the city council"), television's need for ratings and the consequent emphasis on the upbeat or the spectacular, and a feeling that people have had enough of "bad news," such as famines and gang fighting.

USA Today pioneered the new attitude. Colorful, upbeat, filled with graphics, *USA Today* was a tremendous hit, especially with people on the go across the country. Many journalists, eager to find the solutions to the problem of a declining audience, have followed *USA Today*'s lead. These journalists believe that readers are bored with government news, with endless stories about

squabbles over cable television companies, sewage plants, urban development, and zoning laws.

Other journalists argue that the press has a role to play and society needs the same kind of news that it always has, with emphasis on government. Yet many acknowledge that the changes that have taken place are based on economic realities. They wonder if it comes down to a choice between a newspaper that compromises its definition of news or no newspaper at all.

So what is news at the start of the 21st century? It's "all of the above." Events and trends are still covered. To these you can add lifestyles of the rich and famous, fashion, health, the arts, leisure, exercise, sex, parenting, recreation, nutrition, film, video, music. The list is endless because it encompasses all of modern life.

Following this lead, scholastic journalists also have broadened their approaches to the news. News of homecoming dances, international exchange students, new teachers, football games, and current events is still covered, but today there is much more. It's not uncommon to find student journalists examining school budgets, performance on standardized tests, teacher-tenure cases, and lifestyle issues. Teens worry about getting into college, about pregnancy, about how to fit in at school, about abortion—and teen journalists respond with information on such issues.

This change makes some people nervous. They don't like to see stories about the dangers of drug use or sexually transmitted diseases. Yet these are realities for teenagers today.

The Internet has added a new and as yet undefined element to news gathering. Now, for good or ill, the world is a few keystrokes away. It can be easier to download a document from a library in South Africa than to get an appointment with a school administrator. Whereas once student journalists had to scour their exchange papers for story ideas, all they have to do today is conduct a Net search, and in no time at all hundreds of documents on any subject are on their screens.

The information superhighway can be chaotic, and only Web-wise travelers should venture on to it. It's easy to find information today. Making sense of it, sorting it out, is the challenge. Journalists need to be as skeptical as ever when dealing with the Internet: Just because something is in cyberspace doesn't make it true or accurate.

News Judgment

It is the journalist's job to evaluate what's "out there" and to select what will interest, inform, educate, amuse, or amaze the audience. Decisions have to be made about what's important and what's not, about balancing what the audience wants against what it needs.

How do journalists do this? They use news judgment, their own good sense in determining, for example, which of a dozen items should be included in a story, and which should be in the first paragraph or first on the newscast. No one is born with news judgment. That's something one absorbs through experience, attending to the mass media (reading newspapers and magazines; watching newscasts; surfing the Internet), and hard work.

The so-called elements of news, or news values, include such factors as timeliness, proximity, and prominence. These elements and others will be examined in detail shortly.

The "Who Cares?" Method

A quick shortcut to news judgment can be found in the "Who cares?" method. That merely means asking yourself who cares about this story, person, event, or issue. If you are convinced that there is genuine interest or that the story, person, event, or issue is important for the audience . . . you have news. If there is neither interest nor need, skip it.

Let's try the "Who cares?" method in evaluating two simple events; one is news, one is not.

A. The mayor signs a proclamation designating next week Clean-up, Paint-up, Fix-up Week.
B. The mayor announces an investigation into the disappearance of $75,000 from the city's general fund.

An event that directly affects your school, such as the introduction of closed-circuit broadcasting, would pass the "Who cares?" test for inclusion in the school paper.

Now, who cares about Clean-up, Paint-up, Fix-up Week? Practically no one. Politicians constantly issue such proclamations, mostly at the urging of special-interest groups. In this case the special week is a lure for newspaper advertising from lumberyards, nurseries, seed stores, and paint stores. The media pay scant attention to such designations.

Who cares about event B? Nearly everyone in the community. For taxpayers, and that includes practically every citizen, the handling of public money is a critical issue. The conduct of public officials draws intense concern in a democratic society. So, yes, event B is news. Obviously, few news decisions in a journalist's life present such a clear-cut choice as those in this example. As a starter, however, always ask yourself who cares about the story and you will be on your way to developing good news judgment.

Not all events are subject to such evaluation. If your instructor had a fight with a neighbor, you might get a positive answer to the "Who cares?" question, but you wouldn't have news. Why? Because some things are personal. The journalist's duty is to rise above the level of spreading ugly stories that invade the privacy and upset the lives of innocent people. Like so many things in journalism, taste is the issue. One of your jobs as a journalist is to cull items that would offend the audience's taste. This too is part of news judgment.

The Elements of News

A warning bell should go off in your head when you come across an item in bad taste. Another bell should ring when an item is legitimate news. This is just another way of saying that news judgment is, to a great extent, intuitive. Seasoned journalists don't need such guidelines as timeliness, proximity, or prominence. Instead, they rely on the bells in their heads. This is no help, you say, because you don't have bells yet. You haven't acquired the intuitive judgment, a sort of sixth sense that allows you to weigh, often in a split second, the news value of an event. This is where the classic elements of news come in.

Depending on which authors you read, there are anywhere from five to twelve elements of news. Here are some of the most generally recognized.

Timeliness

Timeliness relates to the newness of the facts. It's this element that makes a story about football more timely in November than in June. A story lacks timeliness for the school newspaper if the daily newspaper downtown already covered the story at great length two weeks earlier. Instead, the school paper might concentrate on advance items, stories about coming events.

Proximity

Proximity refers to the nearness of a given event to your place of publication. Events occurring in your school generally have more news value than those occurring on the other side of the world. People like to read

about things they are familiar with, and they are more likely to be familiar with those things closest to home.

This explains the reliance of most journalists on local news, about which a great editor once said, "A tomcat on the steps of City Hall is more important than a crisis in the Balkans." This is no longer true, of course, as we all witnessed during NATO's war against Serbia in 1999. Today such a crisis is recognized as having potentially far-reaching consequences that may dramatically affect the lives of your audience. What the editor said still makes a good deal of sense, however. To paraphrase him, "A minor dropout problem in our school is more important than a major drug problem in a school 500 miles away."

A story about the homecoming parade is timely if it's published near the time the parade occurs— not two months later.

Prominence

Prominence refers to the "newsworthiness" of an individual or organization. It's true that names make news, but some names make more news than others. Why? Because they are more prominent. Thus, if the star quarterback flunks a math exam and is ineligible for the big game, his troubles are newsworthy. Suppose you flunk the same exam. Is that news? Not unless some other issue is involved. The quarterback, like it or not, is more prominent than you, and his failure has more far-reaching impact. "There goes the ball game," will be the reaction to the news of his failure.

When people learn that you flunked, they will shrug, mutter "How about that?" and go on about their business.

The element of prominence explains a great deal about how news is handled. It explains, at least partly, why the press follows movie stars, why it interviews the governor, and why it runs story after story about well-known people and organizations.

Most newspapers put the most important news of the day on the front page. In the front-page sample in the **ON DISPLAY** feature on page 65, you can clearly see the issues of significance for this edition of the paper.

Consequence

The element of consequence refers simply to the importance of an event. To go back to our star quarterback, his failure on the exam is more important to more people than is your failure on the exam because of the consequences. The team may lose the big game. Hundreds, maybe thousands, of football fans may be disappointed—or they may be thrilled at the performance of the substitute who gets his big chance and makes good.

The element of consequence, incidentally, offers many opportunities for stories that do not, on the surface at least, seem to have any news value. For example, if the state legislature passes a bill providing state financial aid to local school districts, you should recognize that this action, even though it took place in the state capital, has important consequences for your school. Ask school officials how much money will come to your school and what will be done with it.

This is an example of localization, the act of bringing out the local angle in a story. Another example would be the effect on construction plans for a new school in your town if steel or railroad workers were to go on strike. It's important to keep up with the news outside your school; you never know when an item in a daily newspaper, newscast, or periodical will lend itself to localization.

Human Interest

As a human being, you're probably most interested in other people and how they behave. Human-interest stories cause readers to laugh or cry, to feel emotion. If a little girl is trapped for days in an abandoned well, that's a human-interest story. If a dog mourns at his master's grave, that's a

Front-Page Coverage

The Spartan Shield, Pleasant Valley Community High School, Pleasant Valley, Iowa

The front page of this student newspaper offers a good idea of the topics of importance at the time it was published.

December 19, 1997
Volume 38 ☐ Issue 4

Sports, 15, 16   News, 4-6, 10-12

Non-Profit Org.
U.S. Postage Paid
Pleasant Valley, IA 52767-0332
Permit No. 4-B

Winter Sports

December marked the official start of winter sports. Here sophomore Seth Mahler competes in a recent swim meet.

Interact Club

Sponsoring a pie-throwing contest helped the club to raise money for the local Angel Tree.

The Spartan Shield

Pleasant Valley Community High School
PO Box 332,
Pleasant Valley, IA
52767-0332
Forwarding and Return Postage Guaranteed
ph. (319) 332-5151
fax (319) 332-8525

Youth and the Law

The adult community and recent legislation have been sending a clear message to teens about their behavior

Despite feelings of discrimination, restrictions enacted to protect all

By Thomas Kroeger
Editor-in-Chief

The teenage years are an unavoidable aspect of human biological maturation, and dating back to the days of Shakespeare, and of course since the advent of the 1960's, adults have grown progressively distrustful of the coming generations. Commonly branded as "out of control," "gangs of delinquents," recent legislation such as curfews, random locker searches, and proposed driving license restrictions continue to stress a feeling of discrimination.

A recent article in the Washington Post cited numerous surveys that detailed the adult community's increasing fear that today's children will fail to make the world a better place. Some students agree that recent trends in society don't portray youth and teenagers fairly.

"I think that society will always stereotype teenagers as being wild and irresponsible, when in reality there is just a small percentage of out of control teens," senior Jon Mcgee said.

Youth and the law *continued on page 5*

➤ INSIDE
Curfew ordinances, their effectiveness, and student opinions are discussed on page 4.

Administration threatens increased penalties for parking violations

■ **Administrators seek to encourage legal parking through increased penalties for violators**

By Nick Mohr
News co-Editor

Responding to an increase in illegal parking in student lots, administrators have instigated a new "no-tolerance policy" to deter students from parking illegally.

"The new policy really doesn't change the existing regulations. We are just enforcing those rules already in place more strictly," Assistant Principal Deb Menke said.

The new restrictions include penalties for parking in teachers' parking zones, utilizing more than one parking space per vehicle, and parking in authorized delivery areas. For the first offense, a record is made of the vehicle's identification and a warning sticker is placed on the car. Additional infractions are punishable by the vehicle's being towed at the owner's expense.

Student's views are divided as to the impact of how the new disciplinary policy is being handled.

"If everyone would park where they are supposed to, there wouldn't be a problem. It's all a question of common courtesy," junior Jeff Haut said.

"It's a good idea to discourage illegal parking, but sometime the administration will have to address the real issue. We need more parking," senior Kris McCulloh said.

"We need to only allow juniors and seniors to drive to school. Don't issue school permits to freshmen and sophomores, and the problems will be reduced," senior Beth Parsons said.

A lack of parking doesn't seem to be a problem, however. "We have enough parking in our student lots. The problems come when parking is a long distance from the door and students choose to park

Parking *continued on page 5*

Photo by Thomas Kroeger

Encouraging students to park legally and obey existing regulations remains the focus of the new "zero-tolerance" parking policy.

Animals or children are usually good topics for human interest stories. Photos can draw readers' attention to the page.

human-interest story. If that substitute quarterback mentioned earlier throws five touchdown passes, that's a human-interest story. In other words, human-interest stories are unusual. They're about the shortest basketball player, the fastest track runner, the youngest teacher, or the oldest custodian. They tickle the funny bone or evoke feelings of sorrow, warmth, pity, or amazement.

The element of human interest explains why newspapers run a story when a 15-year-old genius graduates from college or when a bride on her way to the wedding gets lost and ends up at the wrong church. The fact that the world has one more college graduate is of no particular significance in itself, nor is the fact that someone got married. But wouldn't you want to read a story about a 15-year-old college graduate or a lost bride? Yes, and so would many other people. These stories have human interest.

Conflict

An element of news that enters into many stories is conflict. Why do so many people attend sports events? Conflict. Why are so many people interested in elections? Conflict, at least partly. Why are wars, to take the most extreme case, news? Conflict. Conflict involves tension, surprise, and suspense. (Who will win the game? Who will win the election?) People are in an almost constant state of conflict with their environment. Former husbands and wives fight over custody of their children; homeowners fight to keep taverns out of their quiet neighborhoods; scientists fight to discover cures for deadly diseases; countries fight for supremacy in the world arena.

Other Factors

There are many other elements of news, including progress, money, disaster, novelty, oddity, emotions, drama, animals, and children. It would serve little purpose to

TIPS ✓ **worth taking**

News arithemetic. Here's one way to sum up what is and isn't news, from *Editing the Day's News* by George Bastian and Leland Case:

1 ordinary person + 1 ordinary life = 0

1 ordinary person + 1 extraordinary adventure = news

1 husband + 1 wife = 0

1 husband + 3 wives = news

1 bank cashier + 1 spouse + 7 children = 0

1 bank cashier - $20,000 = news

1 person + 1 achievement = news

1 ordinary person + 1 ordinary life of 79 years = 0

1 ordinary person + 1 ordinary life of 100 years = news

discuss each of these at length here. Just keep in mind that news judgment rarely involves simply checking off items in a list of elements to determine whether the event is news. Professional journalists may not be able to define news, but they know it when they see it. As a student, you just have to develop a system of warning bells. Determining news value is not an exact science. You can't expect to rely on formulas.

Look for news items that will satisfy readers' curiosity, and remember, there are no shortcuts. Saying that "it isn't news if a dog bites a man, but it is if a man bites a dog" is oversimplification. If a dog bites the President of the United States, that's news. If a dog with rabies bites a child, that's news. Nor does it help to talk about having a "nose for news." Some reporters seem to make a career through being in the right place at the right time because they have trained themselves to know where the right place is. Their noses have little to do with it.

Generating News Story Ideas

To begin developing interesting, newsworthy stories, your first step is to come up with possible story ideas. One way to generate ideas is for the newspaper staff to hold a brainstorming session.

Getting On Line

What are some basics I need to know to get started on the Internet?

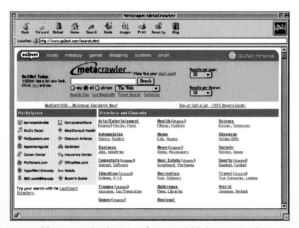

Metacrawler is one of several high-powered search engines that allow users to find specific information on the Internet.

Maybe you're one of those people who's on line every night and could be writing books about it yourself. Then again, maybe you're not. If you're in the second category, read on. What follows are answers to some very basic Internet questions.

How do I get on the Internet? Besides a computer and a modem, you need to subscribe to an Internet service provider (ISP) through which you can get on line. Large national ISPs, such as America Online and Flash Net, provide you with software and a service that gives you simple, user-friendly access to the Internet. Other ISPs just provide the connection and let you find your way through the Net on your own. Your local Yellow Pages probably lists many such companies; just be sure they offer local phone access so you don't have to make a long-distance call to get on line.

What is the World Wide Web? The Web is an interface that hooks up a great number of sites on the Internet and lets users have easy access to them. Web sites are "pages" that may contain text, pictures, sound, and even animation. On any particular page you can connect to other pages by clicking on-screen links (usually words in color). For example, clicking on the link "Turkey" in an on-line news story about earthquakes will take you to stories about the 1999 earthquake in that country.

Access to the Web is available through nearly all ISPs via a browser, a program that lets you get to the information on the Web. Netscape Navigator and Microsoft Internet Explorer are two commonly used browsers, but there are others.

What do those labels beginning with "http" mean? The labels are really addresses of sites—or home pages of individuals or groups—on the Web. For example, the newspaper *USA Today* can be found at http://www.usatoday.com/. The *http* part stands for the means the browser must use to get to the source; it's short for hypertext transfer protocol. The *www* stands for the Web; and *usatoday* is the host name, the computer where that newspaper is physically located. The *com* at the end lets you know that the computer is run by a company rather than an educational institution (*edu*), organization (*org*), or government agency (*gov*).

If there's so much information out there, how can I find what I'm looking for? If you know the exact address of a site, you can simply enter it on your server screen. Most servers also let you "bookmark" a site; just click on its name in a list and the page will appear on the screen.

If you're just looking for, say, information on stress, you can go to various search engines (or directories), enter your category, and find a list of web sites that pertain to it. Search engines include Yahoo!, Lycos, and Webcrawler. All engines can be accessed at their own site addresses on the Web.

FOLLOW-UP

1. In groups, share what you know about the Internet. Answer any questions that non-Internet users in the group may have.
2. Use a search engine to research a topic your teacher assigns to you. Report to the class on how you went about seeking the information and the usefulness of the sites that your search produced.

Most newspaper and yearbook staffs meet for an hour a day; some meet only once or twice a week. There is not a lot of time for discussions that end in long arguments without resolving the problems at hand. The brainstorming technique is a fast method of getting a lot of solutions, ideas, or alternatives for action in a very short amount of staff time. You can use this technique with large groups or with only two or three participants.

Brainstorming Sessions

Here is one proposal for staging a productive brainstorming session. You can adapt it to your own needs and situations.

First, have the group leader—editor, business manager, or adviser—explain the problem to be considered. (Example: We are planning a special issue of the paper on problems facing today's graduate. What stories should be assigned?)

Give people a few minutes of "think time" in which to consider the problem. They might jot down two or three ideas.

Now have the group leader call on each participant individually to raise an issue or make a proposal for action in one short sentence. Participants need not explain their thoughts or elaborate on them. There should be no discussion or criticism of any idea presented. (To continue the example: How does one hunt for a job? What are additional opportunities for education? How about military opportunities? How does a person establish residency for voting, in-state tuition fees, and

Brainstorming is an excellent way to come up with story ideas for the newspaper.

Brainstorming. Become familiar with these basic steps in the brainstorming process:

1. Announce the topic, problem, or goal for the brainstorming session.

2. Allow participants a few minutes to think.

3. Encourage each participant in turn to offer a brief idea or suggestion. Assign a person as a recorder to write down all ideas as presented. Refuse to allow criticism of any idea.

4. Participants offer additional suggestions, in turn or randomly.

5. All participants receive copies of the list of ideas, which they rank in order of importance.

6. Compile all rankings; discuss top ideas further or act on them.

other benefits?) Each idea is briefly stated; each can be the basis for a story.

As each idea is given, a group member records it. You might want to write the ideas on the chalkboard or an overhead-projector transparency.

Go around the group two or three times. Don't let people get by with stating what has already been said. Tell participants always to have more than one idea in mind, and urge them to let their imaginations run wild. Generally, the wilder the ideas the more productive the results. No idea is a bad one unless it's not expressed. Participants can use ideas as springboards for expanding or building on suggestions of others. (Example: The original idea might have been, How does a recent graduate hunt for a job? Follow-up ideas might be, How important is the résumé? How do you arrange for and act during an interview? How do you know if the employer is really interested in you? Are job-placement services available at our school?)

After you seem to have exhausted the ideas from the group, begin to narrow your list to one of top priorities. Here is where you can lose control, unless you are careful about procedure.

Still without discussing the list, have the group look over the suggestions. (If meeting time is a problem, have the recorder type the list and make each member a copy.) Have each participant select the five best ideas from the list—or, if the list is small, the best two or three—and write his or her choices down in order of priority. Don't let people try to influence each other; each person must evaluate the list individually.

Now compile the answers. Some common preferences will emerge quickly. Take the best choices as determined by "secret ballot" and put them into action.

The editors may need a brainstorming session on each of the best ideas to think them through to their final conclusions. You may also want to have a quick brainstorming session on photos or graphics to accompany your chosen stories.

Advantages of Brainstorming

By now the advantages of this system should be obvious. To begin with, no one person can dominate the discussion; every idea is important and equal for purposes of group evaluation. Furthermore, a large number of ideas can be generated in fewer than five minutes; and the more you use the system, the better you get at it. Finally, brainstorming conserves valuable time for more vital functions.

Now, for what planning tasks can the brainstorming system be used? Why not brainstorm that question through for a starter?

Information from Polls

Some of the most interesting news stories are based on the results of polls, but getting legitimate information from polls can be tricky. Consider the following:

Not long ago, ABC's *Prime Time Live* aired a compelling story about a reporter who hitchhiked across America. Shots of breathtaking scenery contributed to a lovely video experience. As he journeyed across the country, the reporter made it a point to get close to the people who offered him rides, and he asked them all the same series of questions: Is America a better place or a worse place than when you were growing up? Is America more dangerous now than then?

To be accurate, polls must involve a carefully selected sample of participants who are asked thoughtfully constructed questions.

On the night the show aired, anchor Diane Sawyer announced that 90 percent of the people the reporter interviewed had said yes, the country has gone downhill. That would be scary except for one thing: The reporter's information and the opinions of those he interviewed are worthless except as anecdotes. They show nothing of any real value. Why?

For starters, the reporter's sample—the number of people interviewed—was far too small to provide any clue about how the population as a whole might feel. He interviewed 31 people! You don't have to interview a million people to make a good generalization in this situation, but 31 is just not enough.

Furthermore, the reporter's sample was biased. It systematically excluded huge numbers of Americans: those too young or too old to drive, those who do not own motor vehicles, shut-ins, people in hospitals, people in class or at work. It also excluded all Americans who weren't driving the roads upon which he was hitching.

It's OK to report what 31 people said about America. It's bad journalism and bad science to suggest that the opinions of those 31 people have broad meaning.

Getting a Fair Sample

Polls are popular, and therefore widespread, in student publications, but unless done right they can spread just as much misinformation as good information. The key is this: For a poll or survey to have a statistically high chance of representing not just those surveyed but the population at large, *every* member of the group to be surveyed must have an *equal* possibility of being included in the survey sample. A sample so drawn is called a random sample, an important concept for would-be pollsters to know.

A properly created sample—one that complies with the definition just provided—will yield results at what is called the 95-percent confidence level; that is, in 95 of 100 cases, the population sampled will respond the same way as the total population the group is intended to represent.

This is why polls that, for example, predict the outcome of an election always say the poll can be expected to be accurate plus or minus a number of points. The doubt stems from the 5 percent of the time (in our example) that a random sample will not accurately represent the whole group.

What this means can be summed up easily: Be careful about leaping to conclusions about polls or surveys. If you go into the hall and ask the first

10 people who walk by a simple yes-no question, that's fine. You may discover that 8 of the 10 received e-mail last weekend. You can safely report that. You cannot, however, say that 80 percent of the student body received e-mail last weekend, because you don't know that. After talking with 10 people who just happened to be walking by, you have no information upon which to base a generalization. You need a random sample. What you get with people who just happen to walk by is called an availability sample. It's just an accident. Those were the 10 strolling the halls when you were asking about e-mail.

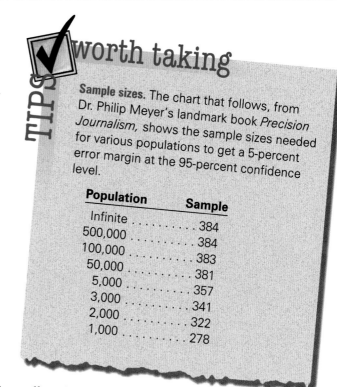

Sample sizes. How many do you need to talk to in order to get a random sample? That's an important question in polls and surveys but not as important as the one overriding principle that everyone in the group to be studied—often called the "universe"—has an equal chance to be in the sample.

Suppose you want to find out what the seniors in your school are going to do after graduation. The first thing you need to know is how many seniors there are. If yours is a small school and there are just 25 seniors, you have no sampling problem. You don't have to worry about setting up a good random sample: Just ask all of them. And forget 95-percent confidence. You are at 100 percent.

If your school is one or two times larger than the first example, you might still survey all the seniors. A questionnaire distributed in a way that allows every senior an equal chance of receiving one would work.

Caution is once again in order. You could ask the senior English teachers to distribute the questionnaire. That would catch most of the seniors—but perhaps not all. Are there seniors who aren't required to take senior English? What about those absent that day? They must have an equal chance to be surveyed, too.

Watch not only for bias built into the process but also your own bias, even if accidental. You want to reach the seniors, so you ask your four favorite teachers who teach senior classes to distribute a questionnaire.

worth knowing

TERMS

Polling. If you really become involved in polling, you will probably use the following terms in analyzing your data:

Mean: Another term for *average*. If the basketball team scores 50 points in one game, 75 in the next, and 100 in the next, compute the mean by adding the three scores and dividing by three. The mean score is 75 points a game.

Median: The number "in the middle." In a series of figures, it's the figure that has the same number higher as lower. In this series of figures the median is 10: 3, 4, 5, 6, 7, 8, 9, 10, 11, 12, 13, 14, 15, 16, 17.

Mode: The most frequent occurrence in a series. Suppose the grades for 200 students divide this way: 25 A's, 50 B's, 100 C's, 15 D's, and 10 F's. The mode is C.

What's wrong with that approach is apparent: Your favorite teachers may all teach social studies, and not all seniors may take social studies.

So what do you do? Go to the school office, get a list of all the seniors, and see to it that each one gets a questionnaire, even if it means sliding one into every senior's locker. An even better idea is to distribute the questionnaires in senior homerooms.

What if the school has 500 seniors? Now the question of sample size is truly relevant. Generally, the bigger the sample, the more trustworthy the results (up to a point). How big is big enough might surprise you. A properly drawn sample of 1,000 people can accurately represent the opinions of 10 million.

Representative sampling. Major public-opinion pollsters routinely generalize to the entire population of the United States based on interviews with 1,600 people. Such a sample must be drawn upon with the population's overall characteristics in mind; that is, if 25 percent of the nation's population is over 65, then 25 percent of the people in the sample must be over 65. If 20 percent are African American, then 20 percent of the sample must be African American as well. However, within that 25 percent of elderly or 20 percent of African Americans people are still selected randomly.

As a scholastic journalist, of course, you have neither the time nor the expertise to define your samples so precisely. Still, you can conduct reliable polls if you stick to the one main rule: Everyone in the sample must have an even chance of being questioned.

So what do you do about those 500 seniors? Well, no sample, random or otherwise, is considered reliable unless it includes *at least* 50 people. That's the minimum number. For a more representative sample, poll 50 people or 10 percent of your universe, whichever is more. (In this case, it's the same.) Using your office list of seniors, therefore, sampling every tenth person on the list would provide a fairly representative random sample.

Formulating Survey Questions

Sampling errors are not the only possible pitfall. The questions themselves must be carefully crafted and unambiguous.

Questions need to be short and simple and should concentrate on only one item. Can you see the problem with a question like "Levi's jeans fit better and last longer. Do you agree or disagree?" A person might agree with the first part of the opening statement but not the second—so how should she answer?

"Do you smoke cigarettes?" is an ambiguous question. Tobacco use among teens, widely believed to be increasing, is a legitimate concern and one a student journalist might want to learn about, but "Do you smoke cigarettes?" won't generate much information. If the respondent—the person you're interviewing—answers yes, does it mean she smokes them every day or just on her birthday? Does it mean one cigarette a day or two packs a day?

Filter questions. "Do you smoke cigarettes?" can be what is called (no pun intended) a filter question. If you ask that question and the respondent filters himself out of the survey by answering no—you're finished with the interview. If the respondent answers yes, now you can zero in: "Do you smoke more or less than one pack per day?" "Do your parents know? If so, do they approve?" "Are you concerned about the health implications of smoking?"

Asking the right questions. Make sure you ask the right people the right questions, so that the people in your universe have a good chance of answering intelligently. For example, don't survey the freshman class on whether teachers in your school should have tenure. It's expecting a great deal of a freshman not only to know what tenure is but to have a reportable response.

Then there's the problem of reporters who stack the deck in the *way* they ask a question: "Are you going to go to college after graduation or just to a technical school?" "Are you going out for football or just joining the choir?"

Respondents can mess things up, too. Think about it: People all like to make themselves seem as cool, important, sophisticated, and well-informed as possible. So if a reporter comes along and asks a certain kind of question, someone might be tempted to stretch things a bit—or even if not, to give the reporter the answer he or she seems to be looking for.

Say that a reporter asks a student, "Did you consume alcohol last weekend?" (probably a filter question, by the way). There may be individuals in your school who would say yes to the question because they think it's cool to drink. So report the results with a large grain of salt or don't ask this sort of question in the first place.

Publishing Poll Results

After conducting a poll or survey, make sure that you publish it in a timely manner so that the results are considered valid. Suppose the football team at a major university in your state loses its first six games. A poll asks if the coach should be fired, and a majority responds yes. A month goes by, in which the team wins four games. Is the poll still valid? Probably not.

Be careful about conclusions. Just because two events occur together does not mean one caused the other. For example, 90 percent of the students randomly surveyed in your school say they rented movies last weekend. At the same time, the school district reports a schoolwide increase in SAT scores. Does that mean that watching movies makes you smarter? What do you think?

Remember also that a survey in your school represents only your school. Even a good sample randomly created still represents only the universe studied. Thus, do not report that 90 percent of all students in the world rented a movie last weekend. You didn't survey all the students in the world.

Graphic presentation. A final word on polls and surveys: Many lend themselves to presentation through charts and graphs. (For an example, see the chart on page 91.) A number of software programs easily convert numbers to charts or graphs. This can cut down the story about the poll to a more readable size than if the results have to be recounted within the story.

Still, sometimes such charts and graphs can be silly: One school ran a pie chart to give the results of a poll that was split 48 percent to 52 percent. Clearly, a little common sense is in order.

The **ON DISPLAY** article on page 77 is based on a poll. In addition to presenting poll results, the story also includes student reaction to the various data compiled.

Story Based on Poll

The Panther, Miami Palmetto Senior High School, Miami, Florida

Teen Smoking Statistics on the Rise Since 1990

by Michele Kavooras and Palak Shah

In the fifth grade when most kids were only studying the dangers of smoking, sophomore Jennifer Klinker was already learning the firsthand effects of nicotine.

"I quit in the sixth and seventh grades and I started again in the eighth grade," Klinker said.

Although most teenage smokers begin smoking later than Klinker, it is estimated by the end of high school 72 percent of high school students will have smoked a cigarette and 32 percent will be labeled as smokers.

Of 183 students surveyed at this school, 19.1 percent said they smoked regularly. However many students feel this statistic is too low.

"I think it is a lot higher than 19 percent. I think at least half the school has tried smoking cigarettes. I think 35 to 40 percent are smokers," junior Alberto Tassenelli said.

According to the survey, most smokers began because they were curious or their friends influenced them. Either way, all smokers agree smoking is a method of relieving stress.

"I've tried to quit three times, but I can't because my friends still smoke around me. It is a stress reliever, and I am allowed to smoke at home," senior Karli Hansen said.

For some students it took a while for the habit to slowly develop over the course of a few years. Yet for others it seems as if they were addicted virtually overnight.

"When I first started smoking my friends would always ask me why I smoked, then they would ask me for a drag. Then it seemed like overnight they were out buying their own packs. They were hooked really quickly," junior Joy Nicholas said.

Many smokers develop an addiction to nicotine, the most addictive substance in cigarettes, and find it very difficult to stop smoking. There are varying methods experts recommend to stop smoking.

"I've tried a nerve pinch in the ear, the patch, the chewing gum, and smokeless cigarettes. None of these methods worked for me," Assistant Principal Marion Rogers said.

Many times the habit cannot be broken and excessive smoking leads to bodily harm. Cigarettes are a carcinogen and many smokers develop lung cancer. It is predicted that there will be about 13,000 new cases of lung cancer in Florida this year and 153,000 people will die of this type of cancer this year. These statistics have been on the rise since 1990. They will continue to grow each year as long as younger people begin to smoke.

"It is very depressing but it is hard to quit. The only way to really influence someone is to see a parent or someone really close to you die of something like that," senior Ryan Baldwin said.

While eating in a restaurant many people are nauseated when a smoker lights a cigarette.

"I think the right to ban smoking in public places is fair. The people who don't wish to smoke have the right to breathe clean air in public places; however, smokers have the right to have a smoking section," Tassenelli said.

Many people do not want to breathe in second-hand smoke because of the harmful ingredients in cigarettes. Recently cigarette companies released a list of 599 possibly harmful ingredients. Among the ingredients is citronella, which is a type of insect repellent, and urea, an excretion from the human body.

With all of the scientific studies most smokers realize their habit is detrimental to their health but still can not kick the habit. "I'm not sure why I smoke. I wish that I didn't, but I do," Nicholas said. ■

Wrap-up

Once-easy ideas of what constitutes news—mostly events and government—have been revised in view of changes in society and in people's interests. Modern readers, with their busy schedules, appear to want shorter stories, often in list form, more color, and less "bad news." Because of *USA Today* and its colorful and upbeat approach, newspapers are changing. As literacy and circulation decline, journalists seek different ways to capture a greater share of an often-mobile audience.

These changes concern some people who believe newspapers have a constitutional role to play that mandates coverage of government. Newspapers apparently must decide whether to compromise or fade. Thus, although once newspapers concentrated on government news, they now deliver information on all aspects of modern life, including fashion, health, the arts, leisure, exercise, parenting, film, video, and music.

Despite these changes, students are urged to read newspapers for knowledge of what editors consider news. Serious journalism students certainly need to be informed about news. Reading newspapers is a good way to hone your news judgment.

Some people decide what is news and what is not by applying the "Who cares?" technique. This means assessing how much reader interest a story has. The more people who care about the informa-

tion in the story, the greater its news value. Of course, there is reader interest in mere gossip, but ethical journalists avoid tasteless items.

Other journalists rely on more formal elements of news to determine a story's importance. Among many, the most-often cited are timeliness, proximity, prominence, consequence, human interest, and conflict.

Once a journalist is trained and experienced, news judgment becomes a matter of instinct. Professional journalists make judgments without reference to techniques that beginners often rely on.

One way to develop ideas for news stories is to make use of the technique of brainstorming, the art of obtaining numerous ideas within a short time. By carefully organizing and controlling brainstorming sessions, the staff can develop new ideas quickly and efficiently.

Many interesting news stories in scholastic publications report the results of polls. These can make interesting reading provided the poll is a random one, which means that every person in the group to be surveyed has an equal chance of being in the poll. Surveys in which a reporter grabs the first 10 people he or she sees are called availability surveys, and while they sometimes make interesting reading, they are valid only as anecdotes. Scientific surveys must be random.

On Assignment

INDIVIDUAL ACTIVITIES

1. Write a brief definition of each of these terms:

advance

brainstorming

conflict

consequence

filter question

human-interest story

localization

news judgment

prominence

proximity

random sample

timeliness

2. Identify three possible school news story ideas for each news element mentioned in this chapter. State the story idea in a single sentence. For example, one idea for timeliness might be that grade averages are rising and causing concern over grade inflation. For each idea identify the news element(s) present. Then identify the audiences to whom the story will appeal.

3. Test your critical thinking. Discuss in class or write an essay on this situation: A 12-year-old student has been involved in a serious crime. As a journalist what do you report? What, if anything, do you leave out about the person? First, answer in terms of "Who cares?" Then consider how your code of ethics affects your decision.

4. Brainstorm these subjects to understand how brainstorming works:
a. What might your school be like in the year 2010?
b. To how many uses can you put a jumbo-size paper clip?
c. What are some possible school yearbook themes?
d. How many photo ideas can you develop to illustrate your school's science program?
e. On what topics could you poll students to develop relevant newspaper articles?

5. Analyze the On Display article on page 77. In your opinion, were enough survey questions asked? What others, if any, might you have included? Make your analysis about one page long.

6. Assume you are totally free to identify a topic for a special issue of your school newspaper. Brainstorm a list of topics; then use the complete process to identify the 10 best ideas. For each idea, brainstorm a list of articles you would assign to cover the topic adequately. Narrow that list to the 10 best subjects for articles. (Keep these lists for use later.)

7. You want to find out how many juniors in your school have ever cheated on a test. How would you go about learning this with reasonable certainty that your facts are correct? Construct a sample and devise a questionnaire to determine scientifically the number who cheat (or who say they do, which might be different from the number who actually do so).

TEAM ACTIVITIES

8. Working in teams, examine the front page of today's local newspaper and identify all the news elements in it. Discuss what you have found out about the news judgment of the paper.

9. On separate cards write a brief summary of each front-page story that you have been studying. Ask six to eight students to rate the stories in order of importance. Is there a general agreement? How do the elements of news affect the raters' decisions? Compare your results with those of the other teams.

10. With a team, find examples of poll results published in local newspapers. Identify the sample used for each one. Decide whether the sample was truly random and whether the conclusions drawn are valid. Compare your findings with those of other teams.

SURF THE NET

11. Identify one story on the Internet that you can localize for your school publication. Good places to start looking are sites such as state agencies or legislative sites.

career profile

Executive Editor

Gilbert Bailon

Most people don't realize how much they need a local newspaper, said Gilbert Bailon, vice president and executive editor for metro at the *Dallas Morning News.*

"Newspapers are still the main source for people to find out everything they need to know in their lives," he said. "CNN isn't going to tell them what happened at the local city council meeting or what the schools are serving for lunch that day.

"Newspapers provide a great deal of the sorts of information and entertainment that people need every day in their lives. Providing that kind of information is needed, and it's a lot of fun. It's very important."

There is another, equally critical role for the media to play, he said—that of watchdog.

"It's essential to the people that someone be able to communicate to them the information they need while at the same time provide accountability to society's leaders," he said. "I feel like I am doing something that's useful, and not just making money for a company."

Bailon entered journalism to find an outlet for his creative writing.

"I have always had this love of writing," he said. "A lot of us in this profession like working with words but are shy when it comes to other people. This lets you find ways to express yourself."

After graduating from the University of Arizona in 1981, Bailon was accepted in the Cap Cities Minority Training internship program and worked at the *Fort Worth Star-Telegram* and the *Kansas City Star.* In 1985 he joined the *Dallas Morning News.*

He is a 1987 graduate of the University of Missouri's Multicultural Management Program and was elected president of the National Association of Hispanic Journalists in 1994. At the *Morning News* he has held positions as a reporter, day city editor, assistant metro editor, and executive editor. He has also worked at the *San Diego Union* and *Los Angeles Daily News.*

Bailon believes there will always be a demand for people who can digest facts and write about them.

"It's not as if the medium of the printed word is going away," he said.

"There will always be a need for journalists in a greater sense. It may not necessarily be in newspapers—although I don't think newspapers are going to go away—but there will always be a need for someone who can think, digest, and put out information."

Bailon loves what he is doing and believes students will too, if they get the proper training.

"The first thing you must do is master the English language," he said. "Learn how to punctuate, learn grammar, and then practice, practice, practice."

He also advises those interested in a journalism career to join a student publication.

"If you have an opportunity to mess around with photos, graphics, and words, do so," he said.

FOLLOW-UP

1. What personality traits would make a person well-suited for a job such as Bailon's—dealing with the "metro," or local, aspects of the news?

2. Survey at least five people about where they get their news. To what extent do they use different types of media to get different types of news? Do they agree with Bailon that newspapers will continue to be an important news source?

CHAPTER 4

Organizing the Staff to Capture the News

KEY CONCEPTS

After reading this chapter, you will

▶ understand both traditional and modern newspaper-staff organization

▶ understand the role of teamwork in news organizations

▶ be familiar with ways to break long stories into more palatable pieces

▶ know some of the basic sources for news

Change—some would say a revolution—has hit the news industry's organizational styles in the last decade or so.

New ways have been devised to organize, and therefore to improve, coverage. Traditional beat systems in which each reporter covered a specific area have given way to what one newspaper describes as "topical beat clusters." From the creation of the story idea through the reporting, photo, design, and production phases, teams often work together in an effort not just to capture the superficial day-to-day material but to get at the heart of readers' information needs. What follows may serve as a guideline.

The Newspaper Staff

Although staff organization has changed at the newsroom level, the lines of authority

Even members of a large city newspaper staff need to work together to keep their readers informed.

and responsibility have remained about the same. The organization of a school newspaper closely parallels that of a commercial newspaper.

The Publisher

At the top is the publisher. In theory the taxpayers of your school district are the "publisher" of your newspaper and yearbook. In practice the taxpayers can't perform that function, so they elect a board of education to oversee the school district, including your publications. Not even the board, however, can be publisher and still perform its other duties, so it appoints a superintendent, who

in turn appoints a principal of your school. The principal functions as publisher.

Just as the publisher of a commercial newspaper is rarely concerned with the minute-to-minute operations of the paper, neither is the principal in most cases. Instead, the principal, usually working with the journalism adviser and the students, sets certain broad guidelines—general policies within which the newspaper staff, like everyone else associated with the school, must function.

Students who grumble that they are not free to publish or broadcast any story they please should remember that the editor of the *New York Times* has the same problem. Sometimes there's not enough space, sometimes stories are not in the public's best interest, and sometimes stories are about unpalatable subjects. This is a fact of journalistic life. Rarely do publishers issue orders that honest journalists can't live with. When it does happen, the journalist—professional or student—has to decide what to do. Take a stand? Resign? Compromise? You should not easily compromise your basic values, but neither should you draw a line in the sand every time you lose an argument.

The Adviser

Sometimes caught between conflicting aims of students and administrators is the journalism adviser. This person serves as liaison to the publisher, the public, the faculty, the students, possibly the printer, and everyone else who wants to talk about the newspaper. The best advisers walk a tightrope and keep all their various publics happy. That's not an easy job.

Department Heads

Next in command in traditional organizations are the heads of the various departments. These include the managing editor, or editor-in-chief, who has the overall responsibility for the editorial department—that is, the news operation. Others may be in charge of business and design.

Subeditors

Under the managing editor are various subeditors. Sometimes these are organized by "page," with each subeditor in charge of a page. This arrangement is often unsatisfactory, because the news can seldom be categorized by page. Some sports stories rate page-one treatment and some so-called hard-news stories may belong on an inside page. Many stories defy simple classification.

Subeditors carry various titles. Sometimes their title is that of a section for which they are responsible, such as entertainment or sports. There may be a news editor, who supervises news coverage or may serve as the chief copy editor and headline writer. There may be an editorial-page editor, who works closely with the managing editor and probably writes the editorials that express the newspaper's opinions.

By whatever names the subeditors go, they form the link between the top person—the managing editor—and the reporters. Under the sports editor, for example, there may be two or three sports reporters.

Traditional Newspaper Staff Organization

Team Newspaper Staff Organization

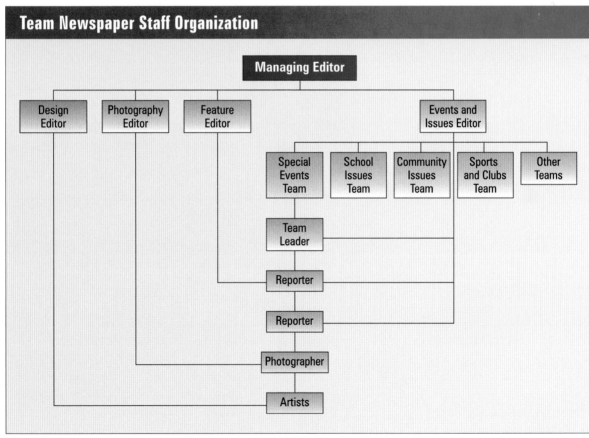

A newspaper staff can be organized in a number of ways. These diagrams show two of the more common ones.

Reporters

In a traditional organization reporters are of two types: beat reporters and general assignment reporters. The beat reporter checks the same news sources for each edition of the paper. If the beat is the fine arts department, for example, the reporter visits each of the art, music, and speech teachers as often as possible, covers the school plays and concerts, writes the story about the annual spring music festival, reports on the new band uniforms, and develops stories about the debate team preparing for its state competition. Beat reporters become specialists; they may not know everything that goes on throughout the school, but they'd better know everything that happens on their beat.

The general-assignment reporter, on the other hand, goes wherever necessary. He or she may be covering the assembly speaker today and writing a piece about the lack of parking space tomorrow. Such a reporter is a jack-of-all-trades, doing the work passed out as the news editor sees fit.

Some people would include a third classification of reporter, the "cub." This is the novice, who may be assigned to pick up brief items from fairly regular sources or to check weekly with three or four teachers to see if they have any news to offer. The cub who does this work willingly and well, and who shows enterprise by coming up with an important story on his or her own initiative, will not remain a cub for long.

Repackaging and Redesigning the Staff

Traditional ways of organizing the staff for coverage and presentation of the news worked well enough until a few years ago. Suddenly, journalists looked up and discovered that a great many of their assumptions about readers were wrong.

When all the audience had to choose from were newspapers, magazines, and the three major television networks, it was fine for journalists to produce long-winded stories about oh-so-serious topics. The audience has more choices now: hundreds of television stations via cable or satellite dish, movies on tape and disk for home viewing, an explosion of niche magazines appealing to small, focused audiences, and the Internet. This explosion of options has forced journalists to take a

One Adviser's Tale of Staff Reorganization

How can a student paper be made more appealing and relevant?

Organizing staffs in new ways can be almost a matter of survival. Here, Deanne Heinen Kunz, adviser at Westlake High School in Austin, Texas, tells of her experience:

We glared, disheartened and forlorn, at the pile of freshly tallied surveys. Discovering that less than 40 percent of our student population read our beloved newspaper caused profound anguish to staff members.

A team organization allows reporters, photographers, and editors a say in choosing stories and deciding the most effective ways to present them.

Although the survey results hurt our egos, we gained valuable information: Our readers looked at the photos and graphics first and remembered them longest. Also, our readers tended to skip over lengthy articles in favor of shorter ones.

So we took the plunge into uncharted waters. Our primary focus became the "packaging" of stories into palatable pieces that we hoped our audience would devour. Our next step was determining what packaging meant to us and how to achieve it. Here is what we came up with.

During the initial phase of planning each issue of the paper, writers work with editors to think through story ideas thoroughly, considering items such as the purpose of the story, the audience, the news values, the possible outcomes, the actual story content, and its placement in a specific section. Beyond this, they provide ideas for graphic enhancement, as well as introduce ways in which the story presentation might entice readers. They prioritize and break the story ideas down into small pieces, or *factor* them.

When packaged into a unit, these factors will provide the reader with multiple entry points into a story, rather than rely on just a headline and photo to grab attention. Entry options include the main story, sidebars, pull quotes, headline and subhead treatments, tip boxes, quick summaries, checklists, schedules, scoreboards, and infographics, as well as photos and art. Treatment may include objective and subjective views, with staffers determining which of these options are suitable for each particular story idea.

Because we chose to package news stories, features, and opinions together, it became necessary to rethink the traditional structure of dividing the paper into four or five sections. Our new system of "Inside," "Outside," and "Sports" gives many options.

The "Inside" section primarily contains stories and visuals linked with events and activities associated with school: clubs, organizations, student or faculty personality profiles, curriculum changes, and similar subjects. "Outside" contains nonschool-related items, such as book, restaurant, music, and college reviews; and teen issues, such as eating disorders, ethics or religion, alcohol and tobacco use, and so forth. "Sports" focuses on school programs and athletes as well as recreational sports, activities, and hobbies. (We have since added a separate section, "Soapbox," which features staffers' columns on a wide range of topics.)

Dividing sections in this manner makes packaging the stories into reader-friendly units much easier. Readers can select one part of the package to read or, if we're lucky, might find themselves engrossed in story after story until they have read the entire paper. And isn't that what they ought to be doing?

FOLLOW-UP

1. How well would the specific organization described in this article work for your school paper? Discuss in class which parts would work well and which would not.
2. Find or prepare a newspaper page in traditional format and one using smaller articles and infographics. Show the two samples to several students and question them about which format they find more appealing and why.

new look at what they do. With fewer resources available to them—yet more sources available to their readers—editors need to discover ways to reach an audience whose interests and lives are quickly changing.

For the most part, this audience doesn't read long stories. Readers skim, jumping from one spot to another on a page. If a story jumps to (is continued on) another page, readers rarely read the jumped part, so long stories are broken into smaller, punchier pieces. Related stories are packaged, not strewn about without a plan. Pull quotes, charts, boxes—all have a more prominent place. Designers strive to provide more points of entry, or spots that attract a reader's eye.

Jack Kennedy, a longtime adviser for publications at City High School in Iowa City, Iowa, wrote the following in the summer 1994 edition of *C:JET* (*Communication: Journalism Education Today*):

> The traditional award-winning feature story is a 30-inch monstrosity that mixes together five authoritative sources, seven local students, three paper sources and the quote/transition formula into a tossed salad that goes "in-depth" on some teen problem. I have never read one of those stories that couldn't be "factored" into several smaller, more compact pieces.

Smaller. More compact. These are words to plan by.

The WED Approach

To produce publications following this new model, many high school journalism departments have replaced top-down planning (Sally, do this story. Juan, get some art. Jim, lay out the page), with all-in-one writing, editing, and design (WED) planning.

It works this way: Teams of editors, reporters, photographers, and designers work together planning stories and graphics before the reporting begins. Some people call this the "maestro" approach to gathering, designing, and packaging news and information. Instead of one writer doing a "30-inch monstrosity," one writes a main-bar (the main story that brings an issue into sharp focus), someone gathers sidebar (related) material for perhaps several short stories, someone else turns some of the sidebar material into charts and graphs for easy reading, and yet another person puts it all together on a page as a complete package. All of the work is done under the direction of a team leader.

The concept requires reporters to think visually—to figure out ways to break long stories into readable chunks, with charts and graphs and other graphic devices. At the same time, it requires designers to understand reporters' problems in telling complete stories: The information is first; how it looks is second. Reporters and photographers must also work together—that is, go out together to get a story. The walls separating the newsroom, darkroom, and production space need to fall, literally and figuratively.

In the **ON DISPLAY** sample on pages 90–91, notice the many means by which information about automobile safety has been presented. Different angles on the same general topic came from many staff members.

News Sources

Both reporters and editors must know where to go to get the news. They cannot sit back with their feet on their desks waiting for someone to walk in and hand them their stories. They must go to the source—and dig, dig, dig, if necessary.

Who are the sources and where are they? Commercial newspapers receive a considerable amount of their news from wire services, organizations such as the Associated Press, United Press International, Reuters, and the *New York Times* News Service. Wire services provide news around the clock from all over the world. No newspaper is fully equipped to cover the world by itself, so newspapers subscribe to services that provide this news for them. Except for these wire services, there is little difference between the types of news sources scholastic journalists use and those the professionals use.

The WED Approach

Featherduster, Westlake High School, Austin, Texas

This sample spread shows how text and graphics can be organized into interesting and inviting packages of information put together by teams of writers, editors, and designers.

---

28   WESTLAKE FEATHERDUSTER   March 26, 1993

From mild fender-benders to massive pile-ups, assorted accidents eventually plague most drivers

COLLISION COURSE

Time slows to a crawl. A foot pushes, painfully slowly, against the brake. The fender of a Pontiac rushes to meet you. A few loose papers on the seat beside you tumble against the dash and falling, as if in ballet, to the floorboards. Metal groans and rubber squeals as you plow head-on into another driver's car. Most drivers have had their share of close calls. Many have had worse. Whether they result from carelessness or malice, car accidents seem nearly inevitable.

Often, close calls on the road result from hot tempers and irrational judgments.

"About a year ago I was driving down First Street when they were building the new convention center, so the road veered off to the right," science teacher Mark Misage said. "And as I turned, there was someone next to me in a big 1971 Buick—just a huge car. As I was coming around the corner, he completely cut me off. My tire hit the curb, and of course I was pretty angry about it. I was honking, yelling and gesturing so they slowed down and almost stopped. As we proceeded on by the river heading to Mopac he tried to stay right next to me. As I came up to the light, I glanced over and there was a chrome-plated .45 leveled right at me. I froze for about three minutes. He was yelling things at me like 'What are you going to do now,' and I just sat there hoping for the best. Then the guy just drove away."

Probably the most dangerous experiences with cars happen in car wrecks. The intensity of wrecks not only causes injuries, but leaves lasting impressions on the lives of the victims involved.

"When I was in seventh grade, we were driving home from school, and it was still drizzling after a hard rain—enough to where the roads were still real wet," senior

Lisa Phipps said. "My mother was driving my friend and me in a Toyota Four Runner. My mom had her seatbelt on, but we didn't. We decided to go home a new way through some winding roads. As we were going around a corner, I looked up and all that I saw was a rock wall rushing towards us. We were totally out of control. My mom slammed on the brakes, but they were locked. We continued towards the rock wall, then for a second were perfectly still. That's when the car began to roll. It rolled onto its top, rocked back and forth a little, and then rolled back upright onto its wheels. The most I remember is being thrown against each side of the car. After realizing what had happened, we got out of the car and another car was there to help us. I had a black eye and a fat lip, and my friend broke her collar bone and her pinky. My mom was okay, but the only thing that saved her life was the seatbelt."

Though injuries are almost inevitable during a wreck, the accidents themselves can often be avoided. Because of the irresponsibility of many drivers, unnecessary wrecks harm innocent people.

"I was riding in my friend's jeep going about 50 mph, and she was showing off," senior Jenny Barrett said. "She took a right into some gravel and swerved back left real fast. I don't remember flipping because I must have flown out first, and I was unconscious. Everyone else was thrown from the car too. My boyfriend jumped out of the car and hurt his foot. Everyone had road burn, and the driver broke her collarbone and a rib. We were all rushed to the hospital and I had to stay the night there, with IVs and staples in my head."

On the other hand, many people fall victim to poor driving on somebody else's

part or something beyond the driver's control. Sometimes in these situations the driver is unfairly responsible for the damages.

"My sister and I were driving in my jeep taking a left into Lost Creek from 360," junior Stephanie Bonner said. "Our light turned green and we started to make our turn, when all of a sudden a car coming in the opposite direction on 360 hit us. I didn't even see him coming because he didn't have his lights on. The driver was drunk and when our cars hit it took off the front end of my car. The wreck was his fault because he ran through a red light. Luckily no one was hurt, but he didn't have insurance so we had to pay for all of the damages. The wreck happened the first of February, and they still haven't been able to repair all of the damage yet."

Other wrecks are no one's fault, but result instead from adverse weather conditions or other uncontrollable factors.

"At 7 o'clock one night, I was rounding a corner on Westlake Drive down by Westlake Beach, and the roads were wet," senior Renick Smith said. "A deer jumped out into the middle of the road and I hit it with the right side of my car. I slammed on my brakes and hydroplaned across the road, hitting a tree with the driver's side of the car. Because I wasn't wearing my seatbelt, I cracked the windshield with my head. Basically the front end of the car was smashed in. I walked home from there. When I went back to get my car, it wasn't there because the cops towed it away, impounded it, and were going to come over to my house and arrest me for leaving my car there. I went to the police station and explained to them what happened, and finally they let me go."

Most of the drivers on the road will at one point in time come face to face with an accident. Though these events are traumatic, many people learn to be more cautious and alert to the drivers around. ■

Angie Thompson

DON'T PANIC

How to keep cool if you are involved in an auto accident

Being in a serious car accident, means that there are injuries, a potential fire hazard involved or an obstruction of Austin property. The driver should, according to the Westlake Police Department, do the following:

•First, try to get your car out of the flow of traffic by pulling your car to the side of the road, in accordance with state law.

•Second, call the police. This is an important step because the officer has to take a report, or a blue form. By that time you should know if there are any injuries. If so you can ask for an ambulance.

•Third, make sure you have your driver's license and proof of insurance to show the officer.

•Fourth, if the damage is severe you may need to call a tow truck. It's wise to keep important numbers in your glove compartment, just in case.

If the car wreck is not serious, the police will not come to the scene of the accident.

The Austin Police Department recommends that as long as a person is not in need of medical assistance, they shouldn't call the police. They recommend exchanging names, addresses, telephone numbers and license plate numbers with the people involved in the accident.

In the Travis County area last year, 1,400 to 1,450 car accidents occurred, some involving students. ■

Valerie Bonner

ROAD TEST

Can you identify these common street signs?

① ② ③

March 26, 1993 WESTLAKE FEATHERDUSTER 29

Safest cars

This table includes the safest vehicles from each manufacturer, the five most popular cars at Westlake and their safety features. An "s" means standard and an "o" means optional. A "-" indicates that this feature is not available.

Make	Model	Price	Air bags	Std/opt	ABS	Auto seat belts
Acura	Legend	$29,500	2	s	s	-
Audi	100 series	35,000	2	s	s	-
BMW	740i	54,000	2	s	s	-
Buick	Roadmaster	23,000	1	s	s	-
Chevrolet	Beretta	12,000	1	s	s	-
Chrysler	Concorde*	19,500	2	s	o	-
Ford	Crown Victoria	22,000	2	s **	s	-
Geo	Prizm	13,000	1	s	o	-
GMC	Sierra pickup	12,900	-	-	s	-
Honda	Accord	17,630	2	s **	o	-
Hyundai	Excel	8,500	-	-	-	s
Isuzu	Trooper	23,000	-	-	s	s
Jeep	Grand Cherokee	25,000	1	-	s	s
Mazda	929	31,300	-	s	s	s
Mitsubishi	Eclipse	13,000	-	-	-	s
Nissan	Sentra	11,000	1	s	o	s
Pontiac	Bonneville	23,000	2	s	s	s
Saturn	SL1	12,700	1	s	o	s
Subaru	Legacy	17,000	1	s	-	s
Suzuki	Swift	9,500	-	-	-	s
Toyota	Camry	18,885	1	s	o	-
Volkswagen	Passat	17,000	-	-	-	s
Volvo	850	26,000	2	s	s	-

Most popular makes and models

Of 193 students surveyed

GAS Chevy 19 percent	GAS Ford 15 percent	GAS Toyota 12 percent	GAS Nissan 10 percent

	Make	Model	Price	Air bags	Std/opt	ABS	Auto seat belts
1.	Chevrolet	S-10 Blazer***	18,000	-	-	s	s
2.	Chevrolet	Full-size pickup	15,000****	-	-	s	s
3.	Honda	Accord	17,630	2	s**	s	s
4.	Ford	Bronco	24,000	1	o	s	
5.	Toyota	Camry	18,885	1	s	o	s

*also sold as Dodge Intrepid & Eagle Vision
.**Driver's side air bag is standard; passenger side is optional.
***also sold as GMC Jimmy
****Several models are available; students did not specify which model they drove.
Note: Reinforced doors roll bars, roll cages, crush zones and other safety-enhancing chassis designs are common and built into most cars.

compiled by Matt Chapin

Insurance rates (per year) for teenagers

Car insurance rates (Full coverage)
New Car (Girl Driver): $1,632
New Car (Boy Driver): $1,672
Used Car (Girl Driver): $1,280
Used Car (Boy Driver): $1,300

Truck insurance rates (Full coverage)
New Truck (Girl Driver): $1,720
New Truck (Boy Driver): $1,800
Used Truck (Girl Driver): $1,520
Used Truck (Boy Driver): $1,600

Safety features on car (Reductions to costs)
Airbag & Anti-lock Brakes: $120-600

Speeding tickets (Added costs)
One: $800
Two: $1,200

How much do the rates drop at one's "mature age"?
Girls (age 21): 25 percent
Boys (age 25): 25 percent

Defensive driving (Reductions to costs)
Girls: 15 percent
Boys: 15 percent

From Cyndee Engal, Gary Russel Farmer's Insurance Co.
compiled by Justin Craycraft

Safety features

Anti-lock braking system (ABS)

Automatic safety belts

Air bags

Answers

1. Bridge or culvert ahead
2. Do not enter
3. Enter either side
4. Steep hill ahead
5. Watch for wet roads
6. Winding road ahead

④ ⑤ ⑥

News Tips

Many ideas for news stories come in the form of tips. No newspaper staff, no matter how large, can be everywhere at once. Often, someone who is not a member of the staff will inform you of an event you may want to cover. Let it be known that you are on the lookout for tips, and you will be surprised at how many people will volunteer valuable information.

Sometimes material for a school newspaper comes from school administrators, teachers, or students who are not on the newspaper staff. These persons may come to the newspaper with ideas for stories or essays. Sometimes they have already written a story or essay. Often these contributions can be valuable additions to the paper.

HISTORY worth remembering

Call for copy. The solicitation of stories or essays dates back to 1721 when James Franklin, brother of printer, inventor, and statesman Benjamin Franklin, announced in his *New-England Courant* that he "earnestly desires his friends may favor him from time to time with some short Piece, Serious, Sarcastick, Ludicrous, or other ways Amusing."

The Future Book

Another valuable source of news comes with the creation of a future book. A future book is a listing, by date, of events coming up that the newspaper might want to cover. If you hear in December that the board of education is going to consider a school bond issue in May, enter that fact in the future book under "May." The future book is simply a long-range calendar of events and ideas. If the paper runs a story this week that mentions an event that will take place next semester or even next year, someone should clip the story and put it in the future book.

School District Public Relations

Many school districts have a public relations representative whose job is to provide newspapers—including yours—with news about what the district is doing and planning. If your school system has such a representative, introduce yourself and make sure the school newspaper is on the mailing list.

Often, the news releases they send about the district will provide the incentive for your newspaper to dig deeper, to get a more complete story. Never assume that a news release is the whole story; always attempt to find out if something is missing. Public relations people have the welfare of their organization uppermost in their minds. Journalists, by contrast, must consider the welfare of the community they serve. (For more information about public relations, see Chapter 16.)

Coverage and Staff Communication

Tips, standard reference works, future books, public relations people—all are potential news sources, but in the end how well the news is covered will depend on what the staff knows about the processes of gathering it. In this area, the reporter is the boss. He or she is on the front lines of journalism, where the action is. No newspaper, radio, or television news department is any better than its reporters.

Reporters are the eyes and ears of the news staff, constantly on the watch for story ideas, but they cannot do the job alone. The entire staff— each person described in this chapter—has an obligation to be on the alert for material.

The people at the top of the organization—the editors—have an obligation to maintain good communication with the whole news organization staff. Editors need to be in constant communication with reporters, photographers, designers, and artists to avoid duplicating assignments and to settle disputes over turf. Memos, bulletin boards, in-house e-mail,

Reporters are on the front lines of journalism, alert and responsive to story ideas.

and staff mailboxes all provide ways for staff members to keep in touch with what others are doing. Frequent staff meetings are helpful. Such meetings are also one way for editors to praise the work of the staff publicly.

In an efficient news-gathering operation all members of the group work together creatively and smoothly to produce accurate, high-quality material—no matter what formal organization is in effect.

Wrap-up

The first requirement for an efficient news-gathering operation is a well-organized staff. In some places, great changes have occurred in news-staff organization.

The organization of most school publications parallels that of commercial publications. At the top is the publisher. The board of education, elected by the public, appoints a superintendent, who in turn appoints a principal for your school. The principal functions as publisher.

The principal, usually working closely with the journalism adviser and the students, sets guidelines—general policies within which the publications staff must function.

Serving as liaison to the publisher, the public, the faculty, the students, and possibly the printer, is the journalism adviser. He or she has a difficult job and is sometimes caught between the conflicting aims of students and administrators.

In the organization of a publication staff, the managing editor (or editor-in-chief) is at the top of the pyramid, determining policies and developing story ideas. Subeditors, sometimes organized by the page or section for which they are responsible, work under the managing editor's direction. Sports editors, chief copy editors, and editorial-page editors are in this group. All help supervise reporters.

Many high school publications have replaced the traditional organization with the notion of teams—editors, reporters, designers, photographers—all working together to package the news effectively.

Reporters can either cover a beat, returning always to the same sources and subjects, or do general assignment work. General assignment reporters cover whatever is necessary.

Where does the news come from? At commercial publications, the wire services provide a great deal of copy. Student publications have no wire services and have to be staffed by people willing to dig for stories.

Tips from readers and a carefully kept future book help keep the news flowing. School public relations people try to keep publications, including school publications, informed. They are advocates of their employers, however, and the material they generate must be viewed accordingly.

The real eyes and ears of any publication are its reporters. They are on the front lines. How good a publication becomes depends on its reporters and how well they are supported. Helpful editors who maintain good communication are great contributors to any publication. Teamwork is essential to a smooth journalistic operation.

On Assignment

INDIVIDUAL ACTIVITIES

1. Write a brief definition of each of these terms:

beat reporter	mainbar
future book	managing editor
general assignment reporter	publisher
jump	sidebar
maestro	WED

2. Test your critical thinking. Why do you think the team approach to staff organization has become so popular? What advantages does it have? What are the possible disadvantages? Do you think the traditional organization works better in certain circumstances? If so, in what circumstances? Discuss your ideas in class.

3. Assume that your editor wants a two-page spread on what to do on a Saturday night in Yourtown, U.S.A. Using WED, or maestro, notions of organization, map out who would do what. What will the mainbar be about? How will the stories be broken down so none is a "30-inch monstrosity"? What elements of the assignment can be done with photos? with charts? graphs? infographics generally? How about a column or other editorial comment? Summarize your ideas in a short report.

4. Now try the same WED, or maestro, breakdown for a story that would be more difficult to make graphic: the budget of your school district. How do you make large figures such as $2.3 million mean something to an average reader? What parts of the story lend themselves to charts and graphs? Can the story be told through the eyes of, for example, one small middle-class family? Write down your ideas and be ready to present them to the class.

5. Write a critique of the On Display spread on pages 90–91. How well do the various parts work together? How effective are the graphics? What changes, if any, would you suggest? Make your critique about one page long.

6. Research the effects of new or recent technology (computers, modems, e-mail, fax transmissions, satellite feeds, digital photography, page-design software) on the media and media organizational patterns. How are the journalists in your town using the Internet? How much do they use computer-assisted reporting to extract information from databases? How do new techniques add to or detract from working in teams? Write a short report on your findings.

7. Interview your journalism adviser or someone on the local newspaper staff to learn the steps involved in newspaper production in precomputer days. Find out about several specific ways in which the computer has made production easier—for writing and editing, for layout, and for photographic reproduction. Report your findings to the class.

TEAM ACTIVITIES

8. As a class, invite your school newspaper editor to talk about the specifics of the paper's organization. Who does what? Do staffers' roles always remain the same? In teams, meet with staff members of other school publications in your town or vicinity, including college and university publications. Ask the questions above about their organization. See whether they have ideas you could borrow or adapt to your special needs.

9. Propose new approaches to the organization of your school newspaper. Develop a staff organization chart. Write a short job description for every person on the chart. What regular beats will you have? What subject-matter teams will you create? What will the adviser's role be? In what specific ways will your plan improve the paper?

SURF THE NET

10. Visit the web sites of several professional or student publications for examples of info-graphics accompanying articles. (*USA Today* is one good source.) Print copies of articles and graphics that you think work effectively together. Be ready to explain your choices to the class.

career profile

Executive Editor

Addie Rimmer

Editors at the *Boulder Daily Camera* were faced with the kind of dilemma editors face every day: whether to run a story on page 1 or somewhere inside the paper.

The story was about a controversial plan to build a large shopping center in a small neighborhood. The editors had put the story on page 1 when the developers announced the plan. The most recent story was the response from neighborhood groups opposed to the plan.

"We had a long discussion about fairness on that one," said Addie Rimmer, then executive editor of the *Daily Camera*. "I wanted the editors to be aware of what the possible conflicts were if they didn't run the response from the neighborhood on page 1."

These kinds of decisions, made several times a day, are what open newspapers to criticism about fairness. Rimmer said that despite what some believe, most papers don't push for certain kinds of stories.

"The news is relative," Rimmer said. "Much of the public doesn't consider what else is competing with certain stories. It may be a day when there are lots of big stories to consider."

Rimmer became executive editor of the *Daily Camera* in November 1995. She previously was editor of the *Boca Raton* (Florida) *News* and deputy features editor of the *Long Beach Press-Telegram.* She is presently assistant managing editor at the *Detroit Free Press.*

Rimmer believes in meeting frequently with city and civic leaders to encourage better communication.

"People have to know that you are accessible," she said. "They know you from your name on the newspaper, but they should feel comfortable enough that they can pick up a phone and talk to the person with the name."

Community meetings also allow Rimmer to find out people's interests.

"It's real important to know what the people who live and work in an area are thinking," she said. "I don't know that you can find that out if you just get in an office every day and talk to other journalists."

An executive editor is in charge of a paper's daily news coverage. The job includes attending news meetings in which editors decide what stories to cover and how much emphasis to give each.

About these meetings, Rimmer has said, "We try to anticipate questions readers might have and make sure we've discussed any balance or fairness issues that might be raised."

The editors also decide at news meetings what stories to put on page 1. In the case of the shopping center, the editors decided the neighborhood position had been covered thoroughly in previous stories and that the story did not warrant front-page play.

"That was OK with me," Rimmer said. "I just wanted to make sure we really thought about the issue and made the correct decision."

FOLLOW-UP

1. An executive editor's job puts more emphasis on meetings and decision making and less on actual reporting. What are the pros and cons of such a job? Discuss your ideas in class.

2. Consider the issue Rimmer faced concerning where the community response to the shopping center should go. Should it be on page 1 regardless of the other news of the day? What sorts of stories might move it off page 1? How could the paper try to ensure fair coverage even if the story were not on the first page?

CHAPTER 5

Making the Interview Work

KEY CONCEPTS

After reading this chapter, you will

▶ know how to conduct an effective interview, including how to research and structure the questions

▶ be familiar with issues related to notetaking and the use of tape recorders

▶ understand the strengths and limitations of conducting interviews on the Internet

▶ know how to prepare and use stock questions

▶ know what to do if the source wants to go off the record or wants to read your story before it's published

▶ know the characteristics of an effective interview-based story

It can be terrifying, edifying, gratifying. You may need a tape recorder, a telephone, e-mail—and a pleasant smile couldn't hurt.

The subject is interviewing. It's the oldest and still the most common technique journalists use to get information.

It's not a perfect technique. When they published their landmark 1966 study on interviewing, Professors Eugene Webb and Jerry Salancik titled it *The Interview, or the Only Wheel in Town*. The second part of the title referred to how a gambler might view a crooked roulette wheel, and it's an apt comparison with interviewing. The process may be flawed—a gamble sometimes—but journalists have to know how to do it.

On the late-late TV show, the reporter crashes into the police chief's office and threatens, "What's going on with that big murder case? Either I get the full story—now—or I'll expose you as the incompetent political hack that you are!"

Even your first experience conducting an interview need not be frightening if you are well prepared and ready to listen.

The chief pleads for time: "Give me until midnight. If we don't have the killer by then, you can go ahead and print the story."

Reporters rarely threaten news sources during interviews. That old movie scene between the chief and the reporter is an interview, however. An interview takes place any time a reporter asks a question. It may be during a quick telephone call, or it may be in an intimate two-hour chat. The type of interview will be determined by what the reporter wants to know: information, facts, opinions, or personal details.

Interviewers need to be courteous and well-mannered; they need to try to accommodate the demands of their deadlines with concern for the needs of sources; and they need to understand and try to stamp out personal biases that can interfere with their own clear thinking. Above all, however, they have to know that their work has a noble side to it, a public-service side. If a question is appropriate and it's in the public's interest to ask, pushing for an answer is appropriate behavior for a journalist.

Conducting your first interview, especially when it's with an intimidating authority figure or celebrity, can indeed be terrifying. Ask any experienced journalist to recount his or her own first interview, and you can expect an anecdote about nervousness, missed follow-up questions—and, often, a kind source who took pity on a novice and saved the day.

Journalists vary in their interviewing skills and techniques, of course. Most agree, however, that there are no great reporters who are not good at the interview. A tough hide, coupled with an open and friendly demeanor, is essential.

General Interviewing Guidelines

The first step in getting ready for an interview is knowing what you want to find out. The second step is deciding whom to ask. This means knowing who can be expected to know what. The rule is to go to the primary source of information, the person whose business it is to have the best and most reliable information about what you want to find out. This seems painfully obvious, but apparently it's not. An instructor was startled when two of his students, sent to get information about a power failure, quoted him in their stories. He had said, "I understand it was caused by construction workers who cut a power line." As it turned out, however, that was not the cause—and the stories looked pretty silly. Ask only what someone is likely to know (unless, of course, you simply want an opinion).

Once you know what you want to find out and whom to ask about it, you can decide what sort of interview is involved. If you want information about plans for a new building, make an appointment to talk to the appropriate administrator. If you want 15 opinions about the grading system in your school, ask 15 instructors or students. Always identify yourself as a reporter before asking questions. (There are exceptions to this on the professional level, but they are not the issue here.) A simple statement such as "I'm ____ of the paper, and I'd like to ask . . ." will usually suffice.

You must be comfortable with people and be able to meet and talk with them. Reporters run the risk of distracting their subject if they are overly nervous. If you're nervous, try to hide it. Remember that most people enjoy being interviewed. They enjoy talking about themselves and expressing opinions to interested people. This works in your favor.

Preparing and Asking Questions

Prepare your questions *before* the interview. Know what you're going to ask. Many times this will require doing some research to get background on your subject or the issues you want to find out about. You can't ask the drama coach intelligent questions about recent productions if you haven't bothered to find out what plays were performed in the last few years. You can't ask the oldest resident in town about the construction of a local covered bridge if it was built 20 years before he was born. Use the local library or historical society, accounts in the professional papers, or any other sources that will provide the background you need.

During the interview, be straightforward. Don't make a speech every time you want to ask a question. Avoid questions that can be answered with a simple yes or no. When you give subjects that choice, too often they will take it. "No" is not the liveliest quote in the history of journalism.

Ask open-ended questions that will get a quotable response. "What do you think about . . . ?" is a better way to start a question than "Do you think . . . ?" In other words, ask good questions. If your questions are superficial, the answers will be too. Ask a school administrator what he or she would do to upgrade the school if unlimited funds were available. Ask how grading policies could be made fairer. Ask if the student government is too powerful or too weak.

Checking through back issues of periodicals is one way to unearth background information on important news stories.

Stock questions. If you find yourself in need of stock questions, remember the following device, invented by Professor LaRue Gilliland. Sometimes known as GOSS, it will give you enough questions to get started:

Goals ("What do you hope to accomplish with this project?")

Obstacles ("What obstacles stand in the way of your achieving your goals?")

Solutions ("How can you solve this problem? How can you overcome these obstacles?")

Start ("How did all this begin? Whose idea was it?")

In lighthearted interviews these stock questions, included in John Brady's *The Craft of Interviewing* (Cincinnati: Writer's Digest, 1976), can be intriguing:

What three books (records, movies, presidents) would you take with you if you were stranded on an island?

If you could live at any time in history, what age would you choose?

If you could be anyone you wanted to be today, whom would you be, and what would you do?

If someone gave you a million dollars, how would you spend it?

If your house were afire, what would you grab on the way out?

-*Est* questions. Some people object to *-est* questions (proudest, saddest, biggest, and so forth) because such questions have a tendency to be "high schoolish," and in their simplicity they can distort people's views. Ask a father his proudest moment, and he may mention the birth of his son—but that doesn't mean he wasn't proud when his daughter was born. (The son came first, that's all.) Ask the football coach to name the "best college football team in history," and you have forced him to pick just one team, when he might list five great teams. In a way, *-est* questions are almost like yes-no questions—they can cut off conversation—and that's not usually what a reporter wants to do during an interview.

Stock questions. When reporters have to interview someone on short notice, some rely on stock questions—all-purpose questions usable in any situation. Because the idea here is how to handle an interview for which you have no time to prepare, sometimes stock questions take the form of *-est* questions, such as What's your biggest worry?

Embarrassing questions. Student journalists often are advised to avoid asking embarrassing questions. This is bad advice. As a journalist, you *must* ask embarrassing questions—but keep good taste in mind. Don't pry; don't snoop. Don't ask hostile or leading or loaded questions. You do, however, have to get the truth if you can; that's almost a definition of journalism. Ask, as politely as possible, what you have to. If you don't get an answer, ask again.

Listening to Responses

Pay attention to how a question is answered. Does the subject answer calmly and easily, as if the question has been asked a thousand times before? Or does he or she grope a bit? Does the subject, perhaps, pay you the finest compliment: "That's a good question"? Note also what questions the source does not answer. Sometimes a "No comment" can be very revealing. Above all, if you don't understand what is said, stop and ask for clarification.

Don't ever threaten your news source or use coercion. Don't challenge what the source says except for clarification (and then don't fail to do so). Don't argue; listen. That's important. You can't hear if you're talking. So be quiet and listen, even when the source seems to be wandering from the subject. Sometimes the digression is more interesting than what you asked about.

Just before the interview ends, ask if there is anything else you should know. Many a routine story has been turned into a good one simply because the reporter had the good sense to leave time for the source to volunteer information.

Conducting the Interview

Much of what we have been talking about so far in this chapter applies to all interviews—that is, all the times when you as a reporter ask questions—but it's particularly true in formal interviews, those that are planned and set up in advance.

When you call to arrange an interview, your choice of language can work in your favor. The very word *interview* can scare off a subject, so perhaps *talk* or *meeting* would be better terms to use.

You have made the appointment, done your research, and arrived on time at the subject's house or office. To start the interview—to get yourself and the subject warmed up to each other—try asking the relatively trivial but necessary background questions. Get down the basic data: exact name (including middle initial), family status (if the interview is to focus mostly on the person), and job title or years in current position (if the interview involves issues).

You might decide to ask the most important questions first (to ensure that they get answered in the time allowed) or you might start with the

Asking relevant, well-thought-out questions often gets your subject talking freely and naturally.

small, unimportant things first and then, as you and your subject become comfortable and the tension fades, get to the bigger, more important questions. Avoid the mistake of a student whose first question to the instructor was "Do you think your contract will be renewed next year?" The question was blurted out as a result of nervousness, and it certainly got the interview off to a rocky start.

Observing the Subject

If you want to make the reader "see" your subject, look for quotes that convey the subject's personality. When the star of a Rose Bowl game of 50 years ago says, "I'm always glad to talk about that game, because it gets better every year," you get a certain insight into his personality. Similarly, a city official who begins every answer with "I'm not sure I should be telling you this . . ." may be revealing not only personal insecurities but internal controversies over what information should be made public.

Actions are important. Does the subject sit on the edge of the chair or pound the desk for emphasis? Does he or she tell a particularly revealing anecdote? (If so, consider putting it in the story.)

Being Friendly and Attentive

How do you get subjects to give you solid, interesting information? How do you get them to open up to you and to talk freely? You already know the answers intuitively from your personal life. Nobody likes a grinch. Nobody likes a smart-aleck or a show-off. Nobody likes people who talk too much or seem to know everything.

Successful interviewers let their pleasant personalities come through. Smile. Relax. Laugh at your subject's jokes. Notice the children's pictures on the desk and say how attractive they are. You want to establish rapport, to connect as a person.

For most ethnic groups in America, good eye contact is considered a sign of interest. So look your subject in the eye—without staring, zombie-like, at him or her. Be aware, though, that in some ethnic groups, eye contact is considered rude—so be sensitive to the other person's views. The same can be said of a firm handshake: Remember that a soft handshake is preferred by some groups (including Native Americans.)

Listen carefully. Listening is often overlooked as a communication tool, and it shouldn't be. Pay close attention to what's being said. There's a famous story of a journalist who covered a speech and then wrote a story about youth in Asia when the speaker really had talked about euthanasia. Listen!

Use the person's name in the conversation. Most people like to hear their name, so use it.

Be polite. Don't ever chew gum during any interview. Don't rearrange the desktop so you can plop down a big notebook or tape recorder. Dress properly. Say "Hmmmmm" and "That's interesting" when the subject speaks. Maintain an alert, not slouching, posture.

If you've prepared well, you should be able to ask thoughtful questions. Express interest in the subject and what he or she has to say. You don't have to agree. You shouldn't agree. (You're neutral, remember?) Besides it's the source's ideas, not yours, that matter. Examine and understand your own biases and set them aside.

Try to develop an atmosphere of trust. There are times when a reporter has to be tough, has to let the source know that it's clear he or she is not being straightforward—but being pleasant works better most of the time.

Taking Notes

How does an interviewer take useful notes? People talk faster than reporters can write, generally. So what journalists do is develop systems that they can rely on and translate after the interview. Skill in shorthand can be helpful, for example. Lacking that, you might invent a system of speedwriting. Then you can fill in the details after you've left the interview. If the source agrees, a tape recorder can also be valuable. Some people freeze up when confronted by a tape recorder, but others are reassured by it, knowing the reporter with a tape recorder has made a commitment to accuracy.

There are pros and cons to the use of tape recorders. On the plus side is the fact that they permit you to get exact quotes, quotes that sound precisely the way the source talks. That's also the minus side. People talk funny. They say "Ya know" a lot, and they start sentences that they never finish, or they switch tenses in the middle of a sentence. You don't want to reproduce all of that (see Chapter 8, "Handling Quotes Fairly and Accurately"). You do want the exact words when they're important, however, and that's what you get with a tape recorder.

Another problem is that tape recorders capture every sound, not just the sound you want. That's why you should be careful not to use a tape

Tape-recording an interview can assure your subject that you have an accurate rendition of what he or she said.

recorder in a crowded restaurant or on a busy street. The sounds you want may be obscured by sounds you don't want.

If you have a tape recorder running, you should be able to listen more attentively than if you're struggling to listen and to take notes at the same time. Nevertheless, always write down the really important information—names, exact figures, dates—just in case the tape recorder fails. Also, keep taking notes throughout the interview. If you stop taking notes, the source will think you're not interested and may stop talking—which usually is exactly the opposite of what you want.

If you use a tape recorder, try to make it a small one, the kind you can easily hold in one hand. Avoid going into an interview carrying a boom-box lookalike.

Conducting Internet Interviews

Nowadays there is a small but discernible trend toward using the Internet as an interview tool. If you and your source both have e-mail accounts, your interview can take place over the Net. In so-called chat mode, you can conduct the interview in real time.

In a sense you can "interview" thousands of people simultaneously on the Net. It's very common these days for student journalists doing research to post a note in a newsgroup to solicit opinions. For example, say you're doing a story about censorship in your school. A common practice would be to post a note in a student journalism group asking other student journalists to relay accounts of their experiences.

Searching for information this way is fine, but remember that not everyone you meet on the Internet is as honest and committed to accuracy as you are. The very fact that so many people on the Internet are anonymous should make you cautious.

There is nothing wrong with using the Internet for interviews. You should be aware, however, that the face-to-face interview is almost always better than one on the telephone or via modem. People send messages in other ways besides words, and you miss the messages sent by smiles, frowns, body language, and gestures if you're not in the same room with your source.

Going off the Record

Sometimes sources suggest providing information to a reporter "off the record." You need to be prepared should that happen.

The first item to ponder is what is meant by *off the record*. Does it mean that the reporter can use the information but not give the name of the source? Does it mean the information cannot be used at all? Before you agree to anything, make sure both parties know the rules.

If you agree to accept off-the-record information, make sure that you and the source agree about when the interview is back on the record. Remember also that no information is off the record unless you agree. No one used to dealing with journalists would ever tell you anything off the record unless you have agreed that it *is* off the record—but then not all sources know the rules.

One thing is certain: If you accept information off the record, you're honor bound to stick by the agreement. If "off the record" in the context of your interview means using the information without giving the name of the source, that's what you have to do. If it means you can't use the information at all, you can't—no matter how much you want to.

Writing the Interview Story

When writing the interview story, try to avoid general descriptions of your subject. Don't for example, say that the store owner is short; tell the reader that he is 5 feet 2 inches tall. Don't say that the executive is lively and efficient; say that she moves about the office, juggling projects while giving an interview. Don't say that the author is intelligent; point out that he has written six books. Don't say that the volleyball coach is athletic; say that she has won four championships and displays the trophies in her office. In other words, be specific in your detail.

Using Details

Here are some examples of detail by Gay Talese, a fine American journalist, writer, and researcher. The first describes a man:

> [He was] fifty years old, a lean and well-tailored man with gray hair, alert blue eyes, wrinkles in the right places . . . . He had an angular face that suggested no special vitality; wavy gray-black hair combed tightly back from his high forehead, and soft, timidly inquiring eyes behind steel-rimmed glasses. His voice was not strong; it was, in fact, almost high-pitched, wavering and imploring when he spoke normally.

The second describes an office:

> Traditional English, thirty-five feet long and eighteen feet wide, trimmed in draperies of a white linen stripe, it is lined with a blue-black tweed rug that conceals the inky footprints of editors who have been up to the composing room. Toward the front of the room is an oval walnut conference table surrounded by eighteen Bank of England chairs. . . . In the rear of the room, a long walk for visitors, is Daniel's big desk and his black leather chair which, according to the decorator, was selected because it produces a minimum of wrinkles in Daniel's suits.

Using Quotes

Use many direct quotes when you write the interview story. Quotes, the person's own words, bring the person or the topic to life. It's through these that your readers come to know the subject best, especially if you've asked the right questions.

Probably the single most important question is Why? Others are Who? What? When? Where? How? As you write, remember to stay out of the story. Don't say, "I asked . . ."; just give the answer.

> **Not this:** When asked how it felt to sky-dive, he replied, "It was exciting and exhilarating."
>
> **This:**   He said sky-diving was "exciting and exhilarating."

Q-and-A Technique

One effective story technique that has won acceptance from readers is what journalists call "Q and A." In this system the reporter's exact questions are reproduced, followed by the source's exact answers. Instead of a story, in the usual sense, the newspaper presents virtually a verbatim transcript of the interview, although sometimes the questions and answers are reordered for a more logical story flow.

In using Q and A, the journalist has no way of signaling to the reader the most important statements in the interview—but that might not be a bad thing. The Q-and-A technique allows the reader to determine, without interference, what is or is not important. It's a good technique, approved by many sources. Don't try it without a tape recorder, though, and reserve it for stories that are not breaking news.

The **ON DISPLAY** article on page 111 is based on an interview with a television reporter in Phoenix. Notice how in this excerpt the writer not only presents details to characterize the interview subject but also, through direct quotes, lets the subject do most of the talking.

Prepublication Checking

What if the person you interview wants to read the story before you print it? At one time, this was considered an open-and-shut case: Tell the source no. That kind of prepublication checking is an intrusion on the journalist's right to print whatever he or she decides. Besides, there's no time. Those are still good arguments, and most journalists operate that way.

There is, however, a trend away from this: More and more journalists are reading back stories to their sources. In at least one course in the School of Journalism at the University of Missouri, students are required to do so.

A reporter may have good reasons to want to read back a story to a source. First, it's good human relations. It shows the source that you care about accuracy. Second, it helps eliminate mistakes. There's a story about a reporter who asked an official in a telephone interview how many people had been killed by a tornado that struck a town. The source answered, "Three to five." The reporter heard and reported "35." Major error! Had the reporter read back the story, this error would have been eliminated. (In fairness, of course, reading back a story to a source is probably impossible when working on deadline on a breaking story.) The small errors that irritate sources will be caught in a readback. If the source says that he graduated from Arizona State University and you write down *University of Arizona*, the readback will reveal the mistake.

Finally, it would be very difficult for a source who sues you for libel to prove actual malice if you had read the story to him or her. As you know, for public officials and public figures to win a libel suit against a journalist, they must show actual malice—that the story was published with reckless disregard for the truth or with a known falsehood. If you read the story to the source, you certainly cut off libel suits based on actual malice.

Advisers and staff members should discuss the issue of prepublication checking and adopt a policy that applies to all staff members. It would not be good for some staffers to read back stories and others not to.

Interview Story

The Phoenix Journalism Monthly, Society for Professional Journalists,
Valley of the Sun Chapter

Professional Profile: *Mary Kim Titla*

by Kara Ritter

From the San Carlos reservation in eastern Arizona, the pattern of Mary Kim Titla's life almost has made a full circle.

The Channel 12 reporter and fill-in anchor was born as a member of the San Carlos Apache Tribe and began her life in a large family within a small Indian community.

Although working as a broadcast journalist for 10 years between Tucson and Phoenix, Titla thinks breaking back into that community and culture on the reservation would be a good move for her family.

"The way Native Americans are described is as people who live in two different worlds. It's as if there is a 'mainstream lifestyle' and an 'Indian lifestyle.' Even though I live in the 'city' now, I miss the freedom, the openness, the culture. I want that for my boys."

The 35-year-old mother of three has worked for KPHX-TV Channel 12 for two years, and prior to that, she hosted a public affairs program for KVOA-TV Channel 4 in Tucson. Titla also was an assistant producer for KTVK-TV Channel 3 in Phoenix.

Being one of a dozen Native American broadcasters, Titla considers herself as a role model.

"I'm the only Native American who is a public figure that people see a lot. I take that seriously. They need to hear and see their own people," she said.

During an interview on the Gila River Reservation, Titla covered a story about some of the NFL players visiting the area. Before the camera crews loaded up, she had more children and people ask for her autograph than the players on the Dallas Cowboys and Pittsburgh Steelers.

"They see me on TV, and I think inside it makes them challenge themselves to say, 'Well, maybe I can do that too.'"

. . . Titla started in the Phoenix journalism market as a news station receptionist.

"It was the only opening, and I had to get my foot in the door. I looked at it as a start, and said to them, 'Well then, I will be the very best receptionist I can.' But they knew I was there because I really wanted to climb the ladder."

The receptionist job was just a small beginning for Titla, who recently was featured in a Super Bowl pre-game show. In a fully beaded buckskin dress, she translated the Star Spangled Banner into American Sign Language as musician Vanessa Williams sang her version.

Although she knows traditional Indian sign language from her past, Titla quickly learned how to interpret American Sign Language, which is a little more complex with its hand signals that represent numbers and letters of the alphabet.

"One of the neat parts about being involved with the production was that the Native American community here nominated me to the pre-game committee. That made me feel pretty good. . . ."

As popular as her name is and as much as people recognize her, Titla originally just wanted to write. . . .

"I really liked writing. That's what hooked me into journalism. I always thought about teaching English because that was my strong subject. . . .

"Going to college was something we all knew was the next step. It wasn't ever an option. I grew up in poverty, and it was really important to our parents to break the cycle of alcoholism. My parents wanted their children to be education-minded and be successful at whatever we choose to do."

Titla's family of seven all have their bachelor's degrees, including her parents.

"They went back to school after we were grown, and my mother now is a social worker and my father is an art teacher. I think it's great they went back. You hardly ever see a family on a reservation with a few graduating from college—let alone a family of seven including the parents.

"I didn't want to be a negative statistic. I'm glad I went and finished. I did think about leaving in the beginning, but I stuck with it, and I'm glad."

Protecting Sources

In what situations may using anonymous sources be appropriate?

Most news stories are the result of interviews with people who have useful or interesting information to impart. Sometimes the person with the story is willing to tell it only if he or she is not revealed as the source of the information. The question then arises as to when, or in what circumstances, a source should be allowed confidentiality.

Sources request anonymity for various reasons. For example, someone telling an interviewer about shoddy practices in a manufacturing company may very well be fired if revealed as the source of the information. Political workers often "leak" information about the motives, opinions, and decisions of their employers, particularly if they disagree with what's going on. One of the most famous political sources was used by reporters Bob Woodward and Carl Bernstein in breaking the Watergate case in the early 1970s. This source, known only as "Deep Throat," provided extremely sensitive information on the Nixon administration's cover-up activities. Although the quality of the information suggested that this source was a high figure in government, his or her exact identity has never been revealed.

Once a source has been promised anonymity, a reporter cannot betray that trust. Besides the moral problem of going back on one's word, there is the very practical consideration of using that source in the future. Most reporters take their promises of confidentiality very seriously; more than one has been jailed for protecting sources in court cases.

But are all sources worthy of protection? Are all equally credible? Suppose a reporter states in an article, "According to a highly placed source, the President had no intention of supporting that legislation." The source's statement may be true; however, that source can't be questioned by other newswriters. The source may be an important, knowledgeable official—or a clerk

With the help of the anonymous source "Deep Throat," *Washington Post* reporters Bob Woodward and Carl Bernstein broke the Watergate story.

in the office of such an official. Because there's no way to know, there's no way to judge the worth of the statement.

Newspapers have sometimes found themselves in the situation where a reporter has promised anonymity to a source whose motives were suspect. An example might be a source who has information about some youthful indiscretion of a middle-aged political candidate. On later investigation, however, it might be found that the source is a financial supporter of the candidate's opponent. As protection from an embarrassing situation such as this, many newspapers have developed strict guidelines about promising anonymity. They include such things as not letting a reporter be the sole determiner of whether anonymity is appropriate, not allowing anonymity to be used for personal attacks, and only permitting its use if there is no way the material can be obtained on the record. Furthermore, papers may decline to publish a story if they feel a reporter has granted anonymity to an unworthy source. Most will also reveal a source's identity if it turns out that he or she has lied. These common-sense practices help ensure that anonymous sources are used appropriately.

FOLLOW UP

1. Think of several recent news stories and decide whether you would have given anonymity to sources in them. Would such a situation ever arise in scholastic journalism? Be prepared to discuss your ideas.

2. Do some research on cases in which journalists have been jailed for protecting sources. Prepare a written report on your findings. Are there any protections for journalists in this situation?

If you decide to incorporate this type of prepublication checking, make it clear to the source that as a journalist you don't have to do it and that you don't have to accept his or her suggestions about your story. In other words, retain control of the story.

Prior review. The purpose of prepublication checking is to ensure accuracy of information. It's not quite the same as prior review, which occurs when a school administrator requires the opportunity to review a publication prior to printing for the purpose of approving (or disapproving) the material. Prior review borders on censorship. It clearly becomes censorship if action is taken by the administrator to change or remove any material. Your school's publication policy should have clear language that addresses prior review.

Wrap-up

Interviewing is an essential journalistic skill. Good techniques can be learned and should be understood before students begin interviewing. The first rule of good interviewing is to go to the primary source. Good reporters select their sources carefully and prepare well for each interview, making up a list of questions and deciding in what order those questions will be asked. They also listen. They realize that they cannot learn anything while doing the talking themselves.

Good questions are clear and understandable, short and to the point. Open-ended questions ("What do you think about . . . ?") usually are better than yes-no questions ("Do you think . . . ?") because quotable responses are needed. So-called *-est* questions ("Who is your greatest hero?") are generally simplistic and not appreciated by some interview subjects. Journalists sometimes have to ask difficult or embarrassing questions to do their jobs well, but this should always be done with care and concern.

Formal interviews require preparation. A reporter needs to research the subject in advance and set up an appointment in a comfortable place to talk. The opening minutes of the interview should permit the source and the reporter to warm up to one another. The reporter should use this time to determine basic data (exact name, age, job title, and so forth).

A reporter should try to establish rapport with the interview subject. It helps to dress properly—that is, not too casually. Try to look directly at the subject and rely on a tape recorder or a shorthand system of note taking to make it seem like you are really conversing with the person. Reporters who are friendly and relaxed with their sources often do better than those who are nervous or artificially tough. It doesn't hurt to smile or to laugh at a source's jokes.

It's also important to leave the door open for another talk. Even with the most careful preparation, a reporter may forget to ask an important question.

Good quotes and concrete details are emphasized in stories based on interviews. Descriptions of people and their surroundings help bring those people to life. The quotes should illustrate the source's personality.

One effective story technique, called the "Q and A," reproduces in question-and-answer form the reporter's exact questions and the source's exact answers. It's a transcript of an interview, rather than a story. The Q-and-A technique allows readers to determine what is important.

Scholastic journalists need to be prepared if a source suggests providing information off the record. Be sure you know what is meant: Can the information be used at all or used only without the source's name? No information is off the record unless the reporter and source agree. One thing is certain: If a reporter accepts information off the record, it must stay that way.

Journalists typically do not permit their sources to read stories before publication, but this practice is changing. Prepublication checking now takes place more frequently, but only if the journalist wants it to and only if the journalist maintains control of the story. Prepublication checking can eliminate inaccuracies in reporting names, dates, and figures.

On Assignment

INDIVIDUAL ACTIVITIES

1. Write a short definition of each of these terms:

-est question	primary source
formal interview	Q and A
off the record	stock question
open-ended question	

2. Test your critical thinking. You have been assigned to interview a person who, in past interviews, has answered basic background questions inconsistently—in other words, the person seems not always to tell the truth. What additional responsibilities, if any, does this put on you as an interviewer? How would you go about interviewing this person?

3. Select one of the following historical figures to interview. Do some research into the person's life and times; then develop your interview questions. You may be asked to role-play the interview with another student.

Dolley Madison	Joan of Arc
Chiang Kai-shek	Paul Robeson
Golda Meir	John D. Rockefeller
Peter the Great	Sitting Bull
Homer	Mary, Queen of Scots

4. Watch one of the Sunday-morning news-interview shows and write a critique. What research went into the reporters' questions? How well did the journalists follow up on vague answers from the guests? How well did they follow up on one anothers' questions? See whether you can find a newspaper account of the interview the next day. Does the story reflect what you saw happening? How would you have written the story? Compare your perceptions with those of classmates who saw the same program.

5. Prepare all the questions you want to ask of someone newsworthy in your school or community, in the order you want to ask them. Exchange your list with that of another student and critique each other's approach. What was missed? Did you include follow-up questions? Keep your refined list handy for writing an interview story later.

6. Record an interview with a classmate, taking notes as you interview. Using only your notes, write a story of the interview, with plenty of quotes. Then listen to the tape of the interview. Are your quotes accurate? If not, what do you think is wrong with your note-taking techniques?

7. Write a critique of the On Display interview story on page 111. How well did the story bring to life the person being interviewed? Do you think that other questions should have been asked? Make your critique about one page long.

8. Do the reporters on TV shows such as *60 Minutes* have an advantage over local reporters? What techniques are available to a network reporter who comes to town for one story that might not be available to a local reporter, who must deal with the same sources over and over? Write a short essay on your thoughts.

TEAM ACTIVITY

9. As a team, brainstorm to develop a list of stock questions. Review your list and select the 8–10 best questions. Compare your list with other teams' lists. Compile the best questions from each list into a class resource book.

SURF THE NET

10. Conduct an e-mail interview over the Internet. Observe how your note taking changes when there is no need for eye contact. What adjustments did you need to make to ensure that you completely understood the interview subject's responses? Write a short report on your observations.

career profile

Columnist

Dinah Eng

Dinah Eng is the first Asian-American columnist whose commentary is available nationwide. Her weekly column, "Bridges," moves on the Gannett News Service wire and through the *Los Angeles Times* Syndicate.

Eng's column runs the gamut from personal relationships to politics. At the heart of every topic, she examines how to create bridges in society. She has written about Asian-American concerns, spiritual values, and women's issues.

"The satisfaction I get from other people is what keeps me in this business," she said. "Because of this business I connect every day with people I might never meet in person."

Eng uses her column to work for better understanding between people.

"It's a vehicle," she said. "By writing, I'm working with other people to promote understanding."

Finding something to write about is not hard, according to Eng.

"The subject matter always varies," she said. "Each week I try to look at something different. I ask myself what issue in the news most affected me that week. Then I try to take my personal reaction to whatever that issue was and turn it into a broader, issues-oriented column that I can use to try to bring people together.

"By sharing my reactions with others, we can find a connection that pulls us together."

Eng has been national president of the Asian-American Journalists Association and was founding president of the Multicultural Journalists Association. She has written for the *Houston Chronicle,* the *National Observer*, and the *Detroit News* and received several writing awards.

Eng started her newspaper career as editor of her junior high school newspaper "because I knew how to run the mimeograph machine" and later was editor of her high school paper.

"One of the biggest reasons I became a journalist is that I had a great teacher in high school," Eng said. "He was a former reporter and taught the class like it was a newspaper. As a result, I was really interested in making journalism a career."

Eng graduated from Syracuse University in 1975 with a degree in journalism and English literature. She earned a master's degree in journalism from Columbia University in 1977 and went to work covering education and county government for the *Montgomery County Sentinel.* She has been special sections editor at Gannett News Service since 1987.

Along the way, she determined she could use a career in journalism to help bring different people together.

"Even though I've stayed in newspapers, my life is not about journalism," she said. "It is about building bridges between people. I write about what goes on in the world and how it relates to who we are, to what's inside of us."

Eng describes herself as "kind of shy" and says newspapers are a way to go places most people cannot.

"A notebook or a camera is kind of an excuse or way to fit in with other people," she said.

FOLLOW-UP

1. How do columnists who write several times a week come up with ideas? For instance, what kind of reading must they do? What other sources might provide ideas?

2. Identify a columnist that you especially like. Record what he or she writes about for at least two weeks. What tendencies do you see? What can you tell about the person's interests or causes?

Putting a Story Together:
From the Idea to Final Film

1 Before going out on a story, the reporter discusses the assignment with his editor to get a clear idea of what is wanted.

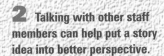

2 Talking with other staff members can help put a story idea into better perspective.

3 If the reporter is planning a formal interview, setting up an appointment in advance is essential.

4 Once the groundwork has been laid, it's time to go out and get the story.

7 Good follow-up questions are essential if the reporter is to get the complete story.

6 The responses to questions need to be recorded carefully. The reporter uses a tape recorder but takes notes as well.

5 Greeting the subject and exchanging pleasantries is the right way to start an interview.

8 After the interview, the reporter reviews his notes to make sure he hasn't missed anything important.

9 Back in the office, the writer discusses the interview with his editor prior to writing the story.

10 The completed story goes to a copy editor for editing and headline writing.

11 At some newspapers, a layout editor positions the final story on the page by hand.

12 Other newspapers do page layout electronically.

13 After the layout is complete, the page is shot as film.

14 The film must be checked carefully for imperfections before it goes for actual printing.

CHAPTER 6

Writing News Story Leads

KEY CONCEPTS

After reading this chapter, you will

▶ understand the elements of lead writing

▶ understand the inverted-pyramid structure

▶ know how to write the traditional "AP" or summary, lead

▶ feel comfortable writing inventive, colorful leads for all kinds of stories

▶ recognize good and bad story leads

▶ know which lead techniques to avoid

Walk into any beginning journalism classroom in the first week of the term and you'll hear this from the instructor:

"The lead is the most important paragraph in the story. It has to get the reader's attention. It has to inform the reader quickly. It has to be honest but colorful. It should have lively verbs. It should be brief, concise, and above all accurate.

"It shouldn't be cluttered with a lot of unfamiliar names, either of people or organizations. It has to represent the best writing you can muster. Depending on the story, the lead probably ought to be attributed. The lead ought to inform sometimes and tease sometimes. It probably ought to include some—but definitely not all—of the five W's and the H."

Sounds easy, but it isn't. Even such a brief overview as the instructor provides

126

CHAPTER 7

Writing News Stories and Headlines

back-up quote	chronological style	stylebook
transition	sexist language	jargon
tieback		redundancy

KEY CONCEPTS

After reading this chapter, you will

▶ know how to use a back-up quote

▶ be able to construct a news story held together with appropriate transitions

▶ understand news-story structures other than the inverted pyramid

▶ be alert to sexist and otherwise inappropriate language

▶ know the importance of conciseness and of avoiding jargon, clichés, and redundancies

▶ understand the various types of headlines and how to write them

▶ understand the role of copy editors in a publication

The proper study of journalism begins not in the journalism class but in the English class. This is because a skill so basic to journalism... doesn't have it, or the w... acquire it, might as we... a career.

That skill is writing... important it is to wr... leads. As you go on... an editorial, a colu... you must continu... an Ernest Hemin... It does, however... comfortable wi... good sentence... you understa... mentals of s... tion. It imp... not just ne... are reader...

...people think is colorful others think is trite. How do I know the difference?"

"What does 'tease' mean? How do I know when to 'tease'?"

"How long is 'brief'?"

"How do I know which names are too unfamiliar to be used in a lead?"

152

CHAPTER 8

Handling Quotes Fairly and Accurately

KEY CONCEPTS

After reading this chapter, you will

▶ understand the need for precision in quotes

▶ know the appropriate uses of direct quotes, partial quotes, and paraphrasing

▶ know the issues associated with taping interviews

▶ know how to handle attribution

▶ understand techniques for reporting on speeches

During a debate between two presidential candidates not long ago, one turned to the other and asked, "Isn't the real question, will we be better off?"

Those are his exact words. Yet when a story about the debate was printed in a newspaper the next day, it came out this way: "The real question is, will we be better off?"

Look at two newspaper accounts about any event and you'll see such discrepancies. They're usually harmless, as in the case of the presidential debate. The sky won't fall over this small error.

Does it matter? Do direct quotations—this is what a person said, in his or her own words—have to be accurate word-for-word? Is there no margin for error?

There probably is—a little. Adrienne Lehrer, a professor of linguistics at the University of Arizona, determined that in 72 percent of these minor discrepancies in

186

124

Writing and Delivering the News

A story about the school board approving funding for a new auditorium might mention the source of the information in the lead and then follow with a back-up quote from that source in the next paragraph.

CHAPTER 9

oing In-Depth Reporting

KEY CONCEPTS

After reading this chapter, you will

- be familiar with the issues teenagers say they care about most, issues that deserve in-depth treatment by students journalists
- understand trends in professional and scholastic journalism leading to new emphasis by students on in-depth reporting
- know how to condense certain items in a newspaper or magazine to find room for in-depth stories
- understand the difference between the lead on a routine news story and this introduction of an in-depth story
- be able to construct in-depth stories by writing an introduction, a nut graph, a body, and an ending

Tremendous change has come t... school journalism. Once mor... trivia, high school publications t... tributes to serious journalism, pr... talented students committed to... serving a modern audience. Ev... casual inspection of the best o... scholastic publications quickl... extent of the change.

If Rip Van Winkle had s... famous nap in the 1970s an... 25 or 30 years later, he wo... Where homecoming quee... and editorials went no fu... school spirit, scholastic... are on top of the news-... complete and detailed,... ists are producing tho... pieces on a wide rang... jects. These days, yo... treatment on everyt... ers to school violen... family crises; from... dardized tests and...

The list is lon... resents the catal...

uirect Quotations

As a beginning journalist, you should pay a great deal of attention to the skills involved in handling quoted material.

206

...y, 100 hands go into ...en he asks, "Were the stories ...etely, totally accurate?" Virtually all

187

CHAPTER 10

Design and Layout

KEY CONCEPTS

After reading this chapter, you will

- understand the basics of design and layout, including page elements common to most publications
- understand the basic principles of design, including dominance, unity, contrast, repetition, balance, and consistency
- understand basic categories of type and appropriate uses for each
- recognize the importance of graphics in modern page design
- know how to go about creating various types of pages, including front pages and double-trucks

A publication's goal of getting information to its readers is only partly achieved when all copy has been turned in. One essential job remaining is the actual design and layout of the issue. Visual communication is now one of the hottest areas of journalism, and in recent years graphic design has become one of the most important aspects of the overall journalism curriculum. Along with news gathering and writing, journalists are learning to become graphic communicators who use technologies such as desktop publishing to reach today's audience more effectively. That audience expects strong visual graphics and stories packaged to attract and hold their attention.

School newspapers, as well as other student-produced publications, must be designed with the visual-reading audience in mind. Publications that still subscribe to the older, more traditional approach to design, featuring numerous small photos and headlines, may lose many of their readers. Strong, story-telling photos, informational graphics, and carefully selected type are what draw in today's audience.

news-brief format   nut graph

KEY TERMS

gutter	grid		eyeline	point	justified	modular format
double-truck		dominant element	leading	pica	dummy	
bleed			foot	ragged	"tombstoning"	miniculume format

KEY TERMS

Basics of Design and Layout

The copy has been read and edited. Now the main articles and sidebars, together with any photographs, are ready to pass on to the designer. It's the designer's job to turn all these pieces into a well-conceived final product.

In producing any type of student publication, a designer must fully understand the content of the publication. In other words, he or she must know how many stories and visuals are available and what types of secondary pieces, such as sidebar stories and informational graphics, need to be included in the layout. The designer must always remember that the content dictates the design.

Page Elements

Every designer works with three basic visual elements: copy, or text, (words set in type); graphics, or art, (photographs, artwork; and devices such as ruled lines); and white space (blank areas on a page). These basic visual elements are combined in various ways to create page elements apparent in every publication, such as a nameplate (which displays the name of the publication), folios

Professional journalists must work together to create effective layouts.

(page numbers), and bylines (credits that identify writers). To work productively on layouts, you should learn the definitions, purpose, and placement of common page elements.

224

225

CHAPTER 6

Writing News Story Leads

KEY CONCEPTS

After reading this chapter, you will

▶ understand the elements of lead writing

▶ understand the inverted-pyramid structure

▶ know how to write the traditional "AP," or summary, lead

▶ feel comfortable writing inventive, colorful leads for all kinds of stories

▶ recognize good and bad story leads

▶ know which lead techniques to avoid

Walk into any beginning journalism classroom in the first week of the term and you'll hear this from the instructor:

"The lead is the most important paragraph in the story. It has to get the reader's attention. It has to inform the reader quickly. It has to be honest but colorful. It should have lively verbs. It should be brief, concise, and above all, accurate.

"It shouldn't be cluttered with a lot of unfamiliar names, either of people or organizations. It has to represent the best writing you can muster. Depending on the story, the lead probably ought to be attributed. The lead ought to inform sometimes and tease sometimes. It probably ought to include some—but definitely not all—of the five W's and the H."

Sounds easy, but it isn't. Even such a brief overview as the instructor provides

lead	five W's and the H	quote lead
inverted pyramid	tease	question lead
summary lead		

KEY TERMS

Other media compete with newspapers for the audience's attention, so leads have to grab readers.

can leave beginners gasping and groping for answers to questions such as these:

"When exactly does a lead need attribution, and when doesn't it?"

"What's a lively verb?"

"What some people think is colorful others think is trite. How do I know the difference?"

"What does 'tease' mean? How do I know when to 'tease'?"

"How long is 'brief'?"

"How do I know which names are too unfamiliar to be used in a lead?"

"What on earth are the five W's and the H—and how do I know when to use all of them and when to use some of them?"

"Why do you keep saying 'probably'? Can't you give us a rule?"

To begin at the beginning: The lead (rhymes with *seed*) most frequently is the first paragraph of the news story. (Some leads, really more like introductions, can run several paragraphs.) It's the do-or-die paragraph, the most important in any story. It's the place where you win or lose the reader. So the lead has to have impact, and it (usually) should come to the point quickly.

127

Everyone knows the problem. The audience is made up of people of all ages and all education levels. They're in a hurry. Television, the VCR, the computer, and the Internet all compete for their attention, so leads have to grab readers.

The Inverted Pyramid

One device journalists have traditionally used to catch readers' attention is the inverted (or upside-down) pyramid. The broad part at the top is where the main facts go. That's the lead. As the pyramid narrows, the facts become less significant until, as you reach the pointed bottom, the facts may not be essential. The (rare) story that springs a surprise at the end doesn't follow this pattern. Nor do the increasingly common feature and in-depth stories, for which no quick diagram can be drawn.

Plenty of evidence today suggests the decline of the inverted pyramid as a news-story device. Although this is true, it's also a fact that the inverted pyramid will be around forever—at least as long as the printed word exists for people in a hurry.

The inverted-pyramid style is used in newswriting for many reasons. First of all, it's a natural way to tell a story. If you want to tell a friend about a football game, you begin by telling who won; you don't start with the kickoff. The final score, therefore, goes into the broad part at the top.

Second, the inverted-pyramid style enables a reader in a hurry to get the essential information without reading the entire story. Suppose this is the lead:

Central High defeated Tech High last night, 23–0.

Readers who have time to read only the first paragraph may not know who scored the touchdowns, or how or when, but they know the essential fact. They know who won.

Third, the inverted pyramid is an aid for the headline writer. Most headlines are based on information contained in the first paragraph, so the most important facts should be in the first paragraph.

Finally, the inverted pyramid makes it easy to trim a story that won't fit into its allotted space. A properly organized inverted-pyramid story

The Inverted Pyramid

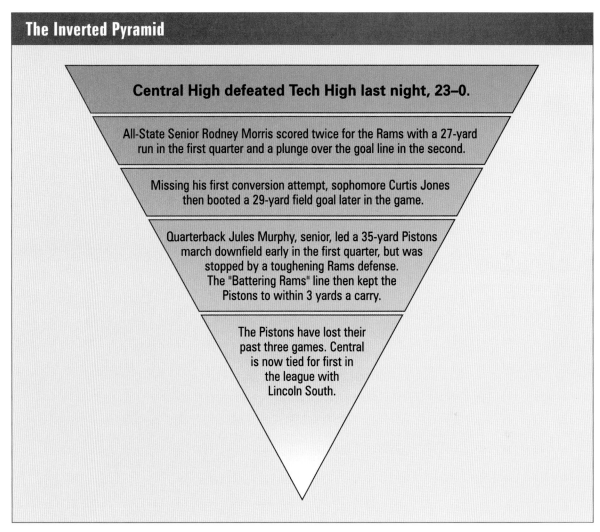

Central High defeated Tech High last night, 23–0.

All-State Senior Rodney Morris scored twice for the Rams with a 27-yard run in the first quarter and a plunge over the goal line in the second.

Missing his first conversion attempt, sophomore Curtis Jones then booted a 29-yard field goal later in the game.

Quarterback Jules Murphy, senior, led a 35-yard Pistons march downfield early in the first quarter, but was stopped by a toughening Rams defense. The "Battering Rams" line then kept the Pistons to within 3 yards a carry.

The Pistons have lost their past three games. Central is now tied for first in the league with Lincoln South.

The inverted pyramid is a traditional yet effective way to organize a news story. The most important facts come at the top, in the lead.

can usually be cut from the bottom up without too much damage.

Sounds easy, doesn't it? Just arrange the facts in descending order of importance and write them down. It seems as if there's nothing very creative about it.

But how do you decide which facts go first? This decision is made on the basis of your news judgment. After you have written the lead, how do you make it flow into the second paragraph, and the second into the third, and so on? Writers using inverted-pyramid style juxtapose related facts in descending order. They must make judgments. They must decide when to weave in some background, when to break the steady flow of the story with some colorful or explanatory material. All this requires practice—and creativity.

The "AP," or Summary, Lead

The Associated Press—or AP—is famous among journalists for its straightforward, no-nonsense writing. These leads usually are short, to the point, and filled with information. They may not be very creative, but they work because they convey information quickly. They work particularly well for traditional inverted-pyramid stories. Here are some AP leads, also widely known as summary leads because they summarize the main facts:

A three-alarm fire Friday destroyed several fuel-storage tanks just outside Centerville, injuring three firefighters and causing an estimated $1 million in damage.

Seniors Jaime Garcia and Mary Jo Shanahan were named King and Queen of Homecoming on Nov. 12.

"A three-alarm fire Friday destroyed several fuel-storage tanks just outside Centerville, injuring three firefighters and causing an estimated $1 million in damage."

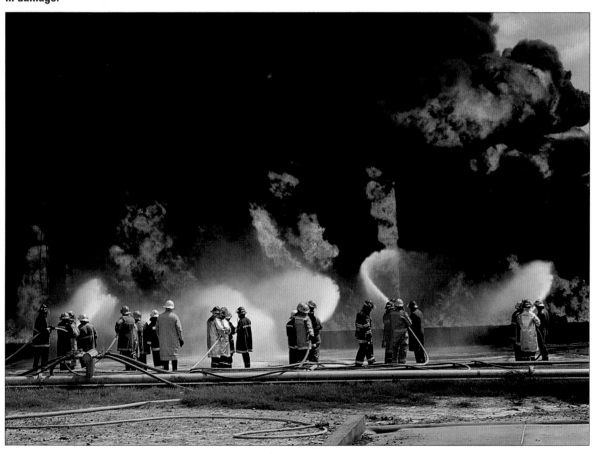

> An airplane bound for New York City skidded off the Cedar Rapids
> Airport runway Tuesday, injuring three passengers slightly.

The AP, or summary, lead—the straightforward inverted-pyramid
lead—is something of a formula. That formula is extremely valuable, especially for plain-vanilla stories that you have to write in a hurry. As a place to
start for a beginning journalist, the formula is fine. Just plug the facts into a
structure: Start quickly with the news ("Traffic is smothering the city") and
follow it with attribution ("an urban-affairs specialist"), give the verb (usually *said;* sometimes a word like *told* or *reported*) and its subject ("Optimist
Club members"), and the time element ("Tuesday"), and the lead is done:

> Traffic is smothering the city, an urban-affairs specialist told Optimist
> Club members Tuesday.

The news, thus, comes to the point in a hurry—which is what it
should do. If a story is about a fire, the first word probably ought to be
"fire." In this sort of approach, it's not enough that the news is in the
lead; it ought to be in the first few words of the lead.

Here is a strong summary lead—packed with clear, solid information—from an edition of *Tiger Tales,* the school paper of Joliet (Illinois)
Township High School, West Campus:

> With a key win against Lockport, the varsity girls' team snapped a
> three-way tie for the SCIA title two weeks ago, then claimed sole pos-
> session of it when Romeoville defeated Joliet Central last week.

Here's another from the Kirkwood (Missouri) *Call:*

> Swing dance classes began in the new dance studio above the small
> gymnasium last Wednesday and will continue throughout the year.

Summary leads can be bright and attractive, but they can also be a
crutch for the lazy journalist because they are relatively easy to write.

As newspapers shift their emphasis from hard to soft news and as TV
and the Internet continue to beat newspapers to the punch on breaking
stories, the inverted-pyramid and the summary lead are waning in importance. Still, every journalist should be able to construct a quick, clean lead
under deadline pressure. Everything else builds on that skill.

Writing the Lead

If you want to write truly effective leads, try picturing a reader over your shoulder. You know what you want that reader to know, and you're aware that readers have choices. They can turn on TV or surf the Net. So don't bore your readers with leads they have seen a thousand times before. Unless the AP, or inverted-pyramid, formula is called for, don't just fill in the blanks. Write.

Be Creative

Suppose your assignment is to write about the appointment of a new drama coach at your school. You could write this:

> Arthur Learned, 42, has been named drama coach at North High School.

That lead comes to the point quickly and certainly conveys the essential information to the reader, but let's face it—it's dull. It's a formula lead, and it lacks luster. Suppose you dig into Learned's biography—you might be able to write a lead like this:

> An Air Force flier with a closetful of medals is the new drama coach at North High School.

Better? Sure, but the objection could be raised that the second lead used more interesting information than the first. Exactly! The best material goes into the lead, provided it doesn't distort the story or emphasize the wrong angle.

Be Objective

Here is another example: The citizens of your town vote to build a new high school. You know that this is big news, and you want to write a good story. You sharpen your imagination and write the following:

> At long last, the citizens of Smithville opened their pocketbooks in recognition of the value of education. Yesterday they demonstrated their faith in the youth of America by approving a $5-million bond issue for a new high school.

Your news editor tosses the story back at you with a curt order: "Rewrite it." Puzzled? Here's the point: The lead is full of clichés ("at long last," "value of education," "demonstrated their faith," "youth of America")—and it's full of opinion. *Your opinion has no place in a news story,* in the lead or anywhere else. The reporter must be *objective.* Clearly, the example shows the writer's own feelings of elation over the new high school.

Here's one way the story could be handled:

> Smiling and relaxed after hearing that a $5-million bond issue for a new high school has been approved, Principal María Ortega today commended Smithville citizens for what she called their progressive attitude toward education.

The facts are all there, and instead of learning the reporter's opinion the reader learns the principal's attitude and viewpoint.

TIPS worth taking

The five W's and the H. Before beginning to write your lead, first write out the answers to these basic questions of journalistic writing. Then put them in order of importance. Your lead should stress the most important of them, usually who and what.

who?	Taneesha Fields and Wendel Chang
what?	Second Place in the National Secondary School Drama Festival
when?	May 17
where?	The Barrington Center for the Performing Arts, New York City
why?	Best Duet Acting
how?	Competed against students at the regional, state, and national levels

Seniors Taneesha Fields and Wendel Chang won second place at the National Secondary School Drama Festival held at New York City's Barrington Center for the Performing Arts on May 17. The two competed in the Best Duet Acting category against high school students in regional, state, and national run-offs.

Find the Right Lead

Some journalism textbooks teach leads by category: summary leads, staccato leads, parody leads, punch leads, cartridge leads, astonisher leads, and so on. Or they say there is a type of lead for each of the parts of speech, and six more for the five W's and the H (who, what, when, where, why, and how). If these methods encourage students to use imagination and creativity, they're worthwhile. Such categories, however, may only cloud the issue. Can you imagine a reporter for the *New York Times* hurrying back from a meeting with the president thinking, Should I write a summary lead or a cartridge lead? It doesn't work that way. The reporter is more likely thinking, I need a smooth, concise, readable, and interesting lead that will pull my reader into the story. Before the reporter gets back to the office to write the story, he or she may have mentally constructed and discarded a dozen leads. Not once do the categories come to mind.

The bottom line is that you need to make the lead work for you. Write it as well as you possibly can and then rewrite it. Writing is rewriting; this is particularly true of leads. Seldom is the first lead that pops into your head the best one.

The five W's and the H are elements that properly belong in nearly every story. Editors once felt that all six belonged in the lead, but this is no longer true. The best lead is the one that tells the story best.

Using the Writing Process in Journalism

Should you use the writing process for newspaper writing? Because you have to plan, draft, and then revise newspaper articles just as you would most other pieces of writing, it certainly makes sense to follow the writing process steps. In fact, it may even be more important in journalistic writing because you're always writing for a real audience, not just your instructor.

Here is how the steps can be applied to newspaper writing.

Prewriting. Prewriting involves gathering and organizing information. For newspaper writing, this means finding out the who, what, when, where, why, and how of the story. It means talking to the right people and following up with the information they give you. It means preparing good questions for an interview and getting good, usable quotes. It means making sure you get the facts about all sides of the story.

Before you start writing, analyze the information you have and see how best to present it. What are the most important details, the ones that should appear in your lead? What order should the rest of the material follow, and where should quotes be inserted? For many news articles, you can use the inverted pyramid as a planning device, jotting down and then rearranging details in descending order of importance.

First-Draft Stage. When you begin writing, follow the plan and order you worked out earlier, and write an article that's as long as or slightly longer than you need. Spend some time on the lead and the transition to the body, but do not labor over any one part. Concentrate on getting the entire story written; then go back and smooth out the rough sections.

Revising/Editing Stage. In the revising/editing stage, spend some time looking at *what* you've said and *how* you've said it. Strengthen your lead if it could be clearer or more interestingly stated. Make sure that all key facts and quotes are accurate and properly attributed. Work on transitions so your ideas flow smoothly. Eliminate any pieces of information that have no direct bearing on your story. Take a careful look at your sentence structure (it should be clear and direct), your language (it should be simple, appropriate, and unpretentious), and your organization (it should generally progress from most to least important).

When you are happy with how your story reads, do a quick check on grammar, spelling, and capitalization, keeping your stylebook handy. A copy editor will probably review your work as well, but there is no reason you can't turn in a story that is as accurate and professional as you can make it.

Good Leads

Here are some examples of good leads that appeared in the *New York Times.* They are good for one simple reason: They make the reader want to read the rest of the story.

Angelo Rafael Luna returns to his Puerto Rican birthplace next week, seven years after leaving, seven months after his Army induction and one week after his death.

They wave one finger, two fingers, a frantic hand; they use a shrill whistle and even a shapely leg. But New Yorkers are finding it as hard as ever to get a taxi, despite reports and studies and public complaints.

"They wave one finger, two fingers, a frantic hand; they use a shrill whistle and even a shapely leg. But New Yorkers are finding it as hard as ever to get a taxi, despite reports and studies and public complaints."

An antipoverty program has gotten happily out of hand here.

In the hot, inhospitable lowland
In the north of Rhodesia, from
The Nafungabusi plateau
Down through dusty river beds to the
Great, roaring Zambesi River.
A party
Of infiltrating
   Black
      African guerrillas
Has disappeared—
Dead
Or in
   Jail or
Lost in the thick, unending bush.

Pay particular attention to the lead beginning "In the hot, inhospitable lowland . . ." It's virtually poetry, evidence that the journalist can be creative and that the writer who wants to may attempt any device as long as it works. There's no rule against writing a news story in iambic pentameter, if it works. Don't be afraid to try, though be prepared to work far harder than you would have to for a more conventional lead.

These inventive leads moved over the wires of United Press International:

> Cape Town, South Africa—A dead woman's heart pumped life Monday through the body of a 55-year-old grocer who gambled on medical history's first human heart transplant even though he is a diabetic.

> London—Psst . . . wanna buy London Bridge?

The Associated Press, mentioned earlier as a wire service with a penchant for no-nonsense leads, can be creative too. Here is an AP lead from a story about an early space shot:

> A black silhouette that is the earth chokes off the sun. As the light dies, it bursts into space with blues and red and pinks and pure white rimming the earth. It's a sight never seen before by man—an eclipse of the sun by the earth. . . .

This AP lead began a story about a tattoo artist:

> People go to him when they want to get something on their chests.

Some leads are so good that they become famous, such as this one by H. Allen Smith on a weather forecast story in the now-defunct *New York World-Telegram:*

> Snow, followed by small boys on sleds.

Collect leads that are creative and informative, using them as models and as inspiration. Here are some good leads collected by Brian Cooper, executive editor of the *Dubuque* (Iowa) *Telegraph Herald* and published in the *American Editor,* magazine of the American Society of Newspaper Editors:

Last year the Arizona Cardinals had a great defense and an awful offense. Coach Buddy Ryan vowed that he would equal things out this year. Now both units are lousy.

—Lee Lewis, *Waterbury* (Connecticut)
Republican-American

Behind a chain-link fence topped with barbed wire, past a handwritten warning that "trespassers will be shot," down a long dirt driveway, beyond two security system signs and two Rottweilers, a man and a woman were found dead early Tuesday.

—Nancy Lawson, *Tampa* (Florida) *Tribune,*
on the deaths of two 26-year-olds

When Princess the miniature schnauzer started rolling over and playing dead without being asked, her owners got worried.

—Carla Crowder, *Albuquerque* (New Mexico)
Journal, on a story about a pacemaker
being implanted into a 7-year-old dog

Maxine Quinn should wear a cape. She can leap eight stories in a single bound and make jaws drop with two words: Going up?

—Cliff Radel, *Cincinnati Enquirer,*
on a story about an elevator operator

It's a hot dog eat hot dog world out there.

—Barbara Chavez, *Albuquerque* (New Mexico) *Journal,*
on a story about heated competition
between rival licensed hot dog carts

A horse led itself to water, but someone else had to pull it from the drink.

—Marshall Wilson, *San Mateo* (California) *Times,*
on a story about a horse that fell into a well

The leads in the **ON DISPLAY** feature on pages 138–139 all come from student newspapers. Some are tease leads—that is, they coax the reader into the story by making him or her want to know what the lead is referring to. Notice that some of the leads are two or more paragraphs long. A good lead can be any length as long as it works.

Leads from Student Newspapers

People stopped talking and slowly turned to face the blackboard as Assistant Superintendent Dr. Robert Jericho wound his way toward the front of the board auditorium.

—*Lakewood* (Ohio) *Times,* reporting on election returns in a school-financing issue

The ferocious winter storm that dropped over a foot of water on parts of the state and sent Bay Area rivers pouring over their banks held a surprise for Saratoga students arriving at school Jan. 10: the heavy winds and rain had forced classes to be canceled for the day.

—*The Saratoga* (California) *Falcon*

We know her as the quiet, patient librarian who is there to organize books and help keep peace and tranquility in the library at all hours of the day, but Nellie Sanders has a wild side.

—*The Chronicle,* Harvard-Westlake School, North Hollywood, California, referring to the librarian's intense interest in ballroom dancing

Hunched over a table, concentrating on the artwork before him, Senior Kevin Box guides his pencil across the paper in careful but loose strokes. Each line is a part of the image in his mind that he brings to life through his hands.

—*The Fourth Estate,* Bartlesville (Oklahoma) High School

It may be chicken feed to some, but for the Schreiber family of Carol, Ken and Pat, it's a serious business. Part of a prizewinning clan of chicken raisers, they've accumulated two grand champions and one reserve champion.

—*Bugle Call,* R. E. Lee High School, San Antonio, Texas

On the day after Thanksgiving, the entire world was Christmas shopping in Houston.

—*The Bear Facts,* Hastings High School, Alief, Texas

Sue's hands were sweating and she "felt funny." Pulling her car quickly off the St. Paul street, she told her friend, "Something's happening to my twin sister Sheri in Chicago."

Then it came to her. Sheri, who was about seven months pregnant, was having her baby prematurely. She drove home, called Chicago and confirmed her "awareness." Sheri had indeed just had a baby.

—*Blue Jay Free Flyer,* Worthington (Minnesota) Community College

I heard loneliness today and I heard courage. I talked to Bill Biggs.

After his Dec. 30 auto accident Bill was in the hospital for three months. Then for three months he was at the Gonzales Rehabilitation Center. Now he's home, learning to cope with paralyzed legs and damaged eyesight.

—*Big Stick,* Roosevelt High School, San Antonio, Texas

Mrs. Lillian McCutcheon was sitting in the housemother's room on the tenth floor with her feet up on the air conditioner giving herself a manicure.

—*The All-Stater,* University of Nebraska Journalism Workshop

The sun creeps up over Stone Avenue Railroad Station. Briefcased urban cowboys cluster around chipping green radiators and iron-grilled ticket windows. There they wait, in the sweet-stale aroma of years past, for their silver stallion.

—*The Lion,* Lyons (Illinois) Township High School

Norman Williams gets paid to do unto others what he would not want others to do unto him.

—*Teen Perspective,* publication of the Marquette University Summer Journalism workshop

While dressed in protective white suits with respirators that looked like something out of a science fiction novel, four trained professionals from ALAMO Incorporated spent the summer removing asbestos from West's pipework.

—*Tiger Tales,* Joliet (Illinois) Township High School, West Campus

Under an almost full Friday the 13th moon, the Red Devils suffered an 18–13 defeat to the second-place York Dukes as York scored the game-winning touchdown with 30 seconds remaining on the clock.

—*The Devils' Advocate,* Hinsdale (Illinois) Central High School

What was once a flourishing, green, spider plant of Kathy McKown, business teacher, in room 222 is now a mere stub in the soil, on the edge of its death bed.

—*The Rustler,* Fremont (Nebraska) Senior High School

As he inched his way around the corner of the mountain, he found himself suddenly staring up at a huge expanse of rock directly in front of him. Looking over his shoulder, he could see the tiny dotted trees of the Colorado landscape thousands of feet below him; the river had become nothing more than a thin, blue line.

—*The Arlingtonian,* Upper Arlington (Ohio) High School

Jim is 16 years old. He is a straight "A" student who rarely gets in trouble and never breaks the law. However, when Jim gets his driver's license, his father's insurance will nearly double.

—*X-Ray,* St. Charles (Illinois) High School

Leads with Problems

You can learn from bad leads too; you can learn what to avoid. Here are some bad leads:

> At a meeting at City Hall Monday evening, which was attended by several residents of the community in addition to the Village Board of Trustees, the council passed an ordinance forbidding the sale of alcoholic beverages within the corporate limits of the village of Cornstock on Sunday.

The news here is the board's action about alcohol on Sunday, and that should have been in the opening words. Instead, readers were told where the meeting was, when the meeting was, what the attendance was, and the name of the body taking action—all before the key words "alcohol on Sunday."

Some writers try to use a chronological approach, much like taking the minutes of a meeting. Unless there are extraordinary reasons to do so—some dramatic turn, perhaps—straight-news stories should never unfold chronologically. Don't do this:

> The Skiler City Council met July 15 with a light agenda. First order of business was a communication to the city clerk from William Pulsey of Pulsey Corp.

Length

Effective leads typically use short sentences. The following lead is too long:

> Seniors would be given the last Friday of May for final examinations, the school colors would be changed from red and blue to crimson and blue, retiring teachers would be given plaques of appreciation from the student body, and the editor of the school newspaper would be elected from the student body under bills introduced in the regular weekly meeting of the Central High School Student Council Friday.

Short leads catch people's attention because they are easier to read. Furthermore, long paragraphs, both in the lead and in the body of the story, are unacceptable for typographical reasons. Since most newspaper

trends and issues

Real Versus Created News

To what extent can individuals and groups manipulate the news?

Unabomber Ted Kaczynski's plan to manipulate the media for his own ends backfired when his brother recognized his writing style, which led to Kaczynski's arrest.

Once upon a time, people thought they could make clear distinctions between public occurrences and news stories. Elements of the public made news, and the media reported on it. Eventually people began to realize that they could use the media to help them create news. Today many would argue that the lines between straight reporting and media manipulation seem to have blurred. Out of this perception an ethical question arises: Are the media allowing themselves to be taken advantage of?

One of the first times this issue arose was in the 1960s, when public protests became common. Although many of these were spontaneous and genuine, a certain number were staged. A small number of protesters would gather and then call in the media to report on their event. Television cameras tended to make the number of protesters look larger than it was, and the public could be led to think that a cause was supported by a large number of people, whether it was or not. Thus a group could use the media to promote its cause.

As time went on, the practice of feeding selective information to the media became fairly commonplace. Current-day presidential-election campaigns, for example, are almost totally engineered in this way. Advisors will plan what topic the candidate will address on a given day and then try to permit media questions and discussion only on that topic. Is the topic newsworthy? Very often it is. Is it necessarily the only issue the candidate should be addressing that day? That really depends on the circumstances. And, to be fair, the technique doesn't always work: It's pretty hard, for example, for a candidate to stick only to welfare issues on a day when a huge airliner has crashed.

Some critics see a problem only when the media allow outside forces to manipulate them uncritically. Before Unabomber Ted Kaczynski was captured late in 1996, he promised to stop his wave of mail-bomb terror only if the *New York Times* and the *Washington Post* published his manifesto on the evils of technology. But his plan backfired; his brother David recognized Ted's writing style from the article, and this eventually led to Ted's arrest. Were the *Times* and the *Post* right to let Kaczynski try to use them for his own purposes? In this case, fortunately, their decision turned out to be correct.

Some events staged for the media can become tragic. In the mid-1990s a seven-year-old girl, along with her father and a flight instructor, attempted to be the youngest person to fly across the United States. The media were notified before the event began, and each refueling stop was carefully publicized so that reporters could update the flight's progress. Unfortunately, the plane crashed at the first refueling stop, and the parents faced a barrage of criticism. Although every large news source in the country had publicized the planned expedition, virtually none had questioned the appropriateness of letting a child attempt such a dangerous feat.

In this incident, as in other similar cases, the media were quick to analyze their coverage and admit their shortcomings. Vigilance and an ability to learn from past mistakes remain the best defenses against manipulation.

FOLLOW-UP

1. Give recent examples in which you think the media was simply informed of coming events and others in which attempts were made to manipulate coverage. What made you think manipulation was happening?
2. In a group, plan and dramatize a media "event," such as a press conference or award presentation. One group member should play a reporter trying to cover the story fairly. The rest of the class should critique each dramatization.

columns are narrow—just over two inches wide—paragraphs must be kept short, usually about two or three typewritten lines. Even a paragraph that appears short on the screen will seem long when it's squeezed into a narrow printed column. Here is one way the preceding lead could be rewritten:

> Bills introduced at the Friday meeting of the Student Council would do the following:
> - give seniors the last Friday in May for final examinations
> - change the school colors from red and blue to crimson and blue
> - provide for plaques to be given by the students to retiring teachers
> - provide for election of the editor of the school paper by vote of the student body

This is a common way of dealing with stories that have more than one "main fact."

Grammar and Content

Can you see what the problem is with this lead?

> Your Student Council is considering several new projects.

The trouble is that it doesn't say enough. What projects are being referred to? The lead must provide information. Another problem is the use of *your*, which should be reserved for direct quotes and editorials, because it puts the writer into the story. The word *the* should be substituted.

Here is another problem lead:

> A reminder to those who enjoy new recordings. The library has 22 new compact discs that it's willing to loan out! All students are invited to come and look them over!

TIPS worth taking

Writing captivating leads. Follow these tips to write leads that will make readers sit up and take notice.

- Make your lead introduce your angle—your unique take on the story.
- Consider using *why* and *how* leads instead of *who* and *what* leads. A *why* lead concentrates on the cause or reason behind the news. A *how* lead explains the way something happened.
- Avoid *when* leads, unless the time something occurred is by far the most important fact.
- Avoid starting with a reference to your school or a school group.
- Avoid stating the obvious—for example, "Winter is here again."
- Avoid starting with *There is/was/are, It is/was, This is/was.*
- Create a question in the reader's mind—without asking a question.

In the first place, the opening sentence isn't even a sentence. There are times when sentence fragments are acceptable, if you use them effectively, but that first sentence isn't one of them. Furthermore, is it news that the library is willing to "loan out" its materials? That's what libraries are for. (The word *out* is unnecessary. And *loan* is an adjective or noun, not a verb. *Lend* would be correct here.) Inviting students to the library, or anywhere else, is not the function of the newspaper. Quote someone as saying that students are invited, if that's appropriate information. Also, avoid exclamation points in newswriting; they are seldom necessary.

Here is a better way to express the thoughts in this lead:

> Twenty-two new compact discs have been placed in the school's lending library, the head librarian announced.

Consider the grammar of this lead:

> Alumni and friends of Iowa State University in the northern California and Nevada area will meet for their annual dinner meeting Friday in Las Vegas, Nev.

Working on a computer makes it easy to revise a lead until it's clear and grammatically correct.

The problem here is the misplaced modifier. Where is Iowa State University, in Iowa or spread over northern California and Nevada? It's the alumni, obviously, who are in California and Nevada, but that's not what the lead says. The solution is simple. Keep modifiers and what they modify close together in the sentence. Careful rereading of your stories will eliminate many such problems.

Remember also to keep the time element clear:

> The lawyer for three persons convicted of contributing to the delinquency of a minor today remained certain that he would win their freedom from jail terms.

When did the three contribute to the delinquency of a minor? Today? That's what the lead says, but common sense tells us otherwise. This lead illustrates the general need to keep the principal verb and the time element together. The following is much clearer:

> The lawyer for three persons convicted today of contributing to the delinquency of a minor remained certain that he would win their freedom from jail terms.

Beware of another pitfall—a lead that contains no meaningful information:

> Principal Mark Takima discussed some of the problems of the school's science program at the Science Club meeting Monday afternoon.

Why not tell your readers which problems were discussed and what was said about them? In stories about speeches, panel discussions, and the like, the emphasis should not be on the fact that someone spoke or that a panel discussion was held. Instead, the lead should emphasize what was said. This lead could have been written before Principal Takima spoke to the Science Club, in contrast to a successful lead, which provides fresh, real information.

The Quote Lead and the Question Lead

Some approaches to lead writing are to be used sparingly. These are the quote lead and the question lead. This is a quote lead:

> "I promise the people of this city that we are going to solve our parking problem next year."

That's not writing or reporting; it's recording. It's lazy and, unfortunately, is used too frequently.

Rare indeed is the story that can be summarized, its essence distilled, in one direct quote. The lead should be something like this:

TIPS worth taking

To "the" or not to "the." Someone once made a "rule" that news stories cannot begin with the word *the.* Although it's preferable to begin leads with words that have more impact, you can certainly begin with *the* when appropriate.

"The United States faces loss of world leadership unless it solves its problems, Sen. Jena Wright said today."

Mayor Glen Rebalchenko promised today that he will solve Oakton's parking problem this year.

Here is another poor quote lead:

"America must solve its problems in this decade or face the loss of world leadership."

A clearer version would read like this:

The United States faces loss of world leadership unless it solves its problems, Sen. Jena Wright said today.

Quote leads can lead to distortion. The reporter pulls one quote out of a speech or interview, slaps it at the top of the story, and the headline is based on that quote. Unless the quote is exactly right, the precise heart of what the person was trying to say, readers will see a lead and a head based on a fraction of an entire event.

The term *quote lead* refers to this construction: "Word word word word word word word"—that is, just a quote without context or information about who spoke. The next example is different—and acceptable (occasionally):

"You've got to send me to a hospital," insisted the 8-year-old boy, "because I'm going to kill myself."

That's compelling and interesting and tells a reader, at least to some extent, what the story is about. Here is another example of an almost-quote lead that works:

"She told us to pray," Tara McCoy recalled softly. "The nun told us to pray, and it would all go away."

The second paragraph quickly wipes out the one weakness of this lead, which is that readers do not know what "it" is. It's a fire.

Question leads also are to be used rarely. A question lead is one that asks a question:

Will the Delta Queen stop at Cape Girardeau's waterfront this year?

The trouble with such a lead is that it contains no information. If a reporter has some information about the Delta Queen's route, he or she should provide it:

"The Delta Queen's a comin'. The popular riverboat is scheduled to dock at Cape Girardeau's Missouri Riverfront Park four times this year."

The Delta Queen's a comin'. The popular riverboat is scheduled to dock at Cape Girardeau's Missouri Riverfront Park four times this year.

Television journalists are addicted to question leads, typified by this one heard almost nightly:

> What kind of weather will we have tomorrow? Dave will tell us when we return.

This style is OK for a TV teaser, but it's not a good idea in print.

As you begin to write leads of your own, or as you comment on your classmates' work, this checklist can be helpful.

EVALUATION CHECKLIST

News Story Lead

- ☑ Does the lead summarize the main facts of the story in one or two sentences?
- ☑ Is it written in a succinct and direct, yet interesting, way?
- ☑ Does the lead avoid expressing the writer's opinion?
- ☑ Has the writer avoided beginning with a question or a quote?
- ☑ Is the lead correctly punctuated and free from capitalization and spelling errors?

Wrap-up

Getting started specifically in newswriting means working on leads, or first paragraphs. If the lead fails, no reader will read on, so leads should grab readers' attention quickly and in few words.

Many news stories are written in inverted-pyramid style. The main facts go at the top. As the pyramid gets smaller toward the bottom, the facts become less important.

The inverted-pyramid style is fading somewhat in the face of changing news values—more soft news, less hard news—and because television almost always has fast-breaking hard news before newspapers. The inverted pyramid is used because it gets to the point quickly and is a natural way to tell a story. The pyramid also makes it easy to trim a story from the bottom up if it's too long for its allotted space.

Leads need to get the reader's attention honestly and quickly. They should be creative and interesting and make use of the best material the writer has. The lead should be objective and not convey the writer's attitudes or beliefs.

One kind of lead often used is the AP, or summary, lead, which conveys the basic information in a simple, straightforward manner. Leads need to be smooth, concise, readable, and interesting—no matter what type they are.

All stories should include the five W's and the H (who, what, when, where, why, and how) but not all in the lead. The best lead summarizes the entire story but uses the best elements—not all of them.

Good leads are creative and make use of various techniques but share one characteristic: They make readers want to continue. Bad leads are slow getting to the point, are too long or contain too many peripheral points (unnecessary times and places, for example), express the writer's opinion, or confuse readers through misplacement of the time element. Other leads that generally should be avoided are direct quotes presented with no context (quote leads) and question leads.

 # On Assignment

INDIVIDUAL ACTIVITIES

1. Write a brief definition of each of these terms:

five W's and the H	quote lead
inverted pyramid	summary lead
lead	tease
question lead	

2. Secure copies of two newspapers and study their stories about the same news event. How do the papers differ in their selection of lead elements? Which approach is more effective? How could each have done a better job? Rewrite the leads to demonstrate your ideas. Attach the stories to your new versions.

3. Test your critical thinking. Compare the leads on radio and television accounts of news stories with those in a newspaper. How do they differ? Do the needs of their different audiences call for different kinds of leads? Discuss your ideas in class.

4. Read through the student leads on pages 138–139. Write a one-page critique telling which you find most and least effective. Give reasons for your choices.

5. Ask the city council, the board of education, or the zoning commission to provide you with the minutes of its last meeting and the agenda for the next meeting. Write a lead based on the minutes. Then write a lead based on the agenda.

6. Write a lead based on the following information:

▶ The Parent-Teacher Association (PTA) is sponsoring a used-book drive during the month of November.

▶ The books will be donated to area hospitals.

▶ Donations may include books for children or adults.

▶ Only books that are in good condition will be accepted. All others will be recycled.

▶ Collection bins for the books will be placed in the school libraries and in local businesses.

▶ Parents, teachers, and students are encouraged to volunteer for the sorting and boxing of donated books.

▶ Science teacher Wade Carter and parent Nina Hagen are cochairs for the used-book drive.

▶ In a phone interview Hagen said, "We wanted to do something that would involve everyone in the community and something that would benefit the community."

▶ Between classes Carter commented, "You can learn from and enjoy books. What better gift could we give to those who are ill?"

▶ You contact Troy LaRue, public relations director at Payton General, one of the area hospitals that will receive the books. He sends you a press release in which he writes, "Books are always welcome here. We are thrilled that our libraries will be supplemented by this book drive. Our patients will certainly appreciate the effort, especially those who have long-term stays in the hospital."

7. Find the questions you developed in Chapter 5 for someone newsworthy in your school or community. Now plan and conduct the interview. Write three possible leads, and attach your questions. In the next chapter you will complete the story.

TEAM ACTIVITY

8. Working in teams, visit a library or newspaper archive and examine old papers. Copy the leads of several stories from these eras: the partisan-press era, the yellow-journalism era, and the World War II era. What changes have been made in lead style? Make a short presentation on your findings to your class. Include examples.

SURF THE NET

9. Find on-line editions of English-language newspapers published outside the United States. To what extent do the leads and general writing styles differ from those of U.S. papers? Prepare a presentation on your findings for your class.

career profile

Managing Editor

Fernando Dovalina

Fernando Dovalina, an assistant managing editor at the *Houston Chronicle,* has been committed to good writing, good editing, and diversity in the nation's newsrooms most of his professional life.

In his mid-50s, Dovalina is one of the highest ranked Hispanics in the newsrooms of Texas major daily newspapers. He is responsible for the daily operations of the news desk, wire desk, copy desk, and the *Chronicle's* bureau in Mexico City. He also supervises most of the *Chronicle's* international coverage.

He was born and grew up in Laredo, Texas, the son of an immigrant mother and father whose roots in Texas predate Davy Crockett's. His first language was Spanish, which he admits embarrassedly he has lost proficiency in over the years. Since he has a reputation as a good editor and has won writing awards, he says that proves that having spoken Spanish or any other language before learning English is no barrier to a successful career in the English-language media.

His parents' emphasis on education was a central theme in his and his two brothers' lives.

"My parents always had reading material in the house," he said. "I was always writing things—fiction, poetry, song lyrics. I just like to play with words."

It was sports and his father's baseball talent that drew him to newspapers.

"My father had been a semi-pro, minor league baseball player," Dovalina said. "Baseball has always been a part of my family. I paid a lot of attention to baseball in the sports sections. I probably got into newspapers that way."

Dovalina worked at the *Beaumont Enterprise* and *Fort Worth Star Telegram* before joining the *Chronicle* in 1968. He has been a police and general assignments reporter, a pop-rock music columnist, copy editor, makeup editor, assistant city editor, wire editor, and news editor. In 1991, he supervised a project for the *Houston Chronicle* that was named a Pulitzer finalist in international reporting.

As an editor, Dovalina frequently spots a common mistake made by reporters.

"Reporters get a lot of information but don't know how to organize their story," he said. "The first thing a reporter should

do is ask 'What's the story I'm trying to tell?'

"If it's a news story the reporter should ask how to tell a coherent story. If it's a feature, the reporter should ask, 'How do I hook the reader with the first paragraph and then tell the story in an interesting and compelling way?'"

Dovalina believes the emergence of new information sources for readers to choose from makes good writing more important.

"There's too much out there competing for our readers' attention," Dovalina said. "If we can't write an interesting tale, we probably ought not be in the business."

Dovalina is one of several *Chronicle* staff members who teach a high school journalism class in the summer. He advises aspiring journalists to read every day.

FOLLOW-UP

1. Dovalina covers international events. What kinds of international news stories seem to be most common? Which kinds, if any, might make international coverage more interesting to you?

2. If you attended a summer journalism class that Dovalina taught, what questions would you want to ask him? Consider his job, his background, and his experience.

CHAPTER 7

Writing News Stories and Headlines

KEY CONCEPTS

After reading this chapter, you will

- ▶ know how to use a back-up quote

- ▶ be able to construct a news story held together with appropriate transitions

- ▶ understand news-story structures other than the inverted pyramid

- ▶ be alert to sexist and otherwise inappropriate language

- ▶ know the importance of conciseness and of avoiding jargon, clichés, and redundancies

- ▶ understand the various types of headlines and how to write them

- ▶ understand the role of copy editors in a publication

The proper study of journalism begins not in the journalism class but in the English class. This is because there is one skill so basic to journalism that anyone who doesn't have it, or the willingness to work to acquire it, might as well look elsewhere for a career.

That skill is writing. You've seen how important it is to write clear, well-crafted leads. As you go on to write a news story, an editorial, a column, or even a headline, you must continue to hone your writing abilities. This doesn't mean you have to be an Ernest Hemingway or a Toni Morrison. It does, however, mean that you must be comfortable with words, that you know a good sentence from a bad sentence, that you understand and can apply the fundamentals of spelling, grammar, and punctuation. It implies that you read a lot—and not just newspapers, either. All writers are readers.

A story about the school board approving funding for a new auditorium might mention the source of the information in the lead and then follow with a back-up quote from that source in the next paragraph.

Writing is not, as many people believe, an inherent talent. It *can* be taught or can be *self*-taught through trial and error. By writing, and by having your writing criticized, you learn to avoid certain errors.

Your instructor can help you become a proficient—even an excellent—writer by preparing you and making you write and rewrite. The writing, however, is up to you.

There's nothing awesome about writing news stories. Your basic writing skills and some specialized information—because, after all, journalistic writing is specialized writing—are all you need.

Building on the Lead

Let's say you've written a good lead and you have readers interested in your story. You have them on the hook; now you want to reel them in. If the lead paragraph or paragraphs are the most important in the story, what immediately follows is the next most important. You don't want your reader losing interest, not after all the effort you put into writing the lead.

One way to hold interest is to use a quote—the sound of a human voice—immediately. Quotes add a personal touch to a story.

Let's begin with this lead:

> The school board has approved funding for a new performing arts center, Board President Elizabeth Anderson announced Wednesday.

Now here's what some people call a back-up quote, one designed to support the lead:

> "We need to support the arts in our schools," Anderson said. "This tells students that we care about their arts education."

What you're doing is linking the lead to the second paragraph, making your story unfold logically and coherently. You're using transitions.

Transitions are one of the indispensable tricks in a writer's repertoire. They are words, phrases, even whole paragraphs that hold a story together. Transitions take your readers from subject to subject, fact to fact, time to time, and place to place without losing or confusing them along the way. News stories without adequate transitions fall apart.

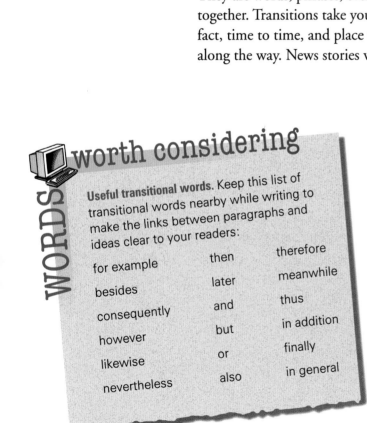

WORDS *worth considering*

Useful transitional words. Keep this list of transitional words nearby while writing to make the links between paragraphs and ideas clear to your readers:

for example	then	therefore
besides	later	meanwhile
consequently	and	thus
however	but	in addition
likewise	or	finally
nevertheless	also	in general

Using Transitions

Transitions come in many forms. For instance, are you able to recognize the transition between these two paragraphs?

> Mayor Sid Goldberg today signed over 40 acres of the Pine Ridge Forest Reserve for the grounds of the new Galileo Observatory.
>
> The observatory, built with federal funds, will provide astronomy research facilities for three area universities.

The transition there is the repetition of the word *observatory.* Because the word appears in both paragraphs, the reader knows the subject hasn't changed.

Here is another, more subtle example from the body of a story:

> "Students should not have to worry constantly about the ceiling falling on their heads," Winston said. "We need to consider the safety of students as well as what they are learning.
> "Of course, building repair will be expensive and may require a referendum," he added.

In this example, the quotation marks at the beginning of each paragraph serve as a signal that the person who was speaking in the first paragraph is still speaking in the second.

Generally, the transition should be unobtrusive. That is, it shouldn't stick out; it should accomplish its job with a minimum of attention. Although this is desirable, it's not always possible. The first duty is to the readers, and if it takes an obvious, blatant transition to help guide them through the story, so be it.

Read the excerpt below and note the transition, set in italics. The transition is necessary because the author is signaling a complete change of subject.

> . . . The battle eventually led to the establishment of the Interstate Commerce Commission for regulation of rates.
> *But that was later. A discussion of the Populist Revolt, a fascinating chapter in the state's history, now seems in order.*

The entire paragraph is a transition; there's nothing subtle about it. See if you can spot the problem in these two paragraphs:

> Rodriguez was more important in the inner workings of the administration of former Governor John P. Henning than his administrative title indicated.
> A native of Central City and holder of business administration and law degrees from State University, Singh is a jet pilot veteran of the U.S. Air Force and presently is a captain in the Air National Guard.

Who is Singh? Readers will assume the subject is still Rodriguez, and the writer gives no clue to indicate a change.

On the other hand, notice how transitions connect the lead and the next two paragraphs in the **ON DISPLAY** sample on page 156.

Lead and Follow-up Paragraphs
The Lion's Roar, Lincoln High School, Gahanna, Ohio

Proficiency Week a New Experience for All

by Erin Profitt

Once again, all the freshmen and various upperclassmen spent a week breaking the tips off their number two pencils while striving to fill in all the Proficiency tests' scan-tron bubbles. The tests, conducted Oct. 25–28, consist of four parts: Writing, Math, Reading and Citizenship. The students also had to be able to distinguish the difference between Great Britain's flag and America's flag.

Yes, believe it or not, several freshmen said there was a question exactly like that on the Citizenship test.

"You had to pick out the American flag from Great Britain's flag and know what continent the U.S. was on," freshman Judd Milton said.

The Body of the Story

Assume that you have written the lead and have hooked it to the second paragraph. Now it's time to write the body—the rest of the story. If you have written a traditional inverted-pyramid lead, you have probably summarized the story in your first sentence or two. Now you must elaborate.

Simply retell the story in more detail in the next few paragraphs, making sure you bring in all the background necessary to give the reader full understanding. If the story is straightforward, with one main fact to convey, the task isn't too difficult. That main fact belongs in the lead paragraph; secondary details follow in subsequent paragraphs, as the pyramid narrows. Use tiebacks, or details that bring in last week's or last month's related development; but do so only as needed for the reader's understanding.

If the story is more complex—that is, if it has more than one main fact—your job is harder. You must summarize, giving all three or four main facts in the lead, if possible. In the next section of the story, give the most important detail of each main fact. After that, provide additional but decreasingly important information on each fact.

In the **ON DISPLAY** sample that follows, the opening paragraph presents the basic facts: the name of the play, and where and when it will be performed. Subsequent paragraphs summarize the plot and then present various reactions to the play. Notice that each successive paragraph is just a little less important than the previous one.

Inverted-Pyramid Story
Crier, Munster High School, Munster, Indiana

Drama Club Presents *Anne Frank*

Marking the 50th anniversary of the Holocaust, the Drama Club will present its winter play, *The Diary of Anne Frank*, tomorrow at 7:30 P.M. and Sunday at 2 P.M. in the auditorium. Admission is $4.

The play tells the true story of a Jewish girl, Anne Frank, played by Jessica Schoen, senior. She is forced to go into hiding with her family from the Germans during World War II and must live in an attic above a warehouse. Anne's dad, Mr. Frank, played by Jason Doherty, senior, luckily knows some people who help the Franks by bringing them necessities.

Several cast members like performing in a more serious play. "I'm glad we're doing *The Diary of Anne Frank*. It's different from our usual comedy or drama. It adds variety," Schoen said.

However, others have mixed feelings. "On one hand, I like the play; it gives an excellent example of how people lived in hiding during the Holocaust," Dave Pesich, junior, said. He is playing the part of Mr. Kraler, a friend of the Franks. "On the other hand, knowing that this was a true story and that many people lived like this for years is sort of depressing."

Some can relate to the play personally. "It has special meaning to me as a person," Jessica Kaufmann, senior, said. She is playing Mrs. Frank. "It's part of our culture. It really makes it [the Holocaust] hit home instead of just hearing numbers."

The cast has been working extremely hard. "It's a very intense play. I can't think of another time in all the years I've been teaching that a cast has tried as hard as these guys have," Drama Club sponsor Mr. Gene Fort, social studies teacher, said.

A story about an event like this blizzard usually unfolds in inverted-pyramid style, with the main facts first and the rest in descending order of importance.

Other Organizational Patterns

Not all stories can be written in inverted-pyramid style. As you have seen, fewer and fewer are being written that way because of the influence of the nonprint media. It makes little sense for a newspaper to announce something that everyone saw on television 10 hours earlier. So newswriters have modified the inverted pyramid; newspaper writing reads more and more like magazine writing.

The Storytelling Style

A popular and effective approach to journalistic writing is the use of a narrative, or storytelling, style. Stories that use this style draw the reader into the drama of the event by telling it as a story. The writer sets the scene, introduces the characters, and narrates the events, weaving in facts and opinions from sources. You may write the story chronologically, or move around from one event to another, gradually revealing the information that fleshes out the story. A hallmark of this style is the use of specific details that bring the story to life, such as in this story:

Mark O'Rourke, a janitor at East High School, is used to cleaning up messes. Last Friday he had a big mess to clean up, created by his own young son, Gerald.

O'Rourke had just buckled four-year-old Gerald into the passenger side of his black Honda Civic, which was parked on a hill outside their home at 222 Claymore Lane. Mark and Gerald were off to pick up a pizza. As O'Rourke made his way around the front of the car to the driver's side, he saw it begin to roll backward down the hill.

"I couldn't believe it was happening at first," O'Rourke said. "I grabbed the hood and tried to hold on, but it just slipped away."

In a panic, O'Rourke ran after his car as it careened backward about 50 feet and slammed into a parked car. When he reached the accident, Gerald's eyes were streaming tears and his mouth was wailing for Daddy, but he was unhurt.

"I pulled him out and hugged him tight," O'Rourke said. Then he saw that the gear in his car was shifted into reverse. "I figured Gerald must have grabbed the gearshift."

Sure enough, after calming down Gerald admitted he had "poowd da stick."

The bumper and hood of the parked car were crumpled.

"That's the kind of mess I can handle," said O'Rourke, grinning. Then he said softly, "But I tell you, if anything had happened to my son, I couldn't handle that."

This story illustrates how an event can be given reader appeal through a novel treatment. Such treatment often means the difference between a story that appears on page 1 and a story that ends up on page 27, buried near the want ads. Never be afraid to try an unusual approach.

Many types of stories call for special treatment. A personality profile, in which the writer sketches with words a portrait of an individual, is a type of story that cannot be handled with the inverted pyramid. Here the writer may back into the story, perhaps with an anecdote or a compelling image that draws the reader into the subject's life. (For a sample of a personality profile, see page 275.)

Combination Style

An increasingly popular way of writing news stories combines the summary lead of the inverted-pyramid style with a chronological storytelling style.

An action story can always be enhanced with a photo, if your photographer happens to be in the right place at the right time.

The writer summarizes in the first paragraph and then tells the rest of the story in the order in which it occurred.

This approach is particularly appropriate for action stories. For instance, if a dog wanders into your school, your story will be more interesting if you don't simply state the facts that the dog appeared, sniffed around for a while, and was finally chased out. You may want to describe how the dog entered the building, then give an account of the activities that followed, telling how the dog stopped first in the journalism classroom and was chased from there to the chemistry lab, where it upset some test tubes, and so on. The last paragraph might be about the dog scurrying out the door and heading home.

Thus, you might begin your story as follows.

> A dog with a cold nose for news strolled into the journalism class last Thursday, saw that his help wasn't needed, and then took the grand tour of the building, upsetting test tubes, disrupting gym classes, and disturbing study halls before being expelled.

After that summary, the next paragraph would start the chronological unfolding of the story.

> The dog's presence became known during fifth period when he stuck his nose into the offices of the *Oracle* . . .

Sidebars

The sidebar, a story related to but kept separate from another on the same subject, also requires some approach other than the inverted-pyramid style. In the case of a major storm, the main story (mainbar) will tell about the number of deaths and amount of damage. A sidebar might be the eyewitness account of a survivor or an interview with an official of the National Weather Service describing how the storm developed. As a supplement to the main story, the sidebar provides extra detail or "color," so it uses whatever approach seems most likely to grab the reader's attention. For example, it may include graphics.

Appropriate Newspaper Style

No matter what sort of story you're writing, you must follow newspaper style for capitalization, abbreviation, spelling, and usage. Your newspaper is very likely to have a stylebook explaining when personal titles are used, which spellings of certain words are preferred, and so on. You need to learn that stylebook and follow it.

Beyond stylistic rights and wrongs, there is also a whole range of do's and don'ts for good journalistic writing. Some of the most important ones follow.

Avoid Offensive Language

Journalism students owe it to their audience to be sensitive to the feelings of others. For lack of a better term, student journalists need to be "politically correct." It's not necessary to carry political correctness to nonsensical extremes (call your cat a cat, not your "feline companion"), but you do need to be respectful. Words hurt. They don't exist in a vacuum. They have overtones that can sometimes be extremely painful.

We've come a long way, actually. Watch a 1930s or 1940s movie on late-night TV, and be prepared to endure stereotyping of people by race, age, and gender—at least. Women stayed home and cleaned; men wore suits and hats and were breadwinners. African Americans were portrayed as childlike and shiftless. The elderly appeared primarily in rocking chairs or in long deathbed scenes.

So, yes, the hurt was real. Every effort must be made to avoid perpetuating it.

Offensive terms relating to racial or ethnic background are absolutely forbidden unless in a direct quote that is—truly and without doubt—essential to the understanding of a story. For example, if the president of the college in your town uses a racial slur and is fired over the incident, journalists will have to use the word in their stories about the case. This would be a rare exception to the rule of avoiding offensive language.

trends and issues

The News On Line

If you are an Internet user, you already know some of the things it can do. You can communicate directly with people all over the world. You can locate and purchase a wide variety of products and services. For a journalism student, however, the most interesting and relevant service the Net provides is the capacity to find—and provide—news.

By the late 1990s there were more than 800 newspapers from around the world on line, and that number has continued to grow. If you want, for example, to get a firsthand account of a work stoppage in Kuala Lumpur, you can probably find an English-language Malaysian newspaper that will give you detailed, up-to-the-minute information. If you want to get a sense of how an important presidential address was received in various parts of the country, you can read accounts of it in newspapers from several regions. On a more down-to-earth level, if you are a Cubs fan in Chadron, Nebraska, you should be able to find reports of last night's game simply by connecting with the *Chicago Tribune* on line.

Most newspapers on line cost nothing to access—at least for the current day's edition. Papers are more apt to charge if you want to search through their archives. You also generally have to pay to get direct access to news wire services such as Knight-Ridder and Reuters, as you do with the Clarinet news service, a Net-originated news service with more than a million subscribers.

Some news on the Net emanates from the considerable number of news groups on Usenet, a large on-line bulletin board. Although these nonprofessional sources have been known to break stories earlier than the traditional news media, their accuracy can sometimes be suspect.

The broadcast media also disseminate news on the Internet. CNN, for example, has had a library of significant video news clips available for some time. The other major networks are

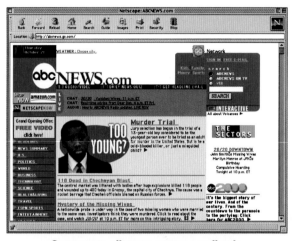

Common to all news sources on line is an interactive capacity—allowing readers to more easily choose their news.

providing news coverage from a variety of angles. ABC, for example, has a web site with late-breaking stories that much resembles a newspaper site. In addition, however, it provides—or leads you to—detailed information on their upcoming TV news specials. There are also links with many of their local affiliates, which give up-to-the-minute coverage on stories relevant to the area. Common to all of these sites is an interactive capability: Readers (and viewers) can respond to polls on news topics or chat with personalities from the news shows.

Student publications can take advantage of the Internet both to circulate their own products and to obtain information. Any number of school newspapers can be found on line, some created expressly for that medium, and many others can be requested by contacting an adviser or other involved party. Additionally, many papers use the Internet as a source of information. Some see this as one of the biggest potential changes in student newspapers. As reporters are able to access more publications from around the country, their stories about student lifestyles and concerns, as well as issues in general, will widen in scope.

FOLLOW-UP

1. Investigate the web sites of four or five large newspapers such as *USA Today* or the *New York Times*. Make a chart showing what information can be had free from the papers and what kind requires you to be a subscriber.

2. Investigate Kidsphere, a listserv (group mailing list) linking K–12 students and teachers around the world. See what you can learn from it about a news event in an African, South American, or Asian country.

The whole class of rude words that ignorant people sometimes use to describe another person's religious faith or ethnic group also is banned from ordinary use, as are stereotypical images in general. Stereotyped references to Native Americans, for example, have offended many Americans recently. Drums, tomahawks, and warpaint thus join our earlier array of offenses against groups: the Irish drink, Asians are inscrutable, fat people are jolly, the elderly can't remember, professors are absent-minded, women are obsessed with shopping, men are obsessed with sports. This list doesn't even touch on the truly outrageous words the races apply all too often to each other.

The stereotypical American housewife of the 1950s no longer exists—if she ever did—so people should not be stereotyped in newswriting either.

As a journalist you should watch carefully for bias—deliberate or accidental—regarding race, age, gender, sexual orientation, or philosophy of life. An environmentalist is an environmentalist, not a tree-hugger. Your grandfather isn't a geezer. Women aren't chicks, babes, or dolls. Men aren't hunks. A woman can be an airline pilot. A man can be a flight attendant. People with disabilities aren't crippled. The elderly can make love. Pictures are meant to illustrate the news, not to titillate. Sneaking words with double meanings into print or on the air doesn't impress intelligent people.

Eliminate sexist language. Don't write as if every person on Earth is a man; on the other hand, writing as if every person were a woman doesn't work either. Notice these examples:

Sexist: For a student to pass the course, he must pass the final exam. [No girls in the class?]

Sexist: For a student to pass the course, she must pass the final exam. [No boys in the class?]

Better: For a student to pass the course, he or she must pass the final exam.

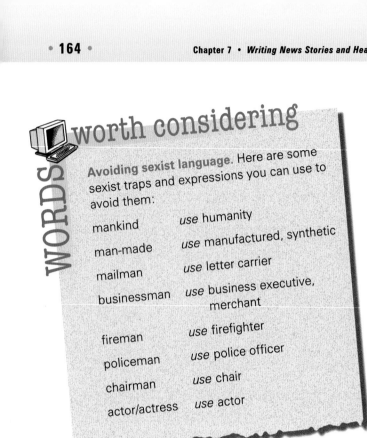

Avoiding sexist language. Here are some sexist traps and expressions you can use to avoid them:

mankind	*use* humanity
man-made	*use* manufactured, synthetic
mailman	*use* letter carrier
businessman	*use* business executive, merchant
fireman	*use* firefighter
policeman	*use* police officer
chairman	*use* chair
actor/actress	*use* actor

The best solution, whenever possible, is to avoid the issue entirely—by making the noun plural or by reworking the sentence:

Best: For students to receive credit for the course, they must pass the final exam.

Or: To receive credit for the course, a student must pass the final exam.

Follow this rule: Don't describe a woman's physical appearance or give her age if you would not in the same circumstance describe a man's appearance and give his age. If the president and the first lady come to your town today, don't write stories about his magnificent speech and her new hairdo. Courtesy titles (Mr., Ms., Miss, and others) are optional and may be governed by local style; however, staff members should make sure that their style isn't dictated by gender. It's not "Jones" if a man and "Ms. Jones" if a woman. That's sexist.

Be Succinct

Because you can never be certain who will read your stories or under what circumstances, you must select words with the utmost care in order to eliminate as much confusion as possible. Develop a clear, simple, concise way of expressing yourself. This doesn't mean that you should write for someone with a sixth-grade reading level. It does mean that you should cull all excess verbiage from every sentence:

Don't write: The Association of the Bar of the City of New York

Write: The New York City Bar Association

Don't write: He was wearing a shirt that was made of cotton and that had been borrowed from a friend of his.

Write: He was wearing a borrowed cotton shirt.

Review every sentence you write, looking for words to cut. The editing process begins with the reporter.

Use Clear, Simple Words

As a journalist, you need to remember that the reason you write is to communicate, not to show off your vocabulary. Here are some examples of pretentious words, with shorter, clearer synonyms in parentheses:

assuage (ease)	fallacious (wrong)
corpulent (fat)	endeavor (try)
circuitous (roundabout)	indisposed (ill)
appellation (name)	purchase (buy)
identical (same)	proceed (go)
erudite (learned)	inebriated (drunk)
conflagration (fire)	terminate (end)
inundated (flooded)	constituency (voters)
edifice (building)	demeanor (behavior)
precipitation (rain, snow)	location (site)

Writers who typically use big words may feel stifled at first, but they should recognize that journalism is "controlled creativity." Because journalists must, above all, communicate, they are not free to fling words around with abandon. They have to watch their language. Besides, it's as easy to be creative with small words as it is with big, pretentious ones. Can you translate the following?

> Objective consideration of contemporary phenomena compels the conclusion that success or failure in competitive activities exhibits no tendency to be commensurate with innate capacity but that a considerable element of the unpredictable must invariably be taken into account.

You may recognize this paragraph if we restore it to its original, simplified form—the way it appeared in Ecclesiastes:

> I returned, and saw under the sun, that the race is not to the swift, nor the battle to the strong, neither yet bread to the wise, nor yet riches to men of understanding, nor yet favor to men of skill; but time and chance happeneth to them all.

You may know the scene-painting technique in which several colors of wet paint are blended into patterns as "scumbling," but don't use the term in newswriting if your audience isn't familiar with it.

Jargon. Another sort of unclear language is jargon, the inside language of groups. Generally, journalists should avoid it, translating it instead into terms everyone can understand.

Players of various sports use jargon. Football players say "blitz" when they mean more players than usual going directly after the passer. Baseball players say "around the horn" when they mean around the bases. Theatre people say "strike" the set when they mean "take it down." Scene painters may say that they are "scumbling," which means they are blending several colors of wet paint into patterns. Members of the military go to "chow" or "mess" instead of to dinner.

Journalists are no different. The say "spike that story," which means "kill that story," which means "do not publish that story." They say "art" when they mean any sort of illustration. They often get their art out of the "morgue," which the rest of the world calls the archive. Sometimes they need art from the morgue to do an obit for the bulldog—which means finding a photo for use with a death notice for the first edition.

The problem with jargon is that it can be so "inside" that people on the outside can't understand what's being expressed. Translate it. If the invitation says "continental breakfast," let your readers know that the expression means juice, a roll, and coffee.

Write Straightforward Sentences

The good newswriter uses short sentences and paragraphs as well as short words—not because the audience is ignorant but because such elements are easier to read. Writing in short sentences doesn't mean adopting a "Dick-and-Jane" style. (The flag is red. It is white. It is blue.) It does mean writing most of the time in simple, declarative sentences rather than complex ones. It means avoiding the semicolon (except in lists) and relying on the period. In this way you not only limit the length of the sentence (and make it more readable) but also reduce the amount of information the reader has to swallow in one gulp.

Don't get the idea that all good writing comes in short words and short sentences; there is no ideal sentence length. Certainly writers who decide never to write a sentence of more than, say, 15 words are in trouble. The result too often will be an unvarying series of choppy, jerky sentences.

Avoid Other Common Hazards

All of the following are problems that crop up in many first drafts of news stories. Be on the lookout for them so you can eliminate them as you revise.

Redundancy. Expressions such as "2 A.M. in the morning" and "the orange is spherical in shape" are redundant. You may write "2 A.M." or "2 in the morning," but there's no sense saying it twice. And it's sufficient to say the orange is spherical. "In shape" isn't needed because the word "spherical" contains the concept of shape. Similarly, don't write "surrounded on all sides," for that's what it means to be surrounded.

Clichés. A cliché is an overworked, overused, old, and trite expression such as "free as a bird" or "since the dawn of time." Clichés reveal to the alert reader that the writer is too lazy to invent bright new figures of speech. A good guideline is this: Never use a figure of speech that you're used to seeing in print. Journalism instructors usually take great delight in spotting clichés in their students' stories. Write "high noon" in a story and you may get a sarcastic note asking, "When is low noon?"

Fear of repetition. A master of the English language, Theodore Bernstein of the *New York Times,* coined a word to describe the next

✓ worth taking

Common clichés. If you've heard it, it's probably a cliché. Avoid these common clichés and be on the lookout for others:

acid test	in the limelight
at long last	in-your-face
avoid like the plague	kicked off the event
beat around the bush	Lady Luck
Been there. Done that.	last but not least
bite the bullet	light as a feather
blunt instrument	little white lie
calm before the storm	milk of human kindness
dead as a doornail	raining cats and dogs
dull thud	sadder but wiser
get down to brass tacks	selling like hotcakes
hands across the sea	smart as a whip
heated argument	take off the gloves
hit the nail on the head	white as a sheet
Hope springs eternal.	with bated breath

writing hazard. The word is *monologophobia*, and it means, roughly, the fear of repeating a word. As Bernstein points out, the ailment leads to such paragraphs as "Sugar Ray flattened Bobo in twelve rounds in 1950, outpointed him in fifteen sessions in 1952, and knocked him out in two heats last December 9." This leaves the reader wondering whether a round, a session, and a heat are the same thing (they are). Have no fear of repeating a word, because if you do you may end up with such silly synonyms as "yellow metal" for "gold," and "grapplers" for "wrestlers."

Passive voice. As much as possible, avoid writing sentences in the passive voice. Passive-voice sentences generally sound weak and often read awkwardly. Here is an example:

All students were requested by the Friends of the Environment committee to use the recycling bins behind the school.

Nearly any sentence can be rewritten so that it's active. Using the active voice makes the message clearer and stronger:

The Friends of the Environment committee requests all students to use the recycling bins behind the school.

State *who* did *what*, not *what* was done *by whom*.

The **ON DISPLAY** article on page 169 elegantly sums up all these points about newspaper style.

A Pro's Opinion: Newspaper Style

Four Bananas Aren't Three Bananas and One Elongated Yellow Fruit

by James L. Kilpatrick

HOLLINS COLLEGE, VA.—The student editors had come from a dozen Southeastern colleges to swap suggestions and receive awards; and now we were assembled on a white veranda, with a spring rain drenching the boxwoods, and the talk turned easily to shop talk.

All of the young writers had read E. B. White's *Elements of Style,* and most of them had browsed in Fowler's *Modern English Usage*. They had profited from Ernest Gowers and Ivor Brown and from courses redundantly styled "creative writing." They put the question to me, as a visiting newspaperman. Would I give them my own set of rules with a few random examples thrown in, for writing newspaper copy? It was a temptation not to be resisted.

I pass these rules along here, for whatever value they may have to fellow workers in the carpentry of words. Every editor in the land could add some admonitions of his own.

1. Be clear. This is the first and greatest commandment. In a large sense, nothing else matters. For clarity embraceth all things, the clear thought to begin with; the right words for conveying that thought; the orderly arrangement of the words. It's a fine thing, now and then, to be colorful, to be vivid, to be bold. First be clear.

2. Love words, and treat them with respect. For words are the edged tools of your trade; you must keep them honed. Do not *infer* when you mean to *imply*, do not write *fewer than* when you mean *less than.* Do not use *among* when you mean *between*. Observe that *continually* and *continuously* have different meanings. Do not write *alternately* when you mean *alternatively*. Tints are light; shades are dark. The blob on the gallery wall is not an abstract. Beware the use of *literally, virtually, fulsome, replica, many-faceted,* and *the lion's share*. Pinch-hitters are something more than substitutes. Learn the rules of *that* and *which*. When you fall into the pit of "and which," climb out of your swampy sentence and begin anew.

3. As a general proposition, use familiar words. Be precise; but first be understood. Search for the solid nouns that bear the weight of thought. Use active verbs that hit an object and don't glance off. When you find an especially gaudy word, possessed of a gorgeous rhinestone glitter, lock it firmly away. Such words are costume jewels. They are sham.

4. Edit your copy; then edit it again; then edit it once more. This is the hand-rubbing process. No rough sandpapering can replace it.

5. Strike the redundant word. Emergencies are inherently acute; crises are grave; consideration is serious. When you exhort your readers to get down to basic fundamentals, you are dog-paddling about in a pool of ideas and don't know where to touch bottom. Beware the little qualifying words: *rather, somewhat, pretty, very.* As White says, these are the leeches that suck the meaning out of language. Pluck them from your copy.

6. Have no fear of repetition. It's better to repeat a word than to send an orphaned antecedent in its place. Do not write *horsehide, white pellet,* or *the old apple* when you mean *baseball*. Members of City Council are not *solons;* they are members of City Council. If you must write *banana* four times, then write *banana* four times; nothing is gained by *three bananas and one elongated yellow fruit*.

7. If you cannot be obviously profound, *try not to be profoundly obvious.* Therefore, don't inform your reader that something remains to be seen. The thought will have occurred to him already.

8. Strive for a reasoned perspective. True crises come infrequently; few actions are outrageous; cities and economies are seldom paralyzed for long. A two-alarm fire is not a holocaust. Not much is imperative or urgent; still less is vital. To get at the size of a crowd, divide the cops' estimate by 3.1416.

9. Style depends in part upon the cadence of your prose. Therefore listen to your copy with a fine-tuned ear. In the prose that truly pleases, you will find that every sentence has an unobtrusive rhythm that propels it on its way. With a little rearranging, you can keep the rhythm going. . . .

10. Beware of long sentences; they spread roots that tend to trip the reader up. The period key lies nicely on the bottom row of your machine, down toward the right-hand end. Use it. Use it often.

Kilpatrick, a political commentator and syndicated columnist, has written two books on the writer's art.

Headlines

Writing a good headline may seem to be a nearly impossible task. From perhaps 500 words of copy in a story, you must select three or four or five that tell the entire story. Not only that, but you must do it according to a rather strict set of rules.

The headline's job is to lure the reader into the story. It must, however, do so honestly; the headline can't promise something that isn't in the story. The headline should be lively and interesting, with sparkling verbs. It must cram as much information into those words as possible, because readers tend to scan headlines looking for something of interest. When they do, they should be able to pick up some information they would not have otherwise.

Headline Styles

Headlines are typeset in various ways. Some are centered:

This Is a Centered Head

A flush-left/ragged-right headline rests squarely against the left side of the column, leaving the lines to run ragged on the right side:

This Represents
Flush Left

Many other varieties of headlines exist. For example, there is the hammer head. Usually the top line is twice as large as the bottom line. One line should be set in a contrasting style. For example, if the top line is set bold, the bottom line might be set italic (type leaning to the right). The hammer is used for important stories where the primary head receives the most attention. Here is one example of a hammer head style:

Hammer Head
Big on top, small on bottom

Another style is the kicker. Featuring one secondary headline over one or more lines of the primary headline, the kicker can be used when the writer wishes to feature a single word or phrase as the main title and add more specific information in the secondary headline, as shown here:

This is a kicker, or overline

Main head indented

In the headline style known as a wicket, several lines of type, up to about six lines, are used as a sort of superlead or introduction. A one-line head set in contrasting Roman or italic type follows, serving more as a magazine-style title than a headline. This is a wicket:

The introductory paragraph, which may run several lines long and offer enticing facts—and even quotes, leads the reader naturally to the

Main Title Here

Headline styles have become quite informal. The following represents a style called a read-out head:

Get their attention here

You can then expand on that in a longer deck, using just about as many words as you need to get a reader really interested. Some publications actually use the lead as a sort of deck, placed like this.

This is called a read-in head:

A phrase that leads readers to a word that captures the story's

Topic!

And one more word about headline style:

AVOID ALL-CAP HEADS

All-cap headlines should be avoided because they are difficult to read. People read not only the letters in words but the words' shapes, which are lost when the letters are all capitalized.

Making Headlines Fit

Before you actually sit down to write a headline for a story, consult with your editor. He or she knows how important your story is compared to the other stories on the page; and the more important the story, the larger

Composing headlines on a computer makes it easier to determine what will fit into the allotted space.

(and often the longer) the headline. Working with your editor, you can decide on an appropriate size and length. Your job then is to write a headline that fits. To make a headline fit in the space allowed on the page's layout, you may have to rewrite it several times.

Headline Writing Do's and Don'ts

As far as the writing itself goes, here are some points to remember.

Telegraphic style. Headline style is telegraphic; that is, all extra words are trimmed. The articles *a, an,* and *the* usually are left out, as shown here:

School wins high state rating

Verb tenses. Headlines are also written in present tense to give readers a feeling of immediacy:

Tigers defeat Tech 7–0

Occasionally a story about something historic will crop up, and then the past tense is acceptable:

Volcano erupted 50 years ago today

Headlines about future events are written with infinitives to indicate future tense, this way:

360 seniors to graduate Sunday

Punctuation. Usually just three marks are used: the comma, the quotation mark, and the semicolon. Whenever part of a headline is enclosed in quotes, to save space a single quote (') is used, not a double quote (").

A comma is used in place of the word *and,* like this:

Smith, Jones win scholarships

Exclamation points are used rarely (and then only for good reason); their value is debased if they are used often. The period is never used except in abbreviations, such as *U.S.* The semicolon is used wherever a period would otherwise seem appropriate:

President announces freeze; Congress to discuss it

Stylistic considerations. Most newspapers prefer not to use headlines that split infinitives or names. It's also not acceptable for a line to end with a preposition. Each line should be a coherent unit by itself:

Wrong: **Smith to go abroad**

HISTORY worth remembering

Memorable headlines. Sometimes significant stories result in memorable headlines. Here are a few examples:

Th-Th-Tha-Tha-That's All, Folks! Dodgers Miss

—in the *Los Angeles Times,* after the Dodgers lost a division championship

Stix Nix Hix Pix

—in *Variety,* when rural Americans stopped attending movies about country living

Up on the Housetop Slick, Slick, Slick

—in an *Omaha World-Herald*'s Christmas storm story

Ford to City: Drop Dead

—in the *New York Daily News*, after President Ford rejected the city's appeal for federal help

Wall Street Lays an Egg

—in *Variety*, after the stock market crash in 1929

Wrong: **Jim Williams, Jane North win elections**

Wrong: **Martin critical of America's journalists**

Parts of the verb *to be* also are to be avoided generally. Lively, active verbs attract more attention than the dull *are.*

Wrong: **15 seniors are chosen**
Right: **15 seniors chosen**

Headline writers should avoid repeating a word in a headline. Avoid this, for example:

Wrong: **Student Council to discuss student rights**

As for capitalization, most newspapers use "down style." That is, all letters except proper nouns and the first letter of the first word are lowercase. Such a headline looks like this:

Library offers amnesty on all overdue books

If you decide to use a style with capital letters, you may either capitalize prepositions and articles or leave them uncapitalized. Both ways are acceptable, although the latter style is preferable.

Aside from all these considerations, the headline writer must cultivate a special vocabulary of short words, such as *panel* for *committee, kin* for *relative, blast* for *explosion, cuts* for *reductions, quits* for *resigns,* and *named* for *selected.*

The headline writer should also cultivate a sense of humor. Puns are

TIPS worth taking

Careless headlines. Be careful when writing headlines or you might end up saying something you never intended, as in these examples:

State pupils below average in raeding

Cold wave linked to temperatures

War dims hope for peace

Grandmother of eight makes hole in one

Man is fatally slain

Iraqi head seeks arms

Milk drinkers turning to powder

considered particularly appropriate for many stories. The play on words often is a handy way to tell a story and draw readers further into it, as demonstrated by these examples:

Phone users have no hang-ups

New spray bugs farmers

Three booked in library dispute

Use alliteration sparingly. A little of this—Tigers Tame Tech Team; Teachers' Tests Trigger Trauma; Bartered Books Bring Big Bundle—goes a long way. The same is true of verse. Unless it's really good, toss it out.

Use the following checklist to evaluate your own news stories or to comment on the stories of others.

EVALUATION CHECKLIST

News Story

☑ Does the story begin with a succinct and direct, yet interesting, lead?

☑ Does a back-up quote or other transition connect the lead with the next paragraph?

☑ Is the style used to develop the story—inverted pyramid, chronological, or a combination—appropriate to the content?

☑ Are the majority of the sentences simple declarative ones?

☑ Has the writer avoided sexist language and other offensive terms, big words, clichés, and jargon?

☑ Has the writer included an interesting, appropriate headline?

☑ Is the story free from errors in sentence structure, capitalization and punctuation, and spelling?

☑ Does the story follow the publication and general AP style?

Copyediting

A publication's goal of getting information to its readers is only partly achieved when reporters have turned in their copy. One job remaining is the copyediting process, an often unglamorous but extremely important side of news work. It's the copy editor's responsibility to prepare the copy for publication. The copy editor edits the story and codes the copy (and sometimes even writes the headline). The job is vital, because if an error has crept into the reporter's copy, it almost certainly will get into the paper unless the copy editor catches it. The copy editor is the last line of defense against inaccuracies.

The Work of the Copy Editor

Copyediting requires a thorough knowledge of grammar and attention to details.

Although all reporters should know the publication's stylebook, copy editors must be masters of it. (Is a man referred to as Mr. Jones or just Jones, after the first reference? Is *re-election* hyphenated?) Copy editors have to know the rules of grammar, spelling, and punctuation. They must be able to catch repetition, dangling modifiers, misplaced pronouns, subject-verb agreement errors, and a whole list of other problems. Every scrap of information, no matter how trivial, that the copy editor can jam into his or her head may come in handy at some point. A copy editor must have a good memory and must know how to locate information—in standard reference books or on the Internet, for example. Very important, too, are matters of organization. The copy editor may change the order of elements in a story to create a more logical style and to make the story read more smoothly.

Copy editors also need excellent judgment and the ability to make fine distinctions in taste and word usage. They must have an ear for rhythm and an understanding of reporting and writing too, because copy editors should never change anything in a story except to improve it. Slavish adherence to rules—

whether of style or of structure—can lead to editing that harms the copy rather than helps it. If a reporter writes a story in unconventional fashion, selects sentence fragments for impact, injects acceptable humor—and can defend doing so—the copy editor should not tinker with it.

Here are some specific areas that copy editors must carefully deal with.

Accuracy. The most essential function of a copy editor is to watch for mistakes. To the reader involved, the smallest mistake may appear enormous.

Good copy editors must know how to spell. For checking spelling, as all computer-wise people know, the spell-checking feature in word processing programs is a blessing. But it's dangerous too. It won't alert you to a wrong word choice. For example, if you want to refer to *guerrilla warfare* and instead write *gorilla warfare,* a spell checker will sail right past it. Human beings, not spell checkers, have to catch that kind of mistake.

WORDS worth considering

Spelling demons. Here are the correct spellings of some of the most frequently misspelled words in the English language:

a lot	extension	Pittsburgh
accordion	fiery	plagiarism
Albuquerque	fluorescent	questionnaire
auxiliary	fulfill	receive
buoy	governor	recommend
calendar	guerrilla	rescind
category	harass	resistance
cemetery	hemorrhage	restaurant
committee	homicide	seize
computer	judgment	separate
consensus	lieutenant	sergeant
defendant	missile	sherbet
definite	misspell	sheriff
dependent	mustache	siege
develop	nickel	silhouette
dormitory	niece	subpoena
dilemma	ninety	suppress
embarrass	occurred	weird
embarrassed	paraphernalia	wield
existence	pavilion	yield

Copy editors must also check facts—and know which facts to check. A relatively harmless error, such as identifying someone as a freshman instead of a sophomore, may cause that sophomore and other readers to doubt every fact in the paper. Obviously there is not time to check every detail in every story. Copy editors must therefore develop a sense, a suspicion, about certain kinds of things.

For instance, they pay special attention to stories with numbers. Does the lead say six students won scholarships, while the story lists only five names? Does the story mention four federal grants to the school totaling $3,600, and then provide figures that add up to only $3,000? Does the story say teacher salaries are going up 3 percent and then name a teacher who is getting a 15-percent pay increase? In all of these cases, something is wrong, and it's up to the copy editor to find out what it is and to correct it.

Accuracy also involves paying special attention to names. Copy editors should not assume that the usual spelling is the correct one. They must check: Is it Patti or Patty? Smith or Smyth? Curtis or Kurtis? The same is true of titles. Is a person assistant superintendent or associate superintendent? counselor or chief counselor? It's never safe to guess.

Special attention also must be given to stories involving police activity and morals. If you incorrectly involve someone in a crime or in any way suggest that his or her moral standards are less than they should be, you will be in deep trouble very fast. High school newspapers don't frequently deal with stories of this nature, but they might. The copy editors who process these stories must be extra careful.

Editing. Besides making sure that stories conform to newspaper style, copy editors check to make sure that the stories read well. They make sure that paragraphs follow each other logically. They watch for loose writing and tighten it. They edit out trivia. They smooth rough passages in the copy, often by breaking long, unwieldy sentences into short, simple ones. They check for common but subtle errors, such as the one in this sentence:

> The committee voted to turn over their profits to the council.

Committee has a singular meaning here and so doesn't agree with the plural *their.*

Because most sentences in a story should be in the active, not passive, voice, a copy editor will change a sentence such as "Suggestions are wanted by the student council" to "The student council wants suggestions."

Attribution. Attribution, providing the source of the facts in the story, is another area that often needs to be checked. Many reporters provide attribution in the lead and then never mention the source again, leaving the reader with the erroneous belief that the opinions are the writer's. In such circumstances the copy editor goes through the story and puts in all the necessary *he saids, she pointed outs,* and so on. The reader must know at all times whose opinion is being expressed or where the information came from. (For a more detailed discussion of attribution, see Chapter 8.)

Copyediting Symbols

Many school publications now use desktop publishing systems that have greatly simplified the mechanical—although not the intellectual—problems of copyediting. Most publications, however, still require staff members to know copyediting symbols, which are essential for marking and correcting copy on paper. These symbols tell those who are making corrections to the copy what to do.

On pages 180–181 is a list of the most commonly used copyediting symbols. Here is how a piece of copy looks after it has been edited, using copyediting symbols:

A torrential downpout last Friday forced the forty-seven members of

(cap) (lc)   donna Florez's Geology class to call off their fieldtrip to Wagners Bluff.

(¶) (cap)   the group has asembled in the North parking lot at dawn but could not

(tr)   maek it across the pools of water that had been formed by the tremendous

rainfall.

"We'll have to go next week," said Florez. The group was planning to

hunt for fossils in an old reiver bed near the bluff, which is sixteen miles

west of town.

Senior Tom Johnson received a break from the rain. He overslpt and

would have missed the busy anyway.

When all the corrections have been made, the copy editor goes over the story one more time, reading it for sense—for total effect rather than for mechanical problems. The editor takes the role of the reader and asks, "Are all the questions answered? Is it clear? easy to read?" If the answer in each case is yes, the story is at last truly finished.

Copyediting Symbols

delete	. . . he ran with the ~~the~~ ball . . .
close up	. . . set up a time table . . .
delete and close up	. . . the studdent council also . . .
insert letter	. . . she told the cro^wd . . .
insert word	. . . something was ^left out . . .
change letter	. . . he ^may go . . .
change word	. . . didn't ~~tarry~~ ^wait long . . .
lowercase	. . . she made the Shot . . . (lc)
capitalize	. . . the drama club will . . . (cap)
set italic	. . . the word poetry has . . . (ital)
set roman	. . . they (refused) to go . . . (rom)
set boldface	. . . Taking Risks . . . (bf)
transpose letters	. . . the fotoball coach said . . . (tr)
transpose words	. . . was also chosen . . . (tr)
spell out	. . . the (gov.) said (7) states . . . (sp)
set in numerals	. . . (thirty-seven) days later . . .
abbreviate	. . . at 244 N. Elm (Street) . . .

insert space	. . . they arrived#on Tuesday . . .
insert period	. . . he said⊙ But Jones . . .
insert comma	. . . never happen again︵she said . . .
insert apostrophe	. . . it̆s always like this . . .
insert quotation marks	. . . ˘Get out,˘ he said . . .
insert colon	. . . the following◇. . .
insert parentheses	. . . on Mars﹙or Venus﹚ . . .
insert hyphen	. . . a well︵dressed person . . .
insert dash	. . . 200 lights︵all blue︵hung . . .
begin new paragraph	. . . talk.⌊Now that she . . . ⑨
no new paragraph	. . . not until then. ⟨no ¶⟩ Later, however, she . . .
begin new line	. . . eagles swept the sky,⌊dipping . . .
set center	⌉At My Wit's End⌈
set flush left	⌊by Jill Wong
set flush right	—Mark Twain (1835–1910)⌉
ignore correction	. . . this is ~~wrong~~ . . . ⟨stet⟩

Wrap-up

If the lead paragraph is the most important in the story, what immediately follows it certainly is next in terms of interest. One way to hold the interest built up in the lead is to follow immediately with a quotation, the sound of a human voice. Some people call this a "back-up quote," a quote designed to support the lead. Such a quote links the lead to the second paragraph, helping the story unfold logically and coherently. This is one type of transition.

Transitions can be entire sentences or even paragraphs, but usually they are one word: *but, also, therefore, however.* To aid the reader, sentences and paragraphs should be tied together logically.

After the lead and back-up quote, the story—told in skeletal fashion in the lead—is then simply retold in greater detail. Besides this inverted-pyramid style of writing, many other techniques are used. They include the storytelling style and a combination style using a summary lead followed by a chronological account. The latter is especially effective in describing action.

Details of style should be kept in mind while writing. The publication's stylebook dictates these decisions, and everyone should follow it. In this way consistency can be guaranteed. In addition, writers should avoid sexist language and racial and ethnic slurs. The use of short words and short sentences can aid busy readers. So can tight writing, and writing that is free from jargon, redundancies, clichés, and the passive voice. Fear of repeating a word ("monologophobia") can lead to inelegant expressions, such as "elongated yellow fruit" for "banana." Have no fear of repeating words.

There are many styles of headlines. Styles such as the hammer head, the wicket, and the kicker are widely used. Well-written headlines use a telegraphic style, mostly present-tense verbs, and limited punctuation. The size and length of a headline is determined by the story's importance on the page, which is typically decided by the reporter and the editor. Reporters may have to write headlines several times before they fit in the space allowed on the page's layout.

When a reporter has finished a story, it goes to the copy editor, whose biggest responsibility is watching for mistakes. There is no such thing as a small mistake; all mistakes undermine the credibility of the publication. Copy editors trim stories, smooth attribution, and correct grammar. Although copy editors may edit stories electronically on the computer, they need to understand and know how to use traditional copyediting symbols whenever they have to edit on hard copy (on paper).

On Assignment

INDIVIDUAL ACTIVITIES

1. Write a definition of each of these terms:

back-up quote	redundancy
chronological style	sexist language
cliché	stylebook
copyediting	tieback
hammer	transition
jargon	wicket
kicker	

2. Test your critical thinking. Recall several recent newsworthy occurrences in your community or school and evaluate possible approaches to handling them. Which could best be treated in an inverted-pyramid story? Of these stories, which would be simplest to write? Which would be hardest to write? Which could best be handled through some other approach? Discuss your ideas and reasons in class.

3. Find five headlines, of different styles, in your school or local newspaper. Clip them out, along with the articles, and then evaluate them. Do the heads fairly represent the articles? Are they well worded? Write a brief evaluation of each headline and then clip it to the head and story.

4. Rewrite this news story to get rid of common style problems. When you have finished, write a headline for the article.

Meeting at 3:45 P.M. in the afternoon, the Centerville High School Student council got down to brass tacks at long last and decided this year's Senior Prom will be Friday, May 11.

Tickets to the event began selling like hotcakes. Students rushed to purchase tickets, and florist shops were inundated with corsage orders.

The location for the prom was not known, but the council promised to hire extra policemen to be on duty in case anyone becomes inebriated. Businessmen also were to be approached and asked to support the prom with donations.

Also wanted by the council was a way to utilize student input in ascertaining which school personnel would attend as chaperones. Approximately five teachers are presently needed.

Future plans made by the council call for the prom queen to receive a bouquet of flowers exactly at the hour of midnight.

After a heated argument in the council meeting, members exhibited the milk of human kindness by pronouncing the dispute dead as a doornail.

On the level of basic fundamentals, council members set aside a large number of issues to be merged together at the next meeting. Qualified experts will be called in as consultants and past records studied carefully for the purpose of finding important essentials.

Council members voted unanimously 14–0 to ask a Jewish rabbi to say the invocation.

"I'm glad this issue is settled," sighed President Sally Smith.

"Me, too," stated the vice president, Chang Lee.

"You can say that again," laughed a new freshman whose appellation was unknown.

5. Write a one-page evaluation of the On Display article on page 157. How well does it follow inverted-pyramid style? What changes, if any, would you make?

6. Complete the stories for which you wrote leads in Chapter 6. Write a headline for each.

7. Complete your interview story from Chapter 5. Write a headline for each.

TEAM ACTIVITY

8. Develop a stylebook for your school publications. You may want to use the *AP Stylebook* as a guide but also include things that stylebook doesn't cover. How will you, for example, refer to women on the second reference in a story? to instructors on the second reference? Does the word *the* in the name of your paper take a capital *T*? Compare your stylebook to those created by other teams and the one currently in use. As a class choose the best version and use it from now on.

SURF THE NET

9. How reliable are various news sources? Identify a current-interest story about an issue on which opinions differ—for example, gun control—and find examples of a balanced and a biased treatment of it on the Internet. Which news sources seemed to have objective presentations and verifiable facts? Which consisted largely of unsubstantiated opinions? What conclusions can you draw about how critically you have to evaluate Internet stories?

career profile
Reporter

Katti Gray

Like many successful journalists, Katti Gray started small. Now a reporter for *Newsday* in Long Island, New York, she began her professional journey in Wichita Falls, Texas.

Armed with a journalism degree and internships at the *Dallas Times Herald* and the *Fort Worth Star-Telegram*'s Washington bureau, Gray began work as a reporter for the *Wichita Falls Record News.*

Gray graduated from Texas Christian University with majors in journalism and political science, an education she feels is a good combination for a journalist. Like many new journalism graduates, she took a job at a midsized daily in a midsized town, hoping to get practical experience reporting a variety of stories.

Covering the social services beat, she learned how to establish and maintain rapport with her contacts on a day-to-day basis, as well as how to dig out underlying issues from daily news.

While at Wichita Falls, she completed a series on the impact of desegregation on minority students and one on alternative schools for troubled and/or disabled students.

Through her more general assignments, she said, she has learned how to be enterprising.

"I learned quickly that you can't come back from an assignment and tell the editor there was no story," she said.

In June 1985 Gray joined the staff of the *Fort Worth Star-Telegram,* where she covered suburban education, social services, and government. Four years later she moved to *Newsday* to cover town government. Today she is a general assignment feature writer. She has also done work for the national, features, and travel desks, and for a now-defunct Sunday magazine.

"I don't have a beat," Gray said. "I cover features—a whole range of topics."

Big-city journalism has also taught her to be "a whole lot more sensitive to how the media exploit people's tragedies."

"We don't respect people's privacy," she said. "There are times when I want to jump up and say I don't want to do this."

Being in New York hasn't changed Gray. "I'm still very much the same person," she said. "I still believe the media have the potential to make a difference in people's lives."

Her New York City bosses, she said, would benefit from visiting smaller newspapers to see the brilliance there. "Good journalism goes on all over the country."

"Kids need to realize that to be important you don't have to be a *New York Times, Washington Post, Chicago Tribune*, or *Newsday* reporter," she said.

College fueled her idealism, pointing out the great power and potential of the media, but she also had to learn to deal with practical realities.

"Not everyone can win a Pulitzer. Every story you write will not liberate or emancipate somebody. You sometimes do things you are intellectually opposed to."

FOLLOW-UP

1. What might be particular problems of working for a big-city paper, such as Gray does? What might be advantages?

2. How would you feel about writing about things you were "intellectually opposed to"? What might some of these things be? How as a reporter would you handle such a situation?

CHAPTER 8

Handling Quotes Fairly and Accurately

KEY CONCEPTS

After reading this chapter, you will

▸ understand the need for precision in quotes

▸ know the appropriate uses of direct quotes, partial quotes, and paraphrasing

▸ know the issues associated with taping interviews

▸ know how to handle attribution

▸ understand techniques for reporting on speeches

During a debate between two presidential candidates not long ago, one turned to the other and asked, "Isn't the real question, will we be better off?"

Those are his exact words. Yet when a story about the debate was printed in a newspaper the next day, it came out this way: "The real question is, will we be better off?"

Look at two newspaper accounts about any event and you'll see such discrepancies. They're usually harmless, as in the case of the presidential debate. The sky won't fall over this small error.

Does it matter? Do direct quotations—this is what a person said, in his or her own words—have to be accurate word-for-word? Is there no margin for error?

There probably is—a little. Adrienne Lehrer, a professor of linguistics at the University of Arizona, determined that in 72 percent of these minor discrepancies in

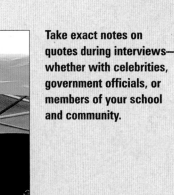

| direct quotation | paraphrase | partial quotation | attribution | KEY TERMS |

Take exact notes on quotes during interviews— whether with celebrities, government officials, or members of your school and community.

quotes, the substitution left the meaning of the quote unchanged. Still, it's bothersome. The world doesn't turn, for example, on the exact phrasing of words spoken by say, a professional football coach. It can, however, turn on the exact phrasing of the words in an important policy statement made by a president, a secretary of state, or a foreign leader. As always, 100-percent accuracy is a goal, a place to start.

One college journalism instructor frequently asks students whether they have had their names in the paper in the past year or two. Typically, 100 hands go into the air. Then he asks, "Were the stories completely, totally accurate?" Virtually all the hands go down. Upon discussion, it turns out that the students feel they were misquoted or their words distorted. In fairness, sometimes (frequently) it's a case of an interview subject saying in hindsight, "Boy, I wish I hadn't said that!" Too often, however, words are misquoted or twisted.

Direct Quotations

As a beginning journalist, you should pay a great deal of attention to the skills involved in handling quoted material.

Ideally, when you enclose a sentence or part of a sentence in quotation marks (quotes), you are telling your readers that the quoted material is exactly what the speaker said. You're not saying it's close or almost. You're saying, "These are the exact words." Anyone who has ever spent any time reporting, however, knows that this ideal is seldom, if ever, reached.

How is it possible to reproduce exactly what people say? People start sentences they never finish; they back up and start again; they say "ya know," "like I said," "ummmm," "ahhhh," and so on. We expect precision and logic in written communications or in a prepared spoken presentation, but extemporaneous human speech doesn't work that way. People think out loud, expressing half-formed thoughts and working out what they want to say as they go. It's virtually impossible to reproduce speech exactly, and why would you want to? The job is to convey information—and there's no information in "ya know."

A Question of Exactness

The journalistic ideal of reproducing speech exactly as it was uttered needs to be reexamined with an eye toward slight and very careful change. Studies indicate that sources care about this issue a great deal less than do journalists. Sources want their thoughts and ideas conveyed accurately to the public. They care less about their exact words. So does this mean journalists can just come close, be almost perfect? Of course not. Regardless of everything that's been written here, most quotes must be 100-percent, absolutely word-for-word perfect. These would include important remarks by politicians (the president's statement about the nation's economy), remarks certain to touch off controversy (a business executive's comments that could be interpreted as racist), or historic words. In 1969, for example, there was discussion by journalists over what Neil Armstrong said as he took the first steps on the moon. Was it "one small step for man . . ." or

WORDS worth considering

A question of meaning. Attention to exact wording—and exact meaning—is vital for handling quotes, as demonstrated in this famous dialogue from *Alice's Adventures in Wonderland* by Lewis Carroll:

> " . . . you should say what you mean," the March Hare went on.
>
> "I do," Alice hastily replied: "at least—at least I mean what I say—that's the same thing, you know."
>
> "Not the same thing a bit!" said the Hatter. "Why, you might just as well say that 'I see what I eat' is the same thing as 'I eat what I see.' "

On the important occasion of the first moon landing in 1969, the media considered it vital to record astronaut Neil Armstrong's exact words: "That's one small step for man, one giant leap for mankind."

"one small step for a man . . . ?" No one was inclined that day just to come close.

You can invent your own scenarios in which the exact language is crucial. Most of the time, journalists simply take out the "ya knows" and the "hmmms," and no harm is done. Faced with a tangled, unclear sentence, most journalists decide not to use a direct quote but to try to convey the source's ideas in clearer words. No one (at least no one with a commitment to ethics) alters quotes a great deal. A bit of sanitizing goes on, but that's about the extent of it.

Use a Tape Recorder

Tape recorders can be a great aid to a reporter for any assignment in which capturing someone's exact words is important. Use a small recorder; some people are intimidated by large ones. If the source agrees, turn on the recorder at the beginning, set it aside, and just let it run. Never, however, tape-record someone without permission, either in person or on the telephone. You can use a tape recorder during speeches and meetings too. In some cities at school board or city council meetings, the area near the speaker's podium is clustered with recorders placed there by print and broadcast journalists.

Remember always to take good notes even if you're using a tape recorder. Sometimes the batteries go dead or the tape breaks or gets twisted in the mechanism. Never rely completely on a tape recorder.

If you're not using a tape recorder and are still concerned about exact quotes, take very careful notes, in shorthand or speedwriting if you know how, and flesh them out from memory as soon as possible. In most cases, no one expects you to reproduce every single word, but your goal is to come as close as possible.

When Not to Quote

Exact quotes are not always appropriate. What if, during a speech or interview, the subject uses a profane four-letter word? What do you do? The easy answer (and frequently the right one) is to simply take it out, ignore it. There are times—rare times, to be sure—when profanity is exactly right, when it conveys the point in the best possible way. If that's the case, quote it. Never, however, sprinkle in four-letter words just to prove your sophistication or your freedom.

Another exception occurs when the subject uses poor grammar. There's no need to reproduce bad grammar exactly as it was spoken. For example, if you are interviewing your elderly custodian who has only a few years of formal education, don't make him seem illiterate. On the other hand, it would be foolish for you to interview a colorful character who uses a lot of quaint phrases and make her sound sophisticated.

Paraphrasing

Often, paraphrasing is helpful. It's perfectly proper, often even desirable, for a reporter to paraphrase a person's words—to put the speaker's ideas into the reporter's own words. Thus, if a direct quote is long or rambling or poorly stated, the writer may revise it, knock off the quote marks, and simply add "he said" or "she said" at the beginning or end of the sentence.

Suppose the speaker, Police Chief Jones, says the following:

> "We are doing everything in our power at police headquarters to see to it that there is a parking place in the school lots or on the street for everyone who drives to school. We hope everyone involved will be patient."

There's little doubt that a journalist could say that more concisely by paraphrasing, in which case it could read like this:

> Chief Jones said that police are trying to find parking space for everyone who drives to school. He urged patience and promised to find a solution for the overcrowded school lots.

One hazard exists in paraphrasing: Certain words must be adjusted. For instance, if the direct quote is "We decided to go to a movie," the paraphrase has to read *They decided to go to the movies, he said.* Notice the shift in pronouns. The word *we* is reserved for direct quotes and editorials; so are *us* and *our.* Journalists speak of *the* country, *the* school, *the* town, not *our* country, *our* school, *our* town.

Paraphrase for Facts

Quotes should not be used to convey facts. Quotes make a story lively, give it a human touch, let readers begin to understand what a source is like. Capture good quotes and use lots of them—but paraphrase when you're simply conveying facts.

Here's why. Let's say you interview the school librarian, Roy Taylor, and he says the following:

> "We have 3,543 books in Room 101 and 4,589 in Room 209, and 400 movies and 250 CDs in the annex—and if we don't pass the bond issue so we can get more room I'm going to resign."

Whatever you do, don't make a quote out of the first part of the statement. Paraphrase it:

> Roy Taylor, the school librarian, said the library houses more than 3,500 books in Room 101 and more than 4,500 in Room 209, plus about 400 movies and 250 CDs in the annex. He said he plans to resign as librarian if voters reject a bond issue to expand the library.

What if the head of the Red Cross says the following?

> "We are going to deliver a planeload of food and supplies to the disaster area. The plane takes off from Municipal Airport at 8:15 A.M."

Don't use that as a direct quote. Paraphrase it:

> The head of the local Red Cross said the Red Cross will airlift food and supplies to the disaster area. The plane takes off at 8:15 A.M. from Municipal Airport.

The direct quote is for color, for impact—not for conveying mere factual information.

Avoid Repetition

Don't present the same information as a paraphrase and a direct quote. Doing so makes copy editors want to tear out their hair. Here's an example:

> The mayor promised today he would never embezzle money from the city again.
> "I will never embezzle money from the city again," the mayor said.

The same information is presented in each sentence. Here's another example:

> The coach said his team could win if it eliminates turnovers, penalties, and mental errors.
> "We have to eliminate turnovers, penalties, and mental errors to win," the coach said.

Hit the delete key!

Partial Quotations

One method for avoiding the overuse of both paraphrased material and long blocks of quoted material is the partial quote. A writer is free to quote part of a sentence directly while paraphrasing the rest. Here are two examples:

> The school needs a dress code, the principal said, because students are becoming "sloppy in dress and sloppy in thought."

Quoting Out of Context

Do all quotes in news stories truly represent the speaker's message?

Direct quotes from a source are the base for many informative news stories. Situations can arise, however, that make their use controversial and, at worst, even the source of lawsuits.

One issue is quoting out of context. Most newswriters are responsible and take pains to explain the situation in which a statement was made. Often, however, the quoted person complains afterward that the spirit of his or her statement was completely misrepresented. For example, a statement such as "When I get this angry, I just don't worry about the consequences" can be taken out of context to characterize the speaker as irresponsible or perhaps even violent. But what if the speaker were talking about how angry he felt as he loudly criticized a neighbor woman for kicking her pet dog? The "consequences" referred to in the quote may simply have been having a public argument with his neighbor, something the speaker ordinarily wouldn't do. Using the quote out of context has taken a probably justifiable act and made it seem like the response of a dangerous person.

Quotes from movie reviews are frequently used in ads. "An appallingly bad script that even Gugliamo's beautifully staged scenes can't overcome" can be quoted out of context as simply "beautifully staged scenes." Here the quote is not only taken out of context; the intended meaning is completely changed.

Occasionally situations arise in which people have no idea that their private comments will be made public. This most often happens to individuals who aren't used to being interviewed or quoted. A case that made headlines several years ago was one in which reporter Connie Chung interviewed the mother of then–Speaker of the House Newt Gingrich on a nationally televised news show. Unused to the media spotlight, Mrs. Gingrich mentioned in the interview that her son not only

Janet Malcolm leaves the court after the lawsuit brought against her by psychiatrist Jeffrey M. Masson. Masson claimed that undocumented quotes used by Malcolm in articles about him constituted libel, but the court declined to award him damages.

disliked First Lady Hillary Clinton but also called her a certain name. Chung cajoled the woman into whispering the name to her, suggesting strongly that it would be kept just between the two of them, but then turned around and quoted her later. Not surprisingly, Chung was strongly criticized.

Sometimes a journalist's alleged distortion of quotations can bring about a lawsuit. One famous example is the so-called Malcolm case, in which reporter Janet Malcolm, in a long article on psychiatrist Jeffrey M. Masson, attributed direct quotes to him that there was no record of his ever having said. (The interview was recorded, but Malcolm had additional notes in which she claimed to have written down the quotes in question.) Masson sued Malcolm, as well as her employer, saying that she fabricated quotes that made him look unscholarly, dishonest, and vain.

Interestingly, the courts in this case sided with Malcolm, saying that her characterization on Masson was not a distortion of the overall impression his interview responses had created. It might be argued that Malcolm was quite lucky to get off. A safer and ultimately more ethical way to handle quotes is to present them accurately and to fully establish their context.

FOLLOW-UP

1. Find ads for several recent movies as well as the reviews quoted in those ads. Create a graph or diagram showing how often the ads accurately represented the reviews.
2. Use a source such as the Congressional Record to find the full text of statements quoted briefly in news articles. How accurately did the articles convey the statements' contexts?

Martinez said he was "ready to do cartwheels" after scoring the winning touchdown.

The material enclosed in quotes in the preceding sentences constitutes partial quotes.

Unnecessary Quoting

Beware, however, that you do not carry the use of partial quotes to absurd extremes. Note the following examples.

Lee said he was "happy" after scoring the goal.

She was in "critical" condition, the hospital spokesperson said.

What purpose do the quotation marks serve in these examples? None at all. Here are some other instances in which quotes are unnecessary:

After three defeats, it appears the season is "down the drain."

The course is "a piece of cake."

The music is "hot."

You get the point. If a slang word or phrase is exactly right, use it and skip the quotes; they will add nothing except confusion. The reader will either understand the slang or not. The quotation marks will not make any difference.

Attribution

Beginning writers often have trouble with attribution. What is meant by attribution is this: Because it's often not possible to know what people really mean or feel or believe, report what they *say* they mean or feel or believe. Report what the person said and make a point of saying who said it. Attribution amounts to giving the reader the name of the source. For example:

The superintendent *said* she will resign.

The police chief *said* Davis had confessed.

Taxes will go down, the governor *promised*.

Police *said* the accident occurred because of slick streets.

There is no way Tech can win, the coach *said*.

Attribution Verbs

The verb you use to indicate your source is important: *stated, declared, noted, pointed out*, and so on. The best of all such words is *said*. It's a neutral word that contains no editorial overtones; it's unobtrusive and rarely becomes tiresome no matter how often it appears in a story.

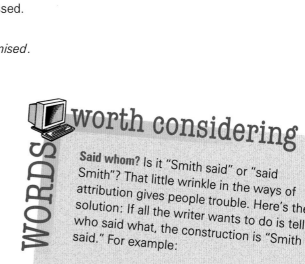

WORDS worth considering

Said whom? Is it "Smith said" or "said Smith"? That little wrinkle in the ways of attribution gives people trouble. Here's the solution: If all the writer wants to do is tell who said what, the construction is "Smith said." For example:

"I love journalism class," Smith said.

If, however, the writer wants to tell a bit about Smith besides his or her name, it goes this way:

"I love journalism class," said Smith, whose mother is the journalism teacher.

Be very careful which verb you select when you depart from *said*. *Stated* is formal. *Pointed out* should be reserved for absolute facts ("The sun rose," he pointed out). *Charge, demand, shout,* and the like have editorial connotations. Whatever you do, stay away from this kind of construction:

"I couldn't care less," he frowned.

"It's no problem of mine," she shrugged.

"How bad is this?" he grimaced.

"Wonderful idea," she smiled.

You can frown, shrug, grimace, or smile all you want, but no words will come out. The verb you use must indicate speech formations by lips, mouth, and tongue.

When reporting on a controversial event such as a car accident, journalists must correctly attribute statements made by witnesses as well as participants.

When, Where, and How to Attribute

When should you attribute? The need for attribution is in direct proportion to the amount of controversy attached to the statement. Thus, a story about a robbery and the arrest of two suspects would need heavy attribution. On the other hand, a story reporting that a downtown street has been closed for repairs would need little attribution, because it's common knowledge and noncontroversial. The best approach is—when in doubt, attribute.

Where should you attribute? Where should you place the "he said" and "she pointed outs"? In general, attribution works best at the end or in the middle of a sentence. Give the quote first and the source of the quote second. In a long quote, attribution should come at the first logical point in the first sentence. Try this lead:

> Professor Pat Brainerd on Thursday told a group of law students that America's poor need free legal advice or they will lose their rights.

This version is easier to read and comes to the point more quickly:

> America's poor need free legal advice or they will lose their rights, Professor Pat Brainerd told a group of law students Thursday.

It's also perfectly acceptable to interrupt a quotation in the middle for attribution. For example:

"Our students are mature," Kuzinski told teachers Tuesday, "but they do not always act that way."

On the other hand, this interruption for attribution is awkward:

"Our students," Kuzinski told teachers Tuesday, "are mature, but they do not always act that way."

It's especially helpful to interrupt in the middle if the quote is long and unwieldy; then the interruption serves as a breath pause for your reader.

Perhaps the most important point concerning attribution is this: Always make it absolutely clear whose opinion is being expressed. Given a choice, the reader may conclude that the opinion is the reporter's—and this is not the impression you want to leave. So don't let quotes float free of their source. This construction, for instance, is wrong:

Schwartz was elated. "It was my first touchdown ever."

And so is this; the reader has to wait too long to find out who is talking:

"It was my best day. I got the ball on a dead run. It was a perfect pass, and I just outran the secondary. One guy dived at me near the goal, but he missed," Schwartz said.

In the latter example, the writer should have identified Schwartz as the speaker right after "It was my best day."

Lest anyone doubt the importance of attribution, consider the embarrassment on the part of the press (and the confusion on the part of the audience) when media across the country reported that prisoners, during a New York prison riot, had slashed the throats of their hostages. Almost without exception the press failed to attribute this "fact" to its source. When it became evident later that no throats had been slashed, the press looked pretty bad, and the public must have wondered how many other statements in the story were false.

Story Based on Interviews

The Echoes, Abraham Lincoln High School, Council Bluffs, Iowa

FOOD FOR THOUGHT

by Holly Wolfe

Hungry students will soon have access to nutritious snacks throughout the day.

Vending machines offering juice and non-candy snacks will be located in the science, social studies, English, and business wings as well as the commons area.

Principal James Lake said these machines, along with the pop and candy machines, will be on all day, giving students a chance to purchase snacks and juice between classes. He said passing periods will be lengthened to eight or nine minutes to accommodate student use of the machines.

Lake and teachers stressed that student cooperation is necessary to do this.

"Students have been pretty good this semester and deserve something," Lake said. "They must be respectful and organized and realize that this is a privilege. As soon as there are wrappers or trash around the campus, the machines will be turned off."

Lake said the decision to permit food in the classroom is entirely up to each teacher. Several teachers already allow food in class.

"I think a lot of kids rush around in the morning and don't have time to eat," said Linda Patton, Spanish instructor. "After it hits them, they just don't function as well. That's why I decided to allow kids to eat in class."

Many students agree with Patton.

"It's easy to be distracted when you're hungry," junior Sarah McLean said. "If you have a break with food, you're able to stay on track longer."

Teachers are hopeful that students will perform better after a snack.

"I'd be willing to give it a try," said Alynn Jaeger, English instructor. "If it really does improve students' academic performances or attention spans, I guess it's a good idea."

Some students feel this might even be an incentive for staying in class.

"I think it's a great idea," senior Sally Christensen said. "It might even help with the problem of skipping because a lot of kids leave school to go get a pop or food."

Teachers were recently asked to consider the idea of a set time during the day where the entire school would get a nutrition break, but they voted down the idea. Many believed it would be impossible to have nearly 1,300 students in the halls or cafeteria at one time.

"I'll try this to see how it goes," said Dennis DeVault, American History instructor, "but they're going to have to earn the privilege of having food in my classroom."

The **ON DISPLAY** example above reports what a number of people said about a new school policy allowing students to buy food all day. As you read it, look for paraphrasing, direct quotes, and the positioning of various attributions.

Use this checklist in evaluating your own and others' news stories.

EVALUATION CHECKLIST

Using Quotes

☑ Are sources clearly identified when they are quoted?

☑ Is the story a mix of text and interesting, relevant direct quotations?

☑ Are paraphrases used in place of rambling speeches and lists of facts?

☑ Are all important, controversial, or opinion-based statements clearly attributed?

☑ Is the story free from grammatical errors and in accordance with the publication and general AP style?

Speech Stories

A fruitful source of news is the speech. Speeches given by newsworthy individuals are almost always covered by the press because journalists know that public pronouncements of great importance—or of great interest to many people—are often made in speech format.

Covering a speech or any oral presentation is, in a sense, one of the easiest of all assignments. On the surface, at least, it consists of one person speaking—and that's quite simple. The reporter must be careful to note exactly what the speaker says. Then the reporter must try to select the speaker's main points for inclusion in the story. There probably has never been a good speech story written in the order in which the speech was given. The lead, the speaker's main point or points, often comes late in the speech, and the writer must tell the reader immediately what the main point is.

The best speech story is a well-designed mixture of direct quotes, paraphrasings, and partial quotes. The lead distills the essence of what the speaker said; it summarizes and explains. The lead gets to the point. It does not waste the reader's time with needless detail, such as where the speech took place. Save that for later—unless there are special circumstances. The lead emphasizes what was said, not the simple fact that a speech was made.

Reporters should be careful to note exactly what speakers say as well as the reaction of the audience.

When you cover a speech, pay close attention to the audience. How many people were there? How many times was the speaker interrupted by applause? Which lines calculated to get applause stirred no one? Were hecklers or protesters present? How many? What was the speaker's reaction?

Watch for the obvious omission, for what the speaker does not say (she did not announce the new budget, she did not announce her candidacy). Realize also that the phrase "she [or he] concluded" can be used only once in a speech story—at the conclusion.

Use the criteria in the checklist below to write and evaluate your own speech stories, as well as when you are asked to evaluate the speech stories of others.

EVALUATION CHECKLIST

Speech Story

☑ Are the time, place, and speaker made clear at the beginning of the story?

☑ Are the most important points from the speech reported in the lead?

☑ Does the rest of the story summarize the speech and quote significant statements directly?

☑ Are noteworthy facts about the audience response included?

☑ Is the story free from grammatical errors and in accordance with the publication and general AP style?

The **ON DISPLAY** feature on page 201 reports on a speech—really a eulogy, a speech praising a dead person—given by Senator Ted Kennedy at the funeral of his nephew John F. Kennedy, Jr., in July 1999. Notice that the article reports on several other aspects of the funeral as well.

Speech Story

The New York Times, New York City, New York

Doors Closed, Kennedys Offer Their Farewells

by N. R. Kleinfeld

In the simple stone church where his mother brought him to worship as a small boy, John F. Kennedy Jr., the country's most famous namesake, was remembered as a young man who shouldered the ponderous weight of legend and was still "becoming the person he would be" in a memorial Mass on Friday that united generations and ideologies.

On a hot, sunshiny morning, an eclectic mix of some 350 mourners—from the eminent figures of his father's administration to his childhood hero, Muhammad Ali, to President Clinton, to many young friends who lived beyond the circumspection of public life—gathered in somber attire at the Church of St. Thomas More on the Upper East Side to honor Kennedy and his wife, Carolyn Bessette Kennedy.

His uncle, Senator Edward M. Kennedy of Massachusetts, delivered an affecting eulogy laced with eloquence and wit in which he said that Kennedy, as the only son of the 35th President of the United States, "seemed to belong not only to our family, but to the American family. The whole world knew his name before he did."

Speaking of the still embryonic stage of his nephew's career, the Senator said: "He had only just begun. There was in him a great promise of things to come."

The death of Mr. Kennedy, 38, along with his 33-year-old wife and her sister Lauren G. Bessette, 34, in the July 16 nighttime crash of the small plane he was piloting over the Atlantic Ocean, has been a weeklong and heartfelt absorption for a nation now both wearied and practiced in mourning Kennedys, and this formal tribute was the culmination, a day after the ashes of the three were poured into the restless waters that claimed them.

The mourners at the invitation-only Mass included a preponderance of family members and political figures. President Clinton attended with Hillary Rodham Clinton and their daughter, Chelsea. Caroline Kennedy came with her husband, Edwin Schlossberg, and their three children. There was Ethel Kennedy, Robert F. Kennedy Jr., Maurice Tempelsman, the longtime companion of Mrs. Onassis, three Kennedy sisters—Jean Kennedy Smith, Patricia Kennedy Lawford and Eunice Kennedy Shriver—and Maria Shriver, Mr. Kennedy's cousin, and her husband, Arnold Schwarzenegger. . . .

In his eulogy, Senator Kennedy thanked the Clintons for their presence and told of how, when they once asked John Kennedy Jr. what he would do if he were ever elected President, Mr. Kennedy had replied, "I guess the first thing is call up Uncle Teddy and gloat."

"I loved that," the Senator said. "It was so like his father."

There were many substrata to Mr. Kennedy's life—fame, power, wealth and expectation—but the eulogy centered on his unpretentious nature and zest for life and adventure, on how he "lived as if he were unrecognizable" and "thought politics should be an integral part of our popular culture, and that popular culture should be an integral part of politics."

The Senator continued: "He and his bride have gone to be with his mother and father, where there will never be an end to love.

"He was lost on that troubled night, but we will always wake for him, so that his time, which was not doubled, but cut in half, will live forever in our memory, and in our beguiled and broken hearts."

Senator Kennedy's voice cracked at two junctures, when he spoke affectionately of Mr. Kennedy and his wife, surrounded by Caroline Kennedy, her family and other relatives, sailing together on Nantucket Sound and when, near the end, he said: "We dared to think, in that other Irish phrase, that this John Kennedy would live to comb gray hair, with his beloved Carolyn by his side. But like his father, he had every gift but length of years."

After Mr. Kennedy's eulogy, the O Freedom Gospel Choir sang, "Amazing Grace," and the 90-minute service came to an end.

Wrap-up

Reproducing accurately what people say is a basic journalistic function. Sometimes sources claim they were misquoted when they really were not, but journalists still need to emphasize accuracy in quoted material.

Too often, there are great differences between what is said and what is published or aired. Words can easily be misquoted or twisted.

Beginning journalists should pay a great deal of attention to the skills involved in handling quoted material. When journalists enclose a sentence or part of a sentence in quotation marks, they are telling readers that this is exactly what the speaker said. They are not saying that it's close to or almost what was said.

It's difficult to reproduce exactly what people say. People start sentences they never finish; they back up and start again; they say "ya know," "like I said," "ummmm," "ahhh," and so on.

The journalistic ideal of reproducing speech exactly as it was uttered needs to be reexamined with an eye toward slight and careful change. Studies indicate that sources care about this issue much less than do journalists. Sources want their thoughts and ideas conveyed accurately to the public. They care less about their exact words.

Most of the time, journalists take out the "ya knows" and the "hmmmms," and no harm is done. Faced with an unclear sentence, most journalists decide not to use a direct quote but to try to convey the source's ideas in the journalist's words.

Tape recorders can aid a reporter. Small, unobtrusive ones are best. Good notes are important, however, even when a tape recorder is used. Sometimes batteries die or the tape breaks. Journalists should never tape-record someone without permission, either in person or on the telephone.

Generally speaking and depending on circumstances, most journalists clean up profanity and bad grammar. Often they simply paraphrase the source's words—that is, they express the source's words in their own way and take off the quotation marks.

Quotes should be used to present interesting or noteworthy statements by speakers. The use of quotes to present facts, such as the number of people attending a school, should be avoided. Also to be avoided is copy that both paraphrases and quotes the same statement.

Journalists must carefully attribute quotes. It's important that readers know at all times where the information they are looking at came from. The verb most favored for attribution is *said* because it has no overtones.

Various rules and suggestions apply to handling quotes, including where to interrupt a sentence to insert attribution.

Stories about speeches, panel discussions, and similar events that are basically about what someone says should be written with a mixture of direct quotes, paraphrased material, and partial quotes. Always remember to write about what was said, not about the simple fact that someone spoke.

On Assignment

INDIVIDUAL ACTIVITIES

1. Write a brief definition of each of these terms:

attribution   paraphrase
direct quotation   partial quotation

2. Clip all the stories from your last newspaper or magazine that quoted someone. Send the stories to the persons quoted to find out whether they were quoted accurately. Conduct interviews—either in person or by phone—with one or more of these people. Write a brief report summarizing your findings.

3. Tape-record an interview; then write a story from it. Discuss your finished stories in class. Was it possible to quote verbatim every time? How did you handle the "ya knows" and the incomplete sentences? What other similar issues arose?

4. Write a story based on a presidential news conference or televised speech. Compare your story with that of a classmate. Did he or she choose to emphasize the same or different topics? Did you both report quotes in the same way?

5. Evaluate the On Display interview story on page 198. How well did the writer handle quotes and attribution? Write a one-page critique of the article.

6. Ask five or more sources for their opinions on a school issue. Choose authoritative sources on the issue as well as a variety of students who may have an opinion on the issue. (Interview students you don't already know well to keep the story balanced.) Write a story suitable for publication, quoting your sources correctly.

7. Find a story on a speech covered by a daily newspaper. Underline the verbs. Is *said* used most? What other words appear frequently? Begin a log of verbs that professional journalists use for attribution and keep it in your notebook. Which ones seem to be used most often? Which are rare?

TEAM ACTIVITIES

8. Invite members of a speech class to give speeches to teams of journalism students. Then write a news story covering the speech given to your team. Compare your story to those of others on your team. Analyze the differences. Have the speech students review the stories and note where they were misquoted or quoted out of context.

9. Simple and short attribution helps keep the focus on the quote. To reinforce this point in an amusing way, you might try writing some Tom Swifties.

   Tom Swift was the hero of a series of children's adventure books who never simply "said" anything. Today, a Tom Swiftie is a humorous exaggeration of an elaborate method of attribution, often with a pun or an allusion thrown in. Here are some samples:

   ▶ "I'll have a hot dog," said Tom frankly.

   ▶ "Let's dig into it," said Tom gravely.

   ▶ "We need a fielder who can hit sixty home runs," he said ruthlessly.

   ▶ "I don't care for fairy tales," she said grimly.

   Working in teams of three or four, try building an extended dialogue of Tom Swifties. Compare your team's dialogue with those of the other teams.

SURF THE NET

10. Find a story in two on-line newspapers about a recent speech given by a government official. Compare the quotes in each story to see whether they match. Now see how the same story was covered by the news group on Usenet. Report your findings.

career profile

White House Correspondent

Helen Thomas

Like a lot of would-be movie stars, Helen Thomas started her career working in a restaurant.

Graduating from Wayne State University during World War II, she moved to Washington, D.C., to be near the center of power. She waited tables for a year before she got her break—as a $17.50-a-week copy clerk at the *Washington Daily News*.

"I've always wanted to be a reporter," said Thomas, who today is the senior member of the White House press corps and has been named one of the 25 most influential women in America. "I got hooked in high school," she said.

Thomas covered several federal agencies and departments until 1960, when she was assigned to cover President-elect John F. Kennedy. She followed him into the White House in January 1961 and has been there questioning presidents ever since. It's the only job she wants.

"This is the seat of power in the world," she said. "There is such an infinite variety of stories."

For nearly three decades Thomas wielded a different kind of power. As senior correspondent it was her job to end the press conferences after 30 minutes—or to keep presidents talking for that long. The tradition of the 30-minute press conference lasted until former President George Bush began to decide himself when to end the questioning.

Covering presidents and the federal government is not easy. Government officials, even presidents, often try to keep information from reporters. A presidential press conference is the only opportunity to ask a president questions and demand answers.

Thomas quotes Thomas Jefferson when asked about the need for a news media to question government. Jefferson noted 200 years ago that a nation ignorant will never be a democracy.

The press-government relationship is often adversarial. Thomas said that no president has ever liked the press and that it doesn't matter whether the press likes the president.

"It is our job to get the facts," she said. "People will never, never know how difficult it is to get information. We're constantly trying to break down the barriers.

That means constant questioning, healthy skepticism, and never giving up. We can't give up because we are the watchdogs for the truth."

Journalists, particularly high-profile ones who cover presidents, are becoming less and less popular with the public, but Thomas is unfazed.

"We didn't get into this business to be loved," she said. "It's our job to keep the government from doing things in secret. We have an important role to play in this country. We can hold our heads high because we seek the truth."

Thomas has had many honors during her career. She was the only print journalist to accompany President Richard M. Nixon on his historic trip to China in 1972. She was the first woman officer of the White House Correspondents Association and also of the National Press Club. She has received several honorary degrees.

FOLLOW-UP

1. White House correspondents such as Thomas have an elite reporting job. Do some research into the qualifications most of them have and the perks that they receive.

2. Has the White House press corps always had an adversarial relationship with presidents? Look into how two recent presidents were covered and report your findings to the class.

CHAPTER 9

Doing In-Depth Reporting

KEY CONCEPTS

After reading this chapter, you will

▶ be familiar with the issues teenagers say they care about most, issues that deserve in-depth treatment by student journalists

▶ understand trends in professional and scholastic journalism leading to new emphasis by students on in-depth reporting

▶ know how to condense certain items in a newspaper or magazine to find room for in-depth stories

▶ understand the difference between the lead on a routine news story and the introduction of an in-depth story

▶ be able to construct in-depth stories by writing an introduction, a nut graph, a body, and an ending

Tremendous change has come to high school journalism. Once monuments to trivia, high school publications today are tributes to serious journalism, produced by talented students committed to their task of serving a modern audience. Even the most casual inspection of the best of today's scholastic publications quickly reveals the extent of the change.

If Rip Van Winkle had started his famous nap in the 1970s and awakened 25 or 30 years later, he would be stunned. Where homecoming queens once reigned and editorials went no further than urging school spirit, scholastic publications today are on top of the news—and the coverage is complete and detailed. High school journalists are producing thoughtful, in-depth pieces on a wide range of important subjects. These days, you're apt to see in-depth treatment on everything from school budgets to school violence; from censorship to family crises; from animal rights to standardized tests and student rights.

The list is long and getting longer. It represents the catalog of interests and concerns

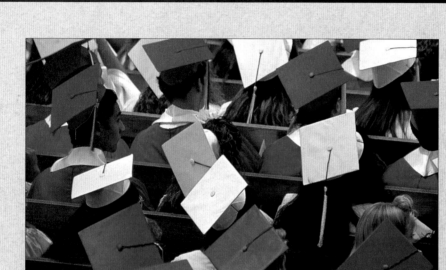

Education is a topic of great interest to teenagers, making it ideal for in-depth coverage.

young people have today. It also represents, in many ways, a catalog of subjects that teens need to know about.

What these and similar subjects have in common is the need for sensitive, objective, in-depth treatment. They do not lend themselves to superficial handling.

A frequent criticism of the professional press is that it is superficial. Critics argue that the lack of space or time forces the press to hit only the highlights—and too often the sensational highlights—of public issues and events. These critics claim that issues laced with subtleties cannot be explored properly under the constraints of speed and brevity.

The critics have a point. Not all stories need in-depth treatment, but many do. Unfortunately many journalists operate superficially even when covering the stories that need deeper treatment. This chapter explores the need for such treatment.

Stories with Substance

In too many newsrooms the reporter who suggests an in-depth story requiring weeks of research and writing is told that there is no time for such a project and no space to run it. It doesn't have to be that way.

207

TIPS worth taking

Topics important to teenagers. Write in-depth stories on topics your readers care about. The information below may help you identify such topics. It presents the results of the 1998 TRU Teenage Marketing and Lifestyle Study, conducted to provide concrete information about teenagers' top three interests. The data shows the percentage of teens listing each topic in his or her top three:

AIDS	29
Education	25
Child abuse	25
Drinking and driving	24
Racism	23
Abortion	21
Drug abuse	18
Violence	15
Sexual assault	13
Environment	12
Cigarette smoking	12
Nuclear war	11
Animal rights	11
Unplanned pregnancy	10
War	8
Suicide	8
Alcoholism	6
Homelessness	6
Women's rights	6
Eating disorders	6
Divorce	5
Unemployment	5
Health care	5

Stories with substance may uncover wrongdoing, but they may also present information on important economic or social issues. Such stories can benefit readers' lives in many ways. Here are some examples of in-depth reporting:

Development of the Boeing 757

At age 28 Peter Rinearson was the newly assigned aerospace writer for the *Seattle Times.* Searching for an interesting, in-depth project that would help him get a grip on his new beat, Rinearson hit upon the idea of preparing "a special report on the conception, design, manufacture, marketing, and delivery of a new jetliner—the Boeing 757."

"I discovered," Rinearson remarked later, "that just as I didn't really understand what Boeing does, the community didn't really understand. Even a lot of people at Boeing didn't know much beyond their direct area of responsibility."

So he went to work. For six months Rinearson did little but work on the Boeing 757 story. He compiled about 1,200 single-spaced typewritten pages of interviews. He talked with 50 to 60 people. His project occupied almost every waking hour. "If I wasn't eating or sleeping, I was reporting or reading in libraries, involved with the story at one level or another," he said.

The *Seattle Times* ran his stories over eight days. The series was 25,000 words long—able to fill 16 full-size newspaper pages. For his efforts Rinearson was awarded the Pulitzer Prize for feature writing.

Some people call the type of stories Rinearson did in-depth reporting. Others argue that such reporting is investigative by nature, and in some quarters investigative reporting is unpopular. Was Rinearson's story investigative? He says no.

"I don't know what that is. Investigative reporting sort of suggests uncovering wrongdoing, and I have done some of that. It pleased me that I was able to win the prize with something other than an account of wrongdoing. . . ."

Watergate

If ever there was an investigative story, it was the story of Watergate, the name applied to an array of deeds and events in the early 1970s that led to the resignation of President Richard Nixon.

The story began with a phone call to Bob Woodward of the *Washington Post*. Five men had been caught inside the offices of the Democratic Party at the Watergate apartment complex. The young reporter, later teamed with Carl Bernstein, was launched on one of the biggest stories of the century—the story that helped topple a president.

It did a lot more too. It stirred a wave of infatuation with investigative reporting on the part of the media.

Two schools of thought exist on such reporting. One says the media have no greater duty than to sniff out and expose wrongdoing and that it is impossible to overdo it. The other says that the media definitely are overdoing it, that they are seeking evil rather than seeking news, and sniffing prizes rather than sniffing wrongdoing.

There is probably truth on both sides. Done right, thorough, in-depth stories represent journalism at its finest. Sometimes there *is* wrongdoing.

Other Examples

There are many examples of investigative reporting that bring out legitimate problems readers need to know about.

Consider Ken Herman. Barely out of college, he was a reporter for the *News*, a small paper in Lufkin, Texas. Covering a story about the death in training camp of a local Marine, Herman was dissatisfied with the official answers to his questions. He discovered that the victim, a young man of limited intellectual ability, had been beaten to death during recruit training. Much of the investigation was done on the telephone. The *News* won the Pulitzer Prize for the story.

Investigative stories on mass murders in Bosnia won David Rohde of the *Christian Science Monitor* commendations from Investigative Reporters and Editors, Inc.

Pat Stith and Jody Warrick of the *News & Observer* in Charlotte, North Carolina, demonstrated through investigative reporting how high-tech hog farms pollute North Carolina's air and water. The group Investigative Reporters and Editors, Inc. (IRE), praised the story this way: "Reporters revealed how the powerful hog industry convinced the government to go easy on environmental controls for the sake of profit. Some of the most powerful writing of the year."

Ignoring personal danger, David Rohde of the *Christian Science Monitor* exposed a massacre in Bosnia. He discovered mass graves and also interviewed survivors in what IRE called "outstanding investigative and foreign reporting in one package." His stories exposed those at fault.

In each of these cases and many more, one theme stands out: Stories with substance do not come easily.

The Role of the Scholastic Press

So what does all this have to do with the scholastic press? Chances are that you could sniff around your school forever and not find scandal. You can, however, decide that superficiality and sensationalism are the enemy. You might not be able to undertake massive investigations (though lots of school papers have), but you certainly don't have to settle for shallow stories that contribute nothing to public understanding.

With a little effort you can explore the news in depth, dig beneath the surface, and report stories that really count. You can concentrate on causes as well as effects; you can ask Why? Why do so many students drop out of school? Why are so many killed in traffic accidents? Why do some of the best teachers leave the profession? Why is our society so violent? You must, in other words, be ready to tackle any subject.

Emphasizing in-depth reporting means better reporting. No longer can a student grab a couple of quick quotes from a school official, dash off six or seven paragraphs, and call it a good news story. On one assignment one reporter—or a team of reporters—may speak with the same sources four or five times, interview a dozen faculty members, attend city council and board of education meetings, and talk to scores of students. Such reporters believe that their publication can inform its readers about what they are most interested in—their school—better than any other newspaper in the world. Even with nonschool-related subjects of interest, student reporters can still do an excellent job of in-depth reporting.

Making Space for In-Depth Stories

Many (though by no means all) in-depth stories are long. Where are you going to get the space to run such stories? Space is too scarce already. The first thing to do (if you haven't already) is eliminate trivia.

Student reporters doing in-depth stories on school-related issues must be willing to interview and reinterview sources.

Condense Minor Stories

Many small stories can be condensed into one "bulletin board" type of column. Instead of publishing three paragraphs on the coming meeting of the Spanish Club, three on the Science Club, and four or five on the class play that you have already devoted half a dozen stories to, combine them into a bulletin board or calendar. Here is an example:

Thursday
>Spanish Club, room 407, 3:45 P.M.
>Science Club, physics lab, 3:50 P.M.
>Repertory Theatre rehearsal, campus center, 6:30 P.M.

Friday
>Pep rally, auditorium, 3:45 P.M.
>Dress rehearsal, senior class play, auditorium, 8 P.M.

Instead of running five stories, which taken together might eat up an entire column of space, you have included all the information in just a couple of inches.

Another way to save space for in-depth stories is condensation of usually lengthy stories into a news-brief format. Thus, a four-paragraph story about band tryouts can be condensed into just one paragraph:

TIPS ✓ worth taking

Quick-read menus. Readers love sidebars, especially those of the type known as "quick-read menus," which offer a brief, well-organized selection of specialized information. Here are some types of quick-read menus you might try:

Quote collection: statements on the story's topic by students and others

Fast facts: the five W's and the H of a story precisely presented

Bio brief: a short profile of a person or group mentioned in the story

Glossary: a list of unfamiliar terms in the story, with definitions

Time line: a chronological list of key dates and events in a story

Step-by-step guide: a succinct summary of a process explained in the story

Quiz: a series of questions about issues related to the story's content

Resource references: a list of places where readers can get more information

Before:

Do you like music, travel, flashy clothes?

Students who can answer yes to these questions should contact Anita Petri, band director.

Petri is seeking new talent to fill out the 100-piece organization that plays at all home games.

Tryouts are scheduled for Sept. 1 at 3 P.M. in the music room.

After:

Band tryouts will be held Sept. 1 at 3 P.M. in the music room, Director Anita Petri announced.

Package Stories Creatively

Once you have space for an in-depth story, you still need to consider how best to present it. One long column of type usually doesn't work in today's visual environment.

Go through the story and decide exactly what it's about. Extract from it a mainbar, or main story, one that gives the pertinent facts that set up other stories. The other stories—the sidebars—are related to the mainbar but elaborate on it, illuminate it. If the story has a lot of numbers making it hard to read, consider pulling the numbers out of the mainbar and translating them into a chart or a graph.

For example, if the mainbar is about drug use, a chart might present information about drug dangers, recent arrests, and so on. One sidebar might be on interviews; the other might be a chart summarizing important facts and statistics about drug use. This sort of in-depth treatment might be produced by a team of students, including writers, researchers, an interviewer, a photographer, and people responsible for graphics.

Finally, teams of writers could independently write several mid-length articles, all on aspects of the same topic. On a topic such as cleaning up a

Invasion of Privacy

How far can the press probe into a person's private life?

Photographers trained powerful telephoto lenses at the church where the memorial service for John F. Kennedy, Jr. and his wife was held, hoping to capture friends, relatives, and dignataries.

A basic right most treasured by Americans is the right to privacy—that is, not to have their lives or affairs disturbed by undue prying. Such prying can be done by government, and it can also be done by the media.

Interestingly, no specific wording in the Constitution guarantees the right to privacy. Louis Brandeis, later to serve on the Supreme Court, wrote an essay defining the concept in 1890, and many judicial scholars have found a legal basis for it in the Bill of Rights. Still, the right to privacy is neither absolute nor perfectly defined, and for the media there is a constantly shifting boundary between the right to privacy and the so-called public's right to know.

The courts have generally found, for example, that public officials cannot use the right of privacy to protect themselves. Yet up until the last 20 years or so, what politicians did in their private lives was allowed to remain private. Exceptions were made only when the politician's private actions had become widely known anyway—for example, when a congressman's private alcohol problem had deteriorated into public drunkenness.

Today, however, any element of a public official's life seems fair game. Candidates for high office especially are scrutinized for the smallest failures—not only in their current activities but often stretching back 20 or 30 years. As a result, many people believe that potentially good candidates have declined to run for office rather than submit to such scrutiny.

Of course, the public does need to know certain things about a candidate. It's clearly newsworthy if he or she has been jailed for embezzlement, for example. It's questionable, however, whether smaller failures, particularly those in the past, need always be publicized.

In the case of public figures such as movie stars, sports stars, and people who work as public servants (those on the government payroll), the line between privacy and the public's rights can be very delicate. A few years ago, some blamed the suicide of a high Navy official on the media's continued probing into his affairs. He did, in fact, kill himself as he waited to be questioned by two *Newsweek* reporters about medals he wore but hadn't earned. Here, however, it's hard to see how the media are responsible. There were legitimate questions to be asked, and his subordinates, as well as others, had the right to answers.

For private citizens who feel that the media have invaded their privacy, a common response is to initiate a lawsuit. Such suits are often the result of a writer reexamining an already well-covered issue: In other words, the public already knows about this—need they know even more? Thus, a West Virginia woman whose husband's death in a bridge collapse had been covered five years earlier sued when a reporter came back and wrote about the family's subsequent poverty.

There are no easy definitions of when right to know crosses over into invasion of privacy. Two possible criteria might be whether the public actually benefits from the information and whether the reporter would feel violated if his or her life were held up to similar scrutiny.

FOLLOW-UP

1. Trace the development of the right-to-privacy concept from Louis Brandeis's essay to the present. Try to find out how the concept was clarified and defined through specific Supreme Court cases.

2. In a group identify two or three recent cases in which the media have probed into individuals' lives. At what point, if at all, did the probing become inappropriate?

local dumping site, one reporter could deal with current clean-up efforts, another could trace earlier uses of the site, another could write about legislation involving use of public land, and someone else might attempt to interview the worst dumping culprits. Charts and other graphics could be added as needed.

Even fairly long articles on unglamorous topics can be made to hold readers' attention if divided into enough different facets, as the **ON DISPLAY** sample on page 215 shows. The articles in this sample are part of a series that won a National Scholastic Press Association Story of the Year competition.

Writing the In-Depth Story

Serious, in-depth stories cannot unfold the same way a story about the sophomore class election might.

When writing longer pieces—in-depth stories—you need to stop thinking of leads and start thinking of introductions. In-depth stories can rarely be summed up in one quick sentence—the traditional lead—the way the class-election story can be.

Good Beginnings

Longer pieces need to be set up. They generally should begin with a scene or an anecdote. For example, if you're writing an in-depth story about the state champion free-throw shooter, you might have something like this at the top:

> Carmen Ruiz first touched a basketball when she was 3. She didn't dribble the ball. She dribbled on it.
>
> When she was 9, she joined a neighborhood team that beat the boys' team every day one winter.
>
> In high school she led Dayton to the state finals, recording a record 27 points per game average. She was named to the all-state team the same day she was elected senior class treasurer.
>
> Last week she learned that she had won the state free-throw shooting title.
>
> "I've been playing with basketballs for 15 years," Ruiz said.

Packaging an In-Depth Story

The Central Times, Naperville Central High School, Naperville, Illinois

ON DISPLAY

The packaging of an in-depth story into smaller, more visual pieces can increase readers' understanding even of complicated issues, as this sample shows.

The ◆Central Times

Vol. 5 No. 6   Naperville Central High School 440 W. Aurora Ave. Naperville, Illinois 60540

Funding cuts threaten science program

District 203 plans to cut the purchase of educational equipment and supplies by 75 percent next year. Teachers, administrators and students anticipate effects of the cut on an already strained Science Department. Fifth priority on the District 203 Budget Reduction Option List, "a 75 percent reduction in acquiring educational equipment" will save the district $450,000. "Right now, I think there is a substantial possibility that this option will...pass," School Board member Marcia Aspinall said.

THE 'BUDGET CRUNCH'

Already, teachers have felt the "budget crunch" as insufficient funding has resulted in a lack of high-tech equipment and up-to-date materials. But, according to Aspinall, the problem isn't poor allocation of resources but simply a lack of funds. "The budget is very lean. Very little, if any, money is wasted. But, we just don't have enough money to both meet our needs and balance the budget," she said.

This lack of funds has hampered the Science Department's ability to purchase new equipment. "There have been [tax] cuts at the state level, and this has led to cuts at the local level," Science Department Coordinator Bill West said. "Taxpayers [must] support technology and its costs."

In the meantime, the Science Department's need for new equipment has been met through a number of fund-raising and cost-reducing methods. The Science Department has been allotted $5 per student for instructional supplies, such as chemicals and glassware. Because this figure has never been adjusted for inflation, the department has had to economize in order to buy the most basic equipment. "We [can] make ends meet because our enrollment increased, and we've instituted lab fees to raise additional revenue," science teacher Sherry Yarema said.

While this additional revenue has been sufficient to purchase basic supplies, more expensive equipment (over $25) is covered by the capital outlay budget of the educational fund — the same budget that the school board is planning to cut. This budget has been inadequate to keep science equipment up-to-date. "I know that we haven't been able to keep up technologically, especially in the area of computers, but the only feasible solution is to raise the tax rate," Aspinall, a former NCHS science teacher, said.

UNORTHODOX FUNDRAISING

Teachers have resorted to unorthodox methods in order to obtain educational supplies. Some science fields such as genetics have grown rapidly and require up-to-date equipment. "Our knowledge of genetics is expanding at a rapid rate," Advanced Biology teacher Gary Slaybaugh said. "We need updated equipment to run labs that utilize this knowledge."

Advanced Biology, along with Advanced Placement Biology, requires specialized equipment to run complex experiments. "The A.P. and advanced science classes are college-level classes with college-level

labs. We need updated equipment in order to run them effectively," A.P. Biology teacher Yarema said.

When Slaybaugh realized that he didn't have enough up-to-date genetic engineering equipment for his students to use, he sought outside assistance. "I've done everything I possibly could to obtain up-to-date equipment. I've enrolled in a class at the University of Illinois because the Howard Hughes Foundation grants free use of equipment to class members," he said.

This equipment is still insufficient for the department's needs. "Even though we have this free equipment, we still need much more. That's why I've been trying to get more teachers, and student teachers, to take this course," Slaybaugh said.

THE TECHNOLOGY GAP

Biology isn't the only area of the department affected by lack of funding. One thing lacking throughout the entire department is computers and computerized equipment such as temperature probes and software. "We want to have computers in all of the science classes with the hardware and software we need—state-of-the-art equipment, not hand-me-downs," physics teacher Allan Etzbach said.

While the administration has outlined a technology plan, little visible effects are seen in the science classrooms, which need new technology. "The District has sent us to workshops that have shown us how to implement computers and other high-tech devices in the classroom," chemistry teacher Sharon Vetter said. "Unfortunately, this equipment is unavailable."

This new equipment would allow teachers to run improved labs. "We've wanted to have a computer at each lab station for quite some time," chemistry teacher Patti Kenton said. "That would allow us to use accurate instruments such as temperature probes to find and record data."

The administration recognizes the need for technological innovation in the classroom. Principal Tom Paulsen said, "We need to keep up with technology because 10-year-old...equipment doesn't help...the students, who will be farther behind students from other schools because of it."

But lack of funds forces the district to sacrifice technology for fiscal responsibility. "Delaying the acquisition of hardware and software" is a higher priority item on the District 203 Budget Reduction Option List than the 75 percent Capital Outlay cut. According to Aspinall, this option has a very good chance of being implemented.

POSSIBLE SOLUTIONS

Science teachers are trying to find a solution to this lack of funding. "The administration should have a liaison to contact local science-based firms like Nalco, Amoco or Bell Labs to get used equipment at little or no charge," Vetter said.

While concerned teachers can help solve the problem, they are not the complete solution. "Teachers receive computers through workshops or donations," West said, "but there is only one source for funding—the public; we're a public school."

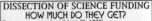

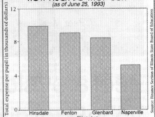

DISSECTION OF SCIENCE FUNDING
HOW MUCH DO THEY GET?
(as of June 25, 1993)

Total expense per pupil (in thousands of dollars) — Hinsdale, Fenton, Glenbard, Naperville (District)

Source: Finance Section of Illinois State Board of Education

WHAT DO THEY NEED?

Computers

"I know that we haven't been able to keep up...especially in the area of computers."
—Board Member Aspinall

"We want ...computers in all of the science classrooms with the hardware and software we need." —Physics teacher Etzbach

Textbooks

Since textbooks need to advance with the technology, "there is a science committee next fall which will request possible replacements. We've used the current ones for six years, and we're on a seven-year replacement curriculum. It used to be a five-year replacement." —Science Department Chairperson West

HOW DOES THIS AFFECT EDUCATION?

• "We are not able to keep up technologically." —Board Member Aspinall

• "The students will be...farther behind students from other schools." —Principal Paulsen

WHAT DOES THE FUTURE HOLD?

75% Cut:

"A 75 percent reduction in acquiring educational equipment [has a] substantial possibility [of being] passed by the board." —Board Member Aspinall

Possible Solutions:

• Referendum: "We want a referendum [to increase taxes] to deal with the future."

• Higher Lab Fees: "We could increase funding by increasing user fees, too, but then [we would be hitting people] twice, and this would turn them off."

—Principal Paulsen

That's why the administration is considering a tax increase to raise funding. "We have the highest IGAP scores in the state of Illinois at the lowest cost," Aspinall said. "Hinsdale has lower scores than us but spends twice as much as we do. We have great teachers, but we haven't had a tax increase since 1976. We need to [give] our teachers the funding they deserve."

Central Times Investigative Report

Investigative Team
Director -Renato Miratti
Writer -Derek
Researchers -Derek Woo, Nicole Dominak
Interviewers -Asad Shaikh, Saif Patel

Genetic Engineering

The Human Genome Project is a $3 billion experiment which will attempt to isolate and crease-quantify identify almost all of the 100,000 genes in the average human being's chromosomes. This will facilitate scientists in the field in their attempts to read the blueprint (DNA) making up the human organism. With this information, more accurate and helpful diagnoses and treatment of many different diseases will be possible.

Research in other areas of genetics will provide information aiding in the development of plant species with the capability to help the environment. Also, fruits and vegetables can be grown, including more prolific vitamins and a much longer shelf life with resistance to disease.

Genetics is one of the last scientific frontiers not fully explored today. New, high-tech equipment makes these types of experiments possible. But at NCHS, the teachers do not have access to this necessary equipment because of funding problems. Science Department Coordinator Bill West said, "Lab fees in the biology classes account for about $2,000. But with the fetal pig dissection itself, we're talking about $1,500." Thus, in the area of genetics, far larger expenditures are needed.

Pencil & Paper Labs

Because of the tight budget, sometimes, necessary equipment is not available to perform experiments in science classes. In these situations, pencil-and-paper labs, simulating a real lab with real data collection, are substituted. Although these experiments are viable for learning, they do not allow for "hands-on" activity.

PERSPECTIVES: How different people view Science Department funding

BY SAIF PATEL

 Marcia Aspinall — School Board Member

Aspinall, a former NCHS science teacher, has first-hand experience with the NCHS Science Department and feels that there will not be many immediate effects of funding cuts.

But in the long run, as increased funding becomes necessary for better technology, Aspinall said, "We should be allowed to keep up the cutting edge.

"Aspinall feels that the board does not "waste a lot of money." But if more money becomes necessary, she says, "people [will become] concerned about their taxes."

Her outlook, though, is that people will benefit, since their "houses will [gain value] because of good schools."

 Tom Paulsen — Principal

Paulsen feels that the public is the main source for the school to turn to. "In the long run, higher tax rates [for the people] are necessary," he said.

Paulsen also feels that the "community would support a higher rate to maintain the levels of funding and even to move forward [with technology]."

Although he favors a referendum to increase taxes is necessary, he says, "only the Board of Education can ask for a referendum," and it has made "no official decision yet."

He is optimistic the referendum will pass.

 Sherry Yarema — Biology Teacher

"We have a first-rate Science Department," Yarema said. "[It] tries to be very up-to-date with emphasis on problem-solving and critical thinking...we [also] believe in hands-on."

But Yarema feels that in the past, although "$5 per student...has been the budget for instructional supplies," this had "no accounting for inflation."

So the only reason "we have been able to survive," according to Yarema, is "because of increasing enrollment [which also increases the money from per-student fees]."

In the future, though, Yarema sees the science program troubled. "[Since] AP classes are college-level courses with college level labs," she said, "equipment should be like students will use in college...[this is] expensive."

The first three paragraphs function together as a lead. They're sort of an introduction, a setup to the rest of the story, which presumably is an exploration of how one becomes a free-throw champion.

If the in-depth story is about, for example, anorexia, it might begin with the story of one victim, detailing how she fought imagined weight gain in unhealthy ways, eating wrongly, exercising fanatically, hiding the secret from friends and family—even from herself.

After several paragraphs—the introduction—the writer would introduce the story's real theme: how the disease affects its victims, how it's treated, what the future holds for treatment options. The paragraph in which the rest of the story is foreshadowed—an internal lead, really—is often called the nut graph. It's the paragraph that says to the reader: I hooked you with my intro; now here's what the story's about.

The **ON DISPLAY** sample below follows this pattern: introduction, nut graph, elaboration on the nut graph.

Introduction and Nut Graph

The Little Hawk, City High School, Iowa City, Iowa

A Pirate's Loot

by Alex Ellis and Ben Schnoor

"I'm not answering any questions about bootlegs," a record store employee states bluntly, looking uncomfortable as customers survey the store's bootleg-infested shelves.

At another store an employee was a little more informative: "Asking a record store if they sell bootlegs is like asking a dope dealer if he sells dope."

Secrecy, questionable activity, and big profits—so begins the journey into the illegal world of bootleg recordings.

Bootlegs, unauthorized recordings of an artist's work, have been around since the late '60s, when they were produced on vinyl, packaged in plain white sleeves and plagued with extremely poor sound quality. In the early '80s, cassette tapes became the most common medium for bootlegs, due to the relatively cheap cost of duplicating equipment. However, it was the introduction of the compact disc in the mid-'80s that helped production of bootlegs progress from a trivial activity into a multimillion dollar underground industry.

Local Angle

To stress the significance of an in-depth story to your readers, incorporate a local angle. This can be as simple as tapping into school or community sources. A story on advances in genetics, for example, might incorporate sources such as students studying genetics in a biology class, a genetics researcher at a local university or hospital, and area farmers who uses hybrid seeds.

Strong Endings

In-depth stories present another structural challenge not usually encountered in shorter, routine stories. In-depth stories need endings. The sophomore election story can just end. It's probably an inverted-pyramid story, and when the writer is finished, he or she just quits. If the last paragraph gets trimmed in production, it's probably OK.

Not so with the in-depth story. It has to be wrapped up; it can't just fade into nothingness. Before journalists came along and invented their particular way of telling stories, stories had beginnings, middles, and endings—and so it is with in-depth stories.

Consider the hypothetical free-throw champion. The ending for her story might be something like this:

Look for an ending to an in-depth story in the story's introduction. It brings the story full circle.

> Ruiz has long since stopped dribbling on basketballs. These days, it's eager college recruiters who are doing the drooling.

An ending that returns to the notion of the lead fulfills the human urge for closure. The story comes full circle. Often the first place to look for an ending to an in-depth story is in the story's introduction. The story about bootlegged music did just that, returning to a quote by a record-store representative:

> For better or worse, bootlegs will be available as long as people are willing to buy them. "It's really no big deal. They've always been out there," Trent said. "We just sell what's available, whatever people want."

In-depth stories often lend themselves to unusual treatment in other respects too. The **ON DISPLAY** example on page 219 introduces a story about the little town in Kansas where four killings led to Truman Capote's book *In Cold Blood* (itself a gripping example of in-depth reporting). Author Jim Pratt, then a student at the University of Nebraska, set out years after the killings to investigate the effects the book and a movie had on the town.

Pratt's dramatic, prize-winning story follows the pattern of introduction, nut graph, and elaboration exactly. First the reader is taken to the scene, where wind and dust mix with the picture of horses shaking their manes and a dog loping down a deserted street—all in all, a compelling opening. From there, the author flashes back to the day of the slayings and captures the mood of the town at the time: police, ambulances, the curious. Finally, in the tenth paragraph (the one beginning "For a while . . ."), comes the nut graph.

Research, organization, time for reflection on what your research uncovers, and writing—these are the elements of in-depth reporting. Use this checklist when evaluating your own in-depth stories and those that others write.

EVALUATION CHECKLIST

In-Depth Story

☑ Does the seriousness or relevance of the topic warrant in-depth treatment of the story?

☑ If the story is one long piece, does it have a full-fledged introduction leading to an internal lead, or nut graph?

☑ Are scenes, anecdotes, and a local angle used to involve the reader in the story?

☑ If the story is broken into several pieces, does each piece deal with a different aspect of the story?

☑ Are charts and other infographics used appropriately and effectively?

☑ Is the story free from grammatical errors and in accordance with the publication and general AP style?

In-Depth Introduction

The Contact Lens, The University of Nebraska, Lincoln, Nebraska

A Kansas Town Remembers

by Jim Pratt

HOLCOMB, KAN.—A harsh north wind whips dust through Holcomb, battering a few worndown stucco dwellings before losing itself in the western Kansas plains. Ponies tied to fence posts shake their manes in the wind and a dog lopes down a deserted dirt street.

Holcomb is a quiet town. Discounting the Mobil gas station (3.2 beer, soda pop, a few groceries), the only gathering place with refreshments is El Rancho Cafe and, in an adjacent room, a bar named Something Else.

Holcomb's few streets, mostly unpaved, are often empty.

Thirteen years ago today, however, the streets were jammed with cars belonging to law enforcement people, ambulance attendants and the curious. For Holcomb had just been stunned by four murders.

Subsequent reverberations would make the town known to millions.

It was early Sunday morning, Nov. 15, 1959, when Herb Clutter, 48, his wife, Bonnie, 45, and their two youngest children, Nancy, 16, and Kenyon, 15, were blasted point-blank with a shotgun by two ex-convicts with no previous records of violence. The motive was robbery.

The murders shocked the town. Herb Clutter was a prominent farmer, and he and his family were well liked. But the murders probably would have been forgotten had author Truman Capote not read a *New York Times* story about the killings and decided to use them as a vehicle for his book *In Cold Blood.*

Capote went to Holcomb shortly after the slayings. He spent nearly a year and a half in the area doing research. He followed the hunt, capture, trial and imprisonment of the two killers, Richard Hickock and Perry Smith, until they were executed April 14, 1965.

The book inspired a movie, also named *In Cold Blood,* which was filmed in the town.

For a while after the killings, Holcomb was gripped by fear, gossip and controversy. But 13 years has allowed the town to relax and to grow, relatively unscarred by the experience. The population is up 25 percent, from about 270 at the time of the slayings to 340 today. The school has a new addition. There are new homes, a new water tower, a new post office.

Curiosity seekers still stop to view the house near town where the Clutters were slain. Once a showcase, the house now seems weatherbeaten.

Townspeople no longer discuss the murders or the aftermath. They would like to forget it.

"It was such a long time ago that it almost seems like it never happened," one woman said.

Wrap-up

High school publications today are tributes to serious journalism. Where homecoming queens once reigned and editorials merely urged school spirit, scholastic publications today are on top of the news and reporting it in depth. The list of stories now developed by high school students represents the wide range of interests of young people. These subjects need sensitive, objective, thorough treatment.

In-depth stories, stories with substance, can present important information that affects people's lives. Some in-depth stories are investigative—rare but not unheard of in high school newspapers. Perhaps the best-known such work was done by Bob Woodward and Carl Bernstein, *Washington Post* reporters widely credited with exposing the Watergate scandal during the Nixon presidency.

Whether stories are called investigative or in-depth, one theme stands out: Reporters dig. They decide that superficiality is the enemy. The changing high school press is putting more emphasis on the *why* of the five W's and the H.

In-depth stories often run longer than routine stories. This can create a space problem. Handling routine club notices and meetings in a list format can help save space for in-depth stories. Furthermore, long articles themselves can be broken up into pieces—a mainbar, two sidebars, and a chart, for example.

Generally, the quality of writing for in-depth stories has to be better than the usual newspaper fare. Careful writing and organization must guide readers through long stories. In-depth stories require introductions, not just leads. Scenes, anecdotes, a first-person approach—all can produce a high-quality introduction.

Essential to the organization of longer in-depth pieces is the notion of the nut graph, the paragraph that functions virtually as an internal lead, the paragraph that follows an introduction and outlines the story's main themes.

Incorporate a local angle on your topic so that readers can relate to your story better.

In-depth stories need endings too. The best place to look for an ending is in the introduction. If that works, the story comes full circle and gives the reader a feeling of closure.

The essential elements of thorough, in-depth reporting are research, organization, time, and good writing.

On Assignment

INDIVIDUAL ACTIVITIES

1. Write a brief definition of each of these terms:

in-depth reporting   nut graph
news-brief format   Watergate

2. Test your critical thinking. Newspapers such as *USA Today* are known for relatively short, one-time articles rather than in-depth reports. Why do you think they take such an approach? Evaluate their audience, the places the paper is sold, and any other factors that might account for the kind of stories they do. Write a brief summary of your ideas.

3. Select one of the topics listed on page 208 for in-depth treatment. How would you go about approaching this topic? How would the one big story be divided into smaller chunks? What opportunities are there for good graphics, charts, and graphs? Write up your ideas. If you wish, include a rough layout.

4. Evaluate this introduction to an in-depth story in terms of its originality and level of interest. Where is the nut graph? Where do you think the story will go from here? Give a grade to the introduction and then write a brief justification of your opinion.

Testing, Testing
by Lynn Roberts

The following questions will test your knowledge of today's college-bound students and tests they take to measure their reasoning abilities.

For some questions there is no single correct answer. Select the answer that best fits the question and proceed to the next question. Begin when you are told and continue until you finish or are told to stop. Go.

1. College-bound students today are (a) smarter than students five years ago, (b) the same as students five years ago, (c) not so smart as students five years ago, (d) none of the above.

Recent declines in scores on the Scholastic Aptitude Test (SAT) and the American College Test (ACT) may indicate (c) as the correct answer, but these scores alone probably do not show the complete picture.

5. Go through your local newspaper. Find at least three stories treated superficially that could be expanded and treated in depth. Interview editors or reporters on the paper. Do they agree? Why or why not? Write an interview story on your findings.

6. Identify a thorough story in any newspaper. Compare it to a magazine article on a similar topic. What similarities and differences appear? Which style do you like better? Why? Write an essay on your findings. Attach the stories.

7. Go through several issues of your school paper. Where will you find the space for a thorough story? What can be eliminated or condensed? What can be put in a bulletin-board column? Can you find a full page of space? Mark your ideas on the papers themselves.

8. Invite to class a local professional reporter who does in-depth or investigative reporting. Ask him or her to explain the techniques. Discuss the pros and cons of this type of reporting. Write a story summarizing the class discussion.

9. Watch a local evening television newscast. Is the station news staff doing any in-depth work? If so, how does the coverage and choice of topics compare with that of newspapers? Discuss in class the differences and possible reasons for the differences.

TEAM ACTIVITY

10. Brainstorm with your team ideas for an in-depth story (or use the list on page 208). Select three. Then brainstorm related sidebar stories for each idea. Consider sources, coverage angles, and questions for each story. Then choose your best story topic. Select a project editor (who is to write also), and assign stories to team members. Research, write, and edit the stories. Keep them for use later.

SURF THE NET

11. What features of on-line newspapers make them good sources for in-depth stories? Think of an important current news story and examine how two or three on-line professional newspapers cover it. Why is on-line coverage inclined to be more thorough than that in the print version of a paper? Discuss your ideas in class.

career profile

Investigative Reporters

Marjie Lundstrom

Sam Stanton

Sometimes it takes a lot of digging to cover a story thoroughly.

That's the way it was for Marjie Lundstrom in 1990, when she and Rochelle Sharpe disclosed in a four-part series that hundreds of child-abuse deaths go unde-tected each year because of errors by medical examiners and coroners. The series won Lundstrom and Sharpe a Pulitzer Prize in national reporting.

Lundstrom's husband, Sam Stanton, earned his reputation in Arizona. His investigative digging led to the indictment and impeachment of former Arizona Governor Evan Mecham in 1987 and resulted in the naming of Stanton as a Pulitzer Prize finalist.

Today, Stanton and Lundstrom work at the *Sacramento Bee*, where Lundstrom is an assistant managing editor and Stanton a senior writer.

Lundstrom is proudest of her first effort at investigative reporting, a series of articles that exposed the fact that gov-ernment officials in Denver, Colorado, had squandered money entrusted to the city by an orphanage.

"I was driving past this really rundown campus one day and just decided to see how it ever wound up in that shape," she said in describing how she got started on that series. "I chipped away at it for months and months."

The series forced city officials to change policies and begin paying back the money.

Stanton made his mark by accepting an assignment that no one else wanted. He was working at the *Arizona Republic* and volunteered to cover political long-shot Evan Mecham's run for governor. Mecham was elected on his fourth try and Stanton found himself covering the governor's office.

It didn't take long for Stanton to begin breaking stories. His digging eventually led to the disclosure that Mecham had accepted an illegal campaign contribution.

"The basis for all that was a reporting affairs class I took in college," Stanton said. "It showed me where to go to look for public records and what kinds of infor-mation you can find. Without that, I don't know if most people can figure out where to find information."

Stanton and Lundstrom both took unlikely paths to their careers. Lundstrom turned to journalism when she decided she didn't want to specialize in one field.

"I had a whole variety of interests," she said. "but I was really a generalist. So I enrolled in journalism out of desperation, and it fit. It was obvious that this is what I love."

Stanton wound up in jour-nalism by getting in the wrong registration line at the University of Arizona. He decided to try journalism anyway.

"I loved it," he said. "That was it. I just fell in love with it and never looked back. It is the most fun you can have and get paid for it. You meet the most interesting people on the planet and witness history at the same time."

FOLLOW-UP

1. Decide on a story in your community that needs investigating, and plot out the steps you would take to get infor-mation. Be sure to list sources, in order of importance, and note what you would expect to learn from each one.
2. Is Lundstrom's background, that of a generalist with many interests, a good one for an investigative reporter? Why or why not?

CHAPTER 10

Design and Layout

KEY CONCEPTS

After reading this chapter, you will

▶ understand the basics of design and layout, including page elements common to most publications

▶ understand the basic principles of design, including dominance, unity, contrast, repetition, balance, and consistency

▶ understand basic categories of type and appropriate uses for each

▶ recognize the importance of graphics in modern page design

▶ know how to go about creating various types of pages, including front pages and double-trucks

A publication's goal of getting information to its readers is only partly achieved when all copy has been turned in. One essential job remaining is the actual design and layout of the issue. Visual communication is now one of the hottest areas of journalism, and in recent years graphic design has become one of the most important aspects of the overall journalism curriculum. Along with news gathering and writing, journalists are learning to become graphic communicators who use technologies such as desktop publishing to reach today's audience more effectively. That audience expects strong visual graphics and stories packaged to attract and hold their attention.

School newspapers, as well as other student-produced publications, must be designed with the visual-reading audience in mind. Publications that still subscribe to the older, more traditional approach to design, featuring numerous small photos and headlines, may lose many of their readers. Strong, story-telling photos, informational graphics, and carefully selected type are what draw in today's audience.

Basics of Design and Layout

The copy has been read and edited. Now the main articles and sidebars, together with any photographs, are ready to pass on to the designer. It's the designer's job to turn all these pieces into a well-conceived final product.

In producing any type of student publication, a designer must fully understand the content of the publication. In other words, he or she must know how many stories and visuals are available and what types of secondary pieces, such as sidebar stories and informational graphics, need to be included in the layout. The designer must always remember that the content dictates the design.

Page Elements

Every designer works with three basic visual elements: copy, or text, (words set in type); graphics, or art, (photographs, artwork; and devices such as ruled lines); and white space (blank areas on a page). These basic visual elements are combined in various ways to create page elements apparent in every publication, such as a nameplate (which displays the name of the publication), folios

Professional journalists must work together to create effective layouts.

(page numbers), and bylines (credits that identify writers). To work productively on layouts, you should learn the definitions, purpose, and placement of common page elements.

225

TERMS worth knowing

Page elements. Become familiar with the page elements listed here, which are common to most publications.

Nameplate or **flag**: copy (often combined with a graphic) that states the name of the newspaper in large, bold letters across the front page; includes the volume and issue numbers, publication date, and city and state where the paper is published

Teaser: boxed copy that promotes stories inside the issue

Index: copy that lists the page numbers on which sections start; in yearbooks, a list of all people, events, groups, sports, and academic areas covered in the book

Headline: a line of copy that serves as a title for a story

Deck: one level of a headline

Subhead: a miniheadline that indicates what the next section of copy contains; breaks up gray blocks of copy in a story

Standing head: a headline for a regular feature in each issue of a publication

Byline: a line of copy that identifies the writer of a story

Dateline: a line of copy that identifies the place where the news occurred; important if the story originated someplace other than the city where the newspaper is published

Jumpline: a line of copy that indicates the page on which a story continues

Refer: a line of copy that refers readers to a related story elsewhere in the issue

Caption or **cutline:** lines of copy placed next to a photo that explain the content of the photo

Photo credit: a line of copy that identifies the photographer of a particular photo

Jumphead: a brief (one- or two-word) headline on a page that shows a reader where to start reading a jumped story again

Pull quote: a quote from a story arranged as a graphic in the layout of the story

Folio: a page number; often includes the name and section of the paper

Gutter: white space that separates columns and facing pages

Screen: shaded area; measured in percentages

Rule: a vertical or horizontal line that serves to accent or separate elements; its width is measured in points

Initial cap or **drop cap:** a large capital letter of the opening word in a story; serves as a graphic

Mugshot or **headshot:** a photo that shows only the shoulders and head of a person

Infographic: a visual representation of statistical information, such as a map, chart, diagram, or time line

Logo: a title with art that identifies a standing feature, such as a column

Spot color: one color applied in strategic places on a page

Clip art: ready-made graphics available for use free of charge or for a small fee

Icon: a symbol or image that identifies a particular feature, perhaps a section or a standing feature, such as a teacher profile

Bleed: the running of color or a photo or other graphic through the external margin and off a page

Overprint: the printing of one item on top of another

Bullet: a large dot that calls attention to a line of copy or sets off items in a list

Facing pages: two inside pages that face each other but are not usually printed on the same sheet of paper; together, they form a spread

Double-truck or **centerspread:** a spread in the center of a publication, printed as one sheet of paper

Internal margin: a consistent margin of white space between copy and graphics; usually one pica in width

External margin: a frame of white space around the layout marked by the outside edge of at least one block of copy or graphic

Fold: the middle of a page, where large-format newspapers are folded

Formats and Grids

The physical size of any page is its format. Most city newspapers use the broadsheet format, which is approximately 14 by 22 inches. School papers typically use a tabloid format, which is approximately 11 by 17 inches. Some school papers use a news-magazine format, which is 8½ by 11 inches, or standard letter-size.

The format you choose will determine, in part, the width of your columns. A broadsheet usually has six columns, a tabloid four or five columns, and a news magazine two or three columns. Most newspapers have one standard column width. To emphasize the difference between stories on a page, however, a wider or narrower width may be used for select stories.

Many designers use a grid to design their pages. A grid is a pattern of lines that forms a base on which you can place page elements. Vertical column lines show the column width and space between columns. Horizontal lines are typically at one-inch increments.

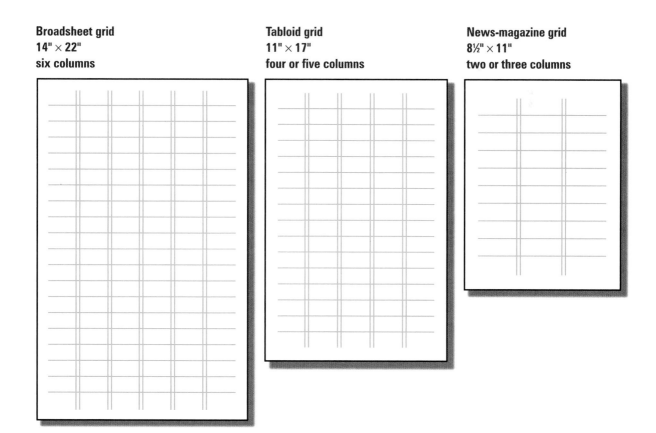

Broadsheet grid
14" × 22"
six columns

Tabloid grid
11" × 17"
four or five columns

News-magazine grid
8½" × 11"
two or three columns

PICAS   INCHES

2
4
6   1
8
10
12 2
14
16
18 3
20
22
24 4
26
28
30 5
32
34
36 6
38
40
42 7
44
46
48 8
50
52

Measurement

Most graphic designers use a system of measurement based on two units of measure: picas and points. A pica measures ⅙ inch; that is, there are 6 picas in 1 inch. The pica can be broken down further into points. One pica is equal to 12 points, so 1 inch equals 72 points. This might make it clearer:

    1 inch = 6 picas
    1 pica = 12 points
    1 inch = 72 points

As you design a page, you will be measuring vertical and horizontal space. Overall dimensions of pages are usually measured in inches or centimeters. Designers use picas and points to measure type and the space between elements on a page.

Basic Principles of Design

Whether designing a palace or a printed publication, you need to be familiar with and make use of the basic principles of design. Here are the six basic principles as they apply to publications.

Dominance

Every single page and every double-page spread should have one dominant element, an element that is at least 2½ times as large as any other element on the spread. The dominant element serves as a visual entry point for the reader—in other words, a place where the reader "enters" the page. Without a dominant element on the page, the reader's eye will either bounce around from element to element, or the reader will skip that page and go on to the next.

During layout, you might find it useful to have on hand a graphic-arts ruler, or pica stick, which shows picas and inches.

The dominant element is usually a large, well-composed photo or other graphic that is representative of the story it illustrates. The content of the dominant element should also be tied to the message expressed in the main headline for the story.

Unity

One way to unify a page or spread is by using consistent internal and external margins. Here are common margin sizes used by designers.

Internal margins: 1 pica between elements
External margins: 3 to 4 picas at page top
4 to 5 picas at page sides
5 to 6 picas at page bottom

For double-page spreads the only difference is a one-pica margin on either side of the interior gutter (the dividing space between two facing pages).

On double-page spreads the placement of the dominant photo can also create unity. Running the photo across the gutter ties the two pages together, making them appear to be one connected page. Another technique is to use an eyeline, one pica of horizontal white space that extends across the spread. An eyeline should run at least six picas above or below the horizontal center of the spread.

Contrast

One of the most important aspects of design is contrast—that is, the use of opposites in size, shape, weight, and color or tone. For example, a design should feature one dominant photo or other graphic contrasted by several smaller photos or graphics, with horizontal as well as vertical photos. Different typefaces and the discreet use of screens also create contrast.

Contrast in headline design. One area where contrast frequently comes into play is in headline design. For stories that feature a headline with primary and secondary components, the primary headline should be at least twice as large in point size as the secondary headline. In other words, if the primary headline is 72 points high, the secondary should be no larger than 36 points high. Usually, the primary headline is set in bold type and the secondary headline in a regular or lighter face.

For special newspaper features, magazine layouts, and yearbook spreads, you may want to choose a special typeface for the primary headline and then choose a more basic typeface for the secondary headline. In standard newspaper design, however, stick with one typeface, using bold for primary headlines and regular for secondary headlines throughout.

The sample headlines that appear in the **ON DISPLAY** feature on page 231 demonstrate more ways to achieve contrast in headline design.

Repetition

Repetition, or rhythm, involves duplicating a color, graphic, or typographic element to hold a design together. For example, the designer of a yearbook or magazine spread may choose a specific headline design and then repeat it in a smaller, modified version for all captions on the spread. This pattern may then be used on each spread throughout a particular section of the book, such as the sports or student life section, to create unity and consistency within the section. The designer of a newspaper spread may repeat a color pulled from a photograph as the background for a secondary coverage box or as a part of a headline design. Either would create unity on the page or spread.

Balance

By using the design principles mentioned above the designer can create a page or spread that features formal or informal balance. Pages that are balanced formally can be folded in half vertically, with each half mirroring the other half of the page. Informally balanced pages feature weight distributed diagonally. Big, bold graphic elements are placed toward the center and white space, story copy, headlines, and captions are pushed to the outside so that pages do not "weigh heavy" to one side or the other. Most designers use informal balance to create variety and dynamic tension. This technique increases the visual interest of the page.

Consistency

Certain elements of a publication should remain unchanged. For example, the staff should establish a byline style, folio style, and standing headline design and should keep these consistent throughout the publication. These elements should also be consistent from issue to issue.

Headline Design

Fans find skyrocketing salaries leave them

Voiceless

The Lakewood Times, Lakewood High School, Lakewood, Ohio

'The Man She Was'
brings Civil War to life

*Drama Department stages
gender-bending production*

The Budget, Lawrence High School, Lawrence, Kansas

IT ISN'T EASY BEING GREEN

The Falconer, Torrey Pines High School, San Diego, California

These headlines are more creative than most. Note the contrast between the primary and secondary heads of the first two examples, as well as the incorporation of illustrations in the second. The third violates a rule (no all-cap heads), yet the novel typeface (appropriate to the story topic—pet iguanas) effectively draws readers' attention and is not overly difficult to read.

Consistency in yearbooks is established by using the same page elements, typography, and graphics throughout the theme pages, on the cover, and on the front and back endsheets. Consistency within each section is established by using the same grid, headline design, caption design, and secondary-coverage design throughout the entire section. These elements provide unity within the section for the reader and allow him or her to recognize when a new section begins.

Selecting and Using Type

From a design standpoint, the basic component of any story is copy—words set in type. There are many typefaces from which to select, with new ones constantly being developed and made available for computer use. The designer's choice of type will often determine if and to what extent a story will be read by the audience.

When choosing typefaces in general, choose a font that's easy to read for body copy—columns of copy for stories. More novel type can be used for display copy—headlines, bylines, captions, copy in advertisements, and so on. Type for display copy is often chosen to convey a mood or to reflect a specific meaning related to the content. For example, for a feature on comedy clubs, you might use a typeface that conveys zaniness.

When choosing typefaces for particular projects, keep the target audience in mind. For example, children and senior citizens may require larger type with extra leading (the white space between the lines) because such text is easy to read. Teenage audiences may not require large type in body copy; however, an interesting typeface in certain layouts may attract and hold their attention.

Using too many different typefaces in one publication creates a "ransom-note" appearance to pages. Establish a strategy to your type choices and stick to it.

Type Categories

Typefaces can be categorized in many ways. A number of experts divide type into these seven classifications.

Oldstyle Roman. This kind of typeface is characterized by its thick, roughly-hewn serifs, or cross-strokes projecting from the end points of each letter, and by the slight difference between the thin and thick parts of the letters. It's a good choice for body copy and for display copy such as headlines and captions, as it is considered easy to read by most experts. The serifs make each letter distinctive, and create subtle horizontal lines at the top and bottom of the letters to guide the reader's eye smoothly across a line of type. For this reason, Oldstyle Roman is the easiest typeface group to read.

Bookman and Caslon are two common examples of Oldstyle Roman typeface.

Bookman
Caslon

worth knowing

TERMS

Type talk. Here are some basic terms used when talking about type.

Character: type letter (such as an *A*), number, or letterform (such as a hyphen)

Typeface: design of a complete set of type characters, specified by a name, such as Arial or Garamond

Font: traditionally, a complete set of characters in one size and style of typeface (e.g., 12-point Gill Sans Italic); used now as a synonym for *typeface*

Family: fonts closely related in style

Roman: characters that are straight up and down

Italic: characters slanted to the right

Light: a thin version of a regular typeface (e.g., Helvetica Light)

Bold: a heavy, dark version of a regular typeface (e.g., Helvetica Bold)

Reverse print: light type on a dark background

Point: a unit of measurement that describes the size of type. (There are 72 points in one inch.)

Pica: a unit of measurement in graphic design. (There are 12 points in a pica and 6 picas in one inch.)

Leading: the white space inserted between lines, normally set an additonal two points. Ten-point type set on a 12-point leading would be referred to as set *10 on 12*, written *10/12*.

Letterspacing: extra space between characters in a line of type

Baseline: the imaginary line on which type rests

Descenders: the parts of characters that extend below the baseline (as in *g, j, p, q,* and *y*)

Ascenders: the parts of characters that rise above the baseline (as in *b, d, f, h, k, l,* and *t*)

***x*-height:** the actual height of the lowercase *x*; may vary from face to face

Type measurement: extending from the highest point of the ascender to the lowest point of the descender. Type measuring 72 points is approximately one inch high from the top of an *h* to the bottom of a *p*.

Small caps: a complete alphabet of capital letters that are the same size as the *x*-height of the lowercase letters

Justified: type that aligns, or is set even, on both sides of a column

Ragged: having uniform word spacing and uneven line length. Type aligned on the left ("flush left") and ragged on the right ("ragged right") is easiest to read.

Centered: type centered within a given horizontal area

Modern Roman. Characterized by thin, precisely attached serifs and dramatic differences between the thin and thick portions of the letters, Modern Roman type is excellent for nameplates, headlines, logos, and display copy in advertisements. Its readability factor diminishes as the type is set smaller; therefore, it should not be used for body copy or captions. It's rarely used in sizes smaller than 14 point.

Bodoni and Modern are examples of Modern Roman typeface.

Bodoni
Modern

Old English
Linotext

Text. Also referred to as Black Letter, Text type was based on the handwriting style popular in the days of Johannes Gutenberg, the developer of movable type. Text type is ornate and difficult to read. It conveys a feeling of formality so is often used for items such as wedding or graduation announcements. In student publications, it might be used as a main headline for a spread on a medieval fair, for example, but not throughout a section. It should never be used in all capital letters.

Old English and Linotext are examples of Text typeface.

Courier
Rockwell

Square serif. Square-serif type is characterized by block-type serifs. It conveys a "steadfast and true" feeling. Square-serif type is good for certain nameplates, logos, or other display copy, but it's rarely used for headlines. A square-serif typeface should not be used for body copy or captions because of its lower readability.

Courier and Rockwell are examples of square-serif typeface.

Helvetica
Futura

Sans serif. The word *sans* means "without" in French, so a sans-serif type has no serifs. Its smooth, clean appearance works well in headlines, logos, nameplates, and advertisements but makes it difficult to read when set in blocks of smaller type, such as body copy. Set bold, it works well for captions. When set regular or light, it can work well for short copy areas, such as sidebars or other types of secondary coverage.

Helvetica and Futura are examples of sans-serif typeface.

Nuptial Script
Brush Script

Scripts and cursives. Both scripts and cursives resemble handwriting. The letters in cursive typefaces usually seem to be "connected," whereas those in script typefaces do not. These typefaces should be used like spices in food—sparingly. Because of low readability, they should never be used for body copy or captions, although they may be used for small headlines or subheadlines. They also should never be set in all caps.

Nuptial Script and Brush Script, respectively, are examples of script and cursive typefaces.

Ad Lib
Whimsy

Novelty. Novelty typefaces are numerous and can look like smoke, neon signs, "down-home country," computer type, or a variety of other objects or ideas. Novelty typefaces should be used with care and only to convey or reinforce a message to the reader. They should rarely be used in all caps and never for type set small, such as body copy or captions.

Ad Lib and Whimsy are examples of novelty typefaces.

Working with Typefaces

Some designers use only one family of type (one typeface) to create a printed piece, changing the styles from regular to bold, italic, outline, or a combination of these. This is called family harmony. Other designers use blending harmony, selecting *one* family of type from three of the seven type groups. The **ON DISPLAY** sample below exhibits blending harmony.

Type Harmony

The Academy Times, Charles Wright Academy, Tacoma, Washington

Blending harmony is exhibited in the choices for the type on this page. See if you can identify the categories of type chosen.

Rules of Typography

Typography experts agree that designers should follow a basic set of rules when selecting types for printed publications. Here are some of their suggestions.

Choosing type sizes and faces. Set body copy in 9-, 10-, or 11-point type. Choose an Oldstyle Roman typeface for body copy, as it's the most readable of all type groups. Use 8-point type for captions, and generally use bold for headlines to provide better contrast for the reader.

For primary headlines, secondary headlines, and subheadlines, select the type style most appropriate for the document. Display copy is often set in type that conveys the "personality" of the printed piece. Some designers choose to mix two typeface groups together in one headline design, one for the primary headline and one for the secondary headline. The contrast in size, weight, and style produces an eye-catching, readable headline design reflecting the document's personality.

Set the leading in body copy at a readable level. Although two points of white space between lines is standard, in special cases, such as theme copy in yearbooks or sidebars in other publications, extra leading may attract readers or enhance readability.

When mixing types, look for typefaces that have strong contrast in characteristics. Mixing an Oldstyle Roman with a sans serif, for example, would work well. Adding a third type, perhaps a script or cursive, would create even greater contrast. If you're not sure that the types look good together, stick to a single face. You can still get variation by changing type size, case, weight, width, or style within that face.

In designing logos and primary headlines, try to connect the verbal and visual elements. For example, if you were creating a headline for the concept "sticking together," you might place the type so that it actually connected, or "stuck" together. Notice how appropriate the graphic is in the nameplate of the **ON DISPLAY** sample on page 237.

TIPS worth taking

Standard type sizes. When choosing type, keep these guidelines in mind:

▶ 6-point (used for indexes and photo bylines)

▶ 8-point (used for captions)

▶ 9-, 10-, 11-, or 12-point (used for body copy; one size used consistently throughout a publication)

▶ 14-, 18-, and 24-point (used for large initial letters, headlines, and subheads)

▶ 30-, 36-, 42-, 48-, 60-, and 72-point type (used for headlines and display copy in ads)

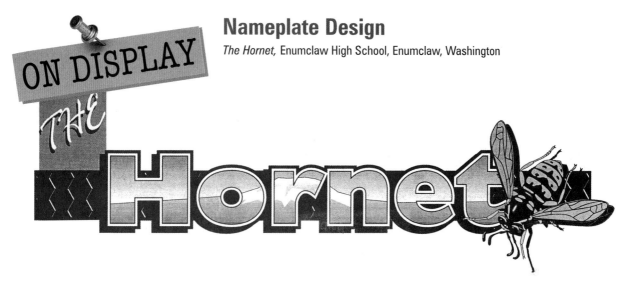

Nameplate Design

The Hornet, Enumclaw High School, Enumclaw, Washington

This nameplate not only makes clever use of a graphic honeycomb to complement the illustration of the Hornet mascot, but also incorporates the mountain background of the school's surroundings into the typeface used for the paper's name.

Establishing column widths and margins. Set body copy at a readable width. Setting 10-point copy wider than 22 picas or narrower than 10 picas causes difficulty for most readers. Try to follow a specific column format and use consistent copy and caption widths to maintain unity in the printed piece. In narrow column widths, consider setting the type flush left and ragged right, rather than justifying it, so as to keep large "rivers" of white space from forming between words or letters within words. Type that is set flush left and ragged right with consistent word spacing is easier to read than type that is justified and variably spaced.

Keep type within the external margin framework of the page. Captions or copy that creep into the external margin look more like mistakes than "planned copy" areas. External margins give the reader room to "breathe" and allow the eye to rest periodically.

When placing boxes around type areas or rules between columns, keep the copy one pica from the rules. If type is allowed to run into a box or rule, reader interference occurs.

Use boxes and rules to "package" copy and headlines together as one unit. Avoid boxing each column of type separately—unless it's a one-column story, such as a sidebar. Also, avoid breaking the reader's eye flow from headline to body copy by inserting extra space or rules between the two elements.

When designing copy-heavy areas, try to help the reader through the materials by using subheads, large initial letters, inset photos, pull quotes, or other graphic devices to break up the gray space. "Rails" of white space strategically placed can also help pull the reader into the copy.

Avoiding common type pitfalls. Remember that the use of all capital letters often lowers readability. Lowercase letters, especially those in the Oldstyle Roman group, are distinctive and allow the reader to see each letter quickly. Lines of copy set in all caps are harder to read because the capital letters have similar characteristics. Furthermore, they tire the reader's eye. If you use all caps, therefore, use them for no more than two or three short lines, and use Oldstyle Roman or Modern Roman faces, which are the easiest to read. Some novelty and square-serif typefaces only offer capital letters. In this case, you can sometimes use small caps for lowercase letters to improve readibility.

Avoid running large blocks of type in color. High contrast between the type and its background is essential for good readability. Reverse type on a dark background can work well for headlines and secondary coverage, but it should be limited to areas of impact rather than used in large, copy-heavy places. For specific effects, color in type for display copy or other emphasis areas can create an interesting, eye-catching effect.

Generally, avoid overprinting or reversing type on photos, patterned screens, or "busy" backgrounds. Always place type in a spot where it can be easily read. Similarly, avoid placing type diagonally or vertically.

Breaking typography rules. Although you should generally try to follow these guidelines, don't be afraid to try something new and different that may stretch or break a rule. After designing a unique typographic element, take a step back and look at it from the reader's point of view. If you are uncertain about the effect, ask impartial sources for their opinions to make sure the design is readable and attractive.

Using Graphics

Once you as a designer have a basic understanding of type and how to use it effectively, you can add graphics—not only rules and boxes, but illustrations, photos, spot color, infographics, and other devices—to enhance the design and to draw the reader into the page.

It's important to remember that graphics must have a specific reason or purpose when used in a printed piece. In general, graphics serve three purposes.

Hot Fonts

What's new and different in the world of type?

If you have any interest in design whatsoever, chances are you also have an interest in fonts. Desktop publishing has given the page designer, and even the writer, access to many more fonts than in the predesktop world. Companies such as Adobe, Bitstream, and URW, to name a few, can make hundreds of different fonts available to you at relatively low cost. These companies, as well as many smaller companies, tend to turn out more new fonts every month or so.

In the design-intensive climate of today, fonts appear, take the marketplace by storm, are used on every possible kind of printed material, become tiresome from overuse, and then seem to disappear almost as quickly as they surfaced. Ten or fifteen years ago, for example, a lovely-looking font called Souvenir made its appearance this way; today it's not often seen. More recently Tekton also grabbed the marketplace by storm. Its influence also is now waning.

Here are a few current trends with fonts.

Grunge fonts. Grunge fonts are novelty fonts that look unplanned. Random rather than consistent in shape and appearance, they often seem to have no baseline. One, named Harding, looks like a bad typewriter ribbon. Type companies such as House Industries and Emigré turn out grunge fonts; and although they can be quite hard to read, certain magazines and alternative publications use them because they bring an exciting informality to a page. They are also now sometimes seen in headlines in yearbooks and news magazines. Remedy, Bevel Broken, Improv, and Good Dog are a few more examples of grunge fonts.

Remedy
Bevel Broken
Improv
Good Dog

Grunge fonts such as these remain popular with teenage audiences but must be handled carefully to ensure readability.

Handwriting fonts. Only a few years ago it was difficult to create and digitize (make electronic) a font that looked like cursive handwriting. Then companies streamlined the technology. Nowadays handwriting fonts are as easy to get hold of as regular fonts.

When might you use a handwriting font? One reason for these fonts' popularity may be designers' needs to convey a softer image, to backtrack from the regularized world of serif type. Or have you ever looked at your own chicken-scratchy handwriting and despaired? Why not solve the problem with a beautiful font created out of someone else's well-formed script that you can use as a replacement for your own?

Fonts from the Internet. These days fonts are easier than ever to come by. Many Internet sites allow you to download them directly. A word of warning: Because fonts are copyrighted, they are not really yours to use in school publications without permission. Be sure to find out who owns any font you decide to use, even if it seems to be freely available.

FOLLOW-UP

1. Research the work and influence of one of these type designers: John Baskerville, Ed Benguiat, Giambattista Bodoni, or Hermann Zapf. Report your findings to the class.
2. Which is easier to read, serif or sans-serif type? Have several volunteers read the same passage in a serif and a sans-serif font. Record their opinions.

To Unify Elements

Boxes, rules, and screens can be used to pull related page elements together. For example, if you were planning to use a series of quotes and photos of the individuals quoted, you might choose to run them vertically, grouped together in a box, aligned beside a rule, or in a screened area. If you were planning to show a sequence of events in a time line, you might use boxes, rules, screens, or a combination of those to pull the events together as a unit.

To Separate Elements

Boxes, rules, and screens can also function to separate page elements. In addition, they serve as "barriers" for the reader, causing the reader's eye to stop at one point and pick up copy at a different point. When used effectively, graphic devices can help guide and direct a reader's eye around a page. When used ineffectively, they can inhibit the reader's ability to fully understand the message.

To Call Attention to Elements

Boxes, rules, screens, large or reverse type, photographs, areas of spot color, and distinctive illustrations allow the designer to attract the reader's eye to specific parts of a layout. When placed in key positions, these graphics can enhance the design of the page and will guide and direct the reader's eye to targeted areas of interest.

The **ON DISPLAY** sample on page 241 shows an effective use of boxes, rules, screens, and bullets.

Establishing an Overall Design

Using basic design principles and an understanding of typography and graphics, the designer arranges the page elements to create the visual "personality" of the publication. Although your publication may already have an established design with a clearly defined personality, the design might still be improved. Many newspaper staffs change their overall design periodically—and yearbook designers create a new design each year.

Boxes, Rules, and Screens

The Lion, Lyons Township High School, LaGrange, Illinois

This page shows how boxes, rules, and screens can unify, separate, or call attention to page elements. A lively use of spot color adds to the effectiveness of the design.

---

16 Lion February 26, 1999

Lunch Ladies

Editor • Jo-jo Belanger
Designer • Sarah Cooper

Lunch Lady Land

Job options explored

Every school day, Marriott employees slave in a hot kitchen to bring students and faculty delicious meals

CafeteriaChecklist

Every day before food is served, the cafeteria must be checked for safety and sanitation. The following is some of the checklist:

* All food prepared must be covered, dated and labeled
* All cutting boards separated
* All refrigerators and freezers maintained at precise temperature
* All washing, rinsing and sanitizing procedures followed
* Periodic checks of all temperatures
* Hands washed before beginning work and between different types of work
* All food handled with gloves or utensils
* Gloves and hair restraints worn at all times

Source: NC cafeteria personnel

HairySituation

A food service worker's requirement of wearing a hair net isn't as bad as one might think.

What do you think of the hair net?

"It's important. I feel more comfortable wearing them, and nobody knows if I'm having a bad hair day."
– *Irene Grzesik*

"I feel more safe wearing them. I even wear them when I'm cooking at my home."
– *Lina Longano*

FoodFacts

Lunch ladies' responsibilities and requirements include the following:

* Monthly safety training dealing with topics such as fire safety, equipment training, chemical hazards, customer service and sanitation.
* Weekly five-minute safety talk dealing with current questions and concerns
* Training in the cafeteria dealing with how food is prepared and how equipment works
* Classes concerning what to throw out, reuse or recycle
* Within first six weeks of working in the cafeteria "Serve Safe" training is required, including temperature safety, bacteriological safety, food preparation and sanitation

Source: Lunch lady Irene Grzesik

Peek into busy day sheds new light on profession

On Feb. 9, I put on a hair net, apron and pair of rubber gloves to go undercover and see what it's like on the other side of the lunch line. When I arrived at the cafeteria around 10 a.m., the staff was already hard at work making sandwiches and preparing for the noon rush. It was hot and noisy, but they all smiled and bustled around having a seemingly good time.

After being introduced to the women, I got a chance to test the lunch lady waters for myself. I helped Ann from the snack line fill the chip rack and snack cake trays. Then, I watched the sandwiches being made and got a chance to talk with some of the ladies.

My first feel of what the staff was like was when they all sat down together to eat in the staff cafeteria. Hoots of laughter and the presence of a bond filled the air. I sat down with a cup of soup and enjoyed the atmosphere. I sat and listened to their stories of their children, husbands and past jobs and had to smile at the reality check. When these women go home at 1:30 p.m., their day is just beginning.

I spent most of my time before first lunch with the head baker learning how the different ovens and fry cookers work. In the middle of all this, and the constant temperature checks on various foods and ingredients, there was a constant banter between all the ladies which showed how much fun they find their jobs.

When the bell rang, and the cafeteria slowly began filling with the buzz of students, I put on safety gloves and went to Irene's hot food "South Line" to make my hair net debut. Every student in the line has overheard their peers giving the lunch

ladies attitude, but the ladies never seem to let it bother them. I got the stares and "Nice hair net" comments which are to be expected. However, the servers, there simply to provide the school with meals, still got harassed. "What in the world is that supposed to be?" one student shot out. "You want me to eat that?" another one exclaimed in disgust.

The ladies simply ignore their comments, as if they weren't even said, and keep smiling at those friendly students who they've come to know since September.

After lunch, the sandwich cashier, Cheryl, proudly relayed a story of one of those friendly students "One of my kids asked me to go to college with them next year," she reported. "Will you come be a server at college for me?' she asked me."

For second and third lunch I was in the sandwich and ice cream line serving soup. This was a little more risky than being behind the hot food lines. A few more odd looks and confused comments were given as I stood in front of the whole lunch room in my apron and hair net. For the most part people seemed to think it was cool that I got to hang with the lunch ladies. I wasn't quite sure how to react in second lunch when a few tables began chanting my name, but the serving process all in all went pretty smoothly.

Throughout the course of my visit, most of our conversations strayed back to the same two topics: safety and why the staff does this for a living. The answers centered around the students. Most everything they do is for the sake of the students' health, and they just love the students.

Jo-jo Belanger
features editor

All Smiles Every school day, Anna Havlik stands infront of a cash register, ready to ring up hungry customers. Havlik is one of the dedicated group of Marriot employees that produces and distributes meals for students.

Val Neylon
staff photographer

BriefBios

Mary Rotrekl

* **Position** – cashier/sandwich maker
* **How long she's been in the business** — two years
* **How she ended up here** — "I started in the Morton food service, then when my son came to LT, my friend told me of the opening."
* **Favorite part of the job** — "Working in the Canteen"
* **Other hobbies** — sports, crafts, biking, singing, and drama

Mary Farmer

* **Position** – cashier/sandwich maker
* **How long she's been in the business** — three years
* **How she ended up here** — The work hours were compatible with her kids' grade school schedules.
* **Favorite part of the job** — contact with all of the kids
* **Other hobbies** – "I drive, drive and drive the kids."

Lunch ladies fond of their job

Cafeteria workers reveal the perks of their jobs

Every day at around 6:45 a.m. lunch lady Patty Hare arrives at work to prepare the day's breakfast. There are only a few of cafeteria staff members who come in early to make breakfast.

Then, for the rest of the day, the entire staff prepares for the lunch hour. She doesn't leave until about 1:45 p.m., after the cleaning process is done.

Despite the unusual hours, Hare loves her occupation.

"If I didn't like my job I wouldn't be here," Hare said.

She explained that one of the major perks of her jobs is working with her fellow lunch ladies. She reflected that her coworkers had provided her with many special memories and experiences of her job at NC.

The most memorable experience of her job was just recently, when the district manager came and worked with the lunch ladies.

"I enjoyed working with him," Hare said. "I learned a lot from working with him."

She also said that her co-workers had taught her a lot about her job.

"I've learned so much from Marcie," said Hare.

She also considered one of the perks of her jobs the silence of her workplace.

"It's really very quiet back here [behind the lunch lines]," Hare said.

Although Hare described the cafeteria

as fairly quiet before lunch, the lunch hour proves to be very different.

Hare said the time when the students and teachers come to the cafeteria is the busiest part of the day.

Lunch lady Joanne Rohlicek also described the lunch ladies' day as being generally very busy. About three staff members arrive at school daily in order to make breakfast.

Hare explained that she makes breakfast daily until 7:15 a.m. Hare describes this part of the day as when the cafeteria is generally the most quiet.

Then, according to Hare, the rest of the lunch ladies arrive and they all prepare the day's food for lunch.

From 11:30 a.m. until 1:30 p.m., the lunch ladies serve the students and teachers. Hare explained that this part of her day was the most stressful.

After the serving of lunch is finished, the rest of the day is comprised of cleaning up from the day's nutritional festivities.

Following that routine, the lunch ladies start to leave. Some of the lunch ladies stay longer than others, Hare said.

Rohlicek explained that the first lunch lady leaves at 1 p.m. and the last one leaves around 2 p.m.

Hare considered her favorite part of her job to be working with the other lunch ladies, and despite popular misconceptions of the profession, claimed that her job is "not that bad."

Ellen Sporleder
staff reporter

If you plan to update or create a new overall design, first review other publications and try out several possibilities. Make brief sketches, and then transfer your best ideas into mockups that clearly show the style of page elements in each potential design. Ensure that all page elements—especially the nameplate—reflect the personality of the paper. You may also want to establish whether your front-page design includes an index or teasers.

Get feedback from the rest of the staff on each potential design and revise as necessary before choosing the one that works best. When the overall design is approved, mark several pages with typefaces and sizes and place these example pages on the wall in the journalism room for future reference. Also, if possible, include information on the typography and design of common page elements in a special section of your stylebook or create a separate design and production manual.

Most desktop publishing programs offer style-sheet options that let you lock in formats for page elements such as headlines, captions, folios, and body copy. Learn how to create such style formats so that they can be easily applied each time a particular page element is needed.

Laying Out Pages

Before designing and laying out an individual issue, meet with editors, reporters, artists, and photographers about the content of the issue so that you can plan the design of each page effectively. Work with your photographers to obtain the types of photos that will best illustrate the stories in the publication.

To begin a design, first draw rough miniature sketches, sometimes called thumbnails, and then transfer these designs to dummies. Dummies are full-size drawings of pages showing where all page elements will appear.

For convenience, use grid sheets to create dummies. Grid sheets are paper forms, the size of the newspaper format, that are lined with light-colored grid marks showing your standard column width. Light-colored lines allow you to see the grid but prevent you from getting grid lines confused with pencil lines as you sketch your dummy. You may have your printer provide grid sheets or print them yourselves from your computer. Some designers do their dummies right on the computer.

On the dummies, indicate where all page elements will be placed, being sure to keep consistent internal margins of one pica. As you place headlines, beware of "tombstoning," headlines placed side by side on a page (or across a spread). "Bumping" heads makes them appear to run together and causes confusion about which copy goes with which headline. You can place headlines on the same horizontal plane only if one headline and its story are boxed.

When you are finished with your dummies, either typeset and paste the copy on the grid sheets or lay out the publication on the computer with a design program. If you are working on a computer, you can print your completed layout on a laser printer and paste it on fresh grid sheets. Or if your publication's printer has the capability, you can send the pages straight to the printer's pre-press department on a disk or through a modem or other delivery system.

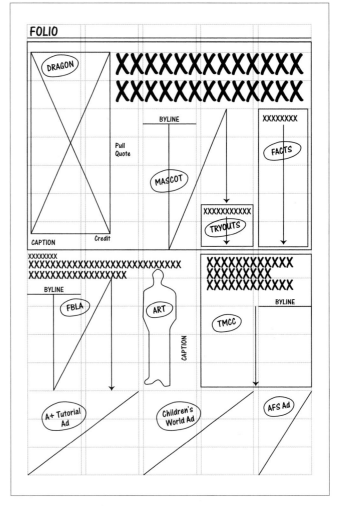

This is a dummy of the front page shown on page 247.

The modular format. Many designers follow a modular format for placing stories on a page. In this format, you package each story, its headline, and its accompanying graphic elements into a neat rectangular unit. A typical modular unit for a story might contain story copy, a headline, a byline, subheads, a pull quote, a photo, a caption, and a photo credit. Each modular unit has a dominant element. One unit is the dominant element on the page or spread.

You can be flexible in the arrangement of page elements within a modular unit provided the end result creates a rectangle with well-defined borders. For one story, you might drop a photo with its caption in the center of your grid, wrap the copy around it, and place a headline over the entire package. For another story you might place an infographic to the right or left of the body copy and a headline over those two elements.

The minicolumn format. For a more open appearance, some papers use the minicolumn format, a format based on a series of narrow or "mini" columns used to create areas of planned white space. In this format a page that normally features 5 standard columns is divided into 10 minicolumns. Specific numbers of mini columns are then combined to create a column width for a particular story. The width of one minicolumn is generally used as a framing device to surround the main story package with a margin of white space. This margin is repeated elsewhere on the page to make these areas of white space appear planned. The use of the minicolumn format in newspaper pages allows the designer to package stories with "breathing room" for the reader. The framing space draws the reader's attention to the main story quickly.

Designing the Front Page

In addition to the paper's nameplate (and possibly an index or teasers), the front page usually includes several major news stories. One of these typically has a large photo or other graphic as the dominant element for the page.

After placing all of the regular items in their predetermined positions, place the main story and the dominant element, which may or may not accompany the main story. Then add the remaining content. Note that advertisements never appear on the front page.

Color is frequently employed on the front page—which means that it can be used on the back page too because the front and back page are printed on the same sheet of paper. Don't overdo the use of color, or it loses its effectiveness. For example, on the front page you might use it in your nameplate and in one or two other places, perhaps for rules around photos and as a colored screen behind teaser copy. On the back page you might use it to punch up an illustration or the headline of a major story.

The **ON DISPLAY** sample on page 245 shows a front page that contains a dominant photo, varied column widths, and a careful use of spot color.

HISTORY worth remembering

The Bauhaus. Members of the artistic movement known as the Bauhaus, founded in Germany in 1919, promoted the ideal, "Form follows function." This principle was integrated into all areas of art and technology, including graphic design, where it resulted most notably in the design of highly readable, streamlined typefaces.

ON DISPLAY

Front-Page Design

Crier, Munster High School, Munster, Indiana

In addition to a varied
column width and practi-
cal use of spot color, this
front page uses a low-key
dotted-rule motif and
generous white space—
all of which combine to
impart a light, modern attitude to the design.

Munster High School CRIER

8808 Columbia Ave. • Munster, IN 46321 • Vol.32 • Issue 13 • March 13,1998

Building a base
Although education is a base for one's life, sometimes the system doesn't deliver.
See Page 4

Quick takes

Parents to meet for College Night
Junior parents will gather next Thursday at 7p.m. in the Food Court to learn about choosing a college and other basic college information.

Test deadline changed
Previously, the deadline for the Advanced Placement (AP) tests was last Tuesday. Fortunately due to inclement weather, the deadline was moved to next Monday.
On that day, students must turn in the application they received at the AP advisory meeting along with the appropriate money.

Concert date moved
Due to adverse weather conditions, the choral concert which was supposed to have taken place last Tuesday, will instead occur next Tuesday.
All choir classes, Womens' Ensembles and Mixed Ensembles will perform at Westminister Presbyterian Church at 7:00 p.m. Tickets can be purchased at the door.

Students can donate blood
The blood drive will be conducted in the Fieldhouse Thursday, April 6 and run by Student Government members. Those who are intravenous drug users, have sport body piercings, or have a sexually transmitted disease will not be eligible to donate blood.
Students qualify to donate blood if they are at least 17 years old and a minimum of 110 pounds.

● **Cover Story**

*Last Monday, unexpected snow forced
students to retreat to powerless homes*

Let it snow

• WINTER CHILL Avoiding foot deep snow, Matt Thompson, sophomore, heads home. A few inches of snow was predicted, but an unanticipated blizzard kept students at home last Monday and last Tuesday.

Trekking through the STORM

Road problems:
● unplowed roads
● I80-94 and I65 closed down

Electric problems:
● almost 135,000 NIPSCO customers were without electricity.
● Lake, Porter and LaPorte county areas were the hardest hit with power outages
● 200 electric linemen and other crews worked to restore electricity.
Source: Mrs. Melissa Long, NIPSCO employee

by Tim Hayes

Winter 's back with a vengeance, dumping at least a foot of snow last Monday, and causing school to be called off both last Monday and last Tuesday.

The last time the school system closed was during January 1994 when subzero temperatures approached dangerously low levels.

At such times, the Superintendent, after consulting with the Director of Transportation, maintenance personnel, road crews and the Munster Police Department, makes the final decision on whether to dismiss school. The decision would optimally be made before 6 a.m. in order to notify the buses and the faculty at the various buildings before they come out to work, according to Mr. Bill Pfister, superintendent of schools.

When students reported to school Monday, they were greeted with an announcement three or four minutes before the first period bell rang, stating school was cancelled due to a power shortage caused by a transformer going out close to the football field.

Power was fully restored to the high school complex at approximately 11:30 a.m., according to Mr. Michael O'Connor, principal. All of the school system's buildings had power as of 9:30 p.m. Monday, according to Mr. Pfister.

Still, problems existed which caused the school closing Tuesday. Even though the high school building had power, NIPSCO was concerned that it could go out again. In addition, only the south parking lot was plowed and parking could have been a problem, according to Mr. Pfister.

see SNOW page 2

Media Center moves to Wrestling Room

Construction chaos will continue as the Library Media Center (LMC) moves to the Wrestling Room.

Last Monday, the library started relocating its materials. Moving should finish during Spring Break, according to Mrs. Cheryl Mason, Media Specialist.

The work was moved up from the end of the school year to start over Spring Break. There is "too much work in there with the heating and electricity," to wait to start construction until June, according to Mr. Bill Ondrovich, construction manager.

Most library services will still be available, according to Mrs. Cheryl

Books, magazines, and other print materials, will be in the Wrestling Room. The LMC is also trying to make at least half of the computers available. However, it is not known whether Internet connections will still be in use.

Unfortunately, since the Wrestling Room has limited space, there's no room for furniture. The chairs are being sent for reupholstering while the tables are put in storage.

Audio-visual (AV) materials will be stored in the TV Studio/Production area by the Commons. AV materials and all other Media Center materials will be together after con-

"I'm hoping it will be worth it," Mrs. Mason said. "We'll have everything in one space, and we'll be able to accommodate everyone."

The new, complete LMC should be ready at the beginning of next school year, according to Mr. Ondrovich.

Other areas of construction are wrapping up and may soon be open for student usage.

"We are hoping for the Music Department, the band, choir, and orchestra areas, to be done after Spring Break," Mr. Ondrovich said.

The auditorium construction is also continuing, and will hopefully

" We'll have everything in one space, and we'll be able to accomodate everyone. **"**
Mrs. Cheryl Mason, Media Specialist

Designing Inside Pages

The same basic approach used to design and lay out the front page is used for inside pages. Identify and place the main story, place the dominant element, and fill in with the remaining smaller story units, which may include sidebars, photos, and graphic devices such as pull quotes.

Inside pages often allow greater flexibility than does the front page because they generally have fewer regular elements. The editorial page, however, is like the front page in that it may have several regular elements, such as the masthead and standing heads for columns or letters to the editor. An editorial cartoon is typically the dominant element. It should be packaged with an accompanying editorial and headline. The masthead, listing newspaper staff members and sometimes editorial policies, should be placed at the bottom of the editorial page. It should be small and inconspicuous but readable. Remember that ads are inappropriate on the editorial page(s). (See page 315 for a sample editorial-page layout.)

Unlike the front page and the editorial pages, many inside pages contain advertising. Ads are usually placed to the outside or across the bottom of the page with one pica of white space between them. The tops of ads placed on the bottom should be even across the page.

The **ON DISPLAY** samples on pages 247 and 248 show layouts for two different kinds of inside pages.

Designing a Double-Truck

Sometimes staff members like to plan an inside double-truck (double-page spread) focused on a specific topic. Because the designer crosses the gutter with copy and graphics on a double-truck, double-truck pages must fall exactly in the middle pages of the paper. In other words, if the paper is eight pages, the double-truck should fall on pages four and five.

The double-truck presents the designer with a unique challenge to create an interesting yet balanced and unified design through the use of related material. It also allows the designer more freedom in working with the space available.

Steps in double-truck design. When designing a spread, use the standard column width for your newspaper grid, with perhaps one variation for interest. Lay out page elements from the inside of the spread and move toward the outside. This strategy will prevent trapping large areas of white space in the interior of the layout.

Inside-Page Design

The Excalibur, Robert McQueen High School, Reno, Nevada

Boxed sidebars, a pull quote, and a dominant photo help to make the stories on this page stand out. The ads are neatly lined up at the bottom of the page.

---

2 *The Excalibur*
DECEMBER 17, 1997 • VOLUME 8, ISSUE 4

SECTION EDITOR • AARON HAYES   **CAMPUS SCENE**

Who is that in the dragon costume?

STAFF PHOTO
Lancerlot (also known as senior Jen Dean, pictured in LSN ad on page 12) waits with other leadership members for the beginning of the first assembly of the school year on Aug. 29.

"Inside the costume, you are a different person. No one really knows it's you, and you can be very outgoing."

SENIOR JEN DEAN

Katrina Smith
REPORTER

Sure we've all seen the cute, grinning dragon that represents our school at football games and assemblies, but have you ever really wondered just who is inside the costume? After a few days of trying to contact Lancerlot, Excalibur finally got to speak to her. Yes, the dragon is a girl...she is McQueen senior Jen Dean.

Dean decided to become mascot because as she said, "I had a few friends from other schools who had been mascots, and they really had a lot of fun doing it.. plus I was the only one who had applied for the position, all I had to do was try out for cheerleading." Besides being the mascot, she is also an editor of the Yearbook.

Dean would recommend being the mascot to others. "Being Lancerlot is a lot of fun. I can pretty much do anything I want to, and I can be as creative as possible. Inside the costume, you are a different person. No one really knows it's

you, and you can be very outgoing."

Dean practices with the cheerleaders and does just about everything that they do except for stunts. "She's as much a part of the team as anyone," said freshman cheerleader Andrea Peterson. "She partakes in every practice and game. She's so interactive," says senior cheerleader Jennifer Tabor.

Most definitely Dean is very busy. In addition to her school responsibilities, she holds a job at Chuckee Cheese as Chuckee himself. Dean hopes to put her experience as an outgoing member of the spirit team by becoming an elementary school teacher; some current schools she's looking at include Michigan State and North Illinois.

**MASCOT TRYOUTS
97-98**

Those interested in becoming next year's mascot should contact Coach Robin Hardesty towards the end of the school year (after basketball season) for the dates of mascot tryouts.

Mascot facts

Who paid for Lancerlot?
Half of Lancerlot's costs were donated by an anonymous donor. The other half of the funds came from the Class of '95

How much does it weigh?
Lancerlot weighs between 25 and 30 pounds.

What's it made of?
Lancerlot is made of thick, spongey foam.

Who made Lancerlot?
Lancerlot is made by the same company that produces the costumes for the Disney characters at Disneyland.

How tall does a person have to be to wear the Lancerlot costume?
The person has to be a minimum of 5'5". The first person to wear the costume was former Principal Mike Whellams, who is about 6'3".

Working towards success...

Future Business Leaders of America re-activated at McQueen

Jennifer Burke
REPORTER

Future Business Leaders of America (FBLA) is a national non-profit organization for students in grades 7-12. FBLA promotes business leadership, the understanding of business enterprise and the establishment of career goals. The Nevada FBLA's biggest annual effort goes toward the March of Dimes.

FBLA has state and national competitions based on speaking and community service. "I went to a conference in Seattle. There were dances and speakers and we dressed up. When the conference was over, we just wandered Seattle. It was a lot of fun," said junior Carrisa Monfalcone.

Assistant Principal Barbara

Creveling started Future Business Leaders of America when she first came to McQueen. The program stopped when she started working in the office but was re-activated this year by computer teacher Kathy Aikin. "I got started again this year when some students showed some interest," said Aikin.

"I participate in the program because it ties in with what I do personally. I also like working with high school students," said Aikin.

Junior Vanessa Wellons participates in FBLA because "[the March of Dimes effort] will help a lot of children and mothers."

"I participate in FBLA because it's a good opportunity to get involved in the business world," said junior Christy Perkins. "Being in FBLA gives me a chance to meet people I normally wouldn't meet."
ILLUSTRATION BY CHRISTIAN OLIVER

MEN WANTED
FBLA participation is open to students in grades 7-12, and male participation is currently underrepresented.

TMCC magnet school gives students an edge

Aaron Hayes
CAMPUS SCENE EDITOR

Truckee Meadows Community College has launched a magnet high school programs which enrolls juniors and seniors, 16 to 18-years-old. The entire school, which is on the TMCC campus in the technology building, consists of 72 students. The program offers the students free college tuition up to three classes each semester as well as program options for most academic, vocational and technical fields of study. "We offer the students free tutoring, computer lab and a library," said TMCC high school secretary Sarah Craperi.

Classes include three required courses (english, math and social studies) taught by high school teachers and three elective classes from TMCC teachers; those classes taught by TMCC instructors count as dual credits for both high school and college. "If you take more than three credits, Washoe County will pay your tuition," said Craperi. The students must provide their own transportation. If a car is not available, the district will provide a Citifare bus pass. Students interested in an application and more information may talk to counselors or call TMCC at 674-7660.

ON DISPLAY

Inside-Page Design

Mt. Carmel Sun, Mt. Carmel High School, San Diego, California

A strong, dominant action photo, plus text wraps around "twin" graphics that lead toward a pull quote draw this sports page together.

Sports

13 | Mt. Carmel Sun Jan. 22, 1999

Allison Vinci

Dillon Brazeal (10) grimaces as he takes down his Escondido opponent. The Sundevils crushed Escondido 51-15, Jan. 6 at home. MC's next match is Thursday at home against Rancho Bernardo at 5:30 pm.

Cougars prove no match for wrestling team

PHIL HIX
Staff Writer

Walking all over Escondido with a score of 51-15, the Sundevil wrestlers — ranked No. 4 by the *Union-Tribune* — look ahead to bigger fish like the undefeated Poway Titans.

Next Thursday the team competes against Rancho Bernardo, and then they look to the big dual match against Poway at 5:30 p.m. Feb. 11 in Sundevil Arena.

Winning against the Cougars with pins were seniors Jon DelaCruz (130 lbs.), Jason Farron (135), and juniors Joe Mueller (171), and Cameron Casper (heavyweight).

Point victories came from Brian Rillo (119), Dillion Brasil (125), Mike Champagne (140), Tommy Figuero (145), Adam Arajo (152), and Jake Morrow (189). Tony Demofonte was awarded a forfeit victory.

"The keys we needed to win were enthusiasm and no one getting pinned— that helped keep the winning streak rolling," captain Tommy Figuero said.

After returning from the Hawaii Tournament over the break the team has molded together.

"After Hawaii, we became tight. Spending the New Year together gave us a chance to bond as a team," senior Jake Morrow said.

The team has eight returners from last year, giving them an experienced team.

"Eight returners is a lot, plus we have a couple of tough sophomores that have stepped it up," Figuero said.

Twins have more in common than looks: hard work

Although their work ethic may be the same, the Cvrks' sports differ

HELEN TRANTER
Staff Writer

Determination, persistence and talent are all skills that are hard to find in one athlete, but even more difficult to find them twice. Senior twin brothers Ronnie and Bobby Cvrk perfect these qualities to a tee, bringing experience and leadership to two varsity teams.

Ronnie a returning midfield varsity soccer player and Bobby, a returning varsity basketball shooting guard, are well respected by their coaches.

"He brings experience, team play, a good attitude and a good work ethic," varsity soccer coach Hank Acquarelli said. "He is an example for the younger players."

According to varsity basketball coach Steve Middleton, Bobby also fits this description.

"Bobby is more persistent than any athlete I have had at MC in five years," Middleton said. "As well as his God-given talent, he has perseverance, dedication, and he works."

The twins' athletic abilities are not their only characteristics that cause them to stand out. Their last name, Cvrk, pronounced like 'Swerk' and rhymes with work, is also unique to their family, coming from their Czechoslovakian roots.

Since they were young, Ronnie and B o b b y h a v e played

soccer, basketball and baseball for at least one season each. They were on the same recreational teams throughout their childhood.

"When we played on the field it was like we had telepathy," Ronnie said. "I always knew where he was and he always knew where I was."

When they reached high school though, their comradeship on teams ended, as each of their favorite sports were offered during the winter season. Each brother chose to go their separate way athletically.

"It was good in a way because we were apart since we usually are always together," Ronnie said. "But I was really used to playing with him."

The twins' relationship extends beyond athletics though. Born only one minute apart and dressed in identical clothes for many years, they have not been separated much since birth.

"We are good friends," Ronnie said. "There is always somebody there, I am never alone."

Ronnie and Bobby have been in several classes together throughout high school. Their twin bond is evident in the classroom.

"It is weird, we think the same way," Ronnie said. "We may be sitting in class and he says something and I was thinking the same thing."

As well as often times thinking the same way, despite them being frater-

nal twins their physical characteristics are very similar.

Ronnie and Bobby are both very actively involved in many of the same extracurricular activities. They are members of the Fellowship of Christian Athletes and the Agape Club as well as being actively involved in the Penasquitos Lutheran Church.

They try to extend their Christian beliefs into games with them.

"I was brought up in the church, I try to carry the church onto the field with me," Ronnie said.

Their characteristics are also very similar, as their lives have been shaped by many of the same experiences.

"We are not really that different," Ronnie said. "We have been in the same atmosphere our whole lives and we have never really been away from each other."

Having so much in common leads to a problem that many twins face, being mistaken for each other.

"It (being called Bobby) doesn't really bother me, you get use to it," Ronnie said.

They are brothers though, so little arguments are not uncommon.

"He loves soccer," Bobby said. "I am sick and tired of watching all soccer games on TV all the time."

Overall, they usually get along pretty well though, they both said.

When they were younger competition among them was pretty fierce because

they faced each other on the same field.

Today though, competition in school sports is not a problem because they play different sports that are hard to compare. Although home sometimes changes that.

"At home one-on-one games are really competitive," Bobby said.

But on the school courts and fields often times the Cvrks can be found at the same time. They regularly attend each others games to cheer on one another.

"His basketball schedule is crazy," Ronnie said. "He is so dedicated to his sport."

The Cvrks will be graduating in June, with hopes of continuing their sports at the college level.

However, they do not plan to attend the same college. Bobby has been accepted to Colorado and is considering San Jose State, the University of Washington, and Long Beach State. Ronnie is hoping to go to Long Beach State, Sonoma State or Westmont.

"Not living together will be different," Ronnie said. "We will definitely keep in touch."

Next September, when Ronnie and Bobby no longer attend MC, the athletic legend and leadership abilities they have created at MC will remain here.

Bobby Cvrk (12)

Photo by Allison Vinci

Ronnie Cvrk

"*When we played on the field it was like we had telepathy. I always knew where he was and he always knew where I was.*"

Ronnie Cvrk (12)

Photo by Liz Mejia

Place the dominant photo or other dominant element near the center and top of the spread. Try to position it so that it crosses the gutter, but avoid placing people's faces in the gutter. Then establish the horizontal eyeline in either the upper third or lower third of the spread.

Now place all other photos or other graphic elements on the spread. The vertical lines of the photos should fall on the vertical grid lines. It's a good idea to contrast the shape of a dominant graphic element with that of smaller ones.

Place captions as close as possible to the photos they describe. Captions may be the width of your standard or alternative column but should generally be the same width throughout the spread. With the exception of related groups of photos, don't put captions between photos.

Finally, add the copy. Place it within your grid using the modular format so that each story creates a rectangular unit. Limit yourself to no more than one mainbar and two sidebars or the spread will appear copy-heavy. When you include the headlines, try to use the primary-secondary style discussed earlier. Incorporate areas of white space (around the edges) for a lighter, more inviting spread.

Study the double-truck in the **ON DISPLAY** feature on pages 250–251 to see how it fulfills these criteria.

Yearbook and Magazine Design

Most of the rules of good design mentioned earlier apply to yearbooks and magazines as well as to newspapers. Here are a few to keep in mind for these types of publications. (For additional discussion of yearbook design, see Chapter 14.)

Setting up a spread. Most yearbooks and many magazines are designed primarily by spreads; therefore, keep the following points in mind as you lay out these types of pages:

As often as you can, create a "photo pinwheel" for the reader. Do this by crossing the gutter with the dominant photo and clustering the other photos around it. The reader's eye will strike the dominant photo first and travel in a clockwise or counterclockwise direction around the page. Thus, the reader's eye won't bounce around the page.

ON DISPLAY

Double-Truck Design

HiLite, Carmel High School, Carmel, Indiana

12 Homecoming
SEPTEMBER 16, 1999

Homecoming

Traditions still thrill students

By Luke McConnell and Jon Campbell

SOCIAL STUDIES
TEACHER
MR. GREG
GOSSARD

With the event figuring prominently in movies such as "Varsity Blues" and TV shows like "South Park," Homecoming has woven itself indelibly into the fabric of the American high school experience. But the traditions we currently follow here leave some wondering how Homecoming started and why it has become such a big deal.

The origins of Homecoming are, for the most part, unknown — no one celebrates the first Homecoming as he would the first Thanksgiving. Mr. James Garretson, social studies department chairperson, speculated that the occurrence started at colleges when graduates returned to the campus for football games. From there, the celebration spread to the high school level and continued to escalate to today's popularity.

SOCIAL STUDIES
DEPARTMENT
CHAIRPERSON
MR. JAMES
GARRETSON

Next Friday, the shortened class schedule will allow the 3,300-person student body time to view the Homecoming parade and floats, cheer on their respective class officers to win Dilly Bars, race tricycles around the track, run in an intramural cross-country race and enjoy live entertainment from student bands while consuming pies from Planet Pizza, all at one of the state's best high school football stadiums. However, this was not always the scene.

Only one tradition from Homecoming past survives today. However, the parade as we know it was remarkably different 40 years ago. The 1959 parade featured floats not just from individual classes but also from clubs and organizations such as the marching band. In addition, the parade highlighted the football team riding on the town's only fire engine, a sharp contrast to the two school buses required to exhibit the squad today. The parade also ended at the old stadium now used for soccer.

> I've been to all the football games and seen people with their bodies painted and filling up the home stands. I think that Homecoming this year could be something really big.
>
> FORMER ASSISTANT
> PRINCIPAL MR. ERIC CLARK

Even the famous floats themselves were not as they are today. Garretson said he remembers when the floats were nothing more than chicken wire with different colored paper napkins threaded through the wire.

"It took more people and really got kids involved in the activity," Garretson said. Garretson, who sponsored the Class of '72, said the majority of the class got involved in the construction of that class's float. Although that class was much smaller than any that has walked across the Deer Creek stage within the last few years, Garretson said that class unity was much greater in those days.

One tradition that has come and gone since the '50s is the Homecoming breakfast. Garretson recalled how the Class of '72 worked all night on its float one night and met for breakfast at a local pancake house the next morning.

"There were about 90 people there," Garretson laughed. "It was a small place, so we were about the only ones there." However, as the school expanded, meeting in one place became impractical.

FORMER
ASSISTANT
PRINCIPAL MR.
ERIC CLARK

Homecoming 1980 became more recognizable by today's standards with the first trike race. In 1982, sophomores participated in an intramural cross-country race to run off demerits accumulated in physical education classes.

However, the festivities almost came to an end in 1984, when the state almost discontinued daytime Homecoming revelry altogether. The Indiana Department of Education contended that the celebrations statewide wasted valuable academic time. Fortunately, the state rescinded its decision, and the yearly tradition was allowed to continue.

The Homecoming hoopla hit another snag the following year when participants in the trike race were required to wear helmets for the first time. Some students were upset at the safety measure, but because it provides a safer environment, the rule persists to this day.

The biggest change in Homecoming, however, came when the new football stadium was built in the early '90s. The new facility offered the space required to house the expanding student body and a new, larger track for the floats and trike race. That student body has grown markedly in 10 years. In 1989, the three-grade enrollment was less than 1,900. This year, this school has become the largest four-grade institution in Indiana, with more than 3,350 students.

The newest addition to the Homecoming schedule was the food court, added in 1996 by that year's Speaker of the House, Joel Zimmerman '97.

"Joel worked his butt off to personally get vendors for the food court, and of all things, it rained. The whole thing had to be moved into the cafeteria, but he'd planned for that, and I was really impressed with how he planned for it," social studies teacher Mr. Greg Gossard said.

Last year's food court included Highflying Pies (now Planet Pizza), Ben and Jerry's and other local food vendors. This year's festivities also will include several carnival games from Party Time Rentals.

Former Assistant Principal Mr. Eric Clark offered his thoughts on this year's Homecoming and school spirit. "I think the spirit this year is better than in the past. I've been to all the football games and seen people with their bodies painted and filling up the home stands. I think that Homecoming this year could be something really big."

Vendors and bands

Food
Candy and drinks
Planet Pizza
Physical education teacher
Mrs. Kathy Buck's
elephant ears

Music
Mulse
Jumpstart

Schedule

Period 1   7:50 to 8:05 a.m.
Period 2   8:15 to 8:30 a.m.
Period 3   8:40 to 8:55 a.m.
Period 4   9:05 to 9:20 a.m.
Period 5   9:30 to 9:45 a.m.
Period 8   9:55 to 10:10 a.m.
Period 7   10:20 to 10:50 a.m.
      (A and B lunches)
      11 to 11:30 a.m.
      (C and D lunches)

Sack lunches and pizza will be served for lunch

Spirit week

During lunches Monday through Thursday
Battle of the Bands, paper chain contest
What would you do for a Klondike bar?
"Best Legs" contest

Class activities
Sing school fight song for monetary prizes
SRT spirit door decorating contest

Dress up days
Monday - Pajama day
Tuesday - '70s day
Wednesday - Crazy hair and socks day
Thursday - Hawaiian day
Friday - Blue and Gold day

(9•24•99)

11:30 a.m.
Students and faculty are dismissed to stadium

11:45 p.m.
Club booths open and bands start playing

1 p.m.
All students must be in stadium for final trike race heats

1:45 p.m.
Parade arrives at stadium

2 p.m.
Dilly Bars distributed and students dismissed

Parade

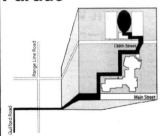

Range Line Road

136th Street

Main Street

Guilford Road

List of participants
Carmel Fire Department
1998 Homecoming queen, Katy Southern '99
Marching band
Choral groups
Senior court
Junior court
Sophomore court
Freshman court
Varsity cheerleaders
Reserve cheerleaders
Freshman cheerleaders
Soccer Hoppers
Thespians and 'drill team"
Head Coach Mr. Keith Fiedler
Senior team members' bus
Junior team members' bus
Sophomore team members' bus
Freshman float
Sophomore float
Junior float
Senior float
Student Senate

Other stuff

Additional information including Homecoming court, club booth information, game results and Homecoming dance will be available at

 **www.hilite.org**

Remember: Don't forget to bring money for the club booths. Games and prizes will be available from various clubs.

GUEST COLUMN

By Katie Mitchell

Issuing a challenge for Homecoming

After school elections ended last May, former student body president Ashley Klein '99 gave me the daunting task of organizing the Senate filing cabinet by determining which files to preserve and to discard. In the process, I came across a folder of the annual Homecoming reports from 1980 to 1998.

Although most probably would read one or two of the ancient archives and then achieve the maximum state of boredom, I reveled in the list of duties, committee reports and overall evaluation each provided. To me, it is more than a glimpse of the past, it is 19 years of precedent that should be respected and occasionally reexamined. However, in this column I simply want to share some of the ways Homecoming here has evolved because I have faith that at least one student in 3,300 will find this insignificant history as fascinating as I do.

The '80s
Seventeen years ago, before the birth of all freshmen and sophomores and many juniors, the third annual trike race took place with psychology teacher Mr. Mark Sutton announcing the heats, just as he will do next Friday. Student body president Chris Sapecky '83 introduced the court during a 9:30 a.m. pep session followed by words of encouragement from Head Coach Mr. Jim Belden. The parade consisted of 13 convertibles, one firetruck, the band, two football team buses and three floats.

In 1984, students went to 26-minute classes with seven-minute passing periods. Unfortunately, student body president Scott Suns '85 couldn't prevent rain. The court got wet at the game, and most of the decorations had to be removed from the cars before half-time. A popular suggestion to improve Homecoming was that the student body should be able to "see" all court candidates before voting on the queen. To conduct an all-school spirit breakfast was another recommendation from the students. In the '80s, helium balloons were released before the kick-off.

The '90s
When the Freshman Class joined the school in 1996, Homecoming was altered significantly. Freshman court members, cheerleaders and football players were added to the parade route. For the Senate, this translates into the responsibility of obtaining four more convertibles and one team bus.

In 1997, vendors sold lunch to students for the first time, but because of the heavy rain, student body president Kari Dunn '97 moved them inside the cafeteria. The parade did not occur, and Principal Dr. William Duke announced Homecoming queen Jenny Kniptash '97 under the protection of an umbrella.

Next week, an entire new year of memories will unravel and then be recorded for the use of senators 20 years from now. Homecoming traditions like the trike race and dilly bar dash will join with new events such as "What would you do for a Klondike Bar?" and the "Best Legs" contest.

My challenge for students this year is to make a Homecoming so memorable that it will forever stand out in the midst of a whole folder of "meaningless" Homecoming reports. *Katie Mitchell is a senior and the student body president.*

Jack Keot / Art

When using a grid with a standard column width (as opposed to using a flexible minicolumn grid format), set all captions and copy in one column to maintain consistency on the spread. Captions may be the width of two columns on your grid, but the type should be increased slightly in size to compensate for the wider measure.

Keep white space to the outside of the page. Working from the inside and progressing to the outside corners of the design will push unplanned white space to the outside of the design.

Remember to place copy and headlines on the spread as a modular unit. The headline should be placed directly over the copy or to the side of the copy so that it leads the reader into the story.

Try to use the eyeline to lead the reader's eye across the page. It's acceptable to break the eyeline; however, the element that breaks it must go at least eight picas above and eight picas below the eyeline to make a formal break.

Plan one high point near the center of the spread and place other elements below that point. If you place a dominant element at the high point it will create a graphic curve in which all elements on either side progress downward from the top of the page. Create the same kind of curve at the bottom of the page by placing another dominant photo near the bottom center and allowing other elements to progress out from that same point across the bottom or to move upward from that point.

Use the same grid format throughout a section, but change grids from section to section. Change also the shape and placement of the dominant photo and other design elements from spread to spread. For example, if you have used a dominant vertical photo or story unit on one spread, stress a horizontal arrangement on the next spread.

The **ON DISPLAY** spread on pages 254–255 shows good positioning of all major page elements—photos, headline, copy, and captions.

Photos and graphics. Here are some pointers for selecting and positioning photos and other graphic devices.

When selecting a photo for the dominant position, choose the photo with the best quality, most news value, and greatest tonal range and contrast.

Make sure that all subjects in the photos face the center of the spread. If subjects seem to look off the page, the reader's eye flow can be interrupted.

If you choose to "bleed" a photo—that is, to let it run off the edge of the page—do so for emphasis only. Limit yourself to no more than one bleed per side of the spread.

When including graphics, always make sure you have a reason and purpose. Avoid random use of "clip art," mascot art, sports art, and other fillers for unplanned white space.

Avoid the use of decorative or heavy borders or rules. Use a one-point border instead.

Designing a "People" section. In the "people" section of a yearbook, use one design style for seniors, another for underclassmembers, and yet another for faculty. The variation could feature the use of a different headline design—perhaps using the same type in a varied manner—or a more obvious difference. Creating these distinctions will add variety to the section and will create a unique personality for each group featured.

When setting up the pages, include a few points of space between rows of portraits, and place names toward the outside. Avoid using one full pica of space between portraits and placing names under individual pictures. This format is considered difficult to read. (For an example of a people section spread and more yearbook layout samples, see Chapter 14.)

When you finish a layout, or are asked to evaluate one prepared by someone else, this checklist may be helpful.

EVALUATION CHECKLIST

Design and Layout

☑ Are body copy and display copy sized appropriately and chosen to complement each other?

☑ Is the dominant element strong and well positioned?

☑ Are copy and other photos placed on the page in a modular format?

☑ Are graphic devices such as boxes, rules, and screens well used but not overused?

☑ Are internal and external margins consistent and not violated by copy or graphics?

Yearbook Spread

The Indian, Shawnee Mission North High School, Overland Park, Kansas

Looking

Ahead

Students focus on preparing for college

By Rachel Blankenship

Carefree lives, no work, lots of fun and parties were what many underclassmen associated with being a senior; the reality was much different.

"Be prepared to fill out lots of applications, write essays and don't procrastinate," advised senior Jessica Yelton.

Many seniors agreed with Yelton.

"You don't want to be stuck at home over winter break filling out applications like I was," said senior Colleen Cunningham.

Starting early was the piece of advice that many suggested. Preparing early, seniors agreed, was the key to success.

"Look for scholarships, get exposure and take classes which relate to your college major," said senior Keith Redmond.

Many seniors believed that looking into several different colleges was the way to find the one that would work for them.

Senior Kathryn Heley-Luedtke said that many factors affected her decision.

"I have visited like eight campuses, but I also looked at tuition, size, location, the dorm's and cafeteria food."

Paying for the immense cost of college was another preparation seniors stressed. Many had a job or a savings account set up specifically for college.

"I'm going to JCCC to get my requirements out of the way, then I am going to transfer to another college," said senior Pamela Hurt. "This way I can save money and go to a college where I can go into a specific field."

Seniors said that it was important to keep an open mind in making a decision about post-graduate learning.

"Keep an open mind when you are choosing your college because you need to choose the one that will work for you," Heley-Luedtke said.

Top Right: During a meeting with her counselor, senior Megan Lubis discusses college options with counselor Kathy Scheve.
photo by Carrie Rowe

Top left: Filling out college forms, senior Alison Griesemer listens to Emporia State University representative, Jim Dean.
photo by Kasi Cooper

Bottom: Learning about the finer points of Carleton College, junior Sara McIntyre listens intently to representative Emily Johnson, who was a valedictorian of SM North last year. "There are so many colleges to weed through, so if you start early you can start concentrating on the ones you're interested in and start planning, taking tests and know what you'll need to succeed at that school," McIntyre said.
photo by Kasi Cooper

Right: "You don't need this!" growls Bravo, the cocker spaniel puppy of senior Brianna Southworth, as he tears into her application to Drew University. The senior class began the college application process in the fall of 1998, many rushing to meet deadlines as early as Nov. 1.
photo by Brianna Southworth

It is a time every senior dreads. Filling out college applications. During late October, senior Megan Lubis consults her counselor on the fine points of filling out college applications. "It's nerve wracking filling out these college applications," Lubis said.
photo by Yvonne Corpus

Deciding which college to attend, junior Rebecca Phipps meets with her counselor, Nancy Silverforb. "She was helping me prepare for college, (with) what classes are better to take at a community college or a four year college," Phipps said.
photo by Carrie Rowe

Stepping Stones...

Senior
Todd Martin

"It takes so much time filling out these applications and looking around at colleges."

Senior
Jamie Precht

"I went on a lot of college visits earlier in the fall, and then kept in contact with colleges about scholarships to make sure they know I am still interested."

College Prep 171

This spread for the academics section of the yearbook shows a clear eyeline and good placement of the major page elements. Notice the use of spot color and the way the headline in the boxed section repeats the design of the main headline.

Wrap-up

Good design is a vital part of contemporary publications. Designers should understand the basics of design and layout, such as the nature of common page elements and how to lay these out on a grid. They must also adhere to the basic design principles of dominance, unity, contrast, repetition, balance, and consistency.

The process of designing pages often begins with type selection. Designers may choose typefaces from seven categories—Oldstyle Roman, Modern Roman, Text, square serif, sans serif, script and cursive, and novelty—although faces from the first four groups are most often used. Designers need to know appropriate sizes of type to use for different situations, as well as ways to package, position, and mix type appropriately.

Graphics such as rules, boxes, illustrations, and photos should only be used for specific purposes, such as to unify, separate, or call attention to elements on a page.

When creating actual page designs, a designer should do an overall plan at the beginning of the year and post samples of it for the staff's benefit. Many newspapers use a modular format in which stories are packaged for better readability.

During layout, designers may build dummies, or full-size drawings of their pages, showing where all page elements will appear. When preparing dummies, designers should beware of "tombstoning," or "bumping," headlines and should ensure consistent internal margins.

Specific page design begins with the placement of the main story (if there is one), followed by the placement of the dominant element (usually a photo), and then the positioning of other photos and copy around the dominant element. Double-trucks, designs that extend across a spread, follow the same general procedure but must be handled carefully.

Columns may be the same width throughout a page or spread or may follow a minicolumn format, which varies column width according to a specific variation on a standard column width.

Although the same basic design principles apply to all publications, yearbooks and some magazines are designed mostly in spreads and need to be especially concerned with a spread's overall unity.

On Assignment

INDIVIDUAL ACTIVITIES

1. Write a brief definition of each of these terms:

bleed	justified
dominant element	leading
double-truck	minicolumn format
dummy	modular format
eyeline	pica
font	point
grid	ragged
gutter	"tombstoning"

2. Brainstorm this question: If you had no concept of what a newspaper was, and someone told you to design one, how would you go about it?

3. Collect samples of typefaces that you find appealing. Note where and how they are used. Compare your collection with those of classmates.

4. To become more aware of graphics and their use in guiding and directing the reader's eye, locate and clip one example of each of the following:

    ▶ an interesting headline design
    ▶ type shadowed in an unusual manner
    ▶ an interesting caption design or a design that could be converted to a caption design
    ▶ creative use of spot color
    ▶ textures and patterns used effectively as graphics
    ▶ eye-catching use of rules
    ▶ pull quotes
    ▶ copy set in an unusual manner
    ▶ use of illustrations or photos in conjunction with headlines
    ▶ infographics
    ▶ creative use of white space
    ▶ Paste the examples in a notebook in the order in which they are listed. In addition, create a cover for the notebook that reflects your personality.

5. Evaluate one of the full-page On Display samples in this chapter. Write a one-page critique of it, citing what you liked and did not like about the layout.

6. Find examples of good and bad page design in school papers or in your local community paper. Bring the samples to class and discuss their strengths and weaknesses.

7. Prepare a dummy for the front page of a newspaper. Include an original nameplate designed specifically for your target audience. Choose a particular format and determine how many columns will be in your grid. Include a dominant element. Keep headlines directly over the copy they relate to. Avoid "bumping" unrelated headlines next to each other. Create a mockup of the completed design, using copy and photos from magazines or newspapers. Then lay out the page on the computer if you have one available.

8. Following the steps outlined in activity 7, prepare a layout for a feature page, an editorial page, or a sports page. Conform these interior pages to show unity with your front page.

TEAM ACTIVITIES

9. Using the in-depth story you prepared in Chapter 9, design a double-truck for your newspaper. Besides mainbars and sidebars, position photos and write captions for them. You may also want to include an illustration, pull quotes, and infographics. Make sure your double-truck reflects the basic principles of design, including consistency.

10. Create an original typeface. Begin by studying the characters in several typefaces to see which features, such as descenders, are generally designed similarly and which characters tend to have the same width. If you use serifs, decide on their shape and learn where they are usually placed in characters. Display your completed typeface to the class and explain what you did and learned in developing it.

SURF THE NET

11. What makes a well-designed web site? Surf the Net to find sites that you think are particularly well-designed. Download samples and bring them to class.

career profile

Art/Technology Coordinator

Bryan Monroe

Bryan Monroe is a storyteller who doesn't rely on words. Photographs, headlines, graphics, art, and design are some of the tools he uses.

"I'm a firm believer that readers don't just read text by itself," said Monroe, assistant managing editor of the *San Jose Mercury News*. "Every mark you make on a page means something. If you don't give it meaning the reader will."

Monroe is in charge of the photo, art, design, and systems departments at the *Mercury News*. He is also the newsroom coordinator for technology, color, and pagination issues. In 1992 he engineered a major redesign of the paper, the third newspaper redesign he has worked on.

Monroe is a regular visiting lecturer at the Poynter Institute for Media Studies in St. Petersburg, Florida. He was a founder, and is on the executive board of the National Association of Black Journalists Visual Journalism Task Force. He is also chair of the Society of Newspaper Design Diversity Committee.

Before coming to San Jose, he was assistant project director for Knight-Ridder Inc.'s 25/43 Project—a newspaper research and development project targeting readers aged 25–43. Monroe and other editors worked out of the Knight-Ridder paper in Boca Raton, Florida, redesigning it into a daily living laboratory for experimentation into the future of newspapers.

As graphics editor and director of photography at the *Myrtle Beach* (South Carolina) *Sun News,* Monroe helped engineer a redesign in 1988 and was responsible for the overall look and visual content of the paper.

"Creating a new newspaper from scratch for most people is a once-in-a-career thing," Monroe said. "I've been fortunate enough to be able to do it three times already."

Monroe got his start as a photographer for the *Seattle Times* but soon was named graphics editor of the *Myrtle Beach Sun News.* It was there that he first got the opportunity to use what he calls his toolbox.

"It was my first chance to learn about growing; to learn about integrating visuals into journalism," Monroe said. "We started using visual elements that tell stories.

"We give readers information, ideas, and emotion. Words are just one tool in your toolbox.

"In the old days newspapers did a great job of getting the information you need and putting it on a page. But it's not good enough anymore to get it to the page. You've got to get it from the page to the reader's head.

"Photos, graphics, headlines, and everything else you can do are more tools for your toolbox. My background and desire is storytelling and I've gravitated to certain tools. I had to learn how to write."

Don't be afraid to experiment is the message Monroe leaves with page designers:

"Go out to the edge of the tree limb and jump up and down. If the limb doesn't break, go out farther and jump up and down some more. Keep doing that until the limb breaks and then step back one step."

FOLLOW-UP

1. Monroe has worked on newspaper design for an audience aged 25–43. What design elements do you think need to be incorporated into designs for both younger and older readers? Discuss your ideas with the class.
2. Is a new design always better? Get older copies of magazines such as *Time* and *Newsweek* and compare the old designs with the current ones. Point out strengths and weaknesses in each version.

Getting the Newspaper Ready for Distribution

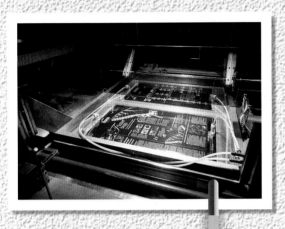

1 The manufacturing process begins by making negatives of the pages that will be used to make metal plates to go on the printing presses.

2 The metal plates are hand-positioned on the presses.

3 As printed paper goes through the press, it is formed and cut into newspapers.

4 Sections of the paper are stacked as they come off the conveyor.

5 The whole process can be monitored from the packaging control room.

6 Preprinted sections await the inserting of advertising supplements.

9 The delivery trucks set out on their daily runs.

8 A worker loads the papers onto delivery trucks.

7 The assembled papers, now wrapped and bundled, are ready to be loaded onto delivery trucks.

263

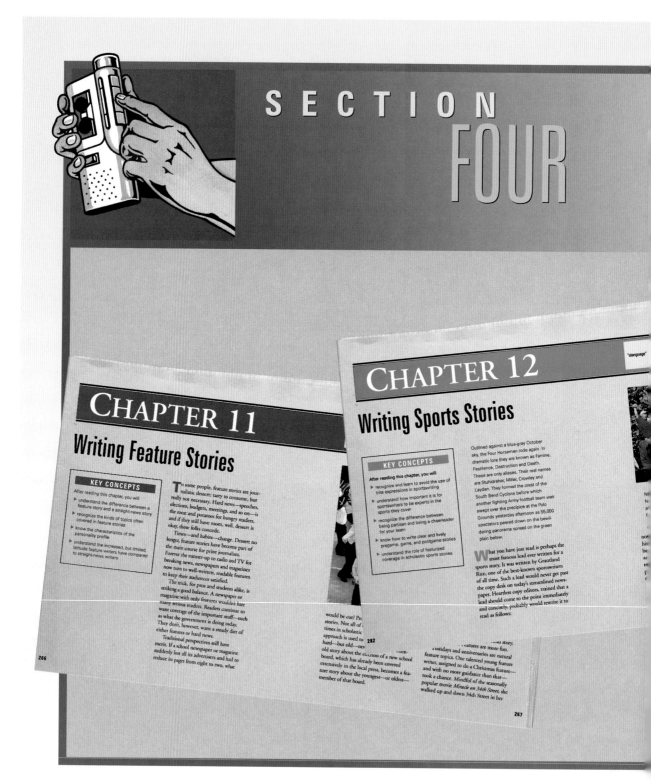

CHAPTER 11

Writing Feature Stories

KEY CONCEPTS

After reading this chapter, you will

► understand the difference between a feature story and a straight-news story

► recognize the kinds of topics often covered in feature stories

► know the characteristics of the personality profile

► understand the increased, but limited, latitude feature writers have compared to straight-news writers

To some people, feature stories are journalistic dessert: tasty to consume, but really not necessary. Hard news—speeches, elections, budgets, meetings, and so on—is the meat and potatoes for hungry readers, and if they still have room, well, dessert is okay, these folks concede.

Times—and habits—change. Dessert no longer, feature stories have become part of the main course for print journalists. Forever the runner-up to radio and TV for breaking news, newspapers and magazines now turn to well-written, readable features to keep their audiences satisfied.

The trick, for pros and students alike, is striking a good balance. A newspaper or magazine with only features wouldn't lure many serious readers. Readers continue to want coverage of the important stuff—such as what the government is doing today. They don't, however, want a steady diet of either features or hard news.

Traditional perspectives still have merit. If a school newspaper or magazine suddenly lost all its advertisers and had to reduce its pages from eight to two, what

would be cut? Pro... stories. Not all of ... times in scholastic ... approach is used to ... hard—but old—nev... old story about the ele...ion of a new school board, which has already been covered extensively in the local press, becomes a feature story about the youngest—or oldest—member of that board.

CHAPTER 12

Writing Sports Stories

KEY CONCEPTS

After reading this chapter, you will

► recognize and learn to avoid the use of trite expressions in sportswriting

► understand how important it is for sportswriters to be experts in the sports they cover

► recognize the difference between being partisan and being a cheerleader for your team

► know how to write clear and lively pregame, game, and postgame stories

► understand the role of featurized coverage in scholastic sports stories

Outlined against a blue-gray October sky, the Four Horsemen rode again. In dramatic lore they are known as Famine, Pestilence, Destruction and Death. These are only aliases. Their real names are Stuhldreher, Miller, Crowley and Layden. They formed the crest of the South Bend Cyclone before which another fighting Army football team was swept over the precipice at the Polo Grounds yesterday afternoon as 55,000 spectators peered down on the bewildering panorama spread on the green plain below.

What you have just read is perhaps the most famous lead ever written for a sports story. It was written by Grantland Rice, one of the best-known sportswriters of all time. Such a lead would never get past the copy desk on today's streamlined newspaper. Heartless copy editors, trained that a lead should come to the point immediately and concisely, probably would rewrite it to read as follows:

...out story.

...features are more fun.

...holidays and anniversaries are natural feature topics. One talented young feature writer, assigned to do a Christmas feature—and with no more guidance than that—took a chance. Mindful of the seasonally popular movie *Miracle on 34th Street*, she walked up and down 34th Street in her

Writing Features, Sports, and Editorials

KEY TERMS

game story   postgame story

Sports fans want more than an announcement of who won and who lost in sports coverage. For an event such as the Ryder Cup, they want an insightful story about holing the long putt that put the U.S.A. team on top.

watch television—and even record games they're keenly interested in. When they pick up a newspaper a day after the game, the last thing they want is a simple announcement of who won and lost.

Thus, Rice's lead, although outmoded, still has appeal. It's colorful and full of action. If all sports leads had these qualities there wouldn't be such a split in the attitudes toward sportswriting. As it is, though, there are two schools of thought: One holds that sportswriting is the worst writing in journalism today. The other holds that sportswriting is the best.

When sportswriting is bad, it's... When it's good, it can be truly en...

CHAPTER 13

Writing for the Editorial Page

editorial
editorial page   subjective writing   editorial policy
masthead   column   point-counterpoint

KEY TERMS

KEY CONCEPTS

After reading this chapter, you will

- understand the opinion function of a newspaper and the various ways in which it is expressed
- know how to write effective editorials for a variety of purposes
- understand the various types of columns
- be able to write reviews of products and performances
- understand the functions of other elements on the editorial page

The newspaper editorial is often referred to as "the voice of the paper." It is up to the staff to make sure this description is accurate, which is no simple task. The editorial page is the only part of the paper that focuses completely on subjective writing—that is, writing that's not necessarily impartial but instead expresses a point of view.

Everyone has opinions. The newspaper, when it expresses its opinions—or the radio or television station that offers opinion features and editorial voices—amplifies its voice by the number of its readers or listeners. When an editorial writer speaks or writes, therefore, the responsibility weighing on his or her expression is extremely heavy. Editorials have the ability to make or break a project or program, to affect the amount of acceptance given a new policy, or to lead to changes in existing policy. Such a degree of influence cannot be taken lightly.

FUR INDUSTRY: THE END IS NEAR
LEHIGH VALLEY
ANIMAL RIGHTS

Editorials have the power to effect changes in our society. School papers often tackle controversial topics, such as animal rights, in editorials.

In the past, student editors were often told they should not editorialize on curriculum, athletics, or school board decisions, or such issues outside the school as politics and the environment. Today, however, student journalists write about almost any issue of interest or importance to their readers. The list of topics on page 208, suggested as possible subjects for in-depth articles, could certainly also be considered as possible editorial topics.

Research is the first essential step in writing a good editorial. Some of that research may include direct interviews with people knowledgeable about the issue. Using these people's quotes as part of the

editorial adds depth and credibility, as well as providing alternative opinions. Other research information may come from surveys and opinion studies, either conducted in the school or done by research firms. Some of these larger studies are available through on-line databases. Other on-line resources, such as newspapers, general and specialty publications, and government information files, can aid in the search for background information.

As an editorial writer, the journalist should first become immersed in all available information on the subject. Only when a position has been reached, and the research completed to support it, should

302

303

CHAPTER 11

Writing Feature Stories

To some people, feature stories are journalistic dessert: tasty to consume, but really not necessary. Hard news—speeches, elections, budgets, meetings, and so on—is the meat and potatoes for hungry readers, and if they still have room, well, dessert is okay, these folks concede.

Times—and habits—change. Dessert no longer, feature stories have become part of the main course for print journalists. Forever the runner-up to radio and TV for breaking news, newspapers and magazines now turn to well-written, readable features to keep their audiences satisfied.

The trick, for pros and students alike, is striking a good balance. A newspaper or magazine with only features wouldn't lure many serious readers. Readers continue to want coverage of the important stuff—such as what the government is doing today. They don't, however, want a steady diet of either features or hard news.

Traditional perspectives still have merit. If a school newspaper or magazine suddenly lost all its advertisers and had to reduce its pages from eight to two, what

KEY TERMS

hard news	soft news	news feature	personality profile
feature story	"evergreen"	news peg	

A story in the local press about a Cinco de Mayo festival could be handled in the school paper with a feature on student perfomers in the event—and thus capture a unique angle on the story.

Features also allow school papers a way to get a unique angle on a story that the local papers might not have. For example, a story in the local press about a Cinco de Mayo festival might be covered in the school paper with a feature on student performers in the event. Student journalists often are forced into such approaches because they cannot compete with daily publications or newscasts.

Features, which may be considered soft news, thus should be of increased interest to the scholastic journalist. Although banging out quick and readable inverted-pyramid stories remains an essential journalistic skill, crafting artful features is just as critical. It takes a real artist to write a clear, concise, balanced 12-inch inverted-pyramid story. Still, let's face it: Features are more fun.

Holidays and anniversaries are natural feature topics. One talented young feature writer, assigned to do a Christmas feature—and with no more guidance than that—took a chance. Mindful of the seasonally popular movie *Miracle on 34th Street*, she walked up and down 34th Street in her

would be cut? Probably most of the feature stories. Not all of them, though: Many times in scholastic settings a feature approach is used to spruce up what really is hard—but old—news. Thus a two-week-old story about the election of a new school board, which has already been covered extensively in the local press, becomes a feature story about the youngest—or oldest—member of that board.

town, knocking on doors and asking people whether they had experienced any "miracles." Lots of people laughed at her and shut the door in her face—but several talked to her about spiritual or unexplained events in their lives. Her feature was a delight to read.

The same young reporter, assigned to do a post-Christmas feature, produced a winning story without saying a word. With permission, she positioned herself at the returns counter of a popular department store the day after Christmas, listened, and wrote down the excuses people used to return Yule gifts they didn't want. The story provided a good laugh to combat the after-Christmas letdown. (Hmmm, there's a feature-story idea right there.)

Then there's the story of the news editor who needed a fresh angle for a St. Patrick's Day feature. At midnight at his paper in the Midwest, he picked up the phone and called the lord mayor of Dublin, Ireland—where it was the middle of the night. The editor didn't get through to the lord mayor, but he did get an aide on the line. A humorous story about the difficulties of transatlantic telephone hookups made a fine March 17 tale. The article was a feature story—and so good that management didn't even complain about the telephone bill.

On another night at the same paper, an enterprising young reporter was assigned to do a Halloween story. Not one to take the easy way out, he walked through a cemetery—at midnight—alone. His feature story made chilling reading.

Another story relates how a young sportswriter at a daily newspaper did something to make the sports editor angry. In retaliation the editor made the following assignment: "Get a feature story. I don't care what it's about or where you get it, but I want it on my desk before you go home tonight." Panicking, the reporter set out to find a feature story. He ended up going water-skiing, even though he had never tried it before and couldn't swim. Pictures taken from the shore clearly showed his fright. The feature story he wrote about the experience was given special treatment in the Sunday edition of the paper and drew many favorable comments (as well as restoring him to the good graces of the sports editor).

TIPS worth taking

Feature headlines. Feature stories need feature headlines. If the story is light, bright, and colorful, the headline should be too. If the story is creative and fun, the head should be too. One famous headline, for a story about a woman who gave birth to quadruplets—all boys—read, "Boy oh boy oh boy oh boy!"

Characteristics of Feature Stories

Just what is a feature story? Would it help to note that a feature story is usually lighter, more "human," possibly funnier than a regular news story? that most feature stories are not related to any current news event? that a feature story is usually not written in inverted-pyramid style? that it may be about anything or anybody?

Judging by this description, you may have guessed that, like news, a feature story is tough to define. Some people say there's no such thing. By that they mean that all stories, feature or otherwise, should be readable. They fear that the only time a reporter will "write bright" is when the assignment specifies a feature story.

Timelessness

Some properties of the feature story can be isolated. The main characteristic of most features is that they're "evergreen." That is, they're just as acceptable for publication in next week's paper as in this week's. There's no time element involved—but even this isn't always true. The news feature, for example, is pegged to a specific item of news and is usually published the same day as the news story, or at least as soon as possible afterward. When your school wins the state science fair competition, for example, the feature story about the student whose exhibit took first place is a news feature, a feature closely tied to the main news story. A feature on how band members feel about the possible elimination of the band is a news feature related to a news story about a school budget cut. Such stories as these are said to have a news peg, a reason for existence on their own.

Creative Style

Feature stories provide latitude but not license. While feature writers are a trifle more free with regard to the use of the language, they certainly are not free to throw away the rule book entirely. Opinion and speculation are not allowed. The same ethical standards that apply to the straight-news story apply to the feature story. The good feature writer soon recognizes, however, that feature stories sometimes provide a better chance than straight news for literary ingenuity. It's hard to write a truly clever, bright story about the student council meeting, particularly if nothing out of the ordinary happens.

Zines

What makes zines so popular? Could you create one, too?

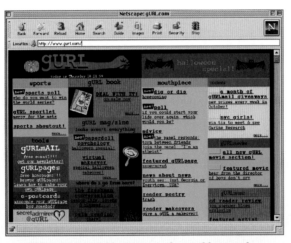

The strong graphic presentation and interactive capacities of gURL magazine are typical of many zines.

Want to create your own publication and circulate it to hundreds, maybe thousands of readers? Join the ranks of zine creators.

"Zines," or "e-zines," are online magazines. Zines fall into two general groups: zine versions of print publications such as *People* or *Newsweek,* and zines created especially for cyberspace. Into this second category fall many publications created by individuals or small groups rather than giant corporations. Zines can be about any topic under the sun; but many, especially the ones found only in cyberspace, are fairly specialized.

Some sources put the total number of zines now in existence at more than 10,000, although many disappear almost as soon as they appear. Trying to keep count is futile, of course, because like all other elements on the Net, zines are growing and changing by the minute. John Labovitz's *E-Zine List* is one useful directory of the various zines out there. Recently it listed more than 4,000 active cyberspace-only publications.

Specialty zines can cover a wide range of topics—games, hobbies, science fiction, geographical regions, government, films and film stars, various types of music, bridge playing, cooking, thrift shopping, and on and on. More than one zine may be devoted to a topic, such as the intricacies of snowboarding. Many are devoted to the wishes and problems of girls and young women. Others focus on political positions or causes. The audiences for these zines may be in the tens, hundreds, or thousands—and as old zines fade away new ones are created.

What makes zines special and different from traditional media is that they're interactive. A zine on snowboarding, for example, may let you call up information on snow conditions in various areas near you. A so-called girlzine might give you a chance to respond directly to an article on anorexia or direct you to where you can find more information about the topic.

The zines put on line by professional publications try to offer materials different from those in their print versions. For example, the print form of a magazine may offer an interview with a rock group. Its zine counterpart may go one step further and, taking advantage of its interactive capabilities, make the star of the group available on line to answer questions directly. Or it may provide a video clip from the group's most recent performance. Because most zines also have screens that function as tables of contents, one click of a button will take you directly to the article you're interested in.

So—how about you? Do you have a topic you know well or feel passionately about? Are you willing to write articles and share your information for little or no financial reward? Numerous web sites offer help in starting your own zine. You might begin with a simple, print-only format that you distribute by e-mail. As you become more skilled and experienced, you might graduate to a graphic-filled publication on the World Wide Web. Your zine might last for three issues—or three years. Nevertheless, you will have had the thrill of offering your ideas to a potential audience of millions of readers.

FOLLOW-UP

1. Locate a student zine on the Internet and contact its founder via e-mail. Ask questions such as the following: Where did the original idea for the zine come from? How long has the zine been in existence? What keeps it going? What does the founder think will happen to the zine in the next six months? Report your findings to the class.

2. Find out more about *Slate,* a professional zine designed specifically for the Internet. Examine the contents of various issues and discuss, in class, reasons for this zine's success.

Truly clever or bright stories can be hazardous too. The danger is that writers, especially (but not exclusively) beginners, will become carried away by the sound of their own words. They will try to be funny, or cute, or even overly somber. Such stories are difficult to pull off, and will be disappointing if they fail. The delightful thing about feature stories is that often the subject matter itself is funny or cute or somber. If the writer doesn't intrude too much, these elements will come through on their own.

Unlimited Subject Possibilities

Another characteristic of the feature story is that its subject matter isn't limited. It may be historical, throwing new light on an old subject or simply reviewing some events of years past. It may be about a remote place or an obscure person. It may be about someone's unusual hobby or someone's interesting relative. It may be written in the first person (as the waterskiing feature was). It may provide background for a developing or continuing news story. It may summarize or wrap up a story that has been told in small pieces over a long span of time. It may rely heavily on the use of anecdotes. In many cases a feature story concentrates on the mood of an event and therefore may convey more accurate information than the straight-news story.

Above all, the feature story is about what people are interested in. That's close to the definition of the human-interest story, and trying to separate the two is difficult. Is an interview with the fifteen-year-old genius who graduated from college a feature story or a human-interest story or both? It doesn't make any difference how you label it as long as you're able to recognize and gather such stories.

Fortunately, examples of good features are easy to come by in the scholastic press. The article in the **ON DISPLAY** feature on page 272 was the lead story on a full page about left-handedness.

TIPS ✓ worth taking

Writing fascinating features. Keep these guidelines in mind as you write your features:

▶ Show, don't tell. Use details that help the reader see, smell, hear, taste, and touch the elements in the story.

▶ Personalize and localize. Whatever the topic, incorporate real people from your school and community.

▶ Draw information from a variety of sources.

▶ Get to the people and events of the story quickly.

▶ Include only one anecdote, example, or quote to get across a single idea.

▶ Hang onto interesting items that don't quite fit in the main story. Add a sidebar to incorporate some of these related facts, quotes, and so on.

▶ Reemphasize your angle in your conclusion.

ON DISPLAY

Feature Story

The Stinger, Emmaus High School, Emmaus, Pennsylvania

Lefties do it right

by Steph Brewer

It isn't often that junior Bea Polanco is put in the same category as Pablo Picasso, Babe Ruth, Marilyn Monroe, Billy the Kid and Queen Victoria.

One might wonder what a high school student, a painter, a baseball player, a movie star, an outlaw and a queen could possibly have in common.

Truthfully, they don't have much in common except for one unusual trait; they are all left-handed.

Fifteen to 20 percent of Americans are left-handed, according to Carol Riddle, marketing and public relations director of the Topeka, KS, based Lefthanders International.

The number of lefties has gone up in recent years, Riddle said, because children are usually not encouraged by teachers to use their right hand instead of their left.

Throughout history, left-handedness has been regarded as a nasty habit and social inconvenience, according to The Lefthander Syndrome by Stanley Coren. It has been associated with traits such as artistic ability, rebellion, creativity, criminality, bed wetting and sports proficiency.

Polanco does not agree with these typical theories.

"I really don't think it makes any difference whether you're left- or right-handed," she said.

Health teacher and lefty George Gibbs attributes the theories of creativity to the number of great left-handed artisans. He said he could not think of a reason why the theory involving criminality was developed. He did, however, offer one explanation.

"I guess being a criminal you would have to be creative," he said.

Although many modern-day lefties don't think anything of their oddity, the lefties of the past were painfully aware of the difference between them and their right-handed counterparts.

In the 1600s, left-handedness was considered a sign of witchcraft, according to Coren. In Morocco, lefties are called s'ga's, which means "devil" or "cursed person." In the Eskimo culture, lefties are thought of as potential sorcerers.

Because of the negative connotations associated with left-handedness, many left-handers have been forced to use their right hands.

Senior Stacey Nagle does many things with her left hand but was forced by her father to write with her right hand when she was young.

"My dad would always switch things, like my fork, to my right hand," she said.

Senior Beth Demers said her left-handed uncle went to parochial school and was hit on the knuckles every time he used his left hand. Eventually, he just learned to write with his right hand.

Left-handed people are more intuitive and creative because they are right brained, according to Riddle.

However, sociology teacher Robert Braun said he would like to see statistics before he believes the theories about lefties.

Area psychologist Dr. Richard Weiss agreed with Braun.

"In my opinion, there isn't enough research to say left-handers are more creative," he said. "It still remains theoretical." Aside from the problem of being stereotyped, lefties also face many other problems, the main one being they live in a right-handed world.

Lefties must use special scissors; they can't use some desks or spiral notebooks; and they have problems writing in pen.

"We live in a right-handed world, but we operate from the left side," Gibbs said.

The goal of Lefthanders International is to make the world easier for left-handed people, Riddle said. They even publish a magazine full of products for left-handed people.

So while Polanco, Picasso, Babe Ruth, Marilyn Monroe, Billy the Kid and Queen Victoria may not have a lot in common, they all faced, or are still facing, the trials and tribulations of being a lefty.

Personality Profiles

Many feature stories deal with individuals, and this makes sense. In fact, it's fair to state that every person on Earth is worth a personality profile—a feature story about that person. Somewhere in the background of every human being is an incident, an idea, a problem, a thought, a relative, an opinion, a hobby, a hope that will make interesting reading. A journalism instructor once decided to prove this notion to his students. On the first day of class he picked a name at random from the roster and called a student to the front of the class. The instructor didn't know her; in fact, he had never seen her until that day. As the class watched, he interviewed her. The next time the class met, the students were amazed at the personality profile he had written. Some even thought the whole thing was rigged. The fact is, the result would have been about the same no matter which student had been chosen. Today, the student the professor chose is a feature writer for *Newsday* in New York.

Although everyone is a possible subject for a personality profile, some people make better stories than others. Perhaps your school newspaper publishes many stories quoting the president of the student body but has never gotten around to doing a personality profile about that person. All of the students may know the student-body president's name, yet they probably don't really know anything about the person. This is a subject ripe for a personality profile.

When you do a personality profile, try to answer the questions Who is this person, anyway? What does he or she do on weekends? What are his or her opinions on politics? the environment? sports? What are his or her goals for your school? If you ask enough questions, you're bound to get an answer that will lead you down the road to a personality profile. In this kind of feature, as in everything else in journalism,

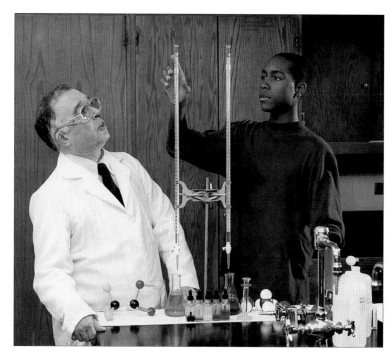

A personality profile of a student who won a science-fair award should aim at revealing interesting facts that make the student a unique individual.

there's no substitute for the hard work of digging for the facts. While actually writing the story, however, the feature writer usually has a chance to exercise more imagination than the straight-news writer.

Notice how the personality profile in the **ON DISPLAY** feature on page 275 uses a combination of details and direct quotes to give the reader a sense of really knowing the person being featured.

From the sample articles, it should be clear that feature stories, including personality profiles, have many qualities in common. When you write yours, use this checklist to guide and then evaluate your work.

EVALUATION CHECKLIST

Feature Story

- ☑ Is the story on a topic of interest for its intended audience?
- ☑ Do the style and tone make it clear from the beginning that this isn't a hard-news story?
- ☑ Does the story use anecdotes and other interesting examples to make its points?
- ☑ If the story is a personality profile, does it focus on interesting or unusual aspects of the person's life?
- ☑ Is the story free from grammatical errors and in accordance with the publication and general AP style?

Features and School Papers

Feature stories play a particularly important role in the scholastic press. Because most such newspapers come out only once a week or every two weeks or even once a month, they should rely heavily on features. The straight news has already been covered by the daily newspaper downtown; as a scholastic journalist, you should be on the watch for feature stories and should featurize even straight-news stories. You might also pay special attention and devote more space to events that are going to happen rather than to those that have already taken place.

Personality Profile
The Echoes, Abraham Lincoln High School, Council Bluffs, Iowa

Artist for Hire

— by Ruvane Kurland

The hope and dream of every artist is to be discovered. For Andrew Johnson, the dream became a reality.

Johnson's mother noticed his talent in third grade when he won Henry Doorley Zoo's poster contest for "Catch Jungle Fever."

In sixth grade, Johnson entered a contest entitled "Written and Illustrated By," a contest in which he had to write and illustrate 28 pages. Johnson placed in the top 100 in the national contest.

Art instructor Randi Kennedy began to guide Johnson's talent when he was still in elementary school.

"I began giving Andy private art lessons when he was in sixth grade," she said. "Andy is one of the most accomplished artists for his age that I have ever taught. He has been involved in many contests and exhibits in the past as well as designing and executing a 40-foot mural at Kirn."

The mural depicts the Kirn Eagle in various activities, such as sports, music and fine arts. After volunteering to paint the mural, Johnson took three months to design it, then the rest of the school year to paint it.

"I procrastinate. That's why it took me so long," Johnson said. "I'd stay after school for a couple hours; then I'd go home, eat dinner, and come back. My mom helped me a little with painting it, but the biggest thing she did was take me back and forth to the school." Like any other artist, Johnson soon faced some complications.

"Some people drew graffiti on it, but for the most part they left it alone," Johnson said. "What we couldn't erase, my mom went over with white paint."

Some may think spending that much time on a mural wouldn't be worth the time. But Johnson said it all paid off in the end when he was paid $200 for the job.

"I wasn't expecting any money; it wasn't talked about in the beginning. I thought it was pretty cool to get out of classes to paint the mural," he said. "Even though it got to be a hassle spending time on it, I think it was worth it because I was happy at what I received. It's nice having the recognition and the money."

With this experience under his belt, Johnson found other offers coming in.

Principal Joy Stein at Lewis and Clark is also interested in his artwork and wants him to paint a mural at his old elementary school. Johnson said he probably would request $200 for the time-consuming job.

"Right now, I want to go into feature animation when I get older, hopefully to work for Disney or Warner Brothers," he said. "But until then I'll stick to drawing cartoon characters."

A feature story can elevate routine news to page-one news—especially if it's a human-interest story, such as the **ON DISPLAY** sample below.

You may detect a note of sympathy in the tone of the story. Part of the latitude allowed in feature writing is that, although you may not come right out and express your opinions openly, you may, through careful choice of words, write a story with an emotional tone.

The **ON DISPLAY** feature on page 277 is an example of a featurized straight-news story on an upcoming event—essentially, a news feature.

Human-Interest Story

Beak 'n Eye, West High School, Davenport, Iowa

Teacher's Pet

by Natalie Hansen

He's West's best teacher's pet. Going from class to class, listening in on the lessons for the day, he loves school so much that he would rather stay in school and chat with faculty members and students than leave the school grounds.

Yes, it's Rocky the squirrel.

Faculty on the first floor call the squirrel Bucky, but faculty on the second floor call it Rocky. So there is no confusion, we'll call him Rocky since newspaper is on the second floor.

Since September Rocky has been living in the main courtyard. The teachers decided that Rocky probably couldn't get out, so Gene Soehl, science, caught Rocky in a live trap and then released it outside the building. In three or four weeks Rocky came back.

Rocky seems to be unable to get out of the courtyard, but head counselor Roger Begthol says if he really wanted out he would find a way. "One thing you should never do is sell a squirrel short," he said.

Faculty and students enjoy feeding Rocky. There are at least four places outside of teachers' windows where food is available for him.

Rocky climbs up to the second floor at least once a day to visit Dave Wessel's history class and then get some of his favorite food, nuts.

Wessel leaves nuts outside of the social studies office for Rocky, and he says that life here is good for Rocky. "He's smart; it's a good retirement in here."

Begthol, who seems to be Rocky's favorite faculty member, even feeds Rocky out of his hand. "You just have to be patient, let them grow accustomed to you," says Begthol.

There are no plans to trap Rocky again, but once school is out something will have to be done with him. Or maybe he will just stay for summer school.

News Feature

The Little Hawk, City High School, Iowa City, Iowa

A Graceful Entrance
Student-run dance company makes its debut

By Meryl McKean

The mid-afternoon sun glides over the polished floors and exercise barres. Natasha Bosma '01, is fitting ballet costumes on fidgety eight-year olds at Terpsichore School of Dance. The small girls laugh and giggle as they are zipped into the sparkling outfits made of satin and gauze. It's not difficult to get these little sprites to become poised when the camera comes out; they seem accustomed to photo sessions. These girls are members of the Southeast Iowa Youth Ballet, a company started last year by Bosma and West High freshman Nina Ordman. Today they are posing with the members of their company to promote their first ballet performance, *Sleeping Beauty*.

But why, with all the effective dance programs in Iowa City, would two high school girls want to start their own company, let alone perform in and direct a ballet by themselves?

"There are many youth arts, but youth ballet doesn't get as many chances to perform or as much recognition as theater, for example," Bosma said. "We wanted to give these kids a chance to know what it's like to perform in front of an audience, so last fall we decided to start the company." Little did these girls know that they would have to sacrifice so much time, effort, and money. But these expenses haven't stopped them from doing what they love.

"I simply cannot imagine my life without dance," said Bosma. "It's my creative outlet, and starting this company just makes me feel better about myself."

Saying you have a company is the first step, but getting dancers and funding is the big leap.

"First we had to get kids to join and dance in *Sleeping Beauty*," said Bosma. "We sent fliers to all the dance studios around Iowa City and held auditions for the girls who responded. We now have a total of 21 girls ranging in age from eight to sixteen."

Once they had the dancers, Bosma and Ordman needed a place to practice. They currently train at Terpsichore School of Dance, but can only practice on the weekends because classes are held there during the week.

"Since we don't have much practice time, everyone works really hard in the time that is allowed to us," said Bosma. "The older girls devote their whole weekends."

The key word is devotion, which has also helped the Southeast Iowa Youth Ballet with its financial problems. Bosma and Ordman didn't do any fund-raising before beginning practices for *Sleeping Beauty*, so they found that paying bills was difficult.

"I never knew how hard it was to get money," said Bosma "We have to pay for rehearsal space, costume dry cleaning, and publicity. It's impossible to imagine the hurdles beforehand, but we just have to remember what's important, and that's the dancing."

The lack of funds has taken a toll on the company's first performance. It originally planned to do full-length production of *Sleeping Beauty*, but had difficulty finding a stage that was affordable and fit to dance on. Southeast Iowa Ballet has had to downsize. It's doing only the Prologue and Act I in conjunction with The Terpsichore School of Dance's spring showing, May 16 at Space Place, in North Hall, at UI.

"Cutting down the ballet isn't what we want," said Bosma, "but it's good that we still get to perform. We'll knock their socks off when we perform the entire production in December."

It has to cut corners now, but the company is applying to the Iowa Women's Foundation to get a fiscal agent. The fiscal agent will be able to give them nonprofit status, which will allow donations to The Southeast Iowa Youth Ballet to be tax-deductible. Hopefully, this will make the company more attractive to potential donators.

Bosma's and Ordman's dedication is impressive, but ask anyone involved with the Southeast Iowa Youth Ballet and it's pretty apparent that dance is life.

"Natasha and Nina are a joy to work with and so dedicated," said Jenny MacFarlane '00, a member of the performance group. "Getting this sort of dance experience is rare for teenagers. I have only been dancing two years, but this experience will stay with me for the rest of my life."

Wrap-up

Feature stories have taken on greater importance in journalism. Although they will never completely replace the inverted-pyramid story, they're essential to good journalism.

Feature stories are generally lighter in tone than regular news stories. They usually are timeless, or "evergreen," unless they're news features and are related to a specific, timely news story. Features permit writers to exercise more creativity in language than do regular news stories, but the rules about objectivity and opinion still apply. Writers have latitude but not license.

Features permit creativity in story ideas too. Topics range from historical events to interesting people and everything between. Features occasionally are written in the first person. They may rely on anecdotes.

All people are possible subjects for a personality profile, a feature story that answers the question Who is this person, anyway? Personality profiles are thorough, in-depth stories about one person. They generally focus on experiences, hobbies or interests, or personal qualities that make a person unique.

Many routine stories have been elevated to page-one status through feature treatment. This treatment does not permit opinion, but it allows a different tone, a different total effect.

Features are important for scholastic publications. Often, the news available to a school paper has already been covered by the commercial press. School newspapers therefore frequently have to rely on features to hold the interest of their audience.

On Assignment

INDIVIDUAL ACTIVITIES

1. Write a brief definition of each of these terms:

   "evergreen"   news peg
   feature story   personality profile
   hard news   soft news
   news feature

2. Test your critical thinking. Go through editions of your local newspaper to find three to five feature stories. After reading each one, evaluate the author's purpose in writing it. Who was the intended audience? In what specific ways did the writer try to reach that audience? How might the article have been improved? Write up your response to each feature and clip it to a copy of the feature.

3. Choose an individual below for a personality profile. Interview the person; then plan and write the story.

   ▶ a disk jockey on an "oldies" radio station
   ▶ a faculty member married to another faculty member
   ▶ a person born on February 29
   ▶ a student who has the same name as a famous person
   ▶ the groundskeeper at a pet cemetery
   ▶ a member of the state champion basketball team from 10 years ago
   ▶ a department-store Santa Claus
   ▶ the clerk at the card counter on Valentine's Day
   ▶ a student who has never missed a day of school

4. Choose one of the topics below for a feature story. Research, plan, and write the story.

   ▶ what your second-grade classroom looks like now
   ▶ how your school's mascot and colors were chosen
   ▶ 10 unusual sites on the Internet
   ▶ the most dangerous intersections in your town for motorists
   ▶ unusual pets owned by students at your school
   ▶ the earliest libraries in your city or county
   ▶ Olympic sports little known in the United States
   ▶ careers in the outdoors
   ▶ names movie stars were born with and why they changed them
   ▶ what people's color preferences tell about them

5. Critique one of the On Display features in this chapter. Use the criteria in the Evaluation Checklist on page 274. Make your critique about one page long.

6. Develop your own list of four to six topics for a personality profile or feature story. After discussing your list with your instructor, choose one topic and then outline your story. Your instructor may ask you to do the research and write the story.

7. Write a feature story based on the following information:

   ▶ A poet gave a speech to an assembly of junior English classes.
   ▶ The speech, first in a series, was given Monday.
   ▶ The poet's name is Guillermo LaFarge.
   ▶ He said that he cuts dictionaries apart and randomly pastes the words on paper. He calls the result poetry.
   ▶ "Because I am a poet, everything I do is poetry by definition," he said.
   ▶ He was dressed in a three-piece light-green suit and socks that didn't match.
   ▶ He is from Princeton, New Jersey.
   ▶ After the speech, no one applauded, and LaFarge left the stage angrily.

TEAM ACTIVITY

8. With a team, stage an argument, play, skit, or other activity that lasts no longer than three minutes. Other class members should watch your production, taking notes as needed. When all productions have been performed, discuss them as a class. Then, with your team, write a feature story about all of the productions.

SURF THE NET

9. Research the history of the Pulitzer Prize for feature writing at the Pulitzer web site (www.pulitzer.org) and write a short report on your findings. Address questions such as the following: When was the prize for feature writing first awarded? What generalizations, if any, can be made about the types of features that win prizes? What kinds of features were runners-up for the prize in the last few years?

career profile

Feature Writer

Nancy Stohs

Milwaukee Journal Sentinel food editor Nancy Stohs wants readers to have fun with her section. On a recent day readers were given a story detailing the pros and cons of Jell-O.

"We don't just print recipes or teach people how to cook," she said. "We try to have fun and teach people how to grasp the basics at the same time."

Stohs has worked in a features department since 1979. She has also worked on a city desk, so she knows the differences in operating styles. Working in features, she said, is a way to do what she loves and get paid for it.

"My story is pretty typical," she said. "I like writing, and journalism was a way to make a living and write."

Prior to becoming food editor of the *Milwaukee Journal Sentinel,* she held positions as suburban reporter, education reporter, features reporter, health columnist, features copy editor, and food reporter.

Generally curious by nature, Stohs feels that journalism gives her the opportunity to find out more about what goes on around her.

"Being in newspapers gives you free rein to ask questions," she said. "No other job lets you ask so many questions and get away with it. It's a fun way to do research and do things you wouldn't get the chance to do in other jobs."

It's also a way to communicate information to readers in a lighter vein.

"We're always trying to be creative," she said. "We're always trying to give readers something fun."

At the same time, however, Stohs believes features reporters are considered in a different light by their counterparts on the city desk.

"The traditional division between the newsroom and features has been very slow to change," she said.

Stohs has won awards for packages of stories on illiteracy and for general reporting on nutrition issues.

She graduated from the University of Nebraska in 1976 and joined the *Lakeland* (Florida) *Ledger* in 1977 as an education reporter. She joined the *Milwaukee Journal* in 1979 and in 1994 was named food editor, a position she held when the *Journal* and the *Milwaukee Sentinel* merged into the *Milwaukee Journal Sentinel.*

Stohs opted for a career in features to get away from the pressure of daily deadlines.

"With no daily deadlines there's more time to give more thought to your stories, to make sure everything in the package goes together," she said. "It's more fun. You can have more freedom with your writing style. You can get into people's personality.

"Our goal is to serve the reader in the best possible way; to make sure the photographs tell a story, the headlines go with the story, and all the other elements mesh. Everything has to fit together."

Stohs advises students who are interested in a career in journalism to read a newspaper every day and to ask questions.

"Keep your eyes open," she said. "Look at people differently."

FOLLOW-UP

1. What differences in operating style does Stohs point out between straight-news reporters and feature writers? Do the differences suggest any kind of rivalry between the two types? Discuss ways in which the work done by each type is equally important.

2. Not many years ago most newspapers had women's sections that contained many kinds of soft features. These sections all but disappeared in the 1970s and 1980s. Are they making a comeback now? Trace the history of women's pages in a brief report.

CHAPTER 12

Writing Sports Stories

Outlined against a blue-gray October sky, the Four Horsemen rode again. In dramatic lore they are known as Famine, Pestilence, Destruction and Death. These are only aliases. Their real names are Stuhldreher, Miller, Crowley and Layden. They formed the crest of the South Bend Cyclone before which another fighting Army football team was swept over the precipice at the Polo Grounds yesterday afternoon as 55,000 spectators peered down on the bewildering panorama spread on the green plain below.

What you have just read is perhaps the most famous lead ever written for a sports story. It was written by Grantland Rice, one of the best-known sportswriters of all time. Such a lead would never get past the copy desk on today's streamlined newspaper. Heartless copy editors, trained that a lead should come to the point immediately and concisely, probably would rewrite it to read as follows:

Sports fans want more than an announcement of who won and who lost in sports coverage. For an event such as the Ryder Cup, they want an insightful story about holing the long putt that put the U.S.A. team on top.

NEW YORK—Led by an all-star backfield, Notre Dame yesterday defeated Army at the Polo Grounds before 55,000 fans, _____.

The blank is for the score. Did you notice that Rice did not include the score in his first paragraph? He can be forgiven because he was writing in a different time and for a pretelevision audience. That audience had time to read on to the second paragraph—or the third or fourth—to get the score. Today's audience doesn't.

In fact, today's audience generally doesn't care much about the score as such in their newspapers. By the millions, people watch television—and even record games they're keenly interested in. When they pick up a newspaper a day after the game, the last thing they want is a simple announcement of who won and lost.

Thus, Rice's lead, although outmoded, still has appeal. It's colorful and full of action. If all sports leads had these qualities, there wouldn't be such a split in the attitudes toward sportswriting. As it is, though, there are two schools of thought: One holds that sportswriting is the worst writing in journalism today. The other holds that sportswriting is the best.

When sportswriting is bad, it's awful. When it's good, it can be truly excellent.

283

The action and excitement of a sports event such as this girls' soccer match can be captured in a colorfully written story.

Sportswriting: The Good and the Bad

For the moment, take the view that sportswriting is some of the best writing there is and try to decide why. One reason is that sportswriters, although they must be objective, are allowed more freedom to be partisan. They're for the hometown team, and everyone knows it. Thus they're able to do a bit more than simply describe an event. They can—they must—interpret it. If the coach rants and raves on the sidelines, or if the spectators boo the officials, sportswriters are free to pick words more descriptive than "angry" (the word most likely to be used in a straight-news story). Sportswriters are expected to convey a word picture of exactly what happened, and this inevitably leads to colorful language.

Further, sportswriters are aware that the events they describe may have been witnessed on television by millions of people. These people don't turn to the sports page to read a play-by-play rehash. They want to know how the coaches and players reacted, what kind of pitch Sammy Sosa hit for the winning home run, or what happened in the third quarter when the officials handed out a 15-yard penalty. Long before the rest of America's journalists had recognized the need for interpretive reporting, sportswriters were forced into it. This led them to be more aware of reporting (they had to have something to offer fans who had seen the game) and of writing.

✓ worth taking

Sportswriters' clichés. Here are some of the trite phrases and terms used by lazy sportswriters that you should strive to avoid:

burn the nets

capped the drive

crushed the opposition

forms the nucleus

under the arcs

scoreless deadlock

tally

canto

stanza

hot corner

banged the apple

booted the pigskin

triple threat

run roughshod

pellet

pilfered sacks

raised (or lowered) the curtain on the season

functioned like a well-oiled machine

local gridiron

the tide shifted

the oval

fought an uphill battle

nailed the three

odds-on favorite

two and 0 on the night

circuit clout (home run)

play one game at a time

freshman phenomenon

paydirt (end zone)

hoopsters (members of the basketball team)

thinclads (members of the track team)

sank the shot from three-point land

tanksters (members of the swim team)

cagers (members of the basketball team)

threw a Hail Mary pass

snagged the aerial (caught the pass)

fans had barely settled into their seats

grapplers (members of the wrestling team)

slammed a homer (hit a home run)

counter (period)

on the heels of controversy

welcome additions to the lineup

brilliant in defeat

Sports fans want the stories they read to reflect the tension, the color, the excitement of the event. They demand colorful, lively writing—which in sportwriting, includes the writer's informed perspective. Let the city council reporter question the mayor's wisdom in vetoing the new city budget, and readers will object that opinion belongs on the editorial page. If, however, the football coach decides to go for it on fourth down deep in the team's own territory and the strategy backfires, eager fans expect to find the writer's opinions about the coach's unwise decision in the coverage.

Sports "Slanguage"

Now here's the argument for why sportswriting is often bad. One reason is that sports reporters tend to be the worst overusers of trite expressions. This apparently stems from two facts: sports has developed some perfectly acceptable semislang of its own, and sports events are action events. The former tends to make writers believe that if some slang expressions are permissible (*knockout, blitz, bomb*), so are others. The trouble, however, is distinguishing between the vivid language of sports and the trite language of mediocre sportswriters. The second fact causes many sportswriters to believe that, because sports is so full of action, they must adopt a special kind of English to capture it. The truth is that action will be evident in the story if it's inherent in the event; special language, such as *toed the ball, split the uprights,* or *whacked a four-bagger* merely disguises the action.

Many sportswriters defend such language on the grounds that it's colorful. They call it sports "slanguage" and say there's nothing wrong with it. What they're doing is confusing legitimate sports terminology (*birdie, eagle,* and so on) with the tired clichés of a past era. Sportswriters should be just as conscious of good English as straight-news reporters. Readers of the sports page appreciate plain English and lively verbs as much as anyone else. Sportswriters need figures of speech, but these should be bright and inventive. For instance, this is how columnist Jim Murray once described the University of Southern California football team:

> The USC varsity hits the field like a broken ketchup bottle. They're not a team; they're a horde. You can't beat them; you must dismember them.

Understanding Sports

Before writing one word about a sport, you must know as much as possible about that sport: all the rules, the various strategies, and the reasons behind them. You need to read the sports pages thoroughly, watch sports events on television, perhaps participate in sports. Immerse yourself in the subject matter. If you don't do your homework, your sports-savvy readers will know it, and you will lose credibility.

Above all, get to know the coaches and players—the sources of information and interviews that brighten the coverage. Bare facts of the contest are seldom enough for the curious fans. They want to know how the coaches and athletes feel, what they think of their opposition, and how they view the big event. This means watching practice sessions as well as sports events, to become as familiar as possible with how the players perform and how the coaches think. It also

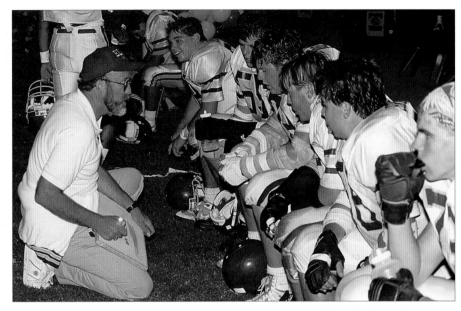

To write compelling sports stories, reporters need to get across the feelings and motivations of coaches and players.

means traveling with the teams. Once you thoroughly understand what you're going to write about, you can plan your coverage.

Sports Coverage

Sports coverage means that you cover winning teams as well as losing teams at your school. The conscientious sports editor doesn't ignore the so-called minor sports—such as gymnastics, swimming, tennis, and golf—either. There is reader interest in these sports, just as there is in freshmen or junior-varsity teams. Even recreational sports, such as snowskiing and skateboarding can be covered on the sports page, although you might want to add a page to your sports section that features these nonschool sports. Certainly, sports activities by both sexes should be covered.

Most schools aim for broad, balanced sports coverage, which may be difficult in schools with many seasonal sports and only two sports pages. One way to achieve this goal is to condense events coverage. Some schools do this by means of sports "shorts," brief articles that capture relevant information and provide a record of events. Other schools incorporate items such as boxes that report scoring records and perhaps a highlight of the event.

Sports Features

The scholastic journalist should generally strive to write sports features, stories not pegged to any specific game or match. Such stories go a long way toward solving the problem most scholastic journalists have: how to provide new information when daily newspapers, radio, and television have already covered specific events.

Sports features are just like any other features except that they're about sports topics. Many sports features take the form of personality profiles of athletes and informative features on topics such as sports technology and training regimens of athletes. The **ON DISPLAY** article on page 289 is an example of an informative and entertaining sports feature.

In addition to sports features, scholastic sportswriters write three types of stories: pregame, game, and postgame, which will be described shortly. Yet even these stories are typically featurized; that is, they are given a feature angle.

The Pregame Story

Because your account of the sports event itself will be old news by the time it gets into print, you need to pay special attention to advance stories, known in sportswriting as pregame stories. This may be the only way you can give readers any information they can't read in the local daily newspaper. To get information for that crucial pregame story, the sports staff will have to organize early, perhaps even before school starts, for fall sports such as football.

Gathering Information on Opposing Teams

The problem is not in getting information about your own team but in finding out about the other team. Letters sent to the coaches of your school's opposing teams asking specific questions almost always produce usable material. The opposing coach usually is glad to tell you how many returning letterholders there are; which of them were all-state or all-city last year; how many starters were lost from last year's team; the size, weight, position, and year in school of everyone on the team; last year's record; and similar information. The coach will also likely cooperate if you ask for an assessment of the team's strengths and weaknesses,

Sports Feature

The Central Times, Naperville Central High School, Naperville, Illinois

Sportuguese baffles fans

by Jocelyn Porzei

Belly back, trap, pinch, dormie, yachtsman, chippy, wing, alley, dink, hook . . .

Baby talk? Senile mumblings? No, simply the jargon used by athletes to describe plays and positions. Fluency in "sportuguese" is a necessary part of communication on and off the field. Senior Brad Mandeville, Varsity football player, said, "It's an easy way of [communicating] without the opposite team knowing what you're doing."

According to the book *The Language of Sport* by Tim Considine, football uses a lot more different play names compared to other sports.

Soccer player junior Scott Vallow agreed but also talked about how the constant communication on the field helps everyone know what's going on. "Being the goalkeeper, you can see who's being marked or remind defenders to mark up so you keep constant communication with the players during the games," Vallow commented.

Along with football and soccer, volleyball uses a lot of plays and formations in its games, but numbers and letters are used to code them.

"It's easy to use one-syllable plays such as colors, letters and numbers because then you have time to call them so the setter knows where to put the ball and who's open," said Varsity volleyball member junior Jayla Ryan.

Although specific language is necessary in games and on the field, it is also helpful off the field during practices. Flag team member junior Mary Kapellen pointed out that "using names for moves and telling the [others] what the timing is for the move help everyone do it faster and quicker and takes up less practice time."

Coaches are primarily responsible for the special jargon. They're the ones who personalize the terms used by athletes. "From high school to college and pro, the techniques are the same, but the names change," explained Varsity football player senior Kyle Buss. "If you've been with a [sport] for a while, you know that year-by-year, the names aren't going to change because you have the same coach. There are some universal terms, but most of it is personal to your team."

Kapellen and Mandeville both added that the coaches will usually name the play after some aspect of the play.

Poms member junior Erin O'Neal summarized that "after the first week, everyone understands everything. It's between the poms, and everybody listens and follows the instructions. All you have to say is leap, jump, and turn!"

although this information will probably be of a general nature. Specific information may come from the sports editor of the school whose team your school is going to play. The coach may be a bit close lipped about the team's chances; the sports editor probably will level with you.

Components of a Pregame Story

Armed with information about the opposing team, you can then turn to your own team to gather material for the pregame story. This story should contain the following information:

- ▶ last year's scores of contests between the two schools
- ▶ condition of athletes (including any injuries)
- ▶ key athletes or starting lineups
- ▶ comparisons of team or individual records
- ▶ comments on styles of play (for example, emphasis on defense or offense)
- ▶ significance of the event in terms of records or future events
- ▶ any history of rivalries between the two schools

It will help the present newspaper staff and future staffs if you compile a complete record of your school's sports history. Old yearbooks and microfilmed copies of the local newspaper on file in the city library should provide the information. Many fans will be interested to learn facts such as that since the rivalry began, Central High School has won 34 games, lost 22, and tied 4 against Tech.

The **ON DISPLAY** article on page 291 is a pregame story that ran at the beginning of girls' basketball season.

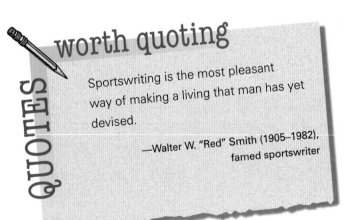

QUOTES

worth quoting

Sportswriting is the most pleasant way of making a living that man has yet devised.

—Walter W. "Red" Smith (1905–1982), famed sportswriter

Pregame Coverage

Pregame coverage should not overlook related spirit activities. The sports page is the proper place for stories about the band's plans for a halftime show, new cheerleaders, pep rallies, and the like. Due to space limitations, these types of stories may be relegated to sports briefs or to periodic sports features.

The Game Story

Covering the sports event is one of the true tests of sportswriters. As a game reporter, you must keep detailed, accurate notes of an event that's happening too fast for the untrained observer to follow. You generally

Pregame Story

The Academy Times, Charles Wright Academy, Tacoma, Washington

Seven seniors jam on court

by Julie Hsu

After three years together, seven senior women begin their final basketball season, and their final chance to win the state title with an undefeated record.

The women's varsity basketball team consists of 11 players, seven of whom are seniors: Molly Wilcox, Heather Meyer, Clara Peck, Laura Lee, Heather Tapp, Sarah Tommervik, and Heather Turner. The majority of the team has played over 90 games together in the last three years.

"After playing with each other for so long, we've learned to play to each other's strengths and avoid our weaknesses," said team member Molly Wilcox.

"Since we all are really motivated and have high expectations for our individual selves, it brings a feeling of unity among the team," said team member Sarah Tommervik.

The team's ultimate goal is to win the state tournament. . . .

"As seniors we've been playing with this team for three years and we all know this is our last chance to meet the goals that have been set," said team member Heather Turner.

The unity and closeness of the team has been formed throughout the years of athletics and friendships that have grown among them. The team believes that this unity is the strongest factor that has aided them through their three years of playing together.

"They love playing basketball with each other, and they do extremely well," said varsity coach Larry Berg.

The players strongly believe in each other's ability, which is apparent in their positive outlook on their teammates. . . .

---

have more comfortable surroundings—the press box—than the fans; make good use of this working space.

Develop a simple, easy-to-read note-taking system; a method of keeping a play-by-play record; and some way to record statistics. (Nothing is more frustrating than searching after the event for a missing fact that you should have written down when it happened.) Watch for turning points in the sports event: the powerful serve that sets up the winning point, the substitute relay runner who pulls ahead to take the lead, the shift from zone to man-to-man defense that bottles up the opponent's top scorer.

As a sports reporter, you're free to analyze the event. If it was a case of your school's offense overpowering the opponent's defense, say so (if

trends and issues

Achieving Gender Equity

What criteria determine which sports get the most media coverage?

In this day and age, there's no question about whether women's sports deserve the same kind of coverage as men's. Attendance at and interest in events such as girls' basketball games is skyrocketing. No scholastic sports page can afford to overlook the trend, for it's no longer a simple matter of trying to be fair to both sexes. These days, fan interest truly drives the coverage.

A highly competitive girls' basketball team will generate a large audience and thus should be given adequate coverage in a school paper.

Determining the appropriate extent of coverage for both sexes, however, can be something of a dilemma. Consider the situation in a big-time college football town such as South Bend, Austin, Lincoln, Tallahassee, College Station, or Columbus. Should every other sports event at a Notre Dame or Nebraska or Ohio State take a back seat to what the football team is doing? Fans of women's sports in such towns often complain about being pushed aside, but should a journalist devote as much coverage to women's archery, played before 50 people, as to football, played before 75,000? Your answer depends on your personal priorities.

Sometimes the situation is reversed. In a state such as Iowa, there has always been intense interest in girls' basketball. The springtime statewide tournament for girls' teams often generates much more interest—and thus more press coverage—than the boys' tournament. Here it might be argued that the boys are getting the short end of the stick. The same situation holds true in Tucson, Arizona, where women's softball often draws larger audiences than men's baseball: The news coverage reflects that fact.

Some would say that the rise in coverage of women's sports began with the Olympics and the star system that Olympic coverage tends to create. Up until 1972, for example, very little attention was paid to women's gymnastics. In that year, however, 17-year-old Russian gymnast Olga Korbut dazzled audiences with her prowess, and coverage of her sport on television increased dramatically. The door then began to open for popular interest in other female athletic events as well: In 1999 the victory of the American women's team in the World Cup of soccer was watched on television by millions throughout the country. Was it fair that the coverage was so extensive and the media hype so intense? This is just the other side of the football coverage question raised earlier. If audience interest in an event is there, sports reporters will write stories about it.

A high school newspaper, of course, is not a commercial enterprise. For a school journalist, the basic goal should be to treat all athletes and all sports equally. Be guided by fairness, not merely by attendance—yet recognize that there will be times when your coverage will be skewed. If a girls' team is winning championships and a boys' team is 5–11, your coverage will have to reflect the situation. Fair or not, there's not much else you can do. A winning team will always be newsworthy.

FOLLOW-UP

1. Track coverage of scholastic sports in the local paper to see how evenhanded it is. Then do the same thing with your school paper. Are there any inequities that need to be addressed?

2. Sports in the 1996 Olympics that were given heavy coverage include men's and women's gymnastics, archery, and women's baseball. How extensive is coverage of these sports today? What sports, if any, have replaced them? Why?

you're sure). If the wet field or the wind played a part, say so. Reiterate the consequences. Tell the fans once more that the winner is the conference champion.

Partisanship

It should be obvious from all this that you will be busy during the sports event. You must watch the contest, the sidelines, the spectators, and the officials, all the while keeping careful, detailed notes. Therefore, you cannot be a cheerleader; you can be partisan, but you can't let this interfere with the job of reporting.

Student reporters have every right to cover events and should resist any attempts by professionals to eject them from the press box. You will find little support, however, from a professional whose notes are soggy from the coffee you spilled as you jumped up exuberantly to cheer your team.

Game Coverage

Given the limited space on the sports pages, sport editors should limit details on game stories because these are old news anyway. Brief accounts, crediting those who scored or who played well, will suffice most of the time.

Comments from athletes about the rigors of training or the stress of competition can add depth to a game story about events such as this hurdle race during a track meet.

If the sports editor decides to run a complete game story even though the local newspaper has already done so, a new angle must be found. The story might, for example, combine a pregame story on an upcoming event with accounts of past events. If the editor can't offer something the local paper didn't, the game story should be featurized.

If you're the reporter assigned to write such a feature, remember not to make the same "mistake" Grantland Rice did. Include the score somewhere; if needed for clarity, tell the name of the event; and make it clear whether the team was the boys' or the girls' and whether it was freshmen, junior-varsity, or varsity.

The Postgame Story

The postgame story could just as easily be called a sideline story, background story, sports interview, or locker-room story. Postgame stories are nearly always featurized. They may include—or focus on—interviews with the players after the event, descriptions of the spectators' actions during the event, historical perspectives on a sport or rivalry, wrap-ups (or reviews) of the season after the last game, and discussions of rule changes.

The postgame story also provides an opportunity to untangle confusing events that occurred during a game—by talking with the official who made the controversial ruling, for instance. In addition, it gives the reporter a chance to update readers on scoring records.

The lead and the tone of postgame stories are usually somewhat different from those of game and pregame stories. The latter are usually written with standard techniques, probably including a summary lead. (The exception would be a game story published two weeks after the game, when a feature angle would be needed.) Postgame stories and other featurized sports stories, on the other hand, follow the same general pattern as feature stories; they should be vivid and colorful, but not overdone.

An effective story about a wrestling tournament may combine straight reporting about the matches with featurized information about players and coaches.

The story opening in the following **ON DISPLAY** sample is a good example of featurized postgame coverage. The outcome of the event is reported—but the story is featurized rather than presented in a straightforward, who-won-and-who-lost fashion. Like many postgame stories, it also includes a wrap-up of the team's record.

Featurized Postgame Story

The Echoes, Abraham Lincoln High School, Council Bluffs, Iowa

Men in Tights

by Jeremy Schnitker

After splitting his head open during a second round match at the Harlan Invitational last Saturday, junior Andy Meyers walked off the mat with blood running down his face. He wondered if he would wrestle again that day.

Before the injury he had won his first round match by pin over Josh Kritenbrink from Tee Jay, who had qualified for State last year. Meyers ended up finishing his second round match, but he lost 7–4 before he was taken to the hospital. He was forced to forfeit the rest of his matches for the day.

Although the rest of the Lynx didn't split their heads open, their day went much like Meyers'. They started off in the first round winning all but two of their matches, but they went on to lose all but two second round matches.

"I thought we did pretty good in the first round, but I could tell that we were all having early season jitters, and we all were nervous, and it showed in the second round," sophomore Dennis Sigafoose said. "But it's nothing that we can't work out towards the end of the season."

As a team, the Lynx placed fifth out of the nine teams in the tournament, but they had to forfeit two weight classes, which hurt their standings.

The grapplers also placed six individuals in the top four: seniors Mike Porter, Aaron Jerome, and Dan Mohatt took first, second and third. Junior Zach Beam and sophomores Nolan Respeliers and Jeremy Schnitker all took fourth.

The fifth place finish was not an accurate reflection of how hard the wrestlers and their coach work. . . .

When analyzing sports stories—be they sports features or pregame, game, or postgame stories—this checklist can be helpful. Use it to evaluate your own stories as well as the stories of others.

EVALUATION CHECKLIST

Sports Story

☑ Does the content of the story reflect support for the local team without being excessively partisan?

☑ If the story is pregame, does it give specific information about the opposition as well as the home team?

☑ For game and postgame stories, has the writer taken essentially a featurized approach?

☑ Is the language fresh and original, with "slanguage" kept to a minimum?

☑ Is the story free from grammatical errors and in accordance with the publication and general AP style?

Sportswriting Today

Most professional sportswriters love their jobs. Harvey Araton, sports columnist for the *New York Times*, said, "One of the more rewarding aspects of being a sports columnist is getting the opportunity to simply ask a question that suddenly, without advance notice, unlocks a door, and allows you to step into a story." This was the case, he said, when he interviewed Roberto Clemente, Jr., son of the late baseball legend. Clemente Sr. died in a plane crash in 1972 on a relief mission to earthquake-torn Nicaragua.

"Clemente Jr. was kind enough to share his childhood memories of the worst day of his life, and the strange premonition he had of his father's death," Araton said. "When the subjects are as giving as Clemente Jr. was that day, there is the tendency to rush home to the computer, to share one's good fortune with the readers."

The **ON DISPLAY** article on page 297 gives another professional's view of some of the pleasures and hazards involved in sportswriting.

A Pro's Opinion: Sportwriters

The Best Seat in the House

— by C. Bickford Lucas

Once upon a time, sportswriters wrote about athletic heroes and heroines and their exploits in grandiose style with the emphasis on adjectives, clichés, and adoration.

Managing editors took a dim view of sports departments, frequently calling them toy shops peopled by undisciplined, unprofessional, beer-guzzling, poker-playing, illiterate journalistic misfits.

The sportswriters took pride in being mavericks, but that's about all they took pride in. Many were unabashed supporters for the schools, teams, or sports they covered. They were often flattered, frequently pampered, and sometimes paid by sports promoters.

And they were envied. Sportswriters were paid to watch events other folks paid to see, and the writers usually had the best seats in the house.

It was exciting and fun.

It still is and probably always will be, even though the business has changed dramatically. Standards for sports departments are as high as or higher than the standards on the city and news desks of most newspapers, particularly the better newspapers.

The excitement of covering a Super Bowl or World Series has to be experienced to be appreciated. For the most part, you are dealing with interesting people doing interesting things. And your audience is virtually guaranteed.

Sometimes the sports reporter must be the bearer of bad tidings. If a writer's team is doing something it shouldn't, the writer must cover—not cover up—the story. The writer's responsibility is to the reader, not the team he or she is covering.

A homer means two things to a sportswriter. One is a four-base hit in baseball. That's okay. The other is a writer who believes in "my team right or wrong." That's not okay, even at the scholastic level. Among responsible journalists there is no reason for hometown bias and boosterism.

That's not to say a writer can or must be totally impersonal. Writers are not made of plastic. It's difficult not to have feelings about teams or individuals you deal with on a regular basis.

A sportswriter without emotions will write colorless, dull stories. But the writer's feelings should not be apparent to the reader. Cheering in the press box is unacceptable.

The positives of being a sportswriter far outweigh the negatives, but students considering this line of work should be aware of the pitfalls.

It is hard work, and the hours can be devastating. Forget weekends—that's when many sports events take place. Forget nights—even baseball usually is played at night these days.

It puts a strain on family life, primarily because of the hours and travel time. Some sportswriters on larger newspapers spend almost as much time on the road as they spend at home. It's a nice way to see the country or the world (with your employer paying the way), but it can create havoc with your family or social life.

An increasing number of athletes are refusing interviews. Some coaches and players verbally, and sometimes physically, abuse writers.

In spite of the recognition and visibility, many sportswriters lead lonely lives. There are lots of parties and press conferences, and hobnobbing with celebrities can be fun, but it's tough to socialize with athletes who may earn more in a week than you earn in a year.

But there is camaraderie in the profession, and the majority of the athletes, coaches, and owners are decent, friendly people. The problem is getting too close. It is difficult to write a story that might cost a friend a job or cause embarrassment. But sometimes it must be done if the writer is to retain credibility.

To be successful, a writer must be enthusiastic, dedicated, devoted, tireless, ethical, imaginative, resourceful, inquisitive, stubborn, flexible, fairminded, thick-skinned, knowledgeable and, above all, accurate. Lazy people looking for an easy way into the stadium need not apply.

Lucas was sports editor of the Denver Post *for 14 years.*

Wrap-up

Two schools of thought about sportswriting exist: One says sportswriting is the best writing in journalism; the other says it's the worst. It can be both. When it's bad, it's awful. When it's good, it's excellent.

Some sportswriters overuse trite expressions such as *tally* for *points* and *cagers* for *basketball players.* The language of sports has color built into it, so there's no need for clichés.

Sports stories often need interpretation, and occasionally judgments can be made by writers to provide this interpretation. Readers want sports stories to reflect the tension, color, and excitement of the contests.

Careful planning is needed for effective and balanced sports coverage. To achieve broad coverage in limited space, some schools condense sports coverage and incorporate items such as boxes that report scoring records.

Few scholastic publications can compete in timeliness with daily newspapers or radio and TV broadcasts. Most sports coverage should therefore be sports features or featurized sports stories (those with a feature angle) because who won or lost is already known.

Student journalists need to develop different angles and approaches, often emphasizing advance stories of sports contests. For these stories and others, schools may exchange information from the coaches or writers at other schools. Good records need to be kept to aid future staff members.

Scholastic journalists follow professional rules and do not cheer in the press box. They keep busy tracking the event, looking for key plays or turning points. Sports stories should be vivid and colorful but not overdone. Open partisanship for one team can damage credibility.

Without sportswriters there would be no record of the grand achievements of athletes, but the work can be difficult and demanding, requiring odd work hours and a great deal of travel. Coaches and players are not always cooperative with the press, particularly after defeats. Despite the demands, most professional sportswriters love their jobs.

On Assignment

INDIVIDUAL ACTIVITIES

1. Write a brief definition of each of these terms:

featurize   pregame story
game story   "slanguage"
postgame story

2. Rewrite the following cliché-filled football story to eliminate trite expressions. *Note:* Not all of the sports expressions are incorrect. Some are legitimate, colorful language of the sport.

Tigers Conquer Cougars
by Josh Rohl

The Trafton High School Tigers clawed their way to the Intercity League football championship Friday with a 14–0 shellacking of the Villa Park Cougars—who played more like kittens.

Playing under the arcs at the local gridiron, the Tigers broke a scoreless deadlock late in the second stanza when quarterback Tommie James threw a Hail Mary pass to wide receiver Corey Campbell, who snagged the aerial for 65 yards and a waltz into paydirt for the tally. Kicker Carlos Sanchez split the uprights. The Tigers took a 7–0 lead into the clubhouse at the intermission.

In the second half the Cougars mounted an aerial attack but it was thwarted by the Tigers' D. Playing out of a 3–4 alignment, the Trafton defenders tagged Cougar mailcarriers for 46 negative yards in the third canto alone.

Meanwhile, James nixed the Tigers' pro set offense with plays out of the I to take Trafton into the red zone three times in the second half. Tiger gridders were able to punch the pigskin into paydirt only once, but that was enough.

Triple threat I-back Dave Williams brought down the curtain on the season with a six-yard scamper into the promised land on a counter play as time ran out in the fourth chapter. Sanchez kicked the extra point.

Williams and James return for their senior season next year, thus forming the nucleus of what should be another well-oiled Tiger machine.

3. Watch a college or professional sports event on television. Make notes of the turning points, the major strategies, the major errors, the star players. Then clip an article about the event from the local paper. Write an essay comparing your list of key elements to those that appear in the paper. What may account for the differences?

4. Test your critical thinking. Assume you know that a member of your school team is ineligible, perhaps for academic reasons or because he or she is too old. The player is a star whose loss would be critical to the team. Should you run a story? Ask the coaches what they think. Write an essay on your position. Does your code of ethics affect your position?

5. Attend your school's major sports event this week and write a feature story about all that happens at the event: the cheerleaders, the band, the crowd, the weather, the excitement, the half-time show, and so on. Do not write about the game itself.

6. Write a story about a school sport with which you are unfamiliar. Choose an upcoming event; then, to become more knowledgeable about the sport, interview the coach and players, observe a practice, and watch an actual game. Read others' stories covering the sport. Write your story and check it with the coach or one of the players for accuracy.

7. Write a one-page critique on one of the On Display articles in the chapter. What makes the article good? What could make it better?

8. Exchange sports stories with another student. Edit each other's writing to make it more lively, exciting, and immediate. Try to make readers feel that they were in the stands participating in the event.

TEAM ACTIVITIES

9. Make a list of so-called minor sports. Each team should select one of the sports, and each team member should identify and write at least one story about it. Make sure the stories explain key parts of the game: scoring, rules, terminology. Include comments from coaches and players. Keep the completed stories for use in a later chapter.

10. Have each team member survey five students on the importance of sports in a scholastic setting. How many students attend sports events? What reasons are given by those who don't? Are sports overemphasized? Do they cost too much? Do athletes' grades suffer because of the time spent at practice and traveling to events? Are boys' and girls' sports financed equally? Compile all the answers into one in-depth story.

SURF THE NET

11. Look for web sites dealing with one or two sports your paper regularly reports on. Bookmark any that you think will provide useful information for the articles you write. Summarize your findings for the class.

career profile

Sports Reporter

Gender and ethnic changes in newsrooms across the country may be best reflected by the increasing number of women moving into the traditionally all-male bastion of sports news.

"More and more African Americans and females are in the business," says Valerie Lister. "We're always going to be challenged. Women aren't supposed to know anything about sports. And racism is a part of society."

Lister joined the staff of *USA Today* in January 1988. She feels that today, when the number of papers is on the decline, the sooner a young person gets started the better. "If you want to go into this business, if you are serious about it, start now," Lister said. "Read and write as much as you can and find a mentor who will help you."

Although she is not trying to discourage people, Lister is realistic. At *USA Today,* as at other papers, minority representation has fallen second to making a profit. Lister encourages students who are serious to apply for any and all scholarships and internships they can find.

Journalism wasn't always Lister's goal. She originally studied civil engineering at the University of Texas at El Paso. "I flunked pre-calculus," she said. "That's when I realized I wasn't going to be an engineer."

She began looking into public relations as a career until a professor read some of

Valerie Lister

her work and convinced her to go into print journalism.

With no high school newspaper experience and only one semester on her college paper, Lister had to work extra hard.

"Most of what you need to know you learn on the job," she said. "You have to expect to start small and work your way up."

Her chance to join *USA Today* came while she was at the *Pensacola* (Florida) *News Journal.* Both publications belong to the Gannett Newspapers group, which brings up journalists from its local publications for four-month training programs with *USA Today.* Lister was one of those brought up.

Coming from a small paper and being an African-American female sportswriter, Lister says she thought she would be "pigeonholed into doing little things."

"It was not as bad as I thought it would be. I was just surprised at how much freedom I was given," she said.

Talking to other writers and reading the newspaper helped her learn more about *USA Today*'s terse writing style.

"I can see now a lot of excess stuff you really don't need. You can be informative in a short space. It's a challenge."

She also has been challenged by the competition and by the needling she sometimes faces as a female sportswriter.

Her interest in sports started when she was a child. Because her father didn't get his first son for several years, she says, she became his "surrogate son." She remembers going to many Atlanta Braves games with him. Even though that changed after her brother was born, the love of sports was ingrained in her.

"Don't give up," Lister advises women aspiring to be sportswriters. "Hang with it. This is not an easy profession."

FOLLOW-UP

1. Do some research on the history of women who cover men's sports. Report your findings to the class.
2. What are some differences between sports coverage in a national paper such as *USA Today* and a local paper? Consider both amount and type of coverage.

CHAPTER 13

Writing for the Editorial Page

KEY CONCEPTS

After reading this chapter, you will

▶ understand the opinion function of a newspaper and the various ways in which it is expressed

▶ know how to write effective editorials for a variety of purposes

▶ understand the various types of columns

▶ be able to write reviews of products and performances

▶ understand the functions of other elements on the editorial page

The newspaper editorial is often referred to as "the voice of the paper." It is up to the staff to make sure this description is accurate, which is no simple task. The editorial page is the only part of the paper that focuses completely on subjective writing—that is, writing that's not necessarily impartial but instead expresses a point of view.

Everyone has opinions. The newspaper, when it expresses its opinions—or the radio or television station that offers opinion features and editorial voices—amplifies its voice by the number of its readers or listeners. When an editorial writer speaks or writes, therefore, the responsibility weighing on his or her expression is extremely heavy. Editorials have the ability to make or break a project or program, to affect the amount of acceptance given a new policy, or to lead to changes in existing policy. Such a degree of influence cannot be taken lightly.

Editorials have the power to affect changes in our society. School papers often tackle controversial topics, such as animal rights, in editorials.

In the past, student editors were often told they should not editorialize on curriculum, athletics, or school board decisions, or such issues outside the school as politics and the environment. Today, however, student journalists write about almost any issue of interest or importance to their readers. The list of topics on page 208, suggested as possible subjects for in-depth articles, could certainly also be considered as possible editorial topics.

Research is the first essential step in writing a good editorial. Some of that research may include direct interviews with people knowledgeable about the issue. Using these people's quotes as part of the editorial adds depth and credibility, as well as providing alternative opinions. Other research information may come from surveys and opinion studies, either conducted in the school or done by research firms. Some of these larger studies are available through on-line databases. Other on-line resources, such as newspapers, general and specialty publications, and government information files, can aid in the search for background information.

As an editorial writer, the journalist should first become immersed in all available information on the subject. Only when a position has been reached, and the research completed to support it, should

303

the editorial be written. Once you have written the editorial, let it sit overnight if you can. Take a look at it the next day—you may see the need to start over or find that some critical information has been left out.

Functions of Editorials

Editorials serve a variety of functions. For example, there are editorials that explain, persuade, answer criticism or a question, express a warning or caution, criticize, entertain, praise, or provide leadership on a subject. A brief discussion of each of these functions follows. An editorial can also be a blend of types: It can praise the board of education for developing new guidelines for graduation but criticize how they're being implemented, while offering constructive solutions to the problems.

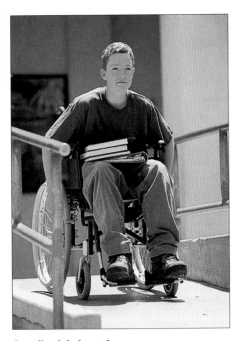

An editorial about the need for better handicapped access in a school may involve explanation as well as persuasion.

Editorials That Explain

A new policy on graduation requirements may have been issued over the summer. Your staff feels the system deserves clarification and an expression of support. Naturally, your paper probably will cover the policy in a news story. That writer is reporting the news, however, not commenting on it. An editorial is the place for comment.

The editorial in the **ON DISPLAY** sample on page 305 explains some of the problems that physically disabled students face in a school, as well as the costs of renovations.

Editorials That Persuade

There are many issues within and outside the student world that require persuasive, responsible voices in order to help readers reach valid resolutions. Maybe your school has just been forced to close the student lounge area because of the mess continually left by students using it. Your editorial might try to persuade the school to reopen the lounge by spelling out guidelines for supervising what goes on there through student service clubs.

Editorial That Explains

Arlingtonian, Upper Arlington High School, Columbus, Ohio

Building needs modifications

In this school, physically disabled students and faculty face challenges most people overlook. Although school officials say the high school attempts to accommodate people with special physical needs, it does not exceed the minimum standards, as would be the Arlington norm.

Whether struggling to open a heavy door, trying to tear a paper towel from a dispenser too high on the wall, or attending a school event without a convenient place to sit, some students and teachers have noticed that high school does not always meet the needs of the physically disabled.

School officials claim not enough money is allotted in each annual budget to fix all of the problems physically disabled people face. If the district would grant the high school enough money, however, some changes could be made to greatly improve the quality of school life for the physically disabled.

To begin the renovations, the high school should lower paper towel dispensers in the restrooms. This will benefit not only the physically disabled, but other students and faculty who cannot easily reach the dispensers. According to the Upper Arlington Accessibility Study Handbook, compiled in May 1994, the district would need to pay approximately $100 for this change.

Unfortunately, other corrections are more expensive, and officials say the high school does not have ready access to large amounts of money.

Providing both gymnasiums, the stadium, the Little Theater and the auditorium with specific wheelchair areas for the physically disabled is one example of costly change. The Accessibility Handbook states this cost at an estimated $5,000. This expense could be achieved, though, by renovating the areas over a selected number of years.

Other needed changes in accessibility for the physically disabled included adding "accessible drinking fountains ($1,800), modifications of one female and one male second floor restroom for the handicapped ($2,400) and volume control for the high school's public telephones ($1,000)."

The physically disabled students and faculty deserve a school which offers them the conveniences most others already take for granted. The district needs to create an annual budget which allows for specific amounts of money to be set aside for these changes, which will enable the physically disabled to learn in an environment of freedom and opportunity.

The persuasive editorial in the **ON DISPLAY** sample on page 306 gives several specific reasons to make its case in favor of a standard academic policy.

Editorial That Persuades

Beak 'n Eye, West High School, Davenport, Iowa

Academic policy should be adopted by the state

The academic policy set for Davenport athletes requiring them to maintain a "C" average and fail no classes has been a successful one, and should become a statewide policy.

The current statewide policy, which requires students to pass four classes the semester before they are to compete, is not strict enough. The State Board of Education is considering raising the standard to a 2.0 grade point average. Not only does the Davenport policy enforce good study habits and self-discipline, but making Davenport schools the only schools under the policy is unfair to Davenport athletes.

This policy enforces good study habits and self-discipline, as well as giving the athletes a little extra motivation to do well academically. Making them put their studies above their extra-curricular activities is a lesson athletes will need to learn as they leave high school and fend for themselves in the real world. Without this policy, many athletes would never learn the self-discipline it takes to become successful off the field.

The whole state would surely benefit from such a policy, and a statewide policy would also ensure equality to all schools competing against each other. Under the present system, however, Davenport athletes are held to higher academic standards than their competition. Someone may be competing against them that would not be eligible under their requirements. We obviously need to establish a level playing field at least in the MAC conference, if not statewide.

Some people fear that such a policy would cause some students to drop out of school or their sports altogether. However, no student has dropped out of school in Davenport as a result of the policy, and there have been many cases of students raising their grades to comply with the policy.

Making athletes keep their grades up before they can participate in interscholastic competition is a good idea because it makes student athletes have their priorities in the right order. The policy adopted by the Davenport school district has been successful, and a similar policy should be adopted statewide to ensure fairness to all competitors.

Editorials That Answer

Suppose that there has been criticism about the conduct of your student delegation at a recent convention. Your job may be to answer that criticism in the form of a defense. If the situations described are true, you may choose instead to answer the criticism with facts and admissions, along with an apology if appropriate.

Editorials That Warn

An alert staff can anticipate problems that lie ahead. (An early warning, for example, might have kept open that student lounge mentioned earlier.) Your reporters should know what's going on around the school or in the community and issue warnings when appropriate. The warning might be a strong one, like a red stoplight, or a mild one, like a yellow caution light.

Editorials That Criticize

Sometimes editorials that criticize the actions of others are appropriate. Writers of critical editorials must remember, however, that the editorial is the voice of the newspaper; therefore, they have a special responsibility to be constructive. If editors aren't able to offer solutions to the actions they criticize, the newspaper will soon lose the respect of its readers. If, for example, the school calendar being considered by the board of education is deemed faulty, the writer should suggest constructive solutions to remedy the problem. Before rushing to write, however, he or she should be sure to understand fully the reasoning behind the proposed changes. Such an understanding could make the criticism invalid. In addition, editorials of criticism should on the issue at hand, not on the personalities involved.

As the voice of the newspaper, an editorial can have considerable influence on its audience. Therefore, even critical editorials should also propose constructive solutions.

Editorial That Criticizes

The Cavalcade, W. T. Woodson High School, Fairfax, Virginia

ADVISORY PERIODS: *Success depends on the changing of attitudes*

This seems to be the year for confusion, since students are being hit with new changes before they have the chance to adjust to the last ones. While most of these changes have gone smoothly, the new advisory period in particular is presenting problems.

In theory, the advisory period is supposed to be a forum for students to connect with their teachers and peers and discuss issues, but that's in theory only. Teachers lecture from a tightly scripted schedule handed down to them, and students either skip the period or fall asleep in class. Something needs to be done about this.

To begin with, the class as a whole should be less structured. As it stands, teachers have a set agenda they can't deviate from, and students have no input. A looser period along the lines of the hugely successful racism seminar last spring would stir more student interest/participation. That activity was popular because of its meaty subject. This year we get to fill out time charts and name different parts of the school. No comparison.

The attitudes of some of the teachers involved need work also. Students are complaining that their teachers are distant or uninterested. These teachers should remember that for this one special period they are more counselor-mediators than teachers. Teachers who don't have an active interest in communicating with their students shouldn't take part in the advisory activity, since students will return indifference with indifference.

We students aren't saints either. Most of us tend to dismiss the period out of hand, which diminishes the class atmosphere. We should be more open to the period and try to make constructive changes instead of griping, and parents shouldn't encourage us by excusing us for skipping, either.

As a concept, the advisory period is fresh and has the potential to revitalize Woodson's student-teacher relations, but that's not going to happen unless we try.

Editorial writers have a journalistic responsibility to balance criticism with suggested solutions or alternative courses of action. Notice how the editorial in the **ON DISPLAY** sample above criticizes both teachers' and students' handling of a new advisory period but, at the same time, offers ways that the situation can be remedied.

Editorials That Entertain

Some issues are just not worth handling with heavy comment or criticism. In such cases, a useful approach may be to create a little humor through an entertaining editorial. Perhaps there was a humorous incident relating to a computer foul-up when your grade reports were issued: 50 student identification numbers got jumbled, and a lot of failures appeared where there should have been passing grades or even A's. You can reconstruct the untangling, report other people's reactions, and comment lightly on the computer age.

Entertaining editorials are not easy to write, but they're rewarding. You may find some good topics in fads and fashions, dating traditions, or the mountain of forms needed to change classes.

Editorials That Praise

Don't forget that you can issue words of praise and congratulations through editorials. When a person or group does something worthy of praise, pass it on, as in the following **ON DISPLAY** example.

Editorial That Praises
Black & White, Walt Whitman High School, Bethesda, Maryland

Recycling Revamped

By taking the steps necessary to establish an effective and well-organized recycling program in county schools, MCPS has made overwhelming improvements over the volunteer and experimental recycling programs formerly done on an individual school basis.

The addition of nine recyclable items and the increased reliability of MCPS' maintenance are significant advances in the county recycling program.

Under a new county mandate, beginning Nov. 1, schools will be required to recycle aluminum cans, newspapers, both white and mixed-color paper, steel cans, glass bottles and jars, corrugated cardboard, plastic containers, polystyrene and grass trimmings. This is an enormous advancement from recycling only white paper and grass, as Whitman has done in past years.

Whitman's former recycling program, sponsored by the SGA, was not maintained on a frequent basis. Paper was taken out for recycling only once a week, a responsibility left to the students, many of whom used it as an opportunity to miss class. Under the new county program, however, the material to be recycled will be picked up two to three times a week by a private recycling company, ensuring that the program will be well-maintained.

Additionally, a new recycling curriculum will be introduced in elementary schools in January, teaching younger students to think of recycling as an effective and necessary measure in preserving the environment. Students in kindergarten through fifth grade will be taught that recycling is something to be taken seriously, and teaching them to recycle early on will ensure that they continue the practice in the future.

MCPS has set a precedent in its efforts to organize and maintain an effective recycling program in county schools. Its attempts to expand and sustain productive recycling programs in all schools, and its foresight in educating a younger generation on the benefits and practicality of recycling should be used as a model for other area school systems.

Editorials That Lead

Since a newspaper can magnify its voice and opinion greatly, it can become a force for change. Many community newspapers have started the wheels turning to recall local politicians, establish commissions or study committees, get schools built or streets beautified. School newspapers can have a similar effect within their own communities. Granted, there may be obstacles such as budget limitations. Nevertheless, student bodies have furnished their own lounges, built their own student centers, provided funds to build Peace Corps schools, established special scholarship funds, initiated or changed laws, and accomplished many other things on their own. Many newspapers have brought together boards, parents, students, and community members to achieve goals. A newspaper that fulfills the leadership role wisely through its editorials will find itself widely respected.

Giving praise for a job well done, such as the development of an effective recycling program, is a legitimate editorial function. An editorial may even lead students to form such a program.

Editorials That Briefly Comment

Finally, in a number of situations opinion may be limited but in need of expression. Many editors will write an occasional "potpourri" editorial in which they comment briefly on a wide variety of subjects. They may commend the freshmen for their excellent clean-up project, the volleyball team for its sportsmanship, the school board or trustees for the new science facilities, and a scholarship winner for his or her academic achievements.

Selecting Editorial Topics

An editorial board often chooses the topics for editorials and who will write them. A typical editorial board includes the adviser, the managing editor, subeditors, the business manager, and the design editor. Sometimes it includes the entire staff. The editorial board not only decides the newspaper's official opinion on issues but also makes decisions about the content of the rest of the editorial pages.

In selecting editorial subjects, choose those important to your readers. Readers are not as likely to care about ecology in Australia as about significant changes in graduation requirements or pollutants recently dumped into the local river. Just as in a news story, proximity and the other elements of news play an important role in determining editorial subjects. If there isn't enough time to write a good editorial, wait until the next issue or don't write one.

If you select controversial subjects, don't be afraid to ask for outside opinions or criticism on the editorial before it is published. Your letters-to-the-editor column will offer the opposition a chance to reply. Be sure your editorial can withstand such criticism without the need for a battle of "can you top this?" with counterletters and editorials.

Writing the Editorial

An editorial is only slightly different from a news story as far as the writing goes. Research your topic; then write a clear, concise, simply worded editorial. Remember that editorials are not written in the first-person singular; never use the pronouns *I, me,* or *my,* but do use *we* . You can also use *you,* but this can cause an editorial to sound "preachy." Develop an informal approach. An editorial should be read as a conversation between two people, the writer and the reader.

Most editorials average 200–500 words, seldom longer. The idea is to reach your readers quickly, to grab their attention about an important issue. After getting readers' attention, you want to carry them with you—smoothly, logically, and consistently—so they begin to think seriously about the issue you're presenting.

Generally you can divide an editorial into three or four parts. Although other organizations are possible, the following usually works well:

- ▶ **Introduction.** Give a brief statement of background concerning the editorial topic. Don't assume your readers already know the basis for your comment.
- ▶ **Reaction.** Explain the position of the editorial and your newspaper.
- ▶ **Details.** Provide support for the position you're taking.
- ▶ **Conclusion.** Comment on recommended solutions, alternatives, and direction, and restate the paper's position.

Introduction

In the introduction, state, as briefly as possible, the background needed for the editorial:

> The student council voted unanimously last week to close the student lounge because it was so filthy. Trash from lunches and notebooks was strewn on tables and floors. Council members had placed warning signs in the lounge for the past few weeks, but they were generally ignored.

This introduction provides a brief history leading to an action. You and your readers are starting off together.

Reaction

Next comes the reaction. You set the reader up to receive your opinion. Continuing the preceding example:

> The council action was justified and necessary. Not only does the lounge require time and effort to clean but it reflects on the school and how students feel about it.

Details

The reader knows your opinion, but you aren't finished. You now go into details that support your reaction and lead to a conclusion. Here, especially if there are strong opinions on the topic, you should acknowledge other views and demonstrate how your idea is preferable:

> The situation became evident several weeks ago when council member Stephen Smith urged the council to establish lounge clean-up patrols. The council responded by appealing to the students' sense of pride, especially those who use the lounge. Signs were posted throughout the school in an effort to capitalize on this "spirit."

TIPS *worth taking* ✔

Effective Editorials. Writers who fulfill the following criteria will generally produce successful editorials:

▶ Be fair.

▶ Be brief.

▶ Do your research.

▶ Come to the point quickly.

▶ Base opinions on fact.

▶ Be sincere.

▶ Don't take yourself too seriously.

▶ Avoid gossip and hearsay.

▶ Admit errors when you have been wrong.

▶ Don't preach; persuade.

Last week, Dr. Jane Robertson, student activities advisor, made an appeal at the honors convocation for students to clean up their mess in the lounge.

All of these efforts and appeals were fruitless. The lounge is an eyesore. We cannot take pride in such a situation. A picture appearing with a story on the closing of the lounge appears (on page one) in this issue. We are sure you will agree—it is a mess.

Conclusion

You have established some background, expanding and repeating in some cases what you briefly mentioned in the introduction. Now conclude your editorial. You may end by criticizing the student body or by applauding the council's decision to take strong action. You may make an effort to lead, compromise, or appeal for a second chance. You may want to offer several alternatives and leave the options up to the council or the student body:

The council should conduct an open forum next week concerning the problem to seek student suggestions on how the lounge might be reopened and kept clean. Among the solutions students and council members might consider are student clean-up patrols, as recommended several weeks ago by council member Smith. It might be possible for several organizations to volunteer for a week of clean-up duty, spreading the job around and making more people aware of the problem.

The decision to close the lounge was right. Now it's time for the council, the administration, and the students to seek solutions that will permit reopening the lounge as soon as possible.

In writing editorials you will find that not all subjects fit into this formula. All four basic elements may be present, but they may be in a different order or require a different emphasis. In some cases, for example, the writer may use much of the editorial to explain a policy and may react only at the end; however, the editorial can still be effectively constructed.

Making Your Point Clear

When you're finished writing, ask yourself whether you can summarize the entire point of your editorial in one or two sentences. If not, you had better start over or forget it, because you have missed the point—and your readers will miss it too. Ask another staff member to read the editorial and write a one-sentence summary. Limit yourself to making just that one essential point.

The following checklist will help you in evaluating your own editorials and those written by others.

EVALUATION CHECKLIST

Editorial

☑ Is the topic a suitable one to take a stand on?

☑ Are there enough specific points to make about that topic?

☑ Does the editorial have a clear purpose, and is that purpose established early in the piece?

☑ Does the editorial follow the introduction-reaction-details-conclusion organization or some other reasonable format?

☑ Is the editorial free from grammatical errors and in accordance with the publication and general AP style?

Other Elements on the Editorial Page

In addition to the editorial, a number of other components may appear on the editorial page. These include columns, reviews, letters to the editor, editorial cartoons, and opinion features. Sometimes so many of these components are included that the editorial "page" in fact runs to two or more pages.

Editorial pages also carry the newspaper masthead. This lists the paper's staff adviser and sometimes the principal, the school address, phone, electronic mail address, fax number, and the names and positions of staff members. The masthead is often headlined with a miniature version of the paper's nameplate. In addition, some newspapers print their editorial policy and their policy on letters to the editor. (For a sample editorial policy, see page 544 of the Appendix.)

The **ON DISPLAY** sample on page 315 shows some of the elements that may appear on an editorial page.

ON DISPLAY

Editorial Page

The A-Blast, Annandale High School, Annandale, Virginia

Editorial pages can contain a number of elements besides editorials and the paper's masthead. This page includes columns, letters to the editor, and a random-opinion poll.

Opinion 3

Is honesty the best policy? I think so.

Public figures are often chastised for being human, but one woman should be commended

It all started with President Clinton admitting at the outset of his first term as president that he smoked marijuana when he was younger.

The public was outraged. How could a man so smart, so revered, and so popular have done something like that? The president stood firm in his position that he had made a mistake and thought using drugs was wrong. His only counter-argument—he promised us he didn't inhale.

Secrets and Lies

This scene was a familiar one when at last week's Kids Against Drugs And Alcohol (KADA) festival which was held at our school; an adult in an esteemed position was asked a challenging question.

Weekend anchor Debbie Lockhart of NBC Channel 4, while speaking to a crowd of students of all ages from the Annandale community about her experiences with drugs and alcohol, was asked by a young boy if she had ever done drugs herself.

Silence fell over the crowd and, for a moment, Lockhart did not quite know what to say. Should she divulge the illegal deeds she had done while an adolescent, or should she put on the guise of a squeaky-clean pillar of the community who never made mistake in her life?

After a few awkward seconds, Lockhart made a difficult decision. She decided to be honest with the children and adults who looked at her as a role model. She told them she had smoked marijuana as a teenager.

Get Out!

Perspectives from

ERIN PERUCCI
Editorials Editor

Oh, no you didn't

As a roar of disapproval and disbelief came from the crowd, Lockhart defended her position by explaining that she had asked her father's permission to try marijuana.

Even though he had consented to the experiment, he made it clear that this was not a good thing to do, and told her that she would not even like it. According to Lockhart, she didn't and never touched the stuff again.

It is most decidedly wrong to use any kind of illegal substance. The president and Ms. Lockhart made a bad decision when they chose to use marijuana, but they should not be chastised for admitting to their wrongdoing and imparting the knowledge and insight they gained from the experience.

Debbie Lockhart put her reputation on the line when she admit-

ted to the community she serves that she had done the unthinkable during her teen years.

This undoubtedly shows that she has a degree of moral character that deserves to be recognized. Many people in the public eye would think of their approval ratings before thinking of integrity and honesty. Lockhart did not and put her goal of bettering the community first.

What's wrong with kids these days?

Drug and alcohol abuse has become more widespread and rampant in these times where children grow up too fast, and are not always taught why these substances are unhealthy. Children learn by example, and when adults cite examples from their lives where they have done wrong and learned from the experience, it is incredibly beneficial.

If Michael Jordan did commercials advocating abstinence from drugs, kids would stop at nothing to be drug free like Mike.

To focus on one event, the KADA festival was an incredible success in informing young children of the dangers of drugs and alcohol, and allowed them to discuss the reasons and ways to be drug free.

And finally, Debbie Lockhart deserves commendation for her honesty and strength of character. Admitting a mistake is not easily done, but this admonition may help some confused kids to make the right decision.

SGA increases activity

With a new advisor, the SGA makes considerable headway

by Jennifer Blahnik
Sports Editor

Two spirit weeks, a scholarship funded by the Winter Ball proceeds, student surveys, sumo wrestling at pep rallies, are just a few of the items the student government can add to its resumé.

This year the SGA has taken strides to increase student involvement in all AHS activities. The student body agrees that this year's student government has been the most involved they have seen at AHS.

In response to the dulling atmosphere around the school building, SGA President Mike Kanach said, "I was kind of bored with school. I figured I would try to spice it up a little."

"They [the SGA] have a greater presence in the school, they're much more active," said sophomore Timur Nowrouz.

In a bold move for next year, the SGA is considering doing away with class elections, and in its place have classroom representatives to diversify the student government.

Moreover, a greater number of students will be able to take an active part in what goes on in their school.

Although an official decision has not been made by the leadership class, this plan would prove to be incredibly beneficial to the ever-diversifying population of AHS.

In addition, the pep rallies, which are held in the beginning of each season, have grown in size and grandeur. At the winter rally, sports teams were allowed to demonstrate some of their abilities. For example, the boys varsity basketball team showed off its dunking talents. And the latest ac-

complishment by the SGA was the addition of the Winter Ball to the usual dance schedule. The proceeds from this occasion are being used to create two $1,000 scholarships for seniors.

The SGA got a boost this year from sponsor Roy Tomlinson. He has offered fresh, new ideas, such as the class murals done during the Homecoming week festivities.

"We've come a long way. The addition of Mr. Tomlinson is another resource, he offers ideas which we may never have thought of before," said Ortiz.

Governing hands

Seniors Sarah Naghdi and Esther Lee put away decorations used during the Winter Ball. The Winter Ball was just one of the new events added by the SGA. *photo by Emily Gardner*

Letters to the Editor

Teacher angered by bathroom smokers

Dear Editor,

I would like to address bathroom etiquette and cleanliness. Each year, I become more appalled at the lack of student concern surrounding an issue that affects all students.

Most students have to visit the bathroom at least once during the school day. What students find in the bathroom would shock most civilized people.

Toilets not flushed, wet toilet paper thrown against the walls, lack of toilet paper, no hot water, smoke filled bathrooms and no doors on the toilet stalls are just some of the many ills that students face.

How long does it take to flush a toilet? Is throwing wet toilet paper around the room a custom of some country I don't know about? Is stopping up sinks and making them overflow really that fun?

I am confident in saying that most of the student population is sick and tired of the bathroom situation at Annandale, but no one is willing to confront the problem.

The entire student body should be embarrassed at their behavior and lack of concern over this issue. Because students use the student bathrooms, bathroom cleanliness should be a *student responsibility*.

Unless students start caring for their school and disciplining themselves, this problem will not go away. Students should tell those who do not follow proper bathroom etiquette, to act grown up and responsible. Adults should

not have to hover around student bathrooms to make sure they act civilized.

I am asking the entire student population to make a concerted effort to improve this horrible situation. For those cigarette smokers, don't smoke in the bathrooms. Everyone should take that extra two seconds to flush the toilet.

For those students who don't know, toilet paper is used for sanitary reasons, not sporting events. And finally, the SGA should address this issue and find answers and solutions to the student body's uncivilized behavior.

—**David Van Vleet**
math teacher

Teacher thanks AHS for support during medical leave

Dear Editor,

Coming back home to Annandale has been just wonderful. I want to take this opportunity to thank all of you for your continuous prayers and the many beautiful plants, cards, letters, books, balloons, calls and visits.

Since my return, every day has been filled with wonderful and caring gestures. My gratitude goes to all of you for not letting me go through this alone.

—**Lillian Arezina**
ESL teacher

Atomic Reactions   *How do you feel about our political conflict with Iraq?*

"I don't think we (the U.S.) should go to war, but if we do, I'll support it. I don't really know anyone it affects, though."
—**David Rey**
freshman

"I have a lot of friends from Iraq, and it puts their families in a difficult position. I don't want anyone to get hurt."
—**Jamie Campbell**
sophomore

"It's not affecting me, but my whole family is in Iraq. I'm not really sure if the U.S. should take action."
—**Alvis Hermes**
junior

"I really don't care. I think we should just take Saddam out because he's becoming a nuisance to the American public."
—**Bobby Wilson**
senior

"I think all sides should be examined before we send anyone to Iraq for war."
—**Valerie Baldwin**
athletic trainer

Columns

An editorial page frequently carries a number of columns written by students—some serious, some amusing. Unlike editorials, which are the voice of the newspaper, these columns, or commentaries, express the personal viewpoints of individual, identified student writers. A column requires the same amount of hard work and research before writing that an editorial does, and columnists must be fair and accurate in the information they use. Columns are often written in an informal, personal style.

Although columnists in major newspapers express their own opinions, few papers run columns by writers with whom they disagree philosophically. For example, a newspaper known for writing editorials that support conservative causes and issues is not too likely to run the editorial views of a nonconservative. This is usually not the case in the student media, where diverse viewpoints are important.

In the **ON DISPLAY** sample on page 317 a student columnist expresses her concerns about the lack of press freedom given to student journalists in her state.

Common Types of Columns

There are as many types of columns as there are prospective writers. With such a variety to choose from, the same type of column need not appear in each issue. Columns usually appear on the editorial pages but may appear elsewhere if topical. A sports column, for example, generally appears in the sports section. Here are some examples of types of columns.

Profile columns. A profile column focuses on an outstanding individual—a student, instructor, or person in the community. The writer discusses the individual's views on current topics and weaves into the column bits of information about him or her: likes and dislikes, postgraduation plans, activities, and community contributions. The column writer can take liberties in drawing conclusions or using opinion-laden phrases that would not appear in a news story or feature (such as *an outstanding sports record, an unsung hero,* or *a sincere concern for people*).

This type of column presents certain problems for which you need to provide solutions. For example, what criteria will be the basis for selecting the students you write about? In a large school the number of candidates for such an honor is considerable. You will receive considerable criticism unless you have firm standards; don't use popularity alone.

Column

Focus, Midland High School, Midland, Michigan

Student freedom of expression vital to future

by Adrian Rogers

When I was in ninth grade, I was allowed to serve as editor for a yearbook and a newspaper, attend Junior Achievement meetings that I could not stand (squeegees and resin owl nite-lites, it turned out, were not for me), produce a district-wide literary magazine, earn straight A's and attend leadership seminars. Other kids with divorced parents and I were allowed to do things like choose between parents, take responsibility for little brothers and sisters and, in some cases, testify in court. And during school, my classmates and I were allowed to listen to AIDS presentations (in graphic detail), view cartoon filmstrips on Mr. Sperm and Ms. Egg (in graphic detail) and hear about each others' sometimes unfortunate weekend adventures (in graphic, gory detail). In ninth grade, we dealt with stuff.

My ninth grade was also the year House Bill 4565, the bill that would restore freedom of the press to high school students, died in the capital, apparently because students weren't mature enough to handle constitutional rights.

The bill was needed because in 1988 freedom of the press for high school newspapers was lost in a Supreme Court case. The Supreme Court ruled that administrators could remove anything from a school publication that they think contradicts the mission of the school. This is called prior review: the principal reviews the stories before the paper is sent to press, and can pull any story.

This made me angry when I was in ninth grade. But it makes me even angrier now, after I have received a top-notch education about a Constitution that barely applies to me at this point. It makes me worried, too, now that I will enter college with the multitudes of other members of my class throughout the state, and very few of us will have practical experience with the rights guaranteed in the Bill of Rights to citizens.

Because the Midland High School administration does not practice prior review, the editorial content of our student newspaper is determined by the editorial board. We are lucky.

But education in the Constitution is distant theory to most students because they are denied any practical application. Our editorial board has faced and succeeded in the challenge of foreseeing consequences of the articles we print and the value and necessity to the entire community of fair reporting and balance of sources. We have learned the importance of the truth, painful and controversial as the truth often is.

That's why it's so disappointing to me when, during journalism conferences and workshops, I hear students from other schools explain that there is no way they could cover the issues being discussed, simply because their administrations would not allow it. Coverage of topics from date rape to ineffective classes is not even considered by many Michigan high school newspaper staffs. This is not because students are incapable of making decisions or taking responsibility for what is printed. The lack of coverage is due to the fact that many school administrators are incapable of "allowing" the Constitutional rights that are preached in classrooms.

Understanding and Recognizing Bias

How evenhanded are reporters in their presentation of issues?

True or False: An editorial, or editorial commentary, is the only place in a newspaper or TV news show where the writer doesn't have to be impartial—in other words, where bias can show. Your answer to a question like this depends not only on how you define bias but on how you view news writers and reporters.

Bias involves slanting information in a way that leads readers or listeners to the conclusion that the presenter wants them to reach. One way bias is expressed is by communicating only information that supports the presenter's opinion. For example, in a biased portrayal of a politician as antienvironment, a reporter would mention only a politician's statements against an environmental policy and ignore those that he or she made in favor of it. Bias can also be conveyed by word choice—for example, by using loaded words such as *misguided* in describing a candidate's stance on a tax issue.

So, does the *New York Times* present biased stories in its news columns? Does CBS News deliberately slant the facts? Some people think so. They point to media studies that show, for example, that the majority of reporters are Democrats and prochoice. They then use this data as evidence that those are the positions these media figures promote in their stories.

Although bias sometimes can occur in news reporting, certain facts should also be considered. First of all, even if reporters do tend to be liberal in their outlook, owners and managers of news media tend generally to be conservative, so a balance is created. Second, just because a reporter holds one political view doesn't mean that he or she cannot give objective coverage to a different point of view. (People whose idea processing was so one-sided wouldn't last long in any business!) Finally, an individual program or publication can't be judged fairly on the basis of one or two selected stories. To be fair and unbiased in your own evaluation of news, you have to take a look at the way a source

Most serious news reporters try hard to write fair, impartial stories. Sometimes, however, bias can creep in through word choice or phrasing.

handles it over a period of time, not just in single, isolated reports.

News programs on radio and television seem particularly susceptible to the bias label. Here, it helps to be aware that different programs have different purposes. A national "nightly news" program is expected to exhibit unbiased reporting in its hard-news stories; but bias is certainly allowed to creep into some of its features.

News commentary programs are a different species altogether. These shows often try to feature a mixture of reporters from across the political spectrum who, like columnists in a newspaper, are not expected to be impartial. You can only determine whether these shows lean toward one side or the other by watching them over a period of time to see whether their coverage ultimately balances out. Don't confuse reporters on these commentary shows with individual talk-show hosts on radio, who have to be considered personalities rather than serious news reporters.

When you read or listen to the news, be alert for bias. You may not find much—and what you do find may be unintentional or only in commentary-type situations. What is important is to not let it stop you from thinking about both sides of an issue as you form your opinions.

FOLLOW-UP

1. Make a list of loaded words that can bias a news presentation. Then, for a two- or three-week period, record uses of such words in the news media.
2. Listen to a news commentary program and try to determine the participants' political stance. Then listen to the same show three more times. How have your views of the politics of the participants changed?

Try to keep trivia out of the column. Focus instead on the subject's views on student activities, the value of being in sports, why he or she has made a particular career choice, or how a teacher contributed to his or her success.

Satirical columns. These are one of the more common types of columns in the student paper. They take a lot of work to be effective. Don't run them unless there's a valid reason. Like an editorial, a satirical column must be able to make its point to the reader. If you write one, be careful to verify any facts you use.

Fashion and fad columns. It is difficult and probably unnecessary to write a column on the changing world of styles very often during the year. An occasional fashion column might be refreshing if it is done with flair and some study of fashion trends. Some publications run columns such as this in special issues containing several fashion-related news features and special advertising.

In-the-clubs columns. A good means for giving credit to clubs or student groups may be a "club" column. In it you write briefly about the activities of various clubs or organizations, urging attendance at groups' dances or other activities and briefly commenting on each. An occasional column of this nature can eliminate several small stories that may be weeks old.

An important note: Don't ignore clubs that have only a few members or ones in which you have no personal interest. It may take more work to come up with comments about the Reptile Lovers' Club than it does to write about the Letter Club, but both clubs deserve coverage.

A clubs column is a good way to cover briefly the activities of various groups or organizations.

Names-in-the-news columns. Another way to wrap up awards and pass out congratulations to officers, groups, or people in or outside your school or the student community is a column about people. Be sure this doesn't degenerate into a gossip column. Never make obscure comments; every reader should be able to understand who and what you're talking about; there should be no inside jokes. Remember that gossip columns reporting all the latest rumors and who had the "wild" party last Saturday have been the reason for some student papers coming under tight supervision by the school or the journalism adviser. Gossip columns can lead to libel lawsuits and can cause serious harm to targeted students. Newspaper columns should be in good taste and in keeping with the canons of responsible journalism.

Question-and-answer columns. You're probably familiar with the "Ann Landers" and "Dear Abby" columns. A question-and-answer column can address student concerns on a number of subjects, such as those related to career or community (for example, How do I enroll in a study-skills program?). Always answer questions carefully and seriously. Be mindful that students are not professional counselors and can be held accountable for advice they give. It's wise therefore to stay away from emotional or legally-sensitive topics.

Other ideas for columns. Look at other student and community newspapers for more ideas, such as hobby columns, sports columns (they're not required to be on the sports page), humorous columns, anecdotal or historical columns, or guest columns—by famous people, other students, alumni, faculty, administrators, or parents.

Use the same approach toward writing any type of column—research, develop your position, write, think, rewrite if necessary, and then publish. When you need to evaluate your own columns or those written by others, use this checklist.

EVALUATION CHECKLIST

Column

- ☑ Does the topic lend itself well to a column?
- ☑ Does the column have a tone—light, serious, humorous, angry—that's appropriate to the subject matter?
- ☑ Are anecdotes or other specific examples included when appropriate to make points?
- ☑ Have all facts—such as names, job titles, and dates—been checked for accuracy?
- ☑ Is the column free from grammatical errors and in accordance with the publication and general AP style?

Reviews

In recent years student newspapers have started to review not only movies and theater performances but also restaurants, web sites, books, music, and computer software and games. Whatever you review, remember that the review should serve to guide and inform your readers, not just serve as a platform for you to complain or rave about an item. Watch performances more than once and use products several times before you formulate final opinions—and support those opinions with specific examples.

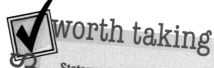

TIPS **worth taking**

Statements about yourself in reviews. How much of yourself should you put into a film review? William Javitz, author of *Understanding Mass Media*, has this to say:

66 When attempting film criticism, especially to an audience that does not know you, making statements about yourself is of limited value. If I tell you that a certain film is 'sickening,' that does not mean that you will find it 'sickening'; you might enjoy the film. . . . A common error is to confuse statements about the film with statements about oneself. 99

Writing Reviews

Several approaches are used to write reviews. These may be used in isolation but are more often used in combination.

Making comparisons. Many reviews require you to make comparisons between one or more products. For example, if you are considering reviewing several local pizza parlors, the focus of the review may be on the quality, flavor, and texture of their crusts and sauces. How do the products differ, if they do? In what ways are the atmosphere of the establishments similar or different? How about the appearance and attitude of the staffs? the other menu items?

Evaluating fulfillment of intended purpose. If you're writing about a new computer game, it may not be necessary to compare it directly with another game. Instead, you may wish to evaluate it on how well it fulfills its intended purpose; that is, on the basis of the excitement in the action it produces, the level of difficulty and challenges it poses, the skill and knowledge needed to play. The evaluation should be based on characteristics that will have meaning to the reader.

Itemizing strengths and weaknesses. You can review the strengths and weaknesses of a product or a performance from a number of directions. For example, if you are reviewing a new CD, you should probably talk about the good and not-so-good tracks on the recording, giving reasons for your opinions. Your comments should address the strengths and weaknesses of the lyrics, musical arrangements, performers' skill, and production quality.

A comprehensive review should evaluate a CD in terms of the artist's entire body of work. It may also compare the CD with recordings made by other artists or groups within the musical category in which it falls.

Reviewing Performances

A review of a film, television production, or play has to tell what the story is about without giving the whole plot away. It may compare the performance to others of its kind and typically evaluates the performance in the following areas:

- ▶ **Acting.** Did the actors play their parts in a believable manner? Were they able to express the emotions that the role required?

- ▶ **Sets.** Were the sets appropriate to the period setting of the production? Did they look realistic? In a stage production using spare and simple sets, how did these sets convey something of the mood, atmosphere, or period of the production?

- ▶ **Dialogue.** Did the dialogue sound realistic for the time and place in which the action was set? Did the lines sound like things people would actually say to each other?

- ▶ **Lighting.** Did the lighting help establish a mood? For a film or television production, were any striking lighting techniques used to convey ideas about characters or situations?

- ▶ **Sound.** Could you hear the lines clearly? If there was background music, how did it add to or detract from the production?

- ▶ **Direction.** Did all the parts of the production work well together? Was the tone consistent? Was it clear that the director knew the story he or she wanted to tell and how most effectively to tell it?

In addition, in film reviews you may want to discuss such elements as editing, camera techniques, and special effects.

The **ON DISPLAY** sample on page 323 focuses mainly on theme—the underlying idea—comparing it with other, similar films.

When you review student products or performances, don't hold them to the same standards as professional ones. Look for good points to go along with any bad points.

Movie Review

Featherduster, Westlake High School, Austin, Texas

War Is Hell: *King of Hearts* Proves There Is More to War Than Violence

BY ZACK JEMISON

Might makes right. Or so we are led to believe. The movies, television shows and books of today are filled with bulked-out men fighting people smaller than themselves and coming up, to no big surprise, the victors. But we still haven't found a film that can be identified as the best war movie. Some contenders might be *Apocalypse Now, Full Metal Jacket* or *Platoon*. However, the most eligible film for this title is also probably the least known about. I'm talking about the French film, *King of Hearts*.

The movie takes place in France during World War One. A German regiment, complete with a young and eager Adolf Hitler, wires a small town to blow up at midnight. All of the villagers evacuate the town, leaving the inhabitants of the local insane asylum to fend for themselves. Charles Plumpick, a Scottish bird expert, is sent in to disarm the explosives and save the town. When he arrives at the scene, the crazies have taken up the various jobs around town where the townspeople left off.

Through his interaction with the then-lunatics, now-villagers, Plumpick discovers the true depth and nature of war. The killing done in wars is senseless as well as useless. There are no winners in these senseless slaughters, only losers.

I think the most powerful scene of the movie is the one in which the lunatics lock themselves into their asylum, subsequently locking all the danger out. We, like the lunatics, sometimes view locked doors as barriers keeping us in or out, depending upon our location. For the lunatics, the door works as a two-way barrier: as their protection from the outside world, as well as the outside world's protection from them.

This cult film examines the extremely touchy subject of war. Along with the film adaptations of the classic anti-war novels *All Quiet on the Western Front* and *Johnny Got His Gun,* I believe that *King of Hearts* should be recognized as a classic by movie-goers. Though similar to these other works in many ways, it differs in a very important vein. The other two plots primarily deal with the effect the war had on the soldier before, during and after the war. *King of Hearts* examines the war from the standpoint of a spectator. The lead characters, instead of going out and actually fighting the war themselves, witness what has happened to the so-called survivors of the war. I especially liked the way that the soldier, in this case Charles Plumpick, was portrayed as the minority.

I wholeheartedly recommend this amazingly touching war movie to anyone. Although it was made in 1966, the ideas presented remain tried and true. While the movie uses subtitles, they don't make this film more difficult to watch. The ideas expressed are visibly liberal, but hey, don't refrain from seeing it just because you're a conservative. Diversity builds character.

Ratings Devices

Ratings devices such as stars or thumbs up–thumbs down may save space and offer a quick way to rate items, but they're no substitute for reviews. You should accompany ratings with written reviews that truly analyze the merits of the product or the performance.

When evaluating your own reviews or those written by others, use this criteria to make sure the review is as good as it can be.

EVALUATION CHECKLIST

Review

☑ Does the review deal with a film, TV show, place, or item with which the writer is clearly familiar?

☑ Does the review explain the basics of the item being reviewed, such as the menu of a restaurant, the plot of a movie, or the rules for a game?

☑ Does the review discuss some of the item's specific strengths and weaknesses, such as good and bad songs on a CD or strong and weak characters in a book?

☑ Does the review make recommendations based on the audience's interests as well as the writer's opinions?

☑ Is the story free from grammatical errors and in accordance with the publication and general AP style?

Letters to the Editor

The editorial page should always contain a place where readers can react to editorial opinions or comment on subjects that concern them. A letter to the editor must be responsible, based on fact, and signed by the writer. The newspaper has an obligation to verify that the person whose name is on a letter actually wrote it. While newspapers allow the use of pen names or initials, all letters should be kept on file for several weeks, whether they're printed or not. If a letter is in bad taste or libelous, you're correct in turning it down. If several letters are received on the same topic, in order to save space, you may select one that's representative and add a note: "We have received several similar letters from . . ."

Editorial Cartoons

Just as a picture is worth a thousand words, one good editorial cartoon may be worth a thousand editorials. An editorial cartoon is typically simple in design, centered on one topic, well drawn, and timely. Usually it relates to a subject or event familiar to readers in their everyday lives. It may stand alone or tie in with a news article elsewhere in the paper or with the lead editorial.

Editorial cartoons often incorporate symbols to represent ideas. A set of scales, for example, typically represents justice. These symbols may be taken from popular culture. A cartoonist may, for example, use Little Red Riding Hood to represent innocence or gullibility. Some general characters may need stereotypic tools or clothing to be properly identified. For example, a construction worker may require a hardhat and a jackhammer.

Editorial cartoons also make frequent use of caricatures, representations of a specific person in which one or more features are exaggerated for comic effect. Before you decide to caricature someone in your school in a cartoon, however, discuss your reasons with your editor.

Editorial cartoonist Steve Kelley, of the *San Diego Union,* says that there are three basic kinds of editorial cartoons:

> ▶ **Cartoon as a symbol.** The cartoon uses an image to represent an attitude, for example, depicting big business as a fat man, swollen with self-importance.
> ▶ **Cartoon as a metaphor.** The cartoon likens one thing to another. School violence, for example, might be portrayed as a snake in the grass, threatening to strike if provoked.
> ▶ **Cartoon as a joke on current events.** The cartoon targets a specific event, for example, an NBA strike in which basketball players earning millions of dollars demand higher wages.

How would you classify the editorial cartoon in the **ON DISPLAY** sample on page 326?

QUOTES worth quoting

A cartoon cannot say, "On the other hand," and it cannot defend itself. It is a frontal assault, a slam dunk, a cluster bomb, a drive-by shooting. It's also a poem, a prayer, a religious experience. It can strike at the heart like a lightning bolt from above and change the way you see and think and feel.

—Doug Marlette, editorial cartoonist at *New York Newsday*

ON DISPLAY

Editorial Cartoon

U-High Midway, University High School, Chicago, Illinois

Editorial cartoons may either stand alone or be related to an editorial or article elsewhere in the paper. This cartoon accompanied an editorial criticizing the teachers' union for opting to continue negotiations rather than taking protest action after being refused a raise.

Karlis Kanderovskis

Random-Opinion Features

Sometimes a paper will want to show opinions on a subject from various people—people not associated with the newspaper staff. The subject can be anything of general interest; often it is the same subject treated else-where in the editorial pages. A typical way to handle this information is to use a roving reporter who asks the same question—for example, What do you think about seniors' rights to choose their own graduation speaker?—of five or six people at random. The views of the people inter-viewed are presented without further comment.

Represent a range of opinions in your poll. If you don't get a range of opinions, ask more people. Choose the opinions that are most interesting.

Strive for equal representation of respondents. You should have a bal-ance of male and female, and represent all grades. Be careful that you don't just poll the most popular or the most outgoing people.

Point-Counterpoint Articles

If you study the editorial pages of leading newspapers, you will see a variety of editorial-page elements. Many newspapers are adopting ways to broaden viewpoints to extend beyond those of the staff and editorial writers. A popular technique is to use a point-counterpoint approach, inviting individuals with opposing views on a topic to express them in side-by-side opinion articles. Going a step further, the paper may then ask four or five people to give a one-paragraph opinion on the same issue, thus ensuring that a variety of viewpoints have been expressed. Often the lead editorial of the newspaper—the newspaper's point of view—addresses the same topic. The reader is served through the variety of opinions expressed and encouraged to look at more than one side of the issue.

Unlike other editorials, point-counterpoint articles must be bylined. Include a lead-in paragraph explaining who the writers are and why they were chosen to represent the two opposing views. If other, briefer views are also included, it should be obvious why those people were chosen. For example, if you're presenting opinions on a proposed plan requiring seniors to pass a state test to graduate, the views of nonseniors (those who will be affected) are expected to be represented.

Finally, make sure guest writers can write. It's a good idea to get their agreement that their copy may be edited as necessary.

Wrap-up

Editorials play an important role in today's media. Along with the opportunity journalists have to express opinions comes the obligation to do the needed research on a subject. You must understand the diverse points of view and background on an issue before presenting the paper's opinion.

Editorials serve a variety of functions. They may explain an issue; try to persuade others to support a viewpoint; respond to statements or positions of others; warn or caution readers, viewers, or listeners about events ahead; entertain; provide leadership by initiating or encouraging action; or offer brief comments on an action or event. One editorial may serve several functions.

One good way to organize an editorial is to begin with an introduction to ensure that the audience understands the background of your subject. Then, clearly state your position. Following that, provide clear and concise detail or background materials that strongly support that position, and address directly or indirectly the possible positions of others. Conclude your editorial by restating your position and spelling out your recommendations or solutions.

Newspaper editorial pages may consist of a number of elements in addition to editorials: columns, reviews, editorial cartoons, and point-counterpoint articles expressing diverse views on a specific subject. Brief opinion sections that use photos of several individuals giving their opinions on an issue of the day are useful editorial elements in many publications. Along with letters to the editor and guest editorials, elements such as these help open the opinion pages of the newspaper to the readers.

Student publications should develop and communicate their editorial policies to their readers and should provide ways for those with differing positions to respond to editorials and other opinion features. The editorial pages should stimulate thought and discussion and should help resolve important issues facing your readership.

To ensure that they serve the important functions for which they were intended, editorials require as much homework and research as news, sports, or any other aspect of journalism.

On Assignment

INDIVIDUAL ACTIVITIES

1. Write a brief definition of each of these terms:

column	masthead
editorial	point-counterpoint
editorial page	subjective writing
editorial policy	

2. Look at the editorials and columns in an issue of your school newspaper. Then examine the news content of the same issue.

   a. Are there background stories to provide information on some or all of the topics covered? If so, clip and attach them.

   b. What evidence do you find that the writers of the editorials or columns did their homework before writing? Write a paragraph to explain your evidence.

   c. Which of the editorial functions does the editorial serve? Write a paragraph explaining your answer and a one-sentence summary of the key position taken.

   d. Rewrite one of the editorials or columns, taking a different approach and an opposite position. Then write a one-sentence summary of your position.

3. Invite the local newspaper editor to visit your class and explain how editorial decisions are made. Discuss the following: Does the newspaper use an editorial board? What is the reporter's role in editorial decisions? Does the paper have a written editorial policy? Who actually writes the editorials? What kind of research does the editorial writer usually do? What is the role of the publisher or owner?

4. Do a comparison of the editorial pages of your local newspaper, your school newspaper, the *Wall Street Journal*, and *USA Today*. What are the differences in the elements used? Is more than one page used? What types of columns appear? Make a chart showing the contents of each one. Then write a brief analysis of the differences you find. Clip the editorial pages to your chart and analysis.

5. Make a list of editorial summary sentences on which you would like to write. Submit the ideas to your instructor, who will select one of the topics. Write the editorial. Mark each key editorial section on your copy. At the top of the page, identify the type of editorial you have written. Attach a summary of the research done before writing.

6. Assume you have total freedom to select a type of column that you want to write for the school paper. Prepare a list of five topics that fit the category you have selected (for example, opinion, profile, entertainment). Your instructor will select one for you to write.

7. Write a review of a current movie or a television show you have recently seen. Then find one or more reviews of the same film or show in another newspaper. How does your review compare with the professional ones? Are there points either you or the professional writers should have covered but didn't? Make copies of all of the reviews and discuss their merits in class.

8. Write a one-page critique of one of the On Display samples in the chapter. Use the appropriate Evaluation Checklist in judging the piece and include any other ideas you have about the editorial as well.

TEAM ACTIVITIES

9. Your team is to be an editorial board setting editorial policy. Study the statement of editorial policy on page 544 in the Appendix. Look for similar statements from other schools. Write out your policy and then compare it with that of other teams. Use ideas from all of the teams to determine one coherent policy. Decide whether it should replace the paper's current policy.

10. Working in a team, develop a new look for the editorial page or pages of your school newspaper. Prepare a mock-up, cutting similar elements from various newspapers to show the desired visual image. Write a brief essay on your team's approach, explaining why you have chosen your design.

SURF THE NET

11. What kinds of editorials and editorial cartoons win awards? Check the Pulitzer Prize on-line site (www.pulitzer.org) and that of the National Student Press Association (http://student-press.journ.umn.edu) and the Columbia Scholastic Press Association (www.columbia.edu/cu/cspa/). Report your findings to the class.

Editorial Cartoonist

When Ed Fischer sits down to draw an editorial cartoon each evening, he doesn't stare at a sheet of clean paper and wait for inspiration to strike.

"It's something that's intuitive," said the syndicated editorial cartoonist, based at the *Rochester* (Minnesota) *Post-Bulletin.* "I don't think anybody can explain how you come up with ideas."

The ideas come to Fischer because he prepares carefully for his daily two-hour stint when an idea is transformed into words and pictures. Fisher wouldn't last long at his job if he didn't prepare carefully, because there are only about 200 jobs for full-time editorial cartoonists at U.S. dailies.

Fischer browses through newspapers, reading national and local news stories. By late in the day, he has picked what he feels is the day's most important news event. Then he watches the evening news shows on television. Finally, he is ready to put his wit and artistic talent to work.

"I think every cartoonist has the urge to sit down and put his or her fantasies in graphic form, but an editorial cartoonist has to make a point," Fischer said.

Although he never earned a degree, Fischer attended classes at three colleges. "I always took things that were related to art and journalism, and that's what cartooning is—a combination of both," he said.

Ed Fischer

Fischer began his career in advertising, a field he saw as "kind of related." He made drawings to "get through to the common person." All the while, though, he pursued a cartooning job.

Persistence paid off. The *Minneapolis Star* began to buy cartoons from him after the paper's cartoonist took an interest in Fischer's work. Soon Fischer was selling the paper three cartoons a week.

"The big things I can offer a paper," he said, "are things that are areawide, statewide, or citywide. Those are my best cartoons. Everybody can relate to them. There is a lot happening in your own area."

"There are some great cartoonists who are not syndicated," said Fischer, who is himself syndicated to 80 newspapers.

"I believe there are many good jobs held by people who are paying attention to what's happening locally."

With so few jobs available on daily newspapers, Fischer admits that prospects aren't all that bright. "It's very difficult to get into this profession, but it's not impossible," he said, adding, "Even if high school and college cartoonists don't go on to become professional editorial cartoonists, they can have a lot of fun."

Even though he likes to make a point in his work, Fischer also wants to make people laugh. So he doesn't always try for biting satire. Once or twice a week, he'll do something a little softer.

Fischer has also produced a number of books on different, less topical subjects: *You're No Spring Chicken* is about getting older, and *Minnesota: A Cold Love Affair* is about what makes his home state unique. Both demonstrate Fischer's distinctive cartooning voice.

FOLLOW-UP

1. Track the cartoons of Fischer or some other editorial cartoonist to detect any patterns or themes in the work. Bring samples to class to support your ideas.

2. What makes a good editorial cartoon? Is it drawing ability, message, or both? Make a class display of strong editorial cartoons.

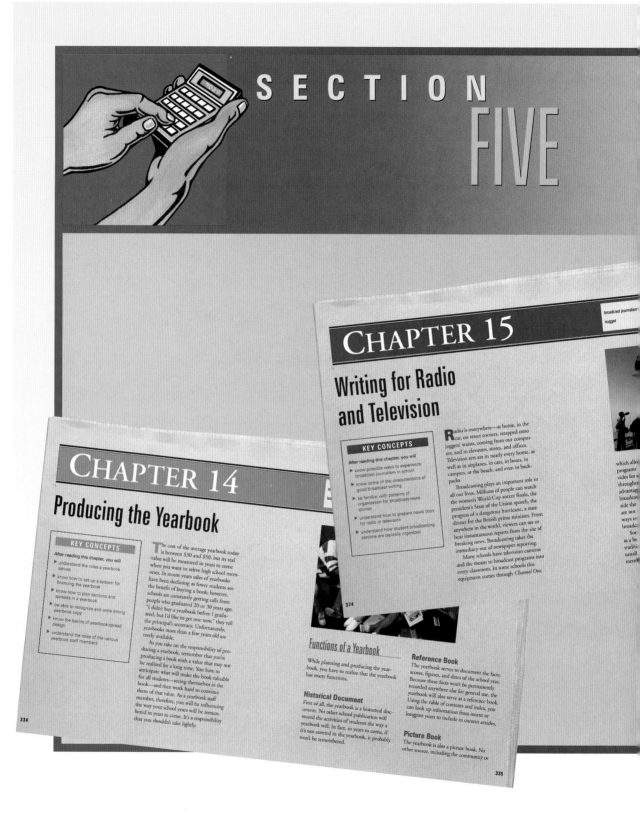

CHAPTER 14

Producing the Yearbook

KEY CONCEPTS

After reading this chapter, you will

▶ understand the roles a yearbook serves

▶ know how to set up a system for financing the yearbook

▶ know how to plan sections and spreads in a yearbook

▶ be able to recognize and write strong yearbook copy

▶ know the basics of yearbook-spread design

▶ understand the roles of the various yearbook staff members

The cost of the average yearbook today is between $30 and $50, but its real value will be measured in years to come when you want to relive high school memories. In recent years sales of yearbooks have been declining as fewer students see the benefit of buying a book; however, schools are constantly getting calls from people who graduated 20 or 30 years ago. "I didn't buy a yearbook before I graduated, but I'd like to get one now," they tell the principal's secretary. Unfortunately, yearbooks more than a few years old are rarely available.

As you take on the responsibility of producing a yearbook, remember that you're producing a book with a value that may not be realized for a long time. You have to anticipate what will make the book valuable for all students—seeing themselves in the book—and then work hard to convince them of that value. As a yearbook staff member, therefore, you will be influencing the way your school years will be remembered in years to come. It's a responsibility that you shouldn't take lightly.

334

CHAPTER 15

Writing for Radio and Television

KEY CONCEPTS

After reading this chapter, you will

▶ know possible ways to experience broadcast journalism in school

▶ know some of the characteristics of good broadcast writing

▶ be familiar with patterns of organization for broadcast-news stories

▶ understand how to prepare news copy for radio or television

▶ understand how student broadcasting stations are typically organized

Radio is everywhere—at home, in the car, on street corners, strapped onto joggers' waists, coming from our computers, and in elevators, stores, and offices. Television sets are in nearly every home, as well as in airplanes, in cars, in boats, in campers, at the beach, and even in backpacks.

Broadcasting plays an important role in all our lives. Millions of people can watch the women's World Cup soccer finals, the president's State of the Union speech, the progress of a dangerous hurricane, a state dinner for the British prime minister. From anywhere in the world, viewers can see or hear instantaneous reports from the site of breaking news. Broadcasting takes the immediacy out of newspaper reporting.

Many schools have television cameras and the means to broadcast programs into every classroom. In some schools this equipment comes through Channel One,

374

which allo programs vides for throughou advantage broadcas side the are not ways to broadca

Sor as a br traditi usuall memb

Functions of a Yearbook

While planning and producing the yearbook, you have to realize that the yearbook has many functions.

Historical Document

First of all, the yearbook is a historical document. No other school publication will record the activities of students the way a yearbook will. In fact, in years to come, if it's not covered in the yearbook, it probably won't be remembered.

Reference Book

The yearbook serves to document the facts, scores, figures, and dates of the school year. Because these facts won't be permanently recorded anywhere else for general use, the yearbook will also serve as a reference book. Using the table of contents and index, you can look up information from recent or longpast years to include in current articles.

Picture Book

The yearbook is also a picture book. No other source, including the community or

335

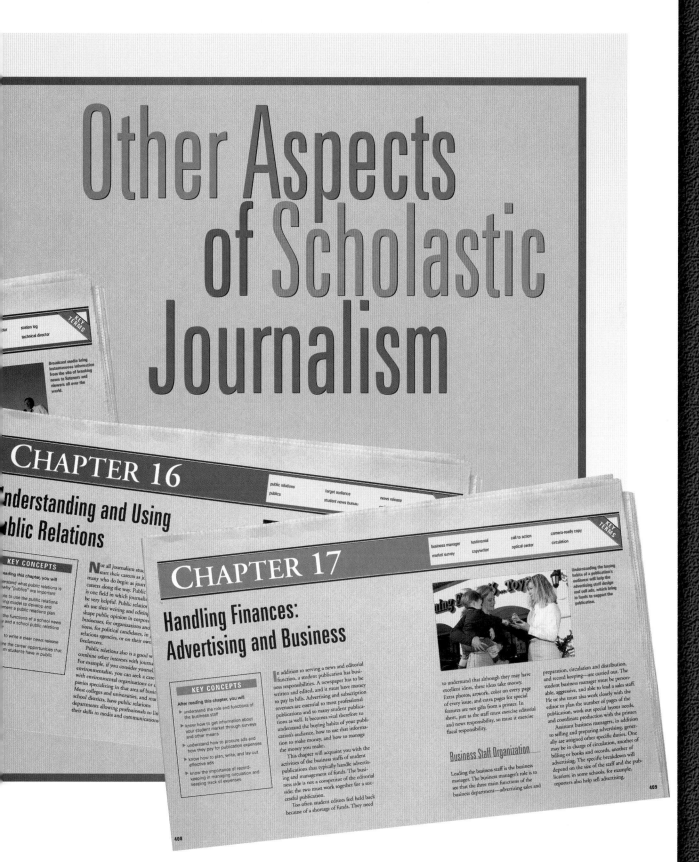

Other Aspects of Scholastic Journalism

CHAPTER 16

Understanding and Using Public Relations

KEY TERMS

station log
technical director

Broadcast media bring instantaneous information from the site of breaking news to listeners and viewers all over the world.

KEY TERMS

public relations
publics
target audience
student news bureau
news release

KEY CONCEPTS

reading this chapter, you will

▶ derstand what public relations is why "publics" are important

▶ le to use the public relations ing model to develop and ment a public relations plan

▶ the functions of a school news and a school public relations

▶ to write a clear news release

▶ re the career opportunities that m students have in public

Nor all journalism stud start their careers as jo many who do begin as journ careers along the way. Public is one field in which journalis be very helpful. Public relatio als use their writing and editing shape public opinion in corpora businesses, for organizations and tions, for political candidates, in relations agencies, or on their own freelancers.

Public relations also is a good w combine other interests with journa For example, if you consider yoursel environmentalist, you can seek a care with environmental organizations or c panies specializing in that area of busin Most colleges and universities, and mar school districts, have public relations departments allowing professionals to lin their skills in media and communications

CHAPTER 17

Handling Finances: Advertising and Business

KEY TERMS

business manager
market survey
testimonial
copywriter
call to action
optical center
camera-ready copy
circulation

Understanding the buying habits of a publication's audience will help the advertising staff design and sell ads, which bring in funds to support the publication.

KEY CONCEPTS

After reading this chapter, you will

▶ understand the role and functions of the business staff

▶ know how to get information about your student market through surveys and other means

▶ understand how to procure ads and how they pay for publication expenses

▶ know how to plan, write, and lay out effective ads

▶ know the importance of record-keeping in managing circulation and keeping track of expenses

In addition to serving a news and editorial function, a student publication has business responsibilities. A newspaper has to be written and edited, and it must have money to pay its bills. Advertising and subscription revenues are essential to most professional publications and to many student publications as well. It becomes vital therefore to understand the buying habits of your publication's audience, how to use that information to make money, and how to manage the money you make.

This chapter will acquaint you with the activities of the business staffs of student publications that typically handle advertising and management of funds. The business side is not a competitor of the editorial side; the two must work together for a successful publication.

Too often student editors feel held back because of a shortage of funds. They need to understand that although they may have excellent ideas, these ideas take money. Extra photos, artwork, color on every page of every issue, and extra pages for special features are not gifts from a printer. In short, just as the staff must exercise editorial and news responsibility, so must it exercise fiscal responsibility.

Business Staff Organization

Leading the business staff is the business manager. The business manager's role is to see that the three main functions of the business department—advertising sales and preparation, circulation and distribution, and record keeping—are carried out. The student business manager must be personable, aggressive, and able to lead a sales staff. He or she must also work closely with the editor to plan the number of pages of the publication, work out special layout needs, and coordinate production with the printer.

Assistant business managers, in addition to selling and preparing advertising, generally are assigned other specific duties. One may be in charge of circulation, another of billing or books and records, another of advertising. The specific breakdown will depend on the size of the staff and the publication; in some schools, for example, reporters also help sell advertising.

CHAPTER 14

Producing the Yearbook

KEY CONCEPTS

After reading this chapter, you will

▶ understand the roles a yearbook serves

▶ know how to set up a system for financing the yearbook

▶ know how to plan sections and spreads in a yearbook

▶ be able to recognize and write strong yearbook copy

▶ know the basics of yearbook-spread design

▶ understand the roles of the various yearbook staff members

The cost of the average yearbook today is between $30 and $50, but its real value will be measured in years to come when you want to relive high school memories. In recent years sales of yearbooks have been declining as fewer students see the benefit of buying a book; however, schools are constantly getting calls from people who graduated 20 or 30 years ago. "I didn't buy a yearbook before I graduated, but I'd like to get one now," they tell the principal's secretary. Unfortunately, yearbooks more than a few years old are rarely available.

As you take on the responsibility of producing a yearbook, remember that you're producing a book with a value that may not be realized for a long time. You have to anticipate what will make the book valuable for all students—seeing themselves in the book—and then work hard to convince them of that value. As a yearbook staff member, therefore, you will be influencing the way your school years will be remembered in years to come. It's a responsibility that you shouldn't take lightly.

signature	theme copy	caption	flat
ladder diagram	endsheets	layout template	

A yearbook serves as a historical document, a reference book, a picture book, and a public relations tool, and provides an educational experience for those who work on it.

Functions of a Yearbook

While planning and producing the yearbook, you have to realize that the yearbook has many functions.

Historical Document

First of all, the yearbook is a historical document. No other school publication will record the activities of students the way a yearbook will. In fact, in years to come, if it's not covered in the yearbook, it probably won't be remembered.

Reference Book

The yearbook serves to document the facts, scores, figures, and dates of the school year. Because these facts won't be permanently recorded anywhere else for general use, the yearbook will also serve as a reference book. Using the table of contents and index, you can look up information from recent or longpast years to include in current articles.

Picture Book

The yearbook is also a picture book. No other source, including the community or

335

✓ worth taking

TIPS

Typical yearbook budget. At the beginning of the year, estimate your expenses and income for this year's book based on last year's budget. Here is a typical yearbook budget:

Expenses

Printing	$15,000
256 pages (16 four-color pages)	
One-color cover + foil	
Photo supplies	$3,000
Computer and production supplies	$1,000
Total estimated cost	$19,000

Revenue

Book sales	
Opening week $30/copy	$1,500
First semester $35/copy	$8,750
Remainder year $45/copy	$2,250
Delivery $50/copy	$1,000
Ad sales	$7,000
Total estimated revenue	$20,500

school newspaper, has as thorough coverage of the year through photos. For many events, it's the photos that tell the story. The copy serves to supplement those photos and explain in detail what the photos can't.

Public Relations Tool

Another function of the yearbook is as a public relations tool. Public administrators and local business executives love to have copies of the yearbook in their offices as a sign of their support for a school. These people are potential financial supporters of the yearbook, and somewhere along the line you may need their help.

Educational Experience

Finally, the yearbook provides an educational experience for those who work on it. Few other courses offer the real-world experience of producing a tangible product that will be remembered for decades to come. Experiences in writing, editing, photography, design, production, desktop publishing, team work, leadership, and attention to deadlines make the yearbook class a unique experience.

Getting Finances in Order

Before beginning the creative experiences involved in producing the yearbook, the yearbook staff has to figure out how to finance its product. Although costs for this year's book will change to reflect printing-cost increases and format changes, the cost of the last year's book will provide a starting point for budgeting. Then you have to plan how to raise enough money to finance the book, including printing and production costs as well as photo and computer supplies.

Funding the Yearbook

The following sources are the usual methods of funding the school yearbook. Your adviser will guide the search for funds.

School funds. The first place to start looking for funds is within the school district's budget. Some schools allocate funds to be used for the production of the yearbook or for photo and computer supplies. Besides these directly budgeted funds, districts may also use funds from sources such as the sale of school portraits as a way to offset costs. Use of these discretionary funds is strictly up to the campus administration.

Although school-budget or discretionary funds can be a dependable source of money, few schools entirely finance a yearbook this way. Most schools use book sales, advertising, and other fundraisers as well.

Yearbook sales. The most obvious source of funding is the sale of the book itself. Students will pay more than $100 for a pair of shoes, but you will have to do market research to find out what they will pay for a yearbook. At the beginning of the year, after last year's book has been delivered, survey students. Will they buy a yearbook this year? If so, how much are they willing to pay? Using last year's cost is always a start—but you will need to justify all cost increases.

To give students an incentive to buy books early—and thus to gain earlier access to funds—many staffs begin selling at the beginning of the year. They offer the yearbook at a discount during the first week of sales; the cost of the book then goes up as the delivery date approaches. For example, you might sell the yearbook for $30 during the first week of sales to encourage people to buy. After that week and until the end of the first semester, the cost might be $35. After the first semester and until the end of the year, the book might cost $45. When the books are delivered, you can sell any extra copies for $50. Selling individual copies will often come close to paying for the printing of the book.

As you're planning for yearbook sales, don't forget to market your product. Put up posters around the school with samples of the pages that will appear in the book. Send out press releases to the local newspapers and radio and television stations. Do a mass mailing to parents. Broadcast your message on the school announcements and marquee. Do the same when the book is delivered. In short, make the yearbook a school event in which everyone wants to participate. Some schools have had great success selling and then later delivering the book at a school dance or schoolwide party.

Selling ads early in the year is one way to ensure having enough money to produce a quality yearbook.

Advertising. Selling ads is an additional source of revenue for many schools. The amount of income that can be raised selling ads varies greatly depending on the aggressiveness of the staff and the willingness of the community to support school activities. Schools that are well organized and that believe the yearbook is a way for businesses to generate revenue can raise several thousand dollars in advertising sales. The key to success is having a professional, organized approach and making the purchase of a yearbook ad different from other fund-raising activities. After all, businesses who advertise in the yearbook will have their company or store remembered for years to come. (For more tips on selling ads, see Chapter 17.)

Senior ads and personal ads are another way for the yearbook staff to generate revenue. For example, a graduating senior's parents could purchase a quarter-page ad as a tribute to their daughter. Such ads can be colorful and include pictures of the individual that wouldn't fit anywhere else in the book. By expanding coverage through this sort of ad, you can ensure that more people will buy a yearbook. These types of ads also provide an opportunity for individuals to purchase space in the yearbook without jeopardizing unbiased coverage of school events.

Fund-raisers. One final source of revenue is various kinds of fund-raisers. You may choose to make holiday greeting cards, using production skills you have learned working on the yearbook. You can sell candy. You can produce programs for the football team, the drama department, or the band. You may sell subscriptions to magazines.

Fund-raisers can be distracting to staff members who are trying to produce the yearbook, so they should be well organized. Encourage fellow staff members to participate and help them understand the importance of raising money to fund the yearbook adequately. More money means more options—such as expanding coverage, increasing your page count, adding color, and so on.

Planning the Yearbook

With the financing plan taken care of, you can get on with thinking about the yearbook itself. Your underlying goal must be to ensure that as many students as possible are included. After all, the more students included, the more likely they are to purchase a book and to support the program.

As you begin to plan how the yearbook will be organized, start with—but don't be limited to—last year's book. The number of pages in the book, the number of pages in each section, and even the number and type of sections can be exactly the same as last year or radically different.

Determining the Sections

The most popular way to divide a yearbook is into sections that ensure balanced coverage of school events, students, and faculty and staff. Some staffs organize their book chronologically. Most, however, divide their book into a combination of the following sections: student life, academics, clubs and organizations, sports, and people.

Student life. The student life section, usually the first section in the book, includes coverage of people and activities not included in other sections. Events such as homecoming, and topics such as students at their jobs, with favorite pets, or on favorite vacations might be found in the student life section. This section also gives you a chance to cover people not directly involved in school activities who might otherwise appear in the yearbook, such as the owner of the corner drugstore where students wait for buses.

Academics. Coverage of academics should go beyond the obvious. Look for teachers who engage in unique activities or students who stand out, but don't forget that many other people have interesting stories too. Include the biology teacher who has been teaching for 35 years or the person who missed being in the top 10 percent of the class by one person.

The biggest challenge to academics coverage is taking pictures that are more than just students sitting behind desks or teachers working at blackboards. Getting unique coverage means having photographers always on the lookout for picture opportunities, even to the extent of carrying their cameras to class regularly. Keep your eyes open for teachers hosting activities such as a Hawaiian luau or computer-science students trying to work while wearing the "clean-room" garb of computer-chip makers.

Organizations and sports. The clubs and organizations and the sports sections are the easiest to complete because coverage is dictated by the activities of the various groups. You still have to work closely with them, however, to get high-quality action photographs of things that are going on. Learning of an event after the fact means that you have missed an opportunity to cover something that can never be re-created.

Provide coverage of these groups in a way that is different from anything done in past years. Look for aspects of events that make this year unique. After all, people aren't paying $35 or more to read the same stories they read in last year's book or to see the same photos. If your cheerleaders got new uniforms, find out why. If your band used an electric guitar during football halftime shows for the first time, find out why. Explore what motivated the student council to work with senior citizens at a local nursing home.

Be sure to leave space when planning this section for the group shots that ensure coverage of a significant number of students. Or make plans to include the group shots in another area of the book, such as the index.

People. The people section, which includes portrait shots of everyone in the school, including faculty and staff, doesn't stop with the portrait shots. It's another opportunity for you to expand coverage by including, for example, personality profiles of the all-state violin player, a student who traveled to the Great Wall of China, or a student who placed first in a Special Olympics event.

Don't limit your coverage to personality profiles. Consider including the results of polls and surveys. Poll students about their favorite vacation spot, fast-food restaurant, television show, computer game, teacher, and class. Work with your student artists to turn this information into interesting art (infographics) to supplement photos and stories.

Also use this section to include stories and photos that don't fit neatly in other sections or to cover topics that don't warrant a full spread (two facing pages) of coverage. Some schools choose not to include anything but portraits in their people section, and that may be

When planning the people section, consider going beyond portrait shots to include interesting personality profiles, such as one on the all-state violin player.

adequate. By including stories and action photos, however, you get people to look at pages they otherwise wouldn't ever see.

Assigning Pages

To figure out how many pages to devote to each section, begin with the total number of pages. This number must be divisible by 8 or 16 because of the bookmaking process. Groups of 8 or 16 pages, called signatures, are printed on large sheets of paper, which are then folded, cut, and bound together into a book.

After deciding the total number of pages, subtract the following:

▶ the title page (page one—also includes the volume number of the book; school's name, address, and phone number; and student enrollment)
▶ number of opening and closing pages (the pages that introduce and conclude the book)
▶ number of division pages (the pages or spreads between each section)
▶ number of advertising pages you plan to sell
▶ number of pages in the index

The result of your calculations will equal the total number of pages available for sections.

Once you know the number of section pages available, use the following percentages to figure out how many pages to devote to each section:

Student life	25–30%
Academics	10–15%
Clubs and organizations	15–20%
Sports	15–20%
People	15–35%

When you plot out exact page counts, you will find that you have the most flexibility in the student life and academics sections. The number and type of groups can dictate the number of pages in the sports and club-organization sections. The number of portraits can dictate the number of pages in the people section. Make the portraits smaller or larger to increase or decrease the people section pages. Combine groups in different ways or run group shots as part of the index for more flexibility with the sports and club-organization sections.

Planning Individual Spreads

After you have mapped out the overall organization for each section of the book, start planning what is going to appear on each individual spread; the facing pages of a yearbook are always related. Decide what the overall topic for the spread will be—what its unifying theme will be. For example, if your yearbook is to include 48 pages of student life coverage beginning on page 10 in the book, decide what will go on pages 10–11, 12–13, and so on until you have a plan for each spread in the book. Do this early in the year—not as you go—or you may miss crucial events to cover.

To decide what to put on each spread, again begin by looking at last year's book. Undoubtedly, there are things you covered last year that you will want to cover this year—but don't stop there. Look at older yearbooks. Look at yearbooks from other schools. Poll students to find out what they would like to see in this year's book that they didn't see last year. Figure out ways to expand coverage and to picture more students.

Using a ladder diagram. As you begin mapping out a plan, write it down on a ladder diagram, a "map" of the yearbook. Your yearbook publisher may provide you with a ladder diagram, or you may make one yourselves. First, write in all the fixed pages, including title page, opening page, division pages, closing page, and other pages that have fixed content, such as ads and index. Then write the topic for each spread on the ladder diagram and note whether the spread will be in black and white or in color. It's also helpful to code the spreads by deadline. For example, you can color-code the first deadline with red ink. When you finish, post the diagram for everyone to see.

Developing a Theme

Another critical task to complete early in the year—in addition to producing a yearbook map—is development of a theme, a unifying concept that gives the book a unique personality. The theme is a common thread that will reappear throughout the book to provide continuity for the reader.

Theme selection. When selecting a theme, realize that it will set the tone for the entire book. It can be built around a word, a phrase, a color, or a graphic element. It should not be gimmicky or cute but should be applicable to the year. It also should be easily developed and easily understood by the reader without jeopardizing coverage.

Yearbook Ladder Diagram

1 title page—black & white	1st deadline
2	**3** opening spread—4-color (bio) + intro copy	1st deadline
4	**5** student life: division page—4-color + copy	1st deadline
6	**7** student life: Places to go—black & white + copy	1st deadline
8	**9** student life: People to know (natural double-page spread)	1st deadline
10	**11** student life: ??
12	**13** student life: The best part of the day—4-color + copy
14	**15** student life: Learning to drive—black & white + copy
16 student life: ??	

A ladder diagram is a useful aid in outlining and organizing the contents of a yearbook.

Note that many phrases from songs, advertising, and movies are copyrighted; you can't use them, no matter how much you want to. Such phrases are often not relevant to the school or specific year anyway.

Because the theme sets the tone for the entire book—sophisticated, spirited, or even serious—take time to decide on a good one. Once you have an idea, play with it. Try using a dictionary of idioms or of phrases to help you find phrases that fit the concept you're trying to convey. Look around the school for what will make this year unique. Look at other yearbooks to see how they have treated themes.

Sometimes themes are obvious. For example, if your school is under reconstruction, the phrase "Growing Pains" may serve as a theme. Or you might choose to use a pile of bricks as a graphic device. Although themes that are stated with a catch phrase such as "Look Who's Talking," "Try This On for Size," or "Let the Spirit Move You" are the most common, there's no rule that yearbooks must have catch-phrase themes. Themes can be developed strictly with graphics or with concepts.

Once you have narrowed the theme down to a couple of ideas, begin exploring how you can develop each of them. Translate your ideas into copy, photographs, and page designs: Pick the theme you like best and try writing some theme copy for it. Think of photos that will support it. Sketch out some graphic elements that will accent the theme without detracting from it.

Inevitably, as you explore development of your top theme ideas, one idea will stand out as the most popular or the most applicable to the school year. That will be the theme you decide to use.

Also consider writing theme spin-offs for each section in the book. Although not required, spin-offs are an easy way to carry the theme throughout the book creatively. For example, if your theme were "Stealing the Spotlight," you could use "In the Light" as the theme spin-off for the student life section, "Sharing the Spotlight" for the people section, "Sore Spot" for the sports section, and "On the Spot" for the clubs-organization section. A dictionary of idioms and a thesaurus can be helpful in suggesting spin-offs.

Theme pages. Certain pages in the book should highlight the theme. These theme pages should stand out as distinct from the rest of the book with a bold design that attracts the reader's attention. Through graphic development and copy, the theme should appear in the following places:

- ▶ the cover
- ▶ the endsheets (the inside front and back covers)
- ▶ the title page
- ▶ the opening section
- ▶ the division pages
- ▶ the closing section

Although you will spend a great deal of time developing the theme, it should only be mentioned on theme pages. You may, however, choose to carry through part of your theme with graphics in the folio at the bottom of the page, which contains not only the page number but information such as the section name, page topic, or page designer. For example, if you used a dotted rule on the cover in your theme logo, you might use a similar dotted rule in your folio.

Theme copy. Theme copy is unlike any other copy in the yearbook. It serves solely to develop the theme and help readers understand how the theme applies to the school year. It may or may not include direct or indirect quotes from sources. It may even read more like advertising copy, with phrases rather than complete sentences. It should be easy and enjoyable to read and should clearly explain how the theme fits the year.

For example, if your school has had a surprising and unusual year in many respects and you choose "Just Imagine" as your theme, your opening copy may read like the following from *Finest Hours,* the yearbook of Winston Churchill High School, Potomac, Maryland:

Just Imagine

Starting school at 7:25 A.M. with each class ending a minute earlier.

Coming to school late and finding a parking space up close, thanks to the new policy.

Studying countless vocabulary words and then finding out a new SAT with no antonym section was developed by the Educational Testing Service.

Having undefeated varsity football, boys' soccer, wrestling, and girls' tennis teams in the regular season.

Seeing your teachers dressed up as anything from a lobster to a jack-in-the-box and being interrupted during class singing "Jack-o-Lantern."

Imagine all this and more!

TIPS **worth taking**

Possible yearbook themes. Look through other schools' yearbooks for possible theme ideas. Here are a few to consider:

It Must Mean Something	It's a Matter of Perspective
Where Do You Fit In?	Ever Been . . .
Outstanding in Our Field	No Boundaries
Rock On	Got It Made
Stay Tuned	People Are Talking
Welcome to the Real World	In a Different Light
Eye of the Beholder	Just Out of Curiosity
Still Waters Run Deep	It All Adds Up
Some Like It Hot	Life Is How You Change It

Theme copy, however, doesn't stop—or even start—with long copy blocks such as this. The headline and captions on the theme pages should also reflect the theme, and the theme should appear in the copy block on every division page or spread. The division spread in the **ON DISPLAY** feature on pages 346–347 features a spin-off of the overall yearbook theme "It's Your Move."

ON DISPLAY

Division Spread

Hiways, Hialeah High School, Hialeah, Florida

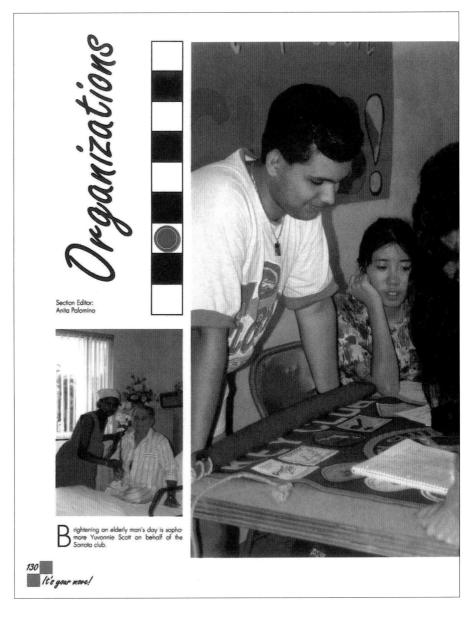

Organizations

Section Editor:
Anita Palomino

B rightening an elderly man's day is sophomore Yuvonnie Scott on behalf of the
Sorrota club.

130

It's your move!

- *Moving the community* -

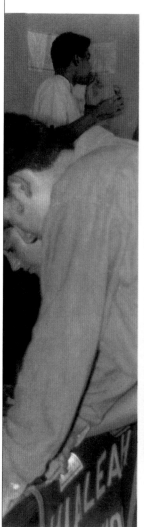

With the vast amount of clubs that existed in the school, practically all interests were represented in one club or another. Clubs established their goals and were formed as soon as the year began. Some organizations focused on community service, while the purpose of others was to inform students, make changes, or provide a place where people of common interests could gather.

The reestablishment of the Interclub Council Association allowed club presidents to join and work on major projects, such as the effort to replant the school's patio that was destroyed by Hurricane Andrew.

The extent to which a student was active in the community was the extent to which that student made his move.

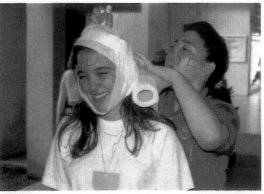

Clubs took advantage of Club Fair Day to recruit members. President senior Antonio Delgado and junior Irene Lui help senior Rebecca Valle and junior Victor Puyada sign up for Key Club.

Senior Yetlanezi Mato can not escape senior Gaby Rodriguez from tapping her to make her membership in A.T.C. official.

131
Organizations

The headline, graphics, and folios on this division spread are based on the overall book theme "It's Your Move."

As the book begins to take shape, periodically do a check to make sure that you're covering the essentials of theme development. Use this checklist to ensure your theme comes through loud and clear.

EVALUATION CHECKLIST

Yearbook Theme

☑ Does the theme reflect the school year?

☑ Is the theme copy interesting? Does it explain in a clever manner how the theme is appropriate to the year?

☑ Are the photographs on the theme pages some of the best in the book, and do they reflect the theme?

☑ Is the design of the theme pages unique yet unified, and do they reflect the theme?

☑ Is the theme depicted graphically on the theme pages?

The Yearbook Spread

Just about every spread in the yearbook will contain several photos and captions as well as a certain amount of copy. These elements need to be drawn together into a cohesive layout. If all the page elements are high quality, the end result is an effective yearbook spread.

Copy

Writing yearbook copy is much like writing feature stories for the newspaper. Yearbook stories should be lively—full of colorful verbs and specific nouns, with just a smattering of adjectives and adverbs. The copy should help readers relive the year each time they read it.

You may wonder, as you start writing copy, why the yearbook can't just be full of pictures. "Who ever reads the copy anyway?" staff members may ask. The truth is that few students *do* read the copy when they pick up their yearbooks. They look at the pictures and read the captions. But yearbook copy isn't written for the present; it's written to help fulfill the yearbook's role as a historical record of the school year. If the book uses good reporting, good interview style and research, and good editing, one day the stories will become as valuable—if not more valuable—than the pictures.

Ask the right questions.

The most common fault staffs have when assigning yearbook stories is that the assignments are not specific enough. It's easy to look at a ladder diagram showing that the story on pep rallies is on page 14 and then to request that someone write a story on pep rallies. A writer with such an assignment will go out and get quotes such as, "The pep rallies were a great way to show school spirit" or "They were a lot of fun." Quotes like these tell nothing about the pep rallies—why the school had them, how many people attended, what the goal of the pep rallies was, and so on.

When making assignments on topic such as pep rallies, be specific about the focus of the story. Reporters can then ask questions that elicit informative, interesting quotes.

Reporters should strive to know *why* things were the way they were. A staff discussion to narrow the topic can focus the kind of information the reporter should seek. Thus, instead of asking sources, "Did you like the pep rallies?" the reporter could ask, "Why did [or didn't] you attend the pep rallies?" or "What do you think of pep rallies?" Such open-ended questions will elicit responses that help the writer develop a story that will aid the reader in remembering what the year was like.

Leads and other devices.

Good leads and good writing are as important in the yearbook as in any other publication. For example, in the student life section of the yearbook, you might have a story about what hairstyles students were exploring during the year. A story about getting a new hairstyle could begin with a lead such as this one:

> The blades came closer and closer to her neck. She tried to remain calm, but her voice began to quiver.

Such verbal descriptions will entice readers into the copy, entertaining them while they relive the school year.

Make no mistake, contemporary yearbook copy is more than just a collection of feature stories. Some yearbooks are not using conventional copy at all in one or two sections of the yearbook. Instead, they're using long photo captions that answer the how and why questions that would traditionally have been answered in a story. Such captions—along with sidebars such as quotes from students and faculty or infographics of survey results—tell the story. Together, these elements give details that help convey what the year was like.

Headlines. Copy blocks and sidebars don't tell the entire story. The headline is important because it serves to tell part of the story while grabbing the reader's attention. Even if students read nothing but the headline, they should end up knowing something about the topic and what happened during the school year.

Many headlines are just one line:

Unexpected events lead to record-breaking year

Some, however, contain a primary headline and a secondary headline:

Students develop personal style
A variety of clubs provide artistic expression

In many yearbooks, headlines are cast in the past tense, reinforcing that these events are part of the year's history rather than current news.

In general, the approach is informal. This informality often leads to headlines that play with words, as in this example:

Cramming for exams
Soda and study-buddies make tests tolerable

Photos

Without high-quality photos, a yearbook can be average at best. The photos are what give the yearbook life. Unfortunately, many yearbooks contain photos that are poor in quality and content. Staffs are willing to write, edit, and rewrite a story a dozen times, yet rarely if ever do they reshoot or reprint photos. Refining photos should become an accepted part of the yearbook routine.

Criteria for good photos.

Good yearbook photographs must show people—and those people should be doing something other than staring at the camera. The more people, and the more action, the better. The hallmark of an outstanding yearbook photograph is that it features someone doing something *unusual*.

In addition, yearbook photos should be storytelling photos. They should show various perspectives on an event and make sense

When selecting yearbook photos, choose those that tell a story and that include people doing something unusal.

of it for the readers. The story of the school play isn't just the performance; it's also the rehearsals leading up to the performance. It's not just about the actors; it's also about the tech staff who does the behind-the-scenes work.

Finally, yearbook photography must be of high technical quality—that is, in focus, not too dark or too light, and so on. Train your photography staff before sending them out to take pictures. It will save you time and money; photo supplies aren't cheap. (For more information on photography, see Chapters 18 and 19.)

Planning photo coverage.

Good photographic coverage should be included in the initial planning of the book. Some spreads may be dictated by events that lend themselves to good photographic coverage—for example, seasonal sports or a drama production. Good coverage, however, doesn't just happen. Just as reporters need direction to focus a story, so photographers need direction to get the best photos. Consult with the staff about the kinds of photos that are required and desired for various events.

Selecting photos.

Some staffs design spreads and then find photos to fit. Although this may save time, it sometimes forces designers to place horizontal photos in vertical spots and vice versa or to use inferior photos as the dominant element—two things that typically result in poor-quality spreads. It's better to select the photos and then design the spread. Depending on your deadline schedule, this may or may not be realistic.

As a compromise, some staffs create 8–12 layout templates, or design patterns, for each section, leaving space for a variety of photo shapes and sizes. After they have selected the photos, all they have to do is pick the layouts in which they work best.

When you select photos for a spread, aim for variety. Include close-ups and long shots as well as photos that offer different perspectives on an event or topic.

The **ON DISPLAY** spread on pages 354–355 is from the student life section of a yearbook. Note the dramatic, well-chosen photos.

Photo Captions

Many people read the photo captions on a spread and nothing else. Every photo caption should therefore fulfill these two goals: to explain what's going on in the photo and to add information.

The first sentence in the caption, the one that explains the activity in the photo, should be written in present tense. As part of this first bit of information, include the names of all easily recognizable people—but don't begin every caption with a name. Other sentences that add information should be written in past tense. This additional information may be statistical information or may be a direct or partial quote from someone involved in the action.

This caption, for example, might accompany a photo of two runners:

> Joining in with the daily practice, Coach Anita Napoli and senior Elizabeth Dominguez begin a two-mile run. The Cross Country team practiced five days a week during the 10-week season.

It's a good caption, but beware of starting all your captions with verbs that end in *-ing*.

This caption describes a photo showing a long line of students looking uncomfortable:

> On a warm August evening, freshmen stand in line waiting patiently to receive their schedules. More than 1,100 freshmen registered for the new school year.

Remember that the photo caption *is* important: It's one more place where you can increase coverage and get more people in the yearbook.

The **ON DISPLAY** spread on pages 356–357, taken from a yearbook academics section, includes a number of longer captions that give useful background information about the photos.

Design and Layout

A complete discussion of design and layout principles and procedures, including tips on laying out yearbook spreads, appears in Chapter 10. What follows are some basic points to keep in mind.

The first rule of yearbook design—as in newspaper design—is that the content of the spread dictates how the pages should be designed. The content must be the principal focus of the spread.

Column grid. To design a yearbook spread using basic modular design (packaging stories and photos in rectangular blocks), begin by establishing a grid, which is based on a specific number of columns per spread. Decide upon a grid that has between 6 and 24 columns. This grid provides a framework within which to work. Once the columns are established, every page element should fall within—not between—them.

Here are a number of layout possibilities for yearbook spreads. In these sample layouts, dark blocks indicate photos; lined areas are for copy; blank areas are white space. A mix of such layouts can add variety to a yearbook.

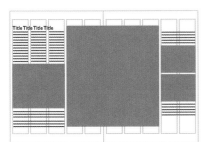

**Modular Format—
10 columns per spread**

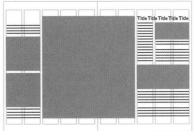

**Modular Format—
10 columns per spread**

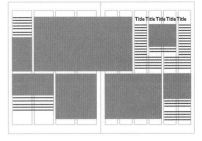

**Modular Format—
10 columns per spread**

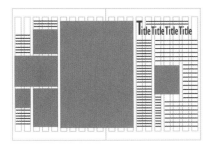

**Minicolumn Format—
20 columns per spread**

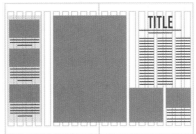

**Minicolumn Format—
20 columns per spread**

**Plus—
full and half-size columns**

Student Life Spread

El Leon, Mansfield High School, Mansfield, Missouri

SENIORS LINE THE edge of the road, watching as police, paramedics, and firemen go about the task of realistically working a drunk driving accident scene. The event was co-sponsored by ESP.

AREA LAW ENFORCEMENT agencies join with a cast of seniors to reenact a drunk driving accident in front of the school. Actors included Scott Corder, who is being extracted from a mangled car by firemen.

PLAYING THE ROLE of a drunk driver, Adam Grubbs is escorted to the police car by a Highway Patrolman. In the background, Jessica Copeland, as the fatality, lies covered in the roadway, while firemen try to extract Scott Corder from a car.

AS PART OF a drunk driving reenactment set up in front of the school, senior Jessica Copeland, covered with fake blood, is pronounced dead at the scene of the two-car accident.

STRAIGHT TALK

"The wreck reenactment was a good experience to be in, and I learned a lot about rescues." - Scott Corder

"I thought it was an actual wreck because I came in second hour and the whole thing looked very realistic." - Bobby Hunsucker

SENIORS ACT 'WRECKLESS' TO MAKE SAD POINT

Blood, alcohol, sirens, and death. These were the details the Senior Class experienced during a mock drinking and driving accident co-sponsored by area law enforcement agencies and Education Supports Prevention.

Five seniors were actors. Jessica Copeland was pronounced dead at the scene, Scott Corder was cut out of a mangled car, and Adam Grubbs, Scott Corder, and Chris Flageolle were taken into police custody.

Police, paramedics, firemen, the Highway Patrol, and prosecuting attorney all took part. The main idea of the accident was to show the students what really goes on after a car wreck involving drinking.

The bloody scene made an impact.

"It looked so unbelievably real," senior Jenny Moody said. "It really made me think after seeing one of my close friends covered with a sheet and pronounced dead."

Despite its seriousness, the event still had a little bit of humor to it.

"It was supposed to be a sad situation," senior Melissa Scott said. "But when the guys started throwing their beer cans and hiding them when the Highway Patrol showed I couldn't help but laugh."

Grubbs, who played the part of the drunk driver, was in the thick of the action.

"It was very realistic," he said. "It was quite an experience riding in the police car and being handcuffed."

The officers, firemen, and paramedics each talked to the students about drinking and driving and the consequences.

The best advice, one said, if your friends are drunk and want to drive, is very simple.

"Stand up at a party," he said. "If you're not drinking then insist that you drive. Your friends may be mad, but at least they'll be there to tell you the next day."

While law officials deal with "drunk drivers," seniors watch emergency workers try to extract Scott Corder from a mangled car. The car used had actually been involved in a drunk driving accident.

STARING UP AT a Highway Patrolman after being taken into "police custody," Chris Flageolle acts the part of a teen involved in a drunk driving accident.

WRECK REENACTMENT 21

Academics Spread

Panther Tale, Duncanville High School, Duncanville, Texas

Words of Wisdom

Guests visit schools to share their life experiences

◆ *Layout and copy by Renee' Gonzales*

Some came to motivate while others came to share their experiences. Guest speakers provided a break from the regular class assignments while teaching valuable lessons.

Cultural awareness was presented in assemblies at the Ninth Grade School.

The Multicultural Studies Club helped bring different cultures to the forefront with such programs as the Trinidad Steel Drum Band and "A World of Culture" for the National Hispanic History Month Celebration.

While the focus was on the Hispanic culture, it had a multicultural background. "It was fun and I wasn't nervous. If I know I can do it, I will. And if I believe I can do it, I will," said freshman Maria Lozano.

Former football player John Randles came to speak to the athletes about setting goals and the importance of education. "They need to hear it from other people beside the coaches," said Coach Bob Alpert. "We try to teach them things besides just athletics. We try to show the difference in right and wrong decisions they can make."

> *The multicultural program was fun and everybody learned about our culture. I think they should do it every year, and I'm sure they would enjoy it to.*
> —Maria Lozano, 9

Susan Dalrymple

Stop signs and transparencies are used as demonstrations in the "Aim for Success" presentation that discusses unsafe sex and the consequences that can change lives. "It's good that we're learning about it (sex) in school than not knowing anything about it," said senior Ryan Montz.

Got ta Say It !

"I really like what people came to talk about. It had a big impact on my life and my actions."
—Jeremy Gordon, 11

"Everybody loved the Steel Drum Band. You didn't have to be a band member or a percussionist to enjoy them."
—Chelsey James, 9

110 Academics

Knowledge of the Hispanic culture gives another taste of a different type of living. Freshmen Sophia Cabido, Michelle Schier, Josie Escobar, and Maria Lozano dance to *Tus Desprecios* by Selena to give everyone a taste of the Hispanic culture at an assembly at the Ninth Grade School.

Randall Knutson

Nascars are the topic of discussion in the auto mechanics class. Del Boren, a representative from Lincoln Tech, shows videos on the making of the Nascar, and students got to inspect a real race car. "It (the presentation) provides future interest, I hope, in a future automotive career," said teacher Wayne Long.

Becca Holmes

Favorite Excuses of '98
Where's your homework?

91. I used invisible ink.
92. Procrastination is the limit to my vocabulary.
93. I'm special.
94. No habla ingles.
95. My mom threw it away.
96. It was accidentally put in the recycle bin.
97. I did the wrong page.
98. We had homework?!

Musically inclined freshman Eric Bryant plays *Mission Impossible* on the tenor steel drums. The Trinidad Steel Band came to let the students experience music from a different culture. "I got to play on an instrument I've never heard of before," said Bryant. The assembly was held in the Ninth Grade School gym as part of the Black History Month celebration.

Curtis Gastin

Champions in life and excellence in relationships are what former football player John Randles promotes. On Feb. 9 he discussed the benefit of smart choices with the football players. "You are the leaders, not the followers," said Randles. Coach Bob Alpert brought in guest speakers to reinforce lessons from the coaches.

Guest speakers **111**

Informative captions add depth to the content of this spread. The boxed sidebar copy—a continuing feature on humorous homework excuses—also adds interest.

Photo placement. With a grid determined, begin placing the photos on the spread. Start with the dominant photo. This photo should be dominant not only in size (at least 2–2½ times as large as any other photo on the page) but also in content: It should be the highest-quality and most-relevant photo on the page. The dominant photo can be placed across the gutter, but be careful to crop photos so that no one's face falls in the gutter.

With the dominant photo in position, decide how to place a subordinate photo of contrasting size and shape. For example, if the dominant photo was large and vertical, the next photo you place should be small and horizontal. This maintains visual variety.

With two photos on the spread, you should have begun to form one of the unifying elements of a yearbook spread—the eyeline, a horizontal line of white space that extends across the spread. If the dominant photo is horizontal, the top or bottom of it will begin the formation of the eyeline. If it's vertical, the first subordinate photo placed in relation to it will begin the formation of the eyeline. The eyeline should fall either above or below the halfway mark on the spread. This eyeline can be broken by the dominant vertical photo or some other vertical element on the page. Don't break the eyeline by only one or two picas, however. If you're going to break it, really break it—by at least eight picas.

Continue placing the photos on the page in a clockwise or counter-clockwise direction until the spread contains five to seven good photos, each either above or below the eyeline.

Notice the strong eyeline and dominant horizontal photo in the sports spread shown in the **ON DISPLAY** feature on pages 360–361.

Copy and graphics. Leave plenty of space for each photo to have a caption. Captions should appear on the outside of the spread, next to the photos they represent. Most captions are at least five picas high and may run as wide as 20 picas. Whatever the height and width, to work effectively, captions must be carefully integrated into the page design.

You will also need space for the copy block and the headline. Remember that all captions, photos, and copy blocks must fall within your column grid. Avoid placing captions between photos or overprinting captions on top of photos; they're hard to read.

After you have the copy, headline, photos, and captions in place, add graphics. Don't choose graphics just because they're cute or cool. Any graphics you use should help unify the section. Unity results not only from your choice of fonts, column grid, story placement, and headline design but from graphic devices such as initial letters, pull quotes, screens, spot color, and rules. Graphic embellishments, if they're chosen to help tell a story and not just fill space, will enhance the page design.

The consistent placement of captions and quotes, along with the similar treatment of headlines and photos, unifies the people spread in the **ON DISPLAY** sample on pages 362–363.

Use this checklist when you're evaluating a yearbook layout that you or one of your fellow students prepared.

EVALUATION CHECKLIST

Yearbook Spread

☑ Is there a strong, well-positioned dominant photo?

☑ Are four or five other people-oriented photos arranged appropriately around the dominant photo?

☑ Has a clear eyeline been established?

☑ Are captions accurate, with as many names as possible included, and are the captions correctly positioned on the spread?

☑ Does the copy contain interesting facts presented in sidebars as well as in regular copy blocks?

☑ Does the headline summarize the content of the page?

The Yearbook Staff

As critical as the organization of the yearbook itself is the organization of the staff, from the editor down to first-year staffers.

The school administration, like the board of directors of an organization, has an indirect role in the yearbook. That role is to work in an oversight capacity, but not in day-to-day oversight. Administrators should get involved as needed to see that the yearbook serves as a forum for student expression and is a true reflection of the school year.

Beyond the administration, many other people play key roles in the yearbook.

Sports Spread

The American, Independence High School, San Jose, California

Cooling Down
Exhausted after just finishing a 2.2 mile run, Alexandra Balagso, 9, pauses a moment to catch her breath. "I joined cross country because it helped me condition for track," said Balagso.

All Together Now
Heading towards the finish line, the runners push themselves every step of the way. "Endurance, strength, determination and the desire to make it through was what made cross country a tough and competitive sport," said Tamika Bush, 12.

A Step Ahead
Heavily focusing on the race, Ken Stachnik, 9, challenges himself to improve his time. "In order to be the best I pushed myself to improve my time every time I ran," said Stachnik.

The Year Sports

78 Sports

Stretching Out
Before the race, Marcelo Caldas, 12, eyes his competition at Alum Rock Park; the last meet of the season. Cross country was a sport which involved rigorous, long-distance running.

Moving Along
After returning from a leg injury, Jenny Do, 12, runs at a constant speed as she makes her way to the finish line. "I was glad I was able to compete for the last time this year," said Do.

This sports spread uses a layout template that was repeated on many spreads. The template allows for many photos and an interesting mix of copy and graphics. Observe how the eyeline leads readers to the main headline.

The runners learned that it all started with a steady pace

& the Scores

On The Go

Copy By Nathan Panganiban, Annamay Rodriguez & Evangeline Toloza

Kris Ajel, 10 Being on the team was a way for me to meet new people, get in shape and apply myself to something I liked. I look forward to a stronger, faster and an injury-free season next year.

Nicole Resendez, 9 The sport really challenged me to make it through the entire course. At one point, Cross Country became really disappointing but it pushed me to do my best.

Edward Chen, 9 Before every race I got butterflies in my stomach. To calm myself I would walk around the park and concentrate on the race. Practice helped to improve the speed and quality of my run.

Girls
James Lick 21-37
Overfelt 28-25
Leland 46-17
Santa Teresa 43-19
Presentation 39-21
Mitty 42-19
Silver Creek 40-20
Mt. Pleasant 29-26

Boys
James Lick 25-38
Leland 48-15
Mt. Pleasant 48-15
Santa Teresa 25-38
Silver Creek 48-15
Overfelt 39-20

& You Played It

Duke Nguyen, 11

I had been in Cross Country for three years now, and I didn't think that there was ever a point where I got tired of running. What I liked best about it was the teamwork. We always tried to stay with each other during the race. Everyone encouraged each other to do their best. I knew it was very beneficial to me because I was able to improve my times at the courses and get through the race. I was proud of everyone who ran this year. They really worked hard and had a positive attitude which kept our spirits high.

Composed mostly of young, inexperienced newcomers, runners searched for stamina and stability to make it through the courses. Running long distances required a tremendous amount of dedication. Coaches, Wendell Bradley and Victor Castillo, always made sure they emphasized the team's accomplishments to keep the runners motivated. The coaches focused on teaching the young team that goals would only be accomplished if they applied themselves. The young team was composed mainly of freshman and yet they still were able to overcome the challenges they faced.

Cross Country **Front Row:** Maria Chunn, Veronica Garcia, Ajene Enriquez. **2nd Row:** Nicole Resendez, Edward Chen, Ngan Nguyen, Duke Nguyen, Lorraine Sanchez, Phuong Nguyen, Anna Almejo, Assistant Coach Kolvira Cheng. **3rd Row:** Coach Wendell Bradley, Marie Madeires, Chin Chi, Casimero Agustin, Tamika Bush, Irene Villanueva, Alexandra Balagso, Ken Stachnik. **Back Row:** Mike Meighan, Barry Chen, Ken Powers, Kris Ajel, Franky Toledo, Ajith Satya, Marcelo Caldas, Harninder Meht, Bac Dang.

ON DISPLAY

People Spread

The Arvadan, Arvada High School, Arvada, Colorado

Cheryl Grant
Jamie Anne Grenz
Joshua Gummersall- Snowboard, Skateboard
Jonathan Gutierrez- Baseball
Nasima Hadi

Eric Hamm
Brandon Hanson- NHS, Thespians, Chorale, Modernaires, Choraliers, "Rehearsal for Murder," "Man Who Cazme to Dinner," "Good Doctor," "You the Jury," "Happily Ever Once Upon," "Frakenstein," "Carousel," "Guys and Dolls," "Music Man"
David Lee Hartman- DECA
Billy Hathorn- Football (9-12), Swimming (11-12)
Jeremy Hatch

Heather Hauer- NHS (11-12), Spanish Club (10-12)
Erin Hausauer
Curt Hay- Football (10-12), Basketball (9-12)
David Heer- Football, Baseball, Wrestling
William Heltzel

Sara Hickey- "Carousel," "Guys and Dolls," "Music Man," Chorale, Modernaires, Choraliers, Chantelles, Swimming (9-12), Cheerleading (12)
Jeremy Hinz
Jeremy Hirsch- Tennis (9-12)
Hue Hoang
Vincent Hodges

Brett Holdaway
Michelle Horn
Jeremy Howland
Anjolie Huizing- Swimming
Jarrod Hurd

146 seniors

stereotypes survey

- 34% of students had been judged by religion.
- 43% of students were discriminated according to race.
- 60% of students had been judged by their gender.
- 64% of students had been judged by their clothes.
- 69% of students were judged by their appearance.
- 75% were grouped by the people they hung out with.

judging originals

"A senior was playing a video game on the internet and would not tell me how to get into it, because he said it was an upperclassmen secret."

-Phillip Page

"Girls come up to me and say they are the better sex; they think they're neat and clean and guys are messy. I don't agree, because I'm pretty clean. Besides, they think they are more intelligent and I think we're equal."

-Josh Gummersall

"I was judged as a gangster, because I am Hispanic and my head was shaved. I 'm nothing like a gangster; I play sports. It made feel bad, because they never met me in person."

-Elijio Martinez

Just because I'm shy and don't know many people, people think I'm stuck up. The way I dress makes people think I'm a snob. I wear nice clothes, but I'm not very outgoing. However, when I go to Hollywood Legends with my sister Mary Gilda (right) and dance, I'm not shy anymore. I love to dance and I'm pretty good, so the guys like me. Then I become more outgoing.

-Mary Grace Ng

Some people will give me dirty looks and look down on me. They can't stand the way I dress, because I'm being myself and they hate that. Most people have to act like everyone else; they want to fit in and they are afraid to be themselves because they wouldn't belong. It used to bother me when I cared what other people thought. Then I realized, I'm going to be who I am.

-Kate Griffin

People hate skateboarders because they think we are hoodlums. They don't like the way we dress. People think we wear chains just for fights and we're sloppy. I like the way I dress, because it's comfortable and I like dark clothes. Just because a few skaters do bad things, they think we are all bad. The cops come all the time to check on us. Over half the time we aren't hoodlums.

-David Edwards

I want to be on the football team, but some people think I can't do it. I've played football for four years at Rocky Mountain Flag Football. Some people make fun of me because I'm small and different. They aren't use to having a girl on the team and some people think I'll wimp out. However, it's cool that some people are excited about me playing freshman football.

-Jessica R. Dimino

looking within
WORTH MORE THAN FACE VALUE

I've been judged by my parents; they expect me to get perfect grades in school. They judge me as a genius because my grades throughout elementary and Jr. high were straight A's. They always expect nothing less. I've also been judged by strangers, because of my previous appearance. I used to have long hair and wear ragged clothes, so people would assume I was a troublemaker.

-Dan Glennon

BY KATHLEEN JEWBY

stereotypes 147

Quotes from seniors, as well as the sidebar of polls results, add interest to this well-designed people spread that supports the theme, "But Always Be Original."

The Adviser

Integral to any staff and at the top of the organizational ladder is the adviser. This individual's role is to facilitate the production of a high-quality book on schedule. Of course, along the way, the adviser has to motivate the staff, give out grades, supervise and teach five or six other classes, organize school portraits, and perhaps do a thousand other things only remotely related to producing a yearbook.

The Yearbook Editor

The student in the highest role on the staff is the yearbook editor. Besides making story, photo, and layout assignments, the yearbook editor is responsible for book content and staff motivation. In recent years, the courts have held that the yearbook editor can be held responsible for the material in the yearbook.

The chief goal of the yearbook editor should be to produce a high-quality book published on time. Secondary goals include supervising the completion of the ladder diagram and deadline schedule; expanding coverage to include as many students as possible; working with staff members to ensure the timely completion of a first-rate product; serving as a liaison between the adviser and the staff; and representing the yearbook staff to the rest of the student body. A good editor leads by example, volunteering to assist any staff members when needed.

This diagram shows a common organizational structure for a yearbook. Other organizational structures and the inclusion of other positions, such as a production editor and staff, are also possible.

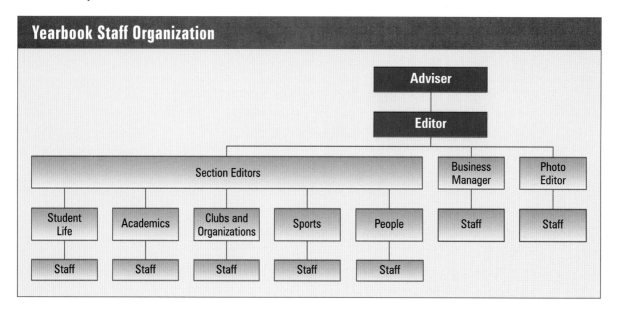

Yearbook Staff Organization

Section Editors

Each section should have one person responsible for the overall look and feel of that section. These section editors have the same responsibility for their sections as the overall editor has for the entire publication: working with other staff members to get the section completed—on time and as close to perfect as possible. The section editor is responsible primarily for dictating the topics to be covered and for the design of the section. On most staffs section editors make specific assignments to the reporters and photographers working for them.

The Production Editor

In addition to, or in lieu of, section editors, some staffs have a production editor and production staff who are responsible for the design and layout of the yearbook pages. The chief responsibility of the production editor is to ensure design consistency for each of the sections. It's the production editor who sets up the templates that will be used as the basis for pages and who worries about design specifics. Often, the production editor helps to maintain the computer equipment as well, assisting with software and hardware problems as needed.

The Photography Editor

Some yearbook staffs have a photo editor who works with the editor and section editors in the assignment of photos and who supervises the photography staff and the use of photos. The role of the photography staff is to complete photo assignments in a timely fashion. This means taking pictures, processing film, and making prints. The entire photography staff is responsible for ensuring that the best photos are used in the dominant positions and that only high-quality pictures are used throughout the book. In some schools the photography staff may work with both the newspaper and yearbook staffs.

Business Manager

The business manager supervises the finances of the publication, including all fund-raising activities, ad sales, and book sales. He or she may work with the editorial as well as the business staff members to raise money for producing the book. The other jobs of the business staff include keeping track of all yearbook receipts and coordinating the distribution of the book on delivery day. Staff members also communicate with potential advertisers and help make the rate card that specifies ad sizes and rates. As with the photography staff, the business staff may work with both the newspaper and yearbook staffs.

Staff Manual

Vital to the smooth running of any yearbook staff is the staff manual. In addition to specific job descriptions for the various positions, a thorough manual will include a general statement of philosophy for the yearbook staff; a statement regarding the inclusion of individual portraits in the yearbook; the advertising policy, including types of ads that can be rejected according to school board policy; and any other policy clarification that may prevent confrontation in the future.

The general statement of philosophy, written and approved by the campus and district administration, should include a policy on prior review, the practice of reviewing publications prior to printing for the purpose of approving—or disapproving—content. Policies on prior review by campus administrators or others vary greatly, and having the policy in writing will avoid potential legal hassles during the year. Understanding any restrictions may save you time and frustration if you must submit material for the administration's scrutiny.

A general statement of yearbook philosophy appears on page 545 in the Appendix. Notice how specifically it spells out content and responsibility issues. You may wish to elaborate on some areas of the document, particularly those that are influenced by school-district policy, local procedures, or state laws. The Student Press Law Center, the Journalism Education Association, and other scholastic journalism organizations can provide further information on writing statements of philosophy.

Working with the Yearbook Company

Obviously, a lot goes into putting together a yearbook—but help is available. Although some yearbooks are printed locally, a handful of national yearbook companies print most yearbooks. Each company also provides a variety of tools to help with yearbook planning and production.

trends and issues

Yearbooks on CD and Video

What can audiovisual technology add to a yearbook?

In these days of multimedia, it may be hard to convince all of your classmates that a hard-copy yearbook is something they need or want. In some schools, however—especially those in which many students have access to VCRs and computers with CD-playing capability—the yearbook can be supplemented by a video or CD addition that adds interest to the package.

The CD is not just an electronic version of the yearbook. Instead, it goes beyond the traditional form, using the CD's capacities for text, audio, photo stills, and video to augment the printed book. For example, a CD may show video footage of homecoming, the school play, prom, academic awards banquets, sports finals, and various other events. Instead of only one story on some of these activities, it may have two or three, presented from different angles. The CD, which often incorporates interactive sections, may include not only photos of the graduating seniors but also audio accompaniments, in the students' own voices, describing their feelings about graduation and their plans for the future. The possibilities are limited only by the staff's imagination and, ultimately, the budget.

A CD yearbook supplement can be produced in a number of ways. Currently, nearly all schools go to outside producers, as the software used to assemble such multimedia presentations is expensive and complicated to use. Some schools send all their materials—photos, stories, videos, and audiotapes—to an electronic service bureau and let that company handle all stages of production. Others lower the cost a bit by doing the electronic prepress—scanning and digitizing images—themselves. A few staffs actually produce the master CD themselves, an endeavor that requires extensive experience and expensive equipment.

A CD yearbook supplement may include not only photos of graduating seniors but audio accompaniments in which they comment on graduation and their plans for the future.

Like a well-conceived CD, an effective video is more than just a collection of video clips. It's another way to tell the story of the year. Video-yearbook production companies shoot footage and assemble it into a moving series of snapshots of the year. The mix of sound and video helps bring back the memories. Some well-equipped schools choose to shoot and edit their own videos, saving all the expense except duplication of the tapes. Taking this route, however, increases the time commitment involved.

The primary incentive for schools to produce either a CD or video supplement is to increase sales of the printed yearbook. Adding a CD or video raises the total cost, but the package often appeals to a broader audience than just the printed book. If marketed correctly and aggressively, the CD or video supplement can result in dramatically increased sales of the yearbook package.

Will the CD or video yearbook someday replace the print version? Not likely. Even in the technology age, a book, like a printed newspaper, is a more permanent record than a piece of software. Besides, you can't get autographs on a CD or video.

FOLLOW-UP

1. Examine several yearbook videos or CDs and discuss their effectiveness. Which events were best conveyed? Which could be handled better?
2. With a partner select a school activity that you think could benefit from a CD presentation. Make a plan showing just what audio, video, and photos you would include in a CD for the activity.

367

Choosing a Company

In some schools, the yearbook company is the same year after year. In others, the company is selected through a formal process each year, during which each company is asked to bid on the printing of the yearbook. The administration—often with the cooperation of the adviser and staff—then consider cost and other factors as they select a company. Still other schools use a less formal bidding process or some other combination of factors.

Using the Production Kit

After the yearbook company has been selected, the company representative will explain how to use its tools in preparing the yearbook. All companies provide a production kit that contains everything from layout sheets (grid sheets) and picture-cropping tools to marketing materials that will help in selling more yearbooks. These kits contain valuable information that often goes overlooked by the staff.

Submitting Layouts

Your representative will stress the importance of properly labeling everything you submit. Each of the yearbook companies produces thousands of books every year, which adds up to hundreds of thousands of photos to process. That's why it's critical to label every single item with your customer number, including every photo, every envelope, and every layout. Use the stickers or rubber stamps the yearbook company provides to facilitate this labeling. Never send one-of-a-kind materials to your printing company, such as a student's award certificate from an honors program.

Many printers prefer to have layouts submitted in 8- or 16-page signatures; their deadline schedules will reflect this. Be prepared for the fact that for color pages the entire signature must be submitted together on one deadline.

Proofs and Flats

Your yearbook company will provide you with proofs of the book as you go along. Plan for time to review proofs and mark corrections. Keep photocopies of the layouts you submit so you can compare them to the proofs. Also keep copies of the proofs, marked with your corrections, as a record of your changes.

Once signatures have been prepared for printing, the yearbook company will send you flats. A flat is a large sheet of paper that shows one side of a signature. The pages will look out of order because of the way signatures are folded and cut for binding. Your real purpose in reviewing flats is to double-check color and photo quality. You *can* make changes at this point, but they're very expensive.

Working with Your Rep

On a regular basis throughout the year—not just at deadline time— schedule visits with your representative. Have the representative look over what the staff is doing to make sure production will flow smoothly at the plant. There's nothing worse than submitting several signatures on time only to find that they were prepared inaccurately. Pages submitted incorrectly can cause a delay in the printing, and therefore in delivery, of the book.

Keep in close contact not only with your yearbook company representative but with your in-plant representative. Keep them informed and request that they keep you informed. Remember, the yearbook company works for you to print the quality of book that your students and staff demand.

Wrap-up

The yearbook is an important record of what has happened during a school year, but it will become even more important as time passes and people want to remember their school years. Therefore, you should seek to include as many students as possible in the yearbook. Besides providing a historical record, a yearbook also functions as a picture book and a public relations tool, and offers an educational experience for those who work on it.

The first step in planning a yearbook is to make sure that there's enough money to finance it. Although schools may provide some funds, staffs often have to raise additional money by fund-raising and selling advertising space. When selling the yearbook itself, you can give discounts to students who pay early in the year, thereby bringing in needed cash at that point.

Planning the content of the yearbook begins with planning the sections—usually student life, academics, clubs and organizations, sports, and people. Once you decide the total number of pages in the book (based on a number of 8- or 16-page signatures), you can determine how many pages to allot to each section. Then you can use a ladder diagram to help you figure out what will appear on each spread. You can also begin to develop theme ideas, discussing and testing them until you come up with one that will work for the whole book.

Good yearbook copy should be insightful and interesting. It needs the same kind of good leads and good writing as newspaper copy. Headlines and captions are particularly important because sometimes these are all that students read.

High-quality, high-interest photos are a must for any yearbook. Include as many people and as many action shots as possible. Good photographic coverage should be considered in the initial planning of the book.

Page design begins with a consideration of content. Photos placement should begin with the dominant photo. An eyeline should be created, and five to seven photos—as well as captions, a headline, and other copy—should appear on each spread.

Once work begins on the book, designate a staff member to serve as the coordinator for each section. These section editors—together with the production editor, photography editor, and business manager—must work together and with the staff adviser and yearbook editor to ensure consistency and quality within each section. Staff members should also get to know the representative from their yearbook company and follow the procedures and deadlines the company sets up.

On Assignment

INDIVIDUAL ACTIVITIES

1. Write a brief definition of each of these terms:

caption

endsheet

flat

ladder diagram

layout template

signature

theme copy

2. Test your critical thinking. Look at the themes for your school's last five yearbooks and evaluate how well each of them related to the school. Then choose one book and examine it more closely. How well was the theme executed? In what ways was the treatment good? How could it have been improved? (If your school's yearbooks did not have themes, find five books that did and use them as models as you establish procedure.)

3. Design, produce, and distribute a marketing survey to get suggestions for improving this year's book. Include such questions as What were your favorite and least favorite spreads in last year's yearbook? and What one thing would you want to see in this year's book? If respondents did not purchase a book last year, ask what could entice them to buy one this year. Compile and analyze your results, and refer to them as you create a strategy to expand coverage and sell more books.

4. Using the information you obtained in the marketing survey, design a poster that will target one specific population and encourage that group to buy yearbooks. Include an idea for a photo or piece of art, and write all copy for the poster.

5. Write a one-page critique of any of the On Display layouts in this chapter. Explain what you think is good or bad about the layout.

6. Pick any spread in the student life section of any yearbook. Using a rough-draft layout sheet, sketch the page, using boxes for photos and lines for text. Write in the words for headlines. Then, in a different color, label the following elements if present: headline, subhead, caption, eyeline, dominant photo, vertical photo (not dominant), horizontal photo (not dominant), sidebar, white space, folio, rule, screen, initial letter, infographic, and illustration. On the back of the rough draft, write a brief evaluation of the effectiveness of the design. Explain any changes you would make in it.

7. Create a rough layout for a spread in the people, student life, sports, or clubs and organizations section. Choose a topic for the spread; then write a headline and body copy. Choose photos and write captions for them. If no photos are available, describe what kinds you would use and where you would position them. Write captions as well.

TEAM ACTIVITIES

8. In small groups identify 25 things that make your school unique. Then brainstorm five phrases (no longer than six words) that summarize your school this year. Share your phrases with the rest of the class and discuss how each one fits the year. Have the class vote on their favorites. Pick the top three.

9. Divide into three groups, each to develop one of the three phrases from activity 8 by doing the following:

   a. Explain how the phrase is an appropriate theme for the year.

   b. Write an opening and a closing yearbook story based on the theme.

   c. Sketch a design for the cover, endsheet, title page, opening spread, and division pages.

   d. Produce a "theme packet" consisting of an actual mock-up of the cover, endsheet, title page, opening spread, and division pages.

SURF THE NET

10. Find samples of on-line yearbooks on the Internet. Compare and contrast their content with that of printed yearbooks.

career profile

Graphic Designer

A picture may be worth a thousand words, but the tone of a story or power of an idea can also be expressed in choices of color, typography, logos, and the other visual vocabulary created by a graphic designer like Mike Quon.

Self-described as "a graphic designer who illustrates," Quon has influenced modes of visual communication throughout the world since founding the Mike Quon Design Office in New York City in 1972.

Quon has created thousands of designs and illustrations for magazines, books, advertisements, posters, and record-album covers. Among his work for corporate, institutional, and nonprofit clients are the logo for the New York State Lottery; television commercial graphics for Xerox, HBO, Dristan, and IBM; and banners for a World Cup Soccer tournament.

Quon's work—ranging from pen-and-ink and pencil drawings to collage to watercolor to acrylic paintings—is represented in the permanent collections of major museums in the United States and abroad. He also has designed, illustrated, and coedited more than a dozen books, many of them for children.

Quon's father, working as an animator for Disney films, discouraged Quon's study of art and graphic design, pushing his son toward science or medicine. Although he took only one art course in high school, Quon found time to draw after his studies and, at age 16, won

Mike Quon

second place in an art contest sponsored by *Surfer Magazine*.

Quon worked at agencies in Los Angeles and New York before founding his own design studio. He also began visiting Europe regularly, filling sketchbooks with drawings and watercolors.

"Daily sketching keeps me sane," he said. His client base—and his sketchbooks—reflect subsequent trips to various corners of the world.

Having a design firm is not just drawing. It's growing a business, solving problems, and mastering new technology. "Who would have thought that teenage computer nerds working in their garages would come up with stuff so highly sought after by today's corporate designers?" he said.

Much of what Quon still has to wrestle with is finding the creative solution.

"It's hard to tell where your inspiration comes from," he admitted. "Everywhere I look there is feedback and information. Part of the job is to be inspired with the right inspiration at the right time."

Graphic designers must reach into the "vast library" of their minds, of everything they have encountered in their lifetimes, Quon said. "Watch movies. Go to animation festivals. Read lots of books, such as Philip Megg's *History of Graphic Design and Graphic Arts*, a compilation of award-winning designs," he added.

"Students should not become discouraged, however competitive the field becomes," Quon advised, "and don't compare yourself with someone who's been in the business for years. Things that seem impossible now come in due time. You just get better each year."

FOLLOW-UP

1. What kinds of opportunities exist in the journalism world for people with artistic talent? List as many specific tasks as you can that require an artistic touch.

2. Graphic artists such as Quon rely more and more on computer-drawing programs (for example, Adobe Illustrator, Corel Draw, and Macromedia Freehand). Find several such programs and demonstrate them for the class.

CHAPTER 15

Writing for Radio and Television

Radio is everywhere—at home, in the car, on street corners, strapped onto joggers' waists, coming from our computers, and in elevators, stores, and offices. Television sets are in nearly every home, as well as in airplanes, in cars, in boats, in campers, at the beach, and even in backpacks.

Broadcasting plays an important role in all our lives. Millions of people can watch the women's World Cup soccer finals, the president's State of the Union speech, the progress of a dangerous hurricane, a state dinner for the British prime minister. From anywhere in the world, viewers can see or hear instantaneous reports from the site of breaking news. Broadcasting takes the immediacy out of newspaper reporting.

Many schools have television cameras and the means to broadcast programs into every classroom. In some schools this equipment comes through *Channel One,*

Broadcast media bring instantaneous information from the site of breaking news to listeners and viewers all over the world.

which allows schools that broadcast its news programs to use the TV monitors it provides for other educational purposes throughout the day. Other schools take advantage of local-access cable TV and broadcast to a small, specific audience outside the school. Even if such opportunities are not available to you, there are other ways to get practice with the basics of broadcast journalism.

Some schools use the intercom system as a broadcast laboratory. Instead of the traditional bulletin listing school events, usually read by a student or school staff member, student journalists compile the news provided in the bulletin and bring it to life with good reporting and additional stories. They interview students involved in the activities being announced and prepare radio-style commercials to promote upcoming events. In some schools arrangements are made to have wire copy of the top news events of the day faxed from a local radio station. That copy is then summarized to help students keep abreast of current events. Today's on-line news also provides a source for current news.

When the news is ready, it's taped daily for broadcast over the intercom system. Not only is the quality of the basic bulletin

Getting practice with the basics of broadcast journalism can be as simple as reading news and feature stories over the school intercom system.

enhanced, but students gain experience in practical broadcasting laboratory with real deadlines. The equipment needed is minimal—a tape recorder, a tape splicer (to cut and edit sound), a cassette or CD player (for musical introductions and advertising sound effects), a few sound-effects CDs, and an adapter to play into the intercom. (Note that many sound-effect records and CDs are copyrighted, which means you must get permission to use the sounds.)

In addition to in-house broadcasting, journalism students can prepare news and broadcast features about school events and send them to local radio and television stations for use in their programs.

If your school and community don't offer opportunities to broadcast to a real audience, you can still learn and apply broadcasting journalism techniques in the classroom. Reporters can prepare stories in broadcast style, interview students involved in them, and prepare newscasts that can be recorded and played for others in the class to critique.

Writing for Broadcast

When writing broadcast copy, you have to keep your listeners and viewers in mind. Remember that they will hear your words only once. Whereas a reader can reread a printed news story, listeners have no opportunity to review a broadcast story.

So how do you proceed? Begin by applying the principles of good reporting. Dig into the news. Seek to find a "nugget"—a fact or bit of information that will stick in the listener's mind and make your story stand out.

Next, organize the information in a way that makes it easy for listeners to understand. The goal is to create a visual picture in the listener's mind. Pictures in a television story can help you do that, but the words you write and speak are equally powerful in creating a mental picture. The ability to write and speak well is particularly important in radio broadcasting.

To organize a story you must first understand it. Ask yourself some questions: What elements of news make this story important to my listeners? How does the information affect people? The answers to these questions can help you tell a good story. In addition, some basic story patterns can help you organize your information.

Cause-Effect Organization

In this organization the cause is your main point. It's followed up by one or more effects.

Cause: Another heavy snowstorm has brought our city to a standstill.

Effect: Schools will remain closed for a second straight week. Superintendent William Onoda says that students will have to make up the lost time at year's end.

Problem-Solution-Results Organization

In this organization, first state the problem, follow with an explanation of a solution, and then tell the results—whether that solution was acted upon, or whether another solution was proposed. Here's an example:

Problem: The Oakcrest School District is facing serious money troubles.

Solution: School board president Jimmy Langham and two other school board members say the only way around the problem is to cut school programs, but at least one board member disagrees.

Results: Betty Pendleton says that because last year's spending cuts didn't help avert this year's budget crisis, the only real alternative is to raise taxes.

Television and the Courtroom

Does TV influence the kind of trial a defendant receives?

The question of TV coverage of courtroom trials isn't a new issue. People have wondered about its appropriateness almost since the time on-the-spot TV reporting became possible.

In 1965 the U.S. Supreme Court refused to allow television coverage of federal cases but let each state decide whether to cover other trials. California was the first state to allow TV coverage in courtrooms; today more than 40 states permit it.

People in favor of televising court procedures have pointed out the educational value of such programming. When Court TV, the first station devoted entirely to broadcasting trials, came along in the early 1990s, many viewers reported a greater understanding of what goes on in a courtroom. Arguments against televising have had to do with changing the basic nature of the judicial process. Are judges, lawyers, and juries even subtly influenced by the presence of cameras? Is the public being taught that trials are merely another form of entertainment? These are some of the same issues that the Supreme Court raised.

Trials of well-known people proved to be the real test of TV courtroom coverage. The 1991 rape trial of William Kennedy Smith, nephew of Senator Edward Kennedy, probably brought much more attention to the case than if it had been covered only by print media. Smith was ultimately acquitted, but virtually everyone in the country had an opinion on the trial based on what they had seen on television.

The question that can be raised here is, So what? So what if people second-guessed Smith's motives and responses? So what if some disagreed with the verdict? The jury was shielded

The advisability of televising controversial trials was called into serious question after the O. J. Simpson criminal trial. Here journalists watch live broadcasts and wait for a chance to do a live interview.

from outsiders' opinions during deliberations, so Smith's right to a fair trial was not affected.

It was the 1995 O. J. Simpson murder trial that raised the most serious questions about TV in the courtroom. Accused of killing his wife and her friend, Simpson was on trial for months, and the event truly became a media circus. In the end the jury took less than four hours to reach a verdict. Had the length of the trial, dragged out by excessive TV posturing, simply worn the jurors out? No one knows for sure, of course, but many people thought it might have been a factor.

This trial was in some ways a watershed event. It made people newly aware that trials were not staged for the benefit of TV cameras; they were serious affairs requiring dignity and restraint. Judges began to exercise their right not to have TV cameras in their courtrooms for possibly sensational trials. Court TV began a program to educate students about trial procedures and protocol. News stations began using better judgment in how they used courtroom footage. Could it be that the era of excessive TV coverage of trials is over?

FOLLOW-UP

1. Does televising a trial constitute an invasion of the defendant's privacy? Following your teacher's instructions, hold a formal debate on the issue.
2. Watch a minimally publicized trial on Court TV for several days or, if possible, for the entire trial. Take notes on what you observe; then discuss the coverage in class.

Comparison Organization

Use this organization to show similarities and differences between two people, plans, products, or proposals:

Comparison: The two leading candidates for Student Council president have similar backgrounds. Barry Miller and Julia Alegría are both honor students. Both want to make Martin Luther King High a center for student social activities after school hours. On that issue, however, they have different ideas. Miller wants to open a student canteen, where students can gather and talk. Alegría wants to double the number of school-sponsored dances. There's money in the student activity fund but not enough to finance both a canteen and extra dances. Students will decide which idea they prefer when voting next Tuesday.

One of these organization patterns will almost always work for any story. Remember that, as in all newswriting, broadcast stories have a beginning, a middle, and an end. Each should reinforce important facts in the story. You set up the story in the beginning, provide additional details in the middle, and tell what happens in the end.

Writing with Flair

You have already seen that one good way to make your story stand out is to find a nugget of information that makes your story stick in your listener's mind. Writing creative copy is another way to help listeners better visualize and understand your story. This is one of the most enjoyable parts of broadcast newswriting. Keep in mind, however, that being creative doesn't mean being cute or flowery. It just means saying something in an interesting way. Notice the difference between these two samples:

Good: Tropical storm Allison is now a full-fledged hurricane. The National Weather Service upgraded the Florida Gulf Coast storm when its winds topped 75 miles per hour. The Florida coast—from Tampa north to Pensacola—is now under a hurricane warning. The storm is expected to hit tomorrow. Ten inches of rain are likely to fall. Residents are being warned to take precautions, which include possible evacuation.

A creative writing style, with strong verbs and specific nouns, can make a good hurricane story into a better one.

Better: Tropical storm Allison is now hurricane Allison. She's whipping the Florida Gulf Coast with 75-mile-per-hour winds. Allison is expected to hit tomorrow, with 10 inches of rain likely. A hurricane warning is in effect from Tampa north to Pensacola. Storm experts are warning residents to get ready and to prepare for possible evacuation.

During his career at CBS News, the late Charles Kuralt set the standard for broadcast-writing creativity. It's called writing with "flair." Kuralt's story about the *Wabash Cannonball* provides a good example. It's about the last days of a passenger train that had rolled through the Midwest countryside every day since 1884. The flair with which Kuralt wrote is well illustrated in the last few lines of his story:

Set your watch by the *Cannonball* while you may. Pause at the crossroads to let her pass. Take one last look. Tomorrow, the *Wabash Cannonball* won't be a train at all, only a banjo tune.

Kuralt's writing and storytelling skills made his reports stand out. But you can find many other excellent reporters. Just listen to the radio and watch TV news. Pick out some stories that you like. Use a tape recorder; record and transcribe them. That way you can study how the stories were organized and written.

Preparing Copy for Broadcast

Generally speaking, writing for broadcast is similar to writing for newspapers. All the basic principles of good reporting discussed earlier in this book apply. The goal is to write well, clearly, and concisely. Gather your information conscientiously; be accurate and objective in writing about it; edit your work carefully.

Here are some other basic tips.

Style. Be concise. Write short, simple sentences. Use a subject-verb-object pattern. Write one thought to a sentence and activate your sentences by writing in the active voice. Active voice helps make news copy more current, interesting, and easy to understand. Compare these two examples:

Passive voice:	It has been found by school librarians that student interest in reading is on the rise.
Active voice:	School librarians say that student interest in reading is on the rise.

Use present tense if possible. Keep in mind that dates generally are not needed. Broadcast news is immediate; you're there as the news happens. Thus, you can easily dispose of the word *today* almost entirely—and never start a story with the word *yesterday*. If it happened yesterday, it's old news. Find a "today" reason to report the story or don't report it.

A main goal in writing for broadcast is to make the copy clear and easy to read on the air.

Eliminate unnecessary words from sentences. Use adverbs, adjectives, and descriptive phrases sparingly. Remember that words are time. You can only fit about 150–180 words into a minute of broadcast news. Depending on your delivery rate, that figure could go up or down. If you use music or sound effects, you have less time to present stories. In television you have to account for the use of videotapes, film, live reports from the field, or electronic graphics as well.

TIPS worth taking

Broadcast writing in a nutshell. Follow these guidelines for broadcast writing to simplify and improve the process:

▶ Be simple and to the point.

▶ Use the present tense.

▶ Remember your time limits.

▶ If you must use numbers, round them off.

▶ Use the active voice.

▶ Attribute before the statement.

▶ Use phonetic spelling for difficult names and terms.

▶ Use caps and lowercase.

▶ Double- or triple-space copy.

▶ Write television copy to correspond roughly to the pictures.

▶ Position directions on the left, script on the right.

▶ Always read copy aloud before broadcasting it.

Minimize the use of numbers. It's hard for listeners to comprehend numbers in a broadcast story. If a number is important, however, by all means use it. Spell it out in written copy. To make things simpler, round numbers off.

Bad: The student charity dance raised $4,263.50 for the Cohen Homeless Shelter.

Better: The student charity dance raised more than four thousand dollars for the Cohen Homeless Shelter.

An attribution, as you recall, is a phrase that identifies who said something or the source of important information. Your copy should help the listener understand who is saying what. In broadcast writing, the attribution should *always* precede the statement of information, this way:

> Mayor Susan Wong says she's running for reelection.

The same attribution approach holds true for important information that you need to broadcast quickly but can't personally confirm.

> The Associated Press says that shots have been fired at the President's motorcade.

Mechanics. Prepare your broadcast copy in capital and lowercase letters—the same as for newspaper copy. Many people think they should write broadcast copy in all caps. But all-cap writing is much harder to read than caps and lowercase.

Double- or triple-space your news copy. Keep it free of errors and too many edits. Messy copy should be retyped to make it easy to read.

Use phonetic spellings of confusing words or names. Use underlining if necessary to mark the emphasis clearly in your copy so that you can quickly and easily read it. (*McNerny* becomes *Mac-ner-nee*; *DeFloria* becomes *Deh-Flohr-ee-uh*). Verify identifications such as professional titles (*Dr., Associate Professor, Mayor*) and courtesy titles (*Mr., Ms., Miss, Mrs.*).

Without fail, always read your copy out loud before going on the air. If it doesn't flow easily, it needs to be rewritten.

Write television copy to correspond to the pictures—but not too closely. The pictures should illustrate the subject of the copy. The copy should add what is not said by the pictures alone. Strive for the goal suggested by this sentence: "I saw it on the radio."

When writing television scripts, divide the page down the middle. Type the story copy and notes about music or sound effects on the right-hand half of the page. Use the left-hand half for video instructions to the director or the story videotape editor. These instructions should tell what studio shots are called for, or what pictures, video, or graphics go with the copy you have written. Develop a numbering system that coordinates video with audio.

The **ON DISPLAY** feature on page 384 demonstrates how you might set up your copy. It's also an example of good storytelling on a human-interest subject that's relevant to students and other viewers in the community.

TERMS worth knowing

Video and audio terms. Student broadcasters should be familiar with these terms.

close-up (cu): a portraitlike shot showing a person's head and neckline; a camera shot that is very near to a subject to show detail

long shot (ls) or **wide shot (ws):** a camera shot that shows the main subject in its surroundings

establishing shot: a camera shot that shows the subject as well as its position and relation to its entire surroundings; a variation of a long shot

medium shot (ms): a camera shot that shows a person cut off just below the waist

medium-long shot (mls): a camera shot in which an entire subject appears, with a little space above and below

pan: to move the camera to follow the motion of a subject

tilt: to move the camera head up or down in a vertical motion

track: to capture horizontal movement by moving the entire camera

dolly: to move the camera toward or away from the subject

zoom: to manipulate the lens of the camera so as to create the appearance of moving closer or farther away from the subject

fade: to bring the picture from blackness into its full light (*fade in*) or take it from its full light into blackness (*fade out*).

dissolve: to fade in one screen image while fading out a previous screen image

cut: an instant switch from one shot to another without fading

voiceover (VO): a voice heard on the audio track without that person being seen on screen

Broadcast Script

News 101, Española Valley High School, Fairview, New Mexico

The Pojoaque Elk Project

Tape	Video	Audio
1)2604	1. sky, tilt down to studio	1. music . . .
1)2635	2. see kids inside	
1)2636	3. zoom in	
1)2639	4. see all kids with Mike on left	
1)0047	5. pan left to Mike and Agoyo and then to elk, large in plaster	5. VO 1)5550 Keith: . . . we're sculpting an elk
4)14324	6. elk crossing sign, zoom in	6. VO 1)1657 . . . it's our school mascot
1)13059	7. Agoyo Talache, student, artist	7. Everybody got assigned a part of the body.
1)1211	8. Jeremy sits down with head in hands	Jeremy has the head. . . .
1)0307	9. ws body, tilt up to Keith	Keith has the body.
1)0702	10. Jessica with antlers	Jessica has antlers
1)2928	11. four hands on ear, Mike and Agoyo, tilt up to Agoyo	and I carve the ears . . . and after hat we're each going to make a leg.
1)3909	12. Agoyo with knife and ear	VO 1)13120 . . . and at the end we're going to put it
1)0851	13. model of black elk, from side, top, and then pull out	together and put it in our school.
1)2246	14. ws, Mike with antlers, Jessica on right	14. VO 1)10350 Jessica: Michael is an artist and he's been a really good teacher.
1)2258	15. zoom in to Mike's hands on antlers	
1)5131	16. Keith Vigil Carleton, student, artist	16. He teaches by feel, being that he's blind.
1)3129	17. Mike feeling head	17. VO 1)10900 . . . you see more with your hands in
1)3217	18. Mike feels body with Keith	sculpture . . . you may look at something and say that looks really good and then you feel it and realize that
1)0059	19. see ear in hands, tilt up to Michael's face	there's a large bump on the side of it.
1)10913	20. Jessica Lujan, student, artist	20. I mean, I think he sees more than we do a lot of the time.
1)0320	21. circle around Keith working	21. VO 1)4736 Keith: I've learned a lot from Michael. He's taught me to take my time, and gradually you'll
1)0746	22. Keith tilt down, see chips on floor	begin to see it.
1)2711	23. Keith's hand carving, cu	
4)0644	24. see 3 kids, pull out to see all 4 and Mike	24. VO 1)10617 . . . working with a bunch of people is kind of interesting; it makes it more fun.
4)3204	25. Jeremy hits Agoyo with head	
1)0923	26. Jessica and Jeremy from side, working	26. VO 1)10649 . . . we help each other out a lot
1)13909	27. Jeremy Perez, student, artist	27. We start off by carving everything out of styrofoam . . .
1)3645	28. Jeremy sands, OTS	28. and sand it down to give it . . . a rough texture . . .
1)3740	29. cu fingers sanding	
1)3941	30. see small black elk between two dark figures	and then we make it into a mold.
4)3009	31. cu little black elk	and then you cast it in bronze
5)0727	32. large elk hanging	and then it's finally put on top of the pedestal at the
5)0838	33. elk on pedestal with school behind	school.
5)1140	34. Michael Naranjo, artist	34. I think it was a fantastic learning experience for the students as well as for myself. It gave them this
	35. news article	whole feeling that anything is possible if you make the effort.
	36. news article	
6)2656	37. see finished elk in front of school, strobe out	37. For News 101, this is _____ from Española Valley High School.

Use this checklist to evaluate your broadcasting writing or the writing of a classmate.

EVALUATION CHECKLIST

Broadcast Script

☑ Has a standard organization pattern been used to present the story?

☑ Is the story told in an interesting way, built around a nugget whenever possible?

☑ Is the copy made easy to read through phonetic spellings, caps and lowercase letters, and double- or triple-spacing?

☑ Are active voice, present tense, and clear, simple writing used?

☑ If the script is for television, is it set up in standard format, with instructions on the left and copy on the right?

The School Broadcasting Station

School broadcasting stations can vary greatly in size and scope. Many involve only a handful of staff members; others employ numerous students. Some schools even secure licenses for limited broadcasting from the Federal Communications Commission (FCC). The chart on page 386 shows a typical organizational structure for an educational broadcasting station.

At the top of the organization is the board of trustees, board of education, or similar entity; if the station is licensed, it's licensed under the name of this group. This board is ultimately responsible for the station's operations and programming.

In practical terms, day-to-day operations and programming supervision are delegated to a faculty adviser—often someone in communications, journalism, or a related academic department. The adviser may also be a staff member, such as the director of student activities. The adviser oversees the station and serves as liaison between the licensee board and the station itself.

An optional advisory or policy board may consist of representatives from various groups within the school, including students, faculty, and

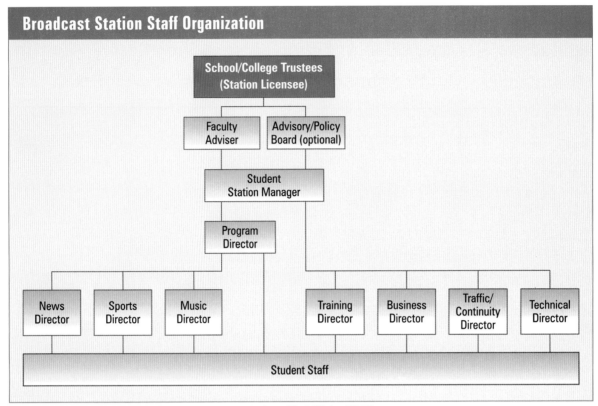

This organization chart was provided by Jeff Tillis, President, Intercollegiate Broadcasting System, P.O. 592, Vails Gate, NY 12584

An educational broadcasting station is often organized into a structure similar to the one shown here.

administrators. It may also include representatives of the community served by the station. The role of this board is generally to advise or to help set overall policy.

From this point, the remainder of the positions shown are normally held by students. Most serve on a voluntary basis, but some may receive a stipend, academic credit, a scholarship, or other appropriate recognition of the enormous amounts of time required to run a successful broadcast station.

Station Manager

The student station manager is the highest-ranking student on the staff. The station manager supervises the department directors and the student staff while also serving as principal liaison with the faculty adviser and advisory or policy board. It's the station manager who balances the individual department interests for the common good.

Program Director

The program director is in charge of all on-air programming. This includes the design of the program schedule, the music format (the type of music played), the selection and assignment of announcers, and the mixture of news, sports, and music to be presented by the station. Working closely with the program director will be one or more production directors, who manage all production and editing for broadcast programs.

News Director

The news director works with the program director to select and schedule news programming, news announcers, reporters, writers, and editors. The news director sets the format to be followed for newscasts and other news and public-affairs programming. This includes story selection, assignment of reporters, writing style, and integration of audio. He or she also selects (within the realistic limitations of the station's budget) equipment and news services to be used by the news department.

Sports Director

The sports director works with the program director to select and schedule sports programming and sports announcers. He or she helps set the sportscast format and helps decide which sports events the station will broadcast play by play. The sports director selects (within budget limitations) portable and remote equipment to be used by the sports department.

Music Director

The music director assists announcers with music selection within the format(s) decided upon by the program director. The music director is responsible for the acquisition of CDs for the station and for maintaining continuing contact with recording companies. Such contact may take the form of periodic playlists to let the companies (and the station's listeners) know what the station is playing. The music director may also be responsible for cataloging new music received by the station, unless there is a music librarian handling that duty. Even in such cases, the librarian is usually supervised by the music director.

Training Director

The training director is responsible for recruiting and training of new station personnel as well as for ongoing training of existing staff.

Business Director

The business director keeps the station's records of income and expenditures, works with appropriate financial authorities within the school, prepares annual operating and capital budgets, and works with the station manager to keep the station's spending within its approved budgetary limits.

Traffic/Continuity Director

The traffic/continuity director prepares and schedules all public service announcements (PSAs) and promotional announcements for programs. He or she also prepares and oversees correction of station logs. The station log is a record of everything that's broadcast during the hours the station is on the air, including regular and special programs, PSAs, and commercials. The date, time, and duration of each item is noted. Complete station logs are required by the FCC.

Careers in broadcasting range from nightly news anchor to such behind-the-scenes jobs as writer, producer, and camera operator.

Technical Director

The technical director (sometimes called the chief engineer) is responsible for the installation, operation, maintenance, and repair of all studio and transmitting equipment, compliance with all FCC technical requirements, and the recommendation of new studio and transmitting equipment.

Station Promotion

In addition to managing the broadcasting and business functions of a station, it's important to build support for station programming. This support usually comes from two areas: contributions and listeners or viewers.

Staffs will usually have a development director, whose job is to seek program underwriting (support) grants and contributions from businesses, foundations, individuals, and other sources. For closed-circuit stations, this position may be called sales director, in which case it involves the sale of advertising time.

A public relations director often is named to promote the station to potential listeners or viewers. He or she writes news releases and places them in appropriate media to attract program interest, prepares spot announcements for use on the air to promote upcoming programs, and develops special events, such as contests, to attract an audience. (For more information on public relations, see Chapter 16.)

Broadcasting Careers

Opportunities in radio and television continue to grow. The number of specialty networks and cable channels, for example, is increasing constantly. More all-news networks are coming into existence, and more all-news-and-talk radio stations are available at the local level. Direct satellite transmission of radio signals and television channels is also growing.

Although few journalists will ever anchor the nightly news, many professionals are needed to keep newscasts on the air—people who gather the news, write, edit, film or tape, or produce the program. There are places for librarians, secretaries, advertising sales personnel, and even pilots.

It's unlikely that television and radio will ever replace print media. Electronic media are, however, important communications vehicles. Many journalists move from one medium to another.

 Wrap-up

Radio and television play an important role in our everyday lives. There are few places you can go where you're not near a radio or TV set. Broadcasts even come through your computer and over the Internet.

Many avenues offer students experience in broadcasting and opportunities to learn how to do broadcast writing. Depending on resources available, students can, for example, prepare stories in broadcast format, using a tape recorder or video camera, to play in class for other students to critique. They may also use the school intercom system to broadcast the day's news and announcements. In some cases students may be permitted to operate a complete radio or television station (licensed or closed circuit) or to prepare news reports for use by local radio or television stations.

Broadcast writing must be clear, concise, and to the point. People hear things differently from how they read them. A story on the radio can't be "reread" if someone didn't hear it correctly.

Writing for broadcasting starts with the same principles of good journalism as writing for print. You do your homework and dig into the story.

Focus on what makes it interesting and how to create a visual image for the listener or viewer. Even on television, words must be well chosen to complement the pictures.

Among the many basic story patterns that broadcast journalists use are cause and effect, problem-solution-results, and comparison.

When writing copy, find the "nugget"—that bit of information that stands out. Finding the "nugget" doesn't mean writing cute copy; it means writing interesting and unique copy. Whenever possible, write in the active voice. Radio and television provide immediacy. The listener is "there"—at the trial, next to the damage caused by the hurricane, with you at the football game, at the scene of the accident, on the floor of the student council meeting. The listener is hearing the words of people making the news as part of your newscast.

Some of the many staff jobs at scholastic broadcasting stations—such as program director, sports director, and technical director—may lead to careers in the ever-expanding field of broadcast journalism.

On Assignment

INDIVIDUAL ACTIVITIES

1. Write a brief definition of each of these terms:

broadcast journalism   program director
flair   station log
music format   station manager
nugget   technical director

2. Tape-record a radio or television news story that you think has been reported with flair. Play the story in class and defend its strong points. What made the story good? Was it only word choice or also the ideas and sequencing of events? Discuss your ideas with others in the class.

3. Clip three news stories from your school newspaper and rewrite them into broadcast style, using the three organization patterns you have learned. Then adjust the stories for television, indicating what visuals you would use to illustrate them. Attach the original stories to your work.

4. Are some stories more effectively handled in one medium than in the other? Watch the local television news tonight. List the stories in the order presented and the time allocated to each. Then read the local newspaper the next morning. How were those same stories treated? Write a news story comparing and contrasting the coverage.

5. Write and record a five-minute newscast on the activities in your school for a single day. Plan two commercials to promote school events (the next sports event, play, or dance). Compare your choice of topics to those of other students.

6. Record a brief interview on a specific topic with a teacher, a student leader, or someone in the community. Before the interview, arrange your questions in logical sequence but be prepared for quick thinking, changes in direction, or following up on new leads as the interview evolves. Ask three students—at least one not involved in journalism—to critique your interview. Were the questions good? Did you follow up? What angles did you miss that would have been interesting?

7. Test your critical thinking. Today there are more news programs on the air than ever before. In addition to 24-hour-coverage on stations such as CNN, all of the major networks have one or more news shows in prime time. Choose one program or news outlet and watch several hours of it. Then write an evaluation of the depth of its coverage and the relevancy of its stories.

8. Write a one-page critique of broadcast script in the On Display feature on page 384. Use the Evaluation Checklist on page 385.

TEAM ACTIVITY

9. As a class, brainstorm topics for documentaries about some facet of your school. Select the top ideas so that there is one for each team. Next, as a team, determine your approach to the story, including whom you will need to talk to. Outline a possible scenario so that you have some established direction. Then set up and conduct interviews, using a tape recorder or video camera. Take good notes to guide your use of the tapes, and prepare introductory and follow-up copy. Produce a 10-minute documentary, and play it for your class to critique.

SURF THE NET

10. Radio and television have found their way onto the Internet. You can find video clips or sound presentations on many company and media web sites. Check out the web sites of such news sources as the major TV networks, as well as local stations and newspapers. Also, go to the web site of the National Press Club (NPC) at www.press.org. to participate in live news conferences as they take place. How easy is it to access audio and video via computer? What types of stories are typically covered? Summarize your experiences with the sites you visited in a short report or review.

career profile

TV Anchor

Katherine Adams

"The biggest advantage of being a journalist is being a witness to history," says Katherine Adams, Emmy Award–winning journalist and former anchor at Detroit's WDIV-TV.

"A journalist is often given a front row seat to events that impact the lives of people," she said.

According to Adams, a journalist has a great responsibility—and she takes that responsibility seriously. Her interest in broadcasting was sparked when she watched classmates at Kent State University prepare for a television program.

"They were putting together a half-hour talk show," Adams recalled. "I was fascinated by the technology, the immediacy, and the creativity displayed. It was then I decided to major in telecommunications."

Adams began her career at Storer Broadcasting Company, starting out as a copy aide and eventually becoming a production assistant.

This exposure taught her a few things. "I realized how much knowledge, intensity . . . were needed to make headway in this field," Adams said. So she concentrated on developing her skills. Soon she showed such promise that she was enrolled in a training program to become a reporter.

In 1976 Adams moved to Cleveland to join the staff at WJKW-TV as a weekend anchor and reporter. After a short time she was promoted to weekday anchor and host of a public affairs program.

Adams gained five years of experience at WJKW-TV before moving to Detroit to WJBK-TV. Within one year she became co-anchor of the six- and eleven-o'clock newscasts. She also has been coanchor of *Newsbeat Today,* the first locally produced morning news hour in Detroit and one of the most consistently watched.

Adams has had half a dozen Emmy nominations, including one for commentary. She won her Emmy for the documentary "Bridge over Troubled Water."

The path to her present success has not always been easy, but Adams has pushed on. "Every experience—whether good or bad—is an experience I've learned from," she said.

Among her many honors, Adams was nominated twice as Outstanding Woman Newscaster by American Women in Radio and Television in Detroit. National American Women in Radio and Television recognized Adams and WJBK-TV for excellence in programming and presentation of a positive and realistic portrayal of women.

Adams gives this advice to aspiring journalists: "Strive for perfection in your writing and delivery. Use your heritage, and don't deny it. Finally, accept the great responsibility of being a role model, and conduct your life . . . in such a way that it will be an inspiration to others, no matter what their race, creed, or color."

FOLLOW-UP

1. Adams's college major was telecommunications. What kinds of courses must one take to complete such a major? Get information from the various colleges and universities in your area.

2. Find out about a news anchor's job by interviewing an anchor or doing library research on the profession. Do anchors write and produce their own stories? How much of their work involves coordinating the work of others? Report your findings to the class.

CHAPTER 16

Understanding and Using Public Relations

Not all journalism students actually start their careers as journalists, and many who do begin as journalists change careers along the way. Public relations (PR) is one field in which journalism skills can be very helpful. Public relations professionals use their writing and editing abilities to shape public opinion in corporations and businesses, for organizations and associations, for political candidates, in public relations agencies, or on their own as freelancers.

Public relations also is a good way to combine other interests with journalism. For example, if you consider yourself an environmentalist, you can seek a career with environmental organizations or companies specializing in that area of business. Most colleges and universities, and many school districts, have public relations departments allowing professionals to link their skills in media and communications

public relations	target audience	news release
publics	student news bureau	embargo

If you're an environmentalist, you can work as a public relations professional with environmental organizations or companies specializing in that area.

with education interests. The list of possibilities is long.

This chapter is intended to give information about how you can use your journalistic abilities in developing public relations skills. Journalists, for example, are inquisitive and know how to get and interpret information. Getting and interpreting information is important to PR professionals. Journalists know how to use the information they gather to write in a manner that communicates effectively. PR requires effective, easily understood writing that will help an organization communicate its views to target audiences.

PR professionals also have to know what the media needs and how it works. Companies and agencies often organize their public relations departments to include specialists in media relations—people who have the ability to think, write, and work effectively with journalists. They work as part of an account or department team to develop the organization's public relations strategy and then use their special expertise to help implement media-related programs.

Student journalists can apply journalistic skills in public relations in many ways. To get started, it's important to understand what public relations is and how the public relations process works.

✓ worth taking

Determining your publics. Make a list of your publics as you prepare a public relations campaign. Post your list in a visible spot to keep these audiences in mind for all you plan. Generally, publics for a school community include the following:

- students
- teachers
- administrators—at the school and in central administration
- office personnel
- support staff—cooks, custodians, bus drivers
- parents of the students
- neighbors (who have no children or grandchildren in school)
- businesses

Lists of publics can easily be expanded or tightened according to the specific audiences to be reached. For example, students might be divided by age, grade level, sex, specific courses being taken, club or specific sports-team membership, or possession of a driver's license.

Defining Public Relations

Public relations may be defined in various ways. The late Edward L. Bernays is credited as one of the founders of this profession in the early 1920s. Bernays saw this new field, which was based on the social sciences, as combining communications and a knowledge of public opinion, human behavior, and motivations to reinforce, modify, or change how groups of people think or act. Each of these groups of people is considered a "public," and there are many of them. On a simple level, therefore, *PR* may be defined as the practice of managing communication between an organization and its publics.

According to Bernays, a public relations professional is guided by a set of ethics and a sense of social responsibility. He or she is not to be confused with press agents and publicists, who use the media as a means for presenting information to the public primarily to promote a cause, a person, or an event.

Today, a number of public relations professionals and public relations firms refer to what they do as "reputation management." Under this definition, an organization's reputation is viewed as an asset to help the organization achieve its objectives while minimizing the resistance of various publics to those objectives.

A Public Relations Model

Regardless of definition, effective public relations strategies are designed along models such as this one, which was developed by Alfred Geduldig, a leading public relations consultant:

- **Objectives.** Determine what you want to accomplish for the organization.

Public Relations Ethics

Where should the line be drawn between business and morals?

Public relations firms should not use phone questionnaires to gather information from consumers about a client's product unless the client is clearly identified as the source of the questionnaire.

Public relations is a worthy and long-established profession, but some people appear to mistrust it. Because PR campaigns try to help companies or organizations put their best foot forward, critics feel that something deceptive must be going on—that the campaign is helping the client hide something.

According to *Media Ethics: Cases and Moral Reasoning* by Christians, Fackler, and Rotzoll (Longman, 1995), public relations workers fill a unique dual function, informing and persuading, but there's no reason why both cannot be done in an honest and ethical manner. Situations arise, though, that require hard decisions. The Public Relations Society of America has a code of standards (see page 547 in the Appendix), but it doesn't cover every situation.

Suppose a conscientious PR professional does the research necessary to give a client an effective campaign. Despite that research, however, the client wants to do the campaign in his or her own way, which promises to be less effective. Should the PR person simply acquiesce, knowing that the client's approach will not achieve the desired results? Is the PR job supposed to be doing things the right way, or is the client's happiness all that matters? Christians, Fackler, and Rotzoll argue that keeping the client happy, although necessary from a business stand-point, causes the PR person to lose a certain moral edge in the process.

One hard question is *how much* of the truth must be told in a PR campaign. Christians, Fackler, and Rotzoll mentions the case of a charitable organization that, while not entirely destitute, would probably have to curtail some services unless more money could be raised. The PR agency decided to institute a campaign that would focus on some of the needy people that the charity helped, suggesting (but not saying directly) that help

for these people might soon be cut off without more funding. Some of the charity's backers objected to the approach, which focused on only one aspect of their work and would make the situation look worse off than it was. The organization *did* help the sort of needy people the ad depicted; therefore, running an ad that viewers would respond to emotionally might not be considered by some a distortion of reality.

Some cases are more clear cut. Say a client wants to disguise itself as the source of a phone questionnaire designed to gather information on attitudes toward its product. The client assumes that it is free to use the names and addresses of the people it questions as leads for new sales. In this case the PR person should refuse to go along with the client. Getting information under false pretenses and using it for gain is unethical.

Ethical questions can be tricky, and the answers can't always be generalized. A PR professional needs to consider each situation carefully and get help when necessary to make the most honest and moral decision possible.

FOLLOW-UP

1. Look for TV ads that involve public relations and jot down their contents to discuss in class. What distinguishes these ads from those that sell products?
2. Think of situations in your own life in which, like the PR worker in the first example, someone was proposing to ignore your research or proposal. Were you able to change the person's mind? If not, what might you have done differently?

▶ **Audiences.** Know which publics are the target for your communications and which groups are important for their ability to influence those target audiences (positively or negatively).

▶ **Desired action.** Define clearly what you want the audiences to do (support, stay neutral, buy a product, and so on).

▶ **Research.** Evaluate what target audiences or publics currently know, think, and believe about an organization, issue, or subject; their motivation for holding the opinions they do; how they get information and who they feel are credible sources (including the media). Engage in fact finding (including database and library research).

▶ **Risks.** Define the risks and barriers that may affect the public relations plan.

▶ **Themes and messages.** Develop information based on the research that will help you affect the behavior of target audiences.

▶ **Action plan.** Determine how you will communicate your messages to these audiences—for example, which media will be used (radio, television, newspapers, newsletters, e-mail, the Internet, direct mail, billboards, posters); timing; meetings, special events, or other nonmedia techniques.

▶ **Budget.** Determine how much the plan will cost in terms of financial resources and the use of people.

▶ **Assessment.** Set measures, in advance, that will help evaluate the effectiveness of your strategy; that is, give ways to measure how successful you are in achieving your objectives with target audiences (Did they receive your messages? Did they take the action you wanted?).

▶ **Course correction.** Take action to change the strategy, messages, or techniques when assessment suggests that the plan is not achieving its objectives as well as it should.

Public Relations for Student Journalists

You can gain public relations experience in a number of ways—on your own time and in school. For example, if you're involved in church, cultural, community, and civic organizations, you can join their PR committees, using your journalism skills to help prepare materials that will further the group's objectives. This may include writing newsletters, conducting research, appearing as a spokesperson before groups or the press, writing speeches, organizing special events, taking photographs, designing brochures, or drafting news releases (information provided to the media for distribution to the public). You can also play a role by planning and implementing campaigns, getting measures through city councils, and supporting issues important to the community.

Working with the School PR Agency

You may also help your school with its public relations. Take a look at all of the things being written about in the school newspaper—musical events, scholarship announcements, fund-raising projects, sports-recognition dinners, class reunions, guest speakers, and so on. Each event may be of interest not only to students but also to one or more of the publics outside the school.

You can even offer to help the school create and implement a public relations campaign. Using the planning model on pages 397–398, you can develop a campaign appropriate to school and outside publics, such as a school-bus safety program.

A public relations campaign to promote safer bus riding for grade-school students may involve parents and teachers as well as the children.

TIPS *worth taking*

Planning PR campaigns. Here are some helpful hints to consider as you plan a PR campaign:

▶ Know the issue inside and out.
▶ Know which community organizations already address the issue and how they do so.
▶ Don't reinvent an existing program.
▶ Determine which are your primary publics and which are secondary.
▶ Consider bringing existing information to your publics in new ways.
▶ Define how you will measure the success of each objective.

Establishing a Student News Bureau

One of the simplest ways to practice the media specialty of PR is through a student news bureau. A news bureau provides information about the school to its publics. For example, the bureau may provide short broadcast "feeds" over the phone for local radio stations to incorporate into their newscasts. Stories can also be put on an Internet home page promoted to and designed for nonstudents. Articles written about students, faculty, activities, and programs for the student media can be submitted as news releases for use in the local daily or weekly newspaper, on radio, and on television. Depending on the situation, news releases can also be offered to church, company, and area business newsletters.

News Releases

News releases are typically written to suit the media in which they will be delivered. If they are adapted from articles in your school paper, they may be released early on the day the newspaper is distributed. Major stories can be sent early with a note that the story is embargoed (not to be published) until a specific day and time, allowing it to appear first in the school newspaper. Instructions for the timing of the release (for example, "For Immediate Release" or "For Release [date]") should appear at the top of the news release.

Writing a news release can be somewhat different from writing a newspaper article. A news release distills the most important information from the article and is usually written in the inverted-pyramid structure. It typically includes quotes from company spokespeople and should be accompanied by contact information for the issuing organization. The **ON DISPLAY** feature on page 401 is a news release adapted from a longer story in the school press.

News Release

The Rampage, Green Mountain High School, Lakewood, Colorado

News from Green Mountain High School
For more information contact Journalism Department, phone 303-555-9500 (weekdays 8 A.M. to 4 P.M.)

Green Mountain student named state's top high school volunteer

Lakewood (Colo.) Feb. 27—Marissa Olson, a Green Mountain High School senior, was named today as one of the top 104 youth volunteers in America and Colorado's top high school volunteer in the Prudential Spirit of Community Awards program, sponsored in partnership with the National Assn. of Secondary School Principals.

Olson was recognized for her work in establishing S.T.A.N.D., Students Taking a New Direction, an organization promoting student involvement in the community. It has been responsible for such activities as Red Ribbon Week and the Neon Drunk Driving Simulator. Olson spent more than two years planning the program before it was launched last January.

As the state honoree, Olson will receive a silver medallion, $1,000, and an expense-paid trip to Washington, D.C., with one of her parents for national recognition events. At those events, 10 of the 104 honorees will be named as the top volunteers in America, and will receive an additional $5,000, a gold medallion, and a trophy.

"There used to be a SADD chapter at GM that dwindled because the leadership was very hypocritical," said Olson. "Many of the students who said 'don't drink' were going out and getting drunk. I was very scared of losing any of my classmates in car accidents."

Scott Peterson, Prudential executive director of the annual awards program, said, "Having seen what they have accomplished has really made us feel that there is a place for this program. We had over 6,000 applicants."

GM Principal Liz Treichler said that Olson "really works to make things happen."

--30--

When assessing your own news releases or those written by your class-mates, use the criteria in this checklist to make sure that the release is as good as it can be.

EVALUATION CHECKLIST

News Release

☑ Does the release include the most noteworthy features of the news story?

☑ Is the information included in the release chosen for its relevance to a particular public?

☑ Have all names, dates, and facts been double-checked for accuracy?

☑ If an embargo is required, are the time and date clearly indicated?

☑ Is the release free from grammatical errors and in accordance with the publication and general AP style?

Public Relations Careers

Careers in public relations can be challenging and rewarding. Although not all PR people have journalism backgrounds, those who do may be able to use their journalistic skills to develop and implement exciting programs designed to motivate target publics.

PR people may be generalists, doing a wide range of things, or specialists in areas such as media relations. Specific tasks for PR professionals may include any or all of the following:

▶ writing, designing, producing company publications for employees, customers, or investors

▶ writing editorial pieces for the company, cause, or client

▶ organizing and managing special events such as trade fairs, receptions, art shows, and tours

▶ arranging for speaking opportunities that will reach target audiences with important company or organizational messages

One function of public relations is helping companies to sell their products in more effective ways. Many companies sponsor festivals and special events that draw in target audiences.

▶ writing speeches for and news releases about speaking events, and coordinating mailings of the speech to other key audiences
▶ serving as official spokespersons for the organizations they represent

Some public relations people specialize in marketing communications—helping companies sell their products more effectively. They may incorporate various media techniques, often coordinating special campaigns and events that supplement paid advertising programs by attracting audience and media interest.

Wrap-up

Public relations and journalism are professions that rely on each other. PR people work closely with the news media to communicate messages about their organization, issue, business, or clients to various audiences that are important to them. At the same time, journalists use public relations people as resources for many of the stories they write. Although not all people who enter the PR profession will be journalists or have journalistic skills, many do.

Public relations is based on blending social sciences with communications. It uses a knowledge of public opinion, human behavior, and motivation to reinforce, modify, or change how groups of people—referred to as "publics"—think or act. Public relations professionals develop programs and events, utilize media, and apply a wide range of communications techniques to get these publics to behave in a certain way as a response to their work. In many ways, PR seeks to accomplish a call to action like that of editorials and advertising.

Public relations strategies are often designed according to a model. The model begins with setting clear objectives that are to be accomplished by a PR program, identifying the target audiences (publics), and determining what action the target audiences are expected to take, such as support-

ing a certain position on an issue. It goes on to study research to understand how to best communicate with the target audience and then develops themes and messages to help achieve the objectives of the program. Finally, it lays out an action plan, summarizes the human and financial resources required to implement that plan, determines how to assess the plan to see whether it's having the desired effects on target audiences, and provides ways to revise the plan if necessary.

Student journalists can apply their writing and editing skills to public relations. One way is to join the PR committees of local nonprofit organizations, political campaigns, or other groups. Another is to work with the school's PR team on a special campaign, such as school-bus safety. Yet another is to be involved in a student news bureau, sending relevant school information to the local media.

Many rewarding PR jobs exist, and a good number of journalists find their way into them. Opportunities exist in businesses, schools, hospitals, government, various community organizations, and many other organizations. There are also specialty PR jobs, such as speechwriter or media spokesperson for a political candidate, an issue, or a cause.

On Assignment

INDIVIDUAL ACTIVITIES

1. Write a brief definition of each of these terms:

embargo	publics
news release	student news bureau
public relations	target audience

2. How well does the news release on page 401 fulfill the requirements of a news release? Write a paragraph explaining your opinion. Use specific examples to support your views.

3. In the last issue of the school newspaper, mark each story that you think would be of interest to one of the nonstudent publics of your school. Specify the top two external audiences for each story. Then determine what would need to be done to make two of the articles acceptable as news releases to those audiences. Rewrite them as needed.

4. Evaluate the various sample articles in this book for their adaptability into news releases. Choose one that contains information that would be of some value to a defined public. Then rewrite the story as a news release. Be ready to explain why you chose the article you did.

5. Choose one of the following topics as a focus for a public relations campaign in your community. Use the PR planning model on pages 396 and 398 to plot the general actions for the campaign. Then compare notes with others who have chosen the same topic. Discuss the strengths and weaknesses of each plan in class:
- ▶ securing volunteer readers for a local senior-citizens center
- ▶ getting young adults registered to vote

- ▶ bringing a greater variety of summertime activities into the community
- ▶ educating children about being cautious with strangers
- ▶ keeping people from cutting down large old trees
- ▶ a school or community issue of your choice

6. If your school has a public relations or public affairs staff member, invite him or her to meet with your class to discuss how public relations is organized and managed. You may also invite a representative from a PR agency in your community. Determine what model the representative relies on to develop a PR plan, and learn how each aspect of the model discussed in this chapter is included in that plan. Write an interview story based on the presentation.

7. Test your critical thinking. Read the Public Relations Society of America's Code of Ethics (page 547 in the Appendix) and compare it with the Society of Professional Journalists' Code of Ethics (pages 541–543). What conflicts, if any, do you see between the two codes? How can an ethical PR person work effectively with journalists? Invite a local media representative and a public relations professional to your school, or arrange a three-way telephone call to discuss these questions. Do your ideas agree with theirs?

TEAM ACTIVITIES

8. Organize the class into teams. Each team should select a school event scheduled for the next couple of months. Learn all you can about the event. Meet with its sponsors or program chairs. (They become your client.) Using the PR planning model, develop a PR plan. Review the plan with the other teams. Then make additions and appropriate changes. Present the plan to the client. If your client is willing, implement the plan.

9. Implement the PR plan you worked out in activity 5. Team up with students who have chosen the same topic as yours. Combine everyone's ideas into a workable, written plan. Do the necessary research, including interviewing people and obtaining approvals as necessary. Then implement the plan.

SURF THE NET

10. From television or newspapers, identify a public relations campaign or event staged by a company or organization in your area. Then find that group's web site and see how it is used to promote the PR activity.

career profile

Public Relations Executive

Elizabeth Krupnick

Although Elizabeth Krupnick's journey to a top corporate communications position has been somewhat circuitous and unorthodox, she says that she had the "journalism bug" from an early age.

Krupnick, chief communications officer for the insurance company New York Life, grew up in New York. The daughter of a journalist, she attributes much of her early interest in journalism to having "four papers on the breakfast table every day."

She graduated from Colby College in Maine with a B.A. in art history, returning to New York to work for a small ad agency. At 25, she went to the prestigious School of Journalism at the University of Missouri in Columbia, where she earned her master's degree.

Although Krupnick always dreamed of working for a newspaper, she originally opted for teaching college journalism. Jobs took her from Massachusetts to Maine to Oregon. She then launched her career in public relations at Aetna Life & Casualty, where she rose to the position of senior vice president of corporate affairs. Later she worked as chief communications officer for The Prudential, another life insurance company.

"In many ways, I got lucky," she says. "I was at the right place at the right time."

Luck may have played a role in her career, but she was clearly prepared each time luck offered an opportunity. Krupnick thinks she was served well by her "academic bent," her development and use of analytical skills, and the knowledge and understanding she gained from traveling at an early age.

Krupnick's responsibilities reflect the diverse role of many of today's communicators. As a chief communications officer, Krupnick has managed public relations, advertising, internal communications, speechwriting, creative services, issues management, and research functions.

Because of the various potential directions for a journalism-based career today, she senses that "a liberal arts education is more important than ever before," adding that in many cases high school education has been inadequate.

"What is most missing today is strength in writing, and it drives me crazy," she said, "but intelligence is as important as education."

Krupnick believes that one of the keys to her success and to her ability as a writer was her work on the University of Missouri newspaper. The newspaper was "run as the town daily" in Columbia, providing a remarkable experience for someone who had "a good nose for sniffing out stuff."

"Covering city government is a great experience for a student. It's mundane, yet something fun is always going on—kind of a potent thing in your twenties. That's good for beginning journalists," she said.

She feels that succeeding in journalism today is tough and that the competition is strong.

"I suggest you go to a big journalism school because the networks [of contacts] you make there are so important," she said.

FOLLOW-UP

1. Krupnick speaks of the importance of analytical skills. What are they, and why might they be important in public relations? Give some examples.
2. Why might city-government stories, though "mundane," offer good experience to new reporters? Bring in some samples from local papers and discuss what was involved in covering them.

CHAPTER 17

Handling Finances: Advertising and Business

KEY CONCEPTS

After reading this chapter, you will

▶ understand the role and functions of the business staff

▶ know how to get information about your student market through surveys and other means

▶ understand how to procure ads and how they pay for publication expenses

▶ know how to plan, write, and lay out effective ads

▶ know the importance of record-keeping in managing circulation and keeping track of expenses

In addition to serving a news and editorial function, a student publication has business responsibilities. A newspaper has to be written and edited, and it must have money to pay its bills. Advertising and subscription revenues are essential to most professional publications and to many student publications as well. It becomes vital therefore to understand the buying habits of your publication's audience, how to use that information to make money, and how to manage the money you make.

This chapter will acquaint you with the activities of the business staffs of student publications that typically handle advertising and management of funds. The business side is not a competitor of the editorial side; the two must work together for a successful publication.

Too often student editors feel held back because of a shortage of funds. They need

Understanding the buying habits of a publication's audience will help the advertising staff design and sell ads, which bring in funds to support the publication.

to understand that although they may have excellent ideas, these ideas take money. Extra photos, artwork, color on every page of every issue, and extra pages for special features are not gifts from a printer. In short, just as the staff must exercise editorial and news responsibility, so must it exercise fiscal responsibility.

Business Staff Organization

Leading the business staff is the business manager. The business manager's role is to see that the three main functions of the business department—advertising sales and preparation, circulation and distribution, and record keeping—are carried out. The student business manager must be personable, aggressive, and able to lead a sales staff. He or she must also work closely with the editor to plan the number of pages of the publication, work out special layout needs, and coordinate production with the printer.

Assistant business managers, in addition to selling and preparing advertising, generally are assigned other specific duties. One may be in charge of circulation, another of billing or books and records, another of advertising. The specific breakdown will depend on the size of the staff and the publication; in some schools, for example, reporters also help sell advertising.

409

The organization of a business staff need not be elaborate. This model shows a simple breakdown based on the primary tasks the staff performs.

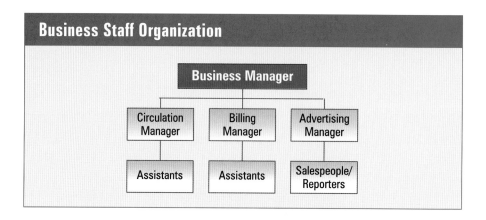

Business Staff Organization

Getting and Using Advertising Information

Advertising generates income for the publication, provides a means of communicating product or sales information from a business to the publication's readers, and assists the reader in selecting that business's products and services. Advertising also stimulates competition and helps keep prices down and the economy active.

Advertising is not a contribution to the student publication. You have a real product to sell. School publications are well read by students, who are today one of the largest single segments of purchasing power in this country. Well-prepared advertising aimed at students will bring many returns to the advertiser.

Unfortunately, some student publications do treat advertising as if it were a contribution by the business. Little boxes that say merely Joe's Pizza or Star Theater, do no one much good. It may not take much effort to get them ready for the printer, but they probably don't sell products. More than likely, they're not even read. The publication that carries this sort of advertising is cheating itself, the reader, and the advertiser.

On the other hand, a publication containing good display advertising that sells products readers like, want, and use regularly is performing a service for all parties concerned. Such advertising also makes student publications more attractive, and good advertising helps attract more good advertising. A successful ad can keep a business using your publication for years to come.

It's your responsibility to make sure that you know as much as possible about your student market. This means knowing how much money students have to spend, where they spend it, and when. If you have done your research, you will be able to go to your advertisers and tell them what potential for success their ads have.

Market Surveys

A very effective way to get information about the size, needs, and wants of the student market is to prepare and distribute a market survey. If your school offers classes in marketing, members may be willing to help conduct a survey for your staff. The questionnaire in the **ON DISPLAY** sample on pages 412–413 shows the types of questions you might ask.

You can also do an Internet search or check the *Readers' Guide* for recent stories on the youth market. You can even poll other teenagers through teen-oriented web sites. Translate what you learn into how much buying power teens have in your own community.

Advertising Sales

Once you know your market, the next step is to prepare a list of prospective advertisers. Ad salespeople should sit down with the business manager to create a list of prospects and a list of existing accounts. Existing accounts will need to be maintained. Prospects will need to be assigned.

If a student has a personal interest in a specific type of product, he or she is a natural to sell ads to stores dealing with that product. For example, if you happen to be an avid CD collector, you will do well selling advertising to music stores. Not all of your accounts will be of special interest to you. Nearly every product or service, however, will likely interest some of your readers, so don't overlook any potential advertiser.

When you have compiled your list of prospects—the advertising beat—contact them on a regular basis. It's always best to show prospects a sample ad to demonstrate your knowledge of the market and of their business. You might also prepare a standard pitch (sales talk) on how your publication operates and how this particular advertising idea will benefit the prospect's business.

A sample pitch. Let's consider how you might use information from the marketing survey in your sale. You could go to the local music store and tell the owner that 81 percent of your school's students have their own CD players and that 73 percent shop downtown where this store is

Market Survey
The Oracle, East High School, Lincoln, Nebraska

This is a marketing survey to aid the *Oracle* in evaluating its advertising efforts. Please answer all questions. Select only one answer for each question.

Marketing Survey

1. Sex

Male_____   Female_____

2. Age

under 14_____   15_____

16_____   17_____

18 or over _____

3. Grade

Freshman_____   Sophomore_____

Junior_____   Senior_____

4. What section of the *Oracle* do you read first?

page 1_____   editorial page_____

sports page _____   inside pages _____

5. Do you take the *Oracle* home?

never_____   always_____

occasionally_____

6. If you take the *Oracle* home, do your parents or caretakers read it?

yes_____   no_____

7. Do you have a part-time job?

yes_____   no_____

8. If you answered yes to number 7, how much do you earn weekly?

under $75_____ $75–$150_____

over $150_____   over $200_____

9. Do you have any other regular sources of income, such as an allowance?

yes_____   no_____

10. If so, how much weekly income do you receive from that source?

$20 or less _____ $21–$25_____

$26–$30 _____   over $31_____

Which items in questions 11–16 do you pay for with your own money?

11. School lunches

yes_____   no_____

12. Clothing

yes_____   no_____

13. Entertainment (movies, dances, etc.)

yes_____   no_____

14. School supplies

yes_____   no _____

15. Gasoline

yes_____   no _____

16. Cosmetics, toiletries, etc.

yes_____   no _____

17. Do you own a CD player?

yes_____   no_____

18. Do you own a VCR?

yes_____   no_____

19. Do you own your own car?

yes_____   no_____

20. Do you have a savings account?

yes_____   no_____

21. About how much money did you (or your parents) spend for clothing at the start of this school year?

up to $100 _____ $100–$200_____

$200–$250_____ $250–$300_____

over $300 _____

22. Where do you do most of your shopping?

downtown_____   Gateway _____

other _____

23. Which radio station do you listen to most?

KFOR_____   KLMS_____

KLIN_____   KFAB_____

KOIL_____   others _____

24. What TV network do you prefer to watch?

ABC_____   NBC_____

CBS _____   Fox _____

cable networks_____   other_____

25. About how often do you go to movies each month?

once_____   2–3 times _____

4 or more times_____   none _____

26. About how much do you spend (away from home and school) each week on food items like soft drinks, snacks, etc.?

less than $10_____ $10–$15_____

$15–$20_____   over $20 _____

27. Did you order a yearbook this year?

yes_____   no_____

28. Do you help make decisions about major family purchases?

yes_____   no_____

29. Do you read the *Oracle* ads?

never_____   occasionally_____

almost always_____

30. If there were a classified ad section in the *Oracle* would you utilize it (read and/or place an ad)?

yes_____   no_____

If you're an avid CD collector, you can use your knowledge and enthusiasm to sell advertising to music stores.

located, according to the survey of your readers. Use the research to point out how much students spend on entertainment, CDs, and similar items. Then show the prospect an ad featuring artists who are currently popular with your readers, pointing out that an ad like this could bring in business.

Discuss how little it costs to reach each student. For example, if a column inch in your newspaper costs $10, a 20-column-inch ad will cost $200. Divide that cost by the 1,200 students who regularly read your paper, and the ad costs 16 cents per reader—a great price for reaching a targeted audience.

When making a pitch to a store owner, be pleasant and answer questions politely. If the answer is no, thank him or her and leave your name, school phone number, and a rate card if you have one. Visit again when the next issue is being prepared. Don't give up.

Your attitude and appearance will have a direct effect on what you sell. Look neat and clean. It cannot be overemphasized that your appearance and attitude reflect the image of your school and your publication.

Ad Contracts

If you want to develop a businesslike relationship between the advertiser and your publication, you should have an advertising contract. It provides proof that the advertiser has agreed to the ad you plan to run, obligating

Tiger Times

Harper High School
24 W. Apple Road, Tarrington, Kansas 74633
Phone: (216) 555-2321

Adviser: _____

Business Manager: _____

AD CONTRACT

for the School Year _____

Date: _____

Advertiser: _____

Contact person and title: _____

Address (City/State/Zip): _____

Phone: _____ Fax: _____ E-mail: _____

Ad staff representative: _____

Publication Date	Size of Ad	Price
	Total Price	
	Minus Discount (if any)	
	Total Price with Discount	

Design
☐ camera-ready ad provided   ☐ custom-design ad per specs provided (attach specs to this contract)

Payment
☐ prepaid; pay at time of contract   ☐ bill after each insertion

The advertiser agrees to purchase advertising space in this newspaper, as indicated above. The advertiser understands the sizes and rates and agrees to the design, payment, and deadline terms specified on the current rate sheet.

Authorized signature (contact person): _____

Advertising contracts such as this one help maintain a businesslike relationship with advertisers and offer a clear explanation of rates and policies of a publication.

his or her company to pay the bills. You may complete contracts with advertisers before the year starts or complete them as each issue is prepared. Develop a contract that best suits your situation and make sure that completed contracts are signed by all appropriate parties.

Figuring Out Ad Revenue and Rates

No hard-and-fast rules exist for determining how many ads you need to sell—beyond making a profit. The overall goals of your staff will determine your sales goals. Be realistic. Some student publications barely break even from one year to the next. Others earn several hundred dollars each year, which are spent on special issues, photography equipment, computers, software, and supplies.

Before considering how to spend extra money, however, your staff must consider how much advertising it will take to pay for your publication. To do this, you must answer a number of questions for each issue: What are the particulars of the issue—number of pages, number of photos, and type of paper on which it will be printed? How much space can be devoted to advertising? These questions can be answered through a process such as the following.

QUOTES — worth quoting

A desirable advertisement . . . will command attention but never be offensive.

It will be reasonable, but never dull.

It will be original, but never self-conscious.

It will be imaginative, but never misleading.

And because of what it is and what it is not, a properly prepared advertisement will always be convincing and it will make people act.

—Fairfax M. Cone:
Foote, Cone & Belding, Inc.

Estimating expenses and advertising revenue. Let's assume that your next newspaper will be an eight-page, full-color homecoming issue. On newsprint, the cost may be as high as $4,000 for printing 2,000 copies of the issue (the cost will vary, depending on the printer). Because this is a special issue, you plan to have four color photos, each about three inches by four inches, for an additional cost of approximately $900. In addition, there will be a number of black-and-white photos, which the printer will factor into the base printing cost. This means that the newspaper will cost about $4,900 to print.

You will also need to factor other costs into the equation. You may determine that it will cost about $150 for photography supplies.

In addition, it will cost about $65 for postage to mail copies of the newspaper to other schools, advertisers, and outside subscribers. If you apply full accounting, you will factor the yearly estimated cost for computer disks, paper, toner, and other office supplies into the overall cost per issue. Assume that these miscellaneous costs average out to an additional $75 per issue. Your total expenses (printing, photography, supplies, and mailing) total $5,190. Let's say that you have $800 per issue in student activity fees as income. This means that the advertising revenue must be $4,390 to break even.

Determining advertising space. Assuming that your paper has five 16-inch columns per page, this issue has a total of 640 column inches of space. Most print media have a ratio of 60 percent advertising to 40 percent news, although a smaller percentage is not uncommon for school media. Let's say that, according to your newspaper policy, you can sell no more than 40 percent of the space in advertising. In this case, that percentage equals 256 column inches.

Calculating the ad rate. To determine the amount you must charge per column inch to break even, divide your advertising revenue estimate ($4,390) by your advertising space (256 column inches). The result is $17.15. Round this amount down to $17 to provide the advertising rate for a column inch. If the newspaper sold more or less than 40 percent, the cost per column inch would change as necessary.

A newspaper would not normally compute its rate on an issue-by-issue basis. In developing the annual budget, the costs for the foregoing items would be estimated for the total number of issues planned in the year ahead. From these estimates, you would establish an advertising rate.

You could also offer discounts to advertisers that agreed to advertise in each issue or purchase a certain number of column inches over the year or semester. Your bookkeeping might be more confusing with variable rates but you might snare larger accounts with such discounts.

Figuring costs for magazines and yearbooks. The process discussed here also applies to school magazines and yearbooks. After you calculate the subscription or sales income, subtract the costs of production—printing, photography, color, supplies, telephones, and postage. The amount that remains must be made up through advertising revenue or other fund-raising activities.

Preparing Advertising Copy

Well-prepared, well-written, well-designed advertising copy appeals to its intended audience and entices them to buy the product. Your ads will be better if you carefully think through audience, purpose, and message in advance. Remember, however, that no matter how creative your ideas, they must always be truthful and never misleading. Before you prepare any ad, become familiar with the Advertising Principles of American Business (see page 549 of the Appendix).

Get Ideas

Writing advertising copy starts with forming the ideas that will sell the products or services of the advertiser. In addition to what you learn from your market research about what appeals to your audience, various other techniques and methods can elicit ideas for copy.

Brainstorm benefits. Most advertising agencies and internal advertising departments have frequent creative meetings at which they brainstorm advertising concepts. The most important thing to sell in an advertisement is how the product benefits the student, so focus on benefits. For example, you don't sell toothpaste; you sell brighter teeth, fresher breath, saving money on dental bills. You don't sell laundry detergent; you sell cleaner, fresher-smelling clothes. Also brainstorm what students miss by not having the product or service. This can help you characterize the benefits. Look at how students can use the product. What makes this product or service better than what the competition offers?

Tap into consumer experiences and emotions. If what is being promoted is a product—or similar to a product—that you use, why do you use it? What has it done for you? How have you felt about it? What makes it a favorite of yours? Your experience as a consumer can help make your copy more vivid and can result in greater impact.

You can also interview customers who use the product or service to discover their personal experiences with and feelings about it. Why did they buy it? How have they benefited from it? Why should others buy it? A good approach for your copy may be to use testimonials from others. Testimonials—written statements describing the value of something—can be very influential, particularly within your peer market group.

Good advertising copy is particularly effective when it's based on personal experience with the product. If you're going to write about an advertiser's pizza, you should try their pizza.

Acquire firsthand information. Even if you have done the research, brainstormed benefits, and thought through your own and others' experiences with this or similar products, you should try the specific product or sample the service to be advertised. It's hard to tell readers about a great pizza if you have never tasted the pizza. Trying it will enable you to better capture in words how you felt as you took the first bite—the rich tomato sauce, the aroma of the sweet Italian sausage and fresh peppers.

Gather information from the source. If possible, you should also interview the seller, manufacturer, or distributor. Ask the same questions you would in your brainstorming session. Ask for copies of fact sheets from catalogs or product sales literature. Get copies of ads used to sell the product or service to adult or other special audiences. Call the 800 number if there is one to see how the salespeople describe their product. Visit the company's web site and the web sites of their competitors as well.

Plan and Write the Ad

To start, make an outline. Once you have the outline, write a letter to a friend in which you tell about the product or services of your advertiser. This may help you to organize your thoughts and focus on benefits in simple, clear, and descriptive language. Some copywriters—as those who write ad copy are called—use this approach to get started and then edit the letters into an advertising format.

All effective ads contain certain features as part of their format.

The headline. The key to successful advertising is the headline. It has to attract the attention of the reader and pull him or her further into the ad. Don't stop with the first headline you write. Write several. Edit them carefully. When you have the text, review your headline ideas. Many good headlines emerge after the copy is complete.

The introduction. Begin the text of your ad with an introductory phrase or sentence that builds on the headline. It should draw the reader further into the ad.

The body. The body of the ad should stress the benefits, linking the reader's interest with that of your advertiser's products or services. Describe what the benefits are to the reader and why these are important to him or her.

The call to action. Finally, tell your reader where and how to get the product, and urge prompt action. Motivate the reader to respond by using an incentive, such as a discount or a time limit on special prices. Make sure the reader has all the information necessary to take action, such as the business hours, address, and phone number. No ad is complete without a call to action.

As you draft an ad, don't worry about whether the copy is long or short. The important thing is the message and how it's expressed. Start with more copy than you need and edit it down to what's essential to do the job.

Study ads in your local paper and in magazines. Many ads are "heavy" with copy, others are very "light," and still others are somewhere in between. Write what you need to sell your product.

Look at the two samples of advertising copy that follow. Both are approaches to selling insurance to a first-time student car owner. One talks about the law and why insurance is needed. This ad emphasizes special rates for, and the importance of, safe-driving records. The other approach addresses benefits to the student in terms of money and convenience. Note the tone and language of each and how the second talks more directly to the reader. Look especially at the difference in the call to action.

	Sample A	**Sample B**
Headline	A Car and Driver's License Aren't Enough—Insurance Is the Law!	What Would You Do with an Extra $60?
Introduction	State law requires that all cars be insured. We offer top-quality, affordable insurance for first-time car owners.	So you're a new car owner! Here's our way of congratulating you: Special insurance rates put that $60 in your pocket if you have had driver's education. And, if you drive safely, you save an additional $60 or more every time you renew your SuperGo insurance policy.
Body	SuperGo Insurance provides special rates for young drivers who have had driver's education. By being a safe driver without accidents or citations, you will save on your premiums each year.	Our new student-driver insurance is unique. We not only save you money—which you can use for that special date or to help you upgrade the speaker system in your new car—but provide coverage with no red tape.
Call to Action	Come to Donovon Hayes SafeGo Insurance Center today! We will provide a free estimate on your insurance costs and show how being a safe driver with a good record saves money.	Call us now, toll free: 1-800-2SafeGo. Or apply on our web site: www.2SafeGo.com. We'll take your information and quickly send you a free estimate and all you need to apply. Why wait? We've made it easy for you!

Use Words That Sell

John Caples, for 40 years a vice president of top advertising agency Batten, Barton, Durstine & Osborn, Inc., made a study of words used in a sampling of good headlines appearing in ad copy. By counting the meaningful words (omitting words such as *and, the,* and *this*), he determined the top 10 words used by copywriters (the number that follows each is how many times the word appeared in headlines he studied):

you 31	who. 8	why. 4
your 14	money. . . . 6	people. . . . 4
how. 12	now. 4	want 4
new. 10		

Caples noted that combining *you* and *your* resulted in 45 mentions in that category, and combining *new* and *now* gave a total of 14 mentions. He noted his surprise that *free, save, quick,* and *easy* did not appear in the top 10, and that *how* scored so well. (Many direct marketers have found the value in *how* as well. Take note of all the "How to . . ." books and pamphlets you have seen.)

With Caples's list in mind, take another look at the ad copy on page 421. Notice how few of the words on the list appear in Sample A and how frequently they appear in Sample B. The words on the list appeal directly to the reader, helping him or her identify with the sales messages and products or services being sold.

After the audience has seen your ad (or heard it on radio or television), you want him or her to take action quickly. Caples suggests copywriters consider using phrases such as *Act now, Don't delay, Get started today, Be the first,* and *While supplies last* to convey a sense of ugency to the audience. The use of coupons, offering a drawing, or providing a special discount on a purchase are also considered useful to support the call to action in an advertisement.

WORDS worth considering

The most persuasive words. Advertising executive and industry leader David Ogilvy has a list of words that he classifies as the most persuasive in advertising. In his book *Confessions of an Advertising Man,* he offers this list of persuasive words:

suddenly	quick
introducing	challenge
sensational	hurry
startling	announcing
offer	amazing
wanted	revolutionary
bargain	magic
now	easy
improvement	compare

Create an Effective Layout

A number of elements may appear in an ad layout. These include the following:

- ▶ the headline and any subheads
- ▶ introductory copy
- ▶ body copy
- ▶ the call to action
- ▶ the company logo
- ▶ the company address, phone number, and business hours
- ▶ photographs and photo captions
- ▶ art—original drawings and computer-generated art
- ▶ prices of products advertised
- ▶ guarantees or warranties
- ▶ testimonials (as part of or separate from copy)
- ▶ coupons or other special discounts
- ▶ white space

Obviously, no ad will contain all of these elements. In preparing your advertisement, however, consider how to blend all the elements you do have into a layout that will attract reader attention. Before you start become a student of other people's ads. You can learn a great deal from what others have done.

When laying out your ad, keep in mind two important elements: the optical center of the ad and white space.

Optical center. The optical center of an ad is not in the middle of the space it occupies but about two-thirds up from the bottom. This is where most readers will perceive the center to be, and where their eyes are usually attracted first. Use art, a headline, or a call to action at the optical center to draw in readers.

White space. White space is another important element of advertising layout. White space helps attract attention to what is important—the headline, an illustration, a price, a unique offer. White space attracts the reader's eye because it's different from the rest of the page.

Most advertisements in student publications are relatively simple; but if they're well presented and laid out, they can still be effective. The samples in the **ON DISPLAY** feature on page 424 demonstrate good copywriting and layout.

Advertisements

The Little Hawk, Iowa City High School, Iowa City, Iowa

Athough not necessarily sophisticated, these ads all use techniques that appeal to a student market.

We know
what you
Didn't
do last
Summer...

No excuses.

Make
your
own
T.V.

338-7035
623 S. Dubuque St.

PUBLIC ACCESS TELEVISION

It's a

sMORPasbord

This Saturday, 8 to midnight

$2 + school supply or $3

Wear the craziest thing you can find!!

Costume contest will be held @ 10 p.m.*

*judging by a panel of five freshmen

Prom Open House

See What's New For '99

Let the professionals at your
**Eastside Hy-Vee
Floral Department**
create the right design
for you.

10% Discount if Order Placed During Open House

April 30-May 2

When you're evaluating ads—both those you create and those created by others—this checklist can be of help.

EVALUATION CHECKLIST

Advertisement

☑ Does the headline pull the audience into reading the rest of the ad?

☑ Does the ad copy use words and ideas that make the product or service appealing to the reader?

☑ Does the ad contain a well-worded call to action?

☑ Is the optical center of the ad space used for the headline, a photo, or other attention-getting element?

☑ Does the ad make effective use of white space?

Work with the Printer

Before preparing ads for layout, discuss with your printer how he or she prefers to receive ad copy and layout. If you're preparing your ad on computer, you probably need only supply a disk. If your disk contains copy only, the printer will want you also to provide a rough sketch (or dummy) of how the ad is to look when done, accompanied by any art or photographs that are to appear in the ad. From this the printer can put together camera-ready copy—a layout ready to be photographed and prepared for printing.

When ads are prepared on the computer, headlines, art, or photos can be inserted and positioned by the student designing the ad.

If you're using a desktop-publishing program, however, you may be able to lay out the entire ad yourself, including any art, before you submit it electronically to the printer. Such ads may even be transmitted to the printer by modem. It's a good idea to get approval from the advertiser before sending the ad off to press.

Circulation and Distribution

Just getting your publication printed is not enough; you must have readers. The number of people and places that receive your publication is your circulation. Management of your paper's circulation and distribution of the publication are another function usually assigned to the business staff.

Paid Subscriptions

Some student newspapers and magazines are sold on a subscription basis. The students purchase a subscription card and take it to a distribution point (usually the cafeteria or student lounge), where it's punched in exchange for the newspaper. People without cards can purchase the issue for a single-copy price. The subscription price should make the per-issue cost low enough to serve as an incentive to the buyer. In some cases, the subscription is sold as part of a total activities ticket.

Free Distribution

One way to broaden your circulation is through total or controlled "free" distribution. ("Free" means that students usually helped pay for the issue through either an activity supplement or funds made available from general school revenue.) Under these conditions, the staff publishes sufficient copies for the entire student population. The copies are placed in student gathering places for free pickup.

Some newspapers have no subsidy but sufficient advertising revenue to be self-supporting, so the paper can be distributed without cost to students. Both types of "free" distribution give advertisers a known circulation for each issue. From this, the advertising cost per hundred can be computed. Many advertisers test your circulation on their sales by running specials only in your publication or by using a coupon so that they can track responses.

Mailing Subscriptions

Part of the responsibility of those in charge of circulation is the processing of mailing newspapers to subsribers, which needs to be done promptly after each issue is published. These subsribers may include alumni, other student publications, students in other schools, parents, and advertisers.

The Editorial Ad

Why do some ads look like editorials? How do these benefit the advertiser?

"Editorial ads," or ads that function as opinion columns on the editorial page, are fairly common, especially in business-oriented papers. Many companies now place such ads, also known as advertorials or advocacy ads, in papers such as the *Wall Street Journal* or in leading business magazines.

The concept is to write strong advertising-style copy on an issue or topic in order to educate and motivate readers to support the company's position on that issue. The issue is often something that involves the public welfare, such as protecting the environment or banning assault weapons, rather than something that relates directly to the company's product. Frequently these ads urge readers to write to their senator immediately, or to join an organization that supports the company's cause.

This type of editorial ad can be an effective means of getting a company's message directly to readers. It's easier to pay for the space to present a viewpoint than to try to get a news article written about it.

The editorial-ad format is also sometimes used to sell products or services. When used to sell, the ads are placed in local and specialty newspapers as well as in large city publications. Sometimes they appear as testimonials by users of the service or product, and their format generally includes a heavy dose of print and little illustration. In other words, such ads look like editorials but are written in advertising language.

Editorial ads of this sort are also finding their way into student publications. A sports-medicine clinic, for example, may place a full-page, print-heavy ad in a yearbook, discussing common types of sports injuries and extolling the strengths of its medical staff in treating them. The ad looks serious and important, and it's effective in attracting readers for that reason.

The owner of a movie theater might advertise the theater by hiring a student to write a review of a movie showing there, hoping to attract a student audience to his business.

An advertiser may try to sell its product using a column written by a student. For example, for a movie being shown at a local theater, a student may prepare copy that summarizes the film and cites various positive reviews. The idea is that more students will believe in the ad because one of their peers wrote it—or the company may simply want to engender goodwill so that students will remember its name later. A real-estate firm, for example, may choose to present a series of outstanding-student profiles in a student publication in hopes of building a future relationship with its readers.

Is it possible to mistake these ads for editorials? Nearly all publications require that they be set off or identified in some way. Many newspapers add a line at the top of the ad labeling it an advertisement, some require that the ad be boxed, and others specify that a typeface be used that is different from the paper. These safeguards are to make clear that the material isn't written by a reporter and that it doesn't represent the opinion of the paper.

The editorial approach adds credibility to the advertiser's cause. As long as it's clearly identified, the selling approach is valid.

FOLLOW-UP

1. Find in the print media a regular product ad, an editorial ad, and an editorial on the same general topic—for example, health products. Prepare a display highlighting similarities and differences in the three.
2. Does the general public actually recognize editorial ads? Show such an ad, in its original context, to various volunteers. Record their reactions.

Subscription lists need to be purged periodically to make sure newspapers are not being mailed to people who have not renewed. Mailing costs also can be kept down by getting second-class mailing permits, designing publications as self-mailers, or preparing bulk mailings.

Every publication maintains a list of free subscriptions. These include prospective advertisers, local news media, school board members, key school administrators, and leaders in the community.

Evaluate your circulation and distribution system often during the year to ensure that it's the best and most cost-effective method for you to use.

Exchange Papers

Naturally, you will want to exchange publications with other schools. Mailing your publication to other schools can be costly. Evaluate the publications you receive and be sure you have a reason for exchanging with a particular school. Publications from schools that are your athletic rivals are useful, for example, in writing sports stories.

Be sure your staff is taking advantage of the publications you receive by reviewing them regularly. It's a waste of money to receive a pile of newspapers and merely hang them on the bulletin board.

Keeping Records

Student-run publications, like small businesses, have to maintain accurate and complete financial records. Although the adviser is ultimately responsible for maintaining and ensuring the accuracy of records, the student business manager and staff often assist in the managing of day-to-day accounts. Regular monthly financial statements should be typed and distributed to the adviser, the editor, and often to the school business office.

Records must be kept of all income and expenses, including advertising revenue, fund-raising monies, newspaper and yearbook sales, "entertainment expenses" (such as work-and-pizza nights), and supplies. To stay on budget, publications need authorization slips or purchase order forms for approving expenditures before money is actually spent.

Maintenance of financial records doesn't require complex accounting methods. A simple spreadsheet created in Microsoft Excel, an accounting package such as Intuit's Quicken, or a paper-and-pencil system based on

	A	B		C	D	E	F
	Date	Description		Expenses	X	Income	Balance
1							
2		Category	Memo	$	X	$	$
3	9/1/--	Opening Balance			X		
4		Activity fees				16,000.00	16,000.00
5	9/5/--	Lajoie Printing					
6		Printing	2,000 copies	4,000.00			12,000.00
7	9/5/--	Diamond Lithography					
8		Photography/Color separations		900.00			11,100.00
9	9/5/--	USPS					
10		Postage		66.00			11,034.00
11	9/6/--	Doctor's Services, Inc.					
12		Advertisement	2 x 8 ad			136.00	11,170.00
13	9/6/--	Candlestick Florist					
14		Advertisement	1/2 page ad			680.00	11,850.00
15	9/6/--	Mac Warehouse					
16		Supplies	toner cartridge	198.00			11,652.00
17	9/9/--	Pizzeria Medici					
18		Advertisement	1/2 page ad			680.00	12,332.00
19	9/9/--	Benjamin's Books					
20		Advertisment	2 x 4 ad			68.00	12,400.00
21	9/9/--	Newspaper sales					
22		September issue				81.50	12,481.50
23						Current Balance:	12,481.50
24							

Sheet1 / Sheet2 / Sheet3

Although budgets can also be handled by low-tech means, a computer spreadsheet is a handy means of keeping a running record of monies coming in and going out. Notice that the $16,000 opening balance in this sample reflects activity fees, which should be distributed evenly across the year.

Summary Report
9/1/-- through 9/30/--

Income	Category	Amount
	Activity fees	$16,000.00
	Advertisements	1,564.00
	Newspaper sales	81.50
Total Income		**$17,645.50**

Expenses	Category	Amount
	Postage	$66.00
	Printing	4,000.00
	Photography/ Color separations	900.00
	Supplies	198.00
Total Expenses		**$5,164.00**
Balance		**$12,481.50**

In a summary report, done at the end of the month, income and expense totals for various categories can be summarized and analyzed.

one of these formats can make record keeping relatively simple. The samples above show a typical monthly accounting sheet done using Excel and then a summary showing only the transactions from that month. Either form can also be set up without a computer program.

Every school district has procedures for spending and collecting money. Some states have laws that also affect activities. Know the rules.

Wrap-Up

Without money, there would be no media. Advertising and subscription revenues are essential for a publication. The number of pages in an edition of the school newspaper, for example, is dependent on revenue from such sources as an activity fund, subscription sales, and advertising. Some publications also hold fund-raising events to raise money for special features. The funding a student publication has determines how many color photos, pages, or special features can be added.

Student media are important to local businesses, linking the businesses with a student market that is known to have strong buying power. To attract advertisers requires a thorough knowledge of the paper's readers. A market research study of the student body will provide important information that can help demonstrate to local businesses the value of advertising to the student market.

In student publications, advertising rates are determined on the basis of an estimate of the money needed to print the publication and the space available for advertising.

Once advertising is sold, it has to be written and designed. Brainstorming techniques can help to identify the benefits of a product. So can firsthand experience with the product. It's also important to interview customers, as well as the seller, manufacturer, or distributor, about product attributes.

When writing advertising copy, start with an outline. Then turn the outline into a letter to a friend telling him or her about the product. Develop several headlines that draw the reader into the ad; then select the best one. Write the ad copy and edit it several times. Pull readers into the copy with text that speaks to them personally, discussing benefits in owning the product or using the service. End the ad with a strong call to action—tell the reader what to do next. Remember to use words that are proven to sell.

When designing the ad, place a strong headline or piece of art at the optical center, about one-third down from the top of the advertising space. That's where most readers will perceive the ad center to be and where their eyes will be drawn first. White space also helps draw attention to key layout elements.

Once the paper is printed it must be distributed. Many publications are distributed by subscription—either directly or by mail.

Businesses don't buy advertising unless they feel assured that the publication will reach its intended audience. Good record keeping is therefore essential. Advertisers must receive timely invoices for their ad space so that the publication receives the funds needed to pay the printing, photography, or other bills. Good books and records must also be kept on all other income received in addition to advertising. A simple accounting system will ensure that each expenditure is carefully entered, that bills are paid on time, and that bills are not paid more than once. Be sure that school business procedures are carefully followed.

On Assignment

INDIVIDUAL ACTIVITIES

1. Write a brief definition of each of these terms:

   business manager   copywriter
   call to action   market survey
   camera-ready copy   optical center
   circulation   testimonial

2. Test your critical thinking. Write an editorial, or column, or an opinion feature about one or more of these statements. Take any position, but provide evidence to support it.
   ▶ Advertising causes people to vote for candidates they should not vote for.
   ▶ Advertising convinces people to buy products they don't need.
   ▶ Advertising has been a leading factor in improving our standard of living.
   ▶ Advertising should be banned from television.
   ▶ Without advertising, the economy of our nation would suffer greatly.

3. Develop an advertisement based on the following information. Supply any additional information needed to complete the ad.
   ▶ A computer store near your school lets students rent computers for home use. The cost is $35 monthly. The computers have built-in modems. A printer is also provided.
   ▶ All rental payments apply to the purchase of the computer should the student decide to buy it later.
   ▶ Rental agreements are for three-month intervals.
   ▶ Students who bring in the ad from your paper will receive free software worth $250 that will allow them to access databases for use in doing research.

   ▶ The equipment is easy to use and comes with an instruction manual. A class is held at the store each Saturday for $10.
   ▶ You have a photo of two students in your school using the equipment and a photo of the store.
   ▶ The store name is ComputeRents & Sales, Ltd.
   ▶ The size is to be 4 columns wide by 12 inches deep.

4. Find articles that discuss research on the buying habits of today's teen and youth markets. Besides surveys from Teenage Research Unlimited, you may find results from large polling companies such as Roper and Gallup or useful information in *American Demographics* magazine. Use the information in a sales letter to businesses currently advertising in your student paper, reinforcing their "good judgment" in advertising with you. Then use the information in a letter to a business that does not use your publication.

5. Using your research for activity 4, prepare an article for your school newspaper on the youth market. If possible, conduct a class interview with one of the professional researchers. He or she may have even more current information for you.

6. Write a one-page critique of the market survey in the On Display feature on pages 412–413. Are any important items missing? Do any of those used seem irrelevant?

7. Write a one-page critique of the On Display ads in this chapter. Use the Evaluation Checklist on page 425.

TEAM ACTIVITY

8. In a team develop a marketing survey for your school's publications. Determine how to conduct the survey (with a random sample or to all students). Compare your team's survey plan and questionnaire with those of the other teams. Develop a combined survey instrument.

    Invite to class someone knowledgeable in testing or evaluation to discuss research techniques and to critique the questionnaire and the plan for securing student opinion. Meet with the appropriate computer expert in your school if you intend to have the results tabulated.

    Make final revisions in the instrument and conduct the study. When the results are tabulated, allow each team to analyze its own data. Write a report summarizing what you learned. Then prepare a letter to advertising prospects about the student market and the benefits of advertising in your publication. Compare your team's interpretations and marketing report with those of the other teams.

SURF THE NET

9. Look on the Internet for examples of good and bad ads. What makes certain ads effective? What kinds of formats seem to work best? What kinds of ads are least appealing? How often do you actually respond to Internet ads? Share your ideas with the class.

career profile

Advertising Director

Kent Matlock

"**P**ractical experience is the lifeline to a position in this industry," says Kent Matlock, president and CEO of Matlock & Associates, Inc., an Atlanta advertising and public relations firm. "I guess it's like the old phrase in politics, which says to vote early and vote often."

Matlock got involved in advertising early. He was a college representative for a major marketing promotion while attending Morehouse College in Atlanta.

That stint in promotion, plus a liberal arts education, helped prepare him to open his own advertising agency. After working for a couple of small agencies, Matlock moved to a Fortune 500 company and then formed his own seven-person firm in 1986.

From his college studies, Matlock gained a general idea of advertising and public relations. He believes, however, that the hard-core realities of the business are encountered on the job. What's more, he believes that timing is the key to success, whether that means developing expertise about a particular market, winning the business of a client or a product that's hot, or landing in a geographical area that's on the upswing. "Pick a growing market, and the opportunities start unfolding professionally and personally," he said.

Matlock's company is a minority firm and naturally does some specialty work in that area, but he urges recent graduates to begin their careers in larger and more generalized corporate environments. "The smaller the agency," he said, "the more likely you are to acquire bad habits," adding that large firms are good places to learn to manage the pitfalls. "It's important to get a neutral orientation in the business," he noted. "Learning the fundamentals is of great value long term."

"Working for a larger firm enhances your appreciation for the business," he said. What you learn there, he adds, can be applied in a small firm, which, by virtue of its size and the number of diverse tasks to be performed, offers a broader scope of opportunities.

Besides pursuing paying clients, Matlock believes there's an oasis of fulfillment in *pro bono publico* work—that is, work done free "for the public good."

"My greatest joy is *pro bono* work, perhaps because they [these projects] tend to be the things we do out of kindness," he explained. He added that part of the satisfaction comes from the opportunity to express creativity and not be "policed," as when a client is paying the bill.

Through the years, Matlock has given professional service to the American Cancer Society, the Atlanta Chamber of Commerce, the Martin Luther King, Jr. Center, the Southern Christian Leadership Conference, the United Negro College Fund, and his alma mater, Morehouse College. "The community loves the insight, guidance, and support," he said, adding that such work often "opens doors" to paying clients. "The most powerful things we cultivate are our relationships," Matlock said.

FOLLOW-UP

1. What may be advantages of beginning your career at a large ad firm, as Matlock suggests? What may be disadvantages? Discuss your ideas in class.

2. Think of an advertising situation in which the timeliness of a campaign is important. Compare it with a situation in which time is not an issue. In what ways might the campaigns be handled differently?

SECTION SIX

CHAPTER 18

Taking and Using Effective Photographs

After reading this chapter, you will

- understand the roles of the photograph in a student publication
- know some simple guidelines for composing a photograph
- understand the role of the photo editor and the photography staff
- know how to plan and do a successful photo shoot
- know how to select, crop, and size the best photos for a layout

A good photograph begins in the mind of the photographer. Photographers begin composing pictures, evaluating lighting, and solving technical problems in their heads long before they put the camera to their eyes.

The ability of photographers to turn what they see in their minds into an image on film is what makes for a great publication. Without good photographs, a publication can be, at best, average. Photographs enable readers to see the action as it occurred without reporter's having to write about it in depth.

The Role of the Photograph

In contemporary publications, the most important role of a photograph is to grab the viewer's attention. Photos are the first thing a viewer sees on a page, and poor-quality or uninteresting photos are an immediate turn-off. Even professional daily publications and nightly news broadcasts realize the impact of a high-quality photograph in capturing viewers and increasing sales. Once viewers have been attracted by a single photo, they're more likely to read the caption (or cutline), the headline, the associated stories, and the ads. Some publications, such as *Life* and *National Geographic*, have built an entire reputation on the quality of their photography.

Good photos can accomplish other goals once they have attracted the viewer's attention. They ... information abou... or a flood in a ne... they serve the sam... news story.

Other photogr... entertain the reade... "wild art" (art not ... simply to provide d... appeal to a greater v... example, a news pag... story about the scho... associated photograp... include a picture of ... concert with a long c...

436

"wild art"   **cropping**   **sizing**

rule of thirds   **halftone**   photo e...

Photography

lens	f-stop	ISO	digital camera	enlarger
aperture	depth of field	back lighting	darkroom	test strip
exposure	shutter speed	flash-synch speed	fixer	

CHAPTER 19

Understanding Technical Aspects of Photography

KEY CONCEPTS

After reading this chapter, you will

- understand the different kinds of camera lenses
- know the f-stops and their relevance to photography
- know the shutter speeds and their relevance to photography
- understand the process of developing film
- understand the process of making a print

The Camera

A good photograph begins in the mind of the photographer. Without a camera,

Professional photographers were once beginners who had to learn the technical aspects of photography.

however, no one else can view that image. A camera is simply a box that holds the medium on which the image can be recorded. In fact, the earliest cameras were literally nothing more than a light-tight box with a tiny hole at one end and a piece of light-sensitive material at the other. Over the last 150 years, the box has evolved into the modern camera body, the hole into the lens, and the material into the film—or in recent years into the solar cell. In digital cameras the light-sensitive surface is a solar cell that transforms light into electronic signals, which are recorded on a computer chip. Regardless of the new technology, the basic principles remain the same. Light shines through the hole (the lens) and registers on the light-sensitive material (the film or the solar cell).

Basic Camera Parts and Terms

An understanding of the basic parts of a camera and their functions is a good way to start learning the technical aspects of photography. If the camera diagrams and terms on pages 460–461 aren't crystal clear immediately, they will become clearer as you read this chapter and work with the camera.

Kinds of Lenses

Some camera lenses are fixed lenses—all you have to do is point the camera at the scene. Everything from about six feet to infinity is in focus. Others can be focused manually, allowing you to zero in on an individual part of the scene.

458

459

Chapter 18

Taking and Using Effective Photographs

A good photograph begins in the mind of the photographer. Photographers begin composing pictures, evaluating lighting, and solving technical problems in their heads long before they put the camera to their eyes.

The ability of photographers to turn what they see in their minds into an image on film is what makes for a great publication. Without good photographs, a publication can be, at best, average. Photographs enable readers to see the action as it occurred without reporter's having to write about it in depth.

The Role of the Photograph

In contemporary publications, the most important role of a photograph is to grab the viewer's attention. Photos are the first

Photos may serve to provide information on news events such as a balloon festival.

thing a viewer sees on a page, and poor-quality or uninteresting photos are an immediate turn-off. Even professional daily publications and nightly news broadcasts realize the impact of a high-quality photograph in capturing viewers and increasing sales. Once viewers have been attracted by a single photo, they're more likely to read the caption (or cutline), the headline, the associated stories, and the ads. Some publications, such as *Life* and *National Geographic,* have built an entire reputation on the quality of their photography.

Good photos can accomplish other goals once they have attracted the viewer's attention. They may, for example, provide information about a festival in the park or a flood in a nearby county. In that sense, they serve the same purpose as part of a news story.

Other photographs may serve simply to entertain the reader. Editors often select "wild art" (art not associated with a story) simply to provide depth to a page—to appeal to a greater variety of viewers. For example, a news page may have a lead story about the school principal and an associated photograph but then may also include a picture of the high school choir concert with a long caption. Although the story about the principal is timely and has consequences for everyone in the school, the picture of the choir concert may do more to attract readers.

By attracting attention, informing, and entertaining, photographs accomplish two broader goals for the publication: they give it an identity, and they establish a link with the reader.

Some publications use large, dramatic photos to show the story. Others use smaller photos. Some use color photos. Some use strictly black-and-white ones. Some use photo essays to tell stories. Others depend on the accurate portrayal of the scene without any manipulation. Each of these approaches gives a publication a look that, when combined with type and layout, is distinctive and can often be recognized even when the name of the publication isn't known.

The identity that photos establish, their ability to grab attention, and the stories they tell help a publication to form a bond with the reader, a bond that strengthens every time a reader has a successful experience with the publication. Readers learn to feel the anger, loneliness, happiness, fear, pain, jubilation, and surprise that the people in the photographs appear to have felt. They share experiences and come to feel a part of the action.

Good Photo Composition

Although establishing a bond and grabbing attention are praiseworthy goals, a poorly composed photograph can seldom accomplish either of them. In fact, a poorly composed photograph can turn off a reader faster than a bad headline or a poorly written lead.

Good composition involves first having good subject matter and the appropriate equipment to shoot it. Beginning photographers should take pictures of things that they're familiar with and that they can shoot with their equipment. A photographer who is in the marching band, for example, may cover band practice for a first assignment. Outdoor band practice can easily be covered with a standard lens during daylight hours.

It's often helpful for beginning photographers to practice with "point-and-shoot" cameras so that they don't have to worry about the technical aspects of photography. This allows them to concentrate solely on composition.

Photographic composition also involves some general guidelines that will help improve any photograph.

Keep It Simple

Good photographs are simple. The best ones involve one, or perhaps two, centers of visual interest to grab attention. They have nothing distracting in the foreground or the background. Include only what's relevant.

Fill the Frame

When you shoot most photographs, move up close to the subject. Getting close is the hardest thing for a beginning photographer to do. Good photographs are filled with the subject, not a lot of wasted space.

Avoid Mergers and Awkward Cuts

Objects that seem to merge into a subject, such as telephone poles growing out of heads, are distracting to the viewer—as are objects that seem disconnected to anything in the photo, such as spare hands floating in from the edge of the frame. Avoid these situations by moving closer to eliminate unwanted parts of the scene—or by moving around to shoot the scene from another perspective. Pay careful attention to potentially distracting objects in the foreground and the background.

Be careful also to avoid awkward cuts, such as trimming off feet, fingers, faces, or the top of a head at the edge of the frame. In addition, don't chop off subjects at the joints of arms and legs, at the waist, or where the neck joins the head or shoulders. Most photographers also try to leave a little space above a subject's head to avoid the impression that the top of the photo is pressing on the top of the head.

The photo on the left demonstrates problems with merging and awkward cuts (in addition to the poor light caused by shooting the subjects in front of a window). Notice the window frame growing out of the boy's head, and the hand apparently not attached to a body. The photographer improved the right-hand photo by repositioning the subjects, shooting from a different angle, and making sure that everyone's face could be seen.

A photo composed according to the rule of thirds doesn't have the subject in the exact center. Instead, the frame is broken into thirds vertically and horizontally and significant elements appear at the intersection of those lines. The horizontal line falls in the top or bottom third of the photo.

Use the Rule of Thirds

Subjects should rarely be placed in the center of the frame. Instead, as you shoot, divide the frame into thirds both horizontally and vertically (into a sort of tic-tac-toe board). Place the subject at the intersection of any two lines. In wide shots place the horizon line either on the top third or the bottom third of the frame—not in the center.

Enhance Posed Shots

In general, avoid posed shots in favor of candid shots of people in action. When you do have to shoot posed groups or individuals, don't be afraid to try something different to enhance such shots. For example, give context to the setting: Shoot the swim team in the pool and the thesbians on stage in costume. Keep people close together to avoid gaps between heads. Don't shoot people in front of a wall, even for quick headshots. Aim for interesting informality. Try settings such as the library or under a tree on campus.

Work with Patterns, Curves, and Leading Lines

Repetition, as any artist will tell you, is an effective composition element. Having a pattern broken by some action (such as a line of dancers with one person out of step) can make for a powerful photo. Similarly, having a subject at the beginning or the end of a leading line or curve—such as a runner at the end of a long path—can draw the reader into the action.

A shot involving a pattern or repetitive action can sometimes be more effective if something breaks the pattern.

Try Various Angles and Viewpoints

For a wider range of shots from which to choose, photograph a scene from different angles—from above, below, to the side, and so on. Be mindful, however, of how angles affect the overall image. Photos taken from above make a subject appear smaller. Photos taken from below make a subject appear larger.

Move around the scene and shoot from different viewpoints. For example, you might take a photo from the baseball dugout to show the other players' viewpoint. You might then take a photo from the press box to show how the baseball diamond looks from above.

The photograph in the **ON DISPLAY** feature below is shot from an angle that gives viewers a unique perspective on the scene.

ON DISPLAY

Unique Viewpoint

Black Hawk, Central High School, Davenport, Iowa

This photo not only demonstrates the effectiveness of using a unique viewpoint to capture the viewers' attention but also the impact of filling the frame.

Photo by Matt Rose

Give Meaning to an Image

A good photograph must do more than just present a subject doing something. It must present a subject doing something in a meaningful way. In other words, a photograph should do more than just record the event—it should give meaning to it. When you compose your photo, therefore, think about how you can use the composition to add depth to the meaning of the action in the photo.

Notice how the photograph in the **ON DISPLAY** feature below is not only well composed but expresses the realtionship between the subject and the action in a meaningful way.

ON DISPLAY

Meaningful Composition

Spectator, Liberty High School, Liberty, Missouri

Photo by Jennifer Cowen

The composition of this photo adds to its meaning. Dynamic tension is created between the golf ball in the foreground and the golfer. Notice how the shadows serve as leading lines.

The Photography Staff

The photography staff in a school publication can function as a separate group that takes on assignments for the whole publication. Its members may instead be assigned to work individually with teams of editors and reporters. Regardless of the organization used, the photography staff must still fulfill basic roles.

The Photo Editor

In general, the photo editor leads the photography staff in taking and developing high-quality pictures. Working closely with other senior staff members, the photo editor supervises the thorough coverage of all school events to obtain all necessary photos. He or she keeps the photography staff informed of such events by recording them on the calendar and by holding regular staff meetings. The photo editor may make photo assignments to the staff and may function as a photographer.

One of the most important responsibilities of the photo editor is to edit photos for quality control—both in the initial negatives and later in the print and electronic versions of the photos.

Although many schools process their film commercially, those schools that continue to use darkroom facilities must ensure that these facilities are maintained. Standard maintenance includes mixing chemicals, distributing film, ordering supplies, and keeping the darkroom clean and safe.

Keeping good photo records and storing images is part of running an effective publication. The photo editor helps staff members maintain a filing system for negatives, contact sheets, prints, and electronic images.

All in all, the photo editor serves as the leader of the photography staff, making sure that staff members' tasks are clear and problems are adequately addressed.

The Staff Photographer

In general, the staff photographer takes pictures, processes film, makes prints, and performs all functions necessary for taking and processing photos in a timely fashion. The staff photographer accepts photo assignments from the editors and helps maintain the equipment and darkroom facilities. He or she should also suggest ideas for photo assignments. In addition, the staff photographers must gather information for the photo captions.

The Photo Assignment

You can take good photographs once you understand basic photographic techniques. When shooting pictures for a publication, however, just taking a good photo isn't enough. The photo must also work with the story it accompanies and fit in with the specific goals of the publication.

Making Specific Assignments

One way to avoid potential problems with photographs is to make sure that photographers have clear assignments. Photographers need to work closely with photo editors, designers, reporters, and others on the staff to make sure everyone is clear about what types of photos are needed.

The best time for a staff or team to discuss photo assignments is during the discussion of story assignments and positioning. As you decide which stories require more prominent positioning and more space, also consider which stories are visually interesting.

After the plan for the newspaper issue (or the yearbook section) is complete, it's time for photographers to get their assignments. Be aware that to tell a photographer to shoot "the football game" is to invite disaster. Do you want pictures of the field action? the sideline action? the fans? the band? the drill team? the concession stand? one player? the coaches? You may need more than one photographer to cover all the action at a football game adequately and each should have a *specific* assignment.

For example, telling a photographer to shoot pictures of the star quarterback at Friday night's game for a personality profile gives the photographer something specific to go on. He or she will be able to concentrate on that one player (on the field and off) and will be likely to bring along the proper equipment. A specific assignment also gives the photographer a chance to think about possible atypical shots, such as the quarterback studying algebra before the game. The more information that the photographer has, the more likely he or she is to return with pictures that supplement the story and provide the reader with a chance to understand it.

Shooting the Photos

When you as a photographer accept assignments, you're doing more than just agreeing to go out to snap a few pictures. You're making a commitment to cover a piece of the school's history. Take your work seriously.

trends and issues

Using Photos Ethically

What kinds of photographs are appropriate in news coverage?

The world has become more and more visually oriented. People read less and depend more on illustrations, particularly photographs, to get information. This reliance on visual images—on what they suggest as well as what they show—means that an ethic must be in place to ensure that they're used appropriately.

Photos are often used in the professional press that make people look bad—or at least foolish. We have all seen photos of presidents and other public figures with silly looks on their faces. Because hundreds of images of these individuals appear regularly, it's fair to assume that some of the pictures will be unflattering. The reality is that public figures sometimes do look foolish. No lasting harm is done by circulating these photos. Sometimes, however, unattractive images can have a direct effect on events. A photo of a candidate looking particularly ridiculous at a campaign stop may make up the minds of some undecided voters.

The audience is much better at reading implications into photos than photo editors sometimes realize. Many people were outraged when *Newsweek* magazine ran a cover photo of Oklahoma bomber Timothy McVeigh looking like a sweet, innocent young man. To the audience the photo suggested that McVeigh was a harmless kid—certainly not a person accused (and later convicted) of so many people's deaths.

Using photos inappropriately—or using inappropriate photos—is one issue. Another is the question of just how much a news photograph should show. Usually we don't see the mangled bodies of airplane fatalities in the mass media, but the results of many other disasters seem to be fair game. At least in some media coverage, it appears that no moment is so private that it can't be recorded by a photographer. As with the shootings at Columbine High School in Colorado, deaths and loved

Media harassment of people during moments of stress or private grief is ethically questionable. Here reporters converge on Columbine High School students after the shooting spree of 1999.

ones' reactions to deaths are often photographed from extremely close range, so the subject almost seems to be captured by the camera. The question, and it doesn't always have an easy answer, is how far the public's right to know—and see—really does go.

Photo editors need to make many decisions about whether to run certain photographs. They also need to be careful about photo positioning. A portrait shot of an innocent individual run next to a headline about a murderer's being arrested will suggest to many casual readers that the person in the photo is the guilty party. Lawsuits have been filed—and won—over this sort of unintentional misrepresentation.

In school publications, photo choice and position also need to be thought through carefully. You may not often deal with life-and-death situations or face potential lawsuits, but you do have people's feelings to consider. Don't operate under the old premise of using a photo just "because we've got it."

FOLLOW-UP

1. Where does the public's right to know end in dealing with the survivors of tragedies? Consider a case that recently was in the news. What images were made available? Did they serve the public's right to know or go beyond it? Discuss your ideas in class.
2. With the class, create a display of appropriate and inappropriate photos from newsmagazines and newspapers. Attach to each a brief note indicating what is praiseworthy or improper about the photo.

A student photographer should prepare for a shoot by bringing along any equipment that might be needed, including lenses, batteries, lighting equipment, extra film, a pen, and a notebook.

Advance preparation. Plan to arrive early and then take pictures before, during, and after the event. If you're taking a portrait of someone, you should make an appointment. Do so well in advance and set aside at least 20 minutes for the shoot.

Whatever your assignment, take a lot of pictures. Remember that coverage of a person or event should include different angles, action shots, horizontal and vertical shots, small-group shots, shots showing the scene, and any others that help tell the whole story. Whenever possible, avoid posed shots. Before going out to cover an event, skim through publications that have covered similar past events. Look for ways to cover the event that haven't been done before.

Finally, note that photographers have to be prepared for a variety of equipment- and weather-related problems that may arise. Being prepared includes bringing along extra film and batteries, carrying other lenses, having extra lighting equipment on hand, and keeping film and supplies in plastic zip-lock bags in case of wet weather.

Captions

When out on assignment, it's also your responsibility to get caption information—the who, what, when, where, why, and how of the action in the photo. Sometimes caption information may be nothing more than the accurate spelling of the names of the people in the photo, but compiling it is an important responsibility for the photographer.

School photographers often think it's easier to go back and find out who the people are after they've printed the pictures. Indeed, in action-packed events that's sometimes true. Generally, however, getting this information on the scene is more efficient than searching for it later.

As you work, record details such as the score of a sports event and the the significance of plays, the location of a special event, and any other information that may not be apparent in the photo. You may also want to get direct quotations from the people involved to add information to a caption.

Writing the caption. Most captions run from two to four lines. Some captions have the first few words set in boldface, so keep that in mind as you write your caption. Those words must be especially engaging.

The first part of the caption explains (usually in the present tense) what's going on in the photo, including the names of all identifiable people. The second part (usually in the past or future tense) adds information that may supplement the story—including quotations.

When writing captions, be specific and use strong action verbs.

Not this: Students participate in the apple-bobbing contest during Harvest Fest.

This: Apple-bobber Andrea Thompson, junior, chomps on her prize during the annual Harvest Fest apple-bobbing contest. Senior Nina Fuentes won the event.

Try to avoid starting with names unless the focus is on a notable person. Another pitfall is the temptation to start too many captions with *–ing* clauses ("Striking a regal pose, sophomore Jamal Davis shows off his costume as the lead in *The Frog Prince*.").

A final important part of the caption is the photo credit, a credit you earn for taking the picture. Attaching your name to a good photo will motivate you to keep taking strong, well-planned pictures.

Selecting and Using the Best Photos

Once the photo assignment is completed, the photo editor—usually in conjunction with the photographer, design editor, and page or section editor—picks the best pictures for a page from a set of prints or from a contact sheet, a sheet of photos printed in negative size. What "best" means differs from page to page, issue to issue, and topic to topic, but some basic principles always hold true.

To begin with, good photojournalism is about *people*. In general, therefore, photos for publications should contain people. When readers flip through the pages of a school newspaper or yearbook, they're looking for pictures of themselves, their friends, and other people with whom they share experiences.

TIPS

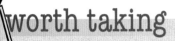

worth taking

Good, better, best. Keep the following comparative definitions in mind as you judge the quality and effectiveness of a photo.

An OK photo: a shot of a chess player rather than of a chess board

A better photo: a shot of the chess player concentrating on her next move

An even better photo: a shot of the chess player with her hands on her head and a look of bewilderment on her face.

Secondly, the people should be *doing something,* not staring at the camera. Photographers capture the best photos when people keep going right on with their lives, totally unaware that they're being photographed.

Finally, whenever possible the action should be *unusual.* The more unusual the action, the more likely the photograph is to make the reader stop and say, "Wow!" Look at the photo in the **ON DISPLAY** feature on page 449 to see how engaging such a photo can be.

Working with the Layout

Besides selecting the best photos, the photo editor also has to make sure they will work on the layout. The best way to do this is to design layouts around the strongest photos. Horizontal photos won't fit in vertical spaces, and redesigning the page is easier than reshooting the photo. Redesigning a page, however, isn't always possible. Good designers and photo editors work together to make sure the needs of both groups are met and a pleasing page results.

Photo editors typically have to lobby for prominent placement of the best photos. The stronger the photo and the better it fits with the entire story-design-photo package, the harder the editor should lobby.

Cropping. Sometimes photos can be cropped. Cropping a picture means removing unnecessary elements from the photo by reproducing only a portion of it. Cropping can serve two purposes: to improve the photo's composition and to make the photo fit a predesigned space.

The first purpose, in general, is good. Removing unnecessary elements from the photo helps draw attention to the center of visual interest and improves the photo.

The second purpose, in general, is bad. Forcing photographs to fit into layout rarely improves them. A vertical picture of a basketball player going for a basket will not work well crammed into a horizontal hole. Similarly, a horizontal picture of a costumer ironing costumes for the school play should not be squeezed into a vertical frame.

ON DISPLAY

People Doing Something Unusual

Hauberk, Shawnee Mission East High School, Prairie Village, Kansas

When selecting photos for use in a publication, choose as many as possible that involve people doing something—ideally, something unusual.

Photo by Brian Provo

One easy technique for cropping is to use two L-shaped pieces of cardboard. Arrange them over your photo until you have the image you want. Remember to maintain the rule of thirds and don't crop too close to the top of a person's head or at their joints (ankles, knees, waist, wrist).

A rectangle is generally the most pleasing shape for photos, so try to maintain rectangular proportions in your cropping. The standard rectangular proportion of a 3 x 5 snapshot is desirable. In some instances, however, nonstandard rectangular cropping can work better to highlight the subject of a photo.

Cropping a photo should increase its impact. In the first photo standard rectangular proportions were maintained while the extraneous portions were cropped out. In the second, unusual cropping highlights the subject.

Preparing photos for the printer. In real life, photographs rarely come ready to run. A little cropping will improve almost any image, and printing photos in the exact size as they will run is time-consuming, expensive, and frustrating. Fortunately, it's easy for production staff members to indicate cropping instructions and to resize photographs early on.

Good photographers crop their pictures in the camera while composing the photo and while printing the picture. Editors can also indicate cropping instructions on the contact sheet when selecting pictures to be enlarged.

Although the method of cropping and sizing depends on the type of publication and publisher, it can be accomplished simply by using a calculator to figure out the size wanted and a ruler and a marker such as a grease pencil to draw crop lines. Proportion wheels and cropping devices make the process easier.

Before a photograph can be printed, it must be made into a halftone—converted into a series of black-and-white (or color) dots so that it can be printed solely in black ink and still pick up the more than 200 shades of gray in the average photo. Halftones are now generally created with computer software after electronically scanning the image. At the same time a photo is made into a halftone, it can be sized and cropped according to instructions marked on the photo—instructions marked by a design staff member or the staff photographer.

To evaluate finished photos, from composition to final production, this checklist can be helpful.

EVALUATION CHECKLIST

Photo Composition

- ☑ Does the subject of the photo fill up most of the space?
- ☑ Has the subject been positioned in the photo according to the rule of thirds?
- ☑ Does the photo show the subject doing something interesting?
- ☑ Is the photo simple, with only one or two centers of visual interest?
- ☑ Has any necessary cropping been done?

Photo Essays

When a photographer shoots an extended assignment, or when a story can be told better through many pictures and few words (instead of many words and few pictures), an editor may choose to print a series of photos as a photo essay. The photo essay serves the same purpose as a copy block—to tell an entire story from beginning to end.

Some photo essays may tell one small portion of a much bigger story, such as the story of one person who has to ride the bus to school all the way across town even though she lives only five blocks from another school. The photo essay could show pictures of the girl hanging around with friends in her neighborhood, pictures of waiting alone for the bus, pictures of her riding the bus, and maybe pictures of her at the other school. Through this series of images, the photographer can tell the entire story.

A photo essay need not always tell a step-by-step story. It might, for example, show a variety of pictures of Spring Fever Week, not isolating any one event. The essay could include everything from the outfits for Nerd Day to the egg toss to the tug-of-war over the mud pit. Most yearbook spreads use this type of photographic coverage over a span of time to illustrate activities of groups during the year. The **ON DISPLAY** feature on page 453 demonstrates this type of photo essay.

A special type of photo essay is the photo series, a group of pictures often taken over time to illustrate how things change or to illustrate a process. These photos typically focus on one person or place and are usually printed side by side. For example, you might show the process of making a breakthrough banner for a football game in a series of photos showing students first getting the supplies, and then painting the banner, followed by the players running through it.

Photo Essay

The Tower, Grosse Pointe South High School,
Grosse Pointe Farms, Michigan

ON DISPLAY

This photo essay presents images of a variety of events that together capture the spirit and excitement of homecoming.

— TOWER — **PHOTO STORY** — Wednesday, October 28 — **3**

Celebrating Freedom

(RIGHT) CLAD IN HIS KILT, Thomas Rourke provides bagpipe music before the parade Saturday morning. Bagpipers were also playing Thursday morning and Saturday night before the dance.
(FAR RIGHT) SWEEPIN' UP in every Homecoming category, Kevin Messacar and Chip Getz, both '99, celebrate during the halftime awards ceremony. The Class of 2002 came in second in every category except the float and penny jar contest, which the Juniors won.

AGONY AND ECSTACY, Josh Lorence '99 is helped off the field by volunteer football Coach Rick Moore, his father Stanley Lorence and Head Coach Mike McLeod. He tore the meniscus in his left knee at the end of the second quarter.

A PERFECT FIT. Homecoming parade Grand Marshall Rod Scott crowns Lauren Pankhurst '99 Homecoming Queen. Pankhurst along with her twin sister Meryl and Kristin Ritter, both '99 were nominated for Homecoming Court by the Senior Class in a vote during third hour two weeks ago.

Photos by Keely Brent and John Sullivan, both '99

IN HIGH SPIRITS, Libby Wayman, Jodie Nyenhuis, Billy Crawford, Rachel Schwanz and Anne Johnson, all '99, cheer during the football game. The team broke their six year Homecoming losing streak by beating Warren Mott 28-0.

Photos by Keely Brent and John Sullivan

Wrap-up

Without good photographs, a publication can be, at best, average. Photographs show the reader what the story tells.

A good photograph attracts a viewer's attention, enticing him or her to take a second look. In addition, photographs provide information and entertain readers, helping them to form a bond with a publication that will keep them waiting for the next issue to come out. Through the use of high-quality photographs, a publication also establishes an identity with which the reader can feel comfortable.

Learning to compose images that are full of people doing unusual things is the first step to getting pictures that are more than just snapshots. This process starts in the mind of the photographer. After beginning photographers have learned to fill the frame with the subject, some simple composition guidelines apply. They include learning to use the rule of thirds, working with repetition and leading lines and curves, and avoiding mergers and awkward cuts. Keeping in mind the need to take photos that have meaning should also guide composition.

The role of the photo editor and photographer goes beyond just taking pictures. It means keeping the photo department organized and the darkroom clean. It means having supplies on hand. It means having working equipment and film. It means gathering information while on assignment to write effective captions. It means knowing how to crop, size, and position photos on a layout. It means communicating with the rest of the staff to ensure thorough coverage of every person and event possible.

Before going out to shoot pictures, photographers must be clear about their assignment. They must know exactly what they are to shoot. The more specific the assignment, the better the results. Once photographers have accepted an assignment, they have made a commitment to record a piece of history, and they should work to cover that piece thoroughly and with as much skill as possible.

Sometimes publications will run photo essays—a series of photos that tell a story or cover various parts of an event. Photo essays work particularly well in situations in which the story comes across more effectively through pictures than through words.

On Assignment

INDIVIDUAL ACTIVITIES

1. Write a brief definition of each of these terms:

cropping	rule of thirds
halftone	sizing
photo essay	"wild art"

2. Brainstorm new ways to cover typical school events or classes with photos. For example, how could you illustrate the school play, a concert, or homecoming? How would you cover physics, world history, or vocational or physical education classes? Discuss your ideas in class.

3. Look at the front pages of several daily newspapers published on the same day. Write a critique of the photo usage on each. Were photos used effectively? Were the layouts well planned to take advantage of the photos? Were the captions written well? Were national photos used differently in different locations? Why? How would you have treated stories that have no photos so as to take advantage of illustrations?

4. Obtain a contact sheet from a photographer or use your own. Crop two or three photos on the contact sheet and arrange to have them enlarged. (Photocopiers can give you an impression of what happens. Enlarge the copies progressively three or four times.) Look at how you cropped the photographs on the contact sheets. How might they have been cropped more effectively? Attach your answers to your contact prints and enlargements.

5. Test your critical thinking. Clip an effective photo and its caption from a magazine. Also clip one that fails to tell the story. Write a short editorial column critiquing the quality of the photos and comparing them according to what you learned in this chapter. Suggest ways to improve the inadequate photo.

6. Find one photograph in newspapers or magazines that fulfills each of these photojournalistic functions: capturing attention, providing information, entertaining, establishing an emotional link, helping to establish a publication's identity. Write a paragraph on the functions each photo performs. Attach the paragraph to the page on which the photo appears.

7. Write a one-page critique of one of the On Display photos in this chapter. Use the Evaluation Checklist on page 451.

8. Take several good photographs of your own. Bring them to class and be prepared to discuss them. Explain what you were trying to do in each photo and whether you feel you were successful. Listen to others' critiques of your work and be prepared to analyze their photos in turn.

TEAM ACTIVITY

9. Working in teams, brainstorm topics for a full-page photo essay for your school newspaper. Select one topic and take the photos. Choose the best shots, crop and size them, mark them for the printer, prepare the layout for a photo page, and write the copy that will accompany the photos (including all captions and appropriate headlines).

   If you have access to a photocopier that enlarges and reduces copy, resize the photos and cut them out. Type the copy and do a dummy of your page if possible. Exchange your essay with those of other teams. In a class discussion, critique one anothers' work.

SURF THE NET

10. Visit the web site of the National Press Photographers Association (www.nppa.org) and report on what it contains. Also, examine one of the collections of news photographs linked to the site. Summarize the work of the photojournalist(s) involved.

career profile

Photo Editor

Some people are writers; some are photographers. A few, like Olga Camacho, are both.

"I could never quite decide. When I was reporting, I wanted to be shooting. When I was a photographer, I wanted to be writing," says the *Honolulu Advertiser* photo editor.

It was Camacho's writing that got her in the door at the *New York Times.* She started in 1986 in the paper's writing program for journalistic newcomers. "I worked as a clerk and a news assistant. You do odds and ends and freelance for the different sections," she said.

After the year-and-a-half-long program, Camacho left to travel. When she returned, she had to find a job.

"I was trying to figure out what I was going to do. I had decided that I wanted to get into photography again," she explained.

Having maintained good relations with the *Times*, Camacho called and asked what was available in photography. "I wanted to know what was—what made—a good photograph. I figured the *Times* was a good place to start," she said. "They sort of invented a position for me." She "bounced around the entire building" for one year, learning picture editing for the paper's various sections. "It was sort of rigorous," she said.

The experience paid off. Camacho became one of three photo editors at the *Times* and remained there for nearly nine years.

Olga Camacho

But Camacho wanted to vary her experience. "I didn't want to stay in one place forever," she said. When she was offered the position at the *Honolulu Advertiser* in 1995, Camacho took it because "it was about as different from the *Times* as I could get."

As the photo editor for the *Advertiser*, Camacho manages a staff of six photographers and two electronic image artists. She is responsible for assigning daily photo shoots, editing film, and working with the staff on ongoing projects. In addition to daily assignments, each photographer is always working on a photo-essay project (usually a feature) that may take a few weeks to complete. This helps to add variety to the staff's routine.

There are pros and cons to working for a smaller paper, Camacho said. Because the *Advertiser* has a smaller staff, Camacho is more likely to see a project through, perhaps being solely responsible for it.

"It's great because you see your work right away. Here, I can come up with a story idea on Tuesday, and it may be the main feature in Sunday's paper," she said.

On the down side, Camacho says she misses being able to bounce her ideas off other people. At a large newspaper such as the *Times*, there are many more hands involved—new ideas are generated and stories improved.

Students interested in journalism should work on their college newspaper, she said. "That's the best place to make all of your mistakes."

The key to getting good jobs, however, is making contacts with editors, Camacho said, adding that internships are best for this. "That's how you get jobs," she said. "You call them up and send them clips all the time."

FOLLOW-UP

1. Camacho brought both writing and photography experience to her photo editor job. Discuss ways a writing background might help a photographer.

2. Contacts are important, according to Camacho. What are some ways you might be able to make contacts with editors on professional publications?

CHAPTER 19

Understanding Technical Aspects of Photography

KEY CONCEPTS

After reading this chapter, you will

▶ understand the different kinds of camera lenses

▶ know the f-stops and their relevance to photography

▶ know the shutter speeds and their relevance to photography

▶ understand the process of developing film

▶ understand the process of making a print

The technical aspects of photography have scared more than one potentially good photographer away. Nevertheless, it's essential to learn the basic underlying principles that serve as a scientific basis for photography. Photographers who understand why things work the way they do will be better suited to preventing problems and fixing them when they do arise.

The ideal way to go through this chapter is not just to sit and read it. You will find it much more helpful to have a camera and film nearby so that you can actually look at the equipment and experiment with processes as they're discussed.

The Camera

A good photograph begins in the mind of the photographer. Without a camera,

lens	f-stop	ISO	back lighting	fixer
aperture	depth of field	flash-synch speed	digital camera	enlarger
exposure	shutter speed		darkroom	test strip

KEY TERMS

Professional photographers were once beginners who had to learn the technical aspects of photography.

cameras the light-sensitive surface is a solar cell that transforms light into electronic signals, which are recorded on a computer chip. Regardless of the new technology, the basic principles remain the same: Light shines through the hole (the lens) and registers on the light-sensitive material (the film or the solar cell).

Basic Camera Parts and Terms
An understanding of the basic parts of a camera and their functions is a good way to start learning the technical aspects of photography. If the camera diagrams and terms on pages 460–461 aren't crystal clear immediately, they will become clearer as you read this chapter and work with the camera.

Kinds of Lenses
Some camera lenses are fixed lenses—all you have to do is point the camera at the scene. Everything from about six feet to infinity is in focus. Others can be focused manually, allowing you to zero in on an individual part of the scene.

however, no one else can view that image. A camera is simply a box that holds the medium on which the image can be recorded. In fact, the earliest cameras were literally nothing more than a light-tight box with a tiny hole at one end and a piece of light-sensitive material at the other. Over the last 150 years, the box has evolved into the modern camera body, the hole into the lens, and the material into the film—or in recent years into the solar cell. In digital

459

worth knowing

Camera parts. All cameras have the same basic parts as described here. Some have a film-advance lever, although many advance film automatically.

body: the light-tight box that houses the camera parts

lens: the part of the camera through which the light enters, is sharpened, and is transmitted to the film (or solar cell). The focal ring on the lens adjusts the focus of the lens.

shutter: a device that slides back and forth (or up and down) to control the amount of time the film or solar cell is exposed to light

shutter-release: a mechanism to release the shutter

aperture: the lens opening that controls how much light gets through the shutter

viewfinder: a framing device that allows the photographer to see the picture before it's taken

In recent years camera manufacturers have incorporated the advantages of these lenses in the autofocus camera, which combines the simplicity of a fixed focus with the flexibility of a 35mm camera. You locate the object you want to have in the sharpest focus through the viewfinder and press the shutter release down halfway; the lens focuses on the object. Some photographers find the autofocus lenses fast enough for average shooting. Others find cameras with manual-focus lenses, or cameras that allow the user to override the autofocus and instead focus manually, more to their liking.

Lens Sizes and Functions

Many 35mm cameras can accept different sizes of lenses. Interchangeable lenses come

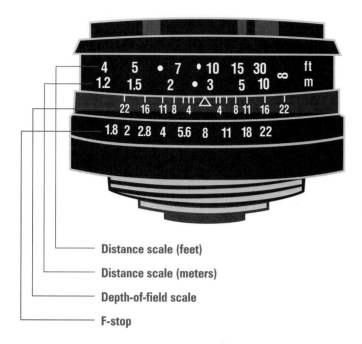

Distance scale (feet)

Distance scale (meters)

Depth-of-field scale

F-stop

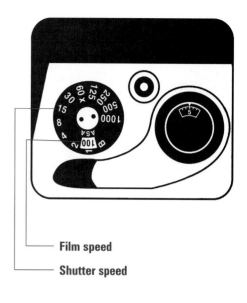

Film speed

Shutter speed

in a variety of sizes. The size of the lens is measured by its focal length in millimeters. The lower the lens number, the shorter the focal length. The shorter the focal length, the wider the lens. A lower lens number equals a wider lens.

Lenses fall into three broad categories. A wide-angle lens takes in more of the scene but stretches perspective (the perception of how objects are placed in a scene). It makes the elements in a scene appear farther apart than they are in reality. A telephoto lens has a long focal length. It magnifies the elements of a scene, making them appear crowded together and closer to the camera than they actually are. A zoom lens is a variable-length lens. It allows the user to vary the focal length between wide-angle and telephoto focal lengths.

TERMS worth knowing

Camera settings. Other parts of a camera may indicate operational settings for some of the basic parts.

f-stop: a scale that indicates the aperture (lens opening) in numbers. The lower the number, the wider the aperture. With each increase in f-stop, half as much light is let in through the aperture.

depth-of-field scale: indicates the depth of field when the camera is focused on a subject at a particular f-stop

shutter speed: indicates how fast the shutter opens and closes, measured in fractions of a second. The higher (or faster) the shutter speed, the less light is let in through the shutter. With each increase in shutter speed, half as much light is let in through the shutter.

Obviously, some lenses are better suited to certain types of photos than others. This chart will guide you.

Lens	Length	Use
Fisheye	7.5 or 15mm	Panoramic landscape shots
Wide angle	28 or 35mm	Large-group shots
Normal	50mm	Candid shots
Short telephoto	85, 105, or 135mm	Informal portraits, sport shots
Long telephoto	200 or 300mm	Spot news, sports shots
Extremely long telephoto	400mm or longer	Wildlife shots

Alternative Cameras

Most of the discussion in the following sections will deal with the manually focused 35mm single-lens-reflex (SLR) camera. Many SLRs include autofocusing and other automatic features. The automatic features usually have a manual override. Although these cameras offer great flexibility and relative ease in getting the desired shots, there are alternatives.

Point-and-shoot cameras. Many newspaper and yearbook staffs use 35mm compact cameras—fully automatic point-and-shoot models. Some feature built-in flashes and zoom lenses. They aren't suited for shooting fast action, but they're good for the average candid shot.

To be successful in using a point-and-shoot model, remember to fill the frame with the action without getting too close. Keep in mind all the other "rules" of composition (explained in Chapter 18) as well.

Digital cameras. These cameras use no film; they transmit images onto a disk for instant viewing and later manipulation and printing from a computer. Used primarily by professionals, they are becoming increasingly popular with amateurs and school journalism programs.

Except for extra bells and whistles, such as preview options and customization for all features, digital cameras resemble other cameras on the market—both the fully functional 35mm SLR and the point-and-shoot models. For publications with a short turnaround time, these cameras have three benefits. First, they eliminate the need for a darkroom. Second, the images can be transmitted across phone lines or satellite uplinks, allowing photographers to transmit images taken in one part of the world to another place in seconds. Third, they allow the photographers to preview images in the field, permitting them to test lighting conditions without having to waste a lot of film.

Video cameras. Using a video camera that can capture still images, a videographer shooting for the nightly newscast can also be taking the pictures for the morning paper or the company's web page. As the quality of these video images becomes suitable for print reproduction, even still photographers may be using video cameras.

Controlling Exposure and Focus

The advantage of a manually focused camera is that it allows more flexibility in shooting and more precision in controlling the lighting and clarity of the photograph. To use one effectively, however, you need to be aware of some of its elements and functions.

F-stops

To get a technically good image, photographers must control the amount of light getting to the film (or solar cell)—the exposure. Too much light can result in an overexposed image (in which the lighter parts of the scene becomes too light) and too little can result in an underexposed image (in which the darker parts of the scene—usually the subject—become too dark).

If the subject reflects bright light, a smaller aperture is used. If the subject reflects little light (if it's dark), a larger aperture is required. That way, an appropriate amount of light reaches the film regardless of the amount of light being reflected.

To quantify the amount of light passing through the lens, photographers have developed the f-stop, the position at which the aperture is set. The widest lens opening, usually f/2, lets in the most light. As the f-stops get higher, the lens opening gets smaller and admits less light. Thus, f/4 lets in *more* light than f/5.6 and f/8 lets in *less* light than f/5.6. In fact, f/4 lets in exactly *twice as much* light as f/5.6 and f/8 lets in exactly *half as much* light as f/5.6. Consecutive f-stops let in either twice as much light or half as much light as their neighbors.

The depth of field in this photo is narrow, with only one student in clear focus.

Depth of Field

The lens aperture (f-stop) also controls the area of the total picture in front of and behind the subject that appears in sharp focus. With smaller apertures such as f/22 or f/16, more of the total picture appears in sharp focus. With larger apertures such as f/2 or f/2.8, less appears in sharp focus. The area in sharp focus in front of and behind the specific spot on which the photographer focused is called depth of field. Of the available depth of field, one-third appears in front of the subject and two-thirds behind it.

Determining depth of field. Some cameras have a depth-of-field preview mode. If your camera doesn't have this feature, you can use the depth-of-field scale on the focus ring of the lens to determine your depth of field for any particular f-stop.

This is done by first twisting the focal ring on your lens to focus on your subject. Then, find the numbers on either side of the depth-of-field scale that match the f-stop you have set. These numbers express the depth of field as a range. For example, if your focal point is about 10 feet, and your f-stop is f/8, the depth-of-field scale will show that everything between about 7 and 15 feet will be in focus.

If you want to increase the depth of field, you can do one of three things (the first is the most common): Use a higher f-stop (narrower aperture), use a lens with a shorter focal length (wider lens), or increase the distance between you and your subject.

Shutter Speed

The f-stop controls the *amount* of light reaching the film. You can also control the *length of time* that the film is exposed to light by controlling the speed of the shutter—the part of the camera that moves, or is "released," to allow light to reach the light-sensitive surface.

The shutter speed, the amount of time the shutter stays open, is measured in fractions of a second. Modern cameras have shutter speeds ranging from B ("bulb"), which indicates that the shutter will stay open as long as the photographer has the shutter release depressed, all the way up to 1/4000th of a second. With a few exceptions, the shutter speeds are measured in multiples of two and are expressed without the fraction. For example, 60 indicates 1/60th of a second. Starting with one second and increasing, the shutter speeds are 2, 4, 8, 15, 30, 60, 125, 250, 500, 1000, 2000, and 4000.

Like the f-stops, each adjacent shutter speed lets in either twice as much or half as much light as its neighbor. For example, 250 (1/250th of a second) lets in twice as much light as 500 and half as much light as 125.

The f-stop/shutter-speed relationship. Because you can set the shutter speed and f-stop on adjustable cameras, you have flexibility in controlling the exposure. If you need more light, use a lower f-stop (wider aperture) to allow *more* light in or decrease the shutter speed to allow more *time* to let in light. If you need less light, do the opposite.

Keep this relationship in mind: Lower f-stops (wider apertures) may require faster shutter speeds. Conversely, higher f-stops (narrower apertures) may require slower shutter speeds.

This diagram will illustrate the relationship more clearly. Any of the combinations shown here would admit exactly the same amount of light to the film:

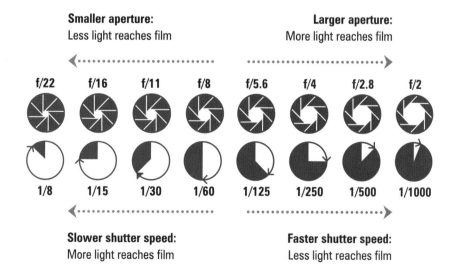

Smaller aperture:
Less light reaches film

Larger aperture:
More light reaches film

f/22   f/16   f/11   f/8   f/5.6   f/4   f/2.8   f/2

1/8   1/15   1/30   1/60   1/125   1/250   1/500   1/1000

Slower shutter speed:
More light reaches film

Faster shutter speed:
Less light reaches film

Setting the shutter speed. There are limits to how much you can play with shutter speeds if you want a sharply focused photo. All photographers tend to move when holding the camera to take a photo. To avoid blur, the slowest shutter speed that can be used with a given lens is approximately equal to the focal length of that lens: 60 for a 50mm lens, 250 for a 200mm lens, and so on. Longer shutter speeds require the use of a device to stabilize the camera, such as a tripod.

Stopping action. When you photograph nonmoving subjects, you can concentrate on depth of field and choose a shutter speed to give you a correct exposure. To stop action requires fast shutter speeds. A lot of movement can occur in 1/60th of a second. To stop most human action, a shutter speed of 500 is needed. All but the fastest action can be stopped with a shutter speed of 2000. If your subject is moving head-on or diagonally, however, you can freeze it at a slower shutter speed than if it's moving horizontally across your field of vision.

You can freeze a moving object and blur the background if you pan. When you pan, you follow the subject by moving the camera at the same pace and direction as the subject.

Stopping action is particularly important for sports photography. The photo in the **ON DISPLAY** feature on page 467 shows the drama of sports action frozen in time.

Proper Exposure

Determining the proper exposure for a scene is more than just choosing an f-stop and a shutter speed. The two must work together to provide enough detail in the light and dark areas of the picture and to stop the action you want stopped but blur the action you want blurred. To ensure good exposure a third variable must be considered: the "speed" of the film that you're using.

Film speed. The speed of film indicates its sensitivity to light, which is rated by a fixed number known as the ISO. The lower the number, the "slower" the film and the less sensitive it is to light. "Faster" film is more light sensitive. Thus, ISO 3200 film is more sensitive than ISO 400 film, which is, in turn, more sensitive than ISO 100 film.

By choosing the right film speed for the lighting conditions of your shoot, you're more likely to get an exposure that preserves the highlights

Stopping Action

Quaker Shaker, Plainfield High School, Plainfield, Indiana
Photo by Becky Butterfield

In sports photography capturing fast-moving action such as this requires a grasp of the importance of the shutter speed.

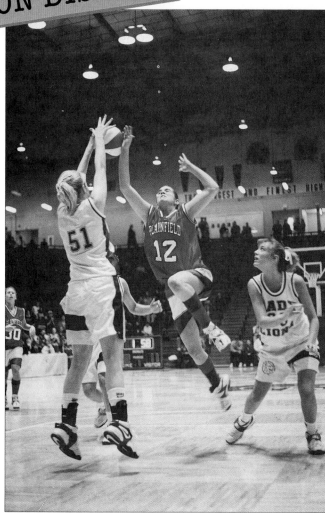

and shadows of the scene. In general, use film with a higher ISO at night and in low light; use film with a lower ISO for bright light or sunny outdoor shoots.

The f/16 rule. A standard rule of exposure is based on taking pictures in bright sunlight. The f/16 (or sunny f/16) rule states that in bright sunlight at f/16, the shutter speed should be nearly equal to the ISO of the film you're using. For example, using ISO 400 film, the shutter speed for f/16 would be 500—or f/16 @ 1/500 (exposures are usually written in this fashion).

It's easy to derive a set of basic exposures from the f/16 rule, remembering that the shutter speed is nearly equal to the ISO:

Bright sun	f/16
Hazy sun	f/11
Weak sun (soft shadows)	f/8
Cloudy (no shadows)	f/5.6
Heavy overcast	f/4
Well-lit interiors	f/1.8

Back lighting. With a modern camera, most of the calculation regarding exposure is automatically determined by a built-in light meter. Under certain lighting conditions, however, camera light meters may be tricked into giving false exposure readings.

The most common false meter reading occurs when the subject is backlit—that is, when the light source is coming from behind the subject instead of behind or to the side of the photographer. The meter attempts to give an exposure that will result in the correct exposure of the "average" part of the scene. To avoid overexposure, the meter tries to make these parts a neutral tone. This results in underexposure.

Using the available light (the natural light of the setting), you can solve the back-lighting problem in one of two ways: You can move yourself, the subject, or the light source; or you can compensate by increasing the amount of light that reaches the film. To do this, either

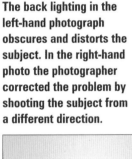

The back lighting in the left-hand photograph obscures and distorts the subject. In the right-hand photo the photographer corrected the problem by shooting the subject from a different direction.

use an f-stop that is two stops wider or a shutter speed that is two stops slower. For example, if the original, backlit scene gave a meter reading indicating a correct exposure of f/8 @ 1/125, your new exposure could be f/4 @ 1/125. This may cause the light area of the scene to be overexposed, but it will prevent underexposure.

Bracketing. To help ensure correct exposure, some photographers bracket their shots. To bracket, shoot one picture at what you think is the correct exposure. Then shoot two more of the same picture, one slightly overexposed and one slightly underexposed. One of the three is likely to be correct.

Artificial light. Although it ends up looking the most natural, using available light is not the only alternative for photographers. Many cameras today come with built-in flashes that create their own, artificial light. Most 35mm SLR cameras come with a way to attach a flash to the top of the camera for perfect synchronization with the camera's shutter.

When using a flash, know the fastest shutter speed you can use with that flash to get a properly exposed picture. That speed is called the flash-synchronization speed (usually 1/60th or 1/250th of a second) and is often marked with a lightning bolt or in red on the camera's shutter-speed dial. Some cameras have automatic synchronization with the flash.

The flash-synch speed is a fairly slow shutter speed, which may not seem fast enough to stop action. Remember, however, that the light for the scene is coming from the flash, which is fast and powerful. If there's ambient light (light from sources such as lamps or the setting sun) in the scene, you may, in effect, get two exposures on the scene, one from the flash and one from the ambient light. This can produce interesting but sometimes unpredictable results. Nevertheless, it's a common technique when taking pictures in front of a bonfire or sunset. The flash lights the subject in the foreground while the bonfire or sunset lights the background.

Because most color films are color-balanced for sunlight, when shooting with color film, you need to take into account the color of the artificial light. Color photos taken under fluorescent light will turn green. Those taken under tungsten light (such as a conventional light bulb) will appear red. Compensating for this color shifting requires either a special film or a color-compensating filter put in front of the lens before taking the picture.

Working in the Darkroom

The day may soon come when digital photography will become so widespread that it will replace the need for a darkroom altogether. For now, however, it's wise to become familiar with basic film development and printing procedures.

Whether it's black and white or color, paper or film, most photographic materials are fundamentally the same: an emulsion consisting of silver halide crystals embedded in a gelatin spread on plastic (in the case of film) or on paper (in the case of photographic paper). The process of exposing and developing images on these materials is also fundamentally the same.

Silver halide (most commonly silver bromide or silver iodide) crystals are sensitive to light and change when exposed to it. The crystals that are changed form a latent image that is invisible until developed.

The process of developing film and making prints from it requires special equipment and skills. Many of the skills are similar to those used in taking pictures with a camera.

A well-equipped darkroom contains, besides running water, the equipment and chemicals necessary to develop film and make prints. Here, a student checks processed film for spots.

Developing Film: An Overview

Before film can be developed, it has to be removed from its canister, rolled onto a reel, and placed into a tank that will allow the developing agent to reach it. The film must be carefully rolled onto a reel that prevents any part of its surface from touching another part. Because film

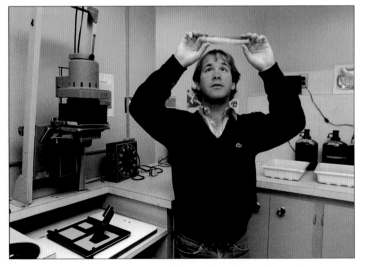

is extremely sensitive to light, this must be done in complete darkness, preferably in a light-tight room, which is part of the larger darkroom.

A darkroom can be an old closet, a bathroom, a kitchen, or a room in the school with easy access to running water. A well-equipped darkroom must have running water and a government-approved drainage system for the chemicals used in development because these chemicals are considered hazardous waste.

The development process acts first on crystals that have been most changed by light. The developing agent starts a chemical reaction. As long as the developer is removed before the unchanged (unexposed) crystals begin reacting, an image made of silver crystals will appear on the film.

Unless the undeveloped crystals are rendered insensitive to light, they can still be changed by light. After the development process is complete, therefore, the film or paper is "fixed" through another chemical process. Fixing renders the silver halide crystals insensitive to light.

Other steps in film development enhance the process and remove the chemicals used in development and fixing. Color film requires more steps, but the basic process is the same as for black-and-white film: develop, stop development, fix, rinse, and dry.

After the film has been dried in a clean environment (so that no dust settles on it), it's cut into strips of five or six frames per strip and stored in plastic sheets for easy filing and access. Contact sheets can then be printed in preparation for photo selection.

Making a Print: An Overview

Once you have developed the film, you can make prints from it. This process requires subjecting the photographic paper to a process much like that used in film development. Making prints also requires working in a room with limited light, although complete darkness is not necessary when working with traditional black-and-white papers.

The negative. The negative is an inverse copy of the photographic image. Where more light hits the film during exposure, more silver crystals are changed, causing a dense buildup of silver. Thus, on a negative, lighter areas in the scene appear more opaque; darker areas appear more transparent. During the print-making process, you expose photographic paper through the negative and make a postive image appear on the paper. Light that shines through the transparent parts of the negative (the dark areas of the scene) exposes the photographic paper, turning it dark. Opaque areas of the negative prevent light from exposing the paper, causing those areas on the paper to remain light.

Because photographic paper is light sensitive, making prints is done in a darkroom. Unlike film, however, which is sensitive to all wave lengths of light, most common black-and-white photographic papers are highly

A photographer must carefully adjust the photo enlarger to make sure the finished print is focused sharply and exposed correctly.

sensitive to light only on the blue end of the spectrum. They're relatively insensitive to red light, so many darkrooms are lit with reddish lights (or safelights), which allows photographers enough light to work.

The enlarger and the easel. The first step to making a print is focusing and cropping the image. This is accomplished with the use of a machine called an enlarger. The enlarger magnifies the negative and projects it onto a baseboard, where the photographic paper will be placed.

For stable positioning the negative is placed in the enlarger's negative carrier—emulsion side down (shiny side up). Once the negative is in position, you turn the enlarger on. Light passes through the negative, through the lens, and onto the baseboard of the enlarger. Using the widest available f-stop, you then focus and crop the image. At this point, no photographic paper is yet on the baseboard. Only when you're ready to expose the image should you use photographic paper. In the meantime, you can use a blank sheet of white paper.

To hold the photo paper securely, use an easel that rests firmly on the enlarger baseboard. Some easels allow you to make prints that aren't fixed sizes. You can make a print measuring 4 ⅓ inches by 5 ¾ inches if you want to; you're not limited to standard sizes, such as 8 inches by 10 inches. These variable easels are handy for publications work and make it easier on the people designing pages because the photographer does the cropping.

Polycontrast filters. To control the contrast of the image, choose a polycontrast filter before choosing the f-stop. The appropriate filter depends on the type of paper you're using and the contrast of the image. Higher-numbered filters raise contrast, as do higher grades of single-contrast paper. Lower-numbered filters lower contrast.

The correct exposure. After choosing the correct filter, you choose an f-stop that will result in a correctly exposed image—one neither too light nor too dark. Note that the f-stops on an enlarger are the same as those on a camera. By doing a test print, you can practice your exposure until you get it right. An f-stop that's too wide open will result in a test print that's too dark overall. An f-stop that's too narrow will result in a test print that's too light overall.

After you have chosen an f-stop, the only variable left to determine is the "shutter speed," which is set with a timer attached to the enlarger. Exposure times for prints are generally 10 to 30 seconds long rather than fractions of a second. If your exposure ends up being longer than 30 seconds, you have chosen an f-stop that isn't letting through enough light. You should then increase the f-stop. Just as on the camera, opening the enlarger's lens by one f-stop lets in twice as much light. To compensate, you have to expose the paper for half as long. For example, if your original exposure was 40 seconds at f/5.6, the equivalent exposure would be 20 seconds at f/4.

Test strips. To determine the exact exposure time without wasting a lot of paper, you can use a test strip—a series of exposures on one piece of paper. Have each successive exposure (in equal intervals of 2–5 seconds) expose the paper to more light, making the image darker. Once you have determined the proper exposure time, you can expose an entire sheet of paper cut to the size of the finished print and can then develop the paper.

Dodging and burning. During the process of making a test print, you may see areas of the image that need to be darker or lighter to reveal adequate detail. With simple homemade tools (or your fingers), you can dodge, or mask, dark areas to prevent them from being exposed to as much light as other parts of the paper. A small cardboard shape taped to a thin wire may serve as a dodging tool. Move it gently over the area to be shaded throughout the exposure.

Conversely, you can burn, or give extra exposure time, to light areas to make them darker, while masking the rest of the print. Hold the masking

trends and issues

Photos from Cyberspace

How can you use the Internet to get high-quality photos and art reproductions?

Looking for a perfect shot of Mount Rainier to accompany a travel feature? Can't find a reproduction of a Picasso painting to go with a story about a new show at a nearby museum? Why not check on the Internet?

It used to be that when a publication wanted a photograph to reproduce, it had to contact a stock house, a company that holds large collections of images for rental. From the several transparencies (slides) that were generally sent back, the publication chose one that best fit its needs. Transparencies had to be treated with care because if any were lost or damaged, the publication was held responsible. Once a selection was made, the transparency then had to be converted for use in the publication.

Today, thanks to the Internet, the whole picture-selection process is much more streamlined. A page designer, a photo editor, or even a sixth-grader doing a science report can visit the web site of a company that purveys images, click on a photo or painting, and download it for use. The cost of using the image varies; for a student needing only a low-resolution image for a school project, it may be free.

Creating this easy access to images took a tremendous amount of effort. Museums had to photograph hundreds of paintings. These and hundreds of thousands of other photographs then had to be scanned, digitized, and indexed.

What kinds of images are available? Well, for example, one company bought the entire Bettman Archive, a 16-million image collection with some of the most famous photographs of the 20th century. That company, Corbis, has scannd and digitized it. Precisely accurate renderings of famous art works from museums around the world are also available. There are also the more run-of-the-mill, but very useful, image collections of various

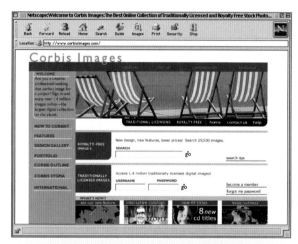

Like most on-line image distributors, the web site of Corbis Images includes a search engine to allow users to explore their image archives for general or specific images.

stock houses on line, which are continually updated.

Here is how a typical transaction of procuring an image could work. An editor might use a company's search engine to look for an appropriate photo or, if the need were more specific, call the company and describe exactly what was wanted. The company researcher would set up an account for the editor and send several samples to a web site so that the editor could make a selection. Then the editor would communicate his or her decision—by phone, fax, or e-mail. The image could be sent via the Internet immediately or be put onto a CD-ROM and sent overnight.

The cost of procuring an image depends both on the image and what it's being used for. Professional publications generally pay for high-resolution scans of images according to the image's size, fame, and popularity. Student publications may pay too—but depending on the supplier, they may pay less. Low-resolution scans are often free.

Procuring photos and other images over the Internet won't put local photographers out of business. Going on line, however, is a good way to fill specific—and especially unusual—needs quickly.

FOLLOW-UP

1. Suppose you needed a particular photo for a student publication. Would it be feasible to procure one via the Internet? Do some research into image companies and the fees they charge.
2. Many Internet sites provide images of famous paintings from around the world. Find at least two such sites and report on what they have available.

tool (generally a larger piece of cardboard) between the light and the paper, moving it gently during the exposure; don't set it directly on the paper, or the result will be a distinct line in the print.

The print-development process. Just as with film, developing prints involves first converting the latent image into a visible image through a chemical process that changes exposed silver crystals by developing the paper, then rendering unexposed crystals insensitive to light by fixing the paper, and finally removing the crystals by rinsing the paper.

To keep prints for a long period of time, one of the most important parts of the printing process is washing the print to remove all the residual fixer and silver halides. Failure to remove any of those chemicals will cause the print to turn brown and the image to fade over time.

Prints are fixed and rinsed in trays large enough to hold the largest print you will be making. It's important to keep fresh chemicals at room temperature in the trays, and it's also extremely important to keep the darkroom clean. Any dust coming from dry chemicals or from book covers or clothes will come to rest on the negative or photo paper, resulting in white spots on the print. In fact, the darkroom should be treated like a chemistry lab. Under no circumstances should food or drink be allowed in the darkroom, and you should arrange for the proper disposal of chemicals, especially fixer, just as chemists do. To ensure correct procedures, Material Safety and Data Sheets (MSDS) should be visible to anyone working in the lab. These are available from photochemical suppliers.

When evaluating prints—either your own or others', use this checklist.

EVALUATION CHECKLIST

Prints

- ☑ Is the print in focus?
- ☑ Was enough light used to bring out the details in the photo?
- ☑ Is the contrast between light and dark areas adequate but not excessive?
- ☑ Are all the necessary details in the highlights and shadows revealed?
- ☑ Is the print free from dust spots?

Wrap-up

Learning the technical aspects of photography can take some time, but having a fundamental understanding of how and why the photographic process works is important. Photography is painting with light: The camera is the brush and the film is the canvas. As a photographer, you control what the brush puts on the canvas by manipulating the f-stop and the shutter speed.

The f-stop is the setting on the lens that indicates the aperture, or lens opening. The f-stop therefore controls the amount of light that reaches the film. Larger f-stops (such as f/2 and f/1.4) allow more light to reach the film. Smaller f-stops (such as f/16 and f/22) allow less light to reach the film.

The f-stop also controls the depth of field, the area of the total picture in front of and behind the subject that appears in sharp focus. With smaller apertures, more of the total picture appears in sharp focus. With larger apertures, less appears in sharp focus.

The shutter, the part of the camera that is released to take the picture, controls the amount of light that reaches the film. The shutter remains open for a very specific duration of time; the longer that time, the more light can reach the film. For example, a shutter speed of 1/60th of a second allows twice as much light to reach the film as a speed of 1/125th of a second.

The shutter speed also impacts what is in focus. To avoid blur, the slowest shutter speed that can be used with a given lens is approximately equal to the focal length of that lens. To stop action requires fast shutter speeds.

To ensure good exposure, photographers must not only consider the f-stop and shutter speed but also the film speed, which indicates a film's sensitivity to light. Film speed is rated by a fixed number known as the ISO. The lower the number, the less sensitive the film is to light.

The shutter speed and aperture work together to expose film to light. This principle works both when taking pictures and making prints.

In the darkroom, photographers have to master the chemical processes involved in both developing film and making prints. A developer converts the latent image to a visible image and a fixative agent "fixes" the image to make it permanent. In the darkroom, photographers can control how light or dark an image, or part of an image, appears. They can also crop off unnecessary portions of the picture, leaving the reader with a powerful photo filled with action.

Most photographers today use a 35mm single-lens-reflex (SLR) camera. Many SLRs include autofocusing and other automatic features, which usually have a manual override. A number of newspaper and yearbook staffs are successful using 35mm compact cameras—fully automatic point-and-shoot models.

Digital cameras are becoming more popular with professionals and amateurs alike. These cameras use no film. They transmit their images onto a disk for instant viewing and later manipulation and printing from a computer, eliminating the need for a darkroom. Photographers can send ready-to-use electronic images across phone lines or satellite uplinks in seconds. They can also preview such images in the field.

On Assignment

INDIVIDUAL ACTIVITIES

1. Write a brief definition of each of these terms:

aperture	flash-synchronization speed
back lighting	f-stop
darkroom	ISO
depth of field	lens
digital camera	shutter speed
enlarger	test strip
fixer	

2. Take a series of pictures of the same scene, experimenting with different f-stops and shutter speeds for each shot. Make note of the settings you used. Then develop the film or have it developed. Examine the results carefully. What differences were caused by using the different settings? Which exposures turned out better—or worse—than you expected? Write a brief report, analyzing the results. Include your photos in the report.

3. Make a list of all the chemicals used in your darkroom. Don't list brand names. Instead, read the packaging and list all the components of, for example, your film developer. Include all chemicals used for both film developing and printing. Then list the chemical compounds common to both processes.

4. If a scene required an exposure of f/16 @ 500 and you exposed it at f/22 @ 1000, would the result be an underexposed negative or an overexposed negative? Why? Without any further manipulation, would a print from this negative be too dark or too light? Why? Explain your answers in a class discussion.

5. Evaluate the photograph in the On Display feature on page 467 strictly on the basis of technical quality. Is it in focus? Is it too high or too low in contrast? If so, how would you correct it?

6. Locate the Material Safety and Data Sheet (MSDS) for one of the chemicals used in the darkroom. What hazards does this chemical have? What can you do to avoid any danger?

7. Using only pictures (no text), diagram the process of exposing and developing film. Illustrate the emulsion, silver halide crystals, latent image, unexposed silver halide crystals, and final image. You may want to refer to a photography manual to clarify steps in the process.

8. Consult a photography manual that explains in detail the process of developing film and making prints. Then compare and contrast the two processes. Consider all chemicals and immersion times, temperatures, and agitation rates for all chemicals.

TEAM ACTIVITY

9. With a team, select the best photos that each member has taken. Then have each team member write a critical analysis of his or her photo, describing the f-stop and shutter speed used and the quality of the print. Combine the analyses, along with the photos, into a display book. Compare your book with those of other teams.

SURF THE NET

10. Use a search engine to find information about technical advances in photography. Report what you learn to the class.

Newspaper Publisher and Editor

A love of sports sparked Don Flores's interest in journalism and helped him score big in a profession that's trying hard to attract more minorities.

From his first bylines as a young reporter covering Little League in his hometown of Goliad, Texas, to his current position as publisher and editor of the *El Paso* (Texas) *Times,* Flores worked his way to the top of the newspaper business.

Although his career has taken him across the country, Flores is happy to be back in his home state. "I think it's great. I grew up in Texas, and I can really blend into the community here. I know its issues," Flores said.

As publisher and editor, Flores says he gets a chance to see the news process from a different perspective. "Being a publisher, you come to see the newspaper as a 'total product.' You're able to see how it fits the community's needs." If the news product is relevant to the community, its members will believe in it and continue to support it, Flores added.

That attitude has helped Flores get where he is today.

When Flores entered Southwest Texas State University in San Marcos, he joined the student newspaper as its sports editor. In 1973, he began working for the *Abilene Reporter-News* and advanced within three years to the position of city editor. His career path took him to the

Don Flores

Dallas Times Herald in 1978 and in 1983 to the *Dallas Morning News.*

During these years Flores also became active in groups and activities designed to bring more minorities into journalism. One such activity was the summer journalism program for minority high school students run by Texas Christian University in Fort Worth.

"That's how we get them [minority journalists] in the newsroom," Flores said. "We track them from high school to college and then snap them up as soon as they are ready."

Flores says he is not a joiner, but his activities contradict that. He regularly attends conventions of both the National Association of Hispanic Journalists, of which he is past president, and the National Association of Black Journalists.

At age 34 Flores left Texas to become assistant managing editor of the *Tucson Citizen* in Arizona, a job that directly involved him in recruiting. After several other jobs, Flores moved back to Texas, where he became publisher and editor of the *El Paso Times* in 1993.

Throughout his career Flores has remained dedicated to minority recruiting. His present job places a greater demand on his time, but Flores intends to continue with that effort. "I try to be as involved as I can," Flores said. Although downsizing in the newspaper industry has hurt minority representation, at least at the *El Paso Times,* he's not discouraged. "I will just have to be more aggressive to make it happen," he said.

Today more and more minority students are learning about career opportunities in journalism. Flores fully acknowledges the importance of his position as a Hispanic journalist in Texas. "I am concerned about being the role model a lot of us didn't have," he said.

FOLLOW-UP

1. What exactly does a publisher-editor job such as Flores's entail? Do some research; then write a brief report describing the job.

2. Find out about some of the professional organizations Flores has belonged to and report to the class about their activities.

CHAPTER 20

The Impact of Technology

desktop publishing	network		photo illustration
CPU	laser printer	pagination software	
RAM	word processing	image editing	scanner

KEY TERMS

KEY CONCEPTS

After reading this chapter, you will

▶ understand the various parts of the computer and their functions.

▶ know the types of printers common on the market today and those that are best suited for desktop publishing.

▶ understand the role of the various types of software used in desktop publishing.

▶ know the various ways an image can be digitized.

▶ be familiar with the development of the Internet and its influence on journalism.

Back in 1988 at a seminar hosted by the American Press Institute (API), some of the top newspaper designers in the United States were surveyed about the paper of the future. They were asked to forecast what they thought newspapers would be like in 2020. About one-third of them said that they believed the traditional newspaper would be replaced with some interactive media that could be delivered electronically.

They cited statistics regarding the viewing of television versus the reading of newspapers to prove their point. "The newspaper is a product that holds the attention of readers for about 24 minutes a day," John Lees, a Massachusetts graphic designer, said at the API seminar. "Meanwhile, television sets are on in American households seven hours a day, although actual viewing time is only three and a half hours. Newspaper circulation has stalled . . . , penetration has declined substantially, and many publishers insist on producing cumbersome products. . . ."

Since 1988, remarkable changes in technology have occurred. Although many newspapers today are distributed electroni-

Newspapers distributed electronically on the Internet, haven't replaced the printed version—the fold-up variety that people can read on the way to work.

cally via the Internet, these papers haven't replaced the printed version—the fold-up variety that people can stick in their briefcases and read on the way to work. In truth, more changes have occurred in the printed version of the paper—at least in the way it's produced.

In 1988 typewriters were just about as common in news offices as computers. Designers laid out pages by hand. Nearly all photos were black and white. The World Wide Web didn't exist. The growth of the personal computer and the Internet, coupled with various other technologically

related products, has radically changed the way all printed materials are produced—and the change continues as new hardware (machinery) and software (computer programs) become available.

Thus it's fitting that this course finishes with a look at technology and the impact it has had on journalism. This final chapter is really a summary; most of the technology described in it involves things you have been using throughout this course. By looking at technology from a historical basis, however, you can get a sense of where things have been and, perhaps, where they are heading.

482

483

Computers
and
Desktop
Publishing

CHAPTER 20

The Impact of Technology

KEY CONCEPTS

After reading this chapter, you will

▶ understand the various parts of the computer and their functions

▶ know the types of printers common on the market today and those that are best suited for desktop publishing

▶ understand the role of the various types of software used in desktop publishing

▶ know the various ways an image can be digitized

▶ be familiar with the development of the Internet and its influence on journalism

Back in 1988 at a seminar hosted by the American Press Institute (API), some of the top newspaper designers in the United States were surveyed about the paper of the future. They were asked to forecast what they thought newspapers would be like in 2020. About one-third of them said that they believed the traditional newspaper would be replaced with some interactive media that could be delivered electronically.

They cited statistics regarding the viewing of television versus the reading of newspapers to prove their point. "The newspaper is a product that holds the attention of readers for about 24 minutes a day," John Lees, a Massachusetts graphic designer, said at the API seminar. "Meanwhile, television sets are on in American households seven hours a day, although actual viewing time is only three and a half hours. Newspaper circulation has stalled . . . , penetration has declined substantially, and many publishers insist on producing cumbersome products. . . ."

Since 1988, remarkable changes in technology have occurred. Although many newspapers today are distributed electroni-

KEY
TERMS

desktop publishing	network	pagination software	photo illustration
CPU	laser printer		scanner
RAM	word processing	image editing	

Newspapers distributed electronically on the Internet, haven't replaced the printed version—the fold-up variety that people can read on the way to work.

cally via the Internet, these papers haven't replaced the printed version—the fold-up variety that people can stick in their briefcases and read on the way to work. In truth, more changes have occurred in the printed version of the paper—at least in the way it's produced.

In 1988 typewriters were just about as common in news offices as computers. Designers laid out pages by hand. Nearly all photos were black and white. The World Wide Web didn't exist. The growth of the personal computer and the Internet, coupled with various other technologically related products, has radically changed the way all printed materials are produced—and the change continues as new hardware (machinery) and software (computer programs) become available.

Thus it's fitting that this course finishes with a look at technology and the impact it has had on journalism. This final chapter is really a summary; most of the technology described in it involves things you have been using throughout this course. By looking at technology from a historical basis, however, you can get a sense of where things have been and, perhaps, where they are heading.

The Beginnings of Desktop Publishing

Paul Brainard, then president of the Aldus Corporation, sat with colleagues around a table in 1985 discussing PageMaker, the new software his company was developing. At that table Brainard and others coined the phrase "desktop publishing" to summarize what could be done with several new products: the recently released Macintosh (Mac) computer with its user-friendly interface; the laser printer, which would provide high-resolution output on conventional paper; and their software.

PageMaker wasn't the first pagination software. It was, however, the first software marketed to bring the "power of the press" to the masses. PageMaker, together with the Macintosh and laser printer, revolutionized the printing business. No longer do you need a $15,000 typesetter, chemicals, and developing equipment to produce high-quality type. Now, with a $1,000 computer, a $500 laser printer, and about $700 worth of software, you can put out your own publication, one that is virtually indistinguishable from a professionally produced publication. In theory at least, a school newspaper can look just as good as the *New York Times*.

Hardware: An Overview

Hardware is, basically, the machinery used in a computer system. This includes the computer itself and various components that may be attached to it, such as a printer.

HISTORY worth remembering

Humble beginnings. Apple Computer, the first company to bring simple-to-use desksize computers to homes and small businesses, had its origins in the bedroom and garage of 20-year-old Steve Jobs. He and his partner, fellow electronics wizard Steve Wozniak, designed and built the Apple I and introduced it in 1976; other computers, including the Macintosh, followed. Both Jobs and Wozniak eventually left Apple Computer, although Jobs later returned.

Computers

In the years since the Macintosh and laser printer hit the market, the user-friendly interface is no longer unique. Now, almost every personal computer (PC) on the market has an easy-to-use interface with which a user can simply point to something with a screen navigating device (the "mouse"), click it, and go. Here is a brief summary of what the various parts of the personal computer do.

The CPU. The central processing unit (CPU) is the brains of the computer. It controls everything that the computer does. The casing that holds the CPU also holds the power supply and slots for items such as accessory cards, which allow the computer to perform specialized functions.

Drives. A computer typically uses two kinds of "drives." One is the built-in hard drive. On the hard drive's hard disk, a user can store any documents created, as well as the software to which access will be needed.

Almost all computers also come with at least one form of accessory drive—a compact disk (CD) drive, a Zip-disk drive, or a floppy-disk drive. Using these drives, you can store ("write") and retrieve ("read") information on the corresponding removable disks—CDs, Zip disks, and floppy disks.

Floppy disks were the sole method of transporting documents between personal computers for

A CD can hold more than 650 megabytes of information.

almost 20 years. Originally called floppy disks because they were made of flexible material, floppies today are still soft, but have hard cases—and at 3 ½ inches square, they are about half the size of the original 6-inch format. However, floppy disks, which traditionally hold about 1 megabyte of information, aren't very reliable and store far less information compared to newer media. Zip disks store up to 250 megabytes of information and a CD can hold more than 650 megabytes of information. Currently, most CDs can't be erased once the information is written on the disk; however, newer hardware and software is making rewritable CDs commonplace. Because CDs store so much information, they're commonly used for archiving back issues of publications, including art files and fonts.

A hard drive might easily contain thousands of documents, so it's important to keep it organized and clean. Related document files should be put into computer-made folders. Unnecessary files should be discarded. Time should be scheduled each week for maintaining the hard drive and checking the various components.

Networks. Efficient maintenance of files becomes even more critical for users on a network, an electronic connection of multiple computers that allows users to share files directly. With the appropriate network software, which comes with most computers today, and a few cables, a system can be set up to allow any user access to any file from any computer—or to restrict access as needed. A network becomes particularly efficient in a publications setting because it allows editors to edit copy and make it available to the person designing the page without the need to switch computers or transfer information via disks.

Modems. A modem is a device that allows information to travel across telephone lines. Some are built in, while others are separate plug-in units. It's the modem that "dials up" the connection between the computer and the Internet.

Input devices. Computers also have keyboards and other input devices—that is, tools to use in creating documents. Most computers ship a keyboard and a mouse with the CPU. Some artists, however, prefer drawing tablets, track balls, or even touch screens to a desktop mouse.

Monitors. The monitor is the screen that shows you what you're doing. Like other hardware, monitors come in different models with different features.

Almost all monitors sold today are color. They may differ in the number of colors they can display and at what resolution, measured in pixels per inch (ppi). The more pixels per inch, the higher the resolution, allowing finer detail to be displayed on the screen.

Monitors also vary in screen size. Large-screen monitors with higher resolution cost more money, but for average use most users don't need monitors that have a screen larger than 13 inches.

Processors. Some computers run faster than others because their CPU contains a faster central-processing chip. Faster processors cost more but allow more operations to be completed in less time. IBM and Macintosh computers (and their respective clones) contain different processors. Therefore, software created to run on an IBM or IBM-compatible can't be run on a Macintosh. The two systems are, however, getting closer. Generally, although programs aren't interchangeable, files are: An IBM can read files (such as newspaper pages) created on a Mac, and vice versa.

Clearly, manufacturers are moving toward having a universal file system, something that will make sharing files even easier—and more productive—for the average user.

Memory. The amount of memory that computers contain also varies. Random access memory (RAM) is the memory reserved for the computer to do things. The more RAM a computer has, the more it can do. Desktop publishing is RAM intensive. That is, it requires more than the average amount of RAM. While 16 megabytes of RAM may be sufficient to run many software programs, those used in desktop publishing may require 24 megabytes of RAM or more to run efficiently. Computers having more than 96 megabytes of RAM are common in businesses doing sophisticated desktop publishing and manipulation of images.

Advantages for publishing. Exploring no further than this, users should be able to recognize certain advantages of the computer. For one thing, it can hold huge numbers of documents that in the past would all have to have been stored on paper. It can be connected through networks that allow people to work together on different aspects of the same project and to easily see each other's work on the screen. Furthermore, although it can be used as a writing machine because of its keyboard, the computer is also capable of being used for other purposes by artists and designers.

Printers

What really made desktop publishing a reality was the capability of printing files created on the computer. Once an individual could quickly produce professional-looking copies of a document rather than having to send manuscript elsewhere for typesetting and printing, whole new worlds of communication possibilities opened up.

Several types of printers can be used in desktop publishing, some of which are more efficient than others.

Dot-matrix printers. Dot-matrix printers use pins that press through a ribbon, much like a typewriter, to form an image on the paper. The more pins the printer has, the higher quality it is. An eight-pin printer for example, is one-third the quality of a 24-pin printer. Although dot-matrix printers are no longer common today, some color printers still use this technology.

Being able to print out copy and page layouts on portable printers has streamlined many publishing operations.

Ink-jet printers. Ink-jet printers squirt ink on the page for a smoother-looking image but one that's still relatively low in resolution. Color ink-jet printers are particularly popular today because of the smoothness of the image they generate, and many black-and-white ink-jet printers are used in home offices.

Laser printers. When the laser printer came along, the real revolution in desktop printing began. Even the earliest laser printers had a resolution much higher than the highest-quality dot-matrix printer.

The resolution of a laser printer, or any high-end printer for that matter, is measured in dots per inch (dpi). A low-end laser printer has a resolution of 600 dpi. This resolution is more than adequate for materials to be photocopied—not only low-end newspapers but even those being printed on newsprint using a 60-lines-per-inch (lpi) screen. High-end laser printers that output to paper have a resolution of 1200 dpi or greater. Because of the coarseness of paper and imprecision of the paper placement, however, printing to paper with such high-end printers is less effective than printing to film.

Many schools that want high-resolution printing—for example, for yearbooks—go directly to the publisher or to a commercial service bureau. These suppliers are capable of taking a disk with all your files, graphics, and fonts, putting the disk in their computer, and printing these files on their imagesetters. The film generated by the imagesetter can be used directly to make the plates that are used to print your pages. Even if your school has only a 300 dpi laser printer for proofing, you can get quality rivaling the best in the publishing industry—2540 dpi or beyond—by having your files output straight to film. Of course, you pay for quality. The cost of printing a page to film is significantly greater than printing direcly to paper.

Software: An Overview

None of the sophisticated things computers and printers can do could be done without the software. The software, written by computer programmers, is what tells the computer what to do. For example, a software program called Excel enables users to create spreadsheets; PageMaker and QuarkXPress facilitate the creation of page layouts; and FileMaker makes creating a database simple. Although it's expensive to replace and update hardware, updating software is relatively easy and inexpensive.

Operating Systems

Every computer requires some basic software just to tell the computer that it's a computer. The operating-system software performs this task, giving the computer its fundamental instructions, such as how to access other programs, how to save files, and how to communicate with other devices, such as printers or monitors.

There are basically two kinds of computer operating systems. One is the Disk Operating System (DOS), the fundamental operating system for IBM-compatible computers. The other is the Macintosh Operating System (Mac OS) for Macintosh computers. These systems are upgraded often to provide better performance. The upgrades contain the features of the previous system as well as new ones.

As you learn about your computer, find out about the operating system, what kind it is, how much memory it uses, and what functions it performs. Information about the system software is stored on your computer's hard drive in a special systems folder. Whatever you do, don't remove or manipulate files in that folder unless you're a skilled computer technician. It contains much of the operating-system software needed to run your machine.

Fonts

Generally, dependable and consistent operation of the operating-system software goes on without a second thought. One exception is in the use of font files, which define how each individual letter of a particular typeface looks on the screen and on the printed page. Each font must be properly installed into the system before it can be used in a document.

Computers Are Important, But . . .

What skills do top editors think aspiring journalists need the most?

Professor Ann Auman of the University of Hawaii surveyed newspaper editors about which skills they consider important in the people they hire. These excerpts from her report tell something interesting about modern-day journalism:

Newspaper editors often complain that journalism students can't spell or write decent headlines, can't locate Puerto Rico on a map, and don't bother to check even the phone book to make sure a store's name is spelled right. But at the same time, editors say they need people who are computer whizzes. What should an aspiring journalist focus on? . . .

I asked top-level editors from around the country to tell me what skills entry-level copy editors should have . . . and about the weaknesses they see. About 160 . . . returned the survey. . . .

Editors ranked grammar, spelling, and punctuation first, followed by accuracy and fact checking. In third place was editing for wordiness, clarity, and sentence structure. General knowledge was fourth, [followed by] story structure, organization, and content. . . .

Editors [also] chose traditional editing skills as the top areas in which entry-level copy editors were found to be the most deficient: grammar, spelling, and punctuation; editing for wording, sentence structure, and clarity; headline writing; and accuracy and fact-checking. . . .

The top-level editors often mentioned general knowledge as an important skill. "Copy editors must have good backgrounds in general knowledge (history, science, the arts, prose, and poetry . . . the list is nearly endless) as well as the use of

Regardless of how much computers dominate publishing, there will always be a need for basic editing know-how such as accurate language skills and careful fact-checking.

language," one editor said. "Copy editors must be able to extract the gem from the story, leaving the rubble behind."

Technical skills, such as the mechanics of computer editing, pagination, and software for graphics, did not even fall among the top ten. . . . Many wrote that computer literacy was assumed and pagination a must. . . .

Anne Glover, assistant managing editor/copy desk (in 1994) for the *St. Petersburg (Florida) Times,* wrote that traditional editing skills are most important even though we must acknowledge the importance of technology. . . . She warned that we shouldn't put technological prowess ahead of journalism, even though "it's easy to think that the people who know how to work the machines and move the papers will be the people who can get the jobs." Glover stressed the importance of analytical thinking too—she needs journalists who can "think about every single piece of information."

So where does this leave students? . . . One editor said it all: "What we need are well-rounded, broad-minded individuals who can argue about story play, present an attractive layout to sell their argument, and then write sparkling heads over tight stories. Is that asking too much? Oh yeah—and on deadline!"

FOLLOW-UP

1. How did you respond to the quotes in this article? Did any surprise you? Share your thoughts with the class.
2. Using information from the article, make an inventory of your own journalistic strengths and weaknesses. Use your list as the basis for setting personal improvement goals.

PostScript fonts. Early in the development of desktop publishing, PostScript fonts were the standard. PostScript, a high-resolution page-description language, gave designers the opportunity to print type that looked as though it had been professionally set—from type almost unreadably small to single letters that filled an entire page. Quickly, type foundries began converting their conventional typefaces to the PostScript format and selling them as part of a desktop-publishing system.

Because PostScript fonts require two file parts—one for screen display and the other for printer output—they're complicated to install and manage. The creation of TrueType fonts simplified things by having only one file part for both screen display and printer output. Nevertheless, thanks to their higher quality, PostScript fonts are still the accepted standard for desktop publishing.

Font development. Today, even the most basic computer comes with 8–10 fonts built into it, and others can be purchased and installed. Companies such as Adobe have set the industry standard in font development, but dozens of others have developed thousands upon thousands of fonts. Having the capacity to use various fonts in a document and to change easily from one font to another is one more technological advantage that could hardly be imagined in predesktop-publishing days.

Word-Processing Programs

Regardless of which fonts are installed in a computer or what operating system it uses, for most people a word-processing program is the most basic type of software. Word-processing programs such as WordPerfect and Microsoft Word are designed to make it easy to type in stories, headlines, and captions—and all have the capacity to perform many other functions as well.

In the predesktop-publishing days reporters or editors had to sit down at a typewriter and approximate the length of a story. Because they could only work on their manuscript in typewriter type, they had little idea what their finished, typeset copy would look like. Errors on manuscript had to be corrected with correction tape or fluid; spellings had to be checked in a dictionary; style inconsistencies had to be found by reading back through completed pages.

Word-processing programs have virtually eliminated the labor associated with these steps in the editorial process. While writing or editing text, you can set the margins and spacing and can format the text exactly as you want it to appear in publication. Additional features allow you to check the spelling in documents and use the search-and-replace function to ensure consistency of style. You can even preset styles so that by pressing a key you can automatically change from, say, a specified headline-size text and typeface to body text. In short, word-processing programs allow you to concentrate on writing and editing without the distraction of laborious corrections or determining whether the story will fit on the page.

Pagination programs, such as QuarkXPress, make professional page layout easy.

Pagination Programs

A word-processing program makes it easy to work with text, but it doesn't help much in laying out pages. Companies such as Adobe and Quark have page-layout (pagination) programs such as PageMaker, QuarkXPress, and InDesign to fill that niche.

Pagination software allows functions previously done by layout people, production people, and designers to be done in one program. With pagination software, you can not only lay out pages but can easily introduce boxes, screens, rules, graphics, and all sorts of type variations into them. You can set type from 4 to 500 points in size. You can fill boxes or other shapes with screens from 0–100 percent in 1-percent increments. You can also define almost any color as a spot color or process-color mixture and apply it to any element on the page.

Besides flexibility, the biggest advantage pagination programs bring to contemporary designers is having complete control of the design process without having to worry about consistency of details. For example, instead of remembering that body copy is 10/11 pt. Palatino, justified, with a paragraph tab set at one pica, all you have to do is define the style "body copy," select the text, and apply the style.

Illustration Programs

Illustration packages such as Adobe Illustrator or Macromedia FreeHand allow you to concentrate strictly on drawing. Artists use such software to draw everything from the infographics to realistic drawings for the cover of a magazine. In the same way as you would with conventional materials, you can change the thickness of lines, shade various areas, and apply color to any portion of the graphic. Unlike using conventional materials, however, if you don't like what you have done, you can simply—and easily—reverse to an earlier version or change it until you do like it. You can even save different versions in case you decide that your first, or tenth, effort was the best one.

Image-Editing Programs

Although some staffs may work with other types of software as well, the last major category of software used in most desktop-publishing set-ups is image-editing software, led in the market by Adobe Photoshop. Anything you can do in the darkroom, you can do with Photoshop—and infinitely more.

National Geographic used image-editing programs to move the Great Pyramids closer together to fit better on the cover. *Texas Monthly* used image-editing programs to put the head of the governor on another person's body.

Image editing involves more mundane things as well. Every day, newspapers and magazines use such software to remove dust spots, eliminate annoying objects in the background, or just bring out the color a little. In any case, the edited image can be saved in Tagged Image File Format (TIFF) or Encapsulated PostScript (EPS) format and placed on the page in the pagination software.

Image-editing software packages require a lot of memory, both RAM and disk space. One four-color snapshot can occupy several megabytes of disk space. Learning how to save and store files so that they take up as little space as possible without sacrificing image quality is vital. A TIFF file, for example, takes up less space than an EPS file.

In addition to knowing how to manage this software, professional image editors also learn all they can about color correction: how the four basic inks—cyan, magenta, yellow, and black—mix together on the press to produce all the colors we see in a typical photo. Note that color photos—and other color graphics—prepared for printing must therefore be set up as CMYK files rather than the default red-green-blue (RGB) color file type. Image editors also learn how to gauge the resolution of an image and how to handle the dozens of effects that the image-editing software allows them to perform.

ON DISPLAY

Photo Illustration

The Budget, Lawrence High School, Lawrence, Kansas

Photo Illustration by Tyler McPheeters

Photo illustrations such as this expand the possibilities for artwork in publications. This photo illustration accompanied a review of the best burritos in the area.

Computer artists can use this technology to create elaborate illustrations, including photo illustrations, which are obviously nonrealistic. The photo illustration in the **ON DISPLAY** feature above is clearly an altered version of reality. Photo illustrations expand the possibilities for artwork in publications, but manipulation of photos must be handled ethically. All photo illustrations should be labeled as such.

The ethics of image manipluation. Anyone involved in image editing must also learn about the ethics of the field—when it's inappropriate to edit an image and when the public should be notified that an image has been edited. As technology makes more and more subtle changes possible, it becomes easier and easier to deceive the public. The National Press Photographers Association, in considering this problem, has made the statement that "accurate representation is the benchmark of our profession." This guideline should be taken to heart by student journalists as well.

The Journalism Education Association position statement on photo manipulation is reprinted on page 550 in the Appendix. It's a good idea to familiarize yourself with it.

Web-Publishing Programs

The widespread growth and influence of the Internet has spurred a new type of software—programs to help make your paper available on the World Wide Web, the graphical interface of the Internet. Programs such as Dreamweaver, for example, eliminate the need to write raw code in HyperText Markup Language (HTML). Without software such as Dreamweaver or the capability of PageMaker and QuarkXPress to write HTML code automatically, creating a web page would require a user to embed HTML codes such as <b> for bold and <h1> for a large headline. Even paragraphing becomes cumbersome with manual HTML coding because every paragraph has to end in <p>.

Although basic text coding is handled by these programs, creating animated characters, moving buttons, and other action on a web page still requires special Java scripts—computer program coding recently developed specifically for Web use—which can be very tedious to write.

Once pages are ready for the Web, they can be uploaded onto the Internet in a few simple steps with a program such as Fetch (which also allows files to be downloaded so they can be changed or updated).

PDF documents. Another way to publish on the Web is to save a document in Portable Document Format (PDF) and then upload it. Although it requires special software to distill the PostScript code from a publication created in pagination software such as PageMaker or QuarkXPress, PDF files are surprisingly small, move across the Web with ease, and retain the original page design, including original fonts. The software to read PDF files on line, Adobe's Acrobat Reader, is commonly available free; any user can download the software quickly and easily from the Internet. PDF publications are largely uneditable and are popular for forms and manuals that the user has no need to edit.

Digital Imaging

Bringing photos and other images quickly and easily into publications is another advantage of desktop publishing. Once upon a time, an image was a separate piece of a page that had to be handled separately. These days, you can integrate photography and artwork into a page layout with ease.

With a scanner, a photo can be digitized and imported directly into a computer document. Until recently, photos were generally not incorporated until the final production stage.

Scanners

Before editing an image electronically, it first has to be digitized—converted into an electronic format. A commercial photo developer can put a photographic image onto a Photo CD. The most popular means, however, is by scanning the image on a flatbed scanner, a piece of hardware that looks—and acts—something like a small photocopier. Using scanning software, you can download into your computer drawings and paintings as well as black-and-white and color prints. What's more, you can bring them in at resolutions more than adequate for newspaper use.

Negative scanners are also popular. Photographers take the pictures and develop the film. Once developed, the film is scanned with no need for a print. Any manipulation—such as dodging, burning, cropping, and sizing—can be done on the computer.

Scanning resolution. To figure out at what resolution you need to scan an image in pixels per inch (ppi), find out from your printer what line screen in lines per inch (lpi) the image will be printed at and then double it. For example, if your printer prints the photos at 150 lpi, which is typical for yearbook reproduction, you need to scan your images at 300 ppi if they're going to be used at actual size. You can usually get by with a little less than that, but twice the lpi offers you a little flexibility. Note that the scanning resolution is for the image at actual size. If you plan to enlarge the image, you need to scan it at a higher resolution. If you plan to reduce the image, you can scan it at a lower resolution. In any case, work closely with your printer to find the optimum scanning resolution.

Digital Cameras

Another way to digitize images is to shoot them with a digital camera (discussed in Chapter 19). Low-resolution digital cameras are inexpensive (less than $500) and adequate for newsletter and small newspaper photos. More expensive, professional digital cameras can be purchased for about $5,000 (for the camera body alone). Only these more sophisticated versions have enough resolution to accommodate output for a magazine or yearbook with photos printed at greater than 85 lpi. As technology advances, the price of such cameras should come down rapidly.

Wire-service agencies such as Associated Press (AP), as well as many newspapers and newsmagazines, use digital cameras to cut down on the time from shooting a photo to getting it in print. Photojournalists can transmit their digital images from anywhere in the world in a matter of moments without having to process film, worry about film damage caused by airport X-ray machines, or risk confiscation of film in hostile countries.

As schools and smaller newspapers and magazines discover the cost savings of digital equipment, more and more will be moving into a completely digital environment.

On-Line Services

The Internet, together with the various services that access it, completely changed communication in the 1990s. Its development is an interesting story.

The Development of the Internet

As a result of a need to communicate during wartime, the telegraph, radio, television, and satellite communications all in their turn became popular. In the late 1960s, however, as government scientists began looking for a way to communicate following a nuclear holocaust, they found that no existing system would work. Electromagnetic pulses from the nuclear fallout would disrupt radio signals, eliminating any possibility of communication via the airwaves. Ground blasts and fires would disrupt land lines, inevitably leaving parts of the country separated from defense headquarters. Over a period of time, therefore, scientists at research institutions all around the world began developing thousands of independent computer networks through which messages could flow freely. If one path was blocked, the message would simply take a different route. Thus was born the Internet (named in 1982), a network of independent computers that can communicate with any other computer in the world that is also on the Internet (or Net).

Initially this network was clumsy and required special coding and expertise to search out information. Even systems such as Gopher and Lynx, which facilitate searching the Internet, didn't make it easy to glean information from the rapidly growing group of interconnected computers. The only people who really got any use of the system were research scientists.

Introduction of commericial user interfaces. To pique the average person's interest in the Internet took the development of commercial Internet service providers (ISPs) such as CompuServe and America Online, whose easier-to-understand user interfaces bypassed any complex coding. People were willing to spend 10 dollars a month for access to hundreds of businesses that had created forums on CompuServe. America Online successfully formed the graphical user interface to on-line communications that's so popular today.

Arrival of Web browsers. While none of the commercial services were watching, along came the development of the graphical World Wide Web (WWW) interface. This system allowed users to access a graphical portion of the Internet and the millions of systems that were the backbone of the network. "Browser" programs such as Mosaic, Microsoft Internet Explorer, and Netscape made navigating, or "surfing," the Net not only popular but downright easy. Increasing numbers of ISPs and the consequent competitive services and pricing gave easy and fairly inexpensive access to anyone with a computer and a modem.

As the 20th century ended, use of the Internet grew at an amazing rate. By 1999 almost 200 million people around the world took advantage of what it could offer, 80 million of them in the United States. More than half of all American classrooms had Internet connections—and the numbers were expected to keep growing.

Journalism and the Web

As soon as the World Wide Web became a reality, journalists immediately started to take advantage of it. They began transmitting their stories to and from the field, making newsrooms almost obsolete, except for copy editors, and allowing writers to spend more time—if not all of their time—in the field. The Web also made transmission of the news to a worldwide audience an instantaneous event. A writer, sitting at his or her computer in France, could transmit a story to millions of users all over the world in seconds. The number of news readers on the Web grew accordingly. In 1995 about 10 million Americans were getting their news from the Internet once a week or more. By the end of 1998 that number had grown to 36 million.

Student journalists are also accessing the Internet in record numbers. They're finding databases filled with useful information. They're establishing contacts with mentors in professional newsrooms. They're sharing their stories through statewide news bureaus and other sites that collect student writing. More and more, they're putting on-line versions of their school papers on the Web.

Many journalists maintain that print media will exist in its traditional form for years to come.

What will happen in the future? Although no one involved in the journalism industry makes light of electronic technology, many still maintain that newspapers and yearbooks in their traditional form will continue to exist for some time. "I believe that people will still want to handle and read a product that looks like a newspaper rather than computer screens of information," Don DeMaio, an Associated Press graphic designer, said.

Marty Petty, executive editor of the *Hartford Courant,* echoed DeMaio's sentiments. "We will still deliver a hard copy of the newspaper to our readers' homes and businesses in 25 years . . . ," she said. Editor after editor and designer after designer, with few exceptions, still believe that the print media will continue to exist but each will be supplemented in electronic form.

Nevertheless, technology is here to stay, and it's waiting for you to benefit from it. So surf the Web, pop a CD in your computer, do a database search at the local library. Look at what's out there. It's amazing, and it's only the beginning.

 # Wrap-up

Computers and Internet technology revolutionized—and will continue to revolutionize—the publishing industry. They have made almost instantaneous reporting of the news a reality.

The computer has certain basic parts, such as the central processing unit (CPU), accessory disk drives for CDs and floppy disks, a keyboard, a mouse, and a monitor. The brand of computer is as important as the type of operating system and the amount of random access memory (RAM), for not all computers are compatible with each other. Computers have greatly facilitated information storage and retrieval, among other things.

Various types of printers are available, including dot-matrix, ink-jet, and laser printers. Most desktop publications with school-size or larger circulations are printed on laser printers.

Although learning about the hardware is important, you need to know less about it than about the software, which is what allows you to create documents. Software allows you to change fonts easily. Word-processing software gives you the capability to write, edit, and fit copy right on the screen. Pagination software, illustration software, and image-editing software allow you to design and lay out pages, create illustrations, and adjust photos. Web-publishing programs let you post your newspaper onto the World Wide Web.

Photographs and artwork can now easily be brought into pages electronically. Scanners allow you to download a digitized image into a computer program. Digital cameras transmit their images onto a disk to be printed directly from a computer.

Since its beginnings as a system used mainly by scientists, the Internet has grown into a huge communication system. In the last few years, millions of computers have been connected to it through the World Wide Web. Journalists, both professional and scholastic, are using the Web both to gather and to disseminate information.

On Assignment

INDIVIDUAL ACTIVITIES

1. Write a definition or each of these terms:

CPU	pagination software
desktop publishing	photo illustration
image editing	RAM
laser printer	scanner
network	word processing

2. Pick one of the computers you have access to and write up your findings on the following:
a. how much RAM it has (for example, 64 megabytes)
b. what type of central-processing chip it uses (for example, G4 or Pentium 3)
c. the size of its hard drive (for example, 5 gigabytes or 5,000 megabytes)
d. type and version of system software (for example, Mac OS 8.5)
e. number of colors or gray levels the monitor can display (for example, millions)

3. Make a list of all of the software applications on one of your computers—for example, Word, QuarkXPress, Photoshop. Then write a short summary of what you like and dislike about the program with which you're most familiar.

4. If you have access to Internet e-mail, get an e-mail address of someone on a publications staff at another school by looking on the other school's home page or even in the masthead of its publication. Send e-mail to that person and begin exchanging information about your publications.

5. Assume that you're in charge of purchasing a new computer system for the journalism department. You intend to use this computer for digital image manipulation. Working with the staff of your computer science department, local newspapers and other publications, and a local computer store, write out the specifications for such a system, including details of the types of software, CPU, monitor, input devices, and output devices you would like to have. As you decide on your system, work within a budget set by your instructor.

6. Poll some of your staff photographers, as well as the staff photographers of community publications. How do they feel about digital image manipulation, including photo illustrations? Do they think it will enhance or detract from their photographs? To what extent are professional staff photographers using digital cameras?

TEAM ACTIVITY

7. With a team find at least five computer users in the community who use computers for different purposes—for example, to play games, or to run a business. Each team member should interview one or more of these people. Do the individuals anticipate that what they do on the computer will change? Is there new equipment or software that they want or need to buy? What will they want or need from a computer in five years? Take notes on the responses.

   After the interviews, meet to discuss the results. Then prepare a class presentation: "The Computer: Now and in the Future." After the presentations, discuss the similarities and differences in people's findings.

SURF THE NET

8. Check out various on-line student papers you have seen throughout the school year. Decide on a few that seem to have the most sophisticated use of technology. Report to the class on what you have found.

career profile

Electronic Journalist

Robert S. Cauthorn

Before developing the on-line service *StarNet,* Bob Cauthorn made his living as a painter and sculptor. A self-described "free-learner," he also enjoys writing.

Cauthorn enrolled at the University of Arizona in journalism in the late 1970s, with an eye toward writing criticism. He was hired by the *Arizona Daily Star* in 1981.

Although hired to write, Cauthorn quickly got sidetracked. On the verge of the rise of the personal computer, Cauthorn jumped in with both feet. He began using the computer to develop database analyses, which helped to support stories.

There was no turning back. He became the *Star*'s computer guru and technology advocate. When the Internet began to take hold commercially, Cauthorn proposed that the *Star* develop its own Internet service. He had two goals: to extend the *Star's* ability to publish, and to migrate newspapers back to being community-oriented companies.

"I wanted to use a high-tech means to get back to small-town news values," Cauthorn said.

Today the small-town camaraderie created by the daily paper is virtually lost, yet Cauthorn said that most dinner conversations are about what people have read in the news.

"If we're responsible for sparking all the dinner conversation, why don't we try hosting one," he thought.

The Internet was a natural place to do this, and *StarNet* was launched May 5, 1995. As a result, the *Arizona Daily Star* became the second daily newspaper to go on line.

As a full Internet service provider, *StarNet* also runs community forums, newsgroups, and e-mail services. Additionally, subscribers have access to Associated Press wire stories from all 50 states, which are searchable in such areas as national and international news, politics, features, and sports.

Although not the first daily on line, *StarNet* does have a claim to fame—it was the first profitable one. It turned a profit after less than eight months.

For students interested in electronic journalism, Cauthorn says to start now. Many high school newspapers will go on line, he said. Students should participate in newspaper projects on line and learn as much as they can. Multimedia skills are very valuable.

"Computer literacy must extend beyond playing video games," he said.

Students must also be good writers and hold high ethical standards. There are lots of enticements to do bad things with computers now, Cauthorn said, especially when getting caught seems so unlikely. Students must rely on their individual strengths and strong moral character when making decisions, he advised.

What's most important, he noted, is to keep asking Why? Too many people think that just by following a curriculum they will get the tools they need to succeed, he said.

"What distinguishes the people who really succeed is their unending curiosity," he said.

FOLLOW-UP

1. Put yourself in Cauthorn's position as an early computer guru. What specific things might he have needed to do to introduce his staff to the computer world? Discuss your ideas in class.

2. One of many ethical problems associated with the Internet is hacking, or breaking into other people's computer systems illegally. Research information on some well-known hackers and report to the class.

Stylebook
The Associated Press

Newswriting

A

abbreviations and acronyms A few universally recognized abbreviations are required in some circumstances. Some others are acceptable depending on the context. But in general, avoid alphabet soup. Do not use abbreviations or acronyms that the reader would not quickly recognize.

Some general principles:

BEFORE A NAME: Abbreviate the following titles when used before a full name outside direct quotations: *Dr., Gov., Lt. Gov., Mr., Mrs., Rep., the Rev., Sen.* and certain military designations. Spell out all except *Dr., Mr., Mrs.* and *Ms.* when they are used before a name in direct quotations.

AFTER A NAME: Abbreviate *junior* or *senior* after an individual's name. Abbreviate *company, corporation, incorporated,* and *limited* when used after the name of a corporate entity.

WITH DATES OR NUMERALS: Use the abbreviations *A.D., B.C., a.m., p.m., No.,* and abbreviate certain months when used with the day of the month.

Right: *In 450 B.C.; at 9:30 a.m.; in room No. 6; on Sept. 16.*

Wrong: *Early this a.m. he asked for the No. of your room.* The abbreviations are correct only with figures.

Right: *Early this morning he asked for the number of your room.*

IN NUMBERED ADDRESSES: Abbreviate *avenue, boulevard* and *street* in numbered addresses: *He lives on Pennsylvania Avenue. He lives at 1600 Pennsylvania Ave.*

STATES: The names of certain states and the *United States* are abbreviated with periods in some circumstances.

ACCEPTABLE BUT NOT REQUIRED: Some organizations and government agencies are widely recognized by their initials: *CIA, FBI, GOP.*

If the entry for such an organization notes that an abbreviation is acceptable in all references or on second reference, that does not mean that its use should be automatic. Let the context determine, for example whether to use *Federal Bureau of Investigation* or *FBI*.

AVOID AWKWARD CONSTRUCTIONS: Do not follow an organization's full name with an abbreviation or acronym in parentheses or set off by dashes. If an abbreviation or acronym would not be clear on second reference without this arrangement, do not use it.

Names not commonly before the public should not be reduced to acronyms solely to save a few words.

academic degrees If mention of degrees is necessary to establish someone's credentials, the preferred form is to avoid an abbreviation and use instead a phrase such as: *John Jones, who has a doctorate in psychology.*

Use an apostrophe in *bachelor's degree, a master's, etc.*

Use such abbreviations as *B.A., M.A., LL.D.* and *Ph.D.* only when the need to identify many individuals by degree on first reference would make the preferred form cumbersome. Use these abbreviations only after a full name—never after just a last name.

Do not precede a name with a courtesy title for an academic degree and follow it with the abbreviation for the degree in the same reference:

Wrong: *Dr. Pam Jones, Ph.D.*

Right: *Dr. Pam Jones, a chemist.*

When in doubt about the proper abbreviation, follow the first listing in Webster's New World Dictionary.

academic departments Use lowercase except for words that are proper nouns or adjectives: *the department of history, the history department, the department of English, the English department.*

academic titles Capitalize and spell out formal titles such as *professor, chancellor, chairman,* etc., when they precede a name.

Lowercase elsewhere.

Lowercase modifiers such as *history* in *history Professor Oscar Handlin* or *department* in *department Chairman Jerome Wiesner.*

addresses Use the abbreviations *Ave., Blvd.,* and *St.* only with a numbered address: *1600 Pennsylvania Ave.* Spell them out and capitalize when part of a formal street name without a number: *Pennsylvania Avenue.* Lowercase and spell out when used alone or with more than one street name: *Massachusetts and Pennsylvania avenues.*

All similar words (*alley, drive, road, terrace,* etc.) always are spelled out. Capitalize them when part of a formal name without a number; lowercase when used alone or with two or more names.

Always use figures for an address number: *9 Morningside Circle.*

Spell out and capitalize *First* through *Ninth* when used as street names; use figures with two letters for *10th* and above: *7 Fifth Ave., 100 21st St.*

Abbreviate compass points used to indicate directional ends of a street or quadrants of a city in a numbered address: *222 E. 42nd St., 562 W. 43rd St., 600 K St. N.W.* Do not abbreviate if the number is omitted: *East 42nd Street, West 43rd Street, K Street Northwest.*

adviser Not *advisor.*

ages Always use figures. When the context does not require *year* or *years old,* the figure is presumed to be *years.*

Ages expressed as adjectives before a noun or as substitutes for a noun use hyphens.

Examples: *A 5-year-old boy,* but *the boy is 5 years old. The boy, 7, has a sister, 10. The woman, 26, has a daughter 2 months old. The law is 8 years old. The race is for 3-year-olds. The woman is in her 30s* (no apostrophe).

allege The word must be used with great care.

Some guidelines:

—Avoid any suggestion that the writer is making an allegation.

—Specify the source of an allegation. In a criminal case, it should be an arrest record, an indictment or the statement of a public official connected with the case.

—Use *alleged bribe* or similar phrase when necessary to make it clear that an unproved action is not being treated as fact. Be sure that the source of the charge is specified elsewhere in the story.

—Avoid redundant uses of *alleged.* It is proper to say: *The district attorney alleged that she took a bribe.* Or: *The district attorney accused her of taking a bribe.* But not: *The district attorney accused her of allegedly taking a bribe.*

—Do not use *alleged* to describe an event that is known to have occurred, when the dispute is over who participated in it. Do not say: *He attended the alleged meeting* when what you mean is: *He allegedly attended the meeting.*

—Do not use *alleged* as a routine qualifier. Instead, use a word such as *apparent, ostensible,* or *reputed.*

ante- The rules in prefixes apply, but in general, no hyphen. Some examples:

antebellum	antedate

anti- Hyphenate all except the following words, which have specific meanings of their own:

antibiotic	antibody	anticlimax
antidote	antifreeze	antigen
antihistamine	antiknock	antimatter
antimony	antiparticle*	antipasto
antiperspirant	antiphon	antiphony
antiseptic	antiserum	antithesis
antitoxin	antitrust	antitussive

*And similar terms in physics such as *antiproton.*

This approach has been adopted in the interests of readability and easily remembered consistency.

Hyphenated words, many of them exceptions to Webster's New World, include:

anti-aircraft	anti-bias	anti-inflation
anti-intellectual	anti-labor	anti-Semitic
anti-social	anti-war	

Arabic numerals The numerical figures *1, 2, 3, 4, 5, 6, 7, 8, 9, 10.*

In general, use Arabic forms unless denoting the sequence of wars or establishing a personal sequence for people or animals.

army Capitalize when referring to *U.S. forces: the U.S. Army, the Army, Army regulations.* Do not use the abbreviation USA.

Use lowercase for the forces of other nations: *the French army.*

This approach has been adopted for consistency, because many foreign nations do not use *army* as the proper name.

arrest To avoid any suggestion that someone is being judged before a trial, do not use a phrase such *as arrested for killing.* Instead, use *arrested on a charge of killing.*

average, mean, median, norm *Average* refers to the result obtained by dividing a sum by the number of quantities added together: *The average of 7, 9, 17 is 33 divided by 3, or 11.*

Mean commonly designates a figure intermediate between two extremes: *The mean temperature of the day with a high of 56 and a low of 34 is 45.*

Median is the middle number of points in a series arranged in order of size: *The median grade in the group of 50, 55, 85, 88, 92 is 85. The average is 74.*

Norm implies a standard of average performance for a given group: *The child was below the norm for his age in reading comprehension.*

B

bi- The rules in **prefixes** apply, but in general, no hyphen. Some examples:

bifocal	bilateral	bilingual
bimonthly	bipartisan	

biannual, biennial *Biannual* means twice a year and is a synonym for the word semiannual.

Biennial means every two years.

Bible Capitalize, without quotation marks, when referring to the Scriptures in the Old Testament or the New Testament. Capitalize also related terms such as the *Gospels, Gospel of St. Mark, the Scriptures, the Holy Scriptures.*

Lowercase *biblical* in all uses.

Lowercase *bible* as a non-religious term: *My dictionary is my bible.*

Do not abbreviate individual books of the Bible.

The books of the Old Testament, in order, are: Genesis, Exodus, Leviticus, Numbers, Deuteronomy, Joshua, Judges, Ruth, 1 Samuel, 2 Samuel, 1 Kings, 2 Kings, 1 Chronicles, 2 Chronicles, Ezra, Nehemiah, Esther, Job, Psalms, Proverbs, Ecclesiastes, Song of Solomon, Isaiah, Jeremiah, Lamentations, Ezekiel, Daniel, Hosea, Joel, Amos, Obadiah, Jonah, Micah, Nahum, Habakkuk, Zephaniah, Haggai, Zechariah, Malachi.

The books of the New Testament, in order: Matthew, Mark, Luke, John, Acts, Romans, 1 Corinthians, 2 Corinthians, Galatians, Ephesians, Philippians, Colossians, 1 Thessalonians, 2 Thessalonians, 1 Timothy, 2 Timothy, Titus, Philemon, Hebrews, Epistles of James, 1 Peter, 2 Peter, 1 John, 2 John, 3 John, Jude, Revelation.

Citation listing the number of chapter and verse(s) use this form: *Matthew 3:16, Luke 21:1–13, 1 Peter 2:1.*

bimonthly Means every other month. *Semimonthly* means twice a month.

biweekly Means every other week. *Semiweekly* means twice a week.

C

call letters Use all caps. Use hyphens to separate the type of station from the basic call letters: *WBZ-AM, WBZ-FM, WBZ-TV.*

Until the summer of 1976, the format citizens band operators used was three letters and four figures: *KTE9136.* Licenses issued since then use four letters and four figures: *KTEM1234.*

Shortwave stations, which operate with greater power than citizens band stations and different frequencies, typically mix letters and figures: *K2LRX.*

Canada Montreal, Ottawa, Quebec and Toronto stand alone in datelines. For all other datelines, use the city name and the name of the province or territory spelled out.

The 10 provinces of Canada are Alberta, British Columbia, Manitoba, New Brunswick, Newfoundland (includes Labrador), Nova Scotia, Ontario, Prince Edward Island, Quebec and Saskatchewan.

The two territories are the Yukon and the Northwest Territories.

The provinces have substantial autonomy from the federal government.

The territories are administered by the federal government, although residents of the territories do elect their own legislators and representatives to Parliament.

capital The city where a seat of government is located. Do not capitalize.

When used in a financial sense, *capital* describes money, equipment or property used in a business by a person or corporation.

capitalization In general, avoid unnecessary capitals. Use a capital letter only if you can justify it by one of the principles listed here.

Some basic principles:

PROPER NOUNS: Capitalize nouns that constitute the unique identification for a specific person, place, or thing: *John, Mary, America, Boston, England.*

PROPER NAMES: Capitalize common nouns such as *party, river, street* and *west* when they are an integral part of the full name for a person, place or thing: *Democratic Party, Mississippi River, Fleet Street, West Virginia.*

Lowercase these common nouns when they stand alone in subsequent references: *the party, the river, the street.*

Lowercase the common noun elements of names in all plural uses: *the Democratic and Republican parties, Main and State streets, lakes Erie and Ontario.*

POPULAR NAMES: Some places and events lack officially designated proper names but have popular names that are the effective equivalent: *the Combat Zone* (a section of downtown Boston), *the Main Line* (a group of Philadelphia suburbs), *the South Side* (of Chicago), *the Badlands* (of North Dakota), *the Street* (the financial community in the Wall Street area of New York).

The principle applies also to shortened versions of the proper names of one-of-a-kind events: *the Series* (for the World Series), *the Derby* (for the Kentucky Derby). This practice should not, however, be interpreted as a license to ignore the general practice of lowercasing the common noun elements of a name when they stand alone.

DERIVATIVES: Capitalize words that are derived from a proper noun and still depend on it for their meaning: *American, Christian, Christianity, English, French, Marxism, Shakespearean.*

Lowercase words that are derived from a proper noun but no longer depend on it for their meaning: *french fries, herculean, manhattan cocktail, malapropism, pasteurize, quixotic, venetian blind.*

SENTENCES: Capitalize the first word in a statement that stands as a sentence.

In poetry, capital letters are used for the first words of some phrases that would not be capitalized in prose.

COMPOSITIONS: Capitalize the principal words in the names of books, movies, plays, poems, operas, songs, radio and television programs, works of art, etc. See **titles; magazine names;** and **newspaper names.**

TITLES: Capitalize formal titles when used immediately before a name. Lowercase formal titles when used alone or in constructions that set them off from a name by commas.

Use lowercase at all times for terms that are job descriptions rather than formal titles.

ABBREVIATIONS: Capital letters apply in some cases. See the **abbreviations and acronyms** entry.

capitol Capitalize *U.S. Capitol* and *the Capitol* when referring to the building in Washington: *The meeting was held on Capitol Hill in the west wing of the Capitol.*

Follow the same practice when referring to state capitols: *The Virginia Capitol is in Richmond. Thomas Jefferson designed the Capitol of Virginia.*

CD-ROM Acronym for a *compact disc* acting as a *read-only memory* device.

CD-ROM disc is redundant.

Celsius Use this term rather than *centigrade* for the temperature scale that is part of the metric system.

The Celsius scale is named for Anders Celsius, the Swedish astronomer who designed it. In it, zero represents the freezing point of water, and 100 degrees is the boiling point at sea level.

To convert to Fahrenheit, multiply a Celsius temperature by 9, divide by 5 and add 32 (25 x 9 equals 225, divided by 5 equals 45, plus 32 equals 77 degrees Fahrenheit).

When giving a Celsius temperature, use these forms: *40 degrees Celsius* or *40 C* (note the space and no period after the capital C) if degrees and Celsius are clear from the context.

cents Spell out the word *cents* and lowercase, using numerals for amounts less than a dollar: *5 cents, 12 cents.* Use the *$* sign and decimal system for larger amounts: *$1.01, $2.50.*

Numerals alone, with or without a decimal point as appropriate, may be used in tabular matter.

chairman, chairwoman Capitalize as a formal title before a name: *company Chairman Henry Ford, committee Chairwoman Margaret Chase Smith.*

Do not capitalize as a casual, temporary position: *meeting chairman Robert Jones.*

Do not use *chairperson* unless it is an organization's formal title for an office.

See **titles.**

chess In stories, the names and pieces are spelled out, lowercase: *king, queen, bishop, pawn, knight, rook, king-side, queenside, white, black.*

Use the algebraic notation in providing tabular summaries.

In algebraic notation, the "ranks" are the horizontal rows of squares. The ranks take numbers, 1 to 8, beginning on white's side of the board.

The "files" are the vertical rows of squares. They take letters, a through h, beginning on white's left.

Thus, each square vase is identified by its file letter and rank number.

In the starting position, white's queen knight stands on *b1,* the queen on *d1,* the king on *e1;* black's queen knight stands on *b8,* the queen on *d8,* the king on *e8,* and so on.

Other features of the system follow:

—DESIGNATION OF PIECES: The major pieces are shown by a capital letter: *K* for king, *Q* for queen, *R* for rook, *B* for bishop and *N* for knight. No symbol is used for the pawn.

—MOVES BY PIECES: Shown by the letter of the piece (except for the pawn) and the destination square. For instance, *Bb5* means the bishop moves to square b5.

—MOVES BY PAWNS: Pawn moves are designated only by the name of the destination square. Thus, *e4* means the pawn on the e file moves to e4.

—CASTLING: It is written as *0-0* for the kingside and *0-0-0* for the queenside. *Kingside* is the side of the board (right half from white's point of view, let half from black's), on which each player's king starts. The other half is *queenside.*

—CAPTURES BY PIECES: A capture is recorded by using an x after the letter for the capturing piece. For instance, if white's bishop captures the black pawn at the f6 square, it is written *Bxf6.*

—CAPTURES BY PAWNS: When a pawn captures a piece, the players name the file the pawn was on and the square where it made the capture. If white's pawn on a g file captured black's pawn on f6 square, the move would be *gxf6.* If black's pawn on an f file captured white's it would be *fxg5.*

—CHECK: Use plus sign.

—AMBIGUITY: If more than one piece of the same type can move to a square, the rank number or file letter of the origination square is added. Thus, if a rook on d1 were to move to d4, but another rook also could move

there, instead of Rd4 the move would be given as *R1d4.* If there are black knights on c6 and e6, and the one on e6 moves to d4, the move is given as *Ned4.*

The form, taken from a 1993 championship match:

	Short (White)	Karpov (Black)
1.	e4	c5
2.	Nf3	d6
3.	d4	cxd4
4.	Nxd4	Nf6
5.	Nc3	a6
6.	Bc4	e6
7.	Bb3	Nbd7

Chinese names Some Chinese have Westernized their names, putting their given names or the initials for them first: *P. Y. Chen, Jack Wang.* In general, follow an individual's preferred spelling.

Normally Chinese women do not take their husbands' surnames. Use the courtesy titles *Mrs., Miss,* or *Ms.* only when specifically requested. Never use *Madame* or *Mme.*

chip An integrated computer circuit.

Christmas, Christmas Day Dec. 25. The federal legal holiday is observed on Friday if Dec. 25 falls on a Saturday, on Monday if it falls on a Sunday.

Never abbreviate *Christmas* to *Xmas* or any other form.

church Capitalize as part of the formal name of a building, a congregation or a denomination; lowercase in other uses: *St. Mary's Church, the Roman Catholic Church, the Catholic and Episcopal churches, a Roman Catholic church, a church.*

Lowercase in phrases where the church is used in an institutional sense: *She believes in the separation of church and state. The pope said the church opposes abortion.*

city council Capitalize when part of a proper name: *the Boston City Council.*

Retain capitalization if the reference is to a specific council but the context does not require the city name:

boston (ap)—The City Council . . .

Lowercase in other uses: *the council, the Boston and New York city councils, a city council.*

Use the proper name if the body is not known as a

city council: *the Miami City Commission, the City Commission, the commission; the Louisville Board of Aldermen, the Board of Aldermen, the board.*

Use *city council* in a generic sense for plural references: *The Boston, Louisville and Miami city councils.*

co- Retain the hyphen when forming nouns, adjectives and verbs that indicate occupation or status:

co-author	co-chairman
co-defendant	co-host
co-owner	co-partner
co-pilot	co-respondent (in a divorce suit)
co-signer	co-star
co-worker	

(Several are exceptions to Webster's New World Dictionary in the interests of consistency.)

Use no hyphen in other combinations:

coed	coeducation	coequal
coexist	coexistence	cooperate
cooperative	coordinate	coordination

Cooperate, coordinate and related words are exceptions to the rule that a hyphen is used if a prefix ends in a vowel and the word that follows begins with the same vowel.

collective nouns Nouns that denote a unit take singular verbs and pronouns: *class, committee, crowd, family, group, herd, jury, orchestra, team.*

Some usage examples: *The committee is meeting to set its agenda. The jury reached its verdict. A herd of cattle was sold.*

colloquialisms The word describes the informal use of a language. It is not local or regional in nature, as dialect is.

Webster's New World Dictionary identifies many words as colloquial with the label *Colloq.* The label itself, the dictionary says, "does not indicate substandard or illiterate usage."

Many colloquial words and phrases characteristic of informal writing and conversation are acceptable in some contexts but out of place in others. Examples include *bum, giveaway* and *phone.*

Other colloquial words normally should be avoided because they are substandard. Webster's New World notes, for example, that *ain't* is colloquial and not automatically illiterate or substandard usage. But it also notes that *ain't* is "a dialectical or substandard contraction." Thus it should not be used in news stories unless needed to illustrate substandard speech in writing.

See **dialect**.

congress Capitalize *U.S. Congress* and *Congress* when referring to the U.S. Senate and House of Representatives. Although *Congress* sometimes is used as a substitute for the House, it properly is reserved for reference to both the Senate and House.

Capitalize *Congress* also if referring to a foreign body that uses the term, or its equivalent in a foreign language, as part of its formal name: *the Argentine Congress, the Congress.*

Lowercase when used as a synonym for convention or in second reference to an organization that uses the word as part of its formal name: *the Congress of Racial Equality, the congress.*

copyright (n., v. and adj.) *The disclosure was made in a copyright story.*

Use *copyrighted* only as the past tense of the verb: *He copyrighted the article.*

council, councilor, councilman, councilwoman A deliberative body and those who are members of it.

counsel, counseled, counseling, counselor, counselor at law To *counsel* is to advise. A *counselor* is one who advises.

A *counselor at law* (no hyphens for consistency with attorney at law) is a lawyer. See **lawyer**.

county Capitalize when an integral part of a proper name: *Dade County, Nassau County, Suffolk County.*

Capitalize the full names of county governmental units: *the Dade County Commission, the Orange County Department of Social Services, the Suffolk County Legislature.*

Retain capitalization for the name of a county body if the proper noun is not needed in the context; lowercase the word *county* if it is used to distinguish an agency from state or federal counterparts: *the Board of Supervisors, the county Board of Supervisors; the Department of Social Services, the county Department of Social Services. Lowercase the board, the department,* etc., whenever they stand alone.

Capitalize *county* if it is an integral part of a specific body's name even without the proper noun: *the County Commission, the County Legislature.* Lowercase *the commission, the legislature,* etc. when not preceded by the word *county.*

Capitalize as part of a formal title before a name: *County Manager John Smith.* Lowercase when it is not part of the formal title: *county Health Commissioner Frank Jones.*

Avoid *county of* phrases where possible, but when necessary, always lowercase: *the county of Westchester.*

Lowercase plural combinations: *Westchester and Rockland counties.*

Apply the same rules to similar terms such as *parish.* See **governmental bodies.**

courtesy titles In general, do not use the courtesy titles *Miss, Mr., Mrs.* or *Ms.* on first and last names of the person: *Betty Ford, Jimmy Carter.*

Do not use *Mr.* in any reference unless it is combined with *Mrs.*: *Mr. and Mrs. John Smith, Mr. and Mrs. Smith.*

On sports wires, do not use courtesy titles in any reference unless needed to distinguish among people of the same last name.

On news wires, use courtesy titles for women on second reference, following the woman's preference. Use *Ms.* if a preference cannot be determined. If the woman says she does not want a courtesy title, refer to her on second reference by last name only. Some guidelines:

MARRIED WOMEN: The preferred form on first reference is to identify a woman by her own first name and her husband's last name: *Susan Smith.* Use *Mrs.* on the first reference only if a woman requests that her husband's first name be used or her own first name cannot be determined: *Mrs. John Smith.*

On second reference, use *Mrs.* unless a woman initially identified by her own first name prefers *Ms.*: *Carla Hills, Mrs. Hills, Ms. Hills;* or no title: *Carla Hills, Hills.*

If a married woman is known by her maiden name, precede it by *Miss* on second reference unless she prefers *Ms.*: *Jane Fonda, Miss Fonda, Ms. Fonda;* or no title, *Jane Fonda, Fonda.*

UNMARRIED WOMEN: For women who have never been married, use *Miss, Ms.* or no title on second reference according to the woman's preference.

For divorced women and widows, the normal practice is to use *Mrs.* or no title, if she prefers, on second reference. But, if a woman returns to the use of her maiden name, use *Miss, Ms.* or no title if she prefers it.

MARITAL STATUS: If a woman prefers *Ms.* or no title, do not include her marital status in a story unless it is clearly pertinent.

court names Capitalize the full proper names of courts at all levels.

Retain capitalization if *U.S.* or a state name is dropped: *the U.S. Supreme Court, the Supreme Court, the state Superior Court, the Superior Court, Superior Court.*

For courts identified by a numeral: *2nd District Court, 8th U.S. Circuit Court of Appeals.*

See **judge** for guidelines on titles before the names of judges.

D

dangling modifiers Avoid modifiers that do not refer clearly and logically to some word in the sentence.

Dangling: *Taking our seats, the game started.* (*Taking* does not refer to the subject, *game,* nor to any other word in the sentence.)

Correct: *Taking our seats, we watched the opening of the game.* (*Taking* refers to *we,* the subject of the sentence.)

dates Always use Arabic figures, without *st, nd, rd* or *th.* See **months** for examples and punctuation guidelines.

days of the week Capitalize them. Do not abbreviate, except when needed in a tabular format: *Sun, Mon, Tue, Wed, Thu, Fri, Sat* (three letters, without periods, to facilitate tabular composition).

decimal units Use a period and numerals to indicate decimal amounts. Decimalization should not exceed two places in textual material unless there are special circumstances.

See **fractions.**

dialect The form of language peculiar to a region or a group, usually in matters of pronunciation or syntax. Dialect should be avoided, even in quoted matter, unless it is clearly pertinent to a story.

There are some words and phrases in everyone's vocabulary that are typical of a particular region or group. Quoting dialect, unless used carefully, implies substandard or illiterate usage.

When there is a compelling reason to use dialect, words or phrases are spelled phonetically, and apostrophes show missing letters and sounds: *"Din't ya yoosta live at Toidy-Toid Street and Sekun' Amya? Across from da moom pitchers?"*

dictionaries For spelling, style and usage questions not covered in this stylebook, consult Webster's New World College Dictionary, Third Edition, published by Macmillan, a division of Simon & Schuster, New York.

Use the first spelling listed in Webster's New World unless a specific exception is listed in this book.

If Webster's New World provides different spellings in separate entries (*tee shirt* and *T-shirt,* for example), use the spelling that is followed by a full definition (*T-shirt*).

If Webster's New World provides definitions under two different spellings for the same sense of a word, either use is acceptable. For example, *although* or *though.*

If there is no listing in either this book or Webster's New World, the backup dictionary, with more listings, is Webster's Third New International Dictionary, published by G. & C. Merriam Co. of Springfield, Mass.

Webster's New World is also the first reference for geographic names not covered in this stylebook. See **geographic names.**

directions and regions In general, lowercase *north, south, northeast, northern,* etc., when they indicate compass direction; capitalize these words when they designate regions.

Some examples:

COMPASS DIRECTIONS: *He drove west. The cold front is moving east.*

REGIONS: *A storm system that developed in the Midwest is spreading eastward. It will bring showers to the East Coast by morning and to the entire Northeast by late in the day. High temperatures will prevail throughout the Western states.*

The North was victorious. The South will rise again. Settlers from the East went West in search of new lives. The customs of the East are different from those of the West. The Northeast depends on the Midwest for its food supply.

She has a Southern accent. He is a Northerner. Nations of the Orient are opening doors to Western businessmen. The candidate developed a Southern strategy. She is a Northern liberal.

The storm developed in the South Pacific. European leaders met to talk about supplies of oil from Southeast Asia.

WITH NAMES OF NATIONS: Lowercase unless they are part of a proper name or are used to designate a politically divided nation: *northern France, eastern Canada, the western United States.*

But: *Northern Ireland, South Korea.*

WITH STATES AND CITIES: The preferred form is to lowercase compass points only when they describe a section of a state or city: *western Texas, southern Atlanta.*

But capitalize compass points:

—When part of a proper name: *North Dakota, West Virginia.*

—When used in denoting widely known sections: *Southern California, the South Side of Chicago, the Lower East Side of New York.* If in doubt, use lowercase.

IN FORMING PROPER NAMES: When combining with another common noun to form the name for a region or location: *the North Woods, the South Pole, the Far East, the Middle East, the West Coast* (the entire region, not the coastline itself), *the Eastern Shore, the Western Hemisphere.*

dollars Always lowercase. Use figures and the $ sign in all except casual references or amounts without a figure: *The book cost $4. Dad, please give me a dollar. Dollars are flowing overseas.*

E

earth Generally lowercase; capitalize when used as the proper name of the planet. *She is down to earth. How does the pattern apply to Mars, Jupiter, Earth, the sun and the moon? The astronauts returned to Earth. He hopes to move heaven and earth.*

e-mail Short form of *electronic mail.*

equal An adjective without comparative forms.

When people speak of a *more equal* distribution of wealth, what is meant is *more equitable.*

equal, equaled, equaling

ex- Use no hyphen for words that use *ex-* in the sense of *out of:*

excommunicate   expropriate

Hyphenate when using *ex-* in the sense of *former:*

ex-convict   ex-president

Do not capitalize *ex-* when attached to a formal title before a name: *ex-President Nixon.* The prefix modifies the entire term: *ex-New York Gov. Nelson Rockefeller;* not *New York ex-Gov.*

Usually *former* is better.

F

Fahrenheit The temperature scale commonly used in the United States.

The scale is named for Gabriel Daniel Fahrenheit, the German physicist who designed it. In it, the freezing point of water is 32 degrees and the boiling point is 212 degrees.

To convert to Celsius, subtract 32 from the Fahrenheit figure, multiply by 5 and divide by 9 (77 − 32 = 45, times 5 − 225, divided by 9 = 25 degrees Celsius).

In cases that require mention of the scale, use these forms: *86 degrees Fahrenheit* or *86 F* (note the space and no period after the f) if degrees and Fahrenheit are clear from the context.

See **Celsius.**

TEMPERATURE CONVERSIONS

Following is a temperature conversion table. Celsius temperatures have been rounded to the nearest whole number.

F	C	F	C	F	C
-26	-32	19	-7	64	18
-24	-31	21	-6	66	19
-22	-30	23	-5	68	20
-20	-29	25	-4	70	21
-18	-28	27	-3	72	22
-17	-27	28	-2	73	23
-15	-26	30	-1	75	24
-13	-25	32	0	77	25
-11	-24	34	1	79	26
-9	-23	36	2	81	27
-8	-22	37	3	82	28
-6	-21	39	4	84	29
-4	-20	41	5	86	30
-2	-19	43	6	88	31
0	-18	45	7	90	32
1	-17	46	8	91	33
3	-16	48	9	93	34
5	-15	50	10	95	35
7	-14	52	11	97	36
9	-13	54	12	99	37
10	-12	55	13	100	38
12	-11	57	14	102	39
14	-10	59	15	104	40
16	-9	61	16	106	41
18	-8	63	17	108	42

felony, misdemeanor A *felony* is a serious crime. A *misdemeanor* is a minor offense against the law.

A fuller definition of what constitutes a felony or misdemeanor depends on the governmental jurisdiction involved.

At the federal level a *misdemeanor* is a crime that carries a potential penalty of no more than a year in jail. A *felony* is a crime that carries a potential penalty of more than a year in prison. Often, however, a statute gives a judge options such as imposing a fine or probation in addition to or instead of a jail or prison sentence.

A *felon* is a person who has been convicted of a *felony,* regardless of whether the individual actually spends time in confinement or is given probation or a fine instead.

Fourth Estate Capitalize when used as a collective name for journalism and journalists.

The description is attributed to Edmund Burke, who is reported to have called the reporters' gallery in Parliament a "Fourth Estate."

The three estates of early English society were the Lords Spiritual (the clergy), the Lords Temporal (the nobility) and the Commons (the bourgeoisie).

fractions Spell out amounts less than 1 in stories, using hyphens between the words: *two-thirds, four-fifths, seven-sixteenths,* etc.

Use figures for precise amounts larger than 1, converting to decimals whenever practical.

Fractions are preferred, however, in stories about stocks.

When using fractional characters, remember that most newspaper type fonts can set only 1/8, 1/4, 3/8, 1/2, 5/8, 3/4 and 7/8 as one unit; use *11/2, 25/8,* etc. with no space between the figure and the fraction. Other fractions require a hyphen and individual figures, with a space between the whole number and the fraction: *1 3-16, 2 1-3, 5 9-10.*

In tabular material, use figures exclusively, converting to decimals if the amounts involve extensive use of fractions that cannot be expressed as a single character.

See **percentages.**

G

geographic names The basic guidelines:

DOMESTIC: The authority for spelling place names in the 50 states and territories is the U.S. Postal Service Directory of Post Offices, with two exceptions:

—Do not use the postal abbreviations for state names. See **state names** for rules based on when the abbreviations may be used.

—Abbreviate *Saint* as *St.* (But abbreviate *Sault Sainte Marie* as *Sault Ste. Marie.*)

FOREIGN: The first source for the spelling of all foreign place names is Webster's New World Dictionary as follows:

—Use the first-listed spelling if an entry gives more than one.

—If the dictionary provides different spellings in separate entries, use the spelling that is followed by a full description of the location. There are exceptions:

1. Use *Cameroon*, not *Cameroons* or *Cameroun.*
2. Use *Maldives*, not *Maldive Islands.*
3. Use *Sri Lanka*, not *Ceylon.*

The latter exceptions have been made to conform with the practices of the United Nations and the U.S.

Board of Geographic Names. (See the NEW NAMES paragraph below.)

If the dictionary does not have an entry, use the first-listed spelling in the National Geographic Atlas of the World.

NEW NAMES: Follow the styles adopted by the United Nations and the U.S. Board of Geographic Names on new cities, new independent nations and nations that change their names.

CAPITALIZATION: Capitalize common nouns when they form an integral part of a proper name, but lowercase them when they stand alone: *Pennsylvania Avenue, the avenue; the Philippine Islands, the islands; the Mississippi River, the river.*

Lowercase common nouns that are not a part of a specific name: *the Pacific islands, the Swiss mountains, Zhejiang province.*

For additional guidelines, see **addresses; capitalization; directions and regions.**

government Always lowercase, never abbreviate: *the federal government, the state government, the U.S. government.*

governmental bodies Follow these guidelines:

FULL NAME: Capitalize the full proper names of governmental agencies, departments, and offices: *The U.S. Department of State, the Georgia Department of Human Resources, the Boston City Council, the Chicago Fire Department.*

WITHOUT JURISDICTION: Retain capitalization in referring to a specific body if the dateline or context makes the name of the nation, state, county, city, etc., unnecessary: *The Department of State* (in a story from Washington), *the Department of Human Resources or the state Department of Human Resources* (in a story from Georgia), *the City Council* (in a story from Boston), *the Fire Department or the city Fire Department* (in a story from Chicago).

Lowercase further condensations of the name: *the department, the council,* etc.

FLIP-FLOPPED NAMES: Retain capital names for the name of a governmental body if its formal name is flopped to delete the word *of: the State Department, the Human Resources Department.*

GENERIC EQUIVALENTS: If a generic term has become the equivalent of a proper name in popular use, treat it as a proper name: *Walpole State Prison,* for example, even though the proper name is the *Massachusetts Correctional Institute-Walpole.*

PLURALS, NON-SPECIFIED REFERENCES: All words that are capitalized when part of a proper name should be lowercased when they are used in the plural or do not refer to a specific, existing body. Some examples:

All states except Nebraska have a state senate. The town does not have a fire department. The bill requires city councils to provide matching funds. The president will address the lower houses of the New York and New Jersey legislatures.

FOREIGN BODIES: The same principles apply.

H

habeas corpus A writ ordering a person in custody to be brought before a court. It places the burden of proof on those detaining the person to justify the detention.

When *habeas corpus* is used in a story, define it.

Hanukkah The Jewish Festival of Lights, an eight-day commemoration of re-dedication of the Temple by the Maccabees after their victory over the Syrians.

Usually occurs in December but sometimes falls in late November.

heavenly bodies Capitalize the proper names of planets, stars, constellations, etc.: *Mars, Arcturus, the Big Dipper, Aries.*

For comets, capitalize only the proper noun element of the name: *Halley's comet.*

Lowercase sun and moon, but capitalize them if their Greek or Latin names are used: *Helios, Luna.*

Lowercase nouns and adjectives derived from the proper names of planets and other heavenly bodies: *jovian, lunar, martian, solar, venusian.*

his, her Do not presume maleness in constructing a sentence, but use the pronoun *his* when an indefinite antecedent may be male or female: *A reporter attempts to protect his sources.* (Not *his or her* sources, but note the use of the word *reporter* rather than *newsman.*)

Frequently, however, the best choice is a slight revision of the sentence: *Reporters attempt to protect their sources.*

historical periods and events Capitalize the names of widely recognized epochs in anthropology, archaeology, geology and history: *the Bronze Age, the Dark Ages, the Middle Ages, the Pliocene Epoch.*

Capitalize also widely recognized popular names for the periods and events: *the Atomic Age, the Boston Tea Party, the Civil War, the Exodus* (of the Israelites from Egypt), *the Great Depression, Prohibition.*

Lowercase *century: the 18th century.*

Capitalize only the proper nouns or adjectives in general descriptions of a period: *ancient Greece, classical Rome, the Victorian era, the fall of Rome.*

For additional guidance, follow the capitalization in Webster's New World Dictionary, using lowercase if the dictionary lists it as an acceptable form for the sense in which the word is used.

I

inter- The rules in **prefixes** apply, but in general, no hyphen. Some examples:

inter-American   interracial   interstate

intra- The rules in **prefixes** apply, but, in general, no hyphen. Some examples:

intramural   intrastate

IQ Acceptable in all references for *intelligence quotient.*

J

judge Capitalize before a name when it is the formal title for an individual who presides in a court of law. Do not continue to use the title in second reference.

Do not use *court* as part of the title unless confusion would result without it:

—No *court* in the title: *U.S. District Judge John Sirica, District Judge John Sirica, federal Judge John Sirica, Judge John Sirica, U.S. Circuit Judge Homer Thornberry, appellate Judge John Blair.*

—*Court* needed in the title: *Juvenile Court Judge John Jones, Criminal Court Judge John Jones, superior Court Judge Robert Harrison, state Supreme Court Judge William Cushing.*

When the formal title chief judge is relevant, put the court name after the judge's name: *Chief Judge*

John Sirica of the U.S. District Court in Washington, D.C.; Chief Judge Clement F. Haynsworth Jr. of the 4th U.S. Circuit Court of Appeals.

Do not pile up long court names before the name of a judge. *Make it Judge John Smith of Allegheny County Common Pleas Court.* Not: *Allegheny County Common Pleas Court Judge John Smith.*

Lowercase *judge* as an occupational designation in phrases such as *beauty contest judge Bert Parks.*

L

lay, lie The action word is *lay.* It takes a direct object. *Laid* is the form for its past tense and its past participle. Its present participle is *laying.*

Lie indicates a state of reclining along a horizontal plane. It does not take a direct object. Its past tense is *lay.* Its past participle is *lain.* Its present participle is *lying.*

When *lie* means to make an untrue statement, the verb forms are *lie, lied, lying.*

Some examples:

PRESENT OR FUTURE TENSES:

Right: *I will lay the book on the table. The prosecutor tried to lay the blame on him.*

Wrong: *He lays on the beach all day. I will lay down.*

Right: *He lies on the beach all day. I will lie down.*

M

magazine names Capitalize the name but do not place it in quotes. Lowercase *magazine* unless it is part of the publication's formal title: *Harper's Magazine, Newsweek Magazine, Time Magazine.*

Check the masthead if in doubt.

majority, plurality *Majority* means more than half of an amount. *Plurality* means more than the next highest number.

COMPUTING MAJORITY: To describe how large a majority is, take the figure that is more than half and subtract everything else from it: If 100,000 votes were cast in an election and one candidate received 60,000 while opponents received 40,000, the winner would have a *majority* of 20,000 votes.

COMPUTING PLURALITY: To describe how large a plurality is, take the highest number and subtract from it the next highest number: If, in the election example above, the second-place finisher had 25,000 votes, the winner's *plurality* would be 35,000 votes.

Suppose, however, that no candidate in this example had a majority. If the first-place finisher had 40,000 votes and the second-place finisher had 30,000, for example, the leader's *plurality* would be 10,000 votes.

USAGE: When *majority* and *plurality* are used alone, they take singular verbs and pronouns: *The majority has made its decision.*

If a plural word follows an *of* construction, the decision on whether to use a singular or plural verb depends on the sense of the sentence: *A majority of two votes is not adequate to control the committee. The majority of the houses on the block were destroyed.*

man, mankind Either may be used when both men and women are involved and no other term is convenient. In these cases, do not use duplicate phrases such as *a man* or *a woman* or *mankind* and *womankind.*

Frequently the best choice is a substitute such as *humanity, a person* or *an individual.*

months Capitalize the names of months in all uses. When a month is used with a specific date, abbreviate only *Jan., Feb., Aug., Sept., Oct., Nov.* and *Dec.* Spell out when using alone, or with a year alone.

When a phrase lists only a month and a year, do not separate the year with commas. When a phrase refers to a month, day and year, set off the year with commas.

EXAMPLES: *January 1972 was a cold month. Jan. 2 was the coldest day of the month. His birthday is May 8. Feb. 14, 1987, was the target date.*

In tabular material, use these three-letter forms without a period: *Jan, Feb, Mar, Apr, May, Jun, Jul, Aug, Sep, Oct, Nov, Dec.*

movie ratings the ratings used by the Motion Picture Association of America are:

G — General audiences. All ages admitted.

PG — Parental guidance suggested. Some material may not be suitable for children.

PG-13 — Special parental guidance strongly suggested for children under 13. Some material may be inappropriate for young children.

R — Restricted. Under 17 requires accompanying parent or adult guardian.

NC-17 — No one under 17 admitted.

When the ratings are used in news stories or reviews, use these forms as appropriate: *the movie has an R rating, an R-rated movie, the movie is R-rated.*

Mr., Mrs. The plural of *Mr.* is *Messrs.*; the plural of *Mrs.* is *Mmes.*

These abbreviated spellings apply in all uses, including direct quotations.

See **courtesy titles** for guidelines on when to use *Mr.* and *Mrs.*

Ms. This is the spelling and punctuation for all uses of the courtesy title, including direct quotations.

There is no plural. If several women who prefer *Ms.* must be listed in a series, repeat *Ms.* before each name.

N

names In general, people are entitled to be known however they want to be known, as long as their identities are clear.

When an individual elects to change the name by which he has been known, such as Cassius Clay's transition to Muhammad Ali, provide both names in stories until the new name is known by the public. After that, use only the new name unless there is a specific reason for including the earlier identification.

newspaper names Capitalize *the* in a newspaper's name if that is the way the publication prefers to be known.

Lowercase *the* before newspaper names if a story mentions several papers, some of which use the as part of the name and some of which do not.

When the location is needed but is not part of the official name, use parentheses: *The Huntsville (Ala.) Times.*

Consult the International Year Book published by *Editor & Publisher* to determine whether a two-name combination is hyphenated.

nicknames A nickname should be used in place of a person's given name in news stories only when it is the way the individual prefers to be known: *Jimmy Carter.*

When a nickname is inserted into the identification of an individual, use quotation marks: *Sen. Henry M. "Scoop" Jackson. Also: Jackson is known as "Scoop."*

In sports stories and sports columns, commonly used nicknames may be substituted for a first name without the use of quotation marks: *Woody Hayes, Bear Bryant, Catfish Hunter, Bubba Smith,* etc. But in sports stories where the given name is used, and in all news stories: *Paul "Bear" Bryant.*

Capitalize without quotation marks such terms as *Sunshine State, the Old Dominion, Motown, the Magic City, Old Hickory, Old Glory, Galloping Ghost.*

non- The rules of **prefixes** apply, but in general no hyphen when forming a compound that does not have special meaning and can be understood if *not* is used before the base word. Use a hyphen, however, before proper nouns or in awkward combinations, such as *non-nuclear.* Follow Webster's New World Dictionary.

numerals A numeral is a figure, letter, word or group of words expressing a number.

Roman numerals use the letters *I, V, X, L, C, D* and *M.* Use Roman numerals for wars and to show personal sequence for animals and people: *World War II, Native Dancer II, King George VI, Pope John XXIII.*

Arabic numerals use the figures *1, 2, 3, 4, 5, 6, 7, 8, 9* and *0.* Use Arabic forms unless Roman numerals are specifically required. See **Arabic numerals.**

The figures *1, 2, 10, 101,* etc., and the corresponding words — *one, two, ten, one hundred one,* etc. — are called cardinal numbers The term ordinal number applies to *1st, 2nd, 10th, 101st, first, second, tenth, one hundred first,* etc.

Follow these guidelines in using numerals:

LARGE NUMBERS: When large numbers must be spelled out, use a hyphen to connect a word ending in y to another word; do not use commas between other separate words that are part of one number: *twenty; thirty; twenty-one; thirty-one; one hundred forty-three; one thousand one hundred fifty-five; one million two hundred seventy-six thousand five hundred eighty-seven.*

SENTENCE START: Spell out a numeral at the beginning of a sentence. If necessary, recast the sentence. There is one exception—a numeral that identifies a calendar year.

Wrong: *993 freshmen entered the college last year.*
Right: *Last year 993 freshmen entered the college.*
Right: *1976 was a very good year.*

CASUAL USES: Spell out casual expressions:

A thousand times no! Thanks a million. He walked a quarter of a mile.

PROPER NAMES: Use words or numerals according to an organization's practice: *3M, Twentieth Century Fund, Big Ten.*

FRACTIONS: See the **fractions** entry.

DECIMALS: See the **decimal units** entry.

FIGURES OR WORDS?

for ordinals:

—Spell out *first* through *ninth* when they indicate sequence in time or location: *first base, the First Amendment, he was first in line.* Starting with *10th* use figures.

—Use *1st, 2nd, 3rd, 4th,* etc. when the sequence has been assigned in forming names. *The principal examples are geographic, military and political designations such as 1st Ward, 7th Fleet and 1st Sgt.* See examples in the separate entries listed below.

For cardinal numbers, consult the following separate entries [in the complete *AP Stylebook*]:

act numbers	addresses
ages	aircraft names
amendments	betting odds
to the Constitution	century
channel	chapters
congressional districts	course numbers
court decisions	court names
dates	decades
decimal units	district
earthquakes	election returns
fleet	formula
fractions	handicaps
heights	highway designations
latitude and longitude	mile
millions, billions	model numbers
monetary units	No.
page numbers	parallels
percentages	political divisions
proportions	ratios
recipes	room numbers
route numbers	scene numbers
sizes	spacecraft designations
speeds	telephone numbers
temperatures	years

SOME PUNCTUATION AND USAGE EXAMPLES:

—*Act 1, Scene 2*
—*a 5-year-old girl*
—*DC-10* but *747B*

—*a 5-4 court decision*
—*2nd District Court*
—*the 1980s, the '80s*
—*the House voted 230-205.* (Fewer than 1,000 votes.)
—*Jimmy Carter defeated Gerald Ford 40,827,292 to 39,146,157.* (More than 1,000 votes.)
—*Carter defeated Ford 10 votes to 2 votes in Little Junction.* (To avoid confusion with ratio.)
—*05 cents, $1.05, $650,000, $2.45 million*
—*No. 3 choice,* but *Public School 3*
—*0.6 percent, 1 percent, 6.5 percent*
—*a pay increase 12 percent to 15 percent.* Or: *a pay increase of between 12 percent and 15 percent*
Also: *from $12 million to $14 million*
—*a ratio of 2-to-1, a 2-1 ratio*
—*a 4–3 score*
—*(212) 262-4000*
—*minus 10, zero, 60 degrees*

OTHER USES: For uses not covered by these listings: Spell out whole numbers below 10, use figures for 10 and above. Typical examples: *They had three sons and two daughters. They had a fleet of 10 station wagons and two buses.*

IN A SERIES: Apply the appropriate guidelines: *They had 10 dogs, six cats and 97 hamsters. They had four four-room houses, 10 three-room houses and 12 10-room houses.*

O

obscenities, profanities, vulgarities Do not use them in stories unless they are part of direct quotations and there is a compelling reason for them.

olympics Capitalize all references to the international athletic contests held every four years: *the Olympics, the Winter Olympics, the Olympic Games, the Games, an Olympic-sized pool.*

An Olympic-sized pool is 50 meters long by 25 meters wide.

Lowercase other uses: *a pie-eating olympics.*

organizations and institutions Capitalize the full names of organizations and institutions: *the American Medical Association; First Presbyterian Church; General Motors Corp.; Harvard University, Harvard University Medical School; the Procrastinators Club; the Society of Professional Journalists, Sigma Delta Chi.*

Retain capitalization if *Co., Corp.* or a similar word is deleted from the full proper name: General Motors.

SUBSIDIARIES: Capitalize the names of major subdivisions: *the Pontiac Motor Division of General Motors.*

INTERNAL ELEMENTS: Use lowercase for internal elements of an organization when they have names that are widely used generic terms: *the board of directors of General Motors, the board of trustees of Columbia University, the history department of Harvard University, the sports department of the Daily Citizen-Leader.*

Capitalize internal elements of an organization when they have names that are not widely used generic terms: *the General Assembly of the World Council of Churches, the House of Delegates of the American Medical Association, the House of Bishops and House of Deputies of the Episcopal Church.*

FLIP-FLOPPED NAMES: Retain capital letters when commonly accepted practice flops a name to delete the word of: *College of the Holy Cross, Holy Cross College; Harvard School of Dental Medicine, Harvard Dental School.*

Do not, however, flop formal names that are known to the public with the word of: *Massachusetts Institute of Technology,* for example, not *Massachusetts Technology Institute.*

ABBREVIATIONS AND ACRONYMS: Some organizations and institutions are widely recognized by abbreviations: *Alcoa, GOP, NAACP, NATO.* For guidelines on when such abbreviations may be used, see the individual listings and the entry under **abbreviations and acronyms.**

P

people, persons Use person when speaking of an individual: *One person waited for the bus.*

The word *people* is preferred to persons in all plural uses. For example: *Thousands of people attended the fair. What will people say? There were 17 people in the room.*

Persons should be used only when it is in a direct quote or part of a title as in *Bureau of Missing Persons.*

People also is a collective noun that takes a plural verb when used to refer to a single race or nation: *The American people are united.* In this sense, the plural is *peoples: The peoples of Africa speak many languages.*

percent One word. It takes a singular verb when standing alone or when a singular word follows an *of*

construction: *The teacher said 60 percent was a failing grade. He said 50 percent of the membership was there.*

It takes a plural verb when a plural word follows an *of* construction: *He said 50 percent of the members were there.*

percentages Use figures: *1 percent, 2.5 percent* (use decimals, not fractions), *10 percent.*

For amounts less than 1 percent, precede the decimal with a zero: *The cost of living rose 0.6 percent.*

Repeat percent with each individual figure: *He said 10 percent to 30 percent of the electorate may not vote.*

-persons Do not use coined words such as *chairperson* or *spokesperson* in regular text.

Instead, use *chairman* or *spokesman* if referring to a man or the office in general. Use chairwoman or spokeswoman if referring to a woman. Or, if applicable, use a neutral word such as *leader* or *representative.*

Use *chairperson* or similar coinage only in direct quotations or when it is the formal description for an office.

planets Capitalize the proper names of planets: *Jupiter, Mars, Mercury, Neptune, Pluto, Saturn, Uranus, Venus.*

Capitalize *earth* when used as the proper name of our planet: *The astronauts returned to Earth.*

Lowercase nouns and adjectives derived from the proper names of planets and other heavenly bodies: *martian, jovian, lunar, solar, venusian.*

plants In general, lowercase the names of plants, but capitalize proper nouns or adjectives that occur in a name.

Some examples: *tree, fir, white fir, Douglas fir; Scotch pine; clover, white clover, white Dutch clover.*

If a botanical name is used, capitalize the first word; lowercase others: *pine tree (Pinus), red cedar (Juniperus virginiana), blue azealea (Callicarpa americana), Kentucky coffee tree (Gymnocladus dioica).*

plurals Follow these guidelines in forming and using plural words:

MOST WORDS: Add *s: boys, girls, ships, villages.*

WORDS ENDING IN CH, S, SH, SS, X AND Z: Add *es: churches, lenses, parishes, glasses, boxes, buzzes.* (*Monarchs* is an exception.)

WORDS ENDING IN IS: Change *is* to *es: oases, parentheses, theses.*

WORDS ENDING IN Y: If *y* is preceded by a consonant or *qu,* change *y* to *i* and add *es: armies, cities, navies, soliloquies.* (See PROPER NAMES below for an exception.)

Otherwise add *s: donkeys, monkeys.*

WORDS ENDING IN O: If *o* is preceded by a consonant, most plurals require *es: buffaloes, dominoes, echoes, heroes, potatoes.* But there are exceptions: *pianos.*

WORDS ENDING IN F: In general, change *f* to *v* and add *es: leaves, selves.* (There are exceptions, such as *roofs.*)

LATIN ENDINGS: Latin-root words ending in *us* change *us* to *i: alumnus, alumni.*

Most ending in *a* change to *ae: alumna, alumnae* (*formula, formulas* is an exception).

Most ending in *um* add *s: memorandums, referendums, stadiums.* Among those that still use the Latin ending: *addenda, curricula, media.*

Use the plural that Webster's New World lists as most common for a particular sense of that word.

FORM CHANGE: *man, men; child, children; foot, feet; mouse, mice;* etc.

Caution: When *s* is used with any of these words it indicates possession and must be preceded by an apostrophe: *men's, children's,* etc.

WORDS THE SAME IN SINGULAR AND PLURAL: *corps, chassis, deer, moose, sheep,* etc.

The sense in a particular sentence is conveyed by the use of a singular or plural verb.

WORDS PLURAL IN FORM, SINGULAR IN MEANING: Some take singular verbs: *measles, mumps, news.*

Others take plural verbs: *grits, scissors.*

COMPOUND WORDS: Those written solid add *s* at the end: *cupfuls, handfuls, tablespoonfuls.*

For those that involve separate words or words linked by a hyphen, make the most significant word plural:

—Significant word first: *adjutants general, aides-de-camp, attorneys general, courts-martial, daughters-in-law, passers-by, postmasters general, presidents-elect, secretaries general, sergeants major.*

—Significant word in the middle: *assistant attorneys general, deputy chiefs of staff.*

—Significant word last: *assistant attorneys, assistant corporation counsels, deputy sheriffs, lieutenant colonels, major generals.*

WORDS AS WORDS: Do not use *'s: His speech had too many "ifs," "ands" and "buts."* (Exception to Webster's New World.)

PROPER NAMES: Most ending in *es* or *z* add *es: Charleses, Joneses, Gonzalezes.*

Most ending in *y* add *s* even if preceded by a consonant: *the Duffys, the Kennedys, the two Kansas Citys.* Exceptions include *Alleghenies* and *Rockies.*

For others, add *s: the Carters, the McCoys, the Mondales.*

FIGURES: Add *s: The custom began in the 1920s. The airline has two 727s. Temperatures will be in the low 20s. There were five size 7s.*

(No apostrophes, an exception to Webster's New World guideline under "apostrophe.")

SINGLE LETTERS: Use *'s: Mind your p's and q's. He learned the three R's and brought home a report card with four A's and two B's. The Oakland A's won the pennant.*

MULTIPLE LETTERS: Add *s: She knows her ABCs. I gave him five IOUs. Four VIPs were there.*

PROBLEMS, DOUBTS: Separate entries in this book give plurals for troublesome words and guidance on whether certain words should be used with singular or plural verbs and pronouns. See also **collective nouns** and **possessives.**

For questions not covered by this book, use the plural that Webster's New World lists as most common for a particular sense of a word.

Note also the guidelines that the dictionary provides under its "plural" entry.

p.m., a.m. Lowercase, with periods. Avoid the redundant *10 p.m. tonight.*

police department In communities where this is the formal name, capitalize *police department* with or without the name of the community: *the Los Angeles Police Department, the Police Department.*

If a police agency has some other formal name, such as *Division of Police,* use that name if it is the way the department is known to the public. If the story uses *police department* as a generic term for such an agency, put *police department* in lowercase.

If a police agency with an unusual formal name is known to the public as a *police department,* treat *police department* as the name, capitalizing it with or without the name of the community. Use the formal name only if there is a special reason in the story.

If the proper name cannot be determined for some reason, such as the need to write about a police agency from a distance, treat *police department* as the proper name, capitalizing it with or without the name of the community.

Lowercase *police department* in plural uses: *the Los Angeles and San Francisco police departments.*

Lowercase *the department* whenever it stands alone.

political parties and philosophies Capitalize both the name of the party and the word *party* if it is customarily used as part of the organization's proper name: *the Democratic Party, the Republican Party.*

Capitalize *Communist, Conservative, Democrat, Liberal, Republican, Socialist,* etc., when they refer to a specific party or its members. Lowercase these words when they refer to political philosophy (see EXAMPLES below).

Lowercase the name of a philosophy in noun and adjective forms unless it is the derivative of a proper name: *communism, fascism, fascist.* But: *Marxism, Marxist; Nazism, Nazi.*

EXAMPLES: *John Adams was a Federalist, but a man who subscribed to his philosophy today would be described as a federalist. The liberal Republican senator and his Conservative Party colleague said they believe that democracy and communism are incompatible. The Communist said he is basically a socialist who has reservations about Marxism.*

polls and surveys Stories based on public opinion polls must include the basic information for an intelligent evaluation of the results. Such stories must be carefully worded to avoid exaggerating the meaning of the poll results.

Information that should be in every story based on a poll includes the answers to these questions:

1. Who did the poll? (The place to start is the polling firm, political campaign or other group that conducted the poll.)
2. How many people were interviewed? How were they selected? (Only polls based on a scientific sample of a population can be used as a reliable and accurate measure of that population's opinions. Polls based on interviews on street corners,

calling a 900-number or mailing coupons back from magazines may be good entertainment, but such polls have no validity. They should be avoided. In such unscientific pseudo-polls, the opinions come from people who "select themselves" to participate. If such polls are reported for entertainment value, they must never be portrayed as accurately reflecting public opinion and their failings must be highlighted.)
3. Who was interviewed? (A valid poll reflects only the opinions of the population that was sampled. A poll of business executives can only represent the views of business executives, not of all adults. Many political polls are based on interviews only with registered voters, since registration is usually required for voting. Close to the election, polls may be based only on "likely voters." If "likely voters" are used as the base, ask the pollster how that group was identified.)
4. How was the poll conducted—by telephone or in people's homes?
5. When was the poll taken? (Opinions can change quickly, especially in response to events.)
6. Who paid for the poll? (Be wary of polls paid for by candidates or interest groups. The release of poll results is often a campaign tactic or publicity ploy. Any reporting of such polls must highlight the poll's sponsor and the potential for bias from such sponsorship.)
7. What are the sampling error margins for the poll and for sub-groups mentioned in the story? (Sampling error margins should be provided by the polling organization. The error margins vary inversely with the sample size: the fewer people interviewed, the larger the sampling error. If the opinions of a sub-group—women, for example—are important to the story, the sampling error for that sub-group should be included. The sub-group error margins are always larger than the margin for the entire poll.)
8. What questions were asked and in what order? (Small differences in question wording can cause big differences in results. The exact text of the question need not be in every poll story unless it is crucial or controversial.)

When writing and editing poll stories, here are areas for close attention:

—Do not exaggerate the poll results. A difficult situation arises with pre-election polls in deciding when to write that the poll says one candidate is leading another. The rules are: If the margin between the candidates is more than twice the sampling error margin, then the poll says one candidate is leading. If the margin is less than the sampling error margin, the poll says that the race is close, that the candidates are "about even." If the margin is more than the sampling error, but less than twice the sampling error, then one candidate can be said to be "apparently leading" or "slightly ahead" in the race.

—Comparisons with other polls are often newsworthy. Earlier poll results can show changes in public opinion. Be careful comparing polls from different polling organizations. Different poll techniques can cause differing results.

—Sampling error is not the only source of error in a poll, but it is one that can be quantified. Question wording, interviewer skill and computer processing are all sources of error in surveys.

—No matter how good the poll, no matter how wide the margin, the poll does not say one candidate will win an election. Polls can be wrong and the voters can change their minds before they cast their ballots.

possessives Follow these guidelines:

PLURAL NOUNS NOT ENDING IN S: Add 's: *the alumni's contributions, women's rights.*

PLURAL NOUNS ENDING IN S: Add only an apostrophe: *the churches' needs, the girls' toys, the horses' food, the ships' wake, states' rights, the VIPs' entrance.*

NOUNS PLURAL IN FORM, SINGULAR IN MEANING: Add only an apostrophe: *mathematics' rules, measles' effects.* (But see INANIMATE OBJECTS on page 523.)

Apply the same principle when a plural word occurs in the formal name of a singular entity: *General Motors' profits, the United States' wealth.*

NOUNS THE SAME IN SINGULAR AND PLURAL: Treat them the same as plurals, even if the meaning is singular: *one corps' location, the two deer's tracks, the lone moose's antlers.*

SINGULAR NOUNS NOT ENDING IN S: Add 's: *the church's needs, the girl's toys, the horse's food, the ship's route, the VIP's seat.*

Some style guides say that singular nouns ending in s sounds such as *ce, x,* and *z* may take either the apostrophe alone or 's. See SPECIAL EXPRESSIONS, but otherwise, for consistency and ease in remembering a

rule, always use 's if the word does not end in the letter s: *Butz's policies, the fox's den, the justice's verdict, Marx's theories, the prince's life, Xerox's profits.*

SINGULAR COMMON NOUNS ENDING IN S: Add 's unless the next word begins with s: *the hostess's invitation, the hostess' seat; the witness's answer, the witness' story.*

SINGULAR PROPER NAMES ENDING IN S: Use only an apostrophe: *Achilles' heel, Agnes' book, Ceres' rites, Descartes' theories, Dickens' novels, Euripides' dramas, Hercules' labors, Jesus' life, Jules' seat, Kansas' schools, Moses' law, Socrates' life, Tennessee Williams' plays, Xerxes' armies.*

SPECIAL EXPRESSIONS: The following exceptions to the general rule for words not ending in s apply to words that end in an s sound and are followed by a word that begins with s: *for appearance' sake, for conscience' sake, for goodness' sake.* Use 's otherwise: *the appearance's cost, my conscience's voice.*

PRONOUNS: Personal interrogative and relative pronouns have separate forms for the possessive. None involve an apostrophe: *mine, ours, your, yours, his, hers, its, theirs, whose.*

Caution: If you are using an apostrophe with a pronoun, always double-check to be sure that the meaning calls for a contraction: *you're, it's, there's, who's.*

Follow the rules listed above in forming the possessives of other pronouns: *another's idea, others' plans, someone's guess.*

COMPOUND WORDS: Applying the rules above, add an apostrophe or 's to the word closest to the object possessed: *the major general's decision, the major generals' decisions, the attorney general's request, the attorneys general's request.* See the **plurals** entry for guidelines on forming the plurals of these words.

Also: *anyone else's attitude, John Adams Jr.'s father, Benjamin Franklin of Pennsylvania's motion.* Whenever practical, however, recast the phrase to avoid ambiguity: *the motion by Benjamin Franklin of Pennsylvania.*

JOINT POSSESSION, INDIVIDUAL POSSESSION: Use a possessive form after only the last word if ownership is joint: *Fred and Sylvia's apartment, Fred and Sylvia's stocks.*

Use a possessive form after both words if the objects are individually owned: *Fred's and Sylvia's books.*

DESCRIPTIVE PHRASES: Do not add an apostrophe to a word ending in *s* when it is used primarily in a descriptive sense: *citizens band radio, a Cincinnati Reds infielder, a teachers college, a Teamsters request, a writers guide.*

Memory Aid: The apostrophe usually is not used if *for* or *by* rather than *of* would be appropriate in the longer form: *a radio band for citizens, a college for teachers, a guide for writers, a request by the Teamsters.*

An *'s* is required, however, when a term involves a plural word that does not end in *s*: *a children's hospital, a people's republic, the Young Men's Christian Association.*

DESCRIPTIVE NAMES: Some governmental, corporate and institutional organizations with a descriptive word in their names use an apostrophe; some do not. Follow the user's practice: *Actors' Equity, Diners Club, the Ladies' Home Journal, the National Governors' Association.* See separate entries for these and similar names frequently in the news.

QUASI POSSESSIVES: Follow the rules above in composing the possessive form of words that occur in such phrases as *a day's pay, two weeks' vacation, three days' work, your money's worth.* Frequently, however, a hyphenated form is clearer: *a two-week vacation, a three-day job.*

DOUBLE POSSESSIVE: Two conditions must apply for a double possessive—*a phrase such as a friend of John's*—to occur: 1. The word after *of* must refer to an inanimate object, and 2. The word before *of* must involve only a portion of the animate object's possessions.

Otherwise, do not use the possessive form of the word after *of*: *The friends of John Adams mourned his death.* (All the friends were involved.) *He is a friend of the college.* (Not college's, because college is inanimate.)

Memory Aid: This construction occurs most often, and quite naturally, with the possessive forms of personal pronouns: *He is a friend of mine.*

INANIMATE OBJECTS: There is no blanket rule against creating a possessive form for an inanimate object, particularly if the object is treated in a personified sense. See some of the earlier examples, and note these: *death's call, the wind's murmur.*

In general, however, avoid excessive personalization of inanimate objects, and give preference to an *of* construction when it fits the makeup of the sentence. For example, the earlier references to *mathematics'*

rules and *measles' effects* would better be phrased: *the rules of mathematics, the effects of measles.*

prefixes See separate listings for commonly used prefixes.

Generally do not hyphenate when using a prefix with a word starting with a consonant.

Three rules are constant, although they yield some exceptions to first-listed spellings in Webster's New World Dictionary:

—Except for *cooperate* and *coordinate,* use a hyphen if the prefix ends in a vowel and the word that follows begins with the same vowel.

—Use a hyphen if the word that follows is capitalized.

—Use a hyphen to join doubled prefixes: *sub-subparagraph.*

principal, principle *Principal* is a noun and adjective meaning someone or something first in rank, authority, importance or degree: *She is the school principal. He was the principal player in the trade. Money is the principal problem.*

Principle is a noun that means a fundamental truth, law, doctrine or motivating force: *They fought for the principle of self-determination.*

prison, jail Do not use the two words interchangeably.
DEFINITIONS: *Prison* is a generic term that may be applied to the maximum security institutions often known as *penitentiaries* and to the medium security facilities often called *correctional institutions* or *reformatories.* All such facilities confine persons serving sentences for felonies.

A *jail* is a facility normally used to confine persons serving sentences for misdemeanors, persons awaiting trial or sentencing on either felony or misdemeanor charges, and persons confined for civil matters such as failure to pay alimony and other types of contempt of court.

See the **felony, misdemeanor** entry.

The guidelines for capitalization:

PRISONS: Many states have given elaborate formal names to their prisons. They should be capitalized when used, but commonly accepted substitutes should also be capitalized as if they were proper names. For example, use either *Massachusetts Correctional Institution-Walpole* or *Walpole State Prison* for the maximum security institution in Massachusetts.

Do not, however, construct a substitute when the formal name is commonly accepted: It is the *Colorado State Penitentiary,* for example, not *Colorado State Prison.*

On second reference, any of the following may be used, all in lowercase: *the state prison, the prison, the state penitentiary, the penitentiary.*

Use lowercase for all plural constructions: *the Colorado and Kansas state penitentiaries.*

JAILS: Capitalize *jail* when linked with the name of the jurisdiction: *Los Angeles County Jail.* Lowercase *county jail, city jail* and *jail* when they stand alone.

FEDERAL INSTITUTIONS: Maximum security institutions are known as *penitentiaries: the U.S. Penitentiary at Lewisburg* or *Lewisburg Penitentiary* on first reference; *the federal penitentiary or the penitentiary* on second reference.

Medium security institutions include the word *federal* as part of their formal names: *The Federal Correctional Institution at Danbury, Conn.* On second reference: *the correctional institution, the federal prison, the prison.*

Most federal facilities used to house persons awaiting trial or serving sentences of a year or less have the proper name *Federal Detention Center.* the term *Metropolitan Correctional Center* is being adopted for some new installations. On second reference: *the detention center, the correctional center.*

punctuation Think of it as a courtesy to your readers, designed to help them understand a story.

Inevitably, a mandate of this scope involves gray areas. For this reason, the punctuation entries in this book refer to guidelines rather than rules. Guidelines should not be treated casually, however.

pupil, student Use *pupil* for children in kindergarten through eighth grade.

Student or *pupil* is acceptable for grades nine through 12.

Use *student* for college and beyond.

Q

quotations in the news Never alter quotations even to correct minor grammatical errors or word usage. Casual minor tongue slips may be removed by using ellipses but even that should be done with extreme caution. If there is a question about a quote, either don't use it or ask the speaker to clarify.

Do not routinely use abnormal spellings such as *gonna* in attempts to convey regional dialects or mispronunciations. Such spellings are appropriate when relevant or help to convey a desired touch in a feature.

FULL VS. PARTIAL QUOTES: In general, avoid fragmentary quotes. If a speaker's words are clear and concise, favor the full quote. If cumbersome language can be paraphrased fairly, use an indirect construction, reserving quotation marks for sensitive or controversial passages that must be identified specifically as coming from the speaker.

CONTEXT: Remember that you can misquote someone by giving a startling remark without its modifying passage or qualifiers. The manner of delivery sometimes is part of the context. Reporting a smile or a deprecatory gesture may be as important as conveying the words themselves.

R

race Identification by race is pertinent:

—In biographical and announcement stories, particularly when they involve a feat or appointment that has not routinely been associated with members of a particular race.

—When it provides the reader with a substantial insight into conflicting emotions known or likely to be involved in a demonstration or similar event.

In some stories that involve a conflict, it is equally important to specify that an issue cuts across racial lines. If, for example, a demonstration by supporters of busing to achieve racial balance in schools includes a substantial number of whites, that fact should be noted.

Do not use racially derogatory terms unless they are part of a quotation that is essential to the story.

S

satellite communications The following are some generally used technical terms dealing with satellite communications.

—*uplink* The transmission from the ground to the satellite.

—*downlink* The transmission from the satellite to the ground.

—*foot print* The area on the ground in which a transmission from a particular satellite can be received.

—*earth station* Sending or receiving equipment on the ground for a satellite.

—*transponder* The equipment on a satellite which receives from the ground and sends to the ground. A satellite usually has a number of *transponders.*

—*geosynchronous* A satellite orbit in which the satellite appears to always be in the same place in reference to the Earth. Most communications satellites are in geosynchronous orbits. Also *geostationary.*

school Capitalize when part of a proper name: *Public School 3, Madison Elementary School, Doherty Junior High School, Crocker High School.*

semi- The rules in **prefixes** apply, but, in general, no hyphen.

semiannual Twice a year, a synonym for *biannual.*

Do not confuse it with *biennial,* which means every two years.

senate Capitalize all specific references to governmental legislative bodies, regardless of whether the name of the nation is used: *the U.S. Senate, the Senate, the Virginia Senate, the state Senate, the Senate.*

Lowercase plural uses: *the Virginia and North Carolina senates.*

The same principles apply to foreign bodies.

Lowercase references to nongovernmental bodies: *the student senate at Yale.*

sentences Capitalize the first word of every sentence, including quoted statements and direct questions:

Patrick Henry said, "I know not what course others may take, but as for me, give me liberty or give me death."

Capitalize the first word of a quoted statement if it constitutes a sentence, even if it was part of a larger sentence in the original: *Patrick Henry said, "Give me liberty or give me death."*

In direct questions, even without quotation marks: *The story answers the question, Where does true happiness really lie?*

state Lowercase in all *state of* constructions: *the state of Maine, the states of Maine and Vermont.*

Four states—Kentucky, Massachusetts, Pennsylvania and Virginia—are legally commonwealths rather than states. The distinction is necessary only in formal uses: *The commonwealth of Kentucky filed a suit.* For simple

geographic reference: *Tobacco is grown in the state of Kentucky.*

Do not capitalize *state* when used simply as an adjective to specify a level of jurisdiction: *state Rep. William Smith, the state Transportation Department, state funds.*

Apply the same principle to phrases such as *the city of Chicago, the town of Auburn,* etc.

state names Follow these guidelines:

STANDING ALONE: Spell out the names of the 50 U.S. states when they stand alone in textual material. Any state name may be condensed, however, to fit typographic requirements for tabular material.

EIGHT NOT ABBREVIATED: The names of eight states are never abbreviated in datelines or text: *Alaska, Hawaii, Idaho, Iowa, Maine, Ohio, Texas* and *Utah.*

Memory Aid: Spell out the names of the two states that are not part of the contiguous United States and of the continental states that are five letters or fewer.

ABBREVIATIONS REQUIRED: Use the state abbreviations listed at the end of this section:

—In conjunction with the name of a city, town, village or military base in most datelines.

—In conjunction with the name of a city, county, town, village or military base in text.

—In short-form listings of party affiliation: *D-Ala., R-Mont.*

The abbreviations are:

Ala.	Ariz.	Ark.	Calif.	Colo.	Conn.
Del.	Fla.	Ga.	Ill.	Ind.	Kan.
Ky.	La.	Mass.	Md.	Mich	Minn.
Miss.	Mo.	Mont.	Neb.	Nev.	N.H.
N.J.	N.M.	N.Y.	N.C.	N.D.	Okla.
Ore.	Pa.	R.I.	S.C.	S.D.	Tenn.
Va.	Vt.	Wash.	W.Va.	Wis.	Wyo.

PUNCTUATION: Place one comma between the city and the state name, and another comma after the state name, unless ending a sentence or indicating a dateline: *He was traveling from Nashville, Tenn., to Austin, Texas, en route to his home in Albuquerque, N.M.*

sub- The rules in **prefixes** apply, but in general, no hyphen.

subcommittee Lowercase when used with the name of a legislative body's full committee: *a Ways and Means subcommittee.*

Capitalize when a subcommittee has a proper name of its own: *the Senate Permanent Subcommittee on Investigations.*

T

teen, teen-ager (n.) **teen-age** (adj.) Do not use teen-aged.

telecast (n.) **televise** (v.)

temperatures Use figures for all except zero. Use a word, not a minus sign, to indicate temperatures below zero.

> Right: *The day's low was minus 10.*
> Wrong: *The day's low was –10.*
> Right: *The temperature rose to zero by noon.*
> Also: *5-degree temperatures, temperatures fell 5 degrees, temperatures in the 30s* (no apostrophe).
> Temperatures get *higher* or *lower,* but they don't get *warmer* or *cooler.*

titles In general, confine capitalization to formal titles used directly before an individual's name.
LOWERCASE: Lowercase and spell out titles when they are not used with an individual's name: *The president issued a statement. The pope gave his blessing.*

Lowercase and spell out titles in constructions that set them off from a name by commas: *The vice president, Nelson Rockefeller, declined to run again. Paul VI, the current pope, does not plan to retire.*

U

ultra- The rules in prefixes apply, but in general, no hyphen. Some examples:

ultramodern   ultrasonic
ultraviolet   ultranationalism

ultrahigh frequency *uhf* is acceptable in all references.

un- The rules in **prefixes** apply, but in general, no hyphen. Some examples:

un-American   unarmed   unnecessary   unshaven

V

VCR Acceptable in second reference to *videocassette recorder.*

VDT Abbreviation for *video display terminal.* Spell out.

verbs The abbreviation v. is used in this book to identify the spelling of the verb forms of words frequently misspelled.

SPLIT FORMS: In general, avoid awkward constructions that split infinitive forms of a verb (*to leave, to help,* etc.) or compound forms (*had left, are found out,* etc.).
Awkward: *Then she was ordered to immediately leave on an assignment.*
Preferred: *Then she was ordered to leave immediately on an assignment.*

Occasionally, however, a split is not awkward and is necessary to convey the meaning:

> *He wanted to really help his mother.*
> *The budget was tentatively approved.*

vhf Acceptable in all references for *very high frequency.*

vice- Use two words: *vice admiral, vice chairman, vice chancellor, vice consul, vice president, vice principal, vice regent, vice secretary.*

Several are exceptions to Webster's New World. The two-word rule has been adopted for consistency in handling the similar terms.

videotex, teletext Not videotext. Videotex is the generic term for two-way interactive data systems that transmit text and sometimes graphics via telephone lines or cable. User can specify desired information and communicate with host computer or other users through terminal keyboard.

Teletext is a one-way system that transmits text material or graphics via a TV or FM broadcast signal or cable TV system. The user can select material desired but cannot communicate with other users.

W

who, whom Use who and whom for references to human beings and to animals with a name. Use that and which for inanimate objects and animals without a name.

Who is the word when someone is the subject of a sentence, clause or phrase: *The woman who rented the room left the window open. Who is there?*

Whom is the word when someone is the object of a verb or preposition: *The woman to whom the room was rented left the window open. Whom do you wish to see?*

wide- Usually hyphenated. Some examples:

wide-angle	wide-awake	wide-brimmed
wide-eyed	wide-open	

Exception: *widespread.*

-wide No hyphen. Some examples:

citywide	continentwide	countrywide	industrywide
nationwide	statewide	worldwide	

-wise No hyphen when it means in the direction of or with regard to. Some examples:

clockwise	lengthwise	otherwise	slantwise

Avoid contrived combinations such as *moneywise, religionwise.*

The word *penny-wise* is spelled with a hyphen because it is a compound adjective in which *wise* means *smart,* not an application of the suffix *-wise.* The same for *street-wise* in the *street-wise youth.*

women Women should receive the same treatment as men in all areas of coverage. Physical descriptions, sexist references, demeaning stereotypes and condescending phrases should not be used.

To cite some examples, this means that:

Copy should not assume maleness when both sexes are involved, as in *Jackson told newsmen* or *in the taxpayer . . . he* when it easily can be said *Jackson told reporters* or *taxpayers . . . they.*

Sports Guidelines and Style

A

abbreviations Do not spell out the most common abbreviations: NFL, NBA, CART, USAC, AFC, NFC.

athletic teams Capitalize teams, associations and recognized nicknames: *Red Sox, the Big Ten, the A's, the Colts.*

athletics director Not *athletic.*

B

baseball The spellings for some frequently used words and phrases, some of which are exceptions to Webster's New World:

backstop	ballclub
ballpark	ballplayer
baseline	bullpen
center field	center fielder
designated hitter	doubleheader
double play	fair ball
fastball	first baseman
foul ball line	foul tip
ground-rule double	home plate
home run	left-hander
line drive	line up (v.)
lineup (n.)	major league(s) (n.)
major-league (adj.)	major-leaguer (n.)
outfielder	passed ball
pinch hit (v.)	pinch-hit (n., adj.)
pinch hitter (n.)	pitchout
play off (v.)	playoff (n., adj.)
put out (v.)	putout (n.)
RBI (s.),	RBIs (pl.)
rundown (n.)	sacrifice
sacrifice fly	sacrifice hit
shoestring catch	shortstop
shut out (v.)	shutout (n., adj.)
slugger	squeeze play
strike	strike zone
Texas leaguer	triple play
twi-night double-header	wild pitch

NUMBERS: Some sample uses of numbers: first inning, seventh-inning stretch, 10th inning; first base, second base, third base; first home run, 10th home run: first place, last place; one RBI, 10 RBIs. The pitcher's record is now 6–5. The final score was 1–0.

LEAGUES: Use American League, National League, American League West, National League East, or AL West and AL East, etc. On second reference: the league, the pennant in the West, the league's West Division, etc.

BOX SCORES: A sample follows.

The visiting team always is listed on the left, the home team on the right.

Only one position, the first he or she played in the game, is listed for any player.

Figures in parentheses are the player's total in that category for the season.

Use the First Game line shown here only if the game was the first in a double-header.

One line in this example—None out when winning run scored—could not have occurred in this game as played. It is included to show its placement when needed.

First Game

philadelphia	ab	r	h	bi	san diego	ab	r	h	bi
Stone lf	4	0	0	0	Flannry 2	3	0	1	0
GGross lf	0	0	0	0	Gwynn rf	4	0	2	0
Schu 3	4	1	0	0	Garvey 1	4	0	0	0
Samuel 2b	4	0	1	2	Schmidt 1	4	0	0	0
Nettles 3b	3	1	1	0	Royster 3	0	0	0	0
Virgil c	4	2	2	3	GWilson rf	4	0	0	0
McRynl cf	4	0	1	1	Kennedy c	4	0	1	0
Maddox c	3	0	0	0	Martinez lf	4	1	1	0
Jeltz ss	2	0	0	0	Templtn ss	4	0	2	1
KGross p	3	0	1	0	Tekulve p	0	0	0	0
Dravcky p	2	0	0	0	Bmbry ph	1	0		
					Lefferts p	0	0	0	0
Totals	**32**	**3**	**4**	**5**		**33**	**2**	**9**	**2**

Philadelphia	010 200 000 –3
San Diego	000 200 000 –2

None out when winning run scored.

E. Templeton, GWilson. DP — Philadelphia 2. lob — Philadelphia 3, San Diego 6. 2B — Templeton, Gwynn. HR — Virgil (8).

	IP	H	R	ER	BB	SO
Philadelphia						
KGross W, 4–6	7 1–3	9	2	2	0	3
Tekulve S, 3	1 2–3	0	0	0	1	0
San Diego						
Dravecky L, 4–3	7	4	3	1	1	2
Lefferts	2	0	0	0	0	1

HBP — Flannery by KGross. T — 2:13. A-17, 740.

LINESCORE: When a bare linescore summary is required, use this form:

Philadelphia	010 200 000 — 3 4 1
San Diego	000 200 000 — 2 9 1

K. Gross, Tekulve (8) and Virgil; Dravecky, Lefferts (3) and Kennedy. W — KGross, 4–6, LDravecky, 4–3. Sv — Tekulve (3). HRs — Philadelphia Virgil 2 (8).

LEAGUE STANDINGS:

The form:

All times EDT
National League
East

	W	L	Pct.	GB
Pittsburgh	92	69	.571	—
Philadelphia	85	75	.531	61/2
Etc.				

West

	w	l	Pct.	GB
Cincinnati	108	54	.667	—
Los Angeles	88	74	.543	20
Etc.				

(Night games not included)

Monday's Results

Chicago 7, St. Louis 5

Atlanta at New York, rain.

Tuesday's Games

Cincinnati (Gullett 14–2 and Nolan 4–4) at New York (Seaver 12–3 and Matlack 6–1) 2, 6 p.m.

Wednesday's Games

Cincinnati at New York

Chicago at St. Louis, night

Only games scheduled.

In subheads for results and future games, spell out day of the week as: *Tuesday's Games,* instead of *Today's Games.*

basic summary This format for summarizing sports events lists winners in the order of their finish. The figure showing the place finish is followed by an athlete's full name, his affiliation or hometown, and his time, distance, points, or whatever performance factor is applicable to the sport.

If a contest involves several types of events, the paragraph begins with the name of the event.

A typical example:

60-yard dash — 1, Steve Williams, Florida TC, 6.0. 2, Hasley Crawford, Philadelphia Pioneer, 6.1. 3, Mike McFarland, Chicago TC, 6.2. 4, Etc.

100 — 1, Steve Williams, Florida TC, 10.1. 2, Etc.

Additional examples are provided in the entries for many of the sports that are reported in this format.

Most basic summaries are a single paragraph per event, as shown. In some competitions with large fields, however, the basic summary is supplied under a dateline with each winner listed in a single paragraph.

For international events in which U.S. or Canadian competitors are not among the leaders, add them in a separate paragraph as follows:

Also: 14, Dick Green, New York, 6.8. 17, George Bensen Canada, 6.9. 19, Etc.

In events where points, rather than time or distance, are recorded as performances, mention the word points on the first usage only:

1. Jim Benson, Springfield, N.J., 150 points. 2. Jerry Green, Canada, 149. 3. Etc.

basketball The spellings of some frequently used words and phrases:

backboard	backcourt	backcourtman
baseline	field goal	foul line
foul shot	free throw	free-throw line
frontcourt	full-court press	goaltending
half-court pass	halftime	hook shot
jump ball	jump shot	layup
man-to-man	midcourt	pivotman
play off (v.)	playoff (n., adj.)	zone

NUMBERS: Some sample uses of numbers: *in the first quarter, a second-quarter lead, nine field goals, 10 field goals, the 6-foot-5 forward, the 6-10 center. He is 6 feet 10 inches tall.*

LEAGUE: *National Basketball Association* or *NBA.*

For subdivisions: *the Atlantic Division of the Eastern Conference, the Pacific Division of the Western Conference,* etc. On second reference: *the NBA East, the division, the conference,* etc.

BOX SCORE: A sample follows. The visiting team always is listed first.

In listing the players, begin with the five starters—two forwards, center, two guards—and follow with all substitutes who played.

Figures after each player's last name denote field goals, free throws, free throws attempted and total points.

Example:

Los Angeles (114)

Worthy 8-19 4-6 20, Rambis 4-6 0-0 8, Abdul-Jabbar 6-11 0-0 12, E. Johnson 8-14 3-4 19, Scott 5-14 0-0 10, Cooper 1-5 2-2 4, McAdoo 6-13 0-0 12, McGee 4-7 4-5 14, Spriggs 4-7 0-2 8, Kupchak 3-3 1-2 7, Totals 49-100 14-21 114.

Boston (148)

McHale 10-16 6-9 26, Bird 8-14 2-2 19, Parish 6-11 6-7 18, D. Johnson 6-14 1-1 13, Ainge 9-15 0-0 19, Buckner 3-5 0-0 6, Williams 3-5 0-0 6, Wedman 11-11 0-2 26, Maxwell 1-1 1-2 3, Kite 3-5 1-2 7, Carr 1-3 0-0 3, Clark 1-2 0-0 2. Totals 62-102 17-25 148.

Three-point goals — Wedman 4, McGee 2, Bird, Ainge, Carr. Fouled out — None. Rebounds — Los Angeles 43 (Rambis 9), Boston 63 (McHale 9).

Assists — Los Angeles 28 (E. Johnson 12), Boston 43 (D. Johnson 10).

Total fouls — Los Angeles 23, Boston 17. Technicals — Ainge. A — 14,890.

STANDINGS: The format for professional standings:

Eastern Conference
Atlantic Division

	W	L	Pct.	GB
Boston	43	22	.662	—
Philadelphia	40	30	.571	5 1/2

etc.

In college boxes, the score by periods is omitted because the games are divided only into halves.

UCLA (69)

Jackson 1-6 2-2 4, Maloncon 4-7 2-2 10, Wright 4-7 1-5 9, Gaines 4-6 1-2 9, Miguel 5-10 0-0 10, Butler 2-3 6-8 10, Hatcher 3-8 0-0 6, Immel 2-2 1-1 5, Haley 1-1 4-4 6, Miller 0-2 0-0 0, J. Jones 0-3 0-0 0, Dunlap 0-0 0-0 0. Totals 26-55 17-24 69.

St. John's (88)

Berry 10-14 3-5 23, Glass 4-5 3-6 11, Wennington 5-9 4-4 14, Moses 5-6 0-0 10, Mullin 6-11 4-6 16, Jackson 1-3 5-5 7, Stewart 0-3 2-2 2, S. Jones 1-2 2-2 4, Bross 0-1 0-0 0, Rowan 0-2 0-0 0, Shurina 0-0 1-2 1, Coregy 0-0 0-0 0. Totals 32-56 24-32 88.

Halftime — St. John's 48, UCLA 35. Fouled out — None. Rebounds — UCLA 25 (Wright 9), St. John's 39 (Mullin 9).

Assists — UCLA 18 (Gaines 5), St. John's 21 (Moses 8).

Total fouls — UCLA 22, St. John's 20.

A-15,256

The format for college conference standings:

	Conference			All Games		
	W	L	Pct.	W	L	Pct.
Missouri	12	2	.857	24	4	.857

cross country No hyphen, an exception to Webster's New World based on the practices of U.S. and international governing bodies for the sport.

Scoring for this track event is in minutes, seconds and tenths of a second. Extended to hundredths if available.

National AAU Championship
Cross Country
Frank Shorter, Miami, 5:25.67; 2. Tom Coster, Los Angeles, 5:30.72; 3. etc.

Adapt the basic summary to paragraph form under a dateline for a field of more than 10 competitors.

cycling Use the basic summary format.

decathlon Summaries include time or distance performance, points earned in that event and the cumulative total of points earned in previous events.

Contestants are listed in the order of their overall point totals. First name and hometown (or nation) are included only on the first and last events on the first day of competition; on the last day, first names are included only in the first event and in the summary denoting final placings.

Use the basic summary format. Include all entrants in summaries of each of the 10 events.

An example for individual events:

Decathlon

(Group A)

100-meter dash — 1. Fred Dixon, Los Angeles, 10.8 seconds, 854 points. 2. Bruce Jenner, San Jose State, 11:09, 783. 3. Etc.

Long jump — 1. Dixon 24-7 (7.34m), 889, 1,743. 2. Jenner, 23-6 (7.17m), 855, 1,638. 3. Etc.

Decathlon final — 1. Bruce Jenner, San Jose State, 8,524 points. 2. Fred Dixon, Los Angeles, 8,277. 3. Etc.

E

ERA Acceptable in all references to baseball's *earned run average.*

F

football The spellings of some frequently used words and phrases:

ball carrier	ballclub
blitz (n., v.)	end line
end zone	fair catch
field goal	fourth-and-one (adj.)
fullback	goal line
goal-line stand	halfback
halftime	handoff
kick off (v.)	kickoff (adj.)
left guard	linebacker
lineman	line of scrimmage
out of bounds (adv.)	out-of-bounds (adj.)
pitchout (n.)	place kick
place-kicker	play off (v.)
playoff (n., adj.)	quarterback
runback (n.)	running back
split end	tailback
tight end	touchback
touchdown	wide receiver

NUMBERS: Use figures for yardage: *The 5-yard line, the 10-yard line, a 5-yard pass play, he plunged in from the 2, he ran 6 yards, a 7-yard gain.* But: *a fourth-and-two play.*

Some other uses of numbers: *The final score was 21-14. The team won its fourth game in 10 starts. The team record is 4-5-1.*

LEAGUE: *National Football League,* or *NFL.*

STATISTICS: All football games, whether using the one- or two-point conversion, use the same summary style.

The visiting team always is listed first.

Field goals are measured from the point where the ball was kicked—not the line of scrimmage. The goal posts are 10 yards behind the goal lines. Include that distance.

Abbreviate team names to four letters or less on the scoring and statistical lines as illustrated.

The passing line shows, in order: completions-attempts-had intercepted

A sample agate package:

Birmingham-Houston, Stats

Birmingham	7	16	0	7—30
Houston	14	7	0	6—27

First Quarter

Hou — Harrell 23 pass from Dillon (Fritsch kick), 1:00

Bir —Jones 11 run with lateral after Mason, 12 pass from Stoudt (Miller kick), 5:57

Hou — Harrell 6 run (Fritsch kick), 8:07

Second Quarter

Bir — FG Miller, 1:13

Bir — Caruth 6 run (Miller kick) 5:49

Hou – Johnson 36 pass from Dillon (Fritsch kick), 12:12

Bir — FG Miller 43, 14:33

Fourth Quarter

Bir — FG Miller 20, 3:42

Bir — Stoudt 1 run (kick failed), 9:09

Hou — Dillon 8 run (pass failed), 13:58

A —13,202

	Bir	Hou
First downs	21	15
Rushes-yards	46-209	12-70
Passing yards	109	260
Return yards	75	112
Comp-Att	13-24-0	17-33-2
Sacked-Yards Lost	4-23	2-24
Punts	3-38	3-41
Fumbles-lost	1-1	2-0
Penalties-yards	3-25	12-69
Time of Possession	35:57	24:03

Individual Statistics

RUSHING — Birmingham, Caruth 23-84, Coles 14-59, Stoudt 8-50, Gant 1-5. Houston, Harrell, 4-34, Fowler 5-26, Dillon 3-10.

PASSING — Birmingham, Stoudt 13-24-0 133. Houston, Dillon 17-33-2 283.

RECEIVING — Birmingham, Toler 4-53, Jones 3-15, McFaddon 2-38, Coles 2-12, Mason, 1-12, Caruth 1-4. Houston, Johnson 5-108, McGee 3-59, McNeil 3-36, 2-27, Sanders 3-29, Verdin 1-24.

MISSED FIELD GOALS — Houston, Fritsch 32.

The rushing and receiving paragraph for individual leaders show attempts and yardage gained. The passing paragraph shows completions, attempts, number of attempts intercepted, and total yards gained.

STANDINGS: The form for professional standings:

American Conference
East

	W	L	T	Pct.	PF	PA
Baltimore	10	4	0	.714	395	269
New England	9	5	0	.643	387	275
Etc.						

The form for college **conference standings:**

	Conference					All Games				
	W	L	T	Pts.	OP	W	L	T	Pts.	OP
UCLA	6	1	0	215	123	8	2	1	326	233
Etc.										

In college conference standings, limit team names to nine letters or fewer. Abbreviate as necessary.

G

golf Some frequently used terms and some definitions:

Americas Cup No possessive.

birdie, birdies One stroke under par.

bogey, bogeys One stroke over par. The past tense is bogeyed.

caddie

eagle Two strokes under par.

fairway

Masters Tournament No possessive. Use the Masters on second reference.

tee, tee off

U.S. Open Championship Use the U.S. Open or the Open on second reference.

NUMBERS: Some sample uses of numbers:

Use figures for handicaps: *He has a 3 handicap; a 3-handicap golfer, a handicap of 3 strokes; a 3-stroke handicap.*

Use figures for par listings: *He had a par 5 to finish 2-up for the round, a par-4 hole; a 7-under-par 64, the par-3 seventh hole.*

Use figures for club ratings: *a No. 5 iron, a 5-iron, a 7-iron shot, a 4-wood.*

Miscellaneous: *the first hole, the ninth hole, the 10th hole, the back nine, the final 18, the third round. He won 3 and 2.*

ASSOCIATIONS: *Professional Golfers' Association of America* (note the apostrophe) or PGA. Headquarters is in Palm Beach Gardens, Fla. Members teach golf at golf shops and teaching facilities across the country.

The *PGA Tour* is a separate organization made up of competing professional golfers. Use tour (lowercase) on second reference.

The PGA conducts the PGA Championship, the PGA Seniors' Championship, and the Ryder Cup matches as well as other golf championships not associated with the PGA Tour.

The *Ladies Professional Golfers Association* (no apostrophe, in keeping with LPGA practice) or *LPGA.*

SUMMARIES—Stroke (Medal) Play: List scores in ascending order. Use a dash before the final figure, hyphens between others.

On the first day, use the player's score for the first nine holes, a hyphen, the player's score for the second nine holes, a dash and the player's total for the day:

First round:
Jack Nicklaus	35-35 — 70
Johnny Miller	36-35 — 71
Etc.	

On subsequent days, give the player's scores for each day, then the total for all rounds completed:

Second round:
Jack Nicklaus	70-70 —140
Johnny Miller	71-70 — 141
Etc.	

Final round, professional tournaments, including prize money:

| Jack Nicklaus $30,000 | 70-70-70-68 — 278 |
| Johnny Miller $17,500 | 71-70-70-69 — 280 |

Use hometowns, if ordered, only on national championship amateur tournaments. Use home countries, if ordered, only on major international events such as the British Open. If used, the hometown or country is placed on a second line, indented one space:

Arnold Palmer	70-69-68-70—277
United States	
Tony Jacklin	71-70-70-70 — 281
England	

The form for cards:

Par out	444 343 544-35
Watson out	454 333 435-34
Nicklaus out	434 243 544-33
Par in	434 443 454-35 — 70
Watson in	434 342 443-31 — 65
Nicklaus in	433 443 453-33 — 66

SUMMARIES — Match Play: In the first example that follows, the *and 1* means that the 18th hole was skipped because Nicklaus had a 2-hole lead after 17. In the second, the match went 18 holes. In the third, a 19th hole was played because the golfers were tied after 18.

Jack Nicklaus def. Lee Trevino, 2 and 1
Sam Snead def. Ben Hogan, 2-up.
Arnold Palmer def. Johnny Miller, 1-up (19).

gymnastics Scoring is by points. Identify events by name: *sidehorse, horizontal bars,* etc.

Use a basic summary. Example:

Sidehorse—1. John Leaper, Penn State, 8.8 points. 2. Jo Jumper, Ohio State, 7.9 3. Etc.

H

handball Games are won by the first player to score 21 points or, in the case of a tie breaker, 11 points. Most matches go to the first winner of two games.

Use a match summary. Example:

Bob Richards, Yale, def. Paul Johnson, Dartmouth, 21–18, 21–19.

Tom Brenna, Massachusetts, def. Bill Stevens, Michigan, 21–19, 17–21, 21–20.

hockey The spellings of some frequently used words:

blue line	crease	face off (v.)
faceoff (n., adj.)	goalie	goal line
goal post	goaltender	penalty box
play off (v.)	playoff (n., adj.)	power play
power-play goal	red line	short-handed
slap shot	two-on-one break	

The term *hat trick* applies when a player has scored three goals in a game. Use it sparingly, however.

LEAGUE: *National Hockey League* or *NHL.*

For NHL subdivisions: *the Wales Division of the Campbell Conference, the division, the conference, etc.*

SUMMARIES: The visiting team always is listed first in the score by periods.

Note that each goal is numbered according to its sequence in the game.

The figure after the name of a scoring player shows his total goals for the season.

Names in parentheses are players credited with an assist on a goal.

The final figure in the listing of each goal is the number of minutes elapsed in the period when the goal was scored.

| **Philadelphia** | **3 0 0 — 3** |
| **Edmonton** | **2 2 1 — 5** |

First period — 1, Philadelphia, Rick Sutter 1 (Ron Sutter, Smith), :46. 2, Edmonton, Coffey 10 (Huddy, Kurri), 4:22 (pp). 3, Philadelphia, Bergen 4 (Zezel, Crossman), 6:38 (pp). 4, Philadelphia, Craven 4 (Smith, Marsh), 11:32 (sh). 5, Edmonton, Huddy 3 (Coffey, Kurri), 18:23 (pp). Penalties — Poulin, Phi (high-sticking), 3:31; Hughes, Edm (high-sticking), 5:17; Messier, Edm (slashing), 5:59; Crossman, Phl, double minor (holding-unsportsmanlike conduct), 8:32; Hospodar, Phl (slashing), 16:38.

Second period — 6, Edmonton, Anderson 10:21. 7, Edmonton, Gretzky 15 (Coffey, Huddy), 12:53 (pp). Penalties — Tocchet, Phil (roughing), :48; Fogolin, Edm (roughing), :48; Paterson, Phil (hooking), 12:11; Allison Phil (slashing), 17:39; Hunter, Edm (roughing), 17:39; Lowe, Edm (holding), 18:02; Crossman, Phil (holding), 19:07; Hunter, Edm (holding), 20:00.

Third Period — 8 Edmonton, Gretzky 16 (Messier, Anderson), 3:42 (pp). Penalties — Hospodar, Phl (hooking), 2:46; Hunter, Edm (kneeing), 7:58.

Shots on goal — Philadelphia 10-6-7 23. Edmonton 10-12-1 — 32.

Penalty shots — Ron Sutter, Phl 8:47 1st (missed).

Goalies — Philadelphia, Lindbergh at 8:56 2nd; reentered at start of 3rd, 10–9) Edmonton, Fuhr (23-20). A —17,498. Referee — Kerry Fraser.

STANDINGS: The form:

	W	L	T	Pts.	GF	GA
Wales Conference						
Patrick Division						
Philadelphia	47	10	14	108	314	184
NY Islanders	45	17	9	99	310	192
Etc.						

S

scores Use figures exclusively, placing a hyphen between the totals of the winning and losing teams: *The Reds defeated the Red Sox 4-3, the Giants scored a 12-6 football victory over the Cardinals, the golfer had a 5 on the first hole but finished with a 2-under-par score.*

Use a comma in this format: *Boston 6, Baltimore 5.*
See individual listings for each sport for further details.

skating, figure Scoring includes both ordinals and points.

Use a basic summary. Examples:

Men
(After 3 compulsory figures)
Sergei Volkov, Russia, 19.5 ordinals, 44.76 points. 2, John Curry, Britain, 21.5, 44.96. 3, Etc.
Women's Final
Dorothy Hamill, Riverside, Conn., 9.0 ordinals, 215 points; 2, Dianne de Leeuw, Netherlands, 20.0, 236; 3, Etc.

skating, speed Scoring is in minutes, seconds and tenths of a second. Extended to hundredths if available. Use a basic summary.

ski, skis, skier, skied, skiing Also: *ski jump, ski jumping.*

skiing Identify events as: *men's downhill, women's slalom,* etc. In ski jumping, note style where two jumps and points are posted.

Use a basic summary. Example:

90-meter special jumping — 1, Karl Schnabel, Austria, 320 and 318 feet, 234.8 points. 2, Toni Innauer, Austria, 377-299, 232.9. 3, Etc. Also: 27, Bob Smith Hanover N.H. 321-280, 201.29, Etc.

swimming Swimming is in minutes, if appropriate, seconds and tenths of a second. Extend to hundredths if available.

Most events are measured in metric units.

Identify events as *men's 440-meter relay, women's 100-meter backstroke,* etc., on first reference. Condense to *men's 440 relay, women's 100 backstroke* on second reference.

See the **track and field** entry for the style on relay teams and events where a record is broken.

Use a basic summary. Examples, where qualifying heats are required:

Men's 200-meter Backstroke Heats (fastest eight qualify for final Saturday night) heat 1 — 1, John Naber, USC, 2:03.25; 2, Zoltan Verraszio, Hungary, 2:03.50; 3, Etc.

For diving events, adapt the **skating, figure** entry.

T

tennis The scoring units are points, games, sets and matches.

A player wins a point if his opponent fails to return the ball, hits it into the net or hits it out of bounds. A player also wins a point if his opponent is serving and fails to put the ball into play after two attempts (*double faults,* in tennis terms).

A player must win four points to win a game. In tennis scoring, both players begin at *love,* or zero, and advance to 15, 30, 40 and game. (The numbers *15, 30* and *40* have no point value as such—they are simply tennis terminology for *1 point, 2 points* and *3 points.*) The server's score always is called out first. If a game is tied at 40-all, or *deuce,* play continues until one player has a two-point margin.

A set is won if a player wins six games before his opponent has won five. If a set becomes tied at five games apiece, it goes to the first player to win seven games. If two players who were tied at five games apiece also tie at six games apiece, they normally play a tiebreaker—a game that goes to the first player to win seven points. In some cases, however, the rules call for a player to win by two games.

A match may be either a best-of-three contest that goes to the first player or team to win two sets, or a best-of-five contest that goes to the first player or team to win three sets.

Set scores would be reported this way: *Chris Evert Lloyd defeated Sue Barker 6–0, 3–6, 6–4.* Indicate tiebreakers in parentheses after the set score: *7–6, (11–9).*

SUMMARIES: Winners always are listed first in agate summaries. An example:

Men's Singles
First Round

Jimmy Connors, Belleville, Ill., def. Manuel Orantes, Spain, 2–6, 6–3, 6–2, 6–1.

Bjorn Borg, Sweden, def. Jim Green, New York (default).

Arthur Ashe, New York, def. James Peters, Chicago, 6–3, 4–3 (retired).

track and field Scoring is in distance or time, depending on the event.

Most events are measured in metric units. For those meets that include feet, make sure the measurement is clearly stated, as in *men's 100-meter dash, women's 880-yard run,* etc.

For time events, spell out *minutes* and *seconds* on first reference, as in *3 minutes, 26.1 seconds.* Subsequent times in stories and all times in agate require a colon and decimal point: *3:34.4.* For a marathon, it would be *2 hours, 11 minutes, 5:01 seconds* on first reference then the form *2:12:4.06* for later listings.

Do not use a colon before times given only in seconds and tenths of a second. Use progressions such as *6.0 seconds, 9.4, 10.1,* etc. Extend times to hundredths, if available: *9.45.*

In running events, the first event should be spelled out, as in *men's 100-meter dash.* Later references can be condensed to phrases such as *the 200, the 400,* etc.

For hurdle and relay events, the progression can be: *100-meter hurdles, 200 hurdles,* etc.

For field events—those that do not involve running—use these forms: *26 1/2* for *26 feet, one-half inch; 25–10 1/2* for *25 feet, 10 1/2 inches,* etc.

In general, use a basic summary. For the style when a record is broken, note the mile event in the example below. For the style in listing relay teams, note 1,000-meter relay.

60-yard dash — 1, Steve Williams, Florida TC, 6.02, Hasley Crawford, Philadelphia Pioneer, 6.2. 3, Mike McFarland, Chicago TC. 6.2. 3, Etc.

100 — 1, Steve Williams, Florida TC 10.1. 2, Etc.

Mile — 1, Filbert Bayli, Tanzania, 3:55.1, meet record; old record 3:59, Jim Beatty, Los Angeles TC. Feb. 27, 1963; 2, Paul Cummings, Beverly Hills TC, 3:56.1; 3, Etc.

Women's 880 — 1, Johanna Forman, Falmouth TC. 2:07.9. 2, Etc.

1,600-meter relay — 1, St. John's, Jon Kennedy, Doug Johnson, Gary Gordon, Ordner Emanuel, 3:21.9 2.; Brown, 3:23.5 3, Fordham, 3:24.1. 4. Etc.

Team scoring — Chicago TC 32. Philadelphia Pioneer 29, Etc.

Where qualifying heats are required:

Men's 100-meter heats (first two in each heat qualify for Friday's semifinals): Heat 1 — 1, Steve Williams, Florida TC. 10.1. 2. Etc.

W

water polo Scoring is by goals. List team scores. Example:

World Water Polo Championship
First Round

United States 7, Canada 1
Britain 5, France 3
Etc.

water skiing Scoring is in points. Use a basic summary. Example:

World Water Skiing Championships
Men

Overall — 1, George Jones, Canada, 1,987 points. 2, Phil Brown, Britain, 1,756. 3, Etc.

Slalom — 1, George Jones, Canada, 73 buoys (two rounds). 2, Etc.

weightlifting Identify events by weight classes. Where both pounds and kilograms are available, use both figures with kilograms in parentheses, as shown in the examples.

Use a basic summary. Example:

Flyweight (114.5 lbs.) — 1, Zygmont Smalcerz, Poland, 744 pounds (337.5 kg). 2, Lajos Szuecs, Hungary, 728 (330 kg). 3, Etc.

wrestling Identify events by weight division.

Punctuation Marks and How to Use Them

ampersand (&) Use the ampersand when it is part of a company's formal name: *Baltimore & Ohio Railroad.*

The *ampersand* should not otherwise be used in place of *and.*

apostrophe (') Follow these guidelines:

PLURAL NOUNS NOT ENDING IN *s:* Add *'s: the alumni's contributions.*

PLURAL NOUNS ENDING IN *s:* Add only an apostrophe: *the churches' needs, the VIPs' entrance.*

NOUNS PLURAL IN FORM, SINGULAR IN MEANING: Add only an apostrophe: *mathematics' rules.*

NOUNS THE SAME IN SINGULAR AND PLURAL: Treat them the same as plurals, even if the meaning is singular: *one corps' location, the two deer's tracks.*

SINGULAR NOUNS NOT ENDING IN *s:* add *'s: the church's needs, the VIP's seat.*

SINGULAR COMMON NOUNS ENDING IN *s:* Add *'s* unless the next word begins with *s: the hostess's invitation, the hostess' seat.*

SINGULAR PROPER NAMES ENDING IN *s:* Use only an apostrophe: *Achilles' heel, Agnes' book, Ceres' rites.*

SPECIAL EXPRESSIONS: The following exceptions to the general rule for words not ending in s apply to words that end in an *s* sound and are followed by a word that begins with *s: for appearance' sake, for conscience' sake, for goodness' sake.* Use *'s* otherwise: *the appearance's cost, my conscience's voice.*

PRONOUNS: Personal interrogative and relative pronouns have separate forms for the possessive. None involves an apostrophe: *mine, ours, your, yours, his, her, its, theirs, whose.*

Caution: If you are using an apostrophe with a pronoun, always double-check to be sure that the meaning calls for a contraction: *you're, it's, there's, who's.*

Follow the rules listed above in forming the possessives of other pronouns: *another's idea, others' plans, someone's guess.*

COMPOUND WORDS: Applying the rules above, add an apostrophe or *'s* to the word closest to the object possessed: *the major general's decision, the major generals' decisions, the attorney general's request, the attorneys general's request.*

JOINT POSSESSION, INDIVIDUAL POSSESSION: Use a possessive form after only the last word if ownership is joint: *Fred and Sylvia's apartment, Fred and Sylvia's books.*

Use a possesive form after both words if the objects are individually owned: *Fred's and Sylvia's books.*

DESCRIPTIVE PHRASES: Do not add an apostrophe to a word ending in s when it is used primarily in a descriptive sense: *a teachers college, writers guide.*

OMITTED LETTERS: *I've, it's, don't, rock 'n' roll, 'tis the season to be jolly. He is a ne'er-do-well.*

OMITTED FIGURES: *The class of '62. The Spirit of '76. The '20s.*

PLURALS OF A SINGLE LETTER: *Mind your p's and q's. He learned the three R's and brought home a report card with four A's and two B's. The Oakland A's won the pennant.*

colon (:) The most frequent use of a colon is at the end of a sentence to introduce lists, tabulations, texts, etc.

Capitalize the first word after a colon only if it is a proper noun or the start of a complete sentence: *He promised this: The company will make good all the losses.* But: *There were three considerations: expense, time and feasibility.*

LISTINGS: Use the colon in such listings as time elapsed *(1:31:07.2),* time of day *(8:31 p.m.),* biblical and legal citations *(2 Kings 2:14; Missouri code 3:245-260).*

DIALOGUE: Use a colon for dialogue. In coverage of a trial, for example:
> *Bailey: What were you doing the night of the 19th?*
> *Mason: I refuse to answer that.*

Q AND A: The colon is used for question-and-answer interviews:
> *Q: Did you strike him?*
> *A: Indeed I did.*

PLACEMENT WITH QUOTATION MARKS: Colons go outside quotation marks unless they are part of the quotation itself.
MISCELLANEOUS: Do not combine a dash and a colon.

comma (,) The following guidelines treat some of the most frequent questions about the use of commas.
IN A SERIES: Use commas to separate elements in a series, but do not put a comma before the conjunction in a simple series: *The flag is red, white and blue.*

Put a comma before the concluding conjunction in a series, however, if the integral element of the series requires a conjunction: *I had orange juice, toast, and ham and eggs for breakfast.*

Use a comma also before the concluding conjunction in a complex series of phrases: *The main points to consider are whether the athletes are skillful enough to compete, whether they have the stamina to endure the training, and whether they have the proper mental attitude.*

WITH EQUAL ADJECTIVES: Use commas to separate a series of adjectives equal in rank. If the commas could be replaced by the word *and* without changing the sense, the adjectives are equal: *a thoughtful, precise manner; a dark, dangerous street.*

Use no comma when the last adjective before a noun outranks its predecessors because it is an integral component of a noun phrase, which is the equivalent of a single noun: *a cheap fur coat* (the noun phrase is *fur coat*); *the old oaken bucket; a new, blue spring bonnet.*

WITH NONESSENTIAL CLAUSES: A nonessential clause must be set off by commas. An essential clause must not be set off from the rest of the sentence by commas.

WITH NONESSENTIAL PHRASES: A nonessential phrase must be set off by commas. An essential phrase must not be set off from the rest of the sentence by commas.

WITH INTRODUCTORY CLAUSES AND PHRASES: A comma is used to separate an introductory clause or phrase from the main clause: *When he had tired of the mad pace of New York, he moved to Dubuque.*

WITH CONJUNCTIONS: When a conjunction such as *and, but* or *for* links two clauses that could stand alone as separate sentences, use a comma before the conjunction in most cases: *She was glad she had looked, for a man was approaching the house.*

As a rule of thumb, use a comma if the subject of each clause is expressly stated: *We are visiting Washington, and we also plan a side trip to Williamsburg. We visited Washington, and our senator greeted us personally.* But no comma when the subject of the two clauses is the same and is not repeated in the second: *We are visiting Washington and plan to see the White House.*

INTRODUCING DIRECT QUOTES: Use a comma to introduce a complete one-sentence quotation within a paragraph: *Wallace said, "She spent six months in Argentina and came back speaking English with a Spanish accent."* But use a colon to introduce quotations of more than one sentence.

Do not use a comma at the start of an indirect or partial quotation: *He said the victory put him "firmly on the road to a first-ballot nomination."*

BEFORE ATTRIBUTION: Use a comma instead of a period at the end of a quote that is followed by attribution: *"Rub my shoulders," Miss Cawley suggested.*

Do not use a comma, however, if the quoted statement ends with a question mark or exclamation point: *"Why should I?" he asked.*

WITH HOMETOWNS AND AGES: *Mary Richards, Minneapolis, and Maude Findlay, Tuckahoe, N.Y., were there.*
If an individual's age is used, set it off by commas: *Maude Findlay, 48, Tuckahoe, N.Y., was present.*

NAMES OF STATES AND NATIONS USED WITH CITY NAMES: *His journey will take him from Dublin, Ireland, to Fargo, N.D., and back.*

Use parentheses, however, if a state name is inserted within a proper name: *The Huntsville (Ala.) Times.*

WITH YES AND NO: *Yes, I will be there.*

IN DIRECT ADDRESS: *Mother, I will be home late.*

SEPARATING SIMILAR WORDS: Use a comma to separate duplicated words that otherwise would be confusing: *What the problem is, is not clear.*

IN LARGE FIGURES: Use a comma for most figures higher than 999. The major exceptions are: street addresses (*1234 Main St.*), broadcast frequencies (*1460 kilohertz*), room numbers, serial numbers, telephone numbers, and years (*1876*).

PLACEMENT WITH QUOTES: Commas always go inside quotation marks.

dash (—) Follow these guidelines:

ABRUPT CHANGE: Use dashes to denote an abrupt change in thought in a sentence or an emphatic pause: *We will fly to Paris in June—if I get a raise. Smith offered a plan—it was unprecedented—to raise revenues.*

SERIES WITHIN A PHRASE: *He listed the qualities—intelligence, humor, conservatism, independence—that he liked in an executive.*

ATTRIBUTION: *"Who steals my purse steals trash."—Shakespeare.*

IN DATELINES: *NEW YORK (AP)—The city is broke.*

IN LISTS: Dashes should be used to introduce individual sections of a list. Capitalize the first word following the dash. Use periods, not semicolons, at the end of each section. Example: *Jones gave the following reasons:*

> *—He never ordered the package.*
> *—If he did, it didn't come.*
> *—If it did, he sent it back.*

WITH SPACES: Put a space on both sides of a dash in all uses except the start of a paragraph and sports agate summaries.

ellipsis (. . .) In general, treat an ellipsis as a three-letter word, constructed with three periods and two spaces, as shown here.

Use an ellipsis to indicate the deletion of one or more words in condensing quotes, texts, and documents. Be especially careful to avoid deletions that would distort the meaning.

hyphen (-) Hyphens are joiners. Use them to avoid ambiguity or to form a single idea from two or more words.

Some guidelines:

AVOID AMBIGUITY: Use a hyphen whenever ambiguity would result if it were omitted: The president will speak to small-business men. (*Businessmen* normally is one word. But *the president will speak to small businessmen* is unclear.)

COMPOUND MODIFIERS: When a compound modifier—two or more words that express a single concept—precedes a noun, use hyphens to link all the words in the compound except the adverb *very* and all adverbs that end in *-ly; a first-quarter touchdown, a*

bluish-green dress, a full-time job, a well-known man, a very good time, an easily remembered rule.

TWO-THOUGHT COMPOUNDS: *serio-comic, socio-economic.*

COMPOUND PROPER NOUNS AND ADJECTIVES: Use a hyphen to designate dual heritage: *Italian-American, Mexican-American.*

No hyphen, however, for *French Canadian* or *Latin American.*

AVOID DUPLICATED VOWELS, TRIPLED CONSONANTS: Examples: *anti-intellectual, pre-empt, shell-like.*

SUSPENSIVE HYPHENATION: The form: *He received a 10- to 20-year sentence in prison.*

parentheses ( ) In general, be sparing with them.

Parenthesis are jarring to the reader.

The temptation to use parentheses is a clue that a sentences is becoming contorted. Try to write it another way. If a sentence must contain incidental material, then commas or two dashes are frequently more effective. Use these alternatives whenever possible.

There are occasions, however, when parentheses are the only effective means of inserting necessary background or reference information. When they are necessary, follow these guidelines:

PUNCTUATION: Place a period outside a closing parenthesis if the material inside is not a sentence (*such as this fragment*).

(An independent parenthetical sentence such as this one takes a period before the closing parenthesis.)

When a phrase placed in parentheses *(this one is an example)* might normally qualify as a complete sentence but is dependent on the surrounding material, do not capitalize the first word or end with a period.

INSERTIONS IN A PROPER NAME: Use parentheses if a state name or similar information is inserted within a proper name: *The Huntsville (Ala.) Times.* But use commas if no proper name is involved: *The Selma, Ala., group saw the governor.*

NEVER USED: Do not use parentheses to denote a political figure's party affiliation and jurisdiction. Instead, set them off with commas.

periods (.) Follow these guidelines:

END OF DECLARATIVE SENTENCE: *The style-book is finished.*

END OF A MILDLY IMPERATIVE SENTENCE: *Shut the door.* Use an exclamation point only if greater emphasis is desired: *Be careful!*

END OF SOME RHETORICAL QUESTIONS: A period is preferable if a statement is more a suggestion than a question: *Why don't we go.*

END OF AN INDIRECT QUESTION: *He asked what the score was.*

INITIALS: *John F. Kennedy, T.S. Eliot* (No space between *T.* and *S.*, to prevent them from being placed on two lines in typesetting.)
   Abbreviations using only the initials of a name do not take periods: *JFK, LBJ.*

ENUMERATIONS: After numbers or letters in enumerating elements of a summary: *1. Wash the car. 2. Clean the basement.* Or: *A. Punctuate properly. B. Write simply.*

PLACEMENT WITH QUOTATION MARKS: Periods always go inside quotation marks.

question mark (?) Follow these guidelines:

END OF A DIRECT QUESTION: *Who started the riot?*

INTERPOLATED QUESTION: *You told me—Did I hear you correctly? —that you started the riot.*

MULTIPLE QUESTION: Use a single question mark at the end of the full sentence: *Did you hear him say, "What right have you to ask about the riot?"*
   Or, to cause full stops and throw emphasis on each element, break into separate sentences: *Did he plan the riot? Employ assistants? Give the signal to begin?*

CAUTION: Do not use question marks to indicate the end of indirect questions:
   He asked who started the riot. To ask why the riot started is unnecessary. I want to know what the cause of the riot was. How foolish it is to ask what caused the riot.

QUESTION AND ANSWER FORMAT: Do not use quotation marks. Paragraph each speaker's words:
   Q: Where did you keep it?
   A: In a little tin box.

PLACEMENT WITH QUOTATION MARKS: Inside or outside, depending on the meaning:
   Who wrote "Gone With the Wind"?
   He asked, "How long will it take?"

MISCELLANEOUS: The question mark supersedes the comma that normally is used when supplying attribution for a quotation: *"Who is there?" she asked.*

quotation marks (" ") The basic guidelines for open-quote marks (") and close-quote marks ("):

FOR DIRECT QUOTATIONS: To surround the exact words of a speaker or writer when reported in a story:
   "I have no intention of staying," he replied.
   "I do not object," he said, "to the tenor of the report."
   Franklin said, "A penny saved is a penny earned."
   A speculator said the practice is "too conservative for inflationary times."

RUNNING QUOTATIONS: If a full paragraph of quoted material is followed by a paragraph that continues the quotation, do not put close-quote marks at the end of the first paragraph. Do, however, put open-quote marks at the start of the second paragraph. Continue in this fashion for any succeeding paragraphs, using close-quote marks only at the end of the quoted material.
   If a paragraph does not start with quotation marks but ends with a quotation that is continued in the next paragraph, do not use close-quote marks at the end of the introductory paragraph if the quoted material constitutes a full sentence. Use close-quote marks, however, if the quoted material does not constitute a full sentence. For example:
   He said, "I am shocked and horrified by the incident.
   "I am so horrified, in fact, that I will ask for the death penalty."
   But: *He said he was "shocked and horrified by the incident."*
   "I am so horrified, in fact, that I will ask for the death penalty," he said.

DIALOGUE OR CONVERSATION: Each person's words, no mater how brief, are placed in a separate paragraph, with quotation marks at the beginning and the end of each person's speech.
   "Will you go?"
   "Yes."
   "When?"
   "Thursday."

NOT IN Q-AND-A: Quotation marks are not required in formats that identify questions and answers by *Q:* and *A:*.

NOT IN TEXTS: Quotation marks are not required in full texts, condensed texts or textual excerpts.

IRONY: Put quotation marks around a word or words used in an ironical sense: *The "debate" turned into a free-for-all.*

UNFAMILIAR TERMS: A word or words being introduced to readers may be placed in quotation marks on first reference:

Broadcast frequencies are measured in "kilohertz."

Do not put subsequent references to *kilohertz* in quotation marks.

AVOID UNNECESSARY FRAGMENTS: Do not use quotation marks to report a few ordinary words that a speaker or writer has used:

Wrong: *The senator said he would "go home to Michigan" if he lost the election.*

Right: *The senator said he would go home to Michigan if he lost the election.*

PARTIAL QUOTES: When a partial quote is used, do not put quotation marks around words that the speaker could not have used.

Suppose the individual said, *"I am horrified at your slovenly manners."*

Wrong: *She said she "was horrified at their slovenly manners."*

Right: *She said she was horrified at their "slovenly manners."*

Better when practical: Use the full quote.

QUOTES WITHIN QUOTES: Alternate between double quotation marks (" or ") and single marks (' or '):

She said, "I quote from his letter, 'I agree with Kipling that "the female of the species is more deadly than the male," but the phenomenon is not an unchangeable law of nature,' a remark he did not explain."

Use three marks together if two quoted elements end at the same time: *She said, "He told me, 'I love you.'"*

PLACEMENT WITH OTHER PUNCTUATION: Follow these long-established printers' rules:

—The period and the comma always go within the quotation marks.

—The dash, the semicolon, the question mark and the exclamation point go within the quotation marks when they apply to the quoted matter only. They go outside when they apply to the whole sentence.

semicolon (;) In general, use the semicolon to indicate a greater separation of thought and information than a comma can convey but less than the separation that a period implies.

The basic guidelines:

TO CLARIFY A SERIES: *He leaves a son, John Smith of Chicago; three daughters, Jane Smith of Wichita, Kan., Mary Smith of Denver, and Susan, wife of William Kingsbury of Boston; and a sister, Martha, wife of Robert Warren of Omaha, Neb.*

Note that the semicolon is used before the final *and* in such a series.

PLACEMENT WITH QUOTES: Place semicolons outside quotation marks.

Appendix

Document A

Society of Professional Journalists' Code of Ethics

Preamble

Members of the Society of Professional Journalists believe that public enlightenment is the forerunner of justice and the foundation of democracy. The duty of the journalist is to further those ends by seeking truth and providing a fair and comprehensive account of events and issues. Conscientious journalists from all media and specialties strive to serve the public with thoroughness and honesty. Professional integrity is the cornerstone of a journalist's credibility.

Members of the Society share a dedication to ethical behavior and adopt this code to declare the Society's principles and standards of practice.

Seek Truth and Report It

Journalists should be honest, fair and courageous in gathering, reporting and interpreting information.

Journalists should:

- Test the accuracy of information from all sources and exercise care to avoid inadvertent error. Deliberate distortion is never permissible.
- Diligently seek out subjects of news stories to give them the opportunity to respond to allegations of wrongdoing.
- Identify sources whenever feasible. The public is entitled to as much information as possible on sources' reliability.
- Always question sources' motives before promising anonymity. Clarify conditions attached to any promise made in exchange for information. Keep promises.
- Make certain that headlines, news teases and promotional material, photos, video, audio, graphics, sound bites and quotations do not misrepresent. They should not oversimplify or highlight incidents out of context.
- Never distort the content of news photos or video. Image enhancement for technical clarity is always permissible. Label montages and photo illustrations.
- Avoid misleading re-enactments or staged news events. If re-enactment is necessary to tell a story, label it.
- Avoid undercover or other surreptitious methods of gathering information except when traditional open methods will not yield information vital to the public. Use of such methods should be explained as part of the story.
- Never plagiarize.
- Tell the story of the diversity and magnitude of the human experience boldly, even when it is unpopular to do so.
- Examine their own cultural values and avoid imposing those values on others.

- Avoid stereotyping by race, gender, age, religion, ethnicity, geography, sexual orientation, disability, physical appearance or social status.
- Support the open exchange of views, even views they find repugnant.
- Give voice to the voiceless; official and unofficial sources of information can be equally valid.
- Distinguish between advocacy and news reporting. Analysis and commentary should be labeled and not misrepresent fact or context.
- Distinguish news from advertising and shun hybrids that blur the lines between the two.
- Recognize a special obligation to ensure that the public's business is conducted in the open and that government records are open to inspection.

Minimize Harm

Ethical journalists treat sources, subjects and colleagues as human beings deserving of respect.

Journalists should:

- Show compassion for those who may be affected adversely by news coverage. Use special sensitivity when dealing with children and inexperienced sources or subjects.
- Be sensitive when seeking or using interviews or photographs of those affected by tragedy or grief.
- Recognize that gathering and reporting information may cause harm or discomfort. Pursuit of the news is not a license for arrogance.
- Recognize that private people have a greater right to control information about themselves than do public officials and others who seek power, influence or attention. Only an overriding public need can justify intrusion into anyone's privacy.
- Show good taste. Avoid pandering to lurid curiosity.
- Be cautious about identifying juvenile suspects or victims of sex crimes.
- Be judicious about naming criminal suspects before the formal filing of charges.
- Balance a criminal suspect's fair trial rights with the public's right to be informed.

Act Independently

Journalists should be free of obligation to any interest other than the public's right to know.

Journalists should:

- Avoid conflicts of interest, real or perceived.
- Remain free of associations and activities that may compromise integrity or damage credibility.
- Refuse gifts, favors, fees, free travel and special treatment, and shun secondary employment, political involvement, public office and service in community organizations if they compromise journalistic integrity.
- Disclose unavoidable conflicts.
- Be vigilant and courageous about holding those with power accountable.
- Deny favored treatment to advertisers and special interests and resist their pressure to influence news coverage.
- Be wary of sources offering information for favors or money; avoid bidding for news.

Be Accountable

Journalists are accountable to their readers, listeners, viewers and each other.

Journalists should:

- Clarify and explain news coverage and invite dialogue with the public over journalistic conduct.
- Encourage the public to voice grievances against the news media.
- Admit mistakes and correct them promptly.
- Expose unethical practices of journalists and the news media.
- Abide by the same high standards to which they hold others.

Sigma Delta Chi's first Code of Ethics was borrowed from the American Society of Newspaper Editors in 1926. In 1973, Sigma Delta Chi wrote its own code, which was revised in 1984 and 1987. The present version of the Society of Professional Journalists' Code of Ethics was adopted in September 1996.

Document B

Editorial Policy (sample)

The following policy was established for the Hi-Spot, *the student newspaper of Waverly High School, Waverly, Nebraska.*

Hi-Spot members will, at all times, be working under the code of ethics that has been set down as journalistic standards. Freedom of the press, honesty, accuracy, impartiality, decency, and equality will be used to benefit reporter and story subjects. Never will a statement be considered true just because an accusation is made.

All editorials will reflect views that are backed by research and fact. Questions on story content, editorial policy and controversial issues will be interpreted by the executive board, which will consist of the editor, managing editor, photography editor, page editors, business manager, advertising manager, and adviser.

Hi-Spot editorials will never be by-lined because they represent the ideas of a part of the staff with whom others may disagree. The *Hi-Spot* will protect the rights of any person submitting editorials. The executive board will decide when editorials are suitable for publication.

All letters to the editor will require a signature (or signatures) of those who submitted them. The names may not be published but pen names will be substituted upon request of the writer. Again, signatures are required on the original for the protection of the *Hi-Spot.*

Speak-outs and letters to the editor are encouraged from staff and non-staff members alike. All letters must be signed and turned in to the mailbox provided in the journalism room (room 18S) or to a *Hi-Spot* staff member. The *Hi-Spot* reserves the right to edit all letters, with regard to libel, without changing the substance of the letter. The *Hi-Spot* also reserves the right not to publish any letter for incriminating reasons or that person will be given a chance to respond in the same issue. The *Hi-Spot* will not publish obscene or libelous material; rulings will be made by the executive board.

Money for the publication of the *Hi-Spot* will come from advertising sales. No ads are to appear on the cover page nor the editorial page.

In accordance with Nebraska law, staff reporters may not be required to show a completed story to the source for the source's approval. If a question comes up about a story, the source will be contacted to verify information and direct quotes.

The *Hi-Spot* will not reveal a minor's name in a story (a Nebraska minor being any person under the age of 19 years old) who attends Waverly High School and is involved in a felony crime. But the *Hi-Spot* may include the name of students involved in misdemeanors serious enough to stimulate permanent expulsion from Waverly High School.

Document C

Yearbook Statement of Philosophy (sample)

The yearbook is a staff-produced publication, a product of a co-curricular publication class and extracurricular involvement. In general, the yearbook will provide memories, a record of historical events, data regarding the year, and educational opportunities for the staff, including a chance for staff members to plan, to write, to take pictures, and to design the yearbook.

As a public forum for student expression, the yearbook attempts to inform and entertain its audience in a broad, fair, and accurate manner on subjects that affect readers. The entire student body constitutes the primary audience for the book, with secondary audiences including faculty, staff, administrators, parents, and other members of the community.

The content of the book will focus on covering the school year, meeting the needs of the majority of the students. While the staff allows and encourages constructive criticism of any part of the book before and after publication, final authority for the content of the book rests in the hands of the yearbook adviser and student editorial board. Any controversial decisions will be made by the editor, staff, and the adviser. Despite the court ruling in *Hazelwood v. Kuhlmeier*, administrators rely on the adviser and staff to make content decisions.

Students working on the publication will strive to produce a publication based upon professional standards of accuracy, objectivity, and fair play. They will check all facts and verify the accuracy of all quotations. They will not publish or distribute any material that is construed to be obscene, in accordance with state law. They will not publish any libelous material or any material which could cause a material and substantial disruption of school activities. Material that stimulates heated discussion or debate does not constitute the type of disruption prohibited.

The school assumes no liability for the content of the yearbook.

Document D

Broadcast Standards for On-the-Air Personalities, Narrators, Color Commentators, & Others Appearing Before the Microphone (sample)

The purpose of this station is to provide information in the broadest sense. The channel exists to serve the students, staff, and community as a medium of communication. Additionally, the channel provides a learning experience in all facets of video production for students.

In producing programs for this station, technical crews, and on-the-air persons should strive for the highest degree of professionalism possible. Commentators should abide by the following standards:

1. No person is to be slandered through on-the-air commentary or libeled by on-the-air signs or character generated text.
2. Basic conversational good taste should be adhered to at all times. Vulgarities; sexual innuendoes; obscenities; racial, sexist, or ethnic slurs; or language in poor taste are not permitted.
3. Nothing should be broadcast that is disruptive to the school routine or purpose.
4. In unstructured programs ("freewheeling interviews," sporting events, etc.), commentary should be restricted to the subject, game, or meet. Conversation or dialogue unrelated to the event or subject is not permitted and is unprofessional. Remember, the program may be "freewheeling," but that does not mean that anything goes.
5. News reporters, interviewers, and sports commentators should be prepared to discuss the subject, game, or meet prior to going on the air (i.e., have team rosters and player statistics at hand).
6. Stage directions and conversation between crew and commentators should not become part of the taped program as it is amateurish and unprofessional.
7. Balance, accuracy, and fairness should be the aim of every reporter/commentator.
8. In covering events or activities involving this school and other schools, commentators should strive to show no partiality to their home school.
9. Personal viewpoints that are not expressed in a forum for sharing opinion or presented as analysis should be kept to a minimum in sports reporting and should not be part of news reporting.
10. "On-the-air" persons shall not use this station as a personal instrument to aggrandize themselves or to control, intimidate, or unduly influence others.

Failure to adhere to these standards may result in a suspension or restriction of programming privileges.

Document E

Code of Professional Standards for the Practice of Public Relations

Declaration of Principles

Members of the Public Relations Society of America base their professional principles on the fundamental value and dignity of the individual, holding that the free exercise of human rights, especially freedom of speech, freedom of assembly, and freedom of the press, is essential to the practice of public relations.

In serving the interests of clients and employers, we dedicate ourselves to the goals of better communication, understanding, and cooperation among the diverse individuals, groups, and institutions of society, and of equal opportunity of employment in the public relations profession.

We pledge:

To conduct ourselves professionally, with truth, accuracy, fairness, and responsibility to the public;

To improve our individual competence and advance the knowledge and proficiency of the profession through continuing research and education;

And to adhere to the articles of the Code of Professional Standards for the Practice of Public Relations as adopted by the governing Assembly of the Society.

Code of Professional Standards for the Practice of Public Relations

These articles have been adopted by the Public Relations Society to promote and maintain high standards of public service and ethical conduct among its members.

1. A member shall conduct his or her professional life in accord with the **public interest.**
2. A member shall exemplify high standards of **honesty** and **integrity** while carrying out dual obligations to a client or employer and to the democratic process.
3. A member shall **deal fairly** with the public, with past or present clients or employers, and with fellow practitioners, giving due respect to the ideal of free inquiry and to the opinions of others.
4. A member shall adhere to the highest standards of **accuracy and truth,** avoiding extravagant claims or unfair comparisons and giving credit for ideas and words borrowed from others.
5. A member shall not knowingly disseminate **false or misleading information** and shall act promptly to correct erroneous communications for which he or she is responsible.
6. A member shall not engage in any practice which has the purpose of **corrupting** the integrity of channels of communications or the processes of government.
7. A member shall be prepared to **identify publicly** the name of the client or employer on whose behalf any public communication is made.

8. A member shall not use any individual or organization professing to serve or represent an announced cause, or professing to be independent or unbiased, but actually serving another or **undisclosed interest.**

9. A member shall not **guarantee the achievement** of specified results beyond the member's direct control.

10. A member shall **not represent conflicting** or competing interests without the express consent of those concerned, given after a full disclosure of the facts.

11. A member shall not place himself or herself in a position where the member's **personal interest is or may be in conflict** with an obligation to an employer or client, or others, without full disclosure of such interests to all involved.

12. A member shall **not accept fees, commissions, gifts, or any other consideration** from anyone except clients or employers for whom services are performed without their express consent, given after full disclosure of the facts.

13. A member shall scrupulously safeguard the **confidences and privacy rights** of present, former, and prospective clients or employers.

14. A member shall not intentionally **damage the professional reputation** or practice of another practitioner.

15. If a member has evidence that another member has been guilty of unethical, illegal, or unfair practices, including those in violation of this Code, the member is obligated to present the information promptly to the proper authorities of the Society for action in accordance with the procedure set forth in Article XII of the Bylaws.

16. A member called as a witness in a proceeding for enforcement of this Code is obligated to appear, unless excused for sufficient reason by the judicial panel.

17. A member shall, as soon as possible, sever relations with any organization or individual if such relationship requires conduct contrary to the articles of this Code.

This Code was adopted by the PRSA (Public Relations Society of America) Assembly in 1988. It replaces a Code of Ethics in force since 1950 and revised in 1954, 1959, 1963, 1977, and 1983.

Document F

The Advertising Principles of American Business

Truth

Advertising shall tell the truth, and shall reveal significant facts, the omission of which would mislead the public.

Substantiation

Advertising claims shall be substantiated by evidence in possession of the advertiser and advertising agency, prior to making such claims.

Comparisons

Advertising shall refrain from making false, misleading, or unsubstantiated statements or claims about a competitor or his products or services.

Bait Advertising

Advertising shall not offer products or services for sale unless such offer constitutes a bona fide effort to sell the advertised products or services and is not a device to switch consumers to other goods or services, usually higher priced.

Guarantees and Warranties

Advertising of guarantees and warranties shall be explicit, with sufficient information to apprise consumers of their principal terms and limitations or, when space or time restrictions preclude such disclosures, the advertisement should clearly reveal where the full text of the guarantee or warranty can be examined before purchase.

Price Claims

Advertising shall avoid price claims which are false or misleading, or savings claims which do not offer provable savings.

Testimonials

Advertising containing testimonials shall be limited to those of competent witnesses who are reflecting a real and honest opinion or experience.

Taste and Decency

Advertising shall be free of statements, illustrations or implications which are offensive to good taste or public decency.

Adopted by the American Advertising Federation Board of Directors, March 2, 1984; reprinted with permission.

Document G

Position Statement on Photo-Manipulation

Given the rapid growth brought about by photo-manipulation software and the reliance scholastic journalism programs are placing on it, the Journalism Education Association urges students and advisers to follow these principles:

Advisers of student media should not make decisions about the suitability or legality of images in question. Instead, advisers should empower students to make such decisions and to counsel students to avoid deceptive practices in all aspects of publication work.

Advisers should also counsel students to seek professional legal advice in all legal and ethical questions.

Students working on publications should consider the following tests devised by University of Oregon professors Tom Wheeler and Tim Gleason about "whether and how to manipulate, alter or enhance" images:

The viewfinder test—Does the photograph show more than what the photographer saw through the viewfinder?

The photo-processing test—A range of technical enhancements and corrections on an image after the photo is shot could change the image. Do things go beyond what is routinely done in the darkroom to improve image quality—cropping, color corrections, lightening or darkening?

The technical credibility test—Is the proposed alteration not technically obvious to the readers?

The clear-implausibility test—Is the altered image not obviously false to readers?

If any of the above tests can be answered "yes," JEA urges student journalists to
- not manipulate news photos;
- not publish the image(s) in question; or
- clearly label images asphoto-illustrations

when student editors decide they are the best way to support story content.

Adopted by the Journalism Education Association Board of Directors, April 1997.

Glossary

advance: a story about a coming event.

anecdote: a short account of an interesting, powerful, or humorous event

angle: the approach a reporter takes to a story

aperture: in a camera, the lens opening that controls how much light gets through the shutter

ascenders: the parts of characters that rise above the baseline (as in *b, d, d, f, h, k, l,* and *t*)

attribution: the citing of the precise source of information

back lighting: having the light source behind the subject instead of behind the photographer

back-up quote: a quotation intended to support the lead in a story

balance: the design principle that reflects the stable, yet dynamic distribution of elements in a design

banner: a bold headline that runs the entire width of the page

baseline: the imaginary line on which type rests

beat: an area or source of news that's regularly covered by a specific reporter

beat reporter: a reporter assigned to check the same news source for each issue of the paper (for example, art, music, theater, police administration)

bleed: the running of color or a photo or other graphic through the external margin and off a page

body: in a camera, a light-tight box that houses the camera parts

body copy: columns of text for stories

bold: a heavy, dark version of a regular typeface (e.g., Helvetica Bold)

bracketing: a method by which a photographer shoots one picture at the perceived correct exposure, then overexposes one picture and underexposes another. The basic idea is that one of the three exposures will likely be correct.

brainstorming: a method of obtaining many ideas in a short time

broadcast journalism: journalism produced for radio or television

broadsheet: a newspaper format that measures approximately 14 by 22 inches

bullet: a large dot that calls attention to a line of copy or sets off items in a list

business manager: the person on the staff of a publication who is in charge of advertising sales and preparation, circulation, and record keeping

"by authority": the designation given to most early American newspapers, which meant they had the government's approval. The papers were published with this statement.

byline: a line of copy that identifies the writer of a story

call to action: that part of an advertisement urging the reader to take some specific action, such as calling for information or buying the product

camera-ready copy: text prepared so that the headlines, body type, and art are already set, positioned, and ready to be photographed

caption: lines of copy placed next to a photo that explain the content of the photo; also called a cutline

caricature: in cartooning, a representation of a specific person in which one or more features are exaggerated for comic effect

censorship: the restriction or suppression of material by an authority

centered alignment: type centered within a given horizontal area

character: type letter (such as an A), number, or letterform (such as a hyphen)

chronological style: having events written in the order in which they occurred

circulation: the number of people who receive a publication

civil libel: written defamation of an identified individual, group, or corporation

cliché: an overused, trite expression (for example, *busy bee*)

clip art: ready-made graphics available for use free of charge or for a small fee

close-up (cu): in video, television, or film, a portrait-like camera shot showing a person's head and neckline; a camera shot that is very near to a subject to show detail

column: a bylined article expressing the opinions of the writer, usually signed, and appearing on the editorial page; vertical section of printed copy in a publication

column inch: a measurement for newspaper space. A column inch is one inch high and the width of a newspaper's standard column.

"composite characters": fictional characters a news writer creates by using characteristics of several real people. This practice is frowned upon by ethical journalists.

computer-assisted reporting: the use of various news databases and other resources on the Internet to facilitate the gathering of certain kinds of news information

conflict: an element of news that involves tension, surprise, and suspense, and arises with any good news topic—sports, war, elections

consequence: an element of news that refers to the importance of the event. The greater the consequence, the greater the news value.

consistency: the design principle reflects the application of an identical design to elements that are identical and application of a similar design to elements that are similar

contact sheet: a sheet of photographs, printed negative size, from which photo selection is made

contrast: the design principle that reflects the use of opposites in color, size, and shape to create emphasis and to distinguish one element in a design from another

copy: all words that will be set in print

copyediting: the review of manuscript for errors in mechanics, facts, and style

copy editor: the person who checks copy before it goes into pages to make sure it's factually accurate and conforms to the newspaper's style

copyright: the exclusive legal right to material someone has created

copywriter: one who writes material for advertising

CPU: the central processing unit of a computer; it controls everything the computer does

credibility: the ability to inspire belief and trust

criminal libel: defamatory statements that might bring about public anger, revolt, or disturbance of the peace

cropping: the cutting or marking of a photograph to eliminate unnecessary material and highlight important elements

cub reporter: a novice reporter assigned to pick up brief items or do weekly checks with sources for news

cut: in video, television, and film, an instant switch from one shot to another without fading

darkroom: a room having little or no light, in which film can be developed and prints made

dateline: a line of copy that identifies the place where the news occurred; important if the story originated someplace other than the city where the newspaper is published

deck: one level of a headline

depth of field: the area of clear focus in front of and behind the subject of the photograph

depth-of-field scale: in a camera, a scale that indicates the depth of field when the camera is focused on a subject at a particular f-stop

descenders: the parts of characters that extend below the baseline (as in *g, j, p, q,* and *y*)

desktop publishing: using a desktop computer to set and design type, edit, produce graphics, and determine page layout

digital camera: a camera that transmits electronic images onto a disk for printing from a computer rather than onto film

direct quotation: the exact words of a speaker. Direct quotes are set off in type with quotation marks.

display copy: text for headlines, bylines, captions, advertisements, and so on. Type for display copy is often chosen to convey a mood or to reflect a specific meaning related to the content.

dissolve: in video, television, or film, to fade in one screen image while fading out a previous screen image

distribution: the delivery of a newspaper into the hands of its readers, achieved by various methods

dolly: in video, television, or film, to move a camera toward or away from the subject

dominance: the design principle that reflects the use of one visual focal point, or dominant element in each design

dominant element: the strongest element on a page, usually a large photo, which leads the reader into the page

double-truck: a spread in the center of a publication, printed as one sheet of paper; also called a centerspread; referred to as a double-page spread in yearbook design

downstyle: a headline style in which all letters, except the first letter of the first word and proper nouns, are set lowercase.

dummy: a full-size drawing of a page showing where all page elements will appear

duotone: a photograph printed in two colors. One is almost always black; the other may be any color.

edit: to make changes to copy that improves it

editorial: a short article that expresses opinions on a topic. By strict definition, an editorial expresses the official opinion of the newspaper and so doesn't have a byline.

editorial board: members of a newspaper staff who meet regularly to discuss the newspaper's content and to plan future issues

editorial cartoon: a type of editorial that uses pictures to get a point across. It may illustrate a written editorial or stand alone. Unlike other editorials, it's signed (by the artist).

editorialize: to include personal opinions in a supposedly objective story

editorial page: a section of the newspaper reserved for editorials and various other pieces that contain opinion rather than objective reporting

editorial-page editor: the person who works closely with the managing editor to plan the editorial page. This person writes or directs staff to write the editorials that express the newspaper's opinions, the columns, and other editorial features.

editorial policy: a statement of the position of the paper on various editorial issues, such as whose viewpoint the editorials represent, how the newspaper handles letters to the editor, how monies from ads will be handled, etc.

editor-in-chief: the person who has overall responsibility for a news operation or publication; also called managing editor

elements of news or **news values:** characteristics that define whether something is newsworthy or not. These elements include timeliness, human interest, proximity, prominence, consequence, and conflict.

embargo: to request delay of a news story or release until a specified date and time

endsheets: the inside front and back covers of a book

end sign: 30 or pound sign #. Either symbol placed at the end of copy signifies "the end" of the copy.

enlarger: a device used to shine light through a negative, magnifying the image onto light-sensitive photographic paper, where the image is focused and imprinted

entry point: a visual element that draws readers into a story or page

establishing shot: in video, television, or film, a camera shot that shows the subject as well as its position and relation to its entire surroundings; a variation of a long shot

***-est* question:** a question built around a word ending in *-est* —*biggest, proudest, greatest,* and so forth. Such questions are generally avoided by good interviewers.

ethics: a system of moral principles

"evergreen": a term applied to material acceptable for publication at any time, with timeliness not a factor

exposure: in photography, the amount of light that strikes the film (or solar cell)

external margin: a frame of white space around the layout marked by the outside edge of at least one block of copy or graphic

eyeline: a pica of white space that extends horizontally across a spread

facing pages: two inside pages that face each other but are not usually printed on the same sheet of paper; together, they form a spread

fade: in video, television, or film, to bring the picture from blackness into its full light (*fade in*) or take it from its full light into blackness (*fade out*).

fair comment and criticism: a libel defense that protects a journalist's expressed opinion of public figures or reviews of books, records, and the like

family: fonts closely related in style

feature story: a story that focuses more on entertaining than on informing; soft news. Feature stories may be written on virtually any topic.

featurize: to make a hard-news story into a feature by injecting anecdotes, background, and similar information

film speed: a film rating, indicated by a number, that reflects a film's sensitivity to light. The lower the number, the "slower" the film and the less sensitive it is to light. See *ISO.*

filter question: a question, posed at the beginning of a survey, designed to eliminate people who do not belong to the desired population. "Are you 18 years old?" would be an appropriate filter question in a survey designed to find out about students' voting habits.

five W's and the H: Who, What, When, Where, Why, and How. These elements belong in nearly every newspaper story.

fixer: in photo development, a bath that sets a film or print image permanently. The film coating not blackened during development is dissolved away in this solution, and the film emulsion is hardened to prevent scratching of the finished negatives or print.

flair: the quality of writing that makes it creative, original, and memorable

flash-synchronization speed: the fastest shutter speed that can be used with a flash to obtain a properly exposed picture

flat: a large sheet of paper that shows one side of a signature

flush-left alignment: a positioning of copy so that it rests squarely against the left-hand side of the column

flush-right alignment: a positioning of copy so that it rests squarely against the right-hand side of the column

focal length: in a camera, the measurement of the lens in millimeters. The lower the lens number, the shorter the focal length. The shorter the focal length, the wider the lens.

focus: to adjust the camera lens closer to or farther from the film so that the subject will appear sharp (in focus) on the developed film

fold: the middle of a page, where large-format newspapers are folded

folio: a page number; often includes the name and section of the paper

follow-up question: an interview question intended to get a source to further explain or expand upon a previous answer

follow-up story: a story that focuses on an event in the recent past

font: traditionally, a complete set of characters in one size and style of typeface (for example, 12-point Gill Sans Italic); used now as a synonym for *typeface*

formal interview: an interview set up and planned in advance

format: the physical size of a publication's page

forum theory: the idea that once a forum (or place where ideas are exchanged) is created, the ideas expressed there cannot later be controlled

f-stop: a scale that indicates the aperture (lens opening) in numbers. The lower the number, the wider the aperture. With each increase in f-stop, half as much light is let in through the aperture.

future book: a chronological list of upcoming events that might be worth covering; a long-range calendar of events and ideas

game story: a sports story recounting the play-by-play activities of a game

general assignment reporter: a person who writes articles or does the work on any subject assigned as the editor sees fit

global village: the concept, so named by Marshall McLuhan, of the world as having become a more tightly interrelated community because of simultaneous broadcast of significant events

graphic (or art): a photograph, illustration, or device such as a rule, box, chart, graph, diagram, map, or arrow

grid: a pattern of vertical and horizontal lines that forms a base on which to place page elements

grid sheet: a sheet, the size of a specific newspaper format, lined with light-blue grid marks. Grid sheets are used as a form on which to make dummies.

gutter: white space that separates columns and facing pages

halftone: a screen that prepares a photographic image for reproduction by converting it into a series of tiny dots

hammer head: a headline style that features one or more lines of a primary headline above one or more lines of a secondary headline

hard news: the news that involves timely, significant events, such as an election, a speech by a public official, or a report on a budget meeting; also called straight news

headline: a line of copy that serves as a title for a story. The headline is usually printed in larger type above the story

human-interest story: a story that causes the reader to feel such emotions as sorrow, pity, or amazement

icon: a graphic symbol or image that identifies a particular feature, perhaps a section or a standing feature, such as a teacher profile

image editing: changing, adjusting, or cleaning up of photographic images by means of certain computer programs

in-depth reporting: reporting that uses extensive research and interviews to provide a detailed account of a significant story. In-depth stories require extensive research, many interviews, and dozens of sources.

index: copy that lists the page numbers on which sections start; in yearbooks, a list of all people, events, groups, sports, and academic areas covered in the book

infographic: a visual representation of statistical information, such as a map, chart, diagram, or time line

initial cap: a large capital letter of the opening word in a story; serves as a graphic; also called a drop cap

in loco parentis: the legal idea that school authorities act "in place of the parent" and assume a parent's rights, duties, and responsibilities. This concept was apparently struck down in the Tinker case.

internal margin: a consistent margin of white space between copy and graphics; usually one pica in width

interview: a situation in which a reporter asks a source questions and records the answers, which may be used later in a news story

invasion of privacy: unlawful prying by the government and the media into the lives of private citizens

inverted pyramid: a style of newswriting in which the main facts appear at the top of the article (the lead) and less-significant facts follow until the end, where the facts may be dispensable. This gives the reader the essential facts first and permits expansion or contraction in editing and page layout.

investigative reporting: a type of in-depth reporting that seeks to uncover and expose something hidden. In many cases, what is revealed is illegal activity or information that has been purposely kept from the public.

ISO: a standard measure (formerly called ASA) of the speed of film. A film with a higher ISO is more light sensitive than one with a lower ISO.

issue number: a number that refers to the consecutive number of issues of a publication during one calendar year.

italic: characters slanted to the right

jargon: the special language of a specific group, such as that applicable to a particular profession—generally to be avoided in student publications

jump: to continue a story from one page to another

jumphead: a brief (one- or two-word) headline on a page that shows a reader where to start reading a jumped story again

jumpline: a line of copy that indicates the page on which a story continues

justified alignment: type that aligns, or is set even, on both sides of a column

kicker: a headline style that features one secondary headline above one or more lines of primary headline

ladder diagram: a planning device designating what goes on specific pages (as in a yearbook)

laser printer: a printer in which a laser beam forms characters and graphic images onto paper, similar to the way a photocopier works

layout template: a pattern for a page design

layout: the design stage where all the elements of a newspaper's pages are arranged; the physical arrangement of the elements on a page

lead: the beginning of a news story, often consisting of just one sentence

leading: the white space between lines of type. Leading is normally set an additional two points. Ten-point type set on a 12-point leading would be referred to as set *10 on 12,* written *10/12.*

lens: the part of the camera through which the light enters, is sharpened, and is transmitted to the film (or solar cell). The focal ring on the lens adjusts the focus of the lens. Lenses vary from single pieces of ground and polished glass to complex and expensive groupings of several glass elements.

letter to the editor: a letter from a reader expressing an opinion

letterspacing: extra space between characters in a line of type

libel: written defamation; damaging false statements against another person or institution that appear in writing or that are spoken (broadcast) from a written script

light: a thin version of a regular typeface (e.g., Helvetica Light)

"limited effects": the notion that consumers have psychological defenses by which they resist and mold messages from the mass media to fit their own needs

local angle: someone or something that connects a story's topic to the local readers

localization: the writing of a regional, national, or even international story to bring out the local angle

logo: a title with art that identifies a standing feature, such as a column, in a newspaper a distinctive graphic treatment of a brand or company name. It's also known as the signature, slug, or nameplate and is an important layout element in advertisements.

long shot (ls): a camera shot that shows the main subject in its surroundings; also called a wide shot (ws)

maestro: the concept of joint planning of pages or sections of publications by writers, editors, and designers; also called the team or WED approach

mainbar: the main story of several stories about a topic on one page of a paper; the story that brings the issue into sharp focus

managing editor: the person who has overall responsibility for a news operation or publication; also called editor-in-chief

market survey: a series of questions designed to elicit information about specific habits or preferences of a particular audience (market)

masthead: a statement printed in all editions of a newspaper, generally on the editorial page, identifying pertinent information about the publication, such as name, publisher, editor, and staff members

medium shot (ms): in video, television, or film, a camera shot that shows a person cut off just below the waist

medium-long shot (mls): in video, television, or film, a camera shot in which an entire subject appears, with a little space above and below

minicolumn format: a style of page layout based upon a series of narrow or "mini" columns used to create areas of planned white space

modem: a device that converts copy and graphics into signals that can be sent and received over phone lines

modular format: a style of page layout that uses rectangular units, each of which consists of all the visual elements that make up the layout for a particular story

monologophobia: a term coined by Theodore Bernstein to describe the fear of repeating a word; also called the "elongated yellow fruit" (rather than "banana") school of writing

morgue: a collection of back issues of the newspaper, needed for reference and historical record

muckraking: journalism that crusades for social justice or to expose wrongdoing

mugshot: a photo that shows only the shoulders and head of a person; also called a headshot

music format: the type of music played by a radio station

nameplate: copy (often combined with a graphic) that states the name of the newspaper in large, bold letters across the front page; includes the volume and issue numbers, publication date, and city and state where the paper is published; also called a flag

negative: a section of film that has been chemically processed

network: a means of connecting computers together so that information can easily pass between them

news: information about events, people, or issues that the public wants or needs to know

news-brief format: a condensation of a lengthy story into a sentence or two (usually used to summarize routine stories when space is needed)

news feature: a feature story related to a breaking or developing news story

news editor: the person in charge of hard-news stories, and often the supervisor of the copy editors

news judgment: the knowledge and instinct a reporter calls on to determine whether an event is news

news magazine: a newspaper format that measures 8 1/2 by 11 inches

newspaper style: guidelines that include standardized forms for capitalization, abbreviation, and spelling. They are set forth in a publication's stylebook and establish consistency for the reader.

news peg: a sentence or paragraph connecting a news-feature story to a specific item of news

news release: information about an organization provided to the news media by that organization

novelty: a class of type that reflects a particular mood or historic period

nugget: a fact or bit of information that will stick in the audience's minds and make the audience remember a story

nut graph: the paragraph within the introduction to an story that foreshadows the rest of the story; a sort of internal lead

objectivity: the ability to make fair, neutral observations about people and events

obscenity: material considered offensive by community standards and lacking any serious literary, artistic, political, or scientific value

off the record: an agreement reached, before an interview begins, that the interviewer will not print the information that the interviewee provides

open-ended question: a question that is structured to allow the interview subject latitude in answering. The structure of an open-ended question does not allow for a simple one-word answer.

optical center: a point about two-thirds of the way up from the bottom of an ad (not the physical center of the space)

overprint: the printing of one item on top of another

page proof: a version of edited copy that has been placed in a designed page. A page proof shows how the page will look when it's printed or photocopied.

pagination software: a computer program designed for page layout

pan: in video, television, film, or photography, to move a camera to follow the motion of a subject

paraphrase: to put speakers' own words into the reporter's words without changing the meaning or inserting opinion. A paraphrase is used to clarify lengthy, fuzzy, or complicated thoughts. Paraphrased material is not enclosed in quotation marks.

partial quotation: a quotation that uses just a few words from a speaker's statement

partisan press: early American newspapers that aligned themselves with one political party. This was commonplace during the Revolutionary period.

pasteup: to affix type to a grid sheet in preparation for printing. The pasteup shows what the page will look like when printed. See *layout*.

penny press: newspapers, from the mid-19th century, that were filled with news and read by a mass audience, included advertising, and sold for a penny

personality profile: a thorough, in-depth feature story about one person

photo credit: a line of copy that identifies the photographer of a particular photo

photo essay: a story told in pictures—generally involving three to seven photographs with captions

photo illustration: a photograph that has been edited or manipulated in an image-editing program so that it deviates markedly from reality and becomes instead an illustration. Photo illustrations should be clearly labeled as such.

photo series: a series of photos that shows how something has changed or developed over time

pica: a unit of measurement in design. There are 12 points in a pica and 6 picas in one inch.

plagiarism: the taking and using as one's own the writings or inventions of another person

point: a small unit of measurement that describes the size of type. There are 72 points in one inch.

point-counterpoint: a technique in which the opinions of individuals with opposing viewpoints on a topic are run in side-by-side opinion articles

postgame story: a follow-up story about a sports event. Such stories are nearly always featurized.

pregame story: an advance story about a sports event, which may include background and other information about both teams. Pregame stories are generally featurized.

press: a word used to refer to the print and electronic media—radio, television, newspapers, magazines, and all other news-gathering and disseminating agencies; the machine that prints the newspaper

press run: the number of copies of a publication printed for a single issue

primary source: a person whose business it is to have the best and most reliable information about the topic; especially important in interviewing

prior restraint: censorship, or restraint in advance of publication. This is illegal in the United States except in the rarest of circumstances, usually pertaining to national security in wartime.

prior review: the practice of reviewing material in advance of publication for the purpose of approving or disapproving content

privileged statements: statements made on the floor of Congress, in the state legislature, or in a courtroom that, if published, are immune from libel suits

program director: the person in charge of all on-air programming; determines the programming schedule and mix and the choice of announcers

prominence: an element of news that refers to how well-known an individual is in the community, school, nation, or world

proof: a version of edited copy

proofread: the process of reading proofs to correct mechanical errors made by a writer or copy editor

proximity: an element of news that refers to the geographic nearness of a given event to your place of publication or your readers

public: one of various groups or audiences to whom public relations goals and activities may be directed

public figure: a person who purposely thrusts himself or herself into the news

public forum: a place to freely exchange ideas. See *forum theory.*

public official: a government official—for example, a mayor, a school board president, and so on

public relations: the communication of information from an organization, company, or group to some particular audience to achieve a specific response

publisher: the person or body that owns, runs, or controls a publication, sets broad guidelines and general policies but is rarely concerned with day-to-day operations

pull quote: a quote from a story arranged as a graphic in the layout of the story

Q and A: a technique for writing an interview story in which the reporter's exact questions are reported, followed by the source's exact answers

question lead: a lead that begins with a question, generally to be avoided. This kind of lead gives little information and is generally to be avoided.

quote lead: a lead that begins with an unattributed quote, usually to be avoided because it is unclear. This kind of lead is unclear and should usually be avoided.

ragged: having uniform word spacing and uneven line length. Type aligned on the left ("flush left") and ragged on the right ("ragged right") is easiest to read.

RAM: the random access memory in a computer, reserved for information being temporarily put into or taken out of a computer. Desktop publishing requires a high amount of RAM.

random sample: a sample of a population to be surveyed in which every member of the population has an equal possibility of being included in the survey sample

rate sheet: a sheet, distributed to advertising clients, that lists ad rates

redundancy: unnecessarily repetitious phrasing (for example, *2 A.M. in the morning*)

refer: a line of copy that refers readers to a related story elsewhere in the issue

repetition: the design principle that reflects the recurring use of visual arrangements to create order in a design

reporters: the people who carry out the assignments that have been determined by the various subeditors in conference with the managing editor and the publication's adviser

reverse print: light type on a dark background

review: a bylined opinion article focusing on the relative worth of a product or performance

right of reply (or simultaneous rebuttal): the opportunity for permitting a person criticized in a story to respond to that criticism in the same story

roman: characters that are straight up and down

rule: a vertical or horizontal line that serves to accent or separate elements; its width is measured in points

rule of thirds: a method of composing photographs in which the field of vision is divided into thirds horizontally and vertically and the image is placed at the intersection of any two lines

sans serif: a class of type without serifs

scanner: digitizing equipment that scans and transfers visual material, such as illustration or type, to a computer

schedule: a list compiled by the editor of everything on each page, including lengths of stories and sizes of pictures

screen: shaded area; measured in percentages

screen: devices the printer uses when preparing pictures for printing. Halftone screens are used to prepare photos for reproduction, as well as textured screens for special effects.

script: a class of type that resembles handwriting

sensationalism: the tendency to publish information that creates intense but brief interest or emotional reaction

serif: a class of type with small "feet" or strokes at the end of most letters

sexist language: terms and general word choices that categorize all people according to sex—for example, "mail*man*," "wait*ress*"

shock jock: a radio disk jockey who entertains his or her audience by saying outrageous, often vulgar or offensive, things about people or situations

shutter-release: in a camera, a mechanism to release the shutter

shutter speed: in a camera, a scale that indicates how fast the shutter opens and closes, measured in fractions of a second. The higher (or faster) the shutter speed, the less light is let in through the shutter. With each increase in shutter speed, half as much light is let in through the shutter.

sidebar: a story supplementing, but separate from, another story on the same subject in the same issue of the paper

signature: a set of 8 or 16 pages printed on a large sheet of paper, which is folded, cut, and bound (with other signatures) into a book

simultaneous rebuttal: See *Right of reply.*

sizing: reducing or enlarging a cropped photo to fit exactly a space on the layout

slander: a damaging false statement against another person or institution spoken or broadcast extemporaneously

"slanguage": in sportswriting, trite expressions stemming from the jargon of sports (for example, *pigskin* for *football*)

slug: brief identifying name (usually one or two words) for a story. Used on copy, page layouts, and the schedule.

small caps: a complete alphabet of capital letters that are the same size as the x-height of the lowercase letters

soft news: the stories that are considered not of immediate importance or of significance to a wide audience, such as personality feature stories or "news you can use" columns

spot color: one color applied in strategic places on a page

spread: a set of facing pages

standing head: a headline for a regular feature in each issue of a publication

station log: a complete record of everything broadcast during the hours a station is on the air

station manager: the highest-ranking student on a broadcast staff; the one who supervises the various department directors and acts as liaison between them and the faculty advisory board

stock question: an all-purpose question usable in any situation—for example, "What are your immediate and long-term goals?"

storytelling format: a form of reporting in which the information is presented as a narrative story

student news bureau: an organization set up to provide information about a school to its publics

style: the way copy should be written to be consistent within a publication. Rules for a publication's style are included in a stylebook.

stylebook: a guide setting forth style decisions specific to a publication—for example, when to abbreviate, preferred spellings, and punctuation. The stylebook is to be followed by all writers.

subhead: a miniheadline that indicates what the next section of copy contains; breaks up gray blocks of copy in a story

subjective writing: writing that expresses the writer's opinion and viewpoint. Subjective writing in a newspaper belongs on the editorial page.

subscription: an arrangement in which a reader pays in advance to receive a publication on a regular basis for a certain period of time

summary lead: a lead that provides the briefest possible summary of the major facts of a story in the first sentence

tabloid: a newspaper format that measures approximately 11 by 17 inches

target audience: the particular audience selected to receive a message

tease: to use a lead that coaxes readers into a story by encouraging them to read further to see what the lead really means

teaser: boxed copy that promotes stories inside the issue

technical director: the person in charge of installation and maintenance of all broadcast equipment at a station

testimonial: a written statement attesting to the value of something

test strip: in photo development, a series of print strips made at different exposures to determine the most appropriate one for the final print

theme copy: text in a yearbook that explains and develops the theme chosen for the book

thumbnail: a small, rough sketch representing a page layout

tieback: a detail or details that relate a news story to a previous development

tilt: in video, television, or film, to move the camera head up or down in a vertical motion

timeliness: an element of news that has to do with how new or current the event is

tip: a piece of information that leads a reporter to a potential story

"tombstoning": the placing of two headlines side by side on a page or spread

track: in video, television, or film, to capture horizontal movement by moving the entire camera horizontally

transition: words, phrases, or even whole paragraphs that hold a story together and smooth the shift from one topic to another

type measurement: extending from the highest point of the ascender to the lowest point of the descender. Type measuring 72 points is approximately one inch high from the top of an *h* to the bottom of a *p*.

typeface: design of a complete set of type characters, specified by a name, such as Arial or Garamond

typography: the way printed letters are handled on a page

unity: the design principle that reflects a striving for a sense of wholeness—so each part of a design looks different, yet all have the same visual tone, or feeling

upstyle: a headline style in which every major word is capitalized.

verbatim transcript: a technique, often called the "Q and A" system, in which the reporter's exact questions are reproduced, followed by the source's exact answers. A verbatim transcript of an interview requires a tape recorder for accuracy. The term can also refer to printing the exact text of a speech or message.

viewfinder: in a camera, a framing device that allows the photographer to see the picture before it's taken

voiceover (VO): in video, television, or film, a voice heard on the audio track without that person being seen on screen

volume number: a number that refers to the number of years a newspaper has been in existence

Watergate: the term applied to the whole series of events that developed from the break-in at the Democratic Party headquarters at the Watergate apartment complex and that led to the resignation of U.S. President Richard M. Nixon

WED: the concept of joint planning of pages or sections of publications by writers, editors, and designers; also called the team, or maestro, approach

white space: blank areas in ads or page design. Used effectively, white space attracts the reader's eye.

wicket: a headline design that consists of two or more lines of a secondary headline above one or more lines of a primary headline

"wild art": art not associated with any particular story. These pictures are usually feature-oriented and are published principally because they are entertaining and catch the reader's attention. They also break up otherwise heavy layouts.

wire services: a service that provides, for a fee, news from around the world to publications that subscribe to it

word processing: the editing, storage, and reproduction of words by means of certain computer programs

x-height: the actual height of the lowercase *x;* may vary from face to face

yellow journalism: a sensational brand of journalism given to hoaxes, altered photographs, screaming headlines, frauds, and endless promotions of the newspapers themselves. The term derives from the name of the Yellow Kid, a cartoon character popular in the late nineteenth century.

zine: an newspaper or magazine published on the Internet

zoom: in video, television, or film, to manipulate the lens of the camera so as to create the appearance of moving closer or farther away from the subject

Acknowledgments

The authors thank the following for their generous contributions to this edition of *Journalism Today:*

Student Publications

The A-Blast, Annandale High School, Annandale, Virginia

The All-Stater, The University of Nebraska, Lincoln, Nebraska

The Academy Times, Charles Wright Academy, Tacoma, Washington

The American, Independence High School, San Jose, California

The Arvadan, Arvada High School, Arvada, Colorado

Arlingtonian, Upper Arlington High School, Columbus, Ohio

Beak 'n Eye, West High School, Davenport, Iowa

The Bear Facts, Hastings High School, Alief, Texas

Black & White, Walt Whitman High School, Bethesda, Maryland

Black Hawk, Central High School, Davenport, Iowa

The Budget, Lawrence High School, Lawrence, Kansas

Bugle Call, R. E. Lee High School, San Antonio, Texas

Call, Kirkwood High School, Kirkwood, Missouri

The Cavalcade, W. T. Woodson High School, Fairfax, Virginia

The Central Times, Naperville Central High School, Naperville, Illinois

The Chronicle, Harvard-Westlake School, North Hollywood, California

Crier, Munster High School, Munster, Indiana

The Contact Lens, The University of Nebraska

The Echoes, Abraham Lincoln High School, Council Bluffs, Iowa

El Leon, Mansfield High School, Mansfield, Missouri

Featherduster, Westlake High School, Austin, Texas

The Excalibur, Robert McQueen High School, Reno, Nevada

The Falconer, Torrey Pines High School, San Diego, California

Finest Hours, Winston Churchill High School, Potomac, Maryland

Focus, Midland High School, Midland, Michigan

The Fourth Estate, Bartlesville High School, Bartlesville, Oklahoma

Hauberk, Shawnee Mission East, Prairie Village, Kansas

The Hornet, Enumenclaw High School, Enumenclaw, Washington

Inklings, Staples High School, Westport, Connecticut

Hi-Lite, Carmel High School, Carmel, Indiana

Hi-Spot, Waverly High School, Waverly, Nebraska

Hiways, Hialeah High School, Hialeah, Florida

Indian, Shawnee Mission North High School, Overland Park, Kansas

The Lakewood Times, Lakewood High School, Lakewood, Ohio

The Lion's Roar, Lincoln High School, Gahanna, Ohio

The Lion, Lyons Township High School, Lyons, Illinois

The Little Hawk, City High School, Iowa City, Iowa

Mt. Carmel Sun, Mt. Carmel High School, San Diego, California

News 101, Española Valley High School, Fairview, New Mexico

Oracle, East High School, Lincoln, Nebraska

The Panther, Miami Palmetto Senior High School, Miami, Florida

Panther Tale, Duncanville High School, Duncanville, Texas

The Phoenix Journalism Monthly, Society for Professional Journalists, Valley of the Sun Chapter

Quaker Shaker, Plainfield High School, Plainfield, Indiana

The Rampage, Green Mountain High School, Lakewood, Colorado

The Rustler, Fremont Senior High School, Fremont, Nebraska

The Saratoga Falcon, Saratoga High School, Saratoga, California

The Spartan Shield, Pleasant Valley Community High School, Pleasant Valley, Iowa

The Spectator, Liberty High School, Liberty, Missouri

The Stinger, Emmaus High School, Emmaus, Pennsylvania

Teen Perspective, Marquette University Summer Journalism Workshop

Tiger Tales, Joliet Township High School, West Campus, Joliet, Illinois

The Tower, Grosse Pointe South High School, Grosse Pointe Farms, Michigan

U-High Midway, University High School, Chicago, Illinois

X-Ray, St. Charles High School, St. Charles, Illinois

Professional Publications and Organizations
American Advertising Federation
American Society of Newspaper Editors
The Associated Press
Chicago Tribune
Dubuque Telegraph Herald
Journalism Education Association
The New York Times
Public Relations Society of America
Society of Professional Journalists
Southfield Public Schools/Kenson Siver
United Press International

Literary Credits
Page 201: "Doors Closed, Kennedys Offer Their Farewells," N.R. Kleinfeld, *The New York Times,* July 24, 1999. Copyright © 1999 The New York Times.

Page 208: "Teen Social Concerns." Reprinted with permission from *Wise Up to Teens: Insights into Marketing and Advertising to Teenagers.* Copyright © 1999 by Peter Zollo, <www.teenresearch.com>.

Page 422: "Top Ten Words" and "Words That Copywriters Use" from *How to Make Advertising Make Money* by John Caples, pgs. 66, 77. Copyright © 1983. Published by Prentice Hall.

Page 422: "Most Persuasive Words" from *Confessions of an Advertising Man* by David Ogilvy. Copyright © 1963. Published by Simon and Schuster.

Pages 505–540: Excerpted from *The Associated Press Stylebook and Libel Manual,* Sixth Trade Edition. Norm Goldstein, ed. Reading, Mass.: Addison-Wesley Publishing Company, Inc., 1996. Reprinted with permission of the Associated Press.

Photographs
The authors wish to thank the students and staff of Larkin High School (Elgin, Illinois), Niles West High School (Skokie, Illinois), and Evanston Township High School (Evanston, Illinois), for their cooperation in the photographic illustration of this text.

Allsport: page 187, Peter Taylor; page 283, Craig Jones. AP/Wide World Photos: pages 41, 49, 108, 141, 193, 210. Chicago Daily Defender: page 12. Chicago Tribune: pages 83, 118–123, 260–263. Corbis-Bettmann: pages 8, 14, 163. Corbis: pages 437, 485; page 16, Tim Page; page 135, Bruce Burkhardt. Corbis Sygma: page 378, Bill Nation; page 380, Les Stone. Delta Queen: page 146. Bob Daemmrich Photo, Inc.: page 267. Jeff Ellis, photographer, pages 21, 32, 66, 68, 69, 87, 99, 104, 143, 145, 160, 166, 172, 176, 217, 273, 307, 338, 351, 425, 446, 472, 483, 488, 490, 492, 496. Finley Holiday Film/NASA: page 189. Gamma Liaison/Liaison Agency Inc.: pages 39, 388, Michael Schwarz; page 59, Walter Stricklin; page 318, Cynthia Johnson; page 375, Stephen Ferry; page 445, Renato Rotolo. The Image Works: page 31, Joe Sohm; pages 153, 319, 395, Bob Daemmrich; page 303, Richard Lord; page 403, Steven Rubin. IPOL: page 213, Giorgio Cosulich. PhotoEdit: page 63, David Conklin; page 71, Kate Denny; pages 106, 225, Michael Newman; page 196, Robert Brenner; pages 207, 284, 287, 293, 294, Tony Freeman; pages 304, 310, 349, 367, David Young-Wolff. St. Louis Post-Dispatch: page 47. Stock Boston: pages 61, 130, 211, 292, 459, Bob Daemmrich; page 101, Laimute Druskis; page 419, Lawrence Migdale; page 427, Michele Burgess; page 409, Spencer Grant; page 450 (b), Mark Burnett; page 470, Richard Pasley. The Stock Market: page 3, Bill Binzen; page 29, Thomas Ives; page 158, David Pollack; page 414, Chuck Savage; page 450 (t), Mark A. Johnson. Tony Stone Images: page 27, J.P. Williams; pages 93, 200, 381, 397, Bob Daemmrich; page 127, Don Smetzer; page 335, Mitch Kezar; page 340, Charles Gupton; page 399, Frank Cezus; page 499, Frank Clarkson. Bradley Wilson, photographer, pages 376, 439, 440, 464 (all), 468 (all).

Individuals
Terry Anderson; Jody Beck; Jack Botts; Linda Butler; Alfred Geduldig; Dr. Loyal N. Gould; Jimmy Langham; C. Bickford Lucas; Mike Patten; Susan Bridges Patten; Thomas L. Pendleton; Laura Plachecki; Mary Kay Quinlan; B.C. Rafferty; Barbara R. Sarnataro; Jacqueline Sharkey; Lynn Silhasek; Lynn Smith; Stephen A. Smith; and Holly Spence.

Index